Quantitative Modelling for Management and Business

A problem-centred approach

Mike Carter and

PITMAN
PUBLISHING

D1337939

PITMAN PUBLISHING
128 Long Acre, London WC2E 9AN

A Division of Pearson Professional Limited

First published in Great Britain in 1996

© Mike Carter and David Williamson 1996

ISBN 0 273 60510 0

British Library Cataloguing in Publication Data

A CIP catalogue record for this book can be obtained from the British Library

10 9 8 7 6 5 4 3 2 1

Printed and bound in Great Britain by Clays Ltd, St Ives plc

The Publishers' policy is to use paper manufactured from sustainable forests.

Contents

About the book

The following pages will describe the approach the book will take to develop your skills and knowledge in quantitative management. This will include the way in which you will interact with the text to demonstrate that you are competent in the areas of quantitative management. This section will also relate the book to the National Standards laid down for managers and consider the level at which the book can be used. There are three main organising principles of the text, these being problem-centred, capability and competence:

1   Problem-centred

The various areas of quantitative management will be introduced wherever possible through the use of problems taken from a wide variety of industries, including manufacturing, service and the public sector. This will allow you to directly relate the theory and underpinning knowledge to the reality of the real managerial world in which you operate or plan to operate. The majority of the problems are based on our experience and have been structured so that they enable you to develop and practise the competences in the area of quantitative modelling. All of the examples have been simplified so that you can build and practise one set of competences at a time without being diverted by other managerial issues. Once you have developed the competences you will be encouraged to test these against problems in your own work environment. Here you will need to integrate all your studies in management (marketing, operations, accounting, human resource management, etc.) but you will be able to carry this out with the confidence that you have competence in quantitative modelling.

2   Capability

Stephenson & Weal, in their book *Quality of Learning – A Capability Approach in Higher Education* (1992), describe the idea of capability as:

> ... *an all round human quality, an integration of knowledge, skills and personal qualities used effectively and appropriately in response to varied, familiar and unfamiliar circumstances.*
>
> *Capable people have confidence in their ability to (1) take effective and appropriate action (2) explain what they are about (3) live and work effectively with others and (4) continue to learn from their experience, both as individuals and in association with others, in a diverse and changing society.*
>
> *Capability is a necessary part of specialist expertise, not separate from it. Capable people not only know about their specialisms, they also have the confidence to apply their knowledge and skills within varied and changing situations and to continue to develop their specialist knowledge and skills long after they have left formal education.*

Capability is not just about skills and knowledge. Taking effective and appropriate action within unfamiliar and changing circumstances involves judgements, values, the self-confidence to take risks and a commitment to learn from the experience. Involving students in the decisions which directly affect what they learn, and how they learn, develops a sense of ownership and a high level of motivation.

The aim of this text to develop (through the underpinning knowledge and demonstrating competence on the problem examples) your capability. One word of warning in the form of a modified proverb: the text will enable you to grasp firmly the tail of a very tame tiger. We have engineered the problems so that only one area of quantitative management is covered in each one. When you practise the competences on problems based on your working environment then you will need to grasp firmly the tail of a wild tiger. To avoid being mauled you should ensure you have built your confidence and skills by demonstrating competence on all the examples in the text. Then, when attempting to demonstrate competence on your own examples, use both the underpinning knowledge and the evidence you have produced in demonstrating the competence on the text examples to help you show capability in varied and new situations. You may need to be prepared at this stage to demonstrate competence from a series of areas on a particular work-based problem. In some areas of quantitative management the tigers are particularly wild and you may well need additional help from the game warden (the tutor on your course or somebody in your organisation with quantitative management skills). We will give you a health warning when we come across these areas.

3 Competence

The final organising principle is that of competence. The text will identify general and specific quantitative management competences at the beginning of each chapter or section. Then, based around a problem, the competences you will have to develop will be demonstrated, and this will be underpinned with the knowledge you need to understand the operation of these competences. At the end of each section or chapter there is a structure of the competence you will be asked to demonstrate and provide evidence of. Figure A gives an example of how the competence examples are structured within the chapters.

The first part of the structure lists the *competences* that are going to be demonstrated. This is then followed by the *procedures* which will help you to demonstrate these competences. The *problem* and a *solution format* to the problem from the text will then be given. So that you can identify the evidence from the solution that will demonstrate the particular competence there are numbers down the right-hand side of the structured solution. Procedure points are noted down the left-hand side.

It is then your turn to provide the evidence that you have developed competence in the area. In the first instance attempt to demonstrate competence on the problem recommended in the text. When you have produced your evidence of competence on this problem turn to the back of the book and you will find a complete competent solution. If your evidence matches the competent solution you may judge yourself *competent* and move on to practise competence on the

COMPETENCES

1

2

3

PROCEDURES

1

2

3

4

PROBLEM

SOLUTION FORMAT

1   **1**

2   **2**

3

Figure A   Format for competence examples

remaining problems for the section or chapter (brief answers for these will be found at the end of the book). Then, for the majority of the areas in the book, you will be asked to practise your competence on problems from the work environment. Your tutor may ask you to produce evidence of competence in these work-based examples. If you find your evidence does not match the complete competent solution at the end of the book, don't panic – this does not mean you have failed. What it means is that you are *not yet competent* in one or more of the elements of competence. To help you gain competence in the areas you are not yet competent in you need to refer to the text again and revisit the underpinning knowledge. If you look down the right side of the complete competent solution given at the back of the book you will find the page numbers of the text to refer back to. When you have done this attempt to produce the evidence of competence for the problem again and then check against the complete competent solution. If you find after repeated attempts that you are still not producing competent evidence then you should contact your tutor or somebody in your organisation who has quantitative management skills.

For many areas of the book there is a supporting Lotus and Excel-based disk. Once you have demonstrated competence in an area you will be able to automate the arithmetic elements of the competence using this disk. You should find it particularly useful when working on problems from your own working environment.

National standards for managers

There exists a framework of national standards that have been developed for managers. Within this framework participants are judged 'competent' or 'not yet competent' in terms of the national standards of performance. These standards are general to all areas of management (not specific to quantitative management as in this text) and have been produced by the Management Charter Initiative (MCI) as the lead body. They have been produced at two levels: Level I at the certificate level (now NVQ4) and Level II at the diploma level (now NVQ5). The Level III standards are currently under development. The documentation of these standards is achieved by specifying *units of competence*, each of these units describing in broad terms what is expected of a competent manager in a particular aspect of the job. Each unit consists of a number of *elements of competence*. These show the skills, knowledge and abilities that managers at a given level are expected to have. Elements form the basis of assessment. Each element is then described by *performance criteria* which specify the outcomes that a manager has to achieve in order to demonstrate competent performance. For each of these elements there is a set of range indicators that will describe the range of instances and situations in which the element is applied. The following tables give the units of competence at Level I and Level II.

There are limited explicit standards on quantitative management within these national standards. Where they do exist they are contained within the key role of 'Manage Information'. However, quantitative management skills are implicit in many areas where the manager has to demonstrate effective decision making and planning. This book will provide the basic knowledge and skills in the area of quantitative management for both levels of the national standards. Also, due to the three underlying principles of the book, it is compatible with competency-based programmes as well as with more traditional programmes.

National Standards at Level I

Unit of competence	Key role
Maintain and improve service and product operations.	Manage Operations
Contribute to the implementation of the change in services, products and systems.	Manage Operations
Recommend, monitor and control the use of resources.	Manage Finance
Contribute to the recruitment and selection of personnel.	Manage People
Develop teams, individuals and self.	Manage People
Plan, allocate and evaluate work carried out by teams, individuals and self.	Manage People
Create, maintain and enhance effective working relationships.	Manage People
Seek, evaluate and organise information for action.	Manage Information
Exchange information to solve problems and make decisions.	Manage Information

National Standards at Level II

Unit of competence	Key role
Initiate and implement change and improvement in services, products and systems.	Manage Operations
Monitor, maintain and improve service and product delivery.	Manage Operations
Monitor and control the use of resources.	Manage Finance
Secure effective resource allocation for activities and projects.	Manage Finance
Recruit and select personnel.	Manage People
Develop teams, individuals and self to enhance performance.	Manage People
Plan, allocate and evaluate work carried out by teams, individuals and self.	Manage People
Create, maintain and enhance effective working relationships.	Manage People
Seek, evaluate and organise information for action.	Manage Information
Exchange information to solve problems and make decisions.	Manage Information

Level of the book

This book is designed mainly for use on management development programmes to provide the basic knowledge and skills in the area of quantitative management. These programmes will include courses at certificate and diploma levels in management, management studies or business administration. The book can also be used to underpin programmes at the Masters level (MBA, MSc, Marketing etc.), as it provides a range of core skills and competences that can be applied to subject areas at this higher level. It can also be used very effectively in the under-graduate business area. However, it will not always be possible for you to find examples from your own work experience.

Managers who are not undertaking a specific course of study will also be able to use the book effectively given the interactive nature of the competences. Managers who use the book as a development guide in this way may find it useful to identify someone with quantitative management skills to act as a mentor in the situations where they prove to be not yet competent.

Computer support disk

Provided with this book is a computer support disk (CSD). It is not necessary to use this disk to be able to work through the book and develop competence in quantitative modelling, but it is a useful and helpful extra. The computer disk contains a series of spreadsheets that are based on both the Lotus 1-2-3 version 2.3 and Excel version 4.0a spreadsheet packages. The spreadsheets have been provided in both of these formats to give you the choice of which of these popular spreadsheets to use. They have been designed to require the minimum spreadsheet skills and to take away the burden of some of the calculations within the book. You will be advised in the text when to use the disk, but do remember that it is an optional extra. It is very important that a copy is made of the CSD and that is used as your working copy. Put the original disk in a safe place. Full details on how to use the computer support disk are given in Chapter 2 of the text.

Using the disk with Lotus 1-2-3   Call up Lotus 1-2-3 on your computer (this is not included on your CSD) and carry out the following instructions:

/	(type / to call up menu)
File	(type F to call up file menu)
Directory	(type D to call directory menu)
a:	(type this and press enter to change directory)
/	(type / to call up menu)
File	(type F to call up file menu)
Retrieve	(type R to retrieve file menu)
Start	(type this and press enter to call up initial file)

You can now follow the instructions on the screen and the examples on the disk

Using the disk with Excel   Call up Excel on your computer (this is not included on your CSD) and carry out the following instructions:

File	(select File from top tool bar and click with mouse)
Open	(select Open from drop down menu and click with mouse)
Drives	(select a:)
List Files of Type	(go to List Files of Type bar and with the mouse click on the arrow and then use the mouse to select Lotus 1-2-3 (*.wk*))
Start	(scroll through list and select Start Wk1)
OK	(go to OK box and click with mouse)

You can now follow the instructions on the screen and the examples on the disk

---

1 Quantitative modelling

why and where we start

1.1 Introduction

This book is concerned with quantitative modelling for management and business – both the private and the public sector, including the manufacturing and the service industry. The underlying approach of this book is to explain modelling through a series of practical management and business examples.

By the end of this chapter you should be able to demonstrate basic competence in:

- the reasons why managers should use modelling
- the different types of models that can be used
- the basic mathematics of straight line equations

This chapter will also use practical examples to develop the underpinning knowledge in the area of modelling.

At the end of each section the required competence will be specified and described. A typical problem format with the competences highlighted will also be given to help you demonstrate the competences on the problems at the end of the chapter. At the end of the book a full solution will be given for the first of these problems as well as the answers for the rest.

1.2 What is modelling?

This chapter will develop general competence in understanding models and detailed competence in linear equations. Let us start by asking the question: what is modelling?

Consider the problem of a manager requiring to lay out a production facility. If you want to change the layout of your lounge it can be carried out by moving furniture around until you obtain the layout that suits you best. The only cost involved will be a little extra backache on the part of the person moving the furniture. This 'try and see' method cannot be used in the layout of production facilities – large production machines cannot be moved round several times until a layout that suits is found. The relocation costs would be prohibitive for such an approach and it would be unlikely any right-thinking manager would ever consider it.

The modelling of layout problems has been carried out successfully for many years. The basic approach in such problems is to produce a scale drawing of the area in which the new layout is to be planned, making a careful note of floor levels, supporting pillars, roof heights, service availability, etc. The machines, conveyors, transport systems can then be produced to scale as separate templates (produced in card ideally). These templates can then be added to the scale drawing to form a model on which many alternative layouts can be tried. The aim would be to produce a layout to give efficient production flows and efficient utilisation of space and services, within the scope of such constraints as fire regulations and the Safety at Work Act. Other models may also be needed to achieve the correct balance of machines to avoid bottlenecks. The cost of trying alternative layouts on a model is only a fraction of the cost of actually moving the machines themselves. Computers are now taking the drafting skills out of such modelling approaches and good, reasonably priced packages are available on micro computers.

An important part of modelling is ensuring the validity of the model, so that it replicates the real world. I remember an incident from my own experience concerning a major layout of a production facility. All the machines were installed with extensive conveyor systems to bring raw material to the machines and to transport the finished goods to the warehouse, packaging and despatch. The final conveyor connecting the production facility and the warehouse was being installed when a worried installation engineer appeared in the project office. Across the path of the conveyor was a supporting column for the floors above, some ten metres long by just under one metre thick. Unfortunately this supporting column had been missed because two scale drawings had been used for the layout, one for the warehouse and one for the production area. The column was in between the two and was forgotten until the time came to connect the two systems together. This problem was due entirely to the fact that the model did not fully replicate the real world. The validity of all models is vital if they are to be of use and value to management. The problem with the conveyor system was solved by making a tunnel through the supporting column to take the conveyor, the finished goods disappearing through a hole in the wall to the warehouse. This hole in the wall proved to be quite a talking point among people being shown round the factory. Most considered it a good idea, and a few even copied it to solve problems of their own. Very few knew that if the column had been taken into account at the planning stage, the hole in the wall could have been avoided completely at a cost saving. The hole was remembered for a long time as 'Frank's Folly', after the unfortunate project engineer.

It should always be remembered that the consequence of models failing to replicate the real world can be much more severe than having to make a hole in the wall. It can lead to major financial loss or bankruptcy.

1.3 Categories of models

Models can be categorised into three types: **iconic**, **analogue** and **symbolic**.

1.3.1 Iconic models

An iconic model represents a certain aspect of a system pictorially or visually, on a different scale than its actual size. A model aircraft or car in a wind tunnel is an iconic model. Iconic models can be used to display a company's product range when the products are either too large to be carried around (a power station or a new motorway) or too small to be seen by eye (small valves used as human heart valve replacements). They can be of great value when used to provide information of this type. They can also, in a limited sense, be of value in prediction. For example, in the case of an aircraft it is far cheaper to make design changes at the model stage of development than at the prototype stage. This type of model construction is beyond the scope of this book and will not be considered. It is the realm of the model maker, a craft occupation.

1.3.2 Analogue models

An analogue model employs one set of properties to represent some other set of properties which the system being studied possesses. Maps, graphs and flow charts are examples of analogue models, where colours are used to show physical or other characteristics of the entity being modelled. These types of models have a considerable value in the provision of information but like the iconic model, this is mainly in the provision of visual information and only to a small degree in prediction and control. An example of an analogue model used in prediction is the production facility layout discussed previously.

1.3.3 Symbolic models

A symbolic model is one which employs symbols to represent properties of the system under study by means of a mathematical equation or set of such equations and mathematical rules. The symbolic model is, of the three, the most difficult to conceive and the most general and abstract. This problem can be overcome in part by using a corresponding analogue model, whose function is more often explanatory than predictive. Symbolic models are well suited to the prediction of effects of changes on the actual systems. Symbolic modelling is the type frequently used in quantitative modelling where effects of change etc. need to be discovered. This type of modelling can either be carried out manually or on a computer. In practice, the majority of quantitative modelling applications are carried out with the use of a computer, which has a greater speed of operation and greater accuracy. The type of problems where solutions have been found by quantitative modelling includes stock control, forecasting and corporate modelling to name but a few. The most popular will be developed in this text.

1.4 A cost revenue model

This section of the chapter will enable you to:

- construct simple straight line equations
- manipulate straight line equations
- graph straight line equations

- construct break-even graphs
- apply sensitivity analysis to break-even graphs

The section will also provide underpinning knowledge in the areas of linear models and break-even graphs.

Let us now expand the relationship between analogue and symbolic models with another example. This example is concerned with the cost and revenue of a product.

The fixed cost of producing the product is £1,000 and this will be incurred no matter how many are produced or even if none are produced. The variable cost of production (materials etc.) is only incurred as the units are produced and is £10 per unit. The cost model will be as follows:

Let y_1 = the total cost of production
and x = the number of units produced

For every unit made a cost of £10 will be incurred. The contribution to the total cost of this variable cost element can be calculated by $10 \times x$ i.e $10x$. To this must be added the £1,000 fixed cost before we arrive at the total cost.

This will give the following cost model:

$y_1 = 1,000 + 10x$

This model is a symbolic model and can be used to predict the cost for any level of production, and can also be shown as an analogue model by producing a graph. Figure 1.1 shows this analogue cost model from no production to producing 200 items.

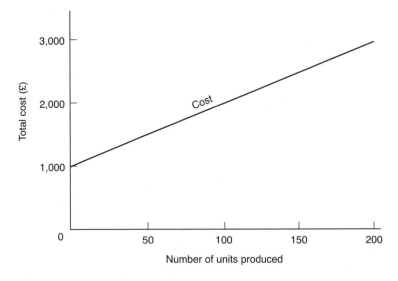

Figure 1.1 Cost model

The analogue cost model is more visual and is the more powerful way to present the model but the symbolic cost model is the best way to predict cost. This is carried out by substituting the number produced for x and calculating the value of y, the total cost.

The revenue element can now be added to the model. The product sells for £20.

> Let y_2 = the total revenue of items produced
> and x = the number of units produced

Note: The assumption has been made that all items produced will be sold and converted to revenue.

For every unit made and sold a revenue of £20 will be received. The total revenue can be calculated by $20 \times x$ (i.e. $20x$). This will give the following revenue model:

$$y_2 = 20x$$

If this symbolic model of revenue is converted to an analogue model and added to the cost model we will have a cost revenue model often referred to as a **break-even chart**. This is shown in Figure 1.2.

The cost revenue analogue model indicates that at production levels of less than 100 the product will make a loss. At exactly the level of 100 the revenue equals cost and the product will break even and at production levels in excess of 100 the product will make a profit.

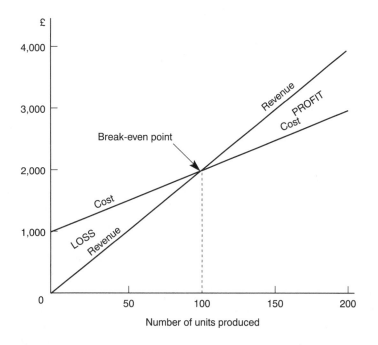

Figure 1.2   Cost revenue model

The cost revenue model can be represented in a symbolic form as follows:

$$y_1 = 1,000 + 10x$$
$$y_2 = 20x$$

where y_1 = the total cost of production
y_2 = the total revenue of items produced
x = the number of units produced

The break-even point can also be calculated from this model. The break-even point will occur when the total revenue equals the total cost. In symbols this will be:

$$y_1 = y_2$$

knowing that $y_1 = 1,000 + 10x$ and $y_2 = 20x$

then
$$1,000 + 10x = 20x$$
$$1,000 = 20x - 10x$$
$$1,000 = 10x$$
$$\frac{1,000}{10} = x$$
$$100 = x$$

Note: To find x we move elements of the equation until the x is left. As part of the equation moves across the = sign we change the sign of that part of the equation (+ changes to − and vice versa).

Therefore, the break-even point occurs at a production level of 100. To determine the revenue and cost at which this break-even point occurs, the production level of 100 can be substituted into either equation of the model:

$$y_2 = 20x$$
$$= 20 \times 100$$
$$= £2,000$$

∴ break-even occurs at production of 100 with a revenue of £2,000 and a cost of £2,000

Again it can be seen that the analogue model is the most effective for *presenting the model* and the symbolic is most effective for *calculating predictions*.

Having now built a cost revenue model have we produced an answer to the situation? From an early age we are taught there is only one answer to a problem and this is especially so with mathematical problems. With management problems there can be many answers to a problem and this is also true of quantitative modelling for management. Looking at the cost revenue model we have just built, the variable cost of production was taken to be £10 and the fixed cost £1,000. The costs in a lot of organisations are determined by the accountants, who produce accounts of the past to help make predictions for the future. The further into the future forecasts go, the more uncertain they become.

In the example we have just calculated, the break-even point for the fixed cost is £1,000. This cost is required before production starts and therefore is likely to be a reasonably accurate estimate and not subject to change. The variable cost of £10 per unit produced may not be quite so accurate. Such a cost may be affected by wage rates, inflation or changing commodity prices to name but a few. A more realistic view would be within a *range* of values. For example, £10 is considered to be the best estimate of the future variable cost, but the cost may fall as low as £8 if there is a low pay award, or the cost could rise as high as £12 if commodity prices rise more than anticipated. Such a range of cost values rather than a single point value provides a more realistic forecast of cost. Such a range of values added to a model is called a **sensitivity analysis**.

This analysis can be carried out by modifying the cost equation of the cost revenue model. The modified equations can then be used to calculate a range of break-even points for the range of variable cost values:

Variable cost	Modified cost equation	Break-even point
8	$y_1 = 1,000 + 8x$	$= 83.33 \cong 84$
9	$y_1 = 1,000 + 9x$	$= 90.91 \cong 91$
10	$y_1 = 1,000 + 10x$	$= 100$
11	$y_1 = 1,000 + 11x$	$= 111.10 \cong 112$
12	$y_1 = 1,000 + 12x$	$= 125$

The break-even points have to be whole numbers in this case because products must be in whole numbers. The more usual term for whole number solutions is an **integer solution**. Usual rounding rules have not been used in this analysis. Break-even points need to be rounded up in all cases because any rounding down will move the solution into a loss situation.

This is only part of any sensitivity analysis, and it would be necessary to carry out a similar analysis by varying the selling price of the product and recalculating the break-even point for each price. With a large model the sensitivity analysis can be considerable, with a range of results being needed on several variables within the model. This approach will provide not just a single point answer but a range of answers given the variable nature of the real world.

Competence Example 1.1

At the end of this section you should now be able to demonstrate how to:

1 construct simple straight line equations

2 manipulate straight line equations

3 graph straight line equations

4 construct break-even graphs

5 apply sensitivity analysis to break-even graphs

To practise and demonstrate these competences, complete problems 1.1 and 1.2 at the end of this chapter. To help you to develop these competences, a description of the procedure you will need to follow is now given, along with a typical problem format. This problem format is based on the example we have just considered:

PROCEDURE (COST REVENUE MODELS)

❶ Define and annotate the variables in the problem.

❷ Construct the cost and revenue equations.

❸ Determine the break-even point.

❹ Construct the break-even chart.

❺ Determine the ranges of the sensitivity analysis.

❻ Carry out sensitivity analysis.

PROBLEM

This example is concerned with the cost and revenue of a product. The fixed cost of producing the product is £1,000 and this will be incurred no matter how many are produced or even if none are produced. The variable cost of production (materials etc.) is only incurred as the units are produced and is £10 per unit. The product sells for £20.

A description of the layout of the solution format is given at the beginning of the book.

SOLUTION FORMAT

❶ Let y_1 = the total cost of production
Let y_2 = the total revenue of items produced
and x = the number of units produced

❷ This will give the following cost model:

$$y_1 = 1,000 + 10x$$

This will give the following revenue model:

$$y_2 = 20x$$

❸ The break-even point will occur when the total revenue will equal the total cost:

$$\therefore y_1 = y_2$$

knowing that $y_1 = 1,000 + 10x$ and $y_2 = 20x$
then $1,000 + 10x = 20x$

$$1,000 = 20x - 10x$$
$$1,000 = 10x$$
$$\frac{1,000}{10} = x$$
$$100 = x$$

Therefore the break-even point occurs at a production level of 100. To determine the revenue and cost at which this break-even point occurs the production level of 100 can be substituted into either equation of the model.

Thus $y_2 = 20x = 20 \times 100 = £2,000$

8

❸ ∴ break-even occurs at production of 100
with a revenue of £2,000
and a cost of £2,000

❹

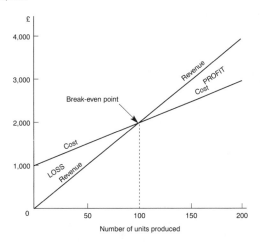

❺ The £10 is considered to be the best estimate of the future variable cost. But the cost may fall as low as £8 if there is a low pay award and the cost could rise as high as £12 if commodity prices rise more than anticipated.

❻

Variable cost	Modified cost equation	Break-even point
8	$y_1 = 1,000 + 8x$	$= 83.33 \cong 84$
9	$y_1 = 1,000 + 9x$	$= 90.91 \cong 91$
10	$y_1 = 1,000 + 10x$	$= 100$
11	$y_1 = 1,000 + 11x$	$= 111.10 \cong 112$
12	$y_1 = 1,000 + 12x$	$= 125$

Practise your competence now on problems 1.1 and 1.2 at the end of the chapter. When you have demonstrated competence in this area you can use the computer disk provided to automate the arithmetic elements of the competences. You may choose to use either a Lotus or an Excel spreadsheet depending on the package you have access to. With the spreadsheet you will be able to input the elements of cost and revenue and the spreadsheet will calculate the break-even point and produce the break-even chart. The spreadsheet will enable you to carry out 'what if' calculations to produce the sensitivity analysis. The operation of this spreadsheet is developed in more detail in Chapter 2. You may now demonstrate the competence in this area against problems from your own work environment. You should do this with care – you now know the basics of break-even analysis but in some cases you may need a more sophisticated view to costing.

1.5 Graphing linear models

This section of Chapter 1 will enable you to:

- construct straight line resource constraints
- identify and construct maximisation functions

- optimise simple resource-constrained models
- apply sensitivity analysis to simple resource-constrained models

This section will also provide underpinning knowledge in the area of linear programming by graphical methods.

Let us develop the ideas of quantitative modelling through another example. A manufacturer can make two products. Both are fancy fire surrounds – one is called the Cotswold, the other the Mendip. The Cotswold requires two square metres of copper and one square metre each of wood and stainless steel. The Mendip requires one square metre of copper, two square metres of wood and one square metre of stainless steel. The profit on a Cotswold is £48 and on the Mendip is £40. The production of the fire surrounds is limited by the availability of raw material. The following materials are available: 90 square metres of copper, 80 square metres of wood and 50 square metres of stainless steel. The manufacturer wishes to use this material to make fire surrounds in a product mix that will maximise the profit. The model in this case will have more elements than the revenue model, taking account of the factors that constrain the situation and the variable elements. Examining the problem, two factors are variable – the number of each of the fire surrounds produced. There are constraining factors concerning the availability of raw materials and the amount of raw materials required to produce the different fire surrounds. The objective will be to make the maximum profit. Taking all these factors and putting them in a table will help the clarity of the problem.

Let x = the number of Cotswold fire surrounds produced
y = the number of Mendip fire surrounds produced

	Requirements		
Materials	COTSWOLD (x)	MENDIP (y)	*Available*
Copper	2	1	90
Wood		1	280
Stainless steel	1	1	50
Profit		£48	£40

This gives a clear view of the material required and available for the production of the fire surrounds. Each Cotswold made requires two square metres of copper and if x are made then the Cotswolds will need $2 \times x$ ($2x$) copper. Each Mendip made requires one square metre of copper and if y are made then the Mendips will need $1 \times y$ (y) copper. If we now add these two elements together ($2x + y$) we will have the total requirement for copper, but this must be less than or equal to ($\leqslant$) the amount of copper available, which is 90. This gives the first of the constraint equations for copper.

Copper $2x + y \leqslant 90$

In the same way the constraint equations for wood and stainless steel can be produced.

Wood $x + 2y \leqslant 80$
Stainless steel $x + y \leqslant 50$

There is another constraint that needs to be added – the production of the fire surrounds must not go below zero, i.e. x and y must be greater than or equal to ($\geqslant$) zero. This stops the model making negative numbers of fire surrounds.

The last part of the model is the element that gives the direction to the model – the objective function. The object of this model is to maximise profit (Z). For each Cotswold made there is a profit of £48 and x Cotswolds are made so that the profit on the Cotswold is $48 \times x$ ($48x$). Similarly, the Mendip has a profit of £40, therefore the profit on the Mendip is $40 \times y$ ($40y$). Adding these two elements together will give the total profit (Z).

The total model will be as follows:

Maximise $Z = 48x + 40y$

subject to $2x + y \leqslant 90$ copper constraint
$x + 2y \leqslant 80$ wood constraint
$x + y \leqslant 50$ stainless steel constraint
x and $y \geqslant 0$

To understand the constraints further it is best to turn them from a symbolic model to an analogue model. Let us first take the copper constraint and produce a graph of it.

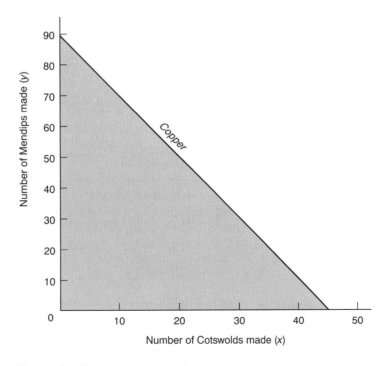

Figure 1.3   The copper constraint

This graph is produced by taking the copper constraint equation $2x + y \leq 90$ and first taking it to the limit $(2x + y = 90)$. To give the first point on the line calculate the number of Mendips (ys) that can be made if no Cotswolds (xs) are made:

If $x = 0$ then $2 \times 0 + y = 90$
$$y = 90$$

Similarly if only Cotswolds are made:

If $y = 0$ then $2x + 1 \times 0 = 90$
$$2x = 90$$
$$x = \frac{90}{2} = 45$$

If only Mendips are made then 90 can be made and if only Cotswolds are produced 45 can be made. These give the two extremes on the copper constraint graph. This is given in Figure 1.3.

This graph was produced assuming that the limit was to be produced, but the equation stated that the production would be less than or equal to ($\leq$). This means that production plans up to but within the line will satisfy the copper constraint, i.e. inside the shaded area.

Copper is only one constraint – there are the other constraints of wood and stainless steel. These constraints can be added to the copper constraint using the same process. The graph of all constraints is shown in Figure 1.4.

Feasible solutions can only exist inside all the constraint lines and will therefore only be inside the shaded area of Figure 1.4. In this problem we are searching for the feasible solution that gives the maximum profit referred to as the **optimum solution** (i.e. best solution). The optimum solution will lie on the boundary of the feasible region, and for reasons that will be outlined later the optimum solution will occur at points where constraints intersect on this boundary. Considering Figure 1.4, this gives four possible solutions: A (0,40) 0 xs produced and 40 ys produced; B (20,30); C (40,10); and D (45,0). To find which of these solutions is the optimum solution, they must be evaluated in the objective function $Z = 48x + 40y$ to determine the profit in each case.

Evaluation of possible optimum solutions:

A $Z_A = 48 \times 0 + 40 \times 40 = 0 + 1,600 = £1,600$

B $Z_B = 48 \times 20 + 40 \times 30 = 960 + 1,200 = £2,160$

C $Z_C = 48 \times 40 + 40 \times 10 = 1,920 + 400 = £2,320$

D $Z_D = 48 \times 45 + 40 \times 0 = 2,160 + 0 + £2,160$

The solution that gives the largest profit will be *optimum*. Therefore the optimum solution is C – 40 Cotswold fire surrounds and 10 Mendip fire surrounds giving a maximum profit of £2,320.

Let us now consider why this optimum solution should lie along the boundary of the feasible region and in particular lie at a point of intersection. The objective

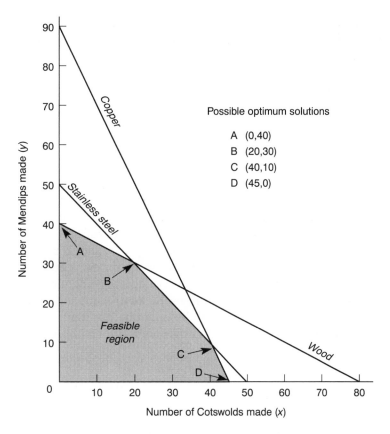

Figure 1.4   Copper, wood and stainless steel constraints

function is a linear (straight line) expression and can be added to the graph if a value for profit is added (i.e. replacing Z with a value for profit). The line produced is called an **Iso profit line** and shows production solutions that give the same profit. This profit will be the value chosen.

To construct an Iso profit line add the required profit into the objective function $Z = 48x + 40y$.

Iso profit £1,200

$$1,200 = 48x + 40y$$

The same procedure is used to add this line onto the same graph as the constraints. To give the first point of the line calculate the number of Mendips (*y*s) that need to be made to make a profit of £1,200, given that no Cotswolds (*x*s) are made.

$$1,200 = 48\ 0 + 40y$$
$$1,200 = 40y$$
$$\frac{1,200}{40} = y$$
$$30 = y$$

Similarly, the second point of the line can be calculated by finding the number of Cotswolds (x's) that need to be made to make a profit of £1,200, given that no Mendips (y's) are made.

$$1,200 = 48x + 40 \times 0$$
$$1,200 = 48x$$
$$\frac{1,200}{48} = x$$
$$25 = x$$

These two points will give the **Iso profit line** for £1,200 and it is added to the graph in Figure 1.5. Also added to the graph in this figure are the Iso profit lines for £1,800 and £2,320 (the optimum solution profit).

It can be seen from Figure 1.5 that Iso profit lines form a series of parallel lines moving away from the origin as the profit increases. The Iso profit line for £2,320 goes as far as an Iso profit line can go while still remaining in the feasible region. It also shows graphically why the optimum solution must lie at a point of intersection of constraints and that there will be only one optimum solution for a given set of conditions. The exception to the single solution is when the optimum Iso profit line

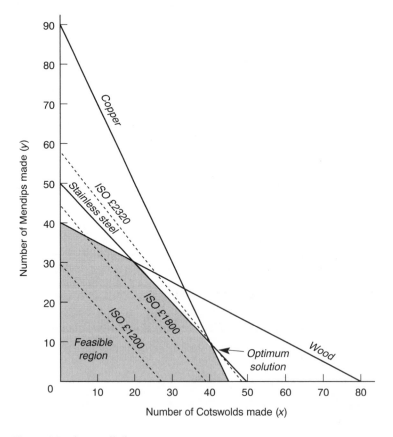

Figure 1.5   Iso profit lines

runs along one of the constraint lines. This will give two optimum solutions when the points of intersection are evaluated. Also, all the points along the constraint line between the two optimum solutions will also be optimum. This situation is not common.

It has already been said that modelling is about the production of a range of values and not single point answers. But the model we have just produced arrives at a single point optimum solution. This optimum solution is only valid for *exactly* the conditions used in building the model. The maximum value from the model is derived when a range of solutions are provided for a series of different conditions, i.e. sensitivity analysis. If solutions for a range of profit figures are required this will change the objective function for each of the profit figures. The graph will remain unchanged but the evaluation will have to be recalculated. Such an analysis will give the point where it becomes more profitable to make a different product mix. If the raw material requirements of the product are altered, this will change the constraint equations and therefore the graph. Similarly, if the availability of raw materials changes then this will also change the constraint equations and the graph.

This shows that even the value of optimising models producing a single answer lie in producing ranges of solutions for varying conditions. As a demonstration of how to carry this out let us consider one element of change. Suppose that it would

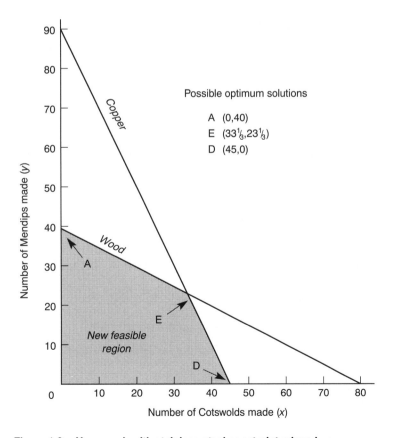

Figure 1.6   New graph with stainless steel constraint relaxed

be possible to obtain further supplies of stainless steel: would this increase profits? If stainless steel is no longer a constraining factor then the stainless steel constraint line will be removed from the graph. The new graph with the removed stainless steel constraint line is shown in Figure 1.6.

In relaxing the stainless steel constraint, solution A (0,40) and D (45,0) have remained but solutions at B and C have been replaced by solution E $(33\frac{1}{3}, 23\frac{1}{3})$. This creates a problem. With solution E it may be possible to make 33 Cotswolds but nobody wants a third of a Cotswold. Normal rounding cannot be used (it is not possible to ever round up or this will take the solution out of the feasible region). The only way rounding can be used is to round *down* in every case to give the integer solution required, i.e. E now becomes (33,23). This is an integer solution that could represent E but it may not be the best. It is therefore necessary to search the immediate vicinity of E to see if there is a better integer solution. The way to do this is to search for the first integer solution along each of the two constraints concerned (it is possible not to find any however).

This will give two possibilities for the best integer solution to represent point E. If a line is drawn between these points then the integer solutions inside this triangle are also considered. It is difficult to see this procedure at the scale of Figure 1.6 so an enlargement of solution point E is given in Figure 1.7.

Searching along the wood constraint the first integer solution is found at δ and is (32,24). Searching along the copper constraint the first integer solution is found at ϕ and is (34,22). If a line is drawn between these two points the only integer point within this triangle is γ and is (33,23), the solution that would have come from rounding E.

To find the integer solution to represent point E these possible integer solutions must be evaluated using the objective function $Z = 48x + 40y$.

$$\delta \ (32,24) \quad Z_\delta = 48 \times 32 + 40 \times 24 = 1,536 + 960 = £2,496$$

$$\gamma \ (33,23) \quad Z_\gamma = 48 \times 33 + 40 \times 23 = 1,584 + 920 = £2,504$$

$$\phi \ (34,22) \quad Z_\phi = 48 \times 34 + 40 \times 22 = 1,632 + 880 = £2,512$$

The best of these integer solutions (34,22) can now be used to represent point E, and the evaluation of the new situation can be carried out. With the relaxed stainless steel constraint there are three feasible solutions to be evaluated in order to determine the new optimum solution A(0,40), D(45,0) and E(34,22).

$$A \ \ Z_A = 48 \times 0 + 40 \times 40 = 0 + 1,600 = £1,600$$

$$D \ \ Z_D = 48 \times 45 + 40 \times 0 = 2,160 + 0 + £2,160$$

$$E \ \ Z_E = 48 \times 34 + 40 \times 22 = 1,632 + 880 = £2,512$$

Therefore, the new optimum solution if more stainless steel is available will be to produce 34 Cotswolds and 22 Mendips at a maximum profit of £2,512. The profit on this new solution is £192 more than that of the first solution, so a more profitable solution *does* exist if more stainless steel can be obtained.

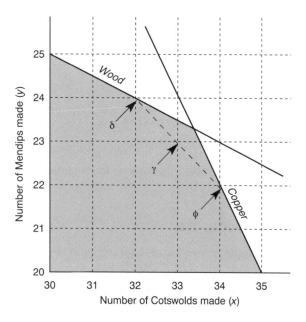

Figure 1.7   Enlargement of solution point E

This is just one example of how these linear models can be used to provide the predictions of what can occur under different conditions. This technique of modelling is called **linear programming** and we have solved this class of problem by graphical methods. Linear programming will be discussed later in Chapter 14 under the more general heading of Mathematical Programming.

Competence Example 1.2

At the end of this section you should now be able to demonstrate how to:

1 construct straight line resource constraints

2 identify and construct maximisation functions

3 optimise simple resource-constrained models

4 apply sensitivity analysis to simple resource-constrained models

To practise and demonstrate these competences complete example problems 1.3. to 1.6 at the end of this chapter. To help you to develop these competences, a description of the procedure you will need to follow is now given, along with a typical problem format. This problem format is based on the example we have just considered.

PROCEDURE (GRAPHICAL LINEAR PROGRAMMING)

❶ Identify and annotate the variables.

❷ Tabulate the problem with the constraints, the requirements, the availability and the monetary considerations.

❸ Construct the objective function.

❹ Construct the constraint equations.

❺ Determine where the equations cut the axis on the graph.

❻ Construct the graph.

❼ Identify the feasible region.

❽ Identify possible optimum solutions (you may need to use the integer solution sub-routine).

❾ Use the objective function to determine the optimum solution.

❿ Identify the range of sensitivity analysis to be carried out.

⓫ Carry out the sensitivity analysis.

INTEGER SOLUTION SUB-ROUTINE

1. Identify non integer solution at an intersection on the graph.

2. Search along each axis to find the first integer solution. (WARNING: it is possible although unlikely that you may not find an integer along an axis.)

3. Form a triangle between two solutions on the axis and identify other integer solutions in or along the bottom line of the triangle.

4. Use the objective function to determine the best integer solution to represent the intersection on the graph.

PROBLEM

A manufacturer can make two products. Both are fancy fire surrounds – one is called the Cotswold, the other the Mendip. The Cotswold requires two square metres of copper and one square metre each of wood and stainless steel. The Mendip requires one square metre of copper, two square metres of wood and one square metre of stainless steel. The profit on a Cotswold is £48 and on the Mendip is £40. The production of the fire surrounds is limited by the availability of raw material. The following materials are available: 90 square metres of copper, 80 square metres of wood and 50 square metres of stainless steel. The manufacturer wishes to use this material to make fire surrounds in a product mix that will maximise the profit.

A description of the layout of the solution format is given at the beginning of the book.

SOLUTION

❶ Let x = the number of Cotswold fire surrounds produced

    y = the number of Mendip fire surrounds produced

❷

Materials	Requirements		Available
	COTSWOLD (x)	MENDIP (y)	
Copper	2	1	90
Wood	1	2	80
Stainless steel	1	1	50
Profit	£48	£40	

❸ Maximise $Z = 48x + 40y$

18

4 subject to $2x + y \leqslant 90$ copper constraint
$\qquad x + 2y \leqslant 80$ wood constraint
$\qquad x + y \leqslant 50$ stainless steel constraint
$\qquad x$ and $y \geqslant 0$

1

5 Determine intersections with the x and y axis:

Cut x	Cut y	Constraint
45	90	Copper
80	40	Wood
50	50	Stainless steel

3

6 7 8

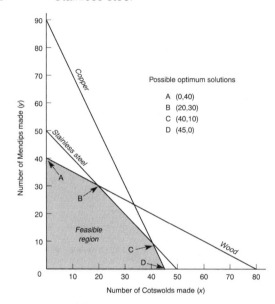

Possible optimum solutions

A (0,40)
B (20,30)
C (40,10)
D (45,0)

9 Evaluation of possible optimum solution:

$\qquad$ A $Z_A = 48 \times 0 + 40 \times 40 = 0 + 1{,}600 = £1{,}600$

$\qquad$ B $Z_B = 48 \times 20 + 40 \times 30 = 960 + 1{,}200 = £2{,}160$

$\qquad$ C $Z_C = 48 \times 40 + 40 \times 10 = 1{,}920 + 400 = £2{,}320$ (maximum value)

$\qquad$ D $Z_D = 42 \times 45 + 40 \times 0 = 2{,}160 + 0 = £2{,}160$

Therefore the optimum solution is C to make 40 Cotswold fire surrounds and 10 Mendip fire surrounds giving a maximum profit of £2,320.

10 Suppose that it would be possible to obtain further supplies of stainless steel. Would this increase profits? Remove stainless steel constraint and evaluate new solutions. (Please refer to Fig 1.6 on p. 15 and Fig 1.7 on p. 17)

4

11 To find the integer solution to represent point E evaluate possible integer solutions against the objective function:

$\qquad$ $Z = 48x + 40y$

$\qquad$ δ (32,24) $Z_\delta = 48 \times 32 + 40 \times 24 = 1{,}536 + 960 = £2{,}496.$

$\qquad$ γ (33,23) $Z_\gamma = 48 \times 33 + 40 \times 23 = 1{,}584 + 920 = £2{,}504$

$\qquad$ ϕ (34,22) $Z_\phi = 48 \times 34 + 40 \times 22 = 1{,}632 + 880 = £2{,}512$

⑪ The best of these integer solutions (34,22) can now be used to represent point E. The **4** evaluation of the new situation can now be carried out. With the relaxed stainless steel constraint there are three feasible solutions to be evaluated to determine the new optimum solution A(0,40), D(45,0) and E(34,22).

A $Z_A = 48 \times 0 + 40 \times 40 = 0 + 1,600 = £1,600$

D $Z_D = 48 \times 45 + 40 \times 0 = 2,160 + 0 = £2,160$

E $Z_E = 48 \times 34 + 40 \times 22 = 1,632 + 880 = £2,512$

Therefore the new optimum solution if more stainless steel is available will be to produce 34 Cotswolds and 22 Mendips at a maximum profit of £2,512. The profit on this new solution is £192 more than that of the first solution so a more profitable solution does exist if more stainless steel can be obtained.

Practise your competence now on problems 1.3 to 1.6 at the end of the chapter. Linear programming is not contained on the computer disk provided with this book. The reasons for this and a brief further development of linear programming into the more general mathematical programming will be considered as part of Chapter 10 at the end of the book. It is not advised that you attempt to demonstrate the competence you have developed in this area on problems from your work environment. This is best left until you have worked through Chapter 10 and completed the remainder of the book, and even then only attempted with extreme care.

1.6 Validation and implementation of models

The validation and implementation of models are closely linked. The validation of a model is the testing to ensure that the model replicates the situation being modelled. The modelling process can be illustrated using the diagram shown in Figure 1.8.

The process shows that the route from the real world problem is not direct to a real world solution. The problem first has to be structured to allow a model to be constructed. It is important to validate the model against the real world to ensure that these initial stages have been carried out correctly. Mistakes and false

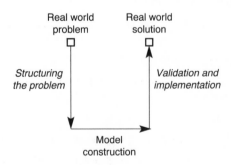

Figure 1.8   Modelling process

assumptions can be made at either the problem structuring or model construction stage. The validation process means running the model with a set of conditions from the real world for which the results have already been observed. The results from the model are then tested with the real world results to ensure that there is no significant difference. If a significant difference is observed, the structuring or model must be modified until it is removed.

The validation process is therefore an important part of implementation. An issue concerning implementation is very neatly summed up with the following saying:

'Managers would sooner live with a problem they cannot solve rather than accept a solution they cannot understand.'

This says that managers will only accept a 'black box' providing they understand the process it is using and believe it will produce *real* solutions. This means there are two vital elements needed in a successful implementation.

First, the manager must have sufficient understanding of the process of the model to realise its potential and recognise its value. This is not necessarily a detailed knowledge that enables them to *build* models, but sufficient knowledge to enable them to understand the models that have been built. This book is aimed to provide the latter. This also means that the providers of models are not just in the business of modelling but also in the provision of some of the knowledge about how to use them.

The second important element is the belief by the manager that the model will provide valid answers. The problem of validity has already been considered but the need of managers highlights how important it is to validate the model. This validation of the model can play a major part in convincing managers that the model will produce valid real world solutions. These two key elements are extremely important for successful implementation.

The skills required for the modelling process are varied. To take real world problems and structure them in such a way as to allow the construction of models requires considerable knowledge of the organisation or area being modelled. Contrary to myth, successful modelling is not carried out in organisations by individuals with little knowledge of that organisation. There is also a considerable 'art' to the structuring of problems for model construction. The model construction stage will require skills in the mathematical and computing stage. This will be to take the structured problem and turn it into a model and then to validate the model. There will also be considerable behavioural skills needed to implement the model. For the model to be used by managers it will almost certainly need to be sold to management, so selling skills will be needed.

There are very few individuals with all these skills. The best approach for modelling in most organisations is to use a team of individuals to provide all these skills. Although the team may not work full time on the building of models, the people with the appropriate skills will be involved. An important member of the team must be an end user of the model. This will help considerably with the implementation of such a model. Working on the building of a model will give the commitment to its implementation.

This important stage of validation and implementation will be highlighted again when the various modelling areas are discussed in detail.

1.7 Predicting with models

One of the main uses of modelling is that of predicting. The model is there to provide not a single answer but a range of solutions for a series of differing conditions. What makes the whole process attractive for management is that the experimenting with the different conditions can be carried out at a fraction of the cost of experimenting directly with the real world. The time taken to carry out the experimentation with models will also be considerably less than experimenting with the real world. Also, with some situations it is not possible to experiment with the real world; therefore in these cases only models can be used. The power and value of models comes from using them to give a range of solutions for varying conditions.

There are dangers in using models in prediction and again this can be best seen from an example. This example is the only one in the book that is not related to management but it will provide a saying which is useful when placing predictions in perspective for reality. The example concerns a television programme that appeared on BBC Television a few years ago called *Before the Ark*. The programme was produced in conjunction with the British Museum and was about dinosaurs. An expert from the British Museum introduced an expert from one of the American universities. This pedigree would suggest credibility for any ideas developed in the programme.

The American expert in the programme took a variety of lizards living today. He measured the length of the lizards' leg and recorded how fast they could run. The data was then used to produce a relationship between the length of leg of lizards and the speed at which they can run. The expert then said that dinosaurs were large lizards and used his models for the lizards living today to predict how fast dinosaurs could run.

He started with Tyrannosaurus, which was about 12 metres long and when standing on its rear legs stood five metres tall and probably weighed about eight tons (almost the weight of two elephants). He measured the length of leg of Tyrannosaurus and using the lizard model predicted the speed at which it could run. The speed came to 65 mph! He then moved on to Diplodocus, which was about 27 metres long and probably weighed about 10 tons (although some of its close relatives could weigh up to 80 tons, the weight of 16 elephants). Diplodocus and its relatives have shorter legs and our American expert predicted their speed at only 45 mph. Imagine a 27 metre long, 80 ton dinosaur travelling at 45 mph – it may give you some new and rather original ideas as to why the dinosaurs died out.

The original lizard model had a largest leg length of 20 centimetres and yet it was used to predict speeds for leg lengths of three metres. This is some 15 times more than the largest lizard leg used to develop the model. This example clearly shows the danger of predicting a long way away from the range of conditions for which the model was validated. The prediction of dinosaurs travelling at 65 mph also puts a considerable strain on reality.

Making bad predictions in the case of dinosaurs has little effect on the world of today. However, bad predictions made in management situations can have catastrophic results, causing considerable loss or bankruptcy.

This example gives an important moral to predicting with models. Wherever predictions are made with a model always take a moment to think of reality. Ask the question, 'Is this prediction a 65 mph dinosaur?', a question which should always remind you of the dangers that are possible when using models for predicting incorrectly.

Summary

Modelling can prove a powerful and extremely valuable aid to management in the decision-making and planning process. It can provide predictions at an economic rate and allow experimentation on processes difficult or very costly to change in reality.

Care should be taken when reading the rest of this book. To structure the book it has been divided into chapters covering different areas. These are not watertight compartments in modelling and any model may use ideas from several areas. Therefore wherever possible the connections between areas will be shown.

This first chapter of the book will have developed your understanding of models and linear equations. The following problems will provide the opportunity for you to practise and demonstrate these competences. You will find that these are manufacturing examples – the reason for this will be explained when linear programming is looked at again in Chapter 10.

Problems for Chapter 1

1.1 To produce a particular product there exist two elements of cost: a fixed cost of £2,000 and a variable cost of £50 for each unit produced. The revenue for each unit sold is £70. Carry out a break-even analysis for this product. It has also been estimated that the variable cost could be as low as £42 or as high as £64. Carry out a sensitivity analysis on the effect of this variability on the break-even analysis.

1.2 To produce a particular product there exist two elements of cost: a fixed cost of £385,000 and a variable cost of £15 for each unit produced. The revenue for each unit sold is £23. Carry out a break-even analysis for this product. It has also been estimated that the variable cost could be as low as £10 or as high as £20. Carry out a sensitivity analysis on the effect of this variability on the break-even analysis.

1.3 A light engineering firm has the following material available: 16 square metres of sheet steel, 11 square metres of sheet copper and 15 square metres of sheet brass. The firm produces high quality barbecues in two varieties – the 'old Western' style (Rawhide) and the 'old Spanish' style (Seville). The Rawhide requires two square metres of steel, one square metre of copper and one square metre of brass. A Seville requires one square metre of steel, two square metres of copper and three square metres of brass. The Rawhide returns a profit of £30 and the Seville returns a profit of £50 for each item.

a) How many of each product should the firm make to obtain the maximum profit?

b) If an unlimited amount of sheet copper is available would it pay the firm to buy more and if so, how much more would be required?

1.4 Taper pins are processed in a factory on two lathes, A and B (in that order) and also on a grinder. The taper pins are produced in two sizes – small and large. The following table shows the processing time in hours per load required on each machine for the two types of pins. It also gives the net profit per load for each type and the maximum time available on each of the machines weekly.

| | Pin type | | Hours |
	Small size	Large size	Available
Lathe A	4	5	50
Lathe B	3	6	50
Grinder	6	3	60
Profit per Load	£60	£90	

a) Using the graphical method of linear programming determine how many loads of each size taper pin the factory should produce in order to obtain maximum profit for the week's operation. Processing is essentially continuous, so the optimum schedule can be in terms of fractional loads.

b) If, because of sales commitments, the factory must produce at least six loads of the small size, how would the production schedule and the profit change?

1.5 A chemical company owns two salt extraction facilities. The Dunsmoor facility produces ten tons of table grade salt, 30 tons of food-processing grade salt and 50 tons of road grade salt each day. The Hillhouse facility produces 20 tons of each of the grades of salt each day. The company requires 800 tons of table grade salt, 1,600 tons of food-processing grade salt and 2,000 tons of road grade salt.

a) Using the graphical approach to linear programming determine how many days each facility should be operated to minimise the cost given each facility costs £200,000 each day to operate. *Be careful with this problem because it is a minimisation problem. The constraint equations will need to be greater than or equal to ($\geq$) rather than less than or equal to ($\leq$) and the feasible region will be unbounded on the outside of the graph rather than on the inside.*

b) How much salt will be left after the requirements have been met and what type is it?

c) If the requirement for food-processing grade salt could take any value how would this affect the original solution?

1.6 A manufacturer has the following raw materials available: 240 units of wood, 370 units of plastic and 180 units of metal. Product A requires 1, 3 and 2 units of wood, plastic and steel respectively. Product B requires 3, 4 and 1 units of wood, plastic and steel respectively. If product A returns a profit of £40 and product B returns a profit of £60 how many of each should be made to maximise profit? If more plastic could be obtained would this have a significant effect on the optimum solution?

2 The role of IT
help from a friendly PC

2.1 Introduction

This chapter will explore the way in which quantitative modelling can be supported and helped by using a personal computer. In particular it will examine the role of the spreadsheet in quantitative modelling. Spreadsheets will be looked at in two ways: first from a general use perspective to help you develop the basic skills of spreadsheet construction; and second as an introduction to the spreadsheet disk provided with this book. Given the popularity of both Lotus and Excel both are considered in this chapter and the book. The choice is yours. If you have access to Lotus, then work through the first part of the chapter then move to the final section on the Computer Support Disk ignoring the section on Excel. If you have access to Excel, then ignore the first section on Lotus and move to the section on Excel and on to the section on the Computer Support Disk. This chapter will be different to the other chapters, it will specify the detailed competences being developed but it will develop these using a short open learning package we have found to be very successful in developing these skills in managers. The example used in this package is a very general one, not based on a particular area of quantitative modelling. You will not be asked to practise and demonstrate these competences at the end of the chapter but in the later parts of the book when you have developed the skills and underpinning knowledge in these modelling areas. If you are already confident you have the required skills in spreadsheets you may proceed to the last section of this chapter which suggests the way in which the disk provided with the book should be used.

2.2 Computer spreadsheets using Lotus 1-2-3

This section of Chapter 2 will enable you to:

- understand the use of spreadsheets
- start up Lotus 1-2-3
- exit from Lotus 1-2-3
- move about the spreadsheet
- enter labels
- enter numbers
- construct formulae

- save and retrieve files on disk
- use the HELP function
- use the SUM and AVERAGE functions
- print worksheets
- create line graphs
- create bar graphs
- create pie charts
- save and retrieve graphs on disk
- print graphs

This section will also provide the underpinning knowledge in the area of spreadsheets.

A spreadsheet is just like a large sheet of squared paper where you would write down numbers in rows and columns and perform calculations on them. On paper you would add some numbers together, subtract some and multiply others until you found an answer. Managers use spreadsheets to work out a whole range of calculations in many areas of their work. Before computer spreadsheets, hundreds of sales figures, costs and expenses would be written down on paper and then a calculator would be used to work out the final profit etc., from all the figures. This could take hours, and what happened if one of the numbers was entered into the calculator wrongly? You'd have to start again!

Also, and more importantly, before the use of computer-based spreadsheets company profit forecasting was done in the same way. Instead of actual figures, a forecast shows what a company expects to sell or expects things to cost over a certain period of time.

When all these hours of work have been done, and many large sheets of paper have been filled with numbers, the company may suddenly think, 'What will our final profit be if we can reduce some costs in May or increase sales in June?' They would then have to go back to their sheets of paper, change the costs in May, change the sales in June, and work out all the numbers again until they reached the profit figure – many hours of work every time they wanted to change some of their sales or cost estimates.

A computer-based spreadsheet will do these hours of work in seconds or minutes. Once you have typed in the numbers and told it which numbers to add together, subtract, multiply, etc., it will automatically work out the final profit figure, thousands of times faster than you could work it out on paper with a calculator.

Now, if the company wants to know what will happen to the final profit if some costs are reduced or sales are increased, all they have to do is change some numbers on the computer spreadsheet and, in seconds, all the numbers will automatically be worked out again.

They can do this over and over again for many different costs and sales forecasts, saving many hours each time they use the computer spreadsheet.

This power to change numbers and still have the answer automatically worked out is one of the main reasons companies first bought personal computers and spreadsheets. In just a few days, the time they saved and the more accurate forecasts they could make would more than pay for the computer.

Apart from forecasts, the computer spreadsheet can be used for scientific calculations, balancing your cheque book account, and any other application where you would write numbers on a sheet of paper and perform calculations on them. In this book we are going to use them to automate the calculation elements of the modelling approaches and to allow us an easy way of producing a sensitivity analysis on the models used. It is not essential to use spreadsheets but you will find it makes life so much easier.

2.3 The spreadsheet learning package using Lotus 1-2-3

The spreadsheet we will look at in this part of the chapter is called Lotus 1-2-3. It's one of the most powerful spreadsheets on the market for a personal computer and is one often used as an industry standard. Lotus is in fact much more – it can provide graphical information of figures in a variety of forms. It even has a built-in database. Once you have developed the ability to use Lotus you will find the transfers to other spreadsheet packages easy. You have an idea of what a spreadsheet is by now, so let's get started on Lotus 1-2-3. The way to work through this package is with the computer switched on and the book open in front of you – it is a package to *do*, not just to read.

Where you are required to enter a series of alpha or numeric characters from the text into the machine they will be given in bold type, e.g. **LOTUS**. This requires you to type in **LOTUS**.

Where a single function key is to be entered this will be given in bold type followed by the word 'key'.

e.g. press **RETURN** key

Simple italics will be used to show you what should appear on the screen.

2.4 Creating a spreadsheet using Lotus 1-2-3

2.4.1 Starting up

This package assumes you have a personal computer with a hard disk. It can be used on a computer without a hard disk but you will need to amend the text to use the A: drive.

Switch on your hard disk computer.

To begin with, check that Lotus 1-2-3 has been installed onto the hard disk within a directory named 123. To carry out this installation follow the directions given in the Appendix or in your Lotus 1-2-3 manual.

When C> appears on the screen type in:

cd 123 and press the **RETURN** key

This changes the directory on the hard disk to the directory allocated to Lotus. C> will then reappear on the screen. Then type in:

LOTUS and press the **RETURN** key

The Lotus 1-2-3 main menu now appears on your screen. 1-2-3 is already highlighted in the top left-hand corner of the screen. Simply press the **RETURN** key to enter the spreadsheet.

Wait until the blank Lotus spreadsheet appears. You will notice in the top left-hand corner of the spreadsheet a highlighted cell with a flashing symbol which is called the *cursor*.

2.4.2   Moving about the spreadsheet

Now locate the cursor arrow keys ← ↑ → ↓ on the right-hand side of the keyboard. Use these to move the cursor around the spreadsheet. When you have finished experimenting, press the **HOME** key to return to cell A1. (A *cell* is the basic unit of a spreadsheet and each cell has its own individual reference or address – just like a home.)

Now press the **F5** key, a special function key on the left-hand side or top of your keyboard. At the top of the screen you will see *Enter address to go to A1*. Type **E7** and press the **RETURN** key. The cursor automatically jumps to cell E7. The display in the top left-hand corner of the screen now shows E7, which is the current address of the cursor.

Next, press the **END** key and the down arrow key (↓). This takes you to the bottom of the spreadsheet. Note how many rows the spreadsheet contains. Press the **END** key again, followed by the right arrow key (→). This will take you to the right-hand edge of the spreadsheet. Note the letters displayed at the top of the spreadsheet. You have now seen the full extent of the Lotus 1-2-3 spreadsheet. Press the **HOME** key to return to cell A1.

2.4.3   Exiting from Lotus 1-2-3

In order to leave Lotus 1-2-3 and return to the operating system, press the slash key (/) which is just above the right-hand edge of the spacebar. This will bring up the command menu. Move the cursor using the right arrow key until QUIT is highlighted. Press the **RETURN** key to accept it. Lotus 1-2-3 again asks if you are sure you want to leave. Press **Y** for yes, which returns you to the opening menu. Move the cursor with the right arrow key until EXIT is highlighted and press the **RETURN** key. This exits you from Lotus 1-2-3 and returns you to the C> display in the top corner of the screen.

2.4.4   Construction of a simple spreadsheet

Load up the Lotus 1-2-3 spreadsheet as before. Move the cursor to cell B5 using the arrow keys. Type in **Rent** and press the down arrow key to enter.

Note that when you are typing in the titles in the top right-hand corner of the screen the box changed from READY to LABEL because Lotus 1-2-3 assumed that you were entering a label. It returns to READY when the label has been entered.

Next type in **Water** and press the down arrow key (if you make any typing errors use the back-space key to correct them).

Type in **Electricity** – press the down arrow key
Type in **Phone** – press the down arrow key twice
Type in **Total** – press the **RETURN** key

Now move to cell C3.

Type in **1992** – press the right arrow key
Type in **1993** – press the **RETURN** key

Now move to cell C5.

Type in **1023** – press the down arrow key
Type in **348** – press the down arrow key
Type in **211** – press the down arrow key
Type in **161** – press the **RETURN** key

If you have entered a wrong number, move the cursor back to that cell, re-type the number and press the **RETURN** key. You will also notice that the last part of **Electricity** has gone missing. Do not worry – this problem will be dealt with later in the learning package.

Now move to cell D5.

Type in **1053** – press the down arrow key
Type in **432** – press the down arrow key
Type in **198** – press the down arrow key
Type in **183** – press the down arrow key twice

2.4.5   Entering formulae

To add the numbers in column D and enter the amount in cell D10, leave the cursor at cell D10 and type:

+ **D5** + **D6** + **D7** + **D8**

Note the + sign which tells Lotus 1-2-3 you are entering a formula. Now press the **RETURN** key. The total for row D has been summed and entered in the cell D10. Move the cursor to cell C10 and type in:

+ **C5** + **C6** + **C7** + **C8** and press the **RETURN** key

Also note that the formula is displayed in the top left-hand corner of the screen, even though the value is in cell C10.

Now try entering other values and watch the totals change automatically as they are recalculated by Lotus 1-2-3.

Move the cursor to cell E3.

Type in:

Change £ and press the down arrow key twice

Type in:

+ **D5-C5** and press the **RETURN** key

This time use Lotus 1-2-3's copy function to repeat the formula into the other cells. Press the slash key (/) and then type in **C** for copy. To enter the range to copy from, simply press the **RETURN** key to accept the cell you are in (cell E5). Then type a **full stop** (.) to anchor the cursor and press the down arrow key until the highlighting includes cell E8. Press the **RETURN** key to enter. Note that all the values have been calculated automatically. Also notice the formulae displayed in the top left-hand corner of the screen. Even though we copied the formula from cell E5, Lotus 1-2-3 adjusts the formula appropriately.

Now go to cell F3 and type in **Change %** and press the down arrow key twice. Type +**E5/C5** and press the **RETURN** key. Press the slash key (/) and type **C** for copy. Press the **RETURN** key for the range to copy from and then type a **full stop** to anchor the cursor. Move the cursor to cell F8 to highlight the range to copy to, and press the **RETURN** key.

To format values to percentages, type /**r** for range, then press the **RETURN** key to accept format. Type in **p** for percentage and **0** for the number of decimal places. Press the **RETURN** key and enter F5..F8 as the range of cells to format. Press the **RETURN** key and the values are now displayed as percentages.

2.4.6 Saving your work to disk

Finally, in order to save the spreadsheet, type **/** for the command menu, **f** for file, **s** for save, and enter an appropriate filename and press the **RETURN** key. The filename must not be more than eight characters long and cannot have any spaces. Now **EXIT** from Lotus.

2.4.7 Retrieving your files from disk

This time load up Lotus 1-2-3 the quick way, without going through the opening menu, by simply typing **123** and pressing the **RETURN** key. Type /**f** and press the **RETURN** key to accept RETRIEVE. The prompt line asks *Name of file to retrieve*: C:\123*.wk?

Underneath the prompt line is a menu of worksheets stored on the data disc. Move the cursor along to the file you wish to retrieve and press the **RETURN** key. The worksheet file is now displayed on the screen.

To obtain a blank worksheet again type **/** and press the **RETURN** key to accept WORKSHEET. Then type **e** for erase and **y** to confirm you want to erase the worksheet. This only erases the worksheet on the screen – it is still stored on your data disk.

2.4.8 The HELP function

Look at the function keys on the left of your keyboard. You should have a Lotus 1-2-3 template over them. If you haven't, ask. This should be with your manual.

Press the **F1** key (the 'help' key). After you have read the help screen titled READY MODE, move the cursor using the down arrow key until HELP INDEX is highlighted. Now press the **RETURN** key. Then press the **RETURN** key again to accept *Using the Help Facility*. Read the screen and when you have finished, return to the HELP INDEX. Now, using the cursor, select additional help screens on some other topics. Spend some time exploring the help facility – after all, it is there to help you! When you have finished, return to the current worksheet by pressing the **ESCAPE** key.

2.4.9 Exploring the menus

Press / and move the cursor along using the right arrow key to highlight each title in turn – note that the line beneath the menu changes to display the various options available when that option is selected.

When you are at the end of the top line menu press **w** to select WORKSHEET. Again move the cursor along the top menu line and look at the line beneath for a description of each option. When you have reached the end of the line, press **s** to select STATUS. This displays the current status of the worksheet. It shows the available memory, the recalculation mode (the default setting is automatic), various cell display information, and that the ***global protection*** is set off. We will explore these areas more fully in more advanced packages later. For now, simply note that the entries on a worksheet can be protected to prevent values being changed. (The default setting is the setting the computer assumes when the user has not specified a different setting.)

Now, return to the worksheet by pressing the **ESCAPE** key. This key is useful to remember if you make a mistake in selecting an option; by pressing it you 'escape' from the latest option selected to the previous one.

2.4.10 Continuing with your example worksheet

Retrieve your worksheet as before. Move the cursor to cell B10. You are now going to practise using the ERASE command. Type in **/re**. Enter **range** to erase: B10..B10 appears at the top of your screen. Press the right arrow key twice to highlight the range to be erased and press the **RETURN** key. Now move the cursor up to cell B9.

Type in **Stationery** – press the down arrow key
Type in **Equipment** – press the down arrow key
Type in **Petrol** – press the down arrow key
Type in **Purchases** – press the down arrow key twice
Type in **Total** – press the **RETURN** key

Now move to cell C9.

Type in **56** – press the down arrow key
Type in **569** – press the down arrow key
Type in **66** – press the down arrow key
Type in **2065** – press the **RETURN** key

So that the titles are not covered up by the numbers, we need to widen column B. Move the cursor to cell B12, type **/** and press the **RETURN** key, then type **c**. *Set width of current column* now appears above the worksheet. Press the **RETURN** key again. *Enter column width (1..240):9* now appears. Type **11** and this will change the column width to 11 after you press the **RETURN** key. The titles are now all visible. Note that even though the numbers in column C overlaid part of the titles from column B, the ends of the titles were still 'there'.

2.4.11   Using the summing function

Move the cursor to cell C14. Type in **@SUM(C5..C12)** and press the **RETURN** key. The value of adding cells C5 to C12 now appears in cell C14, and the formula is still being displayed at the top of the spreadsheet. This is a more efficient way of summing a set of cells than constructing your own formulae, particularly when it is a large set.

Now move to cell D9.

Type in **71** – press the down arrow key
Type in **611** – press the down arrow key
Type in **53** – press the down arrow key
Type in **3053** – press the down arrow key twice

Use the **copy** command to copy the formula from C14 to D14. Type **/c** and **C14** for the range to copy from. Press the **RETURN** key twice. Now copy the formula from E8 to E9:E12 and from F8 to F9:F12.

2.4.12   Using the average function

Go to cell E18. Type **AVERAGE** and press the down arrow key. Now type in **CHANGE %** and press the **RETURN** key. Move the cursor to cell F19. Enter the formula **@AVG(F5..F12)** and press the **RETURN** key. Now format the cell by typing **/r** and press the **RETURN** key. Type **P** to select per cent, enter ϕ for the number of decimal places and press the **RETURN** key. Now press the **RETURN** key to accept the cursor position as the range to format.

2.4.13   Saving your updated worksheets

Now save your worksheet as before. Type in **/f** for FILE, then **s** for SAVE. Lotus 1-2-3 will ask you to *Enter save filename C:\123*wk1*. Press the **RETURN** key to accept the highlighted filename, which is the only one on your data disk at present. You will now be asked if you want to cancel or replace. Type in **r** for REPLACE. Lotus 1-2-3 will now replace the original worksheet with the updated one you have just produced. (Note that the original worksheet is now deleted.)

2.4.14 Printing your worksheet

Only attempt this part of the learning package if you have a printer attached to your computer. Check first that the printer is ON LINE.

To print your spreadsheet, first ensure that the cursor is in the top left-hand corner of your spreadsheet. Type in **/** for the command menu, type in **p** and then type **p** again to select the ***printer menu***. Type in **r** to enter the range over which you want to print. Type in a **full stop** to anchor the range in the top left-hand comer. Using the arrow keys move the cursor to the bottom right-hand corner of the part of the spreadsheet you want to print (the part that will be printed will be highlighted on the screen). Press the **RETURN** key to accept this range. This will return you to the print menu. Type an **a** to align the printer, then **g** for go and your spreadsheet will be printed.

2.5 Creating graphs from a spreadsheet using Lotus 1-2-3

This section will take you through the process of creating graphs with Lotus. Considerably more time is spent on the competences and underpinning knowledge of data presentation in Chapter 3.

2.5.1 Creating a line graph

Start off by loading up Lotus 1-2-3 and retrieving your worksheet as before. To produce a graph, type in **/g** then press the **RETURN** key to accept TYPE. Lotus 1-2-3 now offers you a selection of graph types to choose from. Press the **RETURN** key to accept LINE. To define the X-axis for the graph, type **x**. Type in **b5..b12** for the X-axis range and press the **RETURN** key. Now define the A data range by typing **a** and then **c5..c12** for the data range. If you now select VIEW by typing **v** you will see a line graph for the 1992 expenses.

2.5.2 Creating a bar graph

Press the **RETURN** key to return to your worksheet. Now select TYPE again by typing in **t** and then **b** to select a BAR graph. Then select VIEW by typing **v**. (The X-axis and data range are still the same but the graph is now displayed as a bar graph.) Press the **RETURN** key to get back to your worksheet. Now select a second data range by typing **b**. Type in **d5..d12** for the second data range. Now type **v** to VIEW the graph. You now have the 1992 and 1993 expenses on the bar graph for easy comparison.

2.5.3 Labelling your graphs

As it stands, the graph is not very clear. To put in some labels and a title press the **RETURN** key to get back to your worksheet and type **o** to select OPTIONS. Press the **RETURN** key to accept LEGEND and the **RETURN** key again to select data range A. Type in **Expenses 1992** and press the **RETURN** key. Now press the **RETURN** key to select LEGEND again and then type **b** to select the data range B. Type in **Expenses 1993** and press the **RETURN** key. Now, to enter a TITLE type **t** and press the **RETURN** key to accept FIRST. Type in your title **Expenses 1992/93** and press the **RETURN** key. Press the **RETURN** key again and then type **x** for the title X-axis. Type in **Type of Expenses** and press the **RETURN** key. Press the **RETURN** key again and type **y** for a title for the Y-axis. Type in **Amount £** and press the **RETURN** key. Now type **q** to select QUIT and then **v** to VIEW your graph with the added labels.

2.5.4 Saving a graph for later use

To save a graph with your worksheet so that you can call it up again the next time you use Lotus 1-2-3, type **n** for NAME and then **c** for CREATE. Type in the title **EXPBAR1**, and press the **RETURN** key. Now press the **RETURN** key to accept NAME and the **RETURN** key again to accept USE. EXPBAR1 is now listed on a menu here – simply press the **RETURN** key to accept the highlighted name as the graph to view. Now if you save your worksheet again, exit from Lotus 1-2-3 and then reload Lotus 1-2-3 and retrieve your worksheet, the graph will still be saved under the name EXPBAR1.

2.5.5 Saving a graph for later printing

Press the **RETURN** key to get back to your worksheet. Now type **s** to select SAVE and type in **EXPBAR1** for the graph filename to be saved. Then press the **RETURN** key to save the graph on your data disk as a 'picture' file. The filename will be EXPBAR1.PIC. Later on we will see how to print this graph.

2.5.6 Creating a pie chart

Finally, to create a pie chart type in **r** for RESET and press the **RETURN** key to cancel all graph settings. Now type **t** for TYPE and **p** to select PIE. Then type x and **b5..b12** for the X-axis range and press the **RETURN** key. Now type in **a** and **c5..c12** to define the A data range. Then type **v** to VIEW your pie graph. You can enter a title as before.

2.5.7 Printing your graph

Only attempt this part of the learning package if you have a printer attached to your computer. Check first that the printer is ON LINE.

To print the graph you have saved earlier as the file EXPBAR1.PIC, exit from 1-2-3 by typing **/q** for QUIT and then **y** to confirm. You will now see the original menu for Lotus, so type in **p** to select PrintGraph. Press the **RETURN** key to accept IMAGE-SELECT, move your cursor to EXPBAR1 and press the **SPACEBAR** to select it as the graph you want to print. Now press the **RETURN** key and type **a** to align the printer. Assuming all is well, type in **g** for GO and the graph will be printed. You will have to wait patiently as the printer can take a while to print out the graph.

Competence Example 2.1

At the end of this section you should be able to demonstrate how to:

1 understand the use of spreadsheets

2 start up Lotus 1-2-3

3 exit from Lotus 1-2-3

4 move about the spreadsheet

5 enter labels

6 enter numbers

7 construct formulae

8 save and retrieve files on disk

9 use the HELP function

10 use the SUM and AVERAGE functions

12 print worksheets

13 create line graphs

14 create bar graphs

15 create pie charts

16 save and retrieve graphs on disk

17 print graphs

You will now be able to practise and demonstrate these basic competences on a range of quantitative modelling approaches throughout the rest of the book. It is more desirable that you develop spreadsheets in areas you will be using later rather than any general areas we could create at this stage in the book. You may, however, wish to demonstrate these competences by creating spreadsheets from your own work experience. It is possible to work through the text without using spreadsheets but we would strongly advise their use, given the way in which they will reduce the burden of calculation.

2.6 Computer spreadsheets using Excel

This section of Chapter 2 will enable you to:

- understand the use of spreadsheets
- start up Excel
- exit from Excel
- move about the spreadsheet
- enter labels
- enter numbers

- construct formulae
- save and retrieve files on disk
- use the HELP function
- use the SUM and AVERAGE functions
- print worksheets
- create line graphs
- create bar graphs
- create pie charts
- save and retrieve graphs on disk
- print graphs

This section will also provide the underpinning knowledge in the area of spreadsheets.

A spreadsheet is just like a large sheet of squared paper where you would write down numbers in rows and columns and perform calculations on them. On paper you would add some numbers together, subtract some and multiply others until you found an answer. Managers use spreadsheets to work out a whole range of calculations in many areas of their work. Before computer spreadsheets, hundreds of sales figures, costs and expenses would be written down on paper and then a calculator would be used to work out the final profit etc., from all the figures. This could take hours, and what happened if one of the numbers was entered into the calculator wrongly? You'd have to start again!

Also, and more importantly, before the use of computer-based spreadsheets, a company profit forecasting was done in the same way. Instead of actual figures, a forecast shows what a company expects to sell or expects things to cost over a certain period of time.

When all these hours of work have been done, and many large sheets of paper have been filled with numbers, the company may suddenly think, 'What will our final profit be if we can reduce some costs in May or increase sales in June?' They would then have to go back to their sheets of paper, change the costs in May, change the sales in June, and work out all the numbers again until they reached the profit figure – many hours of work every time they wanted to change some of their sales or cost estimates.

A computer-based spreadsheet will do these hours of work in seconds or minutes. Once you have typed in the numbers and told it which numbers to add together, subtract, multiply, etc., it will automatically work out the final profit figure, thousands of times faster than you could work it out on paper with a calculator.

Now, if the company wants to know what will happen to the final profit if some costs are reduced or sales are increased, all they have to do is change some numbers on the computer spreadsheet and, in seconds, all the numbers will automatically be worked out again.

They can do this over and over again for many different costs and sales forecasts, saving many hours each time they use the computer spreadsheet.

This power to change numbers and still have the answer automatically worked out is one of the main reasons companies first bought personal computers and spreadsheets. In just a few days, the time they saved and the more accurate forecasts they could make, would more than pay for the computer.

Apart from forecasts, the computer spreadsheet can be used for scientific calculations, balancing your chequebook account, and any other application where you would write numbers on a sheet of paper and perform calculations on them. In this book we are going to use them to automate the calculation elements of the modelling approaches and to allow us an easy way of producing a sensitivity analysis on the models used. It is not essential to use spreadsheets but you will find it makes life so much easier.

2.7   The spreadsheet learning package using Excel

The spreadsheet we will look at in this part of the chapter is called Excel. It's one of the most powerful spreadsheets on the market for a personal computer and is one often used as an industry standard. Excel is in fact much more – it can provide graphical information of figures in a variety of forms. It even has a built-in database. Once you have developed the ability to use Excel you will find the transfers to other spreadsheet packages easy. You have an idea of what a spreadsheet is by now, so let's get started on Excel. The way to work through this package is with the computer switched on and the book open in front of you; it is a package to work on – not just to read.

Where you are required to enter a series of alpha or numeric characters from the text into the machine they will be given in bold type, e.g. **EXCEL**. This requires you to type in **EXCEL**.

Where a single function key is to be entered this will be given in bold type followed by the word 'key'.

e.g. press **RETURN** key

Simple italics will be used to show you what should appear on the screen.

2.8   Creating a spreadsheet using Excel

2.8.1   Starting up

This package assumes you have a personal computer with a hard disk.

Switch on your hard disk computer.

To begin with check that Excel has been installed onto the hard disk within the Windows directory.

When C:\> appears on the screen you will need to get into Windows, where you will be able to click on the icon that has the Excel application within it, and then click on the option Excel.

The blank Excel spreadsheet should now appear on the screen. The cell in the left-hand corner of the screen will be highlighted, as well as an arrow and/or cross that is controlled by the mouse. If you are unfamiliar with using a mouse, practise moving the arrow/cross around the screen, and explore the menus on the top of the screen by clicking on the titles or icons.

2.8.2 Moving about the spreadsheet

In addition to the mouse, the cursor arrow keys ← ↑ → ↓ on the right-hand side of the keyboard can be used to move the cursor around the spreadsheet. When you have finished experimenting, press down the **CNTRL** key which is located bottom left and press the **HOME** key top right simultaneously to return to cell A1. (A *cell* is the basic unit of a spreadsheet and each cell has its own individual reference or address – just like a home.)

Now press the **F5** key, a special function key on the left-hand side or top of your keyboard. A box will appear in the centre of the screen which will ask where the cursor needs to go to. Type **E7** and press **RETURN** key. The cursor automatically jumps to cell E7. The display in the top left-hand corner of the screen now shows E7 which is the current address of the cursor.

Next, press the **CNTRL** key and the down arrow key (↓). This takes you to the bottom of the spreadsheet. Note how many rows the spreadsheet contains. Press the **CNTRL** key again, followed by the right arrow key (→) – this will take you to the right-hand edge of the spreadsheet. Note the letters displayed at the top of the spreadsheet. You have now seen the full extent of the Excel spreadsheet. Press the **CNTRL** and **HOME** key simultaneously to return to cell A1.

2.8.3 Exiting from Excel

In order to leave Excel and return to the Windows menus you will need to use the mouse. Click on FILE (see menu at top of worksheet). A menu will appear, choose option EXIT. The computer will ask if you want to save any changes you have made to that worksheet. Select NO. You should now have exited from Excel and have the Windows menu on the screen.

2.8.4 Construction of a simple spreadsheet

Load up the Excel spreadsheet as before. Move the cursor to cell B5 using the arrow keys (remembering that the mouse is always available if you prefer). Type in **Rent** and press the down arrow key to enter.

Next type in **Water** and press the down arrow key (if you make any typing errors use the back-space key to correct them).

> Type in **Electricity** – press the down arrow key
> Type in **Phone** – press the down arrow key twice
> Type in **Total** – press the **RETURN** key

Now move to cell C3.

> Type in **1992** – press the right arrow key
> Type in **1993** – press the **RETURN** key

Now move to cell C5.

> Type in **1023** – press the down arrow key
> Type in **348** – press the down arrow key
> Type in **211** – press the down arrow key
> Type in **161** – press the **RETURN** key

If you have entered a wrong number move the cursor back to that cell, re-type the number and press the **RETURN** key. You will also notice that the last part of **Electricity** has gone missing. Do not worry – this problem will be dealt with later in the learning package.

Now move to cell D5.

> Type in **1053** – press the down arrow key
> Type in **432** – press the down arrow key
> Type in **198** – press the down arrow key
> Type in **183** – press the down arrow key twice

2.8.5 Entering formulae

To add the numbers in column D and enter the amount in cell D10, leave the cursor at cell D10 and type:

> =**D5** + **D6** + **D7** + **D8** and press the **RETURN** key

Note the = sign which tells Excel you are entering a formula. Move the cursor to cell C10 and type in:

> =**C5** + **C6** + **C7** + **C8** and press the **RETURN** key

Also note that the formula is displayed in the top left-hand corner of the screen, even though the value is in cell C10.

Now try entering other values and watch the totals change automatically as they are recalculated by Excel.

Move the cursor to cell E3.

Type in:

> **Change** £ and press the down arrow key twice

Type in =**D5-C5** and press the **RETURN** key.

This time use Excel's copy function to repeat the formula into the other cells. Place cursor on cell E5. Click on the option EDIT with the mouse and choose COPY, move cursor down to cell E6. Click on EDIT again and choose the option PASTE. The calculation should have copied down into cell E6. Now copy both formulae down. Go to cell E5. Use the mouse to cover both cells E5 and E6 by keeping your finger pressed on the click button on the mouse. Now select EDIT and the option COPY. Move cursor to cell E7, select again the option EDIT with the mouse and then PASTE. The formula should now have copied down from E5 to E8.

Take cursor down to cell E8. Select EDIT with the mouse and choose option COPY. Move cursor to cell E10 and select EDIT and option PASTE. The calculation will then have copied into the TOTAL column.

Now go to cell F3 and type in **CHANGE %** and press the down arrow key twice. Type =**E5/C5** and press **RETURN** key. Copy the formulae down as above.

In order to format values to percentages the range needs to be selected. Take cursor to cell F5. Cover the range F5 to F10 by holding down the click button on the mouse. Then with the mouse select FORMAT from the menu then the option PERCENT, then choose the option FIXED. The computer will then ask you how many decimal places to be formatted, type in **0** and then press the **RETURN** key.

2.8.6 Saving your work to disk

Finally, in order to save the spreadsheet, select FILE with the mouse on the menu, then select the option SAVE. Enter an appropriate filename and press the **RETURN** key. The filename must not be more than eight characters long and cannot have any spaces. Now exit from Excel.

2.8.7 Retrieving your files from disk

Load up Excel by clicking on the icon from the Windows menu. When the spreadsheet appears it will be blank. You will need to retrieve the spreadsheet that you were working on.

Use the mouse to click on FILE from the menu and select OPEN EXISTING FILE. A box will appear in the centre of the worksheet with filenames on. Select your worksheet from the list given by highlighting it with the mouse and pressing the **RETURN** key. To obtain a blank worksheet use the mouse to again click on FILE from the menu and choose the option CREATE NEW FILE.

2.8.8 The HELP function

Press the **F1** key (the 'help' key) or click on the Help icon to access the help facility within Excel. Spend some time exploring the Help facility – after all it is there to help you! The help facility is very extensive in Excel and covers all the main functions within the package. It is possible to explore the Help facility either by browsing through the contents page or by carrying out a specific search. When you have finished, return to the current worksheet by clicking on FILE and choosing option EXIT.

2.8.9 Exploring the menus

Explore the various options available to you by using the menu on the top of the spreadsheet. Use the mouse to click on the various selections and look at the options available to you within each selection.

2.8.10 Continuing with your example worksheet

Retrieve your worksheet as before. Move the cursor to cell B10. You are now going to practise using the DELETE command. Press the DELETE button and the data in cell B10 will disappear. To delete more than one cell, place cursor on cell B10 and use the mouse to click on SELECT from the menu, and then choose option CELLS. Use the mouse to cover cells B10–D10 by keeping your finger on the click button. Click on EDIT and then the option CUT. The data in those cells should have now disappeared.

Type in **Stationery** – press the down arrow key
Type in **Equipment** – press the down arrow key
Type in **Petrol** – press the down arrow key
Type in **Purchases** – press the down arrow key twice
Type in **Total** – press the **RETURN** key

Now move to cell C9.

Type in **56** – press the down arrow key
Type in **569** – press the down arrow key
Type in **66** – press the down arrow key
Type in **2065** – press the **RETURN** key

So that the titles are not covered up by the numbers, we need to widen column B. Move the cursor to cell B12, use the mouse to select FORMAT from the menu, choose option COLUMN WIDTH. The computer will then ask you what size the column should be, the standard column width will now appear. Type **11** and this will change the column width to 11 after you press the **RETURN** key. The titles are now all visible. Note that even though the numbers in column C overlaid part of the titles from column B, the ends of the titles were still 'there'.

2.8.11 Using the summing function

Move the cursor to cell C14. Click on option Σ which will total the cells C5..C12 and press the **RETURN** key. This is a more efficient way of summing a set of cells than constructing your own formulae, particularly when it is a large set.

Now move to cell D9.

Type in **71** – press the down arrow key
Type in **611** – press the down arrow key
Type in **53** – press the down arrow key
Type in **3053** – press the down arrow key twice

Use the **copy** command to copy the formula from C14 to D14. Place cursor on cell C14. Click on EDIT from the menu and choose option COPY, move to cell D14. Click on EDIT again from the menu and choose option PASTE. The formula should now be copied into cell D14.

Move to cell E5. The formula for % Change needs to be copied into the other categories which have been added. Use mouse to highlight E5 to E8 by holding down the click button on the mouse. Select EDIT from the menu and then choose option COPY. Place cursor on cell E9, click on EDIT again and then PASTE.

The formula needs to be copied into the TOTALS column. Move cursor to cell E12 choose EDIT and option COPY. Move cursor to cell E14 and click on EDIT and choose option PASTE.

Repeat the process above for the column % Change in column F.

2.8.12 Using the average function

Go to cell E18. Type **AVERAGE** and press ↓. Now type in **CHANGE %** and press **RETURN** key. Move the cursor to cell F19. To access the AVERAGE command click on the FORMULA function at the top of the screen, then click on PASTE FUNCTION and select STATISTICAL. Then click on AVERAGE command, click OK, and type in **f5..f12** and press **RETURN** key. As you get more used to Excel you can type the command =**AVERAGE(f5..f12)** directly into the command line at the top of the screen.

2.8.13 Saving your updated worksheets

Now save your worksheet as before. Using the mouse, click on FILE and choose option SAVE. The computer will automatically save the worksheet using the same name as was previously used replacing the old file. (Note that the original worksheet is now deleted.)

If you want to save the worksheet under a different name then choose FILE and then select option SAVE AS. The computer will then prompt for a file name.

2.8.14 Printing your worksheet

Only attempt this part of the learning package if you have a printer attached to your computer. Check first that the printer is ON LINE.

To print your spreadsheet select option FILE with the mouse and then choose option PRINT. The computer will ask if you want to print all the spreadsheet. Press the **RETURN** key to accept this instruction.

2.9 Creating graphs from a spreadsheet using Excel

This section will take you through the basic steps associated with creating graphs in Excel. Considerably more time will be spent on this competence and its underpinning knowledge in Chapter 3, when we look at data presentation.

The first step involved in creating a graph is to select a data range from your spreadsheet with the mouse. This entails putting a box round the data you want to graph. The next step is to click on the CHARTWIZARD icon in the top left hand corner of the screen, at which point the previously highlighted box will flicker. It is then necessary to create an empty box on the screen, which is where the graph will appear once it is created. When the empty box has been created the chartwizard range box will appear, which specifies the range of the data that is to be graphed, at which point the NEXT button should be clicked. A collection of chart types will then appear on the screen, and it is then simply a matter of selecting an appropriate chart/graph for your data.

2.9.1 Creating a line graph

Following the steps just outlined, but with a data range that includes b5..b12 and c5..c12, select a line graph from the range of graphs on display. Clicking on NEXT then brings up a range of possible line graphs. Clicking on the second icon graph type and then clicking once again on NEXT will bring up a sample graph based upon the data that you previously highlighted. Clicking on NEXT will then enable you to add legends and titles to the graph. The final step is to then click on NEXT, which will produce your graph in the box that you originally drew in your spreadsheet. The graph in the box will be a line graph for the 1992 expenses.

2.9.2 Creating a bar graph

Following the steps just outlined, but with the additional data range of d5..d12, select a bar graph from the range of graphs on display. Clicking on NEXT then brings up a range of possible bar graphs. Clicking on the second icon graph type and then clicking once again on NEXT will bring up a sample graph based upon the data that you previously highlighted. Clicking on NEXT will then enable you to add legends and titles to the graph. The final step is to then click on NEXT, which will produce your graph in the box that you originally drew in your spreadsheet. The bar graph in the box will now have 1992 and 1993 expenses, which facilitates comparison.

2.9.3 Labelling your graphs

As it stands the graph is not very clear. To put in some labels and a title follow these steps:

> Select a range of data on the spreadsheet
> Click CHARTWIZARD
> Chartwizard range box appears – click NEXT
> Click line graph – click NEXT
> Click format 2 – click NEXT
> Sample graph appears – click NEXT
> Sample graph appears – add legend by clicking YES
>> – put cursor in title box and type **Expenses 1992/93**
>> – put cursor in axis titles box 'x' and type **Type of Expenses**
>> – put cursor in axis titles box 'y' and type **Amount £**
>> – click OK
> View graph in worksheet with the added labels.

2.9.4 Saving a graph for later use

To save a graph with your worksheet, so that you can call it up again the next time you use Excel, simply save the worksheet under the name of **EXPBAR1** with the SAVE command in the FILE menu.

2.9.5 Saving a graph for later printing

The graph is saved automatically with your spreadsheet, so to retrieve the worksheet you select FILE and identify your file through the OPEN command.

2.9.6 Creating a pie chart

Finally, to create a pie chart, type following the steps previously outlined. With the data range d5..d12 and c5..c12, select a pie chart from the range of graphs on display. Clicking on NEXT then brings up a range of possible pie charts. Clicking on the second icon graph type and then clicking once again on NEXT will bring up a sample pie chart based upon the data that you previously highlighted. Clicking on NEXT will then enable you to add legends and titles to the graph. The final step is to then click on NEXT, which will produce your graph in the box that you originally drew in your spreadsheet.

2.9.7 Printing your graph

Only attempt this part of the learning package if you have a printer attached to your computer. Check first that the printer is ON LINE.

To print a graph at full size it is necessary to double click on the graph in the worksheet. With the full image now in view you can select FILE and look at PRINTVIEW to see exactly what it will look like prior to printing. To action the print simply click on the PRINT command. The Excel package has an extensive range of features for enhancing the quality of your prints. These include numerous fonts and full colouring, and the reader is encouraged to explore these valuable tools as it is impossible to cover them fully in the present text.

Competence Example 2.2

At the end of this section you should be able to demonstrate how to:

1 understand the use of spreadsheets

2 start up Excel

3 exit from Excel

4 move about the spreadsheet

5 enter labels

6 enter numbers

7 construct formulae

8 save and retrieve files on disk

9 use the HELP function

10 use the SUM and AVERAGE functions

12 print worksheets

13 create line graphs

14 create bar graphs

15 create pie charts

16 save and retrieve graphs on disk

17 print graphs

You will now be able to practise and demonstrate these basic competences on a range of quantitative modelling approaches throughout the rest of the book. It is more desirable that you develop spreadsheets in areas you will be using later rather than any general areas we could create at this stage in the book. You may, however, wish to demonstrate these competences by creating spreadsheets from your own work experience. It is possible to work through the text without using spreadsheets, but we would strongly advise their use, given the way in which they will reduce the burden of calculation.

2.10 Computer support disk

Provided with this book is a computer support disk. It is not necessary to use this disk to be able to work through the book and develop competence in quantitative modelling, but it is a useful and helpful additional extra and we would recommend it to you. The computer disk is based on both Lotus 1-2-3 and Excel spreadsheets and they are a series of interconnected worksheets. You may choose either Lotus or an Excel spreadsheet depending on the package you have access to. It has been designed to require the minimum spreadsheet skills and to take away the burden of some of the calculations within the book. You will have more than sufficient spreadsheet skills if you have worked through the first part of this chapter. You will be advised in the main text of the book when to use the disk. Do remember that it is a very useful but optional extra.

The worksheets we have provided for you based on Lotus use extensively **Macro** commands. These commands are where we have programmed a series of Lotus commands into each Macro command. This makes the spreadsheet easier to use. All of the worksheets contain full instructions on how to use them and they are organised around the chapters of the book. The Macro commands are easy to use because all you need to do is to press the required key. So that the computer knows you want to invoke the Macro, at the same time as you press the letter key, hold down the **Alt** key. You use the **Alt** key in the same way as you use the **Shift** key to obtain a capital letter. Again this is explained on each worksheet.

Before you start to use the disk ensure you make a back-up copy. Always use the back-up copy and keep the disk provided with the book in a safe place as your master copy.

To start and use the disk you have two alternatives. First, you could load the contents of the disk onto your hard disk. This is the best approach as it will operate faster. Second you could use the disk in the A: drive, but you will need to change the file drive in Lotus. This second method will operate a little slower than the first.

Once you are ready to start then load Lotus and move into file RETRIEVE. The file you then need to start is MENU. When you have called up this file you will be able to use Macros to choose the chapter you are working on and then the particular technique you want to work on. You will then find that the spreadsheet will show you how to input data and use each technique.

3 Data reduction and its presentation
sorting the wheat from the chaff

3.1 Introduction

Managers frequently have to prepare reports and give presentations for their organisations. This type of activity reflects a range of skills that are essential for any manager. For instance, it frequently involves gathering or collating data, analysing and interpreting the data, and effectively communicating the results of the analysis to a boss or customer. It also requires, in the light of the penetration of information technology in the business world, the use of computers in the analysis of the data and the generation of presentation material. The chapters that follow provide numerous ways of analysing a situation or a set of data, while the current chapter focuses on the initial task of bringing together what can often be a diverse set of data and presenting it in an easily understood form.

This chapter is therefore concerned with developing competence in data reduction and its presentation. By the end of the chapter you should be able to demonstrate how to:

- build frequency distributions for summarising sets of data
- create a range of graphs to summarise and represent sets of data
- use graphs to estimate and predict events
- appreciate how information technology can be utilised in the analysis and presentation of data

The chapter will use a series of practical examples to develop the underpinning knowledge in the area of data reduction and its presentation.

At the end of each section the required competence will be specified and described. A typical problem format with the competences highlighted will also be given to help you to demonstrate the competences on the problems at the end of the chapter. At the end of the book a full solution will be given for the first of these problems, as well as answers for the rest.

3.2 Summarising a set of data

When investigating a problem the first step is to gather the information. This can be a time-consuming and expensive activity, but it is tremendously important that it is done correctly and that the data collected is truly representative of the area being studied (Chapter 7 looks at this in detail). The quantity of data collected is normally very large, and this presents one of the first hurdles to the person doing the investigating. It can be a frustrating time as the information collected is sometimes not exactly in the form that one wants, and therefore requires further handling before it can be used. The information then needs to be sorted and put in order before any analysis or interpretation can take place. As this type of activity is such an important and frequent task for managers, a detailed example will be used to illustrate the process of data reduction and its presentation:

Tasty Foods Ltd is a relatively small company that produces biscuits and savoury snacks for both large multiple retailers (e.g. Sainsbury's) and small CTNs (confectioners, tobacconists and newsagents). It operates at the low cost end of the market, with its products selling within a price range from 5p to 25p. Due to the low selling price of its products, Tasty Foods has to maintain a high volume of sales in order to generate a respectable level of profit. This high volume is further complicated by a wide range of products, and a production process that is fairly labour intensive.

The plant operates a three-shift production system, i.e. 6 a.m. to 2 p.m., 2 p.m. to 10 p.m. and 10 p.m. to 6 a.m. This is operated five days a week, Monday to Friday, and on Saturday there are only two shifts, from 6 a.m. to 2 p.m. and from 2 p.m. to 10 p.m. There are 152 direct production workers, which account for 12 per cent of the total costs. Although the company has never suffered strikes, sickness and absenteeism are a continuing cause for concern. The senior management of Tasty Foods have therefore asked its personnel department to investigate the problem and provide a preliminary report within the next four weeks.

The first task facing the personnel department was to gather as much information as possible on sickness and absenteeism and its likely causes. The data they collected is shown in Table 3.1.

The management of Tasty Foods were only too aware that this information was in itself unlikely to explain why absenteeism was so high, but they nevertheless hoped that it might provide some insight and direction for any further investigation into the problem.

The first variable, 'Emply', is simply the employee number, and it includes only those employees who are directly involved in the production process. Some of the variables, such as 'Age', are self evident, while others require a little further explanation. The 'MStat' variable provides information on the marital status of the employees, but due to the sensitive nature of this area the company is only able to classify its employees as either *married* (M) or *single* (S). The *single* data is therefore likely to include those who are divorced or separated from their partners. The level of education of the employees is shown under the 'Educ' variable, with 'N' standing for no qualifications, 'O' for O Levels, 'A' for A Levels, 'P' for professional qualifications, and 'D' for a degree. The 'Servic' variable shows how long, in years, they have been employed by the company. The 'Absent' and 'Sick' variables are in days, and it can be seen that in some cases the 'Absent' total is

Table 3.1   Employee data

Emply	Sex	Age	MStat	Child	Salary	Educ	Servic	Absent	Sick
1	F	24	S	2	12000	N	2	17	12
2	F	29	M	2	12100	O	6	12	10
3	F	43	M	3	13200	N	20	5	5
4	F	26	S	1	12300	O	2	13	9
5	F	22	S	1	11500	O	1	10	9
6	M	25	S	0	12100	O	3	15	13
7	F	36	M	4	13100	O	7	6	6
8	M	28	M	2	13000	P	9	5	5
9	F	19	S	0	10300	O	1	8	8
10	F	24	M	3	12200	N	2	9	6
11	F	51	M	2	13500	N	24	27	27
12	F	55	M	1	13500	N	25	5	5
13	F	27	M	2	12200	O	3	6	5
14	F	31	S	1	12100	O	4	7	7
15	M	43	M	2	13700	N	11	3	3
16	F	18	S	0	9200	O	1	5	5
17	F	24	S	2	11700	O	2	13	10
18	F	36	M	3	12600	N	4	8	8
19	F	41	M	2	13100	N	5	8	6
20	F	22	S	3	12300	N	1	11	11
21	F	25	M	2	12500	O	2	10	10
22	F	28	M	4	12900	O	3	5	5
23	F	53	M	2	13700	N	31	4	4
24	M	27	S	0	14900	D	3	0	0
25	M	35	M	2	13500	O	8	12	10
26	F	26	M	0	13600	A	5	3	3
27	M	18	S	0	9300	N	1	6	6
28	F	20	S	2	11900	P	2	14	9
29	F	42	M	2	13300	O	10	2	2
30	F	33	M	1	13900	A	11	5	5
31	F	34	M	2	13700	O	9	13	13

Table 3.1 (*continued*)

Emply	Sex	Age	MStat	Child	Salary	Educ	Servic	Absent	Sick
32	F	34	M	4	13200	O	4	11	6
33	M	21	S	0	11500	O	3	7	7
34	F	34	M	3	12600	N	2	6	5
35	F	19	S	0	9600	O	1	2	2
36	F	25	S	2	12800	P	3	10	10
37	F	22	S	0	12500	O	2	13	13
38	F	31	S	3	12900	A	5	5	5
39	F	35	M	2	12700	O	2	6	6
40	F	27	M	1	12500	O	3	8	8
41	M	40	M	3	13500	N	12	16	16
42	F	20	M	2	11000	O	1	3	3
43	F	37	M	4	13200	O	7	8	4
44	F	24	S	1	12400	O	4	5	5
45	M	28	S	2	13000	O	8	3	3
46	F	26	S	0	12600	O	3	2	2
47	F	31	M	1	12800	A	6	4	4
48	F	43	M	0	13600	N	15	25	23
49	F	36	M	1	13100	O	10	13	10
50	F	24	S	0	12200	A	2	0	0
51	M	23	S	0	11400	O	1	6	6
52	M	29	M	2	13700	A	4	2	2
53	F	22	S	0	11000	O	2	5	5
54	F	33	M	4	12700	N	4	3	3
55	F	44	M	3	13200	N	12	8	8
56	F	25	M	3	12100	P	3	12	12
57	F	32	S	2	12400	O	5	4	4
58	F	30	S	1	12600	N	6	5	5
59	F	27	M	2	12600	O	5	1	1
60	F	18	S	0	9800	O	2	2	2
61	F	32	M	1	12800	O	6	6	4
62	M	29	M	2	13000	N	4	5	5

Table 3.1 (*continued*)

Emply	Sex	Age	MStat	Child	Salary	Educ	Servic	Absent	Sick
63	F	38	M	2	13400	N	11	8	8
64	M	33	M	3	13100	P	6	1	1
65	F	40	M	2	12800	A	13	6	6
66	M	24	M	2	12500	N	3	10	10
67	M	52	M	3	13700	N	9	7	7
68	M	19	S	0	11000	O	2	3	3
69	F	55	M	4	13200	N	13	8	8
70	F	36	M	2	12300	N	6	2	2
71	M	28	M	1	13200	P	5	2	2
72	F	47	M	2	13100	O	12	5	5
73	F	40	M	3	12900	O	12	12	12
74	F	46	S	2	12700	N	7	7	7
75	M	35	M	2	12700	O	3	0	0
76	F	30	S	1	12600	N	4	0	0
77	F	28	M	3	12700	O	7	3	3
78	F	44	M	2	12800	P	8	17	15
79	F	53	M	2	13400	N	12	2	2
80	F	23	M	2	12400	O	4	6	6
81	F	21	S	0	11400	A	3	0	0
82	F	29	S	0	12000	N	3	18	14
83	F	34	M	3	12700	O	5	12	10
84	F	51	M	2	13700	N	13	9	5
85	F	48	M	1	13500	N	9	5	5
86	F	31	S	2	12600	O	3	14	10
87	F	28	M	1	12500	N	3	5	5
88	F	36	M	3	12800	O	6	3	3
89	F	45	M	2	12700	N	2	1	1
90	M	26	S	0	12800	O	3	12	6
91	F	33	M	2	12900	O	4	3	3
92	F	32	M	2	12700	N	3	8	4
93	F	37	M	2	12600	N	2	4	3

Table 3.1   (*continued*)

Emply	Sex	Age	MStat	Child	Salary	Educ	Servic	Absent	Sick
94	F	43	M	3	12900	N	8	0	0
95	F	25	M	1	12500	O	2	1	1
96	F	23	S	0	11800	O	1	2	2
97	M	24	S	0	12400	N	2	5	5
98	F	39	M	1	12800	O	7	4	3
99	F	33	M	3	12600	A	8	3	2
100	F	39	M	2	13400	N	12	2	1
101	F	26	S	0	12400	O	3	7	7
102	M	22	S	0	11800	O	2	5	5
103	F	23	M	1	12200	O	3	8	4
104	F	47	M	2	13100	P	8	3	3
105	M	43	M	2	13800	P	11	13	13
106	F	30	M	3	12700	O	4	6	3
107	F	38	M	4	12800	N	10	24	22
108	F	27	S	1	12300	O	5	5	5
109	F	24	S	0	11500	O	2	3	3
110	F	48	M	2	13500	N	13	7	5
111	F	21	S	0	10900	O	1	0	0
112	F	23	S	0	11500	N	2	4	4
113	F	31	S	2	12600	N	8	14	12
114	F	36	M	5	12500	N	7	10	10
115	F	24	M	2	12200	N	4	5	5
116	F	20	M	2	11200	N	2	3	3
117	F	28	M	1	12300	P	4	6	6
118	M	22	S	0	11300	O	2	7	7
119	F	44	M	3	13300	N	11	22	20
120	F	43	M	2	13000	O	8	12	12
121	M	57	M	2	13500	N	14	3	3
122	F	54	M	4	13400	N	17	0	0
123	F	32	M	2	14500	D	5	5	5
124	F	33	M	2	12500	O	4	1	1

Table 3.1 (*continued*)

Emply	Sex	Age	MStat	Child	Salary	Educ	Servic	Absent	Sick
125	M	30	M	1	13000	O	5	1	1
126	F	22	S	0	11200	A	2	0	0
127	F	25	S	0	11500	O	3	4	4
128	M	21	S	0	10300	O	3	1	1
129	F	38	M	3	12600	N	7	5	5
130	F	46	M	2	13000	N	8	3	3
131	F	27	M	3	12500	O	5	13	10
132	F	25	S	2	12300	N	5	6	6
133	F	18	S	0	8200	O	1	1	1
134	F	31	M	4	12800	N	9	7	4
135	F	35	S	1	12500	O	6	2	2
136	F	38	M	2	12600	N	12	8	8
137	M	40	M	3	13200	N	8	2	2
138	F	42	M	2	13500	N	11	0	0
139	M	24	M	3	12400	P	5	16	10
140	F	36	M	3	12500	N	7	3	3
141	F	23	M	1	12000	O	4	5	5
142	M	21	S	0	12300	N	4	2	2
143	F	34	M	2	12500	A	8	12	12
144	F	27	M	3	12400	N	7	7	7
145	F	20	M	2	11400	N	2	5	5
146	F	37	M	3	12800	O	10	3	3
147	F	41	S	2	12700	N	8	1	1
148	M	33	M	2	13000	O	10	5	5
149	F	56	M	1	13600	N	14	0	0
150	F	50	M	2	13500	P	12	4	4
151	M	45	S	0	13800	N	13	0	0
152	F	24	M	3	12400	N	4	5	5

higher than the 'Sick' total, which simply reflects that people have days off work for non-sickness reasons.

The data in Table 3.1 has been entered into Lotus 1-2-3 and Excel, two well known computer software packages that can be used to organise, analyse and graphically present data (*see* Chapter 2). Lotus 1-2-3 will be used extensively in this chapter as it significantly reduces the amount of time it takes to organise the data to a form that is conducive to analysis and interpretation. The data in Table 3.1 is on your Lotus 1-2-3 and Excel disk, and the majority of the examples and illustrations that follow are available for you to practise with on this data. The use of spreadsheet packages like Lotus 1-2-3 and Excel in organisations is very widespread, and we cannot overstress the importance of using them in the analysis and presentation of data (such skills are now almost mandatory in many organisations). As a consequence of this, the procedures used in Lotus 1-2-3 and Excel in the analysis of the data in Table 3.1 will, where appropriate, be outlined so that you can replicate them if you so wish. The process of analysis will also be explained manually for those who do not have access to a computer or use an alternative spreadsheet package. Such an explanation also aids and reinforces understanding.

3.3 Frequency distributions

It is very difficult to interpret the data as it stands due to its size, and one way of making it simpler to interpret is to reduce its volume by expressing it as a **frequency distribution**. A frequency distribution for the level of salary of the employees is shown in Table 3.2.

It can be seen that there are 152 employees in total, with one employee earning between £8,000 and £8,999, and four employees earning between £9,000 and £9,999, and so on. The benefit of representing the data in this way is that it becomes much more understandable. One can quickly glance at the frequency distribution and get a reasonable impression of the overall situation. It is clear that most employees earn between £11,000 and £14,000, with the highest frequency

Table 3.2   Frequency distribution for level of salary

Salary amount (£)	Frequency
8,000 to 8,999	1
9,000 to 9,999	4
10,000 to 10,999	6
11,000 to 11,999	18
12,000 to 12,999	81
13,000 to 13,999	40
14,000 to 14,999	2
	152

being in the £12,000 to £13,000 range. These ranges are known as classes or intervals (e.g. 10,000 to 10,999), which are non-overlapping so that a data value belongs to one and only one class.

The frequency distribution in Table 3.2 is based on an output from Lotus 1-2-3 (i.e. data, distribution, value range, bin range). The actual output from Lotus 1-2-3 is shown in Table 3.3, and it differs in that for the first class it includes all values up to and including 9,000, with the second class including every value from 9,001 to 10,000, which was four items. To do this manually, as in Table 3.2, you would need to check every data value and record it against its class, which is a much longer and more tedious process than that outlined for Lotus 1-2-3. But regardless of whether one is using Lotus 1-2-3 or not, it is still necessary to decide on the number of classes with which to record the frequencies. It is normal to use classes of equal width (a class width of 1,000 was used for the salary frequency distribution), as this avoids any ambiguity or difficulty when the full frequency distribution is looked at and interpreted. It is also normally the case that between 5 and 20 classes would be used in frequency distributions. The reason behind these guidelines is that if one uses less than five classes it is likely that too much information will be hidden by a few very wide classes. Likewise, if there are too many classes it becomes difficult to interpret due to the amount of information facing the reader. With these guidelines in mind, the approximate number of classes can be found by:

$$\frac{\text{Largest data value} - \text{Smallest data value}}{\text{Class width}}$$

For our employee salary data we therefore find:

$$\frac{14,900 - 8,200}{1,000} = \frac{6,700}{1,000} = 6.7$$

This would then be rounded up to seven classes. If we wanted more classes we would simply reduce the class width of 1,000 to a smaller figure, until we got what was an acceptable number of classes (e.g. if the class width was reduced to 500 we would have $6,700/500 = 13.4$ classes).

Table 3.3   Frequency distribution output from Lotus 1-2-3

Salary	Frequency
9,000	1
10,000	4
11,000	6
12,000	18
13,000	81
14,000	40
15,000	2

3.4 Relative frequency distribution

Sometimes it is convenient to express a frequency distribution in percentage terms, especially when we are dealing in large quantities of data. The frequency distribution is then known as a **relative frequency distribution,** an example of which is shown in Table 3.4 for the salary data. The relative frequency of a class can be found by dividing the frequency of the class by the total frequency and multiplying by 100:

$$\text{Relative frequency of a class} = \frac{\text{Frequency of the class}}{n} \times 100$$

which for the first of the classes is:

$$\frac{1}{152} \times 100 = 0.66\%$$

The relative frequencies in Table 3.4 were again calculated in Lotus 1-2-3 (the above formula was copied across the frequency distribution and the percentage function was applied to the copied fields (i.e. range, format, percentage, two decimal places)).

Table 3.4 Relative frequency distribution for level of salary

Salary amount (£)	Frequency %
8,000–8,999	0.66
9,000–9,999	2.63
10,000–10,999	3.95
11,000–11,999	11.84
12,000–12,999	53.29
13,000–13,999	26.32
14,000–14,999	1.32
	100.00

3.5 Graphical representation of data

Although a frequency distribution is an extremely effective way of summarising and presenting data, it can be enhanced or replaced by a graphical representation. A spreadsheet is particularly useful here as it makes it possible to quickly transform data into a graphical form. Figure 3.1 shows a bar graph for the salary data (i.e. Graph, Type, Bar, X, A, View), and this is a very effective way of graphically representing the frequency distribution salary data.

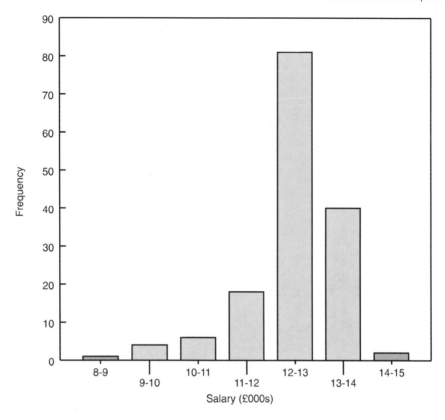

Figure 3.1   Bar graph of salary frequency distribution data

The class limits shown in Figure 3.1 are the apparent limits as opposed to the real limits (e.g. 8,000 to 9,000 as opposed to 8,000 to 8,999), and this was done simply to keep the *x* axis labels as short as possible. For purposes of illustration this is fine as long as one remembers to use the real limits in any further analysis or explanation. Figure 3.1 was created in Lotus 1-2-3 and it is an example of a basic bar graph. Lotus 1-2-3, like many spreadsheet applications, has a number of features to enhance the appearance and effect of graphs. Figure 3.2 shows the same bar graph with perspective. It is also possible to import the data into design packages like Coral Draw and add even more aspects to the graph, as in Figure 3.3.

An effective graph is one that gets the information quickly and efficiently to the reader. Figure 3.4 is an illustration of a graph that is too sophisticated and only succeeds in confusing the reader, and this should be avoided wherever possible.

It is probably becoming apparent that there are many ways to graphically represent a set of data (though they all derive from a frequency distribution), and Figure 3.5 illustrates just four that are available in many spreadsheet packages. Graphs are also very effective when we wish to compare a number of variables, such as say 'salary' and 'length of service'. Figure 3.6 shows the two graphs side by side, and it can be seen that the largest salary frequency is £12,000 to £13,000, while the largest length of service frequency is 0 to 5 years. It appears therefore

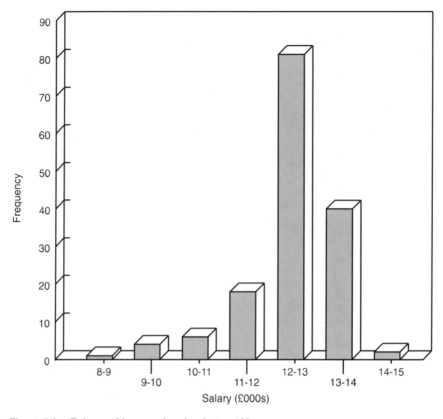

Figure 3.2   Enhanced bar graph using Lotus 123

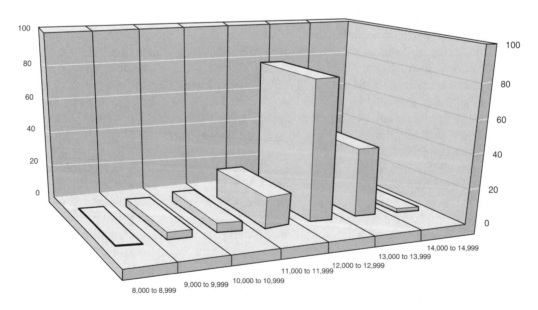

Figure 3.3   Enhanced bar graph using Coral Draw

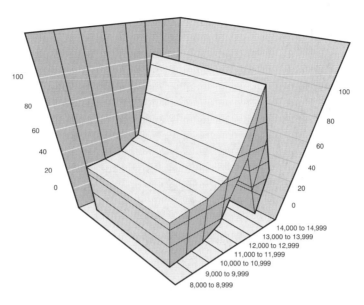

Figure 3.4   An over-sophisticated graph

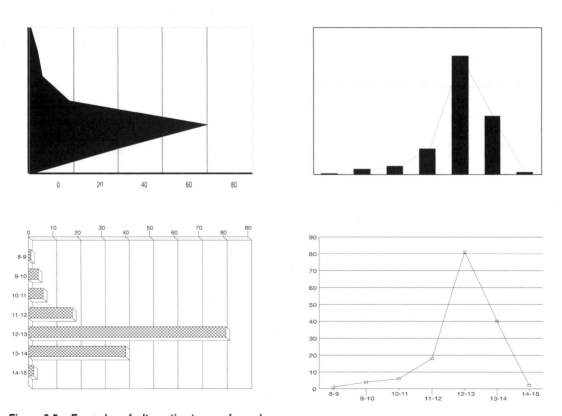

Figure 3.5   Examples of alternative types of graph

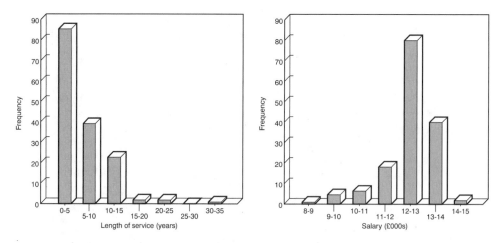

Figure 3.6   Comparison of length of service and salary

that as one decreases the other increases! Figure 3.7 has combined the variables salary and service, and it can be seen even more clearly now that there appears to be an almost inverse relationship between the salary of an employee and their length of service. The type of graph we use can therefore affect the strength of the message we are trying to convey to the reader, and the widespread availability of

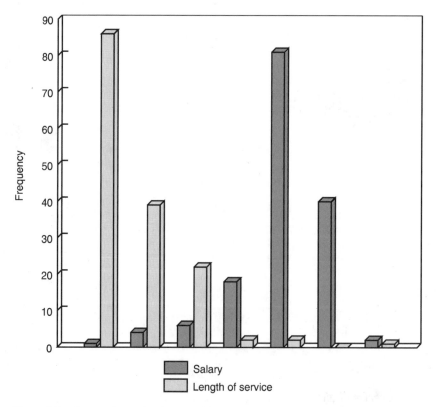

Figure 3.7   Comparison of salary and length of service – a combined graph

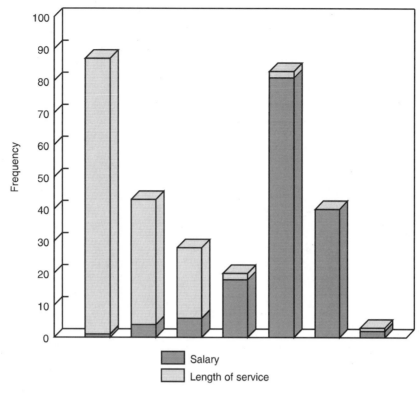

Figure 3.8   Comparison of salary and length of service – a stacked bar graph

appropriate computer software now provides an opportunity for quick and easy graphical manipulations of data. It is quite straightforward, for instance, to convert the information in Figure 3.7 to a stacked bar graph, as in Figure 3.8, if we think this is a more effective way of representing data. This is a very powerful tool for managers, as it enables them to efficiently and professionally summarise data and decide upon what is the most effective way of communicating that information. Before the advent of spreadsheets this would have been a very time-consuming and laborious activity, and not surprisingly it was the exception rather than the rule to see such presentations. Today it is expected that managers have at least a basic competence in the use of such technology and an understanding of how and where it can be used.

Competence Example 3.1

At the end of this section you should now be able to demonstrate how to:

1 reduce a set of data to a more manageable form by creating a frequency distribution

2 graph the frequency distribution data

3 interpret the frequency distribution and graphed data

To practise and demonstrate these competences complete problems 3.1 and 3.2 at the end of this chapter. To help you to develop these competences a description of the procedure you will need to follow is now given, along with a typical problem format. The problem format is based on a problem that is similar to that previously outlined.

PROCEDURE

❶ Decide on number of classes.

❷ Count data against classes.

❸ Create frequency distribution.

❹ Create graph of frequency distribution.

❺ Interpret and report upon your findings.

PROBLEM

For the 'Age' category data in Table 3.1, create a relative frequency distribution and a bar graph and report upon your findings.

SOLUTION FORMAT

❶ ▮

$$\frac{\text{Largest data value} - \text{Smallest data value}}{\text{Class width}}$$

$$\frac{57 - 18}{10} = \frac{39}{10} = 3.9 \text{ rounds up to 4 classes}$$

Since this is only a guideline, we have decided to ignore it and create five classes as these will provide a better framework for the data set.

❷ ❸

Age Class	Frequency
Up to 20	11
21 to 30	63
31 to 40	46
41 to 50	22
51 to 60	10
	152

The above frequencies were actually obtained from Lotus 1-2-3, as previously shown. It was also used to calculate the relative frequencies and to create the bar graph.

Age class	Relative frequency
Up to 20	7.24
21 to 30	41.45
31 to 40	30.26
41 to 50	14.47
51 to 60	6.58
	100.00

❹ With Lotus 1-2-3 it is a straightforward procedure to turn the above relative frequency ▮ distribution into a bar graph, as shown in Figure 3.9.

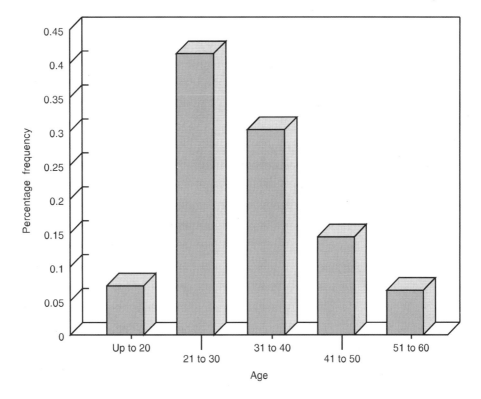

Figure 3.9   Bar graph of relative frequency data of age of employees

It can be seen that the workforce has a youngish age profile, in that 78.95 per cent are aged 40 or less. This might be reflective of the sector within which the company operates and/or the culture that has developed in this particular organisation. It is an interesting feature, and it will be reviewed again later.

Practise your competence now on problems 3.1 and 3.2 at the end of the chapter. When you have demonstrated competence in this area you can use the computer disk provided to automate the labour intensive and arithmetic elements. You may choose either a Lotus or an Excel spreadsheet depending on the package you have access to. The operation of this package was developed in detail in Chapter 2. You may now demonstrate the competence in this area against problems from your own work environment.

3.6   Overview of other types of graphical representations of data

A bar graph is only one way of representing a set of data, albeit the most popular way. The type of graph we use will to some extent depend upon the nature of the data we are handling and the preferences of the user (we will overview the appropriateness of particular graphical methods shortly).

3.6.1 Histogram

A histogram is very similar to a bar graph, and it is distinguishable by the fact that the columns are joined together rather than being separated as in a bar graph, and with the boundaries of the columns corresponding to the real class limits rather than the apparent class limits (e.g. the real upper class limits for the salary data are 8,999, 9,999 etc., rather than 9,000, 10,000 etc.). An example of a histogram for the salary data is shown in Figure 3.10. For most practical situations it does not matter whether one uses a bar graph or a histogram as long as the intended message is effectively transmitted to the reader.

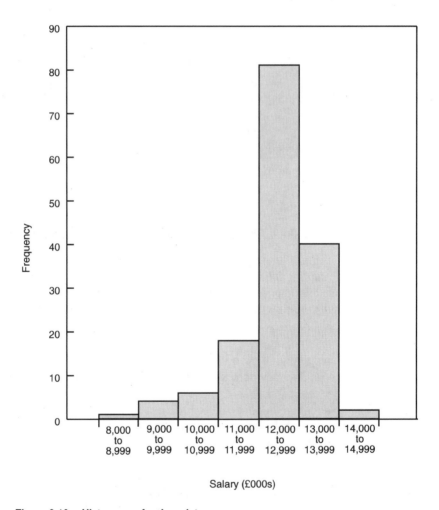

Figure 3.10 Histogram of salary data

For a statistician the histogram is usually the preferred way to represent a set of data, as it is a precursor to one of the most important shapes in statistics – the 'bell' shaped **normal distribution curve** (this is such an important characteristic that a number of the chapters that follow this one will be based upon it).

Frequency	Stem	Leaf
7.00	1	8888999
63.00	2	000011111222222233333344444444444555555566666777777788888889999
46.00	3	0000111111222233333334444455556666666777888899
25.00	4	0000112233333344455667788
11.00	5	01123345567
Stem width: 10.0		

Figure 3.11 Stem-and-leaf display for age data

Frequency	Stem	Leaf
7.00	1	8888999
63.00	2	000011111222222233333344444444444555555566666777777788888889999
46.00	3	0000111111222233333334444455556666666777888899
25.00	4	0000112233333344455667788
11.00	5	01123345567
Stem width: 10.0		

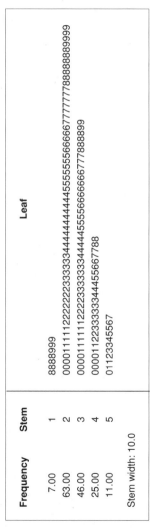

Figure 3.12 Stem-and-leaf display shown as a histogram

3.6.2 Stem-and-leaf displays

An alternative to the histogram is the stem-and-leaf display (created by the respected statistician John Turkey), and like the histogram it provides a quick visual impression for a set of data. The procedure involves putting the last digit of a number to the right of the display (the leaf) and the other numbers to the left (the stem). This has been done for the age data in Figure 3.11, and as can be seen it is similar to the histogram, especially when it is turned on its side as in Figure 3.12, but has the advantage of showing the actual data values.

In most cases the histogram or bar chart is preferred as it can cope more easily with large sets of data and is more amenable for creating relative frequencies and alternative class boundaries.

3.6.3 Pie chart

After the bar graph, this is the most popular way of representing data. It is ideally suited to representing proportions or segments of data, and how these parts contribute to the whole. A good example of this would be the qualification data. Figure 3.13 shows this data in the form of a pie chart, and it can clearly be seen that

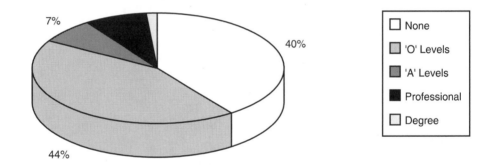

Figure 3.13   Pie chart of qualification data

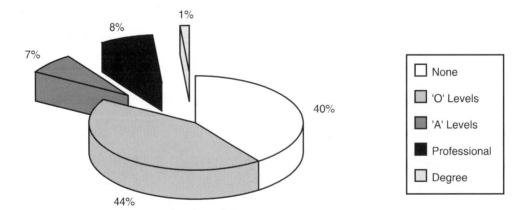

Figure 3.14   Highlighted pie chart

the largest proportions are those with no qualifications and those with 'O' Levels. The effect that these two proportions might have on the sociological and psychological nature of the workforce could be considerable, and might want to be highlighted. A good way of doing this is to 'pull out' a slice of the pie so that it is particularly highlighted. Figure 3.14 has done this by pulling out the 'A' Level, Professional, and Degree slices, to show how small they are in comparison to the other slices.

It is easy to forget just how time consuming the creation of such pie charts are without the aid of computers (or any graphical presentation for that matter). To illustrate this point an example based on a family's weekly expenditure has been done manually:

	£	%	Degrees
Mortgage	$45 = \dfrac{45}{150} \times 100 = 30$	$= \dfrac{30}{100} \times 360 =$	108
Car	$15 = \dfrac{15}{150} \times 100 = 10$	$= \dfrac{10}{100} \times 360 =$	36
Bank loan	$15 = \dfrac{15}{150} \times 100 = 10$	$= \dfrac{10}{100} \times 360 =$	36
Gas & elec	$30 = \dfrac{30}{150} \times 100 = 20$	$= \dfrac{20}{100} \times 360 =$	72
Food	$36 = \dfrac{36}{150} \times 100 = 24$	$= \dfrac{24}{100} \times 360 =$	86
Clothes	$9 = \dfrac{9}{150} \times 100 = 6$	$= \dfrac{6}{100} \times 360 =$	22
TOTAL	£150	100%	360°

Once this part has been carried out it would then be necessary to use a protractor to draw the segments of the pie chart. Thank goodness for computers!

3.6.4 Line graph

The line graph is typically used to show changes over longer periods of time. In terms of our company profile it has been applied to the length of service data, as it clearly shows the downward trend as the years of service increase (*see* Figure 3.15).

The line graph can also be very effective when it is combined with a bar graph or a histogram. To combine a bar graph and a line graph it is necessary to have a common horizontal axis (x axis) for both of the variables you are representing. It would be useful, for example, to compare advertising expenses and sales over a given period of time (*see* Figure 3.16).

3.6.5 Cumulative frequency distributions

A **cumulative frequency distribution** can be quite easily derived from a frequency distribution. A frequency distribution for the number of days absent for Tasty Foods Ltd was created on Lotus 1-2-3 and is shown in Table 3.5.

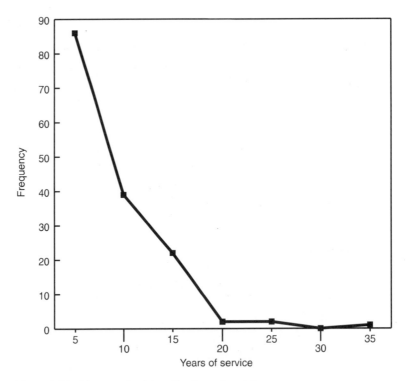

Figure 3.15   Line graph of length of service data

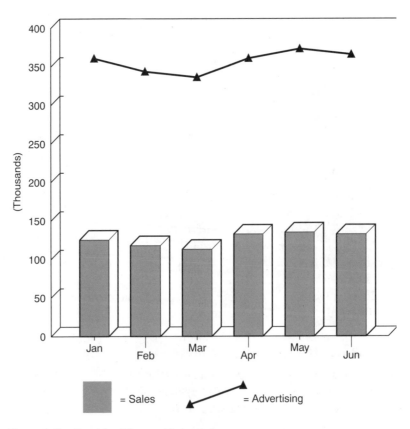

= Sales   = Advertising

Figure 3.16   Combined line and bar graph

Table 3.5 Frequency distribution for number of days absent (Output from Lotus 1-2-3)

Days	Frequency
5	83
10	38
15	21
20	6
25	3
30	1

Once the information is in this format it is then a straightforward matter of adding one class of values to the next class of values until we have a cumulative total, as in Table 3.6 (real class limits are normally used in cumulative frequency distributions).

Table 3.6 Cumulative frequency distribution of number of days absent

Days	Cumulative frequency
5	83
10	121
15	142
20	148
25	151
30	152

It can be seen that there were 83 employees who were absent for five days or less, and 121 employees were absent for ten days or less (this includes the 83 employees who were absent for five days or less) etc. This can be shown graphically as a cumulative frequency curve (also known as an *ogive*) as in Figure 3.17, and it clearly shows that the highest frequencies are at the 5, 10 and 15 day intervals, with a rapid fall off thereafter.

This graph can be used to *estimate* a range of values. For instance, if we wanted to know how many employees were absent for eight days or less from work, we would read from eight days on the horizontal axis and compare it to the number of employees on the vertical axis, as in Figure 3.18, and see that approximately 108 employees were absent for eight days or less.

It is sometimes convenient to have an 'or more' cumulative frequency distribution rather than the preceding 'less than' cumulative frequency distribution. This can be obtained by accumulating upwards from the bottom of the ordinary frequency table, as in Table 3.7. The total is now 140 rather than 152, as it was felt appropriate that those employees with zero absent days should be excluded from the first category of Table 3.7.

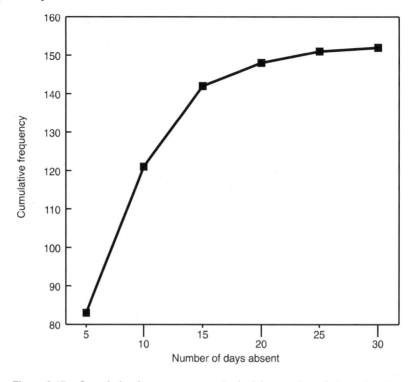

Figure 3.17   Cumulative frequency curve (ogive) for number of days absent

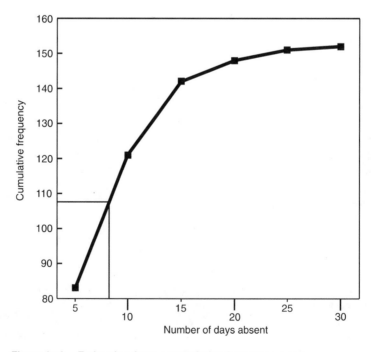

Figure 3.18   Estimating from a cumulative frequency curve

Table 3.7   An 'or more' cumulative frequency distribution

Days	Cumulative frequency
1	140
5	69
10	31
15	10
20	4
25	1
30	0

This can again be shown pictorially as in Figure 3.19. The choice of a 'less than' or 'or more' cumulative frequency distribution is normally dependent on the type of information one is looking for. In terms of our data, the 'or more' might be preferred as it clearly shows that the number of employees falls dramatically as the number of days absent increases.

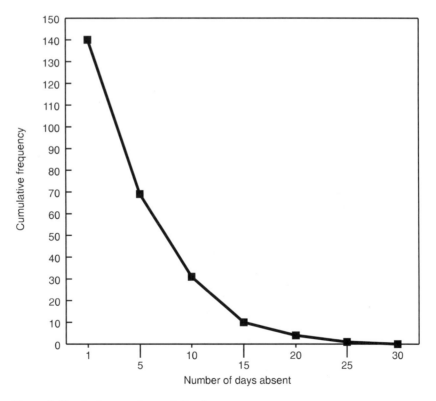

Figure 3.19   An 'or more' cumulative frequency curve

Competence Example 3.2

At the end of this section you should now be able to demonstrate how to:

1 **translate a frequency distribution into a cumulative frequency distribution**

2 **graph the cumulative frequency distribution as a cumulative frequency curve**

3 **use the cumulative frequency curve for estimating values**

To practise and demonstrate these competences complete problems 3.3 and 3.4 at the end of this chapter. To help you to develop these competences a description of the procedure you will need to follow is now given, along with a typical problem format. The problem format is based on a problem that is similar to that previously outlined.

PROCEDURE

❶ Create a cumulative frequency distribution.

❷ Graph the cumulative frequency distribution as a cumulative frequency curve.

❸ Use the cumulative frequency curve to estimate values.

PROBLEM

For the 'Age' category data in Table 3.1, draw a cumulative frequency curve and estimate the following:

a. The number of employees who are 23 years old or less.
b. The number of employees who are 47 years old or less.
c. The number of employees who are least 35 years old but less than or equal to 53 years old.

A description of the layout of the solution format is given at the beginning of the book.

SOLUTION FORMAT

The frequency distribution for the age variable has already been formulated and is shown below:

❶

Age class	Frequency
Up to 20	11
21 to 30	63
31 to 40	46
41 to 50	22
51 to 60	10
	152

The frequency distribution is now converted into a cumulative frequency distribution.

Age	Cumulative frequency
Less than or equal to 20	11
Less than or equal to 30	74
Less than or equal to 40	120
Less than or equal to 50	142
Less than or equal to 60	152

1

❸ ❷ With Lotus 1-2-3 it is now a straightforward procedure to turn the above cumulative **2 3** frequency distribution into a cumulative frequency curve and estimate the values that have been asked for, as shown in Figure 3.20.

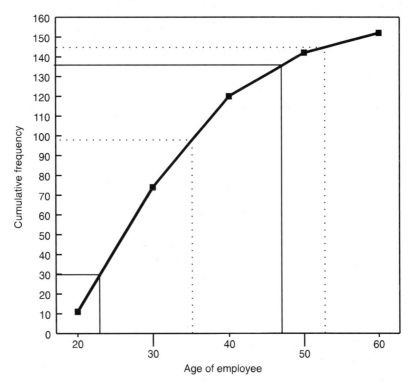

Figure 3.20   Cumulative frequency curve for age of employees

Estimating from the cumulative frequency curve the number of employees who are:

a. 23 years or less = 29
b. 47 years or less = 136
c. at least 35 years and less than 53 years is 145 − 98 = 47

Practise your competence now on problems 3.3 and 3.4 at the end of the chapter. When you have demonstrated competence in this area you can use the computer disk provided to automate the labour intensive and arithmetic elements. You may choose either a Lotus or an Excel spreadsheet depending on the package you have access to. The operation of this package was developed in detail in Chapter 2. You may now demonstrate the competence in this area against problems from your own work environment.

3.6.6 Contingency tables

The methods presented so far have tended to look at only one variable at a time, such as marital status, education or service. A **contingency table** looks at and summarises two or more variables simultaneously. Table 3.8 is a contingency table (also known as a *crosstabs* or *crosstabulation* table) for the age and salary data and it tends to indicate that as the age categories increase so does the level of salary. It also shows that the highest frequencies are in the 21 to 40 age range and the £12,001 to £13,000 salary category. This high concentration indicates that this group is the bedrock of the organisation and that current and future strategies and policies must therefore recognise this and take it into account when any decisions are to be made. The contingency table can thus be a very effective way of summarising a number of variables.

Table 3.8   Contingency table for age and salary data

Age	Salary (£)							Total
	0 to 9,000	9,001 to 10,000	10,001 to 11,000	11,001 to 12,000	12,001 to 13,000	13,001 to 14,000	14,001 to 15,000	
0 to 20	1	4	3	3				11
21 to 30			3	15	41	3	1	63
31 to 40					33	12	1	46
41 to 50					7	15		22
51 to 60						10		10
Total	1	4	6	18	81	40	2	152

3.6.7 Pictograms

Newspapers and magazines often abound with graphs that are designed to catch the eye of the reader. They are visually appealing and attempt to get the message across in one glance. Figure 3.21 shows a pictogram for the age data and it is quite effective in transmitting information. With the emphasis now on managers being equipped and capable of making high impact presentations, it is hardly surprising that more and more people are turning to this type of presentation. It is important to recognise that while these types of presentations can be very effective, they can

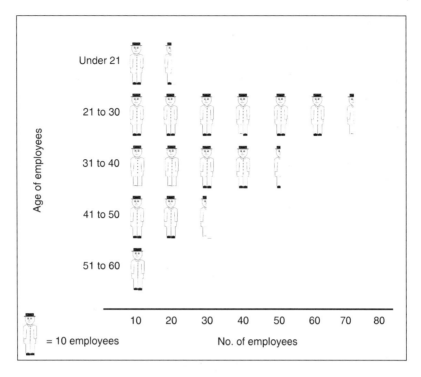

Figure 3.21   Pictogram of age data

also become overcomplicated and alienate the reader. The secret, as in all presentations, is to keep them as simple and interesting as possible.

3.7   A word of caution

Intentionally or unintentionally, bar graphs and other pictorial presentations can sometimes be very misleading. For instance, if we wished to combine the two classes 10,000 to 10,999 and 11,000 to 11,999 for our salary data (Table 3.2) into one class of 10,000 to 11,999, then we would have a new frequency of 24 (6 + 18). If this new frequency was then applied to a bar graph with the area doubled, as in Figure 3.22, then we would get the erroneous impression that this new class contained a higher proportion of the frequencies than is actually the case. To portray the data accurately it is necessary to divide the total of the combined classes by two (i.e. 24/2 = 12), as in Figure 3.23. This has increased the class 10,000 to 10,999 by six and reduced the class 11,000 to 11,999 by six, thus equalising the two classes.

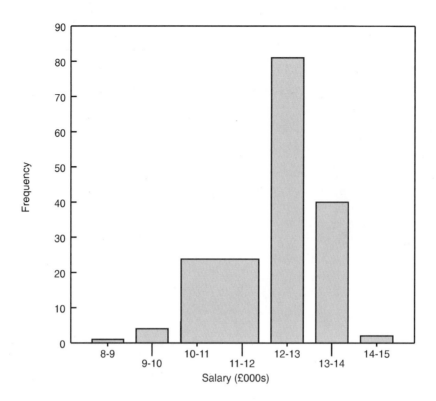

Figure 3.22   Combining two classes incorrectly

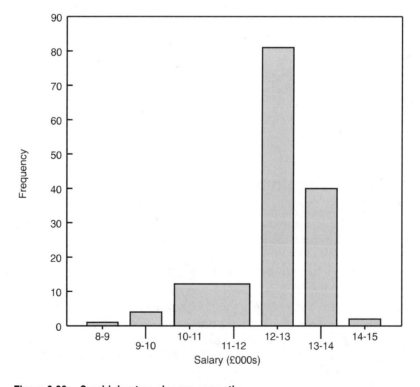

Figure 3.23   Combining two classes correctly

Similar difficulties arise when pictograms of varying sizes are used to illustrate and emphasise differences in the data. For instance, the amount of time that young children watch TV has increased from an average of 14 hours per week in 1970 to 28 hours per week in 1990. Since the amount has doubled, we might draw a pictogram for 1990 that is twice as high and wide as that for 1970, as in Figure 3.24.

This gives the false impression that 1990 viewing was four times (instead of twice) that of 1970, and this is because we have doubled both the height and width of the pictogram. We can rectify the situation if we double either the height or width, but not both (the problem with this is that it will change the shape of the pictogram), or we can increase the height and width proportionally by taking the square root of the growth (this is two as the number of hours had doubled), which is $\sqrt{2} = 1.41$. If we increase the sides of the pictogram by 1.41 rather than by two we thus get a true increase in scale as shown in Figure 3.25.

There might appear to be little difference between Figure 3.24 and Figure 3.25, but when we compare them side by side, as in Figure 3.26, it is clear that the corrected pictogram on the right-hand side is smaller than the uncorrected pictogram.

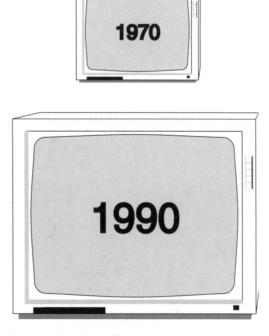

Figure 3.24   Misleading pictogram

Figure 3.25   Corrected pictogram

It is quite possible therefore to convey the wrong impression when one uses graphical presentations, especially when we combine classes or show change by increasing the size of an object. Indeed, a desired impression can be created by purposely manoeuvring the information in this way. Such unscrupulous behaviour would of course never occur to the authors!

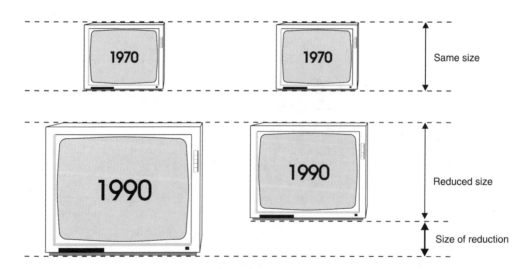

Figure 3.26   Comparison of Figures 3.24 and 3.25

3.8 Choosing the right graph

Unfortunately there are few universal rules about which type of graph is best suited to a given set of data. It is also the case, as this chapter has demonstrated, that a given set of data can be portrayed in many different ways. Having said this, here are a few general rules to help in the selection of an appropriate graph:

Vertical bar

Shows how values change over a time period that is not too long. It is also good at comparing different categories and sets of data.

Stacked vertical bar

Performs a similar job to that of a vertical bar graph, but with the added ability to show how parts contribute to the whole.

Vertical line

Provides an effective means of showing how a set or sets of data change over a longer time period. If there are a number of lines on the graph and they criss-cross a number of times then it might become confusing and difficult to follow and interpret. If this is the case then a vertical bar or area graph might be more appropriate.

Horizontal bar

Is well suited for simple comparisons of a small number of variables at a particular point in time.

Pie chart

Is often the best way to compare the contribution of parts to a whole.

Table chart

Also known as a cross-tabulation or contingency table, and although it is less visually attractive than the above, it can be very effective at comparing two sets of data. It is also one of the few chart types that enable detailed comparison of individual data values or groups of values within the data sets.

Pictogram

This increasingly popular method of presenting data can be very powerful in conveying the main points within the data. It is also potentially misleading if care is not taken in how the pictogram is formulated and presented.

3.9 Guidelines on graphical presentations

The bars, pies and pictograms, etc., are the focal point on any graph and should therefore be as prominent as possible in a presentation. If it is possible to get the message across without the use of axis titles or legends then don't be afraid to do so – let the graph speak for itself. As has been pointed out with line graphs, beware of overcrowding. It is better to have two or three graphs than one that is overcrowded and difficult to interpret.

When using bar graphs keep the bars together if you want to suggest that they belong together. For a graph that is showing a range of variables over a number of years it is quite acceptable to group the bars by years with wider spaces between the years, as this aids interpretation. If there is no need for this then make them as wide and evenly spaced as possible.

Most spreadsheet and presentation packages allow for gridlines on the graph, but these can cause confusion if there are too many, so use only as many as are absolutely necessary to facilitate understanding of the value of the columns etc., on the graph. The gridlines should not be too obtrusive, so use either dotted lines or soft shades of grey or similar that blend into the background.

It is generally recommended that only one typeface should be used on a graph, as sufficient typographical variety can be generated by using bold, italic, and varying text sizes. In the same vein, do not use too many colours on the graph as it only confuses the reader.

Summary

The collection of data and its subsequent reduction to a more manageable size can be both time-consuming and tedious. While acknowledging that this might be true, it must be recognised that it forms the foundation of any investigation and analysis. The skills associated with summarising and presenting a set of data are essential for many managers, and the likelihood is that as one progresses up the managerial ladder the need for those skills will get even greater.

It is not surprising that many students spend a far greater amount of their time on the more difficult areas of a quantitative syllabus, even though on a day-to-day basis they are much less likely to use those skills in an organisation than they are the skills that have been outlined in this chapter. To counter this tendency and build up the necessary competences it is important that you carry out the exercises that follow this section, and in particular that you use Lotus 1-2-3 and Excel to analyse the Tasty Foods data set and so that you are able to produce a range of graphs that support and reinforce the points that need bringing out of the data (remember that the data set is already on the disk).

The competences that have been gained in this chapter are directly transferable to most organisations, and the Lotus 1-2-3 and Excel discs provided can be used to analyse your own company's data. The following exercises provide an opportunity for you to practice and demonstrate these competences, but they are no substitute for the data that needs analysing in your own organisation.

Problems for Chapter 3

3.1 For the absenteeism (Absent variable) data in Table 3.1, construct a relative frequency distribution and a bar graph, and report upon your findings.

3.2 The Sickness and Absenteeism variables in Table 3.1 look as though they might have different characteristics. Summarise and graph these variables and state what differences exist between the two sets of data.

3.3 For the Service variable in Table 3.1 estimate via a cumulative frequency distribution and a cumulative frequency curve the following:
a. the number of employees who have had 12 years' service or less
b. the number of employees who have had 18 years' service or less
c. the number of employees who have had at least eight years' service but less than 14 years' service.

3.4 For the Service variable in Table 3.1 estimate via an 'or more' cumulative frequency distribution and its corresponding cumulative frequency curve the following:
a. the number of employees who have had five years' or more service
b. the number of employees who have had 13 years' or more service
c. the number of employees who have had at least seven years' or more service but less than 16 or more years' service.

3.5 A large manufacturing company is trying to make its employees more aware of the danger of accidents. A survey of the last 50 weeks shows the number of accidents to be as follows:

0	5	9	8	2	10	4	12	14	8
3	8	4	4	0	9	3	10	10	9
1	1	2	14	4	9	1	8	2	7
2	6	2	9	8	5	0	18	8	11
4	6	12	1	12	8	6	6	6	11

Construct a frequency distribution with five classes for this data and represent it graphically as a bar chart.

3.6 Construct a cumulative frequency curve for the following data:

Class Interval	Frequency
3 to under 6	2
6 to under 9	5
9 to under 12	10
12 to under 15	11
15 to under 18	17
18 to under 21	5

3.7 Consumers spend their incomes on a vast array of goods and services. The following data provides a summary of how the average consumer spends their income:

Category	% of Income
Medical care	5
Clothing	5
Entertainment	4
Housing	46
Food	17
Transportation	19
Others	4
Total	100

Summarise the information in the form of a pie chart. What area represents the largest piece of the pie and is it very much larger than the next piece? How much larger is it?

3.8 The United Kingdom balance of trade (exports minus imports) has fluctuated over the last 12 years, as the following data indicates (£m):

1983	106.3	1987	3.6	1991	−577.5
1984	141.1	1988	−111.9	1992	−736.5
1985	137.0	1989	−263.6	1993	−505.5
1986	89.6	1990	−420.5	1994	−104.0

Construct a bar graph to illustrate these figures and interpret its meaning.

3.9 Data has been collected on the times taken by 20 employees to carry out a standard procedure. The times, in minutes, were as follows:

31	25	15	10
22	19	19	35
30	19	27	20
29	26	18	17
20	16	19	14

a. Group the data into five classes.
b. Obtain a cumulative frequency table for the data.
c. Obtain a relative frequency table.
d. Obtain a cumulative relative frequency table.

4 Averages and variability

why an average can represent a thousand numbers

4.1 Introduction

The measures outlined in Chapter 3 tended to use a frequency distribution or a graph to summarise a set of data. Although this is perfectly acceptable, there are many occasions when managers will need to summarise and compare data by a single numerical measure. These numerical measures also provide the foundation for many management reporting and control procedures. The area that this chapter covers therefore represents a set of skills and knowledge that are essential for any manager, and underpins many of the chapters that are to follow. The manual methods used will be explained, although the focus will again be on the use of spreadsheet packages like Lotus 1-2-3 and Excel, as this dramatically increases the speed and flexibility of the user during the analysis of the data.

This chapter is concerned with developing competence in representing and dissecting a set of data by a range of numerical measures and will enable you to:

- represent a set of data by its most typical value
- show how a set of data varies around its most typical value
- compare sets of data by using their most typical value and their associated variation around that most typical value
- rearrange a set of data into different proportions
- compare sets of data by a range of numerical measures
- appreciate how information technology can be utilised in this type of analysis

The chapter will use a series of practical examples to develop the underpinning knowledge in the area that we have called averages and variability.

At the end of each section the required competence will be specified and described. A typical problem format with the competences highlighted will also be given to help you to demonstrate the competences on the problems at the end of the chapter. At the end of the book a full solution will be given for the first of these problems as well as the answers for the rest.

4.2 The size of your data

There is often a need in statistics to distinguish between all the items that are *available* for study and those that are actually *used* in a study. To clearly show which is which it is normal practice to refer to all the items that are capable of being included in an analysis as the **population**, while anything less than all the items is referred to as a **sample**. For the Tasty Foods data that was used in Chapter 3 all the employees were included so it would be known as the population. If we had only looked at say 30 employees, then this would have been a sample. The terms 'population' and 'sample' also depend upon the nature of your investigation, in that if you are looking at all the companies in the snack food industry then the term 'population' now changes to include those companies, with Tasty Foods being a 'sample' of that population. Regardless of the context within which your study operates, the number of items in your population and sample are distinguishable by the following notation:

N = population size
n = sample size

From what we have said it becomes apparent that if we are only looking at 30 employees from a study that has a maximum of 152 employees, then n is 30 and N is 152.

4.3 Measures of location

Most people have an appreciation of the word 'average', which is not surprising when one considers the frequency with which it is used in everyday language. For example:

- the average weight of middle-aged men is 12 stone
- the average rate of inflation is now 3 per cent
- the average wage of hospital cleaning staff is £8,400
- women, on average, are less likely to achieve executive positions in organisations than men
- the average IQ of children in class 3a was 112

If people are asked to explain what the word 'average' actually means they normally have some difficulty in expressing their thoughts and say things like, 'It's when you add up the numbers and divide by the number of numbers,' and 'It's the average.' When this is explored a little further it quickly becomes clear that an average is a number that best represents a set of data. It is also a number that is *most typical* of a set of data. There are a number of averages that can be used to represent sets of data, and some thought is normally required in deciding which is the best to use.

Averages are known as measures of 'location' and 'central tendency' as they are located towards the middle of a set of data. To be precise, we would say they are located towards the centre of a frequency distribution. The types of averages that are used in business, together with their strengths and weaknesses, will now be investigated.

4.3.1 The mean

When people calculate an average they invariably use what is known as a **sample, population** or **arithmetic mean**. We shall simply call it the 'mean', and it is calculated for a sample of data as follows:

Sample mean

$$\bar{X} = \frac{\sum X}{n}$$

Notation like this often causes alarm among students until it is explained that this simply translates as 'the sample mean ($\bar{X}$ is pronounced 'X bar') is equal to the total or summation of ($\sum$ is the Greek letter 'sigma' and means to add up) the individual data values (X) and divided by the number of items in the set of data (n)'. The $\bar{X}$ indicates that this is a sample of data, so for our Tasty Foods data, taking a sample of the first ten employees, the sample mean age is:

Table 4.1   Sample of 'age' data

Employee	Age
1	24
2	29
3	43
4	26
5	22
6	25
7	36
8	28
9	19
10	24

$n = 10$
$\sum X = 24 + 29 + 43 + 26 + 22 + 25 + 36 + 28 + 19 + 24 = 276$

$$\bar{X} = \frac{276}{10} = 27.6$$

The mean age from this sample of data is therefore 27.6 years.

The population mean is denoted by the Greek letter μ (pronounced mew to rhyme with new) and for all the age data in Tasty Foods (i.e. the population) it is:

Population mean

$$\mu = \frac{\sum X}{N}$$

$$\mu = \frac{4919}{152} = 32.36$$

The manual calculation of the population mean is time-consuming because there are 152 items in the data and every one has had to be added together (which lends itself to human error due to missing or duplicating an entry). Lotus 1-2-3 has a specific command (the @ AVG command) and Excel has an equivalent paste function, which can quickly and easily calculate the population mean. Because spreadsheet packages like Lotus 1-2-3 and Excel are well equipped to handle tasks such as these, they will be used extensively in this chapter, as it significantly reduces the amount of time it takes to analyse data. The data in Table 3.1 is on your Lotus 1-2-3 and Excel disk and the majority of the examples and illustrations that follow are available for you to practise with on the Tasty Food data.

The mean is the most widely used average and it forms the basis of many of the techniques that later chapters will explore. The mean has the advantage of being simple to calculate and has widespread acceptance. The main problem with the mean is that it might not be truly representative of the data if very large values occur in what is otherwise a uniform set of data. For example, if we have two sets of data that have the following characteristics:

(a) $\quad \overline{X} = 467 + 451 + 473 + 420 + 436 = \dfrac{2247}{5} = 449.4$

(b) $\quad \overline{X} = 467 + 451 + 473 + 420 + 833 = \dfrac{2644}{5} = 528.8$

it is evident that the unusually high value of 833 in data set (b) has distorted the mean value and it now no longer acts as the best representative value for the rest of the data values. This weakness can sometimes be very important, in that if we wanted the average wage of employees we would not want a very high or low value distorting the true average. It is for this reason that published statistics by professional bodies and organisations always use an alternative average, called the median, when they quote average wage rates.

4.3.2 The median

The **median** is the value of the middle item when the data is arranged in ascending or descending order. If there are an even number of items in the set of data then it is the mean of the middle two items. Applying the median to the data in the preceding example we find:

(a) 420 436 <u>451</u> 467 473
(b) 420 451 <u>467</u> 473 833

When the sample mean was used as the basis of the above example there was a change of 79.4 from (a) to (b). When the median was used there was only a change of 16 from (a) to (b), and it is consequently more appropriate for data set (b) than is the sample mean.

If there had been six items in the list then the median would be 459, as it is the average of the middle two numbers, as shown below:

$$420 \quad 436 \quad \underset{459}{\underline{451 \quad 467}} \quad 473 \quad 483$$

Another way to locate the median is by using $\frac{n+1}{2}$ where n is the number of data values in the set of data. For the above example we have six data items, therefore:

$$\frac{6+1}{2} = 3.5$$

which is between data values 3 and 4. In other words it is the mean of the middle two items, which is 459. When we have a very large number of items the median can be very time-consuming to calculate due to having to arrange the data in ascending or descending order. In these circumstances it is necessary to use a statistical software package to calculate the median. These packages simply replicate the above procedure in that they rank the data in ascending or descending order in order to locate the median. Using Lotus 1-2-3 it is possible to rank the data in either ascending or descending order (e.g. data, sort, range of data to sort, ascending primary sort key) but it is then necessary to apply the $\frac{n+1}{2}$ rule in order to locate the median location. For the age data the median is therefore in position $\frac{152+1}{2} = 76.5$, which is the mean of the values in position 76 and 77, which is $\frac{31+31}{2} = \frac{62}{2} = 31$. This procedure is greatly simplified if you use the Excel spreadsheet package since it has a dedicated 'median' function that can be applied to any set of data.

The mean for all the age data was 32.36 while the median was 31. It is difficult to say that one is more accurate than the other, as they describe the middle of the data in their own way (the median splits the data into two halves while the mean seeks the overall common middle value). The final judgement as to which to use rests, as is always the case, with the person carrying out the analysis. The main benefit of using the median lies in its ability to discount extreme values, and in being able to find middle value non-quantitative phenomena, such as objects and tasks. Its main disadvantage is that it can be time-consuming to calculate and is not as reliable, statistically speaking, as the mean.

4.3.3   The mode

The **mode** is the third main type of average, and it is the value that occurs most often in a set of data. For the age data the value that occurs most often is 24 (there are 11 people aged 24 years). When we compare the three averages:

mean = 32.36   median = 31   mode = 24

it can be seen that the mode is the most divergent of the three measures. This reflects one of the weaknesses of the mode, in that the value that occurs most often might not be, in overall terms, the most representative value for that set of data. It is also quite possible to get two or more modes for a set of data if values occur with the same frequency within the data (i.e. it is not always a unique value). If a set of data has two modes it is called a *bimodal distribution*, and if it has more than two modes it is called *multimodal*. When data is grouped into classes the class with the highest frequency is known as the *modal class*. Bimodal distributions often warn us that there might be more than one factor affecting the data. For instance, if we recorded for a month the number of visits to supermarkets by men and women, we might get a bimodal distribution as shown in Figure 4.1, since women visit supermarkets more frequently than men. This is an important characteristic that supermarket chains might want to exploit, and which could have been missed if only a single mean or median measure had been used. Given this bimodal distribution it is perhaps better for the supermarkets to separate the shoppers by gender before they investigate their buying behaviour.

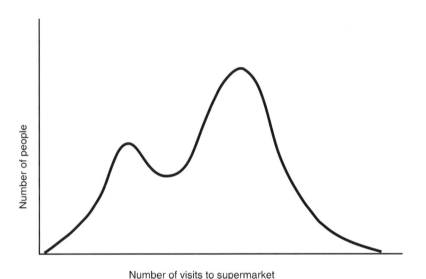

Figure 4.1   A bimodal distribution

Although the mode is of limited use statistically, it does have some applications within business. It is often used for determining sizes, whether it be shoe or dress sizes. If sizes are simply small, medium and large, then it is likely that these represent the modal size for those particular bands. This enables manufacturers to reduce costs by reducing the variety of sizes. The mode is also used in work study, where the average time for a task is often based on the mode.

4.3.4   Comparing the mean, median and mode

When a distribution is perfectly symmetrical as in Figure 4.2, the mean, median and mode are all exactly the same, so they meet in the very centre of the frequency curve.

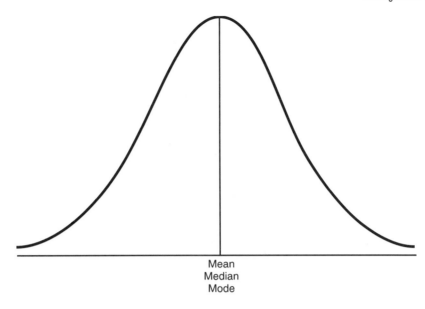

Figure 4.2 A symmetrical distribution curve

If the distribution is positively or negatively skewed however, as in Figures 4.3 and 4.4, then the mean, median and mode are not exactly the same. In fact, the mode (which is the most frequently occurring item) remains in its original position, while the median moves towards the right or left, being positionally in the middle of the data. The mean moves the furthest towards the right or left as it is the average that is affected most by extreme values. Income data is often positively skewed as there are relatively few *very* low wages, a great many middle-income wages, and a small number of *extremely* high wages that push the distribution to the right.

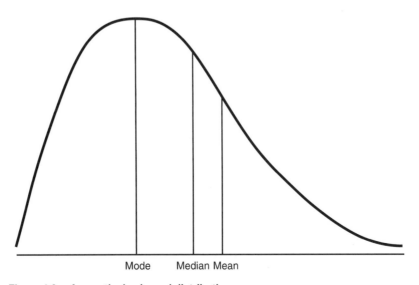

Figure 4.3 A negatively skewed distribution

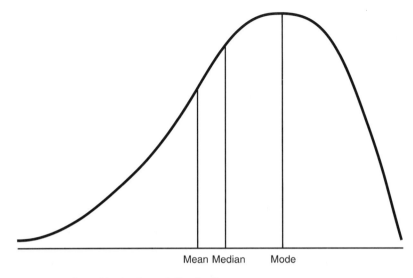

Figure 4.4   A positively skewed distribution

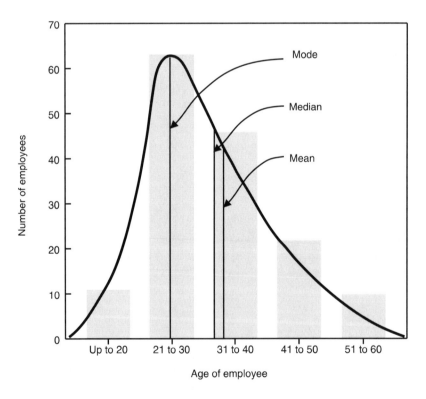

Figure 4.5   Frequency distribution of 'age' data – a comparison of the mode, median and mean

When data is skewed to a marked degree the most appropriate measure to use is normally the median, as it is located between the mode and the mean. In practice, it is probably best to use both the median and the mean, since the difference between the two is an indicator for the level of skewness in the data (the bigger the difference the greater the skewness). The frequency distribution of the age data, with a frequency curve superimposed upon it, is shown in Figure 4.5. It is a negatively skewed distribution that has the mode at the peak of the curve with a value of 24 years. The median and the mean are to the right of the mode, with the mean being the furthest to the right with a value of 32.4 years and the median lying slightly to the left of the mean with a value of 31 years. It is interesting to speculate what the responses of a group of managers would be if Figure 4.5 only had the bar graph on it and they were asked to estimate what the average age was. More likely than not they would have said 35 years since that is the middle of the highest bar (they would have gone for the mode). This has overlooked the fact that the majority of the employees are within the 21 to 30 and 31 to 40 classes, so it is hardly surprising that the median and mean have shifted to the right and are in the lower end of the 31 to 40 class. The more appropriate value would therefore have been the median or the mean. It is more difficult to decide which of these is the best to use, though the discussion would appear to favour the median.

4.3.5 The weighted mean

The weighted mean is used when the values we are using are not equally important (the mean assumes that each value is equally important). For example, if we had three investment accounts which gave us a rate of return of 7 per cent, 8 per cent and 10 per cent respectively, and we wanted to know what the average rate of return was overall, and used the mean as the basis of the calculation, we would have:

$$\overline{X} = \frac{7 + 8 + 10}{3} = 8.33\%$$

This assumes that we have the same amount of money invested in each of the accounts. Since the rate of return is obviously affected by how much money we have invested it seems sensible to take this into consideration when we calculate our average rate of return. To do this we assign the investments weights (to show their relative importance) and calculate a weighted mean:

$$\overline{X}w = \frac{\sum XW}{\sum W}$$

where $\overline{X}w$ is the weighted mean
X is the individual data values
W is the individual weights assigned to each of the data values

Assuming that we had £2,000 in the account that gave 7 per cent return, £6,000 in the account that gave 8 per cent return, and £30,000 in the account that gave 10 per cent return, what would be the weighted average rate of return for the three accounts?

$$\overline{Xw} = \frac{(7 \times 2,000) + (8 \times 6,000) + (10 \times 30,000)}{2,000 + 6,000 + 30,000} = 9.53\%$$

It can be seen that there is a difference of 1.2 per cent between the two measures, and that the correct measure to use was the weighted mean as it has taken the amounts of money invested into proper consideration.

Looking at another example, let's consider a salesman's average rate of commission. If the salesman sells 16,100 boxes of chocolate fingers at 26.6 pence commission per box, 8,800 boxes of cream eggs at 36.9 pence commission per box, 12,200 boxes of truffles at 8.1 pence commission per box, 19,500 boxes of chocolate bars at 10.3 pence commission per box, and 3,400 boxes of chocolate mints at 41.0 pence commission per box, what is the salesman's average rate of commission?

$$\overline{Xw} = \frac{(26.6 \times 16,100) + (36.9 \times 8,800) + (8.1 \times 12,200) + (10.3 \times 19,500) + (41.0 \times 3,400)}{16,100 + 8,800 + 12,200 + 19,500 + 3,400} = 19.87$$

The average rate of commission for this salesman is therefore 19.87 pence, which can then be used by the sales manager, along with other measures, to compare and contrast the sales force's performance.

4.3.6 The geometric mean

It has been shown that the mean can be distorted by very large numbers. The geometric mean has the advantage that it is affected much less by such extreme values. It also has the benefit of being particularly well suited to showing percentage changes in a series of positive numbers. The geometric mean (GM) is calculated by taking the nth root of the product of n numbers:

$$GM = \sqrt[n]{X_1 X_2 X_3 \ldots X_n}$$

If we take three house prices, £115,000, £134,000 and £307,000, the mean is:

$$\overline{X} = \frac{115,000 + 134,000 + 307,000}{3} = £185,333$$

whereas the geometric mean is:

$$GM = \sqrt[3]{(115,000)(134,000)(307,000)} = £167,872$$

It is evident that the geometric mean is smaller than the sample mean and is therefore a more appropriate measure to use since it was influenced less by the much higher third value. Most scientific calculators can be used to calculate the geometric mean (the sequence followed for my calculator was to first multiply the numbers and then press the function key to activate universal root key Y^x, and then input 3 to get the answer of 167872). It is even easier if you use the spreadsheet package Excel, as there is a function called GEOMEAN that calculates the geometric mean automatically.

Although the geometric mean is useful in reducing the influence of high values, its greatest benefit and widest application is in calculating average percentage growth over a given time period, and it is thus widely used in the computation of compounded rates of return in the financial world (it is used extensively in reports on investment returns as well as in population growth, inflation, and several important economic indexes). If you worked in the financial services sector, had financial responsibilities within an organisation, or even had a lump sum of money to invest, how would you evaluate the performance of a mutual investment fund on the basis of an initial investment of £20,000 for a six year period? The mutual fund is kind enough to provide data on how a similar account performed (Table 4.2), and is rather proud that it had an average annual increase of 28.8 per cent. Looking at the revenue returns in Table 4.2 a little closer it is clear that the 28.8 per cent is a mean value.

Table 4.2   Mutual fund account performance data

Year	Fund revenue returns	Fund performance (percentage increase on previous year)
1990	£20,000	–
1991	£24,600	1.230
1992	£35,400	1.439
1993	£39,900	1.127
1994	£46,200	1.158
1995	£68,700	1.487

$$\overline{X} = \frac{1.230 + 1.439 + 1.127 + 1.158 + 1.487}{5} = 1.288$$

The fund performance increase figures in Table 4.2 were calculated by the current year's revenue return divided by the previous year's, which for 1991 was $24,600/20,000 = 1.23$, a 23 per cent increase.

The geometric mean for the fund is:

$$GM = \sqrt[5]{(1.23)(1.439)(1.127)(1.158)(1.487)} = 1.280$$

The geometric mean is 28 per cent as compared to 28.8 per cent when the mean was used, a difference of only 0.8 per cent. If these annual average increase percentages are applied to the initial investment sum of £20,000 we can see that the geometric mean is a much more accurate measure of the final revenue amount:

$\overline{X} = 1.288$

$£20,000 \times 1.288 = £25,760$
$£25,760 \times 1.288 = £33,179$
$£33,179 \times 1.288 = £42,734$
$£42,734 \times 1.288 = £55,042$
$£55,042 \times 1.288 = £70,894$

GM = 1.280

$£20,000 \times 1,280 = £25,600$
$£25,600 \times 1.280 = £32,768$
$£32,768 \times 1.280 = £41,943$
$£41,943 \times 1.280 = £53,687$
$£53,687 \times 1.280 = £68,719$

The actual revenue figure is £68,700, so the geometric mean is 19 above this, while the mean is 2,194 above. The geometric mean is therefore more accurate and is the basis upon which compounded rates of return are calculated.

4.4 Measures of dispersion

The averages we have looked at are known as measures of **central tendency** or **location,** since they tend to be located in the middle of a frequency distribution. If we took ten employees and measured their level of motivation on a scale of 0 to 30 (*see* Table 4.3), the mean value

$$\overline{X} = \frac{\Sigma X}{n} = \frac{150}{10} = 15$$

would tell us that the most representative middle value was a motivation score of 15. This tells us nothing, however, of the way in which the individuals within that group differ from one another in their motivation score. To know how the

Table 4.3   Employee motivation scores

Motivation score
13
18
16
09
11
22
15
17
13
16
$\Sigma X = 150$

individuals vary from one another we need some measure of variability or dispersion. Once we have a suitable measure of central tendency and dispersion it is possible to see how two or more sets of data differ precisely.

4.4.1 The range

This is the simplest of the various measures we could use and it is the difference between the largest and smallest values in the data set. As such it shows how *wide* the distribution of data values is. It can be computed by taking the lowest value from the highest value and adding 1. The range for the motivation scores is therefore:

$$13, 18, 16, 09, 11, 22, 15, 17, 13, 16 \quad 22 - 09 + 1 = 14$$

Using Lotus 1-2-3 on the Tasty Foods data from Table 3.1 in Chapter 3, the range for the 'age' data is $57 - 18 + 1 = 40$ years (use @max and @min to find the maximum and minimum values). The addition of 1 to the calculation allows us to determine the exact limits of the lowest and highest scores in the range.

The problem with the range is that it only tells us what the distance is between the lowest and highest score. If there were an extremely low or high score that was not typical of the majority of the data values then it would not be representative of the data set as a whole. In addition to this it does not tell us how the scores are actually distributed. This can be demonstrated by the following two distributions that have the same range but a very different spread of data values:

$$12, 19, 24, 25, 27, 28, 62 \quad \text{Range} = 51$$
$$8, 19, 25, 33, 41, 47, 58 \quad \text{Range} = 51$$

The range is therefore a crude measure that has limited use in statistics. One important area that uses the range is quality assurance, where it is used to construct control charts. It is also used in the stock market where information is provided daily and weekly on the lowest and highest prices so that price fluctuations can be monitored.

4.4.2 Mean absolute deviation

The mean absolute deviation (MAD) is also sometimes referred to as the *average deviation*. The basis of the MAD and the other measures of dispersion that are to follow is that the most appropriate way of measuring the spread of a set of data is to compare the individual values within that set of data to the mean of that data set. This seems a reasonable thing to do as the mean is the most representative value, so why not compare how the individual values vary or *deviate* in relation to that most typical and representative value?

Looking back to our sample of 10 employees, we found that the mean age for that sample was 27.6 years. If we now compare this mean value to the individual items in the sample, as in Table 4.4, we get the individual **deviations from the mean** $(X - \bar{X})$. The first number in the sample is 24, so the result of $X - \bar{X}$ is

Table 4.4   Mean absolute deviations for sample of 'age' data

X	$X - \bar{X}$	$\lvert X - \bar{X} \rvert$
24	−3.6	+3.6
29	+1.4	+1.4
43	+15.4	+15.4
26	−1.6	+1.6
22	−5.6	+5.6
25	−2.6	+2.6
36	+8.4	+8.4
28	+0.4	+0.4
19	−8.6	+8.6
24	−3.6	+3.6
	$\Sigma(X - \bar{X}) = 0$	$\Sigma \lvert X - \bar{X} \rvert = 51.2$

$24 - 27.6 = -3.6$. This says that the individual value of 24 deviates from the mean of 27.6 by −3.6. The total or sum of these deviations, which is represented by $\Sigma(X - \bar{X})$, will always be zero since the positive and negative deviations will always cancel each other out because the mean is arithmetically in the middle of the data. If the total was not zero we could use it as a basis for an average of the individual deviations, which would then enable us to say what the average amount of spread or deviation was around the mean value. This is important because once we have a measure of central tendency (i.e. the mean), in association with a measure for the spread of the data, we have effectively encapsulated the key attributes of any set of data. It is hardly surprising therefore that these two measures provide the foundations and building blocks of much of statistics and underpin many of the chapters that are to follow.

A way round the problem of a zero total is to ignore the sign of the deviations (when you ignore the sign of a number it is known as an *absolute value*). The average of these absolute deviations is the mean absolute deviation (MAD):

$$\text{MAD} = \frac{\Sigma \lvert X - \bar{X} \rvert}{n}$$

As can be seen from Table 4.4, the sum of the absolute deviations is 51.2, and as there are 10 employees in the sample, we have:

$$\text{MAD} = \frac{51.2}{10} = 5.12$$

The average deviation that the MAD represents is an improvement upon the range, because as Table 4.4 illustrates, it has taken into account all of the items in the data set rather than just the highest and lowest.

The MAD is used to measure the accuracy (error) of forecasts, and this is discussed more fully in Chapter 10. Because the MAD is computed using absolute deviation values, which do not lend themselves to further mathematical manipulation, it is not the preferred method of determining the spread of the data. A more suitable way forward is to use the variance and the standard deviation.

4.4.3 The variance

The variance gets round the problem of negative deviations by taking the square of the deviations. When the square of a number is taken (this is simply the number multiplied by itself) it turns all numbers into positive numbers, as is shown in Table 4.5.

Table 4.5 Squared deviations of 'age' data

X	$X - \bar{X}$	$(X - \bar{X})^2$
24	−3.6	12.96
29	+1.4	1.96
43	+15.4	237.16
26	−1.6	2.56
22	−5.6	31.36
25	−2.6	6.76
36	+8.4	70.56
28	+0.4	0.16
19	−8.6	73.96
24	−3.6	12.96
	$\Sigma(X - \bar{X}) = 0$	$\Sigma(X - \bar{X})^2 = 450.4$

The variance for a sample of data is the total of the squared deviations divided by the number of items in the sample:

$$s^2 = \frac{\Sigma (X - \bar{X})^2}{n - 1}$$

For the sample of age data the sample variance is therefore:

$$s^2 = \frac{450.4}{9} = 50.04$$

It is worth noting that the denominator (i.e. the part below the line) in the sample variance formula is $n - 1$ rather than just n. The reason why we use $n - 1$ instead of n is twofold. Firstly it is to do with degrees of freedom, where degrees of freedom account for any constraints on the data. The constraint we have in a sample of data is that one of the items in the sample is determined by the rest of the items and the sample total. If we have five numbers and we know the first four numbers as well as the total of the five numbers, we have no choice in deciding what the fifth value should be:

$$33 \quad 21 \quad 50 \quad 36 \quad ? = 185$$
$$33 \quad 21 \quad 50 \quad 36 \quad 45 = 185$$

The fifth value has to be 45, which means that there are only four free choices $(n-1)$. The variance formula uses the value of $\bar{X}$, which effectively acts as a constraint and thus reduces the degrees of freedom by 1. The second reason is that a sample of data is slightly less dispersed or spread out than the population from which it is derived. By using $n-1$ we increase the size of the sample spread because it divides into the numerator more often, which brings it more in line with what is happening in the population. In other words it is more accurate to divide by $n-1$ than by n.

The formula for the population variance is:

$$\sigma^2 = \frac{\sum (X - \mu)^2}{N}$$

It is distinguishable from the sample variance by the squaring of the lower case Greek letter sigma (σ^2), which is normally referred to as sigma squared. The population mean also replaces the sample mean in the formula, and this is shown by the Greek letter mu (μ), and with the upper case N replacing the lower case n to show that it is the population of items.

The amount of work involved in calculating the variance can be significantly reduced if we use a spreadsheet. By using the @VAR function in Lotus 1-2-3 it is a straightforward matter of specifying the range of data you want to include in the calculation (e.g. @VAR(A2..A153)).

The variance is an important measure of variability and is used extensively in statistics. For the sample age data it says that the average variability around the mean is 50.04 years. The only problem with this is that 50.04 is the squared value and is thus not of the same magnitude as the original deviations.

4.4.4   The standard deviation

The standard deviation overcomes the magnitude problem by taking the square root of the variance, which brings the outcome of the variance calculation in line with the original data. The standard deviation formula is:

$$s = \sqrt{\frac{\sum (X - \bar{X})^2}{n - 1}}$$

which can also be shown as:

$$s = \sqrt{s^2}$$

The standard deviation for the sample of age data is therefore:

$$s = \sqrt{50.04} = 7.07$$

Our interpretation would now conclude that the sample of ten employees have a mean age of 27.6 years and a standard deviation of 7.07 years. This is a young age profile in that it suggests that the majority of the employees are aged between 20 and 34, with the most typical age being 28 years.

The formula for the population standard deviation is shown below and it is distinguishable from the sample standard deviation by the lower case Greek letter sigma (σ).

$$\sigma = \sqrt{\frac{\sum (X - \mu)^2}{N}} \quad \text{or} \quad \sigma = \sqrt{\sigma^2}$$

The concept and understanding of a mean value and a variance or standard deviation is fundamental to statistics, and as has already been said, underpins much of what follows. As we saw with the variance, the amount of work involved in calculating the standard deviation can be kept to a minimum by using the @STD function in Lotus 1-2-3 (e.g. @STD(A2..A153)).

4.4.5 Shortcut (computational) formulae for ungrouped data

If it is not possible to use a spreadsheet package to facilitate the analysis of the data then the amount of work involved in the calculation of the mean, variance and standard deviation can be reduced if the following formulae are used:

Sample variance $$s^2 = \frac{\sum X^2 - \frac{(\sum X)^2}{n}}{n - 1}$$

Sample standard deviation $$s = \sqrt{s^2}$$

Population variance $$\sigma^2 = \frac{\sum X^2 - \frac{(\sum X)^2}{N}}{N}$$

Population standard deviation $$\sigma = \sqrt{\sigma^2}$$

As an illustration, the first ten employees from Table 3.1 have had their age data recalculated using the shortcut sample variance and standard deviation formulae. The results of this analysis are shown in Table 4.6.

Using the shortcut formula for the variance we find:

$$s^2 = \frac{\sum X^2 - \frac{(\sum X)^2}{n}}{n - 1} \quad s^2 = \frac{8068 - \frac{(276)^2}{10}}{9} = \frac{8068 - 7617.6}{9} = \frac{450.4}{9} = 50.04$$

and for the standard deviation:

$$s^2 = \sqrt{s^2} = \sqrt{50.04} = 7.07$$

Table 4.6 Analysis of 'age' data using shortcut sample formulae

X	X^2
24	576
29	841
43	1849
26	676
22	484
25	625
36	1296
28	784
19	361
24	576
$\Sigma X = 276$	$\Sigma X^2 = 8068$

The variance and standard deviation are exactly the same as previously calculated, with the amount of calculation greatly reduced.

Competence Example 4.1

At the end of this section you should now be able to demonstrate how to:

1 reduce a set of data to a single representative value

2 compare and decide upon the most appropriate representative value

3 decide upon a suitable measure to represent the spread of the data and carry out the appropriate calculations

4 draw suitable conclusions from the analysis and use the results as a basis for comparison

To practise and demonstrate these competences complete problems 4.1 and 4.2 at the end of this chapter. To help you to develop these competences a description of the procedure you will need to follow is now given, along with a typical problem format. The problem format is based on a problem that is similar to that previously outlined.

PROCEDURE

1 Calculate the mean and median for the sample of data.

2 Compare the mean and median.

3 Calculate the variance and standard deviation for the sample of data.

4 Use the mean and standard deviation to describe the sample of data.

5 Compare the results with the sample of ten items used previously in the chapter.

6 Provide an overall review of your analysis.

PROBLEM

For the first 20 items of the 'Age' category data in Table 3.1 (Chapter 3), calculate a mean value, a median value, and a standard deviation value. Comment upon your findings and compare the results of your calculations to the sample of ten 'Age' items that has been used to illustrate the techniques in the first half of this chapter.

A description of the layout of the solution format is given at the beginning of the book.

SOLUTION FORMAT

❶ The mean value was derived from the first 20 items of age data that are shown in Table **1** 4.7. The data in Table 4.7 was also ranked by size to facilitate the identification of the median value.

Table 4.7   Competence exercise sample data

X(age)	X²	Rank order
24	576	18
29	841	19
43	1849	22
26	676	22
22	484	24
25	625	24
36	1296	24
28	784	25
19	361	26
24	576	27
51	2601	28
55	3025	29
27	729	31
31	961	36
43	1849	36
18	324	41
24	576	43
36	1296	43
41	1681	51
22	484	55
$\Sigma X = 624$	$\Sigma X^2 = 21{,}594$	

❶

$$\overline{X} = \frac{\Sigma X}{n} = \frac{624}{20} = 31.2 \text{ years}$$

$$\text{Median} = \frac{n+1}{2} = \frac{21}{2} = 10.5 \text{ position} = \frac{27+28}{2} = 27.5 \text{ years}$$

1

❷ The mean for this set of data is 31.2 while the median is 27.5, which indicates that the mean has been influenced by a few high numbers. The sample also exhibits a slight negative skewness since the mean is to the left of the median (the median has a lower value than the mean). Both the mean and the median indicate a relatively young workforce.

2

❸ The sample variance and the sample standard deviation have been calculated using the shortcut formula:

3

$$s^2 = \frac{\Sigma X^2 - \frac{(\Sigma X)^2}{n}}{n-1} = \frac{21{,}594 - \frac{(624)^2}{20}}{19} = \frac{21{,}594 - 19{,}468.8}{19} = \frac{2{,}125.2}{19} = 111.85$$

$$s = \sqrt{s^2} = \sqrt{111.85} = 10.58$$

❹ The mean for this sample of 20 items is therefore 31.20 years with a standard deviation of 10.58 years. Another way of expressing this would be to say that the mean average age is 31 and that the average amount of variation around this mean age is 10.6 years.

❺ A comparison with the sample of ten items, where the mean was 27.6 years and the standard deviation 7.07 years, shows that the increase in sample size to 20 items has increased the size of the mean to 31.20 and the standard deviation to 10.58. A further comparison with all the 152 employees (Table 4.8) shows that the mean and standard deviation of the sample of 20 items is much closer to the population mean and standard deviation than is the mean and standard deviation of the sample of ten employees. This is not very surprising as we would intuitively expect the mean and standard deviation to get closer to the population mean and standard as the sample size gets larger, and therefore more like the population.

4

Table 4.8 Comparison of sample size 10, sample size 20, and population size 152

$n = 10$	$n = 20$	$N = 152$
Median = 25.5	Median = 27.5	Median = 31
$\overline{X} = 27.6$	$\overline{X} = 31.2$	$\mu = 32.36$
$s = 7.07$	$s = 10.58$	$S = 9.71$

1

❻ Overall, the mean from the sample of 20 items is a better measure than the median as it is very close to both the population mean and median. Since the standard deviation from the sample of 30 items is also very close to the population mean, it is clear that this sample provided very good estimates of what the population values were. The sample data therefore confirms that there is a relatively young workforce with a mean of 31.2 and

⑥ a standard deviation of 10.58. The mean and standard deviation have enabled us to describe and compare the data in a meaningful way, and with the help of the @AVG and @STD functions in Lotus 1-2-3 or the shortcut formulae described above, in an acceptable amount of time.

4

Practise your competence now on problems 4.1 and 4.2 at the end of the chapter. When you have demonstrated competence in this area you can use the Lotus disk provided to automate the labour intensive and arithmetic elements. You may choose either a Lotus 1-2-3 or an Excel spreadsheet depending on the package you have access to. The operation of this package was developed in detail in Chapter 2. You may now demonstrate the competence in this area against problems from your own work environment.

4.5 Measures of location and dispersion: grouped data

In Chapter 3 we saw that data can be very effectively portrayed and summarised by using a frequency distribution based on a number of classes. Since grouped data of this kind is used extensively in government, academic and professional publications, it is important that we have some mechanism by which we can calculate measures of location and dispersion. The problem we face is that the grouped data no longer contains all the information about all the individual items under study. As a consequence of this there is a slight loss in accuracy (but an acceptable level of loss) and the need to use a different set of formulae.

Most spreadsheet packages work on the assumption that individual data values, rather than classes of data, will be the basis upon which calculations will be performed. In this respect this is one of the few areas where spreadsheet packages have limited application.

4.5.1 Calculating the mean from grouped data

The question we face is that if we do not know what the individual values of all the items in the sample or population are, how can we calculate a mean value that is representative of all those individual items? The answer is quite simple – we use the midpoint of the class, for it is the best estimate of what the individual values are within that class. The midpoint is then multiplied by the frequency for that particular class. A frequency distribution for the age data is shown in Table 4.9.

The formulae for computing the mean from a sample or population of grouped data are:

$$\mu = \frac{\sum fM}{N} \quad \text{and} \quad \overline{X} = \frac{\sum fM}{n}$$

where

f = class frequency
M = midpoint of class
N = population frequencies
n = sample frequencies

Table 4.9 Frequency distribution of 'age' data

Age class	Frequency
Up to 20	11
21 to 30	63
31 to 40	46
41 to 50	22
51 to 60	10
	$N = 152$

The work involved in calculating the mean from the frequency distribution of the age data is shown in Table 4.10.

Table 4.10 Computing the mean age from grouped data

Age class	Frequency f	Midpoint M	fM
18 to 20	11	19	209
21 to 30	63	25.5	1,606.5
31 to 40	46	35.5	1,633
41 to 50	22	45.5	1,001
51 to 60	10	55.5	555
	$N = 152$		$\Sigma fM = 5{,}004.5$

The grouped mean age is therefore:

$$\mu = \frac{\Sigma fM}{N} = \frac{5004.5}{152} = 32.92 \text{ years}$$

The true mean is 32.36, which is a loss of accuracy of only 0.56. You will have noticed that we changed the first class from 'Up to 20' to '18 to 20', as it was felt that this was more appropriate and representative of the body of data.

4.5.2 Calculating the variance and standard deviation from grouped data

The variance and standard deviation of grouped data also uses the midpoint of the class as the representative value. The formula for the grouped data therefore becomes:

Sample variance (grouped data) $\qquad s^2 = \dfrac{\Sigma f(M - \overline{X})^2}{n - 1}$

Sample standard deviation (grouped data) $\qquad s = \sqrt{s^2}$

Population variance (grouped data) $\qquad \sigma^2 = \dfrac{\Sigma f(M - \mu)^2}{N}$

Population standard deviation (grouped data) $\quad \sigma = \sqrt{\sigma^2}$

If we apply the population formulae to the grouped age data there is a need to produce an extra three columns to those already shown in Table 4.10. These extra columns are shown in Table 4.11.

Table 4.11 Computing the variance and standard deviation from grouped data

Age class	Frequency f	Midpoint M	fM	$M - \mu$	$(M - \mu)^2$	$f(M - \mu)^2$
18 to 20	11	19	209	−13.92	193.77	2,131.43
21 to 30	63	25.5	1,606.5	−7.42	55.06	3,468.55
31 to 40	46	35.5	1,633	2.58	6.66	306.19
41 to 50	22	45.5	1,001	12.58	158.26	3,481.64
51 to 60	10	55.5	555	22.58	509.86	5,098.56
	N = 152		$\Sigma fM = 5,004.5$			$\Sigma f(M - \mu)^2 = 14,486.37$

$$\text{Where} \quad \mu = \frac{\Sigma fM}{N} = \frac{5004.5}{152} = 32.92 \text{ years}$$

From this the population variance and standard deviation become:

$$\sigma^2 = \frac{\Sigma f(M - \mu)^2}{N} = \frac{14486.37}{152} = 95.30$$

$$\sigma = \sqrt{\sigma^2} = \sqrt{95.30} = 9.76$$

The population standard deviation was previously calculated to be 9.71, so the loss in accuracy is only 0.05. For both the mean and standard deviation the loss of accuracy when using grouped data is therefore very small and does not normally hinder the analysis.

4.5.3 Shortcut (computational) formulae for grouped data

The amount of computation involved in finding the variance and standard deviation for grouped data can be reduced, with no loss of accuracy, if the following shortcut formulae are used:

Sample variance (grouped data) $\qquad s^2 = \dfrac{\Sigma fM^2 - \dfrac{(\Sigma fM)^2}{n}}{n - 1}$

Sample standard deviation (grouped data) $\qquad s = \sqrt{s^2}$

Population variance (grouped data) $\qquad \sigma^2 = \dfrac{\Sigma fM^2 - \dfrac{(\Sigma fM)^2}{N}}{N}$

Population standard deviation (grouped data) $\qquad \sigma = \sqrt{\sigma^2}$

The reduction in computation is clearly seen in Table 4.12, which has two columns less than Table 4.11.

Table 4.12

Computing the variance and standard deviation from grouped data using shortcut formulae

Age class	Frequency f	Midpoint M	fM	fM^2
18 to 20	11	19	209	3,971.00
21 to 30	63	25.5	1,606.5	40,965.75
31 to 40	46	35.5	1,633	57,971.50
41 to 50	22	45.5	1,001	45,545.50
51 to 60	10	55.5	555	30,802.50
	$N = 152$		$\Sigma fM = 5,004.5$	$\Sigma fM^2 = 179,256.25$

Notice that the last column, which is headed fM^2, involves taking the square of M and then multiplying this by f (e.g. $19^2 = 361$, $11 \times 361 = 3971$) rather than taking the square of fM (e.g. $209^2 = 43,681$).

The information in Table 4.12 can now be used to calculate the shortcut variance and standard deviation:

$$\sigma^2 = \frac{\Sigma fM^2 - \frac{(\Sigma fM)^2}{N}}{N} = \frac{179,256.25 - \frac{(5,004.5)^2}{152}}{152} = \frac{179,256.25 - 164,769.87}{152} = \frac{14,486.38}{152} = 95.30$$

$$\sigma = \sqrt{\sigma^2} = \sqrt{95.30} = 9.76$$

As you can see, the standard deviation value of 9.76 is exactly the same as we calculated before.

4.5.4 Calculating the median from grouped data

When data is presented in the form of a grouped frequency distribution we find that the individual data values are lost within the classes of data, and that it is then not possible to calculate the median as shown in section 4.3.2. An alternative method involves converting the grouped frequency distribution to a cumulative frequency distribution. In Chapter 3 the age data was represented as a cumulative frequency distribution, and this is shown again in Table 4.13 and Figure 4.6.

Table 4.13   Cumulative frequency distribution of 'age' data

Age	Frequency	Cumulative frequency
Less than or equal to 20	11	11
Less than or equal to 30	63	74
Less than or equal to 40	46	120
Less than or equal to 50	22	142
Less than or equal to 60	10	152

Figure 4.6   Cumulative frequency curve for 'age' data

To find the median we must convert the cumulative frequency distribution to a relative cumulative frequency distribution (i.e. expressed in percentage terms) and then graph this as a relative cumulative frequency curve. This has been carried out and is shown in Table 4.14 and Figure 4.7.

The median is approximately 30 using this method. Another way of finding the median is to extrapolate it computationally from the frequency distribution. Referring back to Table 4.9, which is shown on page 104, the total was 152 employees, with the middle of the distribution being $N/2 = 152/2 = 76$, the 50th value if the data values were laid out in ascending order.

Since the frequency distribution does have an ascending set of classes, the 76th item will follow and include the 74 items in the first two classes and include two

Table 4.14   Relative cumulative frequency distribution of 'age' data

Age	Frequency	Cumulative frequency	Cumulative relative frequency %
Less than or equal to 20	11	11	$11/152 = 7$
Less than or equal to 30	63	74	$74/152 = 48$
Less than or equal to 40	46	120	$120/152 = 79$
Less than or equal to 50	22	142	$142/152 = 93$
Less than or equal to 60	10	152	$152/152 = 100$

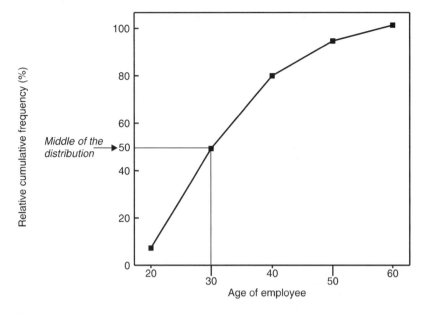

Figure 4.7   Relative cumulative frequency curve for 'age' data

items from the '31 to 40' class. We would expect the two items to be at the lower end of the '31 to 40' class, although we do not know the exact location. A formula that helps to pinpoint the median in these circumstances is:

$$\text{median} = L + \left(\frac{f_1}{f_2}\right)W$$

where

L = the lower limit of the median class
f_1 = the frequency of items interpolated into the median class
f_2 = the median class frequency
W = the width of the median class

For the age data we find

$$31 + \left(\frac{2}{46}\right)10 = 31.43$$

The median is actually 31, so both the relative cumulative frequency curve and the computational approach were very close to the real value.

4.5.5   Finding the mode from grouped data

The mode for a set of grouped data is simply the midpoint of the class with the highest frequency. The highest frequency for the age data is 63, and this is against the '21 to 30' class, which has a midpoint of 25.5. The modal age for this grouped data is therefore 25.5 years.

Competence Example 4.2

At the end of this section you should now be able to demonstrate how to:

■ calculate a mean, median, and standard deviation from a set of grouped data

■ compare and contrast grouped calculations to ungrouped calculations

■ compare and decide upon the most appropriate representative value for a set of grouped data

To practise and demonstrate these detailed competences complete problems 4.3 and 4.4 at the end of this chapter. To help you to develop these competences a description of the procedure you will need to follow is now given, along with a typical problem format. The problem format is based on a problem that is similar to that previously outlined.

PROCEDURE

❶ Calculate the mean and median from a set of grouped data,

❷ Compare the mean and median.

❸ Calculate the variance and standard deviation for a set of grouped data.

❹ Use the mean or median and standard deviation to describe the grouped data.

❺ Compare the grouped calculations to the ungrouped calculations.

❻ Provide an overall review of your analysis of grouped data.

PROBLEM

For the 'Service' category data in Table 3.1 (Chapter 3), create a grouped frequency distribution and from this calculate a mean value, a median value and a standard deviation value. Comment upon your findings and compare the results of your analysis to the ungrouped mean value, median value and standard deviation value (these will have to be calculated separately).

SOLUTION FORMAT

❶ The grouped frequency distribution with appropriate columns for calculating the mean and median for the service data is shown in Table 4.15.

1

Table 4.15

Grouped frequency distribution of service data for calculation of the mean and median

Length of service (Years)	Frequency f	Midpoint M	fM	Cumulative frequency	Cumulative relative frequency (%)
0 to 4	86	2	172	86	$86/152 = 56.58$
5 to 9	39	7	273	125	$125/152 = 82.23$
10 to 14	22	12	264	147	$147/152 = 96.71$
15 to 19	2	17	34	149	$149/152 = 98.02$
20 to 24	2	22	44	151	$151/152 = 99.34$
25 to 29	0	27	0	151	$151/152 = 99.34$
30 to 34	1	32	32	152	$152/152 = 100$
	$N = 152$		$\Sigma fM = 819$		

The mean is:

$$\mu = \frac{\Sigma fM}{N} = \frac{819}{152} = 5.38 \text{ years}$$

The median is:

$$\text{median} = L + \left(\frac{f_1}{f_2}\right)W = 0 + \left(\frac{76}{86}\right)5 = 4.41$$

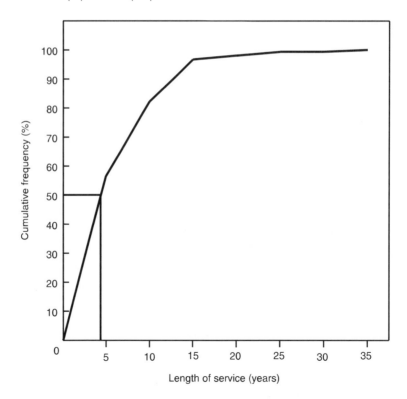

Figure 4.8   Relative cumulative frequency curve for 'service' data

❶ The median has also been estimated from the cumulative frequency curve in Figure 4.8, **■**
where it indicates a value of just over 4.

❷ The frequency distribution clearly indicates that the data is very skewed to the left in that
over half the employees have been employed for under five years. In these circumstances
the median is the better of the two measures to use, as it is not overly influenced by the
few long service employees.

❸ The variance and standard deviation for the service data is based on the information
contained in Table 4.16.

Table 4.16   Variance and standard deviation for service data

Length of service	Frequency f	Midpoint M	fM	fM²
0 to 4	86	2	172	344
5 to 9	39	7	273	1911
10 to 14	22	12	264	3168
15 to 19	2	17	34	578
20 to 24	2	22	44	968
25 to 29	0	27	0	0
30 to 34	1	32	32	1024
	$N = 152$		$\Sigma fM = 819$	$\Sigma fM^2 = 7{,}993$

$$\sigma^2 = \frac{\Sigma fM^2 - \dfrac{(\Sigma fM)^2}{N}}{N} = \frac{7{,}993 - \dfrac{(819)^2}{152}}{152} = \frac{7{,}993 - 4{,}412.9}{152} = \frac{3{,}580.1}{152} = 23.55$$

$$\sigma = \sqrt{\sigma^2} = \sqrt{23.55} = 4.85$$

❹ With a median value of 4.41 and a standard deviation value of 4.85 the evidence is even
stronger that the data is heavily skewed to the left. This characteristic will have an obvious
impact on the culture of the organisation and is also likely to have direct influence on a
number of other areas (e.g. absenteeism).

❺ It is interesting to note that a comparison of the grouped and ungrouped measures (Table **2**
4.17) again reinforces just how close they are. We should feel confident therefore that the
outcome of any analysis that is based on grouped data will be very close to the actual
measures derived from the individual raw data.

3

**Table 4.17   Comparison of grouped and ungrouped service
data measures**

Ungrouped measures	Grouped measures
Mean = 5.95	Mean = 5.38
Median = 4.5	Median = 4.41
Standard deviation = 4.88	Standard deviation = 4.85

6 The overall picture mirrors what has already been said, with the data being highly skewed **3** towards employees who only stay in the organisation for less than five, six or seven years. At the same time there are a small number of employees who have worked within the organisation for more than 15 years. Because the data is skewed it would be appropriate to use the median rather than the mean as the representative value.

Practise your competence now on problems 4.3 and 4.4 at the end of the chapter. When you have demonstrated competence in this area you can use the Lotus 1-2-3 disk provided to automate the labour intensive and arithmetic elements. You may choose either a Lotus 1-2-3 or an Excel spreadsheet depending on the package you have access to. The operation of this package was developed in detail in Chapter 2. You may now demonstrate the competence in this area against problems from your own work environment.

4.6 Other descriptive measures

The statistical measures we have looked at so far are the foundation of any descriptive analysis of data. However, there are a number of other measures that can be useful and supportive in this type of analysis.

4.6.1 Coefficient of variation

The **coefficient of variation**, which is represented by the letters CV, is a ratio. It is the ratio of the standard deviation to the mean (i.e. the amount of times the mean will go into the standard deviation), which is then multiplied by 100 so that it can be expressed as a percentage.

$$\text{Sample coefficient of variation:} \quad \frac{s}{\overline{X}}(100)$$

$$\text{Population coefficent of variation:} \quad \frac{\sigma}{\mu}(100)$$

The value of the coefficient of variation is that the higher the ratio, which is the same as saying that the more times the mean goes into the standard deviation, the greater the spread of the data around the mean. The usefulness of the coefficient of variation can be demonstrated through a simple example:

We want to know what the customers of a fast food chain think about the level of service they have received from its restaurants, so we collect information from two restaurants. The mean for both restaurants is the same but the standard deviations are different:

	Restaurant A	Restaurant B
$\overline{X}$	62	62
s	7	13

This would indicate that there was a much wider range of responses in restaurant B than in restaurant A, even though the means are the same for both restaurants. A comparison like this becomes much more difficult when both the means and standard deviations are different:

	Restaurant A	Restaurant B
$\bar{X}$	62	57
s	9	4

The coefficient of variation for these restaurants is:

$$CV = \frac{9}{62} \times 100 = 14.51\%$$

$$CV = \frac{4}{57} \times 100 = 7.01\%$$

which indicates that although restaurant A has a higher mean than restaurant B, it also has a much wider range of responses. If consistency of service was an important criterion for this organisation then perhaps the lower coefficient of variation in restaurant B is preferable to the higher mean in restaurant A.

4.6.2 Percentiles and the empirical distribution function

Percentiles are used to divide a set of data into specific proportions, and it is possible to separate a set of data into 100 portions by dividing the data into 99 percentiles. The 25th percentile for instance is the position in a set of data, when the data is placed in ascending order, that 25 per cent of the data values are equal to or less than. It also means that 75 per cent of the data values are greater than this locational value. The median, which we have already calculated, is the 50th percentile since it is located exactly in the middle of the data. Since the median was 31 for the age data we can say that 50 per cent of the employees are 31 years of age or less and 50 per cent are over 31 years of age. The formal way of describing percentiles is rather cumbersome, as it says that the nth percentile is the value such that at least n per cent of the items take on this value or less and that at least $(100 - n)$ per cent lie above that value.

There are two ways of determining the value of a given percentile. The first method involves the following steps:

Step 1: Arrange the data values in ascending order
Step 2: Find the position (denoted by i) of the percentile in the above ranked data:

$$i = \frac{P}{100}(n)$$

where: i = the location of the percentile in the ascending set of data

P = the percentile we want to calculate

n = the number of data values in the set of data

Step 3: (a) If i is not a whole number then the percentile is the next value in the ranked set of data (i.e. $i + 1$)

(b) If i is a whole number then the percentile is the average of the value at i and the value next to i (i.e. i and $i + 1$)

To illustrate this, let's suppose that a hospital has monitored and recorded the perceptions of patients in 15 of its wards on the quality of healthcare that was provided. The maximum score that could be scored was 100 while the minimum score possible was 0. The management of the hospital wanted to know, for comparative and performance reasons, what the 30th, 50th and 80th percentiles were. To provide this information it is first necessary to rank the scores in ascending order:

Rank	1	2	3	4	5	6	7	8	9	10	11	12	13	14	15
Score	26	34	39	45	51	58	58	59	61	64	68	69	73	78	81

The next step is to calculate the location of the percentiles in this ranked data:

$$i = \frac{P}{100} (n) \quad = \quad i = \frac{30}{100} (15) = 4.5$$

$$i = \frac{50}{100} (15) = 7.5$$

$$i = \frac{80}{100} = 12$$

For the 30th percentile the location is 4.5, which according to the third step means that the 30th percentile is in position five and therefore has a value of 51. We can now say that 30 per cent of the wards had a score of 51 or less (if you were a manager you might prefer to say that 70 per cent of the wards had a score of more than 51). The 50th percentile is in location 7.5, which again means we go to the next location, which has a value of 59. The 80th percentile is a whole number, so according to the rule in Step 3 it is the average of the values in locations 12 and 13 (i and $i + 1$), which are:

$$\frac{69 + 73}{2} = \frac{142}{2} = 71$$

The 80th percentile is therefore 71, which as the rule states is the average of 69 and 73.

The second and alternative way of determining percentile values is to use a technique that is similar to a cumulative relative frequency curve. It is known as an **empirical distribution function**, and it differs from the cumulative frequency distribution in that it deals with every individual value instead of classes of grouped data. The hospital data has been represented as an empirical distribution function in Figure 4.9, and as you can see it has a number line on the horizontal axis that directly reflects the actual hospital ward scores, while the vertical axis has the now familiar cumulative relative frequency scale. The first task in drawing this graph is to decide on the height of the steps, and this is simply the reciprocal of the number of items of data, which is $\frac{1}{15} = 0.06$. The second stage is to then take the first data value, which is 26, and take this up one step (to a height of 0.06) from its location on the horizontal number line. From the top of this step a line is then drawn horizontally to the next value in the series, which is 34, and then another step of 0.06 etc. Once all the data values have been plotted we can read off the 30th, 50th and 80th percentiles from the graph, which correspond to the previously calculated values of 51, 59 and 71.

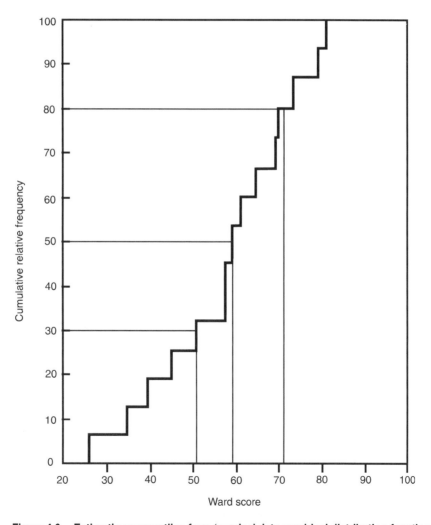

Figure 4.9 Estimating percentiles from 'service' data empirical distribution function

The important point to remember is that a cumulative frequency distribution curve is most suitable for grouped data while the empirical distribution function curve is most suitable for individual items of data.

When data is presented as a grouped frequency distribution, then a similar computational procedure to that for determining the median can be used:

$$n\text{th percentile} = L + \left(\frac{f_1}{f_2}\right)W$$

where

L = the lower limit of the nth percentile class
f_1 = the frequency of items interpolated into the nth percentile class
f_2 = the nth percentile class frequency
W = the width of the nth percentile class

The 60th percentile for the grouped age data is $(N)(.60) = 152(.60) =$ the 91.2nd item in the distribution. Substituting into the formula in the same way as the median we find:

$$\text{The 60th percentile} = 31 + \left(\frac{17.2}{46}\right)10 = 34.74$$

This means that 60 per cent of the workforce are aged 34.74 years or less.

4.6.3 Quantiles

The word **quantile** is a general term that includes percentiles, quartiles and deciles. There are two quartiles, the lower or first quartile and the upper or third quartile, and these correspond to the 25th and 75th percentiles. These percentiles are given special names simply because they are used so much.

A less well known measure of the spread of a set of data is the **interquartile range**. The interquartile range is the distance from the lower quartile to the upper quartile, which for the hospital data corresponds to an interquartile range value of $45 - 69 = 24$. It can be seen that the interquartile range is a restricted version of the range, and like the range tends not to be used in further statistical analysis.

Deciles are perhaps not surprisingly the name given to the 10th, 20th and 30th, etc., percentiles. They have no special importance in their own right but reflect, with percentiles and the interquartile range, the need for a common language to facilitate the comparison of different sets of data.

As with many of the techniques outlined in this book, the amount of computation can be greatly reduced by using spreadsheets. In Excel, for instance, there are percentile and quartile statistical functions that can be applied to a wide range of data types.

4.6.4 Five number summary and box and whisker plots

A **five number summary** and its graphical equivalent, the **box and whisker plot**, are excellent ways of comparing different sets of data. They are shown in

Table 4.18   Five number summary of absenteeism and sickness data

	Absenteeism	Sickness
Median	5	5
Lower quartile	3	3
Upper quartile	8	7
Minimum value	0	0
Maximum value	27	16

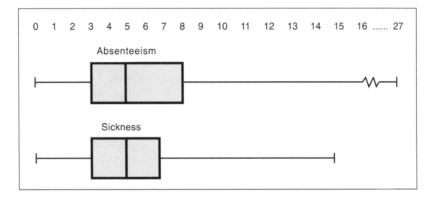

Figure 4.10   Box and whisker plot of absenteeism and sickness data

Table 4.18 and Figure 4.10 for the absenteeism and sickness variables of Tasty Foods Ltd (Table 3.1). From the five number summary and the box and whisker plot it is clear that these two sets of data are very similar, which suggests that absenteeism is primarily a reflection of sickness. When one is looking at a number of sets of data, especially if they are from the same attribute (i.e. such as absenteeism from a number of different locations), this type of comparison can be very useful, for it facilitates a fuller comparison of the main characteristics within the data sets.

4.7   Why standard deviations are so important in quantitative management

The discussion so far has highlighted the important role that the standard deviation plays in describing the spread of the data. Yet the importance of the standard deviation in quantitative management and statistics is much greater than this due to it having a number of other characteristics. Chief among these is the fact that if a set of data is normally distributed (the distribution has a bell shape) then a standard deviation will account for a specific percentage of the values in that distribution. The unit of measure is one standard deviation, and this is taken from the central mean value. Taking standard deviations outwards from both sides of the mean we find that nearly the total number of items within the data set are included once we reach six standard deviations. This is shown in Table 4.19.

Table 4.19   Standard deviations and associated percentage of data

Distance from the mean	Percentage of values falling within distance
$\mu \pm 1\sigma$	68.26
$\mu \pm 2\sigma$	95.44
$\mu \pm 3\sigma$	99.72

This is shown graphically in Figure 4.11, where the standard deviations are shown in terms of the amount of area they occupy under a normal distribution curve.

You may be asking why this characteristic is so important. There are in fact a number of reasons, some of which will become apparent in later chapters. To illustrate just one application, consider the case where the response times to customer enquiries in a busy office are logged, and found to be approximately normal. An analysis of the data shows that the mean response time is 25 minutes with a standard deviation of five minutes. From this we now know that 68.26 per cent of the replies will be between 20 and 30 minutes (25 ± 5, which is one standard deviation), 95.44 per cent of the replies will be between 15 and 35 minutes ($25 \pm 2(5)$, which is two standard deviations), and 99.72 per cent of the replies will be between 10 and 40 minutes ($25 \pm 3(5)$, which is three standard deviations).

If the maximum response time laid down by the organisation is 30 minutes, how many replies exceeded the deadline? Since the mean is the middle of the distribution we know that 50 per cent received a reply within 25 minutes. The deadline of 30 minutes is one standard deviation above the mean, so it accounts

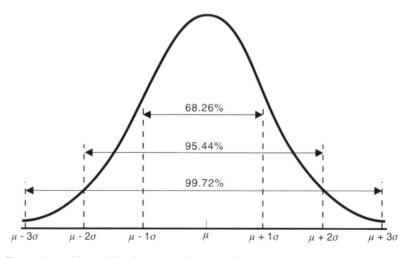

Figure 4.11   Normal distribution and area under the curve standard deviation values

for half of 68.26 per cent, which is 34.13 per cent. We know therefore that 84.13 per cent (50 per cent + 34.13 per cent) of the replies are carried out by the 30 minute deadline and 15.59 per cent (99.72 per cent – 84.13 per cent) exceeded the 30 minute deadline.

The application of this technique is appropriate to any set of data that has a normal type distribution. Since normal distributions are so characteristic of nature (e.g. height and weight of people, intelligence quotients, blood pressure, exam results, shoe sizes), then its potential application is extensive. Many organisations now use $\mu \pm 3\sigma$ as the critical point in accepting batches of work and as the basis of many of their performance indicators. The relationship of standard deviations to the amount of area under a curve does have practical applications (some will be looked at shortly), but it is handicapped by the fact that the data must conform to a normal distribution pattern. An alternative that is not handicapped in this way is known as **Chebyshev's theorem**.

4.7.1 Chebyshev's theorem

The great advantage of Chebyshev's theorem is that it applies to any set of data regardless of its shape (i.e. it does not have to be a normal distribution). The theorem states that for any set of data the proportion of the data that lies within a specified distance of k standard deviations on either side of the mean is *at least* equal to $1 - 1/k^2$, where $k > 1$. A major difference between Chebyshev's values and the normal distribution values is that Chebyshev's values are much less than the normal distribution values. This is clearly shown in Table 4.20.

Table 4.20   Comparison of normal distribution and Chebyshev theorem proportions

Normal distribution (σ)	Normal distribution area	(k)	Chebyshev's theorem area
$\mu \pm 1\sigma$	68.26%	–	–
$\mu \pm 2\sigma$	95.44%	2	$1 - 1/2^2 = 75\%$
$\mu \pm 3\sigma$	99.72%	3	$1 - 1/3^2 = 89\%$
$\mu \pm 4\sigma$	–	4	$1 - 1/4^2 = 94\%$

Because a formula is used to find the proportion of area in Chebyshev's theorem, it is possible to use non-integer standard deviations (e.g. $\mu \pm 2.7\sigma$ becomes $1 - 1/2.7^2 = 86$ per cent).

If we apply Chebyshev's theorem to the salary data in Table 3.1, which has $\mu = 12{,}532$ and $\sigma = 967$, and we work with a value of $k = 3$, then at least 89 per cent of the data should lie between:

$$\mu - 3\sigma = 12{,}532 - 3(967) = -9{,}631$$

and

$$\mu + 3\sigma = 12{,}532 + 3(967) = 15{,}433$$

This says that at least 89 per cent of the salaries lie between £9,631 and £15,433. This illustrates the principle that important statements about a set of data can be made from the summary values of μ and σ without the need, or in the absence of, the individual observations themselves.

4.7.2 Z scores

A **Z score** is a way of representing a number as a standard deviation value. This is not quite as daft as it might first appear, in that if we have a distribution of values on a number line and then superimpose the mean and standard deviations for that distribution on that number line, as in Figure 4.12, it is possible to see that any number could be expressed as a quantity of standard deviations away from the mean. For example, the value of 115 is one standard deviation away from the mean. This could have been calculated by using the following formula:

$$Z = \frac{X - \mu}{\sigma}$$

in which case

$$Z = \frac{115 - 100}{15} = \frac{15}{15} = 1$$

The data in Figure 4.12 actually represents the scores of thousands of applicants on a general intelligence test for a large organisation. If an applicant scores 135 on this test then the applicant is 2.33 ($2\frac{1}{3}$) standard deviations above the mean:

$$Z = \frac{135 - 100}{15} = \frac{35}{15} = 2.33$$

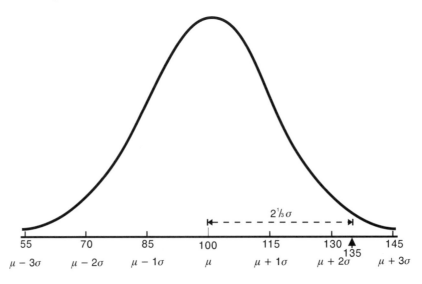

Figure 4.12 Expressing numbers as standard deviations

If this applicant then scored 265 on an accounting and finance test it would be tempting to say that since 265 is nearly twice the size of 135, the applicant did twice as well in accounting and finance than in the general intelligence test. This would only be the case if the mean and standard deviation for all accounting and finance tests were the same as those for the general intelligence tests. If the population mean and standard deviation for the accounting and finance tests had been 250 and 30 then the performance would only have been half a standard deviation above the mean:

$$Z = \frac{265 - 250}{30} = \frac{15}{30} = 0.5$$

Comparatively speaking, this applicant did much better in the general intelligence test than in the accounting and finance test, when the applicant is compared against all the other applicants. The expression of the scores in standard deviations clearly demonstrated this.

Z values can also be negative, which says they are to the left of the mean. We will use Z values in a number of different ways in subsequent chapters, and we will find that the only restriction is that the population must be normally distributed.

Competence Example 4.3

At the end of this section you should now be able to demonstrate how to:

1 **compare sets of data with different means and standard deviations**

2 **dissect sets of data into different sized proportions**

3 **use known frequency distribution characteristics to make statements about the population**

To practise and demonstrate these competences complete problems 4.5 and 4.6 at the end of this chapter. To help you to develop these competences a description of the procedure you will need to follow is now given, along with a typical problem format. The problem format is based on a problem that is similar to that previously outlined.

PROCEDURE

1 Calculate or estimate a range of percentiles for two sets of grouped data.

2 Produce a five number summary, a box and whisker plot and calculate the coefficient of variation for the two sets of data.

3 Compare the two sets of data by the information contained through procedure points 1 and 2.

4 Use Chebyshev's theorem and Z values to provide area under the curve estimates and equivalent standard deviation values.

5 Provide an overall review of your analysis.

PROBLEM

For the 'Service' and 'Age' data in Table 3.1 (page 49), calculate or estimate the 25th, 50th and 75th percentiles. In the light of these and other measures critically compare the two sets of data. Using known characteristics of distributions, what are the values within which 75 per cent, 89 per cent and 94 per cent of the items lie for the two sets of data? If an employee demanded a loyalty bonus and the employee was 36 years old and had been employed by the organisation for 12 years, what would be your response?

SOLUTION FORMAT

❶ The 25th, 50th and 75th percentiles have been calculated using: ⒈ ⒉

$$n\text{th percentile} = L + \left(\frac{f_1}{f_2}\right)W \quad \text{and} \quad \text{median} = L + \left(\frac{f_1}{f_2}\right)W$$

The 'Age' data percentiles are:

$$25\text{th percentile} = 21 + \left(\frac{27}{63}\right)10 = 25.28$$

$$50\text{th percentile (median)} = 31 + \left(\frac{2}{46}\right)10 = 31.43$$

$$75\text{th percentile} = 31 + \left(\frac{40}{46}\right)10 = 39.69$$

The 'Service' data percentiles are:

$$25\text{th percentile} = 0 + \left(\frac{38}{86}\right)5 = 2.20$$

$$50\text{th percentile (median)} = 0 + \left(\frac{76}{86}\right)5 = 4.41$$

$$75\text{th percentile} = 5 + \left(\frac{28}{39}\right)5 = 8.59$$

❷ With this information we can now put together a five number summary for the age and service data (the minimum and maximum values were taken from the midpoint of the lowest and highest classes):

Table 4.21 Five number summary of age and service data

	Age	Service
Median	31.43	4.41
Lower quartile	25.28	2.20
Upper quartile	39.69	8.59
Minimum value	19	2
Maximum value	55.5	32

❷ The graphical representation of this is shown in Figure 4.13.

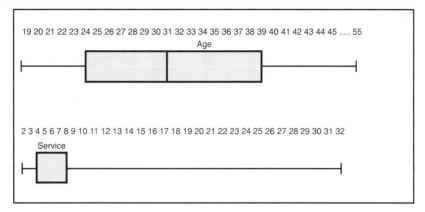

19 20 21 22 23 24 25 26 27 28 29 30 31 32 33 34 35 36 37 38 39 40 41 42 43 44 45 55

Age

2 3 4 5 6 7 8 9 10 11 12 13 14 15 16 17 18 19 20 21 22 23 24 25 26 27 28 29 30 31 32

Service

Figure 4.13   Box and whisker plot of age and service data

❸ The box and whisker plots indicate that the age data is slightly skewed to the left and that the service data is very skewed to the left. Both sets of data show extreme outliers (i.e. the maximum value) that are not typical when compared to the interquartile range. It is clearly visible that the service data interquartile range is bunched to the far left of the number line, which supports earlier claims that the workforce has a very high turnover rate, and that this turnover rate is predominantly in the 25 to 39 years age range.

❷ The coefficient of variation for the two sets of data are:

$$\text{Age data CV} = \frac{\sigma}{\mu}(100) = \frac{9.76}{32.92}(100) = 29.64$$

$$\text{Service data CV} = \frac{\sigma}{\mu}(100) = \frac{4.85}{5.38}(100) = 90.14$$

❸ and they confirm that the service data is more dispersed in relation to the mean than is the age data, although the range of values is smaller in the service data than it is in the age data.

❹ According to Chebyshev's theorem:

At least 75 per cent of employees are aged between

$$\mu - 2\sigma = 32.92 - 2(9.76) = -13.4 \text{ years}$$

and

$$\mu + 2\sigma = 32.92 + 2(9.76) = 52.44 \text{ years}$$

At least 89 per cent of employees are aged between

$$\mu - 3\sigma = 32.92 - 3(9.76) = -3.64 \text{ years}$$

and

$$\mu + 3\sigma = 32.92 + 3(9.76) = 62.2 \text{ years}$$

It does not matter that the limits of these ranges go outside the actual data because Chebyshev's theorem is conservative and thus guarantees that the ages are within these limits rather than to the limits.

④ Applying the same limits to the service data we find:

At least 75 per cent of employees have been employed for between

$$\mu - 2\sigma = 5.38 - 2(4.85) = -4.32 \text{ years}$$

and

$$\mu + 2\sigma = 5.38 + 2(4.85) = 15.08 \text{ years}$$

At least 89 per cent of employees have been employed for between

$$\mu - 3\sigma = 5.38 - 3(4.85) = -9.17 \text{ years}$$

and

$$\mu + 3\sigma = 5.38 + 3(4.85) = 19.93 \text{ years}$$

It is perhaps now appropriate to see how we can convert a number into an equivalent standard deviation value. For the employee who is demanding a loyalty bonus it is necessary to compare his or her services to all the other employees in order to determine if his or her case is justified. Using Z values we find:

$$Z = \frac{X - \mu}{\sigma} = \frac{36 - 32.92}{9.76} = \frac{3.08}{9.76} = 0.31$$

$$Z = \frac{X - \mu}{\sigma} = \frac{12 - 5.38}{4.85} = \frac{6.62}{4.85} = 1.36$$

In terms of the length of service this employee is only 1.36 standard deviations above the mean. Most organisations would expect this to be at least 2 standard deviations above the mean, which means that the employee's demand is unlikely to be met.

⑤ The overall analysis suggests that these two sets of data are skewed, and that one is particularly skewed. This is likely to have a very strong cultural effect on the organisation. The breaking up of the data into percentiles enables proportional comparisons to be made, while Z values provide a way to make individual comparisons.

Practise your competence now on problems 4.5 and 4.6 at the end of the chapter. When you have demonstrated competence in this area you can use the Lotus disk provided to automate the labour intensive and arithmetic elements. You may choose either a Lotus 1-2-3 or an Excel spreadsheet depending on the package you have access to. The operation of this package was developed in detail in Chapter 2. You may now demonstrate the competence in this area against problems from your own work environment.

4.8 Summary

The contents of Chapters 3 and 4 are in many ways the bedrock on which much of statistics and quantitative management is built. They also represent a core of skills and competences that managers and students should have acquired if they are going to be capable of making rational decisions in today's business environment. Chapter 4 has outlined the main measures of location and dispersion, and these will be used extensively in later chapters.

The concept of a standard deviation has led us to consider how a population can be divided into specific proportions, and how these known proportions then enable us to make comments on the population. This is only a short step away from making more widespread statements and inferences. Indeed, the descriptive statistics so far outlined have now paved the way for these more interesting and challenging areas.

Although most of the methods in this chapter have been explained manually, they are nearly all capable of being done on a spreadsheet package, which will reduce the amount of time spent on calculations dramatically.

The competences that have been gained in this chapter are directly transferable to most organisations, and the Lotus 1-2-3 and Excel disk provided can be used to analyse your own company's data. The following exercises provide an opportunity for you to practise and demonstrate these competences, but again they are no substitute for the data that needs analysing in your organisation.

Problems for Chapter 4

4.1 The following daily temperatures (°F) were recorded in the cold room of a large market garden that supplies fresh vegetables to a number of the national food retailers:

9	10	6	7	4	8
7	5	4	7	7	5
12	6	5	9	8	6
4	4	6	8	6	4
5	3	8	4	5	6

a. Calculate the mean, median and standard deviation for this set of data.

b. The recommended temperature for the cold room is 6°F, which is strictly monitored by the food retailers. In light of this, comment on the summary statistics calculated above and their possible implications.

4.2 The Poppy organisation has six main product lines and four sales regions. The rates of commission per garment for each product line, as well as the number of garments sold for each sales region, are:

Product line	Commission (pence per garment)	Regional sales (£000s) A	B	C	D
Daffodil spring wear	1.30	101	98	21	120
Marigold summer wear	1.32	78	150	36	160
Leafy autumn wear	1.55	123	130	49	192
Evergreen winter wear	2.05	119	142	40	192
Brambly everyday wear	1.22	220	491	109	230
Red Rose occasion wear	2.90	22	28	30	60

a. For each sales region calculate the overall average commission, the mean sales, the standard deviation.
b. Based upon the analysis in part (a), compare and discuss the major differences, if any, between the regions.

4.3 The management of a large hospital are aware that public expectations have changed with the introduction of the Citizens Charter. Since the maternity outpatients unit has always been a major part of the hospital's activities it seemed sensible to monitor how long outpatients had to wait to see a paediatrician before any corrective action was taken and public statements made. A sample of waiting times was taken over a four-week period and these revealed the following information:

Time (minutes)	Frequency
0–19	25
20–39	74
40–59	158
60–79	131
80–99	92
100–119	33
120–139	17
140–159	4

Calculate the mean waiting time and its standard deviation and comment on your findings.

4.4 The table below presents sample information about the accounts receivable of a store in a large retail chain:

Size of accounts receivable (£s)	Accounts receivable percentage	Percentage overdue
0 to under 100	35	8
100 to under 200	18	12
200 to under 300	12	8
300 to under 400	10	14
400 to under 500	5	3
500 to under 1,000	12	7
1,000 to under 5,000	8	4

a. Find the mean and median size of an account receivable from the sample data.
b. Comparing the mean and median, what can you say about the shape of the 'Accounts receivable percentage' distribution?
c. Using the information from (b), in association with the variance and standard deviation, comment on the characteristics of this sample of data.

4.5 In a civil servants' capability profiling assessment, 12 candidates obtained fewer than 10 marks, 25 obtained 10 to under 25 marks, 51 obtained 25 to under 40 marks, 48 obtained 40 to under 50 marks, 46 obtained 50 to under 60 marks, 54 obtained 60 to under 80 marks, and only eight obtained 80 marks or more. Marks were out of 100.

The results for previous candidates were:

Marks	No. of candidates
0 to under 15	40
15 to under 30	80
30 to under 45	150
45 to under 60	480
60 to under 75	190
75 to under 90	50
90 and over	10

a. Compare these two sets of marks by way of a five number summary and a box and whiskers plot. In the light of this, what can you deduce about the two sets of data?

b. By using Z values describe and compare the performance of a candidate who scored 64 points, to both groups of scores.

4.6 The time taken to serve customers at the counter of a large insurance broker was recorded for a typical working week:

Minutes	Number of customers
Less than 2	17
2 and less than 4	38
4 and less than 6	69
6 and less than 8	107
8 and less than 10	62
10 and less than 12	35
12 or more	20

The office manager has asked for your help to:

a. determine the average time per customer and the standard deviation.

b. calculate the 30th and 60th percentiles

c. explain how the office manager should use the measures determined in (a) and (b) to monitor the efficiency of the customer service system.

4.7 A friend's investment of £1,000 was invested over a six year period and was valued over that period as:

Year	Value (£s)
1990	1000
1991	1273
1992	1539
1993	1855
1994	2281
1995	2640

a. Find the value of the geometric mean.
b. What would be the expected return if you invested £4,500 at the geometric mean value over an eight year period?

4.8 A cautious-minded investor (likes low risk stocks) has a large amount of clients' money to invest and has narrowed his likely target stocks down to three. The returns on these stocks is shown for the past four years, and bearing in mind his attitude towards risk, which one should he choose?

Year	Stock A (%)	Stock B (%)	Stock C (%)
1992	24	18	12
1993	15	17	21
1994	27	17	25
1995	18	21	16

4.9 The following data gives the distribution of journey times between two production sites of a company:

Journey time (mins)	Frequency
17	6
18	8
19	9
20	12
21	9
22	4
23	2

a. Calculate the mean and standard deviation.
b. What is the 90th percentile value?

4.10 A university finance officer has looked at the number of MBA students who are still owing money and, as part of this analysis, has found that the mean payment of fees is 46 days with a standard deviation of 12 days. Armed with this information, is it possible to say how many MBA students paid between 34 and 58 days as well as between 28 and 64 days?

The finance officer also noted that the number of MBA students had increased steadily over the last four years:

Year	Number of MBA students	Growth rate
1992	27	–
1993	36	33.33
1994	58	61.11
1995	75	29.31

In the light of this, the finance officer would like you to calculate the average annual compounded rate of growth and to estimate the number of MBA students there will be in 1996.

5 Probability
the essential essence of life!

5.1 Introduction

It is important in many areas of management to provide a measure of uncertainty, such as determining the uncertainty of differing levels of sales, determining the uncertainty involved with manpower planning or determining the uncertainty involved in variable process times in the production area. This chapter examines various ways of measuring uncertainty and the calculations involved. The chapter then develops the important area of **subjective uncertainty measurement**, before moving on to **decision analysis**.

By the end of this chapter you should be able to demonstrate how to:

- calculate probabilities
- construct probability trees
- set subjective probabilities
- construct and interpret decision trees

This chapter will also use practical examples to develop the underpinning knowledge in the area of measuring uncertainty and decision analysis.

At the end of each section the required competence will be specified and described. A typical problem format with the competences highlighted will also be given to help you to demonstrate the competences on the problems at the end of the chapter. At the end of the book a full solution will be given for the first of these problems as well as the answers for the rest.

5.2 Probability

In the measuring of uncertainty, managers may use the following phrases:

> *probable*
> *quite certain*
> *unlikely*
> *likely*
> *hoped*
> *possible*
> *not certain*
> *not unreasonable that*
> *expected*
> *doubtful*

P. G. Moore and H. Thomas ('Measuring Uncertainty', Omega, Vol. 3, No. 6, 1975, pp. 657–72) took these ten phrases and asked 250 executives, on middle and senior general management programmes at the London Business School and elsewhere, to rank them in order of certainty. Before reading on, take these ten phrases and rank them in order of certainty on a scale of one to ten (one being most certain and ten being least certain).

As can be seen from Table 5.1, each phrase can be taken to imply a different degree of uncertainty by different managers and only two of the 250 executives arrived at the same ranking. There are of course far more phrases that managers could use to describe uncertainty, thus compounding the problem. Further investigations by Moore and Thomas also showed that managers were not consistent with their ranking over time. Thus it would seem that phrases and words are not a suitable vehicle for measuring uncertainty because of the varying interpretation managers can place on them.

Table 5.1   Results of survey

Phrase	Average rank	Range of ranks
Quite certain	1.10	1–3
Expected	2.95	1–6
Likely	3.85	2–7
Probable	4.25	2–9
Not unreasonable that	4.65	3–7
Possible	6.10	3–9
Hoped	7.15	3–10
Not certain	7.80	3–10
Doubtful	8.60	7–10
Unlikely	8.75	3–10

A better approach would be to use a numeric measure. There are a number of measures that could be used, such as odds, proportions or probabilities. Odds are commonly used in the world of racing and are referred to in the form of 2 to 1 against, 10 to 1 against, 2 to 1 on, etc.

Let us now define probability. The probability of a particular event occurring can be any number from 0 to 1. If the event is part of a steady series, then the probability of the given outcome should equal the proportion of times that event occurs in the series. That is how the numerical value of the probability is often arrived at in the first place.

A probability of 0 represents absolute certainty that an event *will not* occur and 1 represents absolute certainty that an event *will* occur. Probabilities are closely linked to proportions, e.g. a probability of 0.5 corresponds to a proportion of 50 per cent. Probabilities are preferable to proportions for two major reasons: firstly, probabilities are easier to work in a mathematical sense and secondly, probabilities can be used to refer to individual events, whereas proportions can only refer to groups of events.

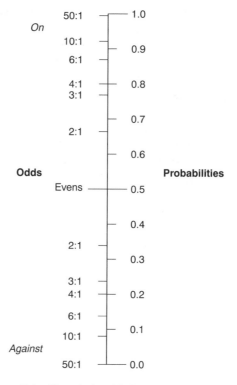

Figure 5.1   The relationship between odds and probabilities

Odds can be used to refer to uncertainty. Figure 5.1. shows graphically how odds relate to probabilities.

Odds can be an advantage when referring to uncertainty if the manager has a good working knowledge of them. However, when both odds and probability are unknown to the manager, then odds are probably less comprehensible than probability. This is because odds are not easily worked mathematically, and odds are thought of only in integer steps. The scale is of a non-linear form and so there are parts of the scale relatively devoid of points unless unusual odds are resorted to. It would therefore seem that the best measure of uncertainty is through the use of probabilities.

5.3   Basic laws of probability

This section of Chapter 5 will enable you to:

- produce basic probabilities of the situation
- construct probability trees
- interpret probability trees to determine probability of events
- use probability in decision making.

The section will also provide the underpinning knowledge in the area of probability and probability trees.

The concept of probability will now be examined in more detail in the following example. A confectionery company has just launched three new products. A market research survey of retail outlets has predicted the following probabilities that retailers will adopt the new products. The acceptance of any of the new products is not dependent on any of the others.

Mother Shipton's humbugs	**0.95**	probability of retailer adoption
Jumping juniper gems	**0.50**	probability of retailer adoption
Shrewsbury extra strong mints	**0.80**	probability of retailer adoption

If a retailer takes at least one of the new products then they will be given a new display stand and if they take all three they will get a special advertising pack. The company wishes to know the proportion of retailers that will need new stands and special advertising packs.

There are three important laws of probability that will need to be considered when exploring this example:

1. *Addition law of probability*: This law states that if A and B are mutually exclusive events, then the probability that either A or B occurs in a given trial is equal to the sum of the separate probabilities of A and B occurring.

   In symbolic terms this law can be shown as:

   $$P(A \text{ or } B) = P(A) + P(B)$$

   This law can be extended by repeated application to cover the case of more than two mutually exclusive events. Thus:

   $$P(A \text{ or } B \text{ or } C \ldots .) = P(A) + P(B) + P(C) + \ldots ..$$

   These events of this law are mutually exclusive events, which simply means that the occurrence of one of the events excludes the possibility of the occurrence of any of the others on the same trial.

2. *Multiplication law of probability*: This law states that the probability of the combined occurrence of two events, A and B, is the product of the probability of A and the conditional probability of B and the assumption that A has occurred. Thus;

   $$P(A \text{ and } B) = P(A \mid B) = P(A) \times P(B \mid A)$$

   where $P(B \mid A)$ is the conditional probability of event B on the assumption that A occurs before or at the same time.

   While this law is usually defined for two events, it can be extended to any number of events.

3. *Independent events*: Events are defined as independent if the probability of the occurrence of either is not affected by the occurrence or not of the other. Thus if A and B are independent events, then the law states that the

probability of the combined occurrence of the events A and B is the product of their individual probabilities. That is:

$$P(A \text{ and } B) = P(A) \times P(B)$$

Given these three laws of probability it is possible to relate multiple events mathematically. We will now explore this with the example. The laws of probability are two basic types: either the addition rule, which is concerned with more than one outcome within the same trial, or the multiplication rule, which is concerned with more than one trial or event which may or may not be independent. In the case of the sweet manufacturer the occurrences are the various products which can be taken. Before we address the main problems of the example let us now explore some of the calculations. The probability for acceptance is given – what then is the probability of *not* accepting? It is possible that the retailer will not take a product, so the total probability must be 1. This is useful because it enables the probabilities of not taking a product to be calculated. We simply take the probability of taking the product away from 1.

	Adoption	Non-adoption
Mother Shipton's humbugs (Product One)	0.95	0.05
Jumping juniper gems (Product Two)	0.50	0.50
Shrewsbury extra strong mints (Product Three)	0.80	0.20

What is the probability that a retailer will take all three products?

The trial in this example is the retailer taking products and this must be made up of whether or not the retailer takes each of the products in turn. Therefore the probability of all three products must be made up of the retailer taking the first and then the second and then the third product. This can be represented in symbols as follows:

$$
\begin{aligned}
P(\text{take all products}) &= P(\text{take product one}) \text{ AND } P(\text{take product two}) \\
&\quad \text{AND } P(\text{take product three}) \\
&= P(\text{take product one}) \times P(\text{take product two}) \\
&\quad \times P(\text{take product three}) \\
&= 0.95 \times 0.5 \times 0.8 \\
&= 0.38
\end{aligned}
$$

This is a use of the multiplication law – you can see in the expression where the AND has been replaced by the multiplication sign.

What is the probability of a retailer taking only one product?

To take only one product this means that the retailer does not take the other two. However, this could happen for each of the three products. This can be represented in symbols as follows:

$$
\begin{aligned}
P(\text{only one product}) &= P(\text{only product one}) \text{ OR } P(\text{only product two}) \\
&\quad \text{OR } P(\text{only product three}) \\
&= P(\text{take one}) \text{ AND } P(\text{not two}) \text{ AND } P(\text{not three}) \text{ OR} \\
&\quad P(\text{not one}) \text{ AND } P(\text{take two}) \text{ AND } P(\text{not three}) \text{ OR} \\
&\quad P(\text{not one}) \text{ AND } P(\text{not two}) \text{ AND } P(\text{take three})
\end{aligned}
$$

$$= P(\text{take one}) \times P(\text{not two}) \times P(\text{not three}) +$$
$$P(\text{not one}) \times P(\text{take two}) \times P(\text{not three}) +$$
$$P(\text{not one}) \times P(\text{not two}) \times P(\text{take three})$$
$$= 0.95 \times 0.5 \times 0.2 + 0.05 \times 0.5 \times 0.2 + 0.05 \times 0.5 \times 0.8$$
$$= 0\ 095 + 0.005 + 0.02$$
$$= 0.12$$

In this calculation the addition law has been used where there was more than one occurrence which would give the same result, i.e. the retailer taking only one product. The ANDs are replaced with a multiplication and the ORs are replaced with an addition.

A useful device to help in the solution of probability problems of this type is a probability tree. A probability tree for this first example is given in Figure 5.2.

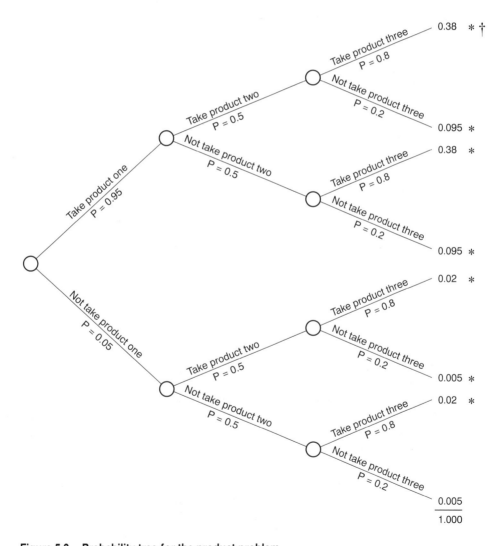

Figure 5.2   Probability tree for the product problem

The probability tree is made up of circles and lines. Each circle marks an occurrence with the lines that come from it. It is important to note that the lines coming from each circle should cover all possibilities from that event – this means that the probabilities on these lines should add to 1. The probabilities at the end of the tree should also add to 1, and this is a further check on both the logic of the tree and the arithmetic calculations. These values at the end of the tree are calculated by multiplying the probabilities along each branch of the tree. By applying the multiplication rule along each branch, the number is the probability of that branch. An example of this can be seen on the top of the tree. The probability of a retailer taking product one *and* taking product two *and* taking product three is the multiple of their probabilities and is 0.38. Because the product acceptances are independent it does not matter in which order they are put on the tree. One, two then three has been chosen but they could have been put on in any order.

Let us now return to the main problems of this example. If a retailer takes at least one of the new products then they will need a new display stand and if they take all three they will need a special advertising pack. The company wishes to know the proportion of retailers that will need new stands and special advertising packs.

To obtain the first probability the probability tree needs to be inspected and all the branches that give at least one product taken need to be identified. These are marked on the tree with a * symbol. These branches are all alternative possibilities, therefore the addition rule is applied to them and they are summed to obtain the required probability.

$$P(\text{at least one product taken}) = 0.38 + 0.095 + 0.38 + 0.095 + 0.02 + 0.005 + 0.02$$
$$= 0.995$$

An alternative way of calculating this probability is to identify that the only branch on the tree that does not give at least one product taken can be found at the bottom of the tree. Product one not taken *and* product two not taken *and* product three not taken. This can then be taken from 1:

$$P(\text{at least one product taken}) = 1 - P(\text{no product taken})$$
$$= 1 - 0.005$$
$$= 0.995$$

This probability can be turned into a percentage by multiplying by 100. Therefore, 99.5 per cent of retailers will take at least one product and a new display stand. If we know the number of retailers, say 3,562, then the expected number of new stands can be calculated by multiplying the probability by the number of retailers.

$$\text{Expected no. of new stands} = P(\text{at least one product taken}) \times \text{No. of retailers}$$
$$= 0.995 \times 3,562$$
$$= 3,544.19 \cong 3,544$$

There is only one branch on the tree that will give retailers who will take all products. This is at the top of the tree and is marked with a † symbol.

P(all products taken) = 0.38

Therefore 38 per cent of all retailers will take all the products and require the special advertising pack.

$$\text{Expected no. of advertising packs} = P(\text{all products taken}) \times \text{No. of retailers}$$
$$= 0.38 \times 3{,}562$$
$$= 1{,}353.56 \cong 1{,}354$$

In this first example the events were independent. Let us now move on to look at an example where events are dependent on previous events:

An electronic system is made up of two sub-systems, A and B. The probability of failure is 0.06 for sub-system A. The probability of failure for sub-system B is 0.05 if A does not fail but due to power surges this rises to 0.15 if A does fail. The result of B is therefore conditional on what happens to A. Management requires the following information to calculate the cost of failure and maintenance. What are the probabilities:

1. of neither sub-system failing?
2. of just one sub-system failing?
3. of both sub-systems failing?

The first stage is to produce the probability tree for this example. This probability tree is given in Figure 5.3.

This probability tree is constructed in a similar manner to the previous example. There are, however, two differences. First, B is conditional on A, therefore on the probability tree A must always come before B. Second, the probabilities must reflect this conditional nature and depend on what has happened to A. Now let's examine the tree to find the required probabilities.

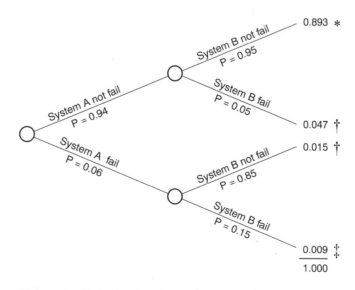

Figure 5.3   Probability tree for systems example

There is only one branch on the tree that gives no fails and this is marked with a * symbol.

$$P(\text{no fails}) = 0.893$$

There are two branches on the tree that give just one fail and they are marked with a † symbol.

$$P(\text{just one fail}) = 0.047 + 0.051$$
$$= 0.098$$

There is only one branch on the tree that gives two fails and this is marked with a ‡ symbol.

$$P(\text{both fail}) = 0.009$$

Competence Example 5.1

At the end of this section you should now be able to demonstrate how to:

1 **produce basic probabilities of the situation**

2 **construct probability trees**

3 **interpret probability trees to determine probability of events**

4 **use probability in decision making.**

To practise and demonstrate these competences complete example problems 5.1. to 5.3 at the end of this chapter. To help you to develop these competences a description of the procedure you will need to follow is now given, along with a typical problem format. This problem format is based on the first example we have just considered.

PROCEDURE (PROBABILITY TREES)

❶ Define the probabilities in the problem.

❷ Construct the logic outline of the probability tree.

❸ Add probabilities to the tree and calculate the probabilities of the branches of the tree.

❹ Check probabilities add to one.

❺ Interpret probability tree to obtain required probabilities.

❻ Use probabilities to make predictions.

PROBLEM

A confectionery company has just launched three new products. A market research survey of retail outlets has predicted the following probabilities that retailers will adopt the new products. The acceptance of any of the new products is not dependent on each other

Mother Shipton's Humbugs	0.95	probability of retailer adoption
Jumping juniper gems	0.50	probability of retailer adoption
Shrewsbury extra strong mints	0.80	probability of retailer adoption

If a retailer takes at least one of the new products then they will be given a new display stand and if they take all three they will get a special advertising pack. The company wishes to know the proportion of retailers that will need new stands and special advertising packs.

A description of the layout of the solution format is given at the beginning of the book.

SOLUTION FORMAT

❶

	Adoption	Non-adoption	▮1
Mother Shipton's humbugs (Product One)	0.95	0.05	
Jumping juniper gems (Product Two)	0.50	0.50	
Shrewsbury extra strong mints (Product Three)	0.80	0.20	

❷❸❹

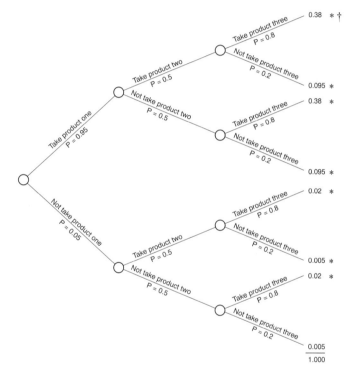

❺ If a retailer takes at least one of the new products then they will need a new display stand ▮3 and if they take all three they will need a special advertising pack. The company wishes to know the proportion of retailers that will need new stands and special advertising packs.

To obtain the first probability the probability tree needs to be inspected and all the branches that give at least one product taken need to be identified. These are marked on the tree with a * symbol.

P(at least one product taken) = 0.38 + 0.095 + 0.38 + 0.095 + 0.02 + 0.005 + 0.02
= 0.995

An alternative way of calculating this probability is to identify from the tree that the only branch on the tree that does not give at least one product taken can be found at the bottom of the tree.

⑤ P(at least one product taken) = 1 − P(no product taken)

   = 1 − 0.005

   = 0.995

3

Therefore 99.5 per cent of retailers will take at least one product and a new display stand.

⑥ There are 3,562 retailers.

Expected no. of new stands = P(at least one product taken) × No. of retailers

   = 0.995 × 3,562

   = 3,544.19 ≅ 3,544

4

⑤ There is only one branch on the tree that will give retailers who will take all products. This is at the top of the tree and is marked with a † symbol.

P(all products taken) = 0.38

3

Therefore 38 per cent of all retailers will take all the products and require the special advertising pack.

⑥ Expected no. of advertising packs = P(all products taken) × No. of retailers

   = 0.38 × 3,562

   = 1,353.56 ≅ 1,354

4

Practise your competence now on problems 5.1 to 5.3 at the end of this chapter. There is not an element on the computer disk for this section due to the problem that each probability tree can be completely different. This makes it very difficult to produce a standard package, but if you have worked through Chapter 2 you should be able to produce a simple spreadsheet to carry out the calculations of the probability tree. This will enable you to carry out a sensitivity analysis on the probabilities on the tree. You may now demonstrate the competence in this area against problems from your own work environment. If you require to set any subjective probabilities from your work environment then you should work through the next section before attempting this.

5.4   Subjective probabilities

This section of Chapter 5 will enable you to:

- set subjective probabilities using heuristics
- ensure the subjective probabilities are estimates and not guesses
- take account of statistical theory using these heuristics
- use techniques like cumulative density function (CDF) to improve estimates

The section will also provide the underpinning knowledge in the area of subjective probability and ways of improving accuracy.

It could be argued that so far the cart has been put before the horse; all that has been considered are the uses and further calculations of probability with little mention of how probability values are arrived at.

The classical statistical approach to the calculation of probability values given in statistical texts is that probability of a particular event occurring is given by the number of occurrences of the event divided by the total number of all occurrences:

$$\text{Probability of event A} = \frac{\text{Number of occurrences of event A}}{\text{Total number of all occurrences}}$$

This method of determination of probability is effective, providing the data required is available. Although this is the case for calculations involving decks of cards, dice, etc., this is not true in connection with the majority of business situations. Consider a typical business problem – that of forecasting future sales.

Past sales information can be used to determine the probabilities of different sales figures by using various mathematical techniques from moving averages to the more mathematically sophisticated Box Jenkins technique (*see* Chapter 10). These methods of forecasting the probabilities of different events are passive in nature. They assume that like the pack of cards, sales will react along fixed lines based purely on past information. Most business situations do not depend completely on the past but on changing conditions in the present. The oil crisis of the early 1970s is a good example of this. This crisis had a dramatic effect on the sales of new motor vehicles, which were considerably less than expected. This was just one factor which could have had an effect on car sales; others could have been government legislation, social changes, environmental issues, etc. An alternative approach to producing a single component forecast is to carry out a **multivariate analysis**. With multivariate analysis, the effect of each factor is estimated individually. This means that when a forecast is produced each factor can be varied individually. This makes the forecast sensitive to changes in individual factors.

The effects of some factors cannot be predicted from the past sales figures but must be estimated in some other way. One possible way is by determining the effect of these factors on the probabilities, which can only be set subjectively as there is no past data from which to work. Another method for the determination of the effects of various factors on probabilities and the generation of probabilities, particularly when there is little past information, is that of **simulation modelling** (*see* Chapter 13). However, because of the uncertainty associated with business, there will always be a need for the subjective estimation of probabilities.

A **subjective probability** may be defined as a probability that has been set by an individual or a group of individuals using his/her or their collective experience and knowledge, due to the fact that there was insufficient data to allow the probability to be calculated in the classical manner (also, the situation may be changeable, which would not allow the probability to be calculated in a classical manner either).

There are many problems which can arise when subjective probabilities are being determined. D. Kahneman and A. Tversky ('Judgement under Uncertainty: Heuristics and Biases', Science, Vol. 185, 1974, pp. 1124–31) have carried out a considerable amount of work in this area. They have put forward the idea that there are three basic heuristics people use when setting probabilities: (1) representativeness (2) availability and (3) anchoring and adjustment.

5.4.1 The heuristic of representativeness

Suppose you are asked one of the following questions: What is the probability that object A belongs to class B? What is the probability that event A originates from process B? What is the probability that process B will generate event A? In the determination of such probabilities the heuristic of representativeness is likely to be used. To think about how representative event A is of events produced by process B is a way of approaching this question. This approach can lead to certain major problems.

Kahneman and Tversky carried out some work with occupations and descriptions of people's characters. For example, read the following description of an individual's character: 'Steve is very shy and withdrawn, invariably helpful but with little interest in people, or in the world of reality. A meek and tidy soul, he has a need for order and structure and a passion for detail.' Look at the following list of occupations:

- farmer
- salesman
- airline pilot
- librarian
- physician

Now rank these from the most likely to the least likely occupation for Steve.

Kahneman and Tversky found that people solving the problem used the representativeness of stereotypes in determining the relative chances of the different occupations.

This method for determining probabilities needs to take account of other factors. If these factors are ignored then the basic laws of conditional probabilities have not been taken into account and the following mistakes could be made:

a) Not allowing for prior probabilities

Prior probabilities are not usually used in the process of representativeness. Take for example the problem of Steve and determining his occupation. The fact that there are more farmers in the population than there are librarians should have affected the relative probabilities of the different occupations. The exact effect of the prior probability is debatable but this is to be expected as we are talking in terms of subjective probabilities. Kahneman and Tversky have carried out some experimental work which suggests that the majority of people ignore prior probabilities when setting subjective probabilities.

Participants in Kahneman and Tversky's studies were given a series of character profiles 'chosen at random' from a group of 100 professionals (30 engineers and 70 lawyers). The character profiles were carefully worded so as to give no information as to the profession of the individual, such as: 'Dick is a 30-year-old man. He is married with no children. A man of high ability and high motivation, he promises to be quite successful in his field. He is well liked by his colleagues.'

Given this type of description (which is completely bland, providing no information) the participants ignored the useful prior probabilities and considered the probability of an engineer 0.5 and the probability of a lawyer 0.5. When they were given no character profile at all and just asked for the probability of an individual chosen at random from the group then they used the prior probabilities and came out with engineers 0.3 and lawyers 0.7.

b) Insensitivity to sample size

Another problem of the technique of representativeness is that of insensitivity to sample size. Kahneman and Tversky showed that when people were presented with a problem that involved sample size, this was ignored. One of the problems they used was concerned with the sampling of a large group of men (average height five feet ten inches in samples of 1000, 100 and 10 men) and then using these to obtain average height figures. The participants were asked to estimate the probability of obtaining samples with average heights in excess of six feet. The majority of participants arrived at the same figure for all three sample sizes, which showed a lack of understanding of the fact that the greater the sample size the smaller the variation in means and therefore the probability of such an event should reduce as sample size increases. They fared no better even when the sample size was emphasised in the formulation of the problem: 'A certain town is served by two hospitals. In the larger hospital about 45 babies are born each day, and in the smaller hospital about 15 babies are born each day. As you know, about 50 per cent of all babies are boys. However, the exact percentage varies from day to day. Sometimes it may be higher that 50 per cent, sometimes lower. For a period of one year each hospital recorded the days on which more than 60 per cent of the babies born were boys. Which hospital do you think recorded more such days?'

When this problem was used the majority of participants still thought the probabilities would be the same in both cases.

c) Lack of understanding of the element of chance

This problem falls into two main parts: the lack of understanding of randomness and the non-appreciation of independence. Kahneman and Tversky showed that the concept of randomness was not fully understood by the majority of their participants. When they asked them which was more likely when tossing a coin six times – H-T-H-T-T-H or H-H-H-T-T-T – the majority said that the first was more likely than the second and only a few came up with the correct answer that they are in fact both equally likely. This shows that people are likely to think that ordered sequenced groups cannot be random whereas this is not necessarily so.

The other problem concerning chance is the lack of understanding of independence. For example, if a coin has been thrown six times and six heads have been recorded, what is the chance of obtaining a head on the next throw? It is an understandable mistake to assume that the chance of a head must be less than that of a tail, i.e. to assume that one throw is related to the next, when in fact each throw is independent (a coin cannot have a memory and remember the prior results). Kahneman and Tversky showed that this was a common failing in their participants.

d) Misconception of validity

A further problem arising from the use of the heuristic of representativeness can be the attribution of too high a validity to subjective probabilities obtained in this way. Most people take insufficient account of the problems caused by lack of information or inaccuracies in the interpretation of the information available.

e) Misconception of regression

Applying incorrect causal relationships can lead to bias and error in the representative heuristic. The following example from Kahneman and Tversky illustrates an incorrectly assumed relationship: 'In a discussion of flight training, experienced instructors noted that praise for an exceptionally smooth landing is typically followed by a poorer landing on the next try, while harsh criticism after a rough landing is usually followed by an improvement on the next try. The instructor concluded that verbal rewards are detrimental to learning while verbal punishments are beneficial, contrary to accepted psychological doctrine.'

This in fact is a spurious relationship. Whatever comments are made to the trainee, the results are likely to be the same due to the fact that performances are distributed about a mean for each trainee and will vary about that mean – some better, some worse. The acceptance of spurious relationships can lead to inaccuracies in the setting of subjective probabilities. This type of mistake is not only made by people with no statistical training but is all too common among people with statistical training.

5.4.2 The heuristic of availability

This technique is used in situations where people assess the frequency of occurrence of a class or the probability of a given event by the number of times and the ease that such occurrences or events can be brought to mind. For example, if you were asked to assess the risk of fatality due to motor vehicle accidents, one way would be to bring to mind any fatalities you have encountered and use this to assess the risk.

This, like the first method of assessing subjective probabilities, can be reasonable. However, it can lead to certain problems which can introduce bias and error:

a) The retrievability of instances

Kahneman and Tversky suggest that when the size of class is judged by the availability of its instances, a class whose instances are easily retrieved will appear more numerous than a class of equal frequency whose instances are less retrievable.

They demonstrated this by presenting the participants with lists of men and women and asking them which of the lists were the larger. Errors were frequently made when smaller lists of famous men or women were used. The participants thought these lists were the larger.

Another problem of retrievability is the way in which the events arrive at the brain. If one actually experiences an event oneself the impact and therefore the retrievability is usually much greater than if one records or is told of such an event. Also the source of one's information (whether read or told) can affect the impact of the information – the more 'reliable' the information, the greater the impact.

How recently the event occurred could also affect the retrievability. Retrievability can be affected by many things and will of course vary considerably from individual to individual.

b) Biases due to the effectiveness of a search set

Biases may be due to the ineffectiveness of certain sets of events stored by people. Due to social, economic, business or other reasons, experiences may be different and this will introduce an element of bias. The search set of managers (i.e. their experience) will vary from manager to manager depending upon such factors as the length of time the person has been a manager, the types of management roles carried out, the management ability of the person, etc.

c) Biases of imagination

Imagination plays an important role in the evaluation of probabilities in real life situations. The risk involved in an adventurous expedition, for example, is evaluated by imagining contingences with which the expedition is not equipped to cope. If many such difficulties are vividly portrayed, the expedition can be made to appear exceedingly dangerous, although the ease with which disasters are imagined need not reflect their actual likelihood. Conversely, the risk involved in an undertaking may be grossly underestimated if some possible dangers are either difficult to conceive of or simply do not come to mind.

The same applies to a large number of business decisions. It can be extremely difficult to imagine and conceive the factors involved and the possible outcomes of events.

Imagination is not only important in terms of different factors – it can also be important in mathematical concepts. For example, if you were to ask a production manager how many schedules it is possible to draw up by putting 50 different jobs through a six-machine sequence, he/she is most likely to grossly underestimate the possible number. This lack of imagination of certain mathematical concepts can cause problems in the setting of some subjective probabilities.

5.4.3   The heuristics of anchoring and adjustment

A possible technique when setting subjective probabilities is to start from an initial value and then adjust this value in the light of experience or knowledge. An example of this type of heuristic could be found in the forecasting field. The initial forecast will be set using mathematical forecasting, this being the **anchoring stage**. This initial value could then be **adjusted** by managers to take into account such factors as increased advertising by the company or competitors, the present economic climate, etc.

There are two main problems with this technique: first, the initialisation value and second, insufficient adjustment from this value. P. Slovic and S. Lichtenstein ('Organizational Behaviour and Human Performance, Vol. 6, 1971, p. 649) carried out a series of studies which involved asking people about certain quantities stated in percentages (for example, the percentage of African countries in the United Nations). They started the process at random for the initialisation value and asked the subjects whether it was too high or too low and to adjust the values. They found that due to the reluctance of the subjects to move far away from the initialisation value, this value had quite an effect on the final estimates even though it had been set at random. This particular effect is likely to be felt in a business situation when initial values have been set by the managing director or a technical expert, whom other personnel would be reluctant to challenge.

5.5   Subjective probability in practice

Where an individual is setting subjective probabilities it is unlikely that just one of three heuristics will be used. It is far more likely that some combination of the three will be used. These techniques can give quite acceptable results, provided that the problems discussed earlier are taken into account. An important contribution to the solving of these problems is to ensure that the manager has a knowledge of the statistical concepts involved. You have already started to overcome these problems by working through this book.

A concept that can be used successfully to supplement the three heuristics is the **cumulative density function** (CDF). This has the advantage that a range of values can be created instead of individual values. To create a CDF, five percentiles have to be estimated – the 1st, 25th, 50th, 75th and 99th. Training may need to be given as to what percentiles are and most people will need some experience at setting them, which can be obtained by using simulation (*see* Chapter 13). In most people there will be a tendency to set the percentiles too close together and to give a CDF with too little range because the majority of people fail to appreciate the uncertainty associated with situations. Experiments have been carried out which suggest that this conservatism is general. With training this natural conservatism can be overcome.

The percentiles required may be defined as follows:

1st percentile   In the assessor's opinion there is a 1 per cent chance that the quantity being assessed will be below this value and a 99 per cent chance that it will be above it (this value could almost be considered the lower limit of the quantity).

25th percentile   In the assessor's opinion there is a 25 per cent chance that the quantity being assessed will be below this value and a 75 per cent chance that it will be above it.

50th percentile   In the assessor's opinion there is a 50 per cent chance that the quantity being assessed will be below this value and a 50 per cent chance that it will be above it.

75th percentile   In the assessor's opinion there is a 75 per cent chance that the quantity being assessed will be below this value and a 25 per cent chance that it will be above it.

99th percentile   In the assessor's opinion there is a 99 per cent chance that the quantity being assessed will be below this value and a 1 per cent chance that it will be above it (this value could almost be considered the upper limit of the quantity).

A useful procedure for the setting of these percentiles is as follows:

1. Select a value for the 50th percentile.
2. Select the values for the 1st and 99th percentiles (i.e. the upper and lower limit).
3. The values for the 25th and 75th percentiles now need to be set. These can be arrived at by dividing the halves of the distribution already obtained. This division must be carried out by dividing probabilities by two and not the distance along the distribution. The value arrived at by this division will be approximately one third of the way along the scale from the 50th percentile (one standard deviation). An alternative approach to the setting of these two percentiles is to produce a range within a range. When the 1st and 99th percentiles are set the range of all values is set. The second range could be set within the first range but containing 50 per cent of values. Individual managers may have a preference for either of the methods depending on their statistical knowledge and training.

Such a procedure is quite useful when used in conjunction with the heuristics and a basic training in statistics.

Gaming simulation can be very useful in the training of assessors of subjective probabilities. It allows individuals to gain experience and allows them to get over some of the problems outlined without any dangers to the organisation of incorrect or biased results. It also allows the organisation to assess the subjective probability setting of different individuals.

Computers will obviously be of value for gaming simulation. Schlaifer took the use of the computer into an interactive role when he designed a series of on-line packages. Initially they provide a tutorial system for the assessor to gain experience and knowledge in the assessing of subjective probabilities. When this has been gained they then go on to assist the assessor in the assessing of actual subjective probabilities and provide built-in consistency checks. The Post Office Corporation (USA) have found that individuals setting subjective probabilities have preferred the computer interaction to having a statistician or decision analyst providing the consistency checks.

The use of groups in the setting of subjective probabilities will only be dealt with briefly here. The methods of using groups will be dealt with separately as they are also important in a number of different areas, including the determination of information needs and design of information systems. One major problem with the use of groups is the bandwagon effect – the group will tend to follow the individual or sub-group of individuals with the stronger personality and/or most power. This would be fine if these were the people who were best at setting these subjective probabilities but this unfortunately is not necessarily the case. A way round this effect is to use techniques like **Delphi**. Within this technique individuals are asked to fill in questionnaires, the results of which are used to produce the next questionnaire and this procedure is continued until a consensus opinion is reached. With this approach it is usual to eliminate a certain amount of the bandwagon effect. The final consensus could be weighted using any of the following methods:

1. Equal weights to each individual.
2. Self weighting.
3. Subjective weighting by a third party (possibly by members of the group or by an 'expert unbiased individual').
4. A weighting based on past experience.

The first method is of no value and the latter three could introduce considerable bias. It should be possible to introduce a combination of the last three so that if used carefully bias could be reduced. Indeed, if it is to be considered a realistic method then some method other than the first *must* be used, although this will not preclude the possibility of equality being arrived at.

Competence Example 5.2

At the end of this section you should now be able to demonstrate how to:

1 set subjective probabilities using heuristics

2 ensure the subjective probabilities are estimates and not guesses

3 take account of statistical theory using these heuristics

4 use techniques like cumulative density function (CDF) to improve estimates.

To practise and demonstrate these detailed competences you will need to use examples from your own work environment. With subjective probability it is important that the probability setters have experience and knowledge of the background of these probabilities. You are much more likely to have this knowledge in your own area of business than in any example we could simulate in this text.

Summary of probability

The only effective way to measure uncertainty is to use a numeric measure such as probability. The phrases used by some managers such as possible, doubtful, etc., are of little value as they mean different levels of uncertainty to different people. Probabilities, being numeric in nature, can be used to extend the knowledge of the situation by using the various rules (these can be of great use in such things as decision analysis, decision trees, etc.).

There is however one major problem with probabilities: that of actually determining a value. The majority of business situations, unlike most situations talked of in classical probability, are *dynamic*. Consider the probability of drawing an ace from a pack of cards – an easy situation. To determine a large number of business situations would be like finding the probability of an ace from a randomly changing pack of cards (not only changing in terms of the number of cards but also in terms of contents with a few jokers for good measure). It is not easy to calculate probabilities under these conditions and it is better to use subjective probabilities, i.e. probabilities assessed by individuals or groups of individuals based on experience, knowledge and information. There are three heuristic methods available which can be used individually or in a combination:

1. The heuristic of representativeness.
2. The heuristic of availability.
3. The heuristic of anchoring and adjustment.

There can be problems in using these methods and assessors will need a certain amount of statistical training and assistance in the setting of probabilities. This can be provided effectively by using simulation gaming in the form of an interactive computer package. It can sometimes be advantageous to use groups of assessors to arrive at a more broadly-based subjective probability, although this again can lead to problems.

5.6 Decision analysis

Decision analysis, as presented in this section of Chapter 5, could be said to consist of a group of analytical techniques which assist managers to make decisions. These techniques provide a framework in which to carry out the majority of problem solving and are an effective way of presenting the decision.

This section will enable you to:

- identify the elements of the decision and produce the outline of the decision tree
- calculate the expected values on the tree
- interpret the decision tree
- if required carry out a sensitivity analysis

The section will also provide underpinning knowledge in the areas of decision analysis and interpretation of such analysis.

The taking of decisions in uncertain conditions involves the following sequence of stages. The range of actions available to the manager must be specified. The outcomes for each action should then be listed, along with their probability of occurrence.

Using these possible outcomes, monetary values may be placed upon the different actions open to the managers, and these may be in terms of returns and costs. The manager then uses this information to try and make the best decision.

Decision analysis as proposed by some writers in the field of Operational Research is concerned only with statistical decision theory. Although this is an important part of decision theory, there is in fact a great deal more to be considered.

5.7 Statistical decision theory

Statistical decision theory applies the concepts of probability and expectation to provide a decision aid for managers.

Expectation is concerned with the establishment of the **expected return** (or in some cases **expected cost**) associated with a series of outcomes resulting from a given action. Providing that the probability and the monetary returns (or cost) are known for each outcome and that the set of outcomes contains *all possible outcomes* for that action, the expected monetary return ($E(M)$) can be calculated as a weighted average by multiplying the probability by the return of an outcome and then summing over all possible outcomes.

Suppose a person receives an amount of money (M_1) if event (Z_1) occurs (M_2 if Z_2, and so on to M_n if Z_n occurs).

$$\text{Expected monetary return} = E(M) = (\text{probability of } Z_1 \times M_1) +$$
$$(\text{probability of } Z_2 \times M_2) + \ldots\ldots +$$
$$(\text{probability of } Z_n \times M_n)$$

given that the sum of all probabilities equals 1

Consider the following example from the field of life insurance:

The probability that a man aged 55 will live for another year is 0.99. How large a premium should he pay for a £2,000 life insurance policy for one year? The amount of premium the man should pay for such insurance must be equal to his expected return from the policy. There are two possible outcomes. Outcome one, that the man lives, has a probability of 0.99 and a monetary return of £0. Outcome two, that the man dies, has a probability of 0.01 and a monetary return to the man's estate of £2,000.

$$\text{Therefore } E(M) = (0.99 \times 0) + (0.01 \times 2000)$$
$$= 0 + 20$$
$$= £20$$

Therefore the premium = £20 + (charges for the insurance company's administration, profit, etc.)

This technique can be applied in situations where a decision needs to be taken. The following example requires a decision:

A woman wishes to sell her car and has two alternatives. Alternative one – to go to a dealer with complete certainty of selling for £1,550. Alternative two – to advertise in a local paper at a cost of £10 in order to sell the car for £1,700 but then only expect a 0.6 probability of a sale. The monetary returns from the actions can be evaluated as follows:

Alternative one: not to advertise

Outcome	Probability	Monetary returns
Sell to dealer	1	£1,550

$$\text{Therefore } E(M_1) = 1 \times 1,550$$
$$= £1,550$$

Alternative two: to advertise in local paper

Outcome	Probability	Monetary returns
Sell through ad	0.6	£1,700
Sell to dealer	0.4	£1,550

Therefore $E(M_2) = (0.6 \times 1,700) + (0.4 \times 1,550)$
$$= 1,020 + 620$$
$$= £1,640 \text{ (this value is a gross return)}.$$

The cost of the action must be deducted
$$E(M_2) = 1,640 - 10$$
$$= £1,630 \text{ (this value is a net return)}.$$

From these figures it would appear that the action giving the greatest return would be to advertise the car in the local paper. This information can be presented in a different form which gives a greatly improved visual impact. This method of presentation is called a **decision tree**. The example of selling the car can be produced in a decision tree form and is shown in Figure 5.4.

It can be seen from this decision tree that the calculations stay the same but the tree has a greater visual impact than the table. This visual impact becomes greater the more complicated the tree.

Decision trees are constructed with four basic steps:

1. Construct the tree to represent the logic of the situation; squares to show a decision point with the actions coming from the square; circles to show points of alternative outcome with the alternative outcomes coming from the circle.

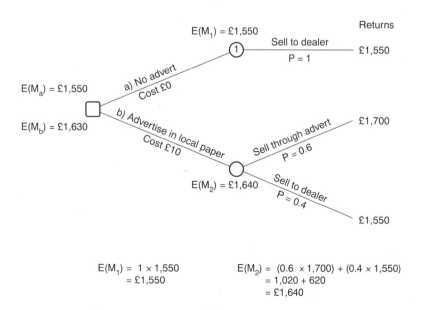

Figure 5.4   Decision tree for car selling problem

2. Write on the tree the return from different alternatives and their probability of occurrence, ensuring that the probabilities on any branch of the tree add to 1. Also place on the tree the costs of the various actions open to the decision maker.

3. Calculate the expected monetary returns starting from the right-hand side of the tree and working to the left.

4. Determine the best decision from the tree. Classical decision theory suggests that the best route through the tree and hence the best decision is the one with the largest monetary return, or if expected costs are being considered the one with the smallest expected cost.

The use of decision trees can be further examined by using of an example closer to the problems facing management. The following example, although still a simplification of reality, has been used by both Moore and Magee to demonstrate how to produce decision trees and has been extended in this chapter.

The following information is available to the manager from three sources:

a. Marketing information

The marketing manager suggests a 60 per cent chance of a larger market in the long run and a 40 per cent chance of a low demand developing as follows:

Initially high, sustained high   60%
Initially high, long term low   10%
Initially low, continuing low   30%   Low 40%
Initially low, subsequently low   0%

2 years   8 years

10 years

b. Annual income

The management accounting section have put forward the following financial estimates:

i. A large plant operating under high market demand conditions would yield £1 million annually in cash flow.

ii. A large plant operating under low market demand conditions would only yield £0.1 million annually in cash flow because of high fixed costs and inefficiencies.

iii. A small plant operating under low market demand conditions would be economic and would yield £0.4 million annually in cash flow.

iv. A small plant operating under high market demand conditions initially (i.e. the first two years) would yield £0.45 million annually in cash flow, but this would drop to £0.25 million annually in cash flow if the high demand market conditions were sustained for eight years of operating.

v. If an initial small plant expanded after two years and was operating under high market demand conditions it would yield £0.7 million annually in cash flow for the remaining eight years and so would be less efficient than a large plant built initially.

vi. If an initial small plant was expanded after two years and was operating under low market demand conditions it would yield £0.05 million annually in cash flow for the remaining eight years and so would be less efficient than a large plant built initially.

c. Capital costs

Estimates from construction companies indicate that a large plant would cost £3 million to build and put into operation. A small plant would cost £1.3 million initially and an additional £2.2 million if expanded after two years.

Management has two possible actions it can take – to build a large plant or a small plant. If the small plant is constructed there is an option to extend it after two years. A series of outcomes of high and low market demands will follow these actions. Given this knowledge and the three sets of information, a decision tree can be constructed as shown in Figure 5.5.

The probabilities after outcome one and two need to be adjusted because from the information the probability of an initial high and then a sustained high is 0.6 and the probability of an initial high and then a long term low is 0.1. This gives a branch on the tree with a set of probabilities that do not add to 1, so this needs to be rectified to ensure they do. This is carried out with a simple weighting process, which means dividing each probability by the sum of the probabilities on that branch, therefore ending with probabilities which add to 1.

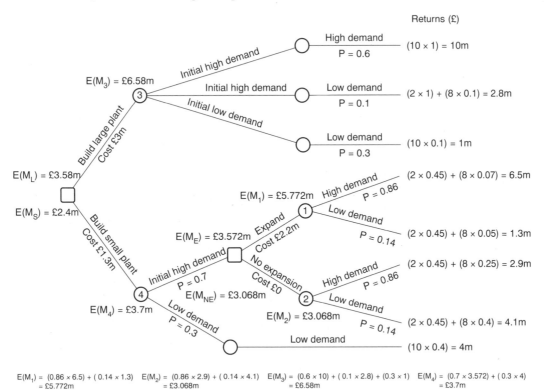

$E(M_1) = (0.86 \times 6.5) + (0.14 \times 1.3)$
$= £5.772m$

$E(M_2) = (0.86 \times 2.9) + (0.14 \times 4.1)$
$= £3.068m$

$E(M_3) = (0.6 \times 10) + (0.1 \times 2.8) + (0.3 \times 1)$
$= £6.58m$

$E(M_4) = (0.7 \times 3.572) + (0.3 \times 4)$
$= £3.7m$

Figure 5.5   Decision tree for plant size problem

Therefore probability of initial high

$$\text{then sustained high} = \frac{0.6}{0.6 + 0.1} = \frac{0.6}{0.7} = 0.86$$

Therefore probability of initial high

$$\text{then long term low} = \frac{0.1}{0.6 + 0.1} = \frac{0.1}{0.7} = 0.14$$

Using classical statistical decision theory the decision giving the greatest return is that of building a large plant.

5.8 The effect of discounting on decision trees

The **discounted cash flow** (DCF) method of appraisal attempts to value projects in terms of the future value of the money returned. The basic philosophy behind DCF techniques is that money invested in a project now could as time progresses be earning interest and so increasing its total value. Therefore the amount of interest that could have been earned must be taken off the money returned from the project.

The present value (discounted cash flow) can be calculated by the following formula:

$$\text{Present value} = \frac{M}{(1 + I)^n}$$

where M = amount of money to be discounted
$\quad$ n = number of periods or times at which interest is calculated
$\quad$ I = the interest rate for calculation of interest in any one of the n periods mentioned above

A discounting factor for any given time period will be given by the following formula:

$$\text{Discounting factor} = \frac{1}{(1 + I)^n}$$

The principal argument *against* the use of discounting is that as it can only be an estimate then the results cannot be considered reliable. In this particular application all the other information tends to be estimated and, therefore, one more estimate can be of little consequence as the solutions are only correct within certain limits. It must be remembered that discounting rates could be expected to

Table 5.2   Discounting factors

Year	Factor
1	0.91
2	0.83
3	0.75
4	0.68
5	0.62
6	0.56
7	0.51
8	0.47
9	0.42
10	0.39

Table 5.3   Discounting returns to plant size problem

Demand		Build large plant					
Initial Long term		High High		High Low		Low Low	
Year	Factor	Return £m	DCF	Return £m	DCF	Return £m	DCF
1	0.91	1	0.91	1	0.91	0.1	0.091
2	0.83	1	0.83	1	0.83	0.1	0.083
3	0.75	1	0.75	0.1	0.075	0.1	0.075
4	0.68	1	0.68	0.1	0.068	0.1	0.068
5	0.62	1	0.62	0.1	0.062	0.1	0.062
6	0.56	1	0.56	0.1	0.056	0.1	0.056
7	0.51	1	0.51	0.1	0.051	0.1	0.051
8	0.47	1	0.47	0.1	0.047	0.1	0.047
9	0.42	1	0.42	0.1	0.042	0.1	0.042
10	0.39	1	0.39	0.1	0.039	0.1	0.039
Total DCF £m			6.14		2.18		0.614
Less cost £m		3		3		3	
Net present value £m		3.14		(0.82)		(2.386)	
Return on capital invested (per £)		1.05		(0.27)		(0.08)	

Note: brackets indicate negative values

Table 5.4 Discounting returns to plant size problem

Demand		Small plant (not extended)					
Initial Long term		High High		High Low		Low Low	
Year	Factor	Return £m	DCF	Return £m	DCF	Return £m	DCF
1	0.91	0.45	0.41	0.45	0.41	0.4	0.364
2	0.83	0.45	0.37	0.45	0.37	0.4	0.332
3	0.75	0.25	0.188	0.4	0.30	0.4	0.300
4	0.68	0.25	0.170	0.4	0.272	0.4	0.272
5	0.62	0.25	0.155	0.4	0.248	0.4	0.248
6	0.56	0.25	0.140	0.4	0.224	0.4	0.224
7	0.51	0.25	0.128	0.4	0.204	0.4	0.204
8	0.47	0.25	0.118	0.4	0.188	0.4	0.188
9	0.42	0.25	0.105	0.4	0.168	0.4	0.168
10	0.39	0.25	0.098	0.4	0.156	0.4	0.156
Total DCF £m		1.882		2.54		2.456	
Less cost £m		1.3		1.3		1.3	
Net present value £m		0.582		1.24		1.156	
Return on capital invested (per £)		0.45		0.95		0.89	

Table 5.5 Discounting returns to plant size problem

Demand		Small plant extended			
Initial Long term		High High		High Low	
Year	Factor	Return £m	DCF	Return £m	DCF
1	0.91	0.45	0.41	0.45	0.41
2	0.83	0.45	0.37	0.45	0.37
3	0.75	0.7	0.525	0.05	0.036
4	0.68	0.7	0.476	0.05	0.034
5	0.62	0.7	0.434	0.05	0.031
6	0.56	0.7	0.392	0.05	0.028
7	0.51	0.7	0.357	0.05	0.026
8	0.47	0.7	0.329	0.05	0.024
9	0.42	0.7	0.294	0.05	0.021
10	0.39	0.7	0.273	0.05	0.020
Total DCF £m		3.86		1.00	
Less cost £m		3.5 (1.3+2.2)		3.5 (1.3+2.2)	
Net present value £m		0.36		(2.5)	
Return on capital invested (per £)		0.10		(0.71)	

Note: brackets indicate negative values

change during the project life span; this will then require the use of several discounting rates. Discounting can be carried out by multiplying the return by the appropriate discounting factor. The factor can be obtained from tables.

The actual choice of a discount rate is difficult and can only be made by managers in conjunction with the accountants looking at economic forecasts to estimate what the rate is likely to be in the future. In Table 5.2 ten per cent was thought appropriate and factors for ten years will be needed.

These discounting factors can then be applied to the returns in the manner shown in the Tables 5.3, 5.4 and 5.5. Having now discounted the returns they can be added to the tree as shown in Figure 5.6. All costs have now been taken from these returns, so the costs now added to the tree are only added as points of information.

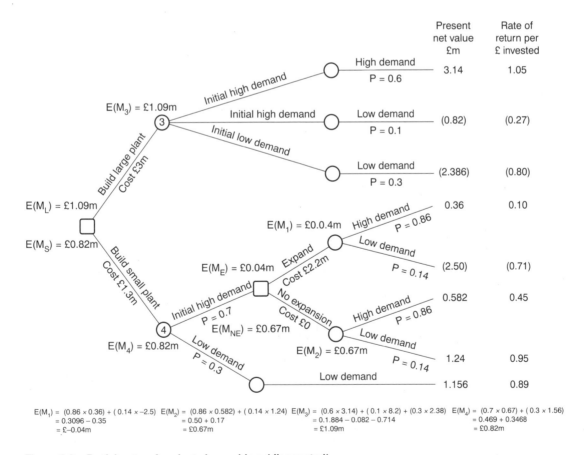

Figure 5.6   Decision tree for plant size problem (discounted)

5.9 The analysis of decision trees

Using a classical decision theory approach, the best decision would appear to be to build a large plant with an expected return at present net value of £1.09 million.

For a manager to use a decision tree to assist him/her in the decision process the whole of the tree must be used. A decision tree is a powerful method of visually presenting the actions that can be taken by the manager and the possible outcomes that can occur when these actions are taken, along with the expected results. The manager must then use all of this information to make the decision. The classical decision theory approach to choose the decision with the largest expected return is only one criterion of choice and is in fact not a very good criterion.

Company policy could well affect the decision. Although building the large plant brings in the greatest return it does have a large risk element to it. With this route there is a 0.6 chance of getting a large return, with 0.4 chance of some amount of loss. With the small plant route, providing that it is not expanded, whatever outcome ensues some form of profit will be made. A large company may well be able to stand the possibility of loss for the greater return but for the small company the only option may be to adopt the safe route as any loss could mean their complete closure.

The financial terms are better considered in the amount of money being returned not purely as an amount but as a rate per point invested to obtain the return. The best possible return on capital invested is £1.05 per £1 invested from the large plant operating with high market demand. Taking into account the probabilities to obtain the expected returns at present net value and then using these values to calculate the return on capital invested, the action to build the large plant gives a rate of return of £0.36 per £1 invested and with the action to build a small plant the rate of return is £0.63 per £1 invested. It would then seem a better decision to invest £1.3 million in the small plant and try to find a project with a higher rate of return from the remaining £1.7 million that could have been invested in the large plant.

It must be remembered that there will be other projects within the organisation all competing for limited resources. Therefore this project cannot be considered in isolation and the returns should be considered along with the returns from the other projects in order to find the project or the group of projects best suited to the firm's requirements.

The decision maker must also take into account the effects of factors which may be difficult to quantify. Factors such as availability of capital, the effect of various actions on the employment of the organisation, the effect of various actions on the 'image' of the organisation, the availability of labour to staff the plants, etc., will all need to be taken into consideration by the decision maker and could well affect the final action to be taken.

Finally, it must be recognised that most of the figures used in a decision tree of this nature are estimated and the rate at which the returns are discounted can only be an estimated rate. Given that the financial estimates and the probabilities are estimated they can only be correct within given limits. These limits need to be considered by the decision maker. They could be written on the tree and then used by the decision maker to apply a sensitivity analysis using statistical techniques. It is likely, however, that the average decision maker could have considerable difficulty with the concepts involved in confidence limits. One way around this problem is to produce three trees:

1. An optimistic tree showing all the values at their best possible, i.e. costs at the lowest, returns at the highest, etc.
2. A pessimistic tree showing all the values at their worst possible, i.e. costs at the highest, returns at the lowest, etc.
3. An expected tree showing all the values at their expected or average value.

This method has a number of advantages to recommend it. It is useful at the stage where subjective values are being set, it allows the manager to produce a series of values instead of just one value and therefore it is likely to improve the manager's ability to set such subjective probabilities. The three trees can then be used by the manager to allow for the effect of inaccuracies in the estimates. Given the average value (expected value) it is possible to estimate the standard deviation from the following formula:

$$\text{Standard deviation} = \frac{\text{Optimistic value} - \text{Pessimistic value}}{6}$$

This formula can be used to determine standard deviations for sales or for expected values. The formula is based on the fact that the optimistic value minus the pessimistic value will give the range of values and that the 99 per cent confidence limits contain six standard deviations. Therefore, an approximate value for the standard deviation will be given by dividing the range by six. This approximation assumes a normal distribution and will become less accurate the more skewed the distribution becomes. The following example shows how this technique is applied:

A manufacturer has the choice of three different types of machine to replace his existing plant. Any money outlaid on machines must be returned in three years, which is the expected life of the machines. The company accountant has produced the following cost per unit estimates for the three types of machines:

Machine type	A	B	C
Pessimistic cost/unit (£)	3.80	2.80	2.20
Expected cost/unit (£)	3.00	2.00	1.50
Optimistic cost/unit (£)	2.60	1.80	1.30

These costs include all costs associated with the production, administration and selling of the product, but excluding the initial purchase cost of the machine. The sales manager has produced the following estimates of sales over the three year

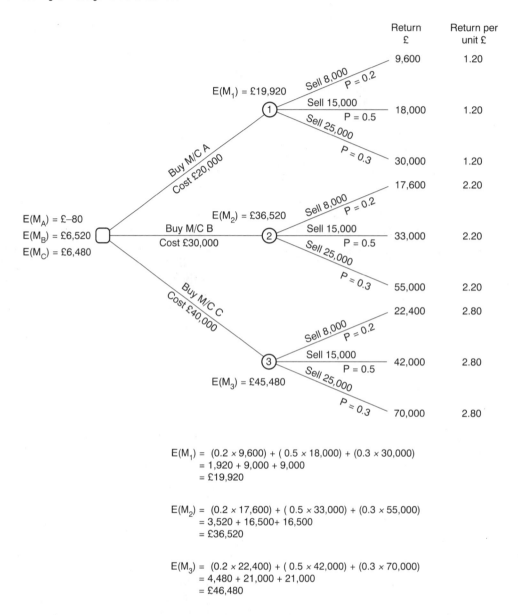

$$E(M_1) = (0.2 \times 9,600) + (0.5 \times 18,000) + (0.3 \times 30,000)$$
$$= 1,920 + 9,000 + 9,000$$
$$= £19,920$$

$$E(M_2) = (0.2 \times 17,600) + (0.5 \times 33,000) + (0.3 \times 55,000)$$
$$= 3,520 + 16,500 + 16,500$$
$$= £36,520$$

$$E(M_3) = (0.2 \times 22,400) + (0.5 \times 42,000) + (0.3 \times 70,000)$$
$$= 4,480 + 21,000 + 21,000$$
$$= £46,480$$

Figure 5.7 Pessimistic decision tree for machine choice problem

period. These sales estimates are independent of machine type and are in unit sales:

Pessimistic estimates			
Sales over three year period	8,000	15,000	25,000
Probability of occurrence	0.2	0.5	0.3
Expected estimates			
Sales over three year period	10,000	20,000	30,000
Probability of occurrence	0.2	0.4	0.4

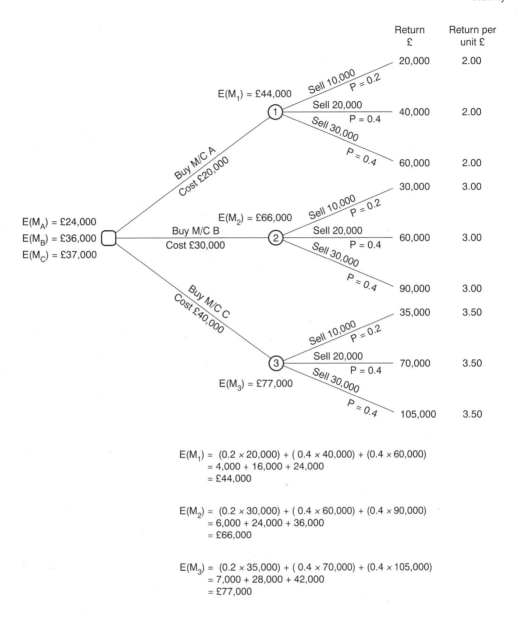

$$E(M_1) = (0.2 \times 20{,}000) + (0.4 \times 40{,}000) + (0.4 \times 60{,}000)$$
$$= 4{,}000 + 16{,}000 + 24{,}000$$
$$= £44{,}000$$

$$E(M_2) = (0.2 \times 30{,}000) + (0.4 \times 60{,}000) + (0.4 \times 90{,}000)$$
$$= 6{,}000 + 24{,}000 + 36{,}000$$
$$= £66{,}000$$

$$E(M_3) = (0.2 \times 35{,}000) + (0.4 \times 70{,}000) + (0.4 \times 105{,}000)$$
$$= 7{,}000 + 28{,}000 + 42{,}000$$
$$= £77{,}000$$

Figure 5.8   Expected decision tree for machine choice problem

Optimistic estimates			
Sales over three year period	12,000	25,000	35,000
Probability of occurrence	0.1	0.5	0.4

The cost of the machines is considered fixed and the price at which the machines can be purchased is as follows: Machine A at £20,000, Machine B at £30,000 and Machine C at £40,000. The selling price of the units is £5 per unit. Splitting the information into three groups (pessimistic, expected and optimistic), the three decision trees can be produced. The figures have not been discounted for ease of calculation but would be in practice. The pessimistic tree is shown in Figure 5.7, the expected tree is shown in Figure 5.8 and the optimistic tree is shown in Figure 5.9.

The results from the tree can be brought together for any point on the tree working on the point of the greatest interest – the final box decision – although it is important in any practical case to consider other points on the tree.

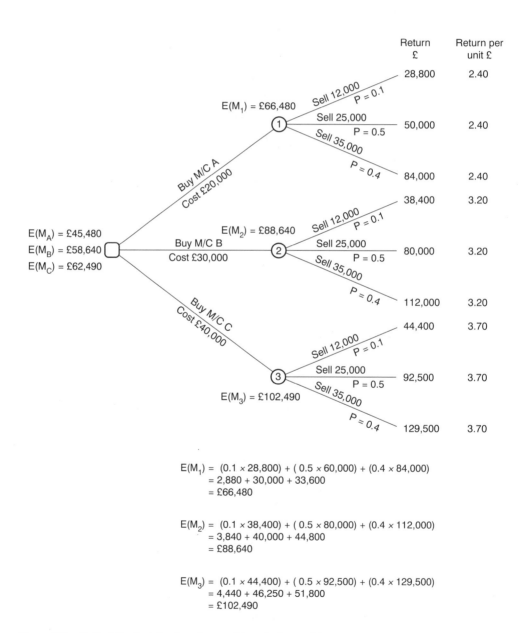

$$E(M_1) = (0.1 \times 28{,}800) + (0.5 \times 60{,}000) + (0.4 \times 84{,}000)$$
$$= 2{,}880 + 30{,}000 + 33{,}600$$
$$= £66{,}480$$

$$E(M_2) = (0.1 \times 38{,}400) + (0.5 \times 80{,}000) + (0.4 \times 112{,}000)$$
$$= 3{,}840 + 40{,}000 + 44{,}800$$
$$= £88{,}640$$

$$E(M_3) = (0.1 \times 44{,}400) + (0.5 \times 92{,}500) + (0.4 \times 129{,}500)$$
$$= 4{,}440 + 46{,}250 + 51{,}800$$
$$= £102{,}490$$

Figure 5.9   Optimistic decision tree for machine choice problem

These final decision box figures can be summarised:

MACHINE A   Pessimistic return = (£80)
                Expected return = £24,000   Standard deviation = £7,760
                Optimistic return = £46,480

MACHINE B   Pessimistic return = £6,520
                Expected return = £36,000   Standard deviation = £8,687
                Optimistic return = £58,640

MACHINE C   Pessimistic return = £6,480
                Expected return = £37,000   Standard deviation = £9,335
                Optimistic return = £62,490

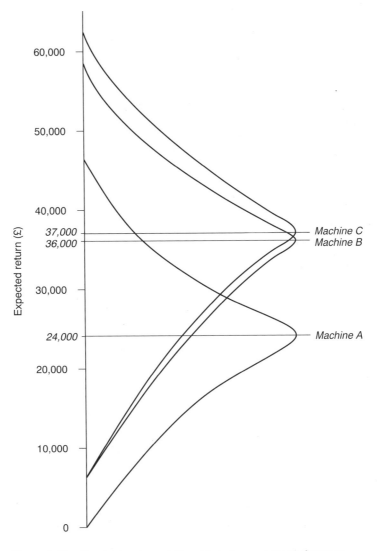

Figure 5.10   Graph showing relationship between expected returns

These results are best presented in a visual form so as to have maximum impact on managers, as shown in Figure 5.10. Such a presentation can be valuable even to managers with little statistical knowledge. The greater the manager's statistical knowledge the more probabilistic the analysis can become. Normal distribution theory can be used to determine the probability of achieving given returns or given expected (average) returns.

The disadvantage of this method is that all the tree is, for example, optimistic whereas the manager may only want part of the tree or some of the values of the tree to be optimistic. This problem could be overcome with the use of an interactive computer simulation package to enable the manager to monitor the effects of various changes in the tree. There is also a problem in the amount of work involved. Such an analysis increases the work in collecting estimates etc., but the time spent gaining a range of values should greatly improve the quality of such estimates. The work in the production of the trees will be increased twofold and the work in analysis will also be increased. Extra benefits gained from the extension of decision trees in this manner, i.e. better estimates, a greater awareness of the variability of decision trees and a measure of this variability, should outweigh this extra work.

5.10 Simulation and other quantitative techniques and decision trees

Simulation can have two major impacts on decision trees. First, it can provide information relating to business decisions. By using simulation models with many parameters, predictions can be made of future events. Models can provide probability elements, costs, returns, etc., to place on the tree. This predictive mode of simulation is discussed in Chapter 13.

The other major impact of simulation is in the provision of an interactive simulation package, almost certainly computerised. The first part of the package would provide, with the use of programmed learning, the manager's introduction to decision analysis. This would then be followed up by providing support for the manager's decision making. This would carry out all the calculation work for the manager although from the first part of the package he would have an understanding of the calculations involved. There would be a question-answer procedure to construct the detail of the decision tree and to enable the manager to ask such questions as, 'What happens if I take the following action?' etc. Managers appear to prefer to work with a computer than a decision analyst in person because they would not have as many consultative problems with the computer, and they would not have to admit lack of knowledge or ask for the help of another member of the organisation.

It must be remembered that many quantitative techniques may be used in the determination of the various actions and associated returns on the decision tree (stock control, mathematical programming, etc.) Decision analysis could be said to involve many quantitative techniques and must also take account of non-quantifiable factors.

Summary of decision analysis

Decision analysis can be of great value to management. Decision trees provide a clear pictorial presentation of any particular decision (whatever quantitative techniques have been used to determine results) and outcomes of the different actions which can be taken. It must be remembered though that decision analysis is only an aid to managers and such an analysis should be considered by the manager along with the non-quantifiable aspects of the decision.

It is possible to use decision analysis as one method of setting a value for a particular set of information.

Competence Example 5.3

At the end of this section you should now be able to demonstrate how to:

1 **identify the elements of the decision and produce the outline of the decision tree**

2 **calculate the expected values on the tree**

3 **interpret the decision tree**

4 **if required carry out a sensitivity analysis.**

To practise and demonstrate these detailed competences complete example problems 5.4 to 5.6 at the end of this chapter. To help you to develop these competences a description of the procedure you will need to follow is now given, along with a typical problem format. This problem format is based on the plant size example we have just considered.

PROCEDURE (DECISION ANALYSIS)

1 Identify probability and decision points.

2 Construct the outline of the decision tree.

3 Carry out the calculations on the decision tree.

4 Interpret the decision tree.

5 If required carry out a sensitivity analysis.

PROBLEM

The following information is available to the manager from three sources:

a. Marketing information

The Marketing manager suggests a 60 per cent chance of a larger market in the long run and 40 per cent chance of a low demand developing as follows:

Initially high, sustained high	60%	
Initially high, long term low	10%	Low 40%
Initially low, continuing low	30%	
Initially low, subsequently low	0%	

```
 2 years              8 years
 ───────►  ──────────────────►
        10 years
 ──────────────────────────►
```

b. Annual income

The management accounting section have put forward the following financial estimates:

i.   A large plant operating under high market demand conditions would yield £1 million annually in cash flow.
ii. A large plant operating under low market demand conditions would only yield £0.1 million annually in cash flow because of high fixed costs and inefficiencies.
iii. A smallplant operating under low market demand conditions would be economic and would yield £0.4 million annually in cash flow.
iv. A smallplant operating under high market demand conditions initially (i.e. the first two years) would yield £0.45 million annually in cash flow, but this would drop to £0.25 million annually in cash flow if the high demand market conditions were sustained for the last eight years of operating.
v.   If an initial small plant expanded after two years and was operating under high market demand conditions it would yield £0.7 million annually in cash flow for the remaining eight years and so would be less efficient than a large plant built initially.
vi. If an initial small plant expanded after two years and was operating under low market demand conditions it would yield £0.05 million annually in cash flow for the remaining eight years and so would be less efficient than a large plant built initially.

c. Capital costs

Estimates from construction companies indicate that a large plant would cost £3 million to build and put into operation. A small plant would cost £1.3 million initially and an additional £2.2 million if expanded after two years.

SOLUTION FORMAT

❶ Management has two possible actions it can take: either to build a large plant or a small plant. If the small plant is constructed there is an option to extend it after two years. A series of outcomes of high and low market demands will follow these actions.

The probabilities after outcome one and two need to be adjusted because from the information the probability of an initial high and then a sustained high is 0.6 and the probability of an initial high and then a long term low is 0.1. This gives a branch on the tree with a set of probabilities that do not add to one so this then needs to be rectified to ensure they do add to one. This is carried out with a simple weighting process by dividing each probability by the sum of the probabilities on that branch so ending with probabilities which add to one.

Therefore probability of initial high

$$\text{then sustained high} = \frac{0.6}{0.6+0.1} = \frac{0.6}{0.7} = 0.86$$

Therefore probability of initial high

$$\text{then long term low} = \frac{0.1}{0.6+0.1} = \frac{0.1}{0.7} = 0.14$$

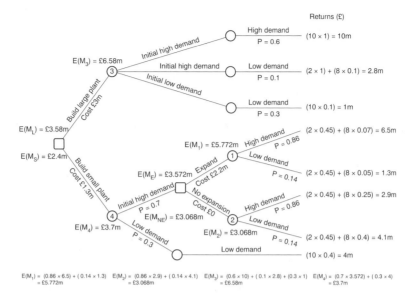

E(M₃) = £6.58m at node 3.

$$E(M_3) = £6.58m$$

Returns (£)

High demand P = 0.6 — (10 × 1) = 10m

Initial high demand

Initial high demand — Low demand P = 0.1 — (2 × 1) + (8 × 0.1) = 2.8m

Initial low demand — Low demand P = 0.3 — (10 × 0.1) = 1m

Build large plant Cost £3m

$$E(M_L) = £3.58m$$

$$E(M_S) = £2.4m$$

$$E(M_1) = £5.772m$$ High demand P = 0.86 — (2 × 0.45) + (8 × 0.07) = 6.5m

Low demand P = 0.14 — (2 × 0.45) + (8 × 0.05) = 1.3m

$$E(M_E) = £3.572m$$ Expand Cost £2.2m

No expansion Cost £0

$$E(M_{NE}) = £3.068m$$ High demand P = 0.86 — (2 × 0.45) + (8 × 0.25) = 2.9m

Build small plant Cost £1.3m

Initial high demand P = 0.7

$$E(M_4) = £3.7m$$ Low demand P = 0.3

$$E(M_2) = £3.068m$$ Low demand P = 0.14 — (2 × 0.45) + (8 × 0.4) = 4.1m

Low demand — (10 × 0.4) = 4m

E(M₁) = (0.86 × 6.5) + (0.14 × 1.3) E(M₂) = (0.86 × 2.9) + (0.14 × 4.1) E(M₃) = (0.6 × 10) + (0.1 × 2.8) + (0.3 × 1) E(M₄) = (0.7 × 3.572) + (0.3 × 4)
= £5.772m   = £3.068m   = £6.58m   = £3.7m

❹ Using classical statistical decision theory the decision giving the greatest return is that of building a large plant with an expected return at present net value of £1.09 million.

For a manager to use a decision tree to assist him in their decision process the whole of the tree must be used. A decision tree is a powerful method of visually presenting the actions that can be taken by the manager and the possible outcomes that can occur when these actions are taken along with the expected results. The manager must then use all of this information to make the decision. The classical decision theory approach to choose the decision with the largest expected return is only one criterion of choice and is in fact not a very good criterion.

Company policy could well affect the decision. Although building the large plant brings in the greatest return it does have a large risk element to it. With this route there is a 0.6 chance of getting a large return, with 0.4 chance of some amount of loss. With the small plant route, providing that it is not expanded, whatever outcome ensues some form of profit will be made. A large company may well be able to stand the possibility of loss for the greater return but for the small company the only option may be to adopt the safe route as any loss could mean their complete closure.

The financial terms are better considered in the amount of money being returned not purely as an amount but as a rate per point invested to obtain the return. The best possible return on capital invested is £1.05 per £1 invested from the large plant operating with high market demand. Taking into account the probabilities to obtain the expected returns at present net value and then using these values to calculate the return on capital invested, the action to build the large plant gives a rate return of £0.36 per £1 invested and with the action to build a small plant the rate of return is £0.63 per £1 invested. It would then seem a better decision to invest £1.3 million in the small plant and try to find a project with a higher rate of return from the remaining £1.7 million that may have been invested in the large plant.

❹ 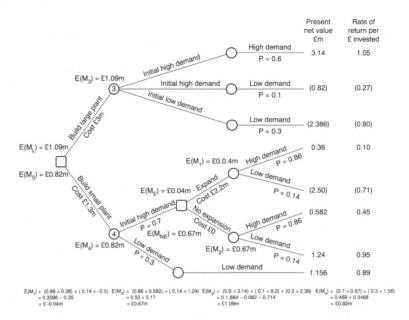 ❸

$E(M_1) = (0.86 \times 0.36) + (0.14 \times -2.5)$ $E(M_2) = (0.86 \times 0.582) + (0.14 \times 1.24)$ $E(M_3) = (0.6 \times 3.14) + (0.1 \times 8.2) + (0.3 \times 2.38)$ $E(M_4) = (0.7 \times 0.67) + (0.3 \times 1.56)$
$= 0.3096 - 0.35$ $= 0.50 + 0.17$ $= 0.1.884 - 0.082 - 0.714$ $= 0.469 + 0.3468$
$= £-0.04m$ $= £0.67m$ $= £1.09m$ $= £0.82m$

It must be remembered that there will be other projects within the organisation all competing for limited resources. Therefore, this project cannot be considered in isolation and the returns should be considered along with the returns from the other projects to find the project or the group of projects best suited to the firm's requirements.

The decision maker must add into the decision-making process the effects of factors which may be difficult to quantify, such as availability of capital, the effect of various actions on the employment of the organisation, the effect of various actions on the 'image' of the organisation, the availability of labour to staff the plants, etc. These may need to be taken into consideration by the decision maker and could well affect the final action to be taken.

❺ Finally it must be recognised that most of the figures used in a decision tree of this nature ❹ are estimated and the rate at which the returns are discounted can only be an estimated rate. Given that the financial estimates and the probabilities are estimated they can only be correct within given limits. These limits need to be considered by the decision maker. They could be written on the tree and then used by the decision maker to apply a sensitivity analysis with the use of statistical techniques. It is likely, however, that the average decision maker could have considerable difficulty with the concepts involved in confidence limits. One way around this problem is to produce three trees:

1. An optimistic tree showing all the values at their best possible, i.e. costs at the lowest, returns at the highest, etc.
2. A pessimistic tree showing all the values at their worst possible, i.e. cost at the highest, returns at the lowest, etc.
3. An expected tree showing all the values at their expected or average value.

Practise your competence now on problems 5.4 to 5.6 at the end of this chapter. There is not an element on the computer disk for this section due to the problem that each decision tree can be completely different. This makes it very difficult to produce a standard package, but if you have worked through Chapter 2 you should be able to produce a simple spreadsheet to carry out the calculations of the decision tree. This will enable you to carry out a sensitivity analysis on the elements of the decision tree. You may now demonstrate the competence in this area against problems from your own work environment. You may have to work with operational level decisions given the sensitive nature of strategic or tactical decisions.

Problems for Chapter 5

5.1 The Highways Committee of a county council has a decision to make concerning three independent road projects. Before the meeting the chief engineer has estimated the following probabilities to help with future planning:

Project A   a road widening scheme   Probability of acceptance   0.9
Project B   a bridge modernisation scheme   Probability of acceptance   0.6
Project C   a new by-pass scheme   Probability of acceptance   0.7

You can assume there is sufficient cash for all three projects. Construct a probability tree and determine the following probabilities:

a) all projects will be accepted
b) at least one project will be accepted
c) at least two projects will be accepted
d) all the projects will be rejected

5.2 A manager has applied for two advertised vacancies in a Sunday newspaper. The first is marketing manager for a frozen food processor, the second is sales manager for an ice-cream manufacturer. The manager believes the probability of gaining an interview for the first position (A) is 0.6 with a subsequent probability of 0.5 of actually being offered the position. For the second position (B) the manager estimates the probability of gaining an interview to be 0.7 with a subsequent probability of 0.8 of actually being offered the position. The interviews are close together so the manager can wait before accepting or rejecting any offers. The two positions can be considered independently. Produce a probability tree of this situation and from the tree determine the following probabilities:

a) of being offered both jobs
b) of being offered at least one job
c) of being offered neither job

5.3 A computer system development house has put in bids for the following four projects and calculates from past performance the following probabilities of acceptance:

Project	A	B	C	D
Probability of acceptance	0.9	0.6	0.7	0.8

The projects are related in two groups, the groups being independent of each other. Group one consists of projects A and D; project A is independent but project D cannot go ahead without A given that it is a possible development from this system.

Group two consists of projects B and C; project B is independent but project C cannot go ahead without B given that it is a possible development from this system. Construct a probability tree of this situation and determine the following probabilities:

a) all the projects will be accepted
b) the projects in group one will be accepted
c) the projects in group two will be accepted
d) at least one project will be accepted
e) at least two projects will be accepted
f) at least three projects will be accepted

5.4 A manufacturer of plastic toys has to decide whether or not to produce and market a new Christmas novelty toy. The life of the product is only expected to be one year in the highly volatile toy business. If the manufacturer decides to produce the toy a special plastic mould will need to be purchased. You can assume that the retirement costs will be balanced out by the scrap value. There exists a choice of moulds to buy. A normal quality mould costs £1,500, with a cost of manufacturing, distribution, advertising, etc., of £1.50 per unit (this cost includes all costs other than the cost of purchase of the mould). A high quality mould costs £2,000 and could be purchased with a cost of manufacturing, distribution, advertising, etc., of £1 per unit (this cost includes all costs other than the cost of purchase of the mould). This mould produces good items to the same quality as the first mould, but it is more efficient and has a lower scrap rate and this is reflected in the cost structure. The selling price is £5 per unit and the following probabilities of sales have been estimated:

Sales	400	1000	2000
Probability	0.4	0.3	0.3

Produce a decision analysis of this situation and advise the manufacturer on alternative decisions.

5.5 Your company is about to purchase a new computer network with a number of magnetic disk units. The company is not sure how many disk units to purchase as this will depend upon the level of sales generated by the competitive edge created by the new network. The following probability distribution has been estimated for the number of disk units required:

Number of disk units required	Probability
1	0.10
2	0.45
3	0.35
4	0.10

If a disk unit is purchased and installed with the main computer network it will cost £1,380 but if a disk unit is purchased and installed after the installation of the main computer network it will cost £2,490. With the aid of a decision analysis present the strategies open to the company.

5.6 A chemical marketing company has a product research and development budget of £600,000 for the coming year and the following possible projects are available:

a) A standard improvement to an existing product costing £300,000 and yielding marginal benefits with the following probability distribution:

Increase in profitability	Probability
£0	0.1
£500,000	0.7
£1,000,000	0.2

b) A high risk development with a 50 per cent chance of a £2,000,000 benefit (otherwise failure and no benefit). The initial investment would be £300,000 and depending on test results a further £300,000 might be needed. This extra investment is thought unlikely and a probability has been assessed at a 0.2 chance of being required.

At the most, one project may be chosen. Unused funds may be invested in other areas of the business with a return of 15 per cent per annum. All benefits listed above and all costs are within a year time span.

Produce a decision analysis of this situation and advise the company on the decision options.

6 Probability distributions
typical patterns and shapes

6.1 Introduction

You should now be getting used to the idea of frequency distributions and the types of shapes they can take, as well as the way that probabilities can be assigned to a variety of different situations. More specifically, Chapter 5 was primarily concerned with how we assign and use probabilities for single events. This chapter tries to extend these ideas by showing that a collection of data can belong to what are known as probability distributions. These probability distributions exhibit a number of characteristics, and it is from these characteristics that we are able to find solutions to a wide range of business problems. The normal distribution is a very important type of probability distribution due to it underpinning a number of other chapters. It can also be used in a very practical way to answer certain types of questions. As a consequence of this the normal distribution is looked at particularly closely and features heavily in this chapter.

Chapter 6 is therefore concerned with developing a competence in the application of probability distributions so that business problems can be more readily solved. By the end of this chapter you should be able to demonstrate how to:

- recognise if a set of data belongs to a discrete or continuous probability distribution
- use probability distributions to solve business problems

The chapter will use a series of practical examples to develop the underpinning knowledge that is associated with probability distributions.

At the end of each section the required competence will be specified and described. A typical problem format with the competences highlighted will also be given to help you to demonstrate the competences on the problems at the end of the chapter. At the end of the book a full solution will be given for the first of these problems as well as the answers for the rest.

6.2 What is a probability distribution?

A probability distribution is all the possible outcomes associated with an experiment (in statistics an experiment is any process or study that has discernible outcomes, such as components produced by a machine and consumer perceptions to a product promotion), as well as the probabilities for each of those outcomes.

Table 6.1   Listing of all customer decisions

	1	2	3	4	5	6	7	8	9	10	11	12	13	14	15	16
A	Y	N	Y	Y	Y	Y	Y	Y	N	N	N	N	N	N	Y	N
B	Y	Y	N	Y	Y	Y	N	N	Y	Y	N	N	N	Y	N	N
C	Y	Y	Y	N	Y	N	Y	N	Y	N	Y	N	Y	N	N	N
D	Y	Y	Y	Y	N	N	N	Y	N	Y	Y	Y	N	N	N	N

A marketing manager, for instance, might want to know what the probabilities are that the company's top four customers will franchise the new 'environmentally friendly' product range. Looking at this simplistically, we have four customers (trials) who can decide either to buy the product or not buy the product (mutually exclusive outcomes). Identifying all possible outcomes shows us that there are 16 ways in which the customers could behave (where Y = buy, N = not buy), and these are shown in Table 6.1.

From Table 6.1 it has been possible to identify the probability distribution of the various outcomes (Table 6.2).

Table 6.2   Probability distribution of customer decisions

Outcome (number of Ys)	Probability
0	1/16
1	4/16
2	6/16
3	4/16
4	1/16

It is also possible, as in Figure 6.1, to depict the probability distribution graphically.

This process can be replicated in the classroom, with students flipping four coins and recording how they land (it's great fun as coins seem to be flying everywhere). These experimental results are then compared to the expected distribution, which is normally very close. This demonstrates that the real world does in fact follow the probabilities we have identified.

In common with a great deal of statistics, there are a number of quite distinct terms used in this area. A **random variable** for instance is the outcome of an experiment, such as heads if you flip a coin. The probability that a random variable (denoted as X) will take on a particular outcome (denoted as x) is $P(X = x)$, in which case the probability that none of the customers will purchase the product is $P(X = 0) = 1/16$.

A probability distribution is, as you can see, very similar to a frequency distribution. Like a frequency distribution it can have a mean and a standard

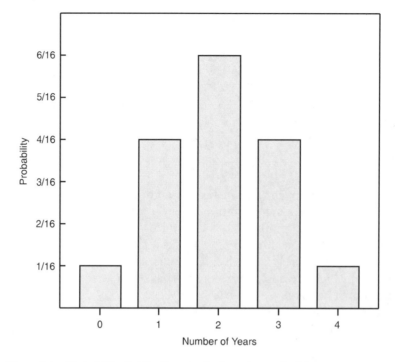

Figure 6.1   Probability distribution graph of customer decisions

deviation. The mean of a probability distribution is called the **expected value** and it is computed as follows:

Mean or expected value: $\mu = E(X) = \Sigma[X \cdot P(X)]$

where $E(X)$ = the long-run average
$\qquad X$ = an outcome
$\qquad P(X)$ = the probability of that outcome

The standard deviation for a probability distribution is computed as follows:

Standard deviation: $\qquad \sigma = \sqrt{\Sigma[(X - \mu)^2 \cdot P(X)]}$

These can be applied to a problem to provide summary values. For example, if a manufacturer of PCBs identified the faults affecting the product over a period of time as:

Number of faults	Probability
0	.221
1	.315
2	.207
3	.112
4	.096
5	.031
6	.018

we could calculate the expected value and standard deviation:

X	P(X)	X · P(X)	(X – μ)²	(X – μ)² · P(X)
0	.221	.000	2.93	.65
1	.315	.315	0.50	.16
2	.207	.414	0.08	.02
3	.112	.336	1.65	.18
4	.096	.384	5.23	.50
5	.031	.155	10.81	.33
6	.018	.108	18.38	.33
		1.712		2.17

$$\mu = E(X) = \Sigma[X \cdot P(X)] = 1.712 \text{ faults}$$

$$\sigma = \sqrt{\Sigma[(X - \mu)^2 \cdot P(X)]} = \sqrt{2.17} = 1.47 \text{ faults}$$

The production manager can therefore expect an average of 1.7 faults with a standard deviation of 1.5 faults.

Returning back to probability distributions, they can be broken down into two main camps: those that come under the heading of **discrete probability distributions** and those that come under the heading of **continuous probability distributions**. Discrete random variables have a distinct and identifiable unit of measure, such as the number of people in a company who have a degree qualification. Continuous random variables do not necessarily have a distinct and identifiable unit of measure because they can have any value associated with them. Examples include people's height, the amount of fluid in a vessel, and the amount of money a company has in a bank. It is ironic that nearly all business data is discrete (for even continuous data normally gets rounded up to full integer values) but that it can, and does, get treated as continuous!

Discrete probability distributions include:

- binomial distributions
- Poisson distributions

and continuous probability distributions include:

- exponential distributions
- normal distributions
- *t* distributions
- chi-square distributions

This chapter will look at binomial, Poisson, exponential and normal distributions. The *t* distributions are looked at in Chapter 7, while chi-square distributions can be found in Chapter 8.

6.3 Binomial distributions

A **binomial distribution** can be used in situations where there are two possible outcomes, such as winning a contract or losing a contract. Although the potential application of the binomial distribution is quite extensive, it is important that any problem that is tackled using it meets the following conditions:

- The problem has a number of trials (an activity or experiment, denoted by n, that is repeatable) that are known and fixed.
- Each trial has only two possible outcomes, often identified as success or failure, and that the probability of success or failure in one trial is totally independent of any other trial.
- The probability of success (p) and failure $(1 - p)$ remains constant from one trial to the next.

An example of a problem that meets the binomial conditions would be a double glazing salesperson who carries out 20 cold calls to randomly selected homes. The double glazing salesperson is judged on whether a sale is won or lost, and experience shows that the probability of success is .15. Relating this back to binomial conditions we find:

- There are 20 identical calls or trials.
- A call results in a sale or a no sale, and these are independent because the homes were selected randomly.
- The probabilities of a sale or a no sale are assumed to be the same for each home, with $p = .15$ and $1 - p = .85$

which meets the binomial conditions.

The benefit of using a binomial distribution is that once we know the probability of success in a trial we can estimate how many successes there will be for any number of trials. The formula for this is known as the **binomial probability function**:

$$\text{Binomial probability function:} \quad P(x) = \frac{n!}{x!(n-x)!} \, p^x (1-p)^{n-x} = {}_nC_x(p)^x(1-p)^{n-x}$$

where x = a particular outcome
$P(x)$ = the probability of that outcome
n = number of trials
p = probability of success
$1 - p$ = probability of failure
${}_nC_x$ = the number of combinations of n trials taken x at a time, which is computed from $\frac{n!}{x!(n-x)!}$

Looking at this formula you might be tempted to finally shred the book into tiny pieces. But don't despair – we will go through the formula step by step, and then show you how you can use tables to simplify the whole process greatly.

Referring back to Table 6.1 and the four customers who might buy the new environmentally-friendly product range, and bearing in mind that the marketing manager is a born worrier, what is the probability that at least one of the customers will buy it? To answer this we need to know all the alternative ways or combinations that one of the customers could buy the product and what the probabilities are for each of those ways (the number of combinations can be obtained from the Excel spreadsheet package by using the 'Combin' command from the formula paste facility). The different ways that one of the four customers could buy the product have been taken from Table 6.1 and are shown in Table 6.3.

If the marketing manager believes that there is a 20 per cent chance that any one customer will buy the product, then there is a $1 - 20\% = 80\%$ chance that a customer will not buy a product. Since each box or event in Table 6.3 represents an independent act, and using the multiplication rule (independent events) that was discussed in Chapter 5, the probability of getting one customer from the four to buy the product is:

$$P(N_A \text{ and } N_B \text{ and } N_C \text{ and } Y_D) = (.80)\,(.80)\,(.80)\,(.20) = .1024$$

Repeating this for each of the different decision alternatives and then summing up the results, as in Table 6.4, shows us that there is a total probability of .4096 that one customer from the four will buy the product.

This way of computing the probabilities of every possible value of a binomial random variable is known as the **method of complete enumeration**. The method is fine as long as the problem is small. When a problem is large the process of identifying every possible permutation and combination, as well as their

Table 6.3 The different ways or sequences
of one customer buying the product

| | | Decisions | | |
Customer	1	2	3	4
A	N	N	N	Y
B	N	N	Y	N
C	N	Y	N	N
D	Y	N	N	N

Table 6.4 Probabilities for customer and decision alternatives

| | | Decisions | | | |
Customer	1	2	3	4	Totals
A	.80	.80	.80	.20	.1024
B	N	N	Y	.80	.1024
C	N	Y	N	.80	.1024
D	Y	N	N	.80	.1024
				Grand Total	.4096

probabilities, is not to be taken on lightly. An alternative way to find the same result is to use the binomial probability function, or as it is often called, the **binomial formula**:

$$_nC_x(p)^x(1-p)^{n-x}$$

$$_4C_1 = \frac{4!}{1!(4-1)!} = \frac{4!}{1!3!} = \frac{24}{6} = 4$$

$$4(.20)^1(.80)^3 = .8 \times .512 = .4096$$

For those readers who are not used to **factorial** notation, the statement 4! means that we carry out the calculation $4 \times 3 \times 2 \times 1$, and in the same way, $3! = 3 \times 2 \times 1$, $2! = 2 \times 1$ and $1! = 1 \times 1$ (it is also necessary to remember that $0! = 1$). Factorial numbers can be obtained from the Excel spreadsheet package following the instructions 'Math', 'Trig' and 'Fact' from the past formula facility. Having shown that the binomial formula does work, let's move on and see how it can be used.

A legal practice that specialises in insolvency knows that if it carries out a postal claim for outstanding debts for a company, there will be a return, under normal circumstances, of 15 per cent. If this is the case, and it sends out 30 bad debt claims, what is the probability that it will get none returned, eight returned, and five or less returned? Is it possible to say how many they would expect to be returned?

Using the binomial formula, with $p = 15$ per cent, $n = 30$, and x at 0 and 8, we find:

$$_{30}C_0 = \frac{30!}{0!(30-0)!} = \frac{30!}{30!} = \frac{2.6525\,k+32}{2.6525\,k+32} = 1$$

$$1(.15)^0(.85)^{30} = 1 \times .0076 - .0076$$

and

$$_{30}C_8 = \frac{30!}{8!(30-8)!} = \frac{30!}{8!22!} = \frac{2.6525\,k+32}{(40320)(1.124\,k+21)} = 5852925$$

$$5852925(.15)^8(.85)^{22} = 5852925(.0000003)(.0280038) = .0420$$

You will have noticed that we have had to resort to scientific notation for the factorials 22! and 30!, and the reason for this is quite simple when you consider that $30! = 2.6525k + 32 = 265252859812191000000000000000000$. Dealing with such large numbers can be difficult, even when we use sophisticated and powerful calculators. An alternative way of arriving at the answer is to use a binomial probability table which has answers for different values of n and p. A section of the binomial probability values is shown in Table 6.5 (a more complete set of values can be found in Table 1 in the Appendix), and it is a simple matter of finding the cell in the table that corresponds to the desired value of n, x, and p that you are looking for.

Table 6.5   Sample of binomial probability table values

n	x	p					
		.05	.10	.15	.20	.25	.30
30	0	.2146	.0424	**.0076**	.0012	.0002	.0000
	1	.3389	.1413	.0404	.0093	.0018	.0003
	2	.2587	.2277	.1034	.0337	.0086	.0018
	3	.1270	.2360	.1703	.0785	.0268	.0072
	4	.0452	.1771	.2028	.1325	.0605	.0209
	5	.0123	.1023	.1861	.1723	.1047	.0464
	6	.0027	.0474	.1368	.1795	.1455	.0829
	7	.0005	.0180	.0828	.1538	.1662	.1219
	8	.0001	.0058	**.0420**	.1105	.1593	.1501
	9	.0000	.0015	.0181	.0676	.1298	.1573

The x values for 0 and 8 have been highlighted and as you can see, they are the same as those calculated using the binomial formula. It is also possible to get these values from a spreadsheet. With Excel the instruction from the formula paste facility is 'Statistical' and then 'Binomdist', where the n, x, p and *cumulative* are then entered. The output for $n = 30$, $x = 8$, $p = .15$ and *cumulative* = false is .0420, which is the same value as previously found.

The final part of the question wanted to know what the probability was that there would be five or less returned. To answer this we add up the probability that none would be returned, one would be returned, two would be returned, etc. The answer is therefore $.0076 + .0404 + .1034 + .1703 + .2028 + .1861 = .7106$ (i.e. there is a 71.06 per cent chance that five or less will be returned).

The sampling of 'bought-out' items that are used in a manufacturing organisation is an important element of quality control, and the decision to accept or reject the goods is normally based upon a binomial decision rule, in that the decision is based upon the number of defects in the shipment. When a manufacturer has a very stringent policy on quality, which is now more common as organisations push for total quality and zero defects, it may have a rule that any incoming parts must not have more than three rejects per 1,000 parts. If a sample of 20 items is then taken from an incoming shipment, and the supplier has stated that their reject rate is not more than 2 per cent, what is the probability that the batch will be rejected?

With $n = 20$ and $p = .02$, we find that the binomial probability for acceptance when $x = 0$ rejects is 0.6676, and that for one, two, and three rejects it is:

$$
\begin{aligned}
p(\text{accepted}) = p(x = 0) &= 0.6676 \\
p(x = 1) &= 0.2725 \\
p(x = 2) &= 0.0528 \\
p(x = 3) &= \underline{0.0065} \\
& \ 0.9994
\end{aligned}
$$

The probability that the batch will be rejected is therefore:

$$p(\text{rejected}) = 1 - p(\text{accepted})$$
$$= 1 - 0.9994 = 0.0006$$

This tells us that there is less than a 1 per cent chance of the batch being rejected, which presumably would satisfy both the supplier and the manufacturer. The same procedure can be followed to obtain acceptance probabilities for different reject percentages. This has been done for $n = 20$ and a range of p values, with the probabilities then being graphed, as shown in Figure 6.2, to form what is known as an 'acceptance probability function'.

An acceptance probability function like this can be useful for a company when it wants to decide on an appropriate acceptance standard, since the costs of returning a batch can be high to the supplier due to extra shipment charges and to the manufacturer because of the potential interruption to production if parts are unavailable. The probability values in Figure 6.2 can easily be obtained from the binomial probability table and graphed on Lotus 1-2-3.

The usefulness of the binomial distribution to business is curtailed to some extent by the difficulty in satisfying the constraints that were outlined at the beginning of this section. It is especially difficult to be sure that the probability of an outcome of a trial remains fixed over time, for even a state of the art machine undergoes wear when it produces a part. In a similar way, the independence

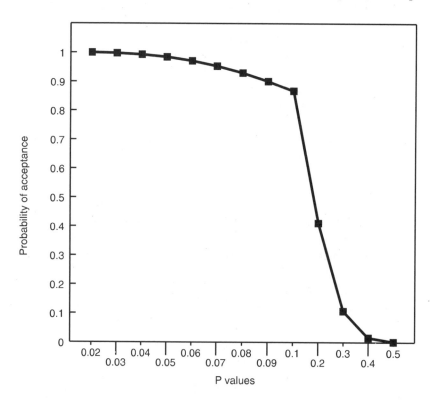

Figure 6.2   An acceptance probability function for $n = 20$ and $x = >3$

between trials (statistical independence) is difficult to maintain in business due to the fact that in many situations our perceptions and actions are influenced by previous actions. When we evaluate suppliers, for instance, it is difficult to ignore their current market standing and past performance. If there are perceptions of this kind then we are unable to say there is statistical independence, and the test, in strict statistical terms, is therefore invalid.

Competence Example 6.1

At the end of this section you should now be able to demonstrate how to:

1 **recognise a binomial type problem**

2 **ascertain probabilities using an appropriate method**

3 **draw suitable conclusions from the analysis**

To practise and demonstrate these competences complete problems 6.1 and 6.2 at the end of this chapter. To help you to develop these competences a description of the procedure you will need to follow is now given, along with a typical problem format. The problem format is based on a problem that is similar to that previously outlined.

PROCEDURE

1 Identify binomial conditions within the problem.

2 Use the binomial formula to determine probabilities.

3 Use the binomial table to determine probabilities.

4 Compare the two methods of finding binomial probabilities.

5 Summarise the outcomes of the analysis.

PROBLEM

A regional gas company estimates that the probability of having a major gas leak on any one day is 0.02. If this is the case, what is the probability that the company will go five days without a major gas leak? The management of the gas company also want to know what the probability is that there will be exactly three days of major gas leaks in a ten day period and at least three days of major gas leaks in a 20 day period.

SOLUTION FORMAT

1 There are three specific questions asked in this problem, and they appear to be binomial **1** type problems because they satisfy the binomial constraints:

- The problem has a number of known and fixed trials, $n = 5$, $n = 10$, and $n = 20$.
- Each day has only two possible outcomes; there is either a major gas leak or there is not a major gas leak, and these are independent because the days are selected randomly.
- The probability of a major gas leak or no major gas leak are assumed to be the same for each day, with $p = 0.02$ and $1 - p = 0.98$.

❷ The first question asks the probability that there will be five days without a major gas leak. **2**
Using the binomial formula, with $x = 0$, $n = 5$, and $p = 0.02$, we find that the probability
value is:

$$_nC_x(p)^x(1-p)^{n-x}$$

$$_5C_0 = \frac{5!}{0!(5-0)!} = \frac{5!}{5!} = \frac{120}{120} = 1$$

$$1(.02)^0(.98)^5 = 1 \times .9039 = .9039$$

Although the second question is worded slightly differently, it is the same but for the fact
that $x = 3$, $n = 10$, and $p = 0.02$:

$$_{10}C_0 = \frac{10!}{3!(10-3)!} = \frac{10!}{3!7!} = \frac{3628800}{(6)(5040)} = \frac{3628800}{30240} = 120$$

$$360(.02)^3(.98)^7 = 120(.000008)(.8681) = 120(.0000069) = .0008$$

The third question is slightly different in that it involves finding the probability of getting **at
least** three days of major gas leaks in a 20 day period ($x = 3$, $n = 20$, and $p = 0.02$). To
answer this we have to find the probability of getting three major gas leaks ($x = 3$), and
then the probability of four major gas leaks ($x = 4$), five major gas leaks ($x = 5$) etc., until
the probability value becomes so small that it is effectively zero, and we stop calculating
any more x values. The answer then involves adding up the calculated probabilities:

$$_{20}C_3 = \frac{20!}{3!(20-3)!} = \frac{20!}{3!17!} = \frac{2.4329 + 18}{(6)(3.5569 + 14)} = \frac{2.4329 + 18}{2.1341 + 15} = 1140$$

$$1140(.02)^3(.98)^{17} = 1140(.000008)(.709322) = 1140(.0000057) = .0065$$

$$_{20}C_4 = \frac{20!}{4!(20-4)!} = \frac{20!}{4!16!} = \frac{2.4329 + 18}{(24)(2.0923 + 13)} = \frac{2.4329 + 18}{5.0215 + 14} = 4845$$

$$4845(.02)^4(.98)^{16} = 4845(.0000002)(.723798) = 4845(.0000001) = .0006$$

$$_{20}C_5 = \frac{20!}{5!(20-5)!} = \frac{20!}{5!15!} = \frac{2.4329 + 18}{(120)(1.3077 + 12)} = \frac{2.4329 + 18}{1.5692 + 14} = 15504$$

$$15504(.02)^5(.98)^{15} = 15504(3.2^{-09})(.738569) = 15504(2.3634^{-09}) = \underline{.0000}$$
$$.0071$$

❸ An alternative way to find these probabilities is to locate the cell in Table 1, Appendix 1,
which corresponds to the parameters of the first question ($x = 0$, $n = 5$, and $p = 0.02$). The
probability, as we would expect, is the same as that found using the binomial formula, a
value of 0.9039. The second question has $x = 3$, $n = 10$, and $p = 0.02$, which provides a
value from the table of .0008, which again corresponds to the calculated value. As
previously pointed out, the third question is worded slightly differently in that it involves
finding the probability of getting **at least** three days of major gas leaks in a 20 day period.
Finding the values of $x = 3$, $x = 4$ etc. from the table and totalling the values up provides us
with the same answer as before, 0.0071.

❸
$x = 3$ .0065
$x = 4$ .0006
$x = 5$ .0000
$\underline{}$
.0071

❷

❹ In comparing the two approaches to finding binomial probabilities it is abundantly clear that it is far easier to use the binomial table than the binomial formula. The only advantage to using the binomial formula relates to the fact that it enables us to calculate probabilities for those x and p values that are not in Table 1.

❺ The binomial probabilities suggest that the likelihood of a major gas leak is remote in terms of the parameters specified within the questions. Specifically, there is a 90.39 per cent probability that they will go five days without a major gas leak, there is only a 0.08 per cent probability of having three major gas leaks in a ten day period, and there is less than a 1 per cent (0.71 per cent) chance of three or more major gas leaks occurring in a 20 day period. In light of this information the gas company might reflect on the resourcing of the emergency service.

❸

Practise your competence now on problems 6.1 and 6.2 at the end of the chapter. When you have demonstrated competence in this area you can use the Lotus disk provided to automate the labour intensive and arithmetic elements. You may choose either a Lotus 1-2-3 or an Excel spreadsheet depending on the package you have access to. The operation of this package was developed in detail in Chapter 2. You may now demonstrate the competence in this area against problems from your own work environment.

6.4 Poisson distributions

A **Poisson distribution** is very useful when we want to know about the number of events that are occurring over time or space. Examples include late arrival of passengers at airports and the number of breakdowns per mile on the London underground railway network. The Poisson distribution, because of the way that it describes events like arrivals, underpins **queuing theory**. Queuing theory can have an important role to play in simulation, and this is looked at in detail in Chapter 13.

The constraints in using the Poisson distribution are that the problem must:

- have discrete data
- ensure that the discrete data is contained within discrete time or space periods (intervals)
- have occurrences that are independent of each other
- ensure that the occurrences remain constant in each time or space interval

The Poisson distribution is really looking for rare events, those that are not typical and can have important implications and/or consequences, such as the number of shutdowns in nuclear plants or the number of times the school bus fails to pick up the children.

When an area is looked at over an extended period it is possible to calculate a long-run mean value which we call **lambda** (λ). A Poisson formula that determines the probability of the occurrence of an event for a particular lambda value is:

$$P(x) = \frac{\lambda^x e^{-\lambda}}{x!}$$

where x = the number of times the event occurs
λ = long-run average (mean)
e = 2.718282, the base of the natural logarithm system

Going back to the airport illustration, suppose British Airways wishes to investigate the problem of passengers arriving late at the airline check-in desk. Having collected data over a long time period it finds that on average six passengers will turn up late. It now wants to know what the probability is that exactly ten passengers will turn up late. Using the Poisson formula we find:

$$P(10) = \frac{(6^{10})(e^{-6})}{10!} = \frac{(60466200)(0.002478752)}{3628800} = \frac{149880.72}{3628800} = 0.0413$$

If we multiply the solution by 100 we see that there is a 4.13 per cent chance that ten passengers will turn up late. With a probability value of this size the airline might decide to build in an extra safety margin to the booking-in time for passengers so that they do not miss their flights and to ensure that aircraft are not delayed.

It is possible to simplify this process by using a table of Poisson probability values. A table of such values is shown in Table 7 of Appendix 1. A section of this table is shown in Table 6.6, and to find the airline passenger probability value we go across the top of the table to $\lambda = 6$ and then down to $x = 10$, where we find the answer of 0.0413.

The answer can also be easily obtained from the Excel spreadsheet package by using the Poisson command from the formula paste function (i.e. 'Poisson (x, mean, cumulative)', which for the above example would be 'Poisson (10,6,0)').

Table 6.6   Sample of Poisson probability table values

			λ			
x	5.7	5.8	5.9	6.0	6.1	6.2
5	.1678	.1656	.1632	.1606	.1579	.1549
6	.1594	.1601	.1605	.1606	.1605	.1601
7	.1298	.1326	.1353	.1377	.1399	.1418
8	.0925	.0962	.0998	.1033	.1066	.1099
9	.0586	.0620	.0654	.0688	.0723	.0757
10	.0334	.0359	.0386	**.0413**	.0441	.0469
11	.0173	.0190	.0207	.0225	.0245	.0265
12	.0082	.0092	.0102	.0113	.0124	.0137

When we are dealing with 'more than' type problems, such as when the airline wants to know the probability of more than 12 passengers arriving late, then we have to find all the values of x greater than 12 and add them up. Since theoretically there is no upper limit to the number of x values (i.e. $x = 13, 14, 15, 16, 17, \ldots \ldots \infty$) we use common sense and stop adding the probability values once they get close to zero. For the airline we find that the values from Table 2 in Appendix 1 are:

$$P(13) = \frac{(6^{13})(e^{-6})}{13!} = .0052$$

$$P(14) = \frac{(6^{14})(e^{-6})}{14!} = .0022$$

$$P(15) = \frac{(6^{15})(e^{-6})}{15!} = .0009$$

$$P(16) = \frac{(6^{16})(e^{-6})}{16!} = .0003$$

$$P(17) = \frac{(6^{17})(e^{-6})}{17!} = .0001$$

$$P(18) = \frac{(6^{18})(e^{-6})}{18!} = .0000$$

$$\text{Total} = \overline{.0087}$$

This tells us that there is less than a 1 per cent chance of more than 12 passengers being late, so the airline is safe in not making contingency plans for such an event.

The Poisson distribution can also be used to provide approximate binomial probabilities when the number of trials, n, is large (if you look at the binomial values in Table 1, Appendix 1, you will see that the largest n value is 30). This approximation can only be used when n is large and p is small, and the guidelines with respect to this are when $n \geq 20$ and $p \leq 0.10$. It is possible to deal with larger values of p by rearranging a success to a failure or vice versa until p becomes the smaller value.

The approximation process involves finding a value of λ so that a corresponding binomial value can be got from the Poisson table. The formula for finding λ is $\lambda = np$. Supposing that we have a situation where $n = 60$ and $p = 0.04$, what therefore is the probability that $x = 5$?

$$\lambda = np = (60)(.04) = 2.4$$

Since $n > 20$ and $p < 10$ we can use the Poisson approximation. Table 2 in Appendix 1 shows us that with $x = 5$ and $\lambda = 2.4$ the value from the table is 0.0602.

The binomial formula says it is

$$_nC_x(p)^x(1-p)^{n-x} = _{60}C_5(.04)^5(.96)^{55} = 0.0592$$

which shows that the Poisson approximation is only 0.001 different from the binomial value.

An important point to finish off with is that the Poisson distribution is dependent on the λ value remaining constant during the life of the investigation. It is not too difficult to imagine for instance that a λ value might change for seasonal consumer products or for behaviour patterns within a day and night rota system. Careful thought and planning should therefore underpin the time intervals used in the investigation.

Competence Example 6.2

At the end of this section you should now be able to demonstrate how to:

1 **recognise a Poisson type problem**

2 **ascertain probabilities using an appropriate method**

3 **draw suitable conclusions from the analysis**

To practise and demonstrate these detailed competences complete problems 6.3 and 6.4 at the end of this chapter. To help you to develop these detailed competences a description of the procedure you will need to follow is now given, along with a typical problem format. The problem format is based on a problem that is similar to that previously outlined.

PROCEDURE

1 Identify Poisson conditions within the problem.

2 Use the Poisson formula to determine probabilities.

3 Use the Poisson table to determine probabilities.

4 Compare the two methods of finding binomial probabilities.

5 Summarise the outcomes of the analysis.

PROBLEM

A social security office has an average of five arrivals per hour of people wanting advice on social security benefits and related matters. Apart from Monday mornings, when there is a rush of people seeking advice, the arrival rate is fairly constant through the week. Because of head office pressure, the senior officer of the social security office wants to calculate the probability of exactly 0, 1, 2, 3, 4 and 5 arrivals per hour. The senior officer also wants to know the probability of more than three arrivals per hour and of more than seven arrivals per hour.

A description of the layout of the solution format is given at the beginning of the book.

SOLUTION FORMAT

❶ The problem appears to satisfy the Poisson constraints in that: **⬛1**

- each arrival is discrete
- the arrivals are contained within the discrete time period of 1
- the arrivals are independent of each other
- the arrivals remain constant in each time period, apart from Monday mornings (although this restriction does not by itself invalidate the use of the Poisson distribution, it does necessitate consideration when we review the results of the analysis)

❷ The probabilities of 0, 1, 2, 3, 4 and 5 arrivals per hour, using the Poisson formula, are: **⬛2**

$$P(x) = \frac{\lambda^x e^{-\lambda}}{x!}$$

$$P(0) = \frac{(5^0)(e^{-5})}{0!} = \frac{(1)(0.0067379)}{1} = \frac{0.0067379}{1} = 0.0067$$

$$P(1) = \frac{(5^1)(e^{-5})}{1!} = \frac{(5)(0.0067379)}{1} = \frac{0.0336897}{1} = 0.0337$$

$$P(2) = \frac{(5^2)(e^{-5})}{2!} = \frac{(25)(0.0067379)}{2} = \frac{0.1684487}{2} = 0.0842$$

$$P(3) = \frac{(5^3)(e^{-5})}{3!} = \frac{(125)(0.0067379)}{6} = \frac{0.8422434}{6} = 0.1404$$

$$P(4) = \frac{(5^4)(e^{-5})}{4!} = \frac{(625)(0.0067379)}{24} = \frac{4.2112169}{24} = 0.1755$$

$$P(5) = \frac{(5^5)(e^{-5})}{5!} = \frac{(3125)(0.0067379)}{120} = \frac{21.056085}{120} = 0.1755$$

❸ Using Table 2 from Appendix 1 to find the cells that correspond to x and λ for these same probability values provides us with the following:

$P(0) = .0067$
$P(1) = .0337$
$P(2) = .0842$
$P(3) = .1404$
$P(4) = .1755$
$P(5) = .1755$

which correspond to those found using the Poisson formula.

❷ ❸ By adding together the probabilities of 0, 1, 2 and 3 we can find the answer to the senior officer's question as to the probability that there are more than three arrivals per hour:

$P(0) = .0067$
$P(1) = .0337$
$P(2) = .0842$
$P(3) = \underline{.1404}$

        $.2650$

❷ ❸ If the maximum probability for all arrivals is 1, and we have calculated arrivals up to and including 3, then the probability of more than three arrivals is:

$$P(3>) = 1 - .2650 = .7350$$

The same procedure is used for determining the probability of there being more than seven arrivals in an hour. Since we have not found the probability values for six and seven arrivals, these have been taken from Table 2 and added to those already listed:

$$P(0) = .0067$$
$$P(1) = .0337$$
$$P(2) = .0842$$
$$P(3) = .1404$$
$$P(4) = .1755$$
$$P(5) = .1755$$
$$P(6) = .1462$$
$$P(7) = .1044$$
$$\overline{}$$
$$.8666$$

$$P(7>) = 1 - .8666 = .1334$$

❹ In comparing the Poisson formula to Table 2 as ways of obtaining probability values, it is clear that Table 2 is both easier and quicker to use. The only drawback to using Table 2 is that one is restricted to the size of the table.

❸ Reviewing the results of this analysis the senior officer now knows the individual probability values of exactly 0, 1, 2, 3, 4 and 5 people arriving per hour. The senior officer also knows that there is a 73.50 per cent chance of more than three arrivals in any one hour, and should therefore ensure that its staff can cover more than three arrivals for three quarters of the time. The probability value for more than seven arrivals is 13.34 per cent, in which case they need only provide cover for more than seven arrivals for 1/7th of the time. These probability values suggest that if the social security office has a human resource level to cover four arrivals per hour, then it is likely to be operating satisfactorily in the sense that it meets the high probability of more than three arrivals per hour. Because the analysis rests upon the principle of a constant and uniform rate of arrivals, it is probably better to ignore the untypical Monday morning rush, in which case the results only apply to the remainder of the week.

Practise your competence now on problems 6.3 and 6.4 at the end of the chapter. When you have demonstrated competence in this area you can use the Lotus disk provided to automate the labour intensive and arithmetic elements. You may choose either a Lotus 1-2-3 or an Excel spreadsheet depending on the package you have access to. The operation of this package was developed in detail in Chapter 2. You may now demonstrate the competence in this area against problems from your own work environment.

6.5 Exponential distributions

The **exponential distribution** is a continuous probability distribution that measures the time period between events or activities. It can be usefully compared to the Poisson distribution in that the Poisson distribution measures the arrival rates of **events** while the exponential distribution measures the **time** between those events.

Not surprisingly, the exponential distribution, like the Poisson distribution, is used in queuing theory, for the time between events is as important as the events themselves. The exponential distribution itself is characterised by the following attributes:

- The data is continuous.
- There is a distinct distribution for every value of λ (λ is the mean number of events per time period).
- x values go from 0 to ∞.

An example of an exponential distribution is depicted in Figure 6.3, and as you can see it shows that as the time interval between events increases, the probability of that time interval occurring decreases (the logic behind this is interesting in that a one hour interval will occur before a two hour interval – it will occur twice as often, and a half-hour interval will occur before a one hour interval – it will occur twice as often, and so on).

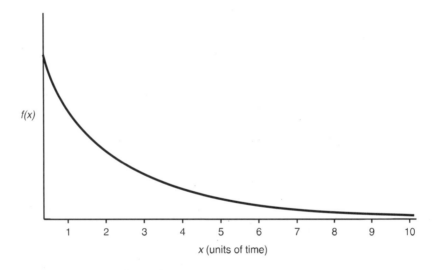

Figure 6.3   Example of an exponential distribution

As was previously pointed out, there is no single exponential distribution. There are in fact a whole family of exponential distributions, the shapes of which are determined by the λ value, as shown in Figure 6.4.

The formula for the exponential probability function is:

$$f(x) = \lambda e^{-\lambda x}$$

where x = number of time intervals

λ = mean number of events per time period

e = 2.71828

$f(x)$ = the probability density function represented by the height of the curve

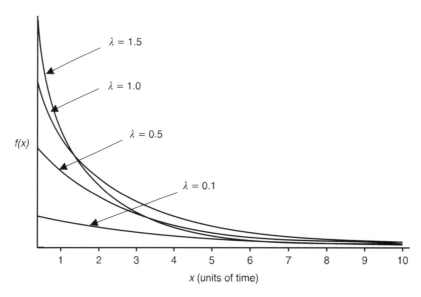

Figure 6.4   Examples of exponential distributions and their λ values

It is possible to find answers to problems that involve an amount of area of the exponential distribution by rearranging this formula (using calculus) so that it becomes:

$$P(x > x_1) = e^{-\lambda x_1}$$

This formula enables us to more easily calculate probabilities from the exponential distribution. Figure 6.5 illustrates this graphically, with the formula providing the probability of the shaded area to the right of x_1 occurring. It also shows the probability of the area to the left of x_1 occurring, which is calculated using $P(x < x_1) = 1 - e^{-\lambda x_1}$, where 1 represents the total area (probability) under the curve.

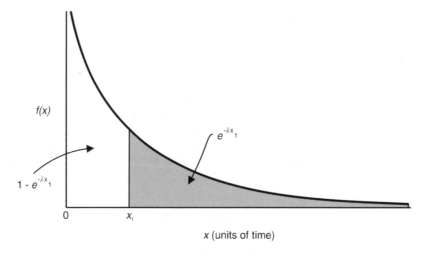

Figure 6.5   Probabilities (areas) of the exponential distribution

Having discussed the exponential distribution, it's now time to see how it works in practice:

Ambulances arrive at the emergency bay of a busy city hospital every 22 minutes on average. Managers at the hospital want to know what the probability is that ambulances will arrive at less than 15 minute intervals. Using Figure 6.6 as a guide, we want to find the area to the left of $x_1 = 15$ minutes.

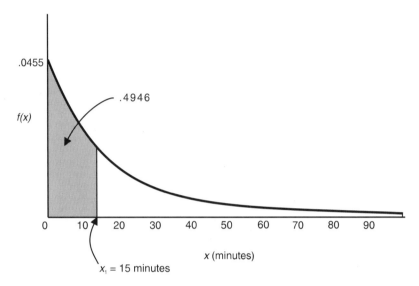

Figure 6.6   Exponential distribution for $x < 15$ minutes

With an arrival rate of 2.73 ambulances per hour $(60/22 = 2.73)$ we get a $\lambda = 2.73/60 = .0455$ per one minute time interval. This provides us with the information to determine the probability that the arrival rate will be less than 15 minutes:

$$P(x < x_1) = 1 - e^{-\lambda x_1}$$

$$P(x < 15) = 1 - e^{-(2.73/60)(15)} = 1 - e^{-.6825} = 1 - .5053 = .4946$$

This tells us that the probability of an ambulance arriving within 15 minutes of the preceding ambulance is 49.46 per cent. The $e^{-\lambda x_1}$ value can be obtained from Table 6 in Appendix 1, a portion of which is shown in Table 6.7.

You will have noticed that the value from the table is slightly less than that which was calculated, i.e. $.4946 - .4934 = .0012$. This is due to the table only working to two decimal places. It is for this reason that calculators are often used to calculate the exponential distribution value (the key on my calculator is e^x). The exponential distribution value can also be obtained from the Excel spreadsheet package by using the 'expondist' function from the 'paste formula' facility (e.g. = expondist $(x,$ lambda, cumulative) which for our example would be = expondist (15, 0.0455, 1) = 0.4946).

Table 6.7 Sample of exponential distribution probability values

λx_1	.05	.06	.07	.08	.09
0.3	0.2953	0.3023	0.3093	0.3161	0.3229
0.4	0.3624	0.3687	0.3750	0.3812	0.3874
0.5	0.4231	0.4288	0.4345	0.4401	0.4457
0.6	0.4780	0.4831	0.4883	**0.4934**	0.4984
0.7	0.5276	0.5323	0.5370	0.5416	0.5462
0.8	0.5726	0.5768	0.5810	0.5852	0.5893

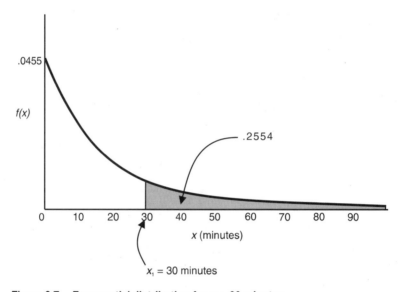

Figure 6.7 Exponential distribution for $x > 30$ minutes

The management of the hospital also want to know what the probability is that the time interval between ambulances will be more than 30 minutes. Using Figure 6.7 and following the previous procedure, we find:

$$P(x > x_1) = e^{-\lambda x_1}$$

$$P(x > 30) = e^{-\lambda x_1} = e^{-(2.73/60)\,(30)} = e^{-1.365} = 0.2554$$

This tells us that there is a 25.54 per cent chance that there will be more than 30 minutes between ambulances arriving at the hospital. Faced with this information the management of the hospital decided that the number of personnel should remain at their current level, a level that was based on an ambulance arriving every 25 minutes!

Competence Example 6.3

At the end of this section you should now be able to demonstrate how to:

1 recognise an exponential type problem

2 ascertain probabilities using an appropriate method

3 draw suitable conclusions from the analysis

To practise and demonstrate these detailed competences complete problems 6.5 and 6.6 at the end of this chapter To help you to develop these detailed competences a description of the procedure you will need to follow is now given, along with a typical problem format The problem format is based on a problem that is similar to that previously outlined.

PROCEDURE

❶ Identify exponential conditions within the problem.

❷ Use the exponential formula to determine probabilities.

❸ Use the exponential table to determine probabilities.

❹ Compare the two methods of finding exponential probabilities.

❺ Summarise the outcomes of the analysis.

PROBLEM

A manufacturer of photocopiers has determined that the switching device within the photocopiers has an average lifetime of five years. If this is the case, what is the probability that the switches will fail after seven years, and what is the probability that they will fail before the warranty period of three years?

A description of the layout of the solution format is given at the beginning of the book.

SOLUTION FORMAT

❶ The problem appears to satisfy the exponential constraints in that: **1**

- the data is continuous
- there is a distinct distribution for every value of λ (λ is the mean number of events per time period), for there will be a distinct distribution when the mean lifetime is five years, a distinct distribution if the mean lifetime had been six years, seven years, etc.
- the number of failures can go from 0 to ∞

❷ With an average lifetime period of five years we get a λ value of $1/5 = 0.2$ per 1 year time   **2** interval (this tells us that the mean time between failures is $0.2 \times 365 = 73$ days). This then enables us to determine the probability of the switches failing after seven years:

$$P(x > x_1) = e^{-\lambda x_1}$$

$$P(x > 7) = e^{-\lambda x_1} = e^{-(.2)(7)} = e^{-1.4} = 0.2466$$

This is shown graphically in Figure 6.8.

Following a similar procedure for the probability that they will fail before three years, we find:

$$P(x < x_1) = 1 - e^{-\lambda x_1}$$

$$P(x < 3) = 1 - e^{-(.2)(3)} = 1 - e^{-.6} = 1 - .5488 = .4512$$

This is shown graphically in Figure 6.9.

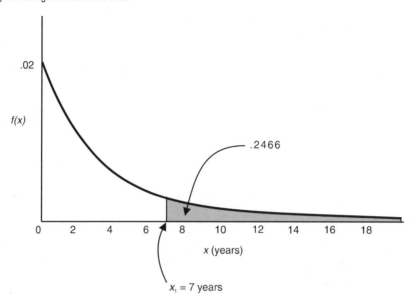

Figure 6.8   Exponential distribution of $x > 7$ years

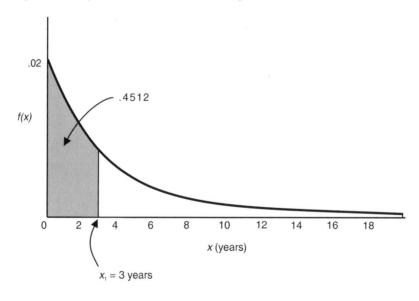

Figure 6.9   Exponential distribution of $x < 3$ years

❸ Using Table 3 from Appendix 1 to find the exponential probability values we find that:

$$P(x>7) = (e^{-\lambda x_1} = -1.4 = .7534) = 1 - .7534 = .2466$$

$$P(x<3) = (e^{-\lambda x_1} = -.6 = .4512) = .4512$$

❹ This tells us that for this set of data there is no difference between the output of the exponential formula and values contained in Table 6 of Appendix 1.

❺ The analysis has shown that 24.66 per cent of the switches will last longer than seven years. It has also shown that 45.12 per cent will fail before the warranty period of three

⑤ years. This has serious implications and justifies a reduction in the warranty period or ▣
♥ steps being taken to extend the average life of a switch.

Practise your competence now on problems 6.5 and 6.6 at the end of the chapter. When you have demonstrated competence in this area you can use the Lotus disk provided to automate the labour intensive and arithmetic elements. You may choose either a Lotus 1-2-3 or an Excel spreadsheet depending on the package you have access to. The operation of this package was developed in detail in Chapter 2. You may now demonstrate the competence in this area against problems from your own work environment.

6.6 Normal distributions

In Chapter 4 we introduced the concept of standard deviations and their corresponding equivalence to specific areas under a normal distribution, and how a number can be represented as a standard deviation value by the conversion of that number into a Z score using the formula below. A summary of this is shown in Figure 6.10.

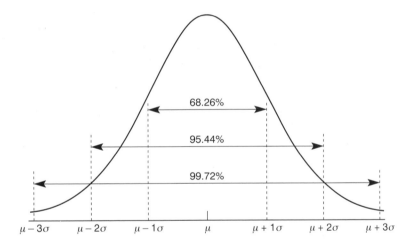

Figure 6.10   Summary of area under a normal distribution

Distance from the mean	Percentage of values falling within distance
$\mu \pm 1\sigma$	68.26
$\mu \pm 2\sigma$	95.44
$\mu \pm 3\sigma$	99.72

$$Z = \frac{X - \mu}{\sigma}$$

The wide-ranging potential application of the normal distribution explains why it is so important in statistics and quantitative management. Example of phenomena that form a normal distribution include people's height and weight, IQ scores, fill quantities in a bottling plant, life span of lightbulbs, the amount people spend when they visit a supermarket, exam scores, and the length of time of telephone calls. Although the normal distribution is a continuous distribution, it is used to approximate discrete data (Figure 6.11 shows that as more discrete data is collected the closer the distribution resembles a continuous distribution and the characteristic bell shape of a normal distribution), which in turn lends itself to

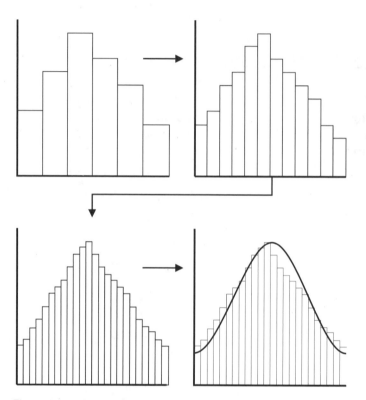

Figure 6.11   Approximation of discrete data to the normal distribution

being approximated to the binomial distribution. It also has the advantage, as we will discover in Chapter 7, that when we take samples of data and plot the means of those samples, we end up with a normal distribution, even if the original data was not normally distributed!

The shape of a normal distribution is determined by its mean (μ) and standard deviation (σ). The mean actually determines the height of the normal distribution while the standard deviation determines its width, as shown in Figure 6.12.

Even though the shape of a normal distribution can vary, the area under the curve always remains constant with respect to the standard deviation value. For instance, we know that plus or minus one standard deviation accounts for 68.26 per cent of the area of a normal distribution, in which case the area to plus one

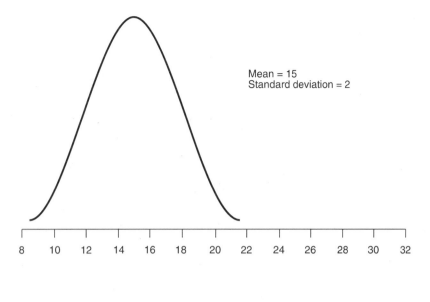

Mean = 15
Standard deviation = 2

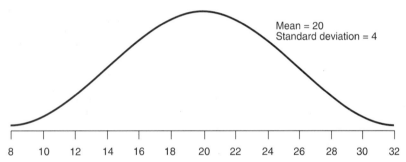

Mean = 20
Standard deviation = 4

Figure 6.12   Examples of how μ and σ determine the shape of the normal distribution

standard deviation must be 34.13 per cent, regardless of the actual value of the mean and standard deviation. Figure 6.13 illustrates this in that the proportion of area for one standard deviation is the same for the two distributions even though the shape is different due to the different mean and standard deviation values.

By equating an amount of area to a standard deviation value it is possible to say what proportion it is of the total distribution (an alternative way of expressing this is as a probability value, a value that will be up to a maximum of 1, since the total area under the curve is 100 per cent). A number can be easily converted to its equivalent standard deviation value by using the Z score formula, and it is because of this that we are able to use the normal distribution to answer a wide range of questions.

For example, if a packing machine produces packets of breakfast cereals with a mean weight of 500 grams and a standard deviation of 2 grams, and the packing weights are normally distributed, what is the probability that a package will weigh between 500 grams and 503 grams? (This probability would normally be expressed as $P(500 < X < 503)$.) To help answer this it is useful to first visualise what the question is asking, as shown in Figure 6.14.

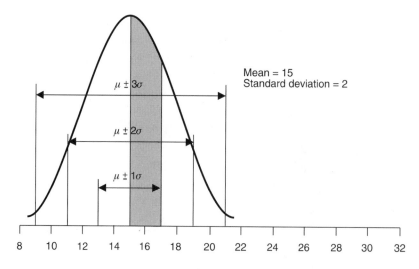

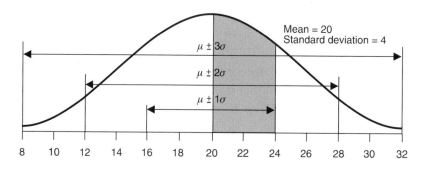

Figure 6.13   Equivalence of one standard deviation across two normal distributions

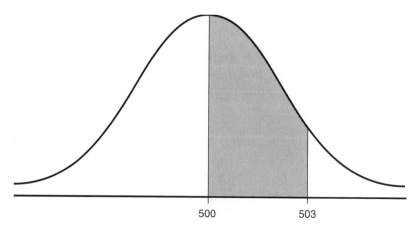

Figure 6.14   Area between 500g and 503g

To find the shaded proportion from 500 to 503 we must calculate how many standard deviations away from the mean the point 503 lies:

$$Z = \frac{X - \mu}{\sigma} = Z = \frac{503 - 500}{2} = 1.50$$

Because the proportion of the area is always constant between the mean and a specified number of standard deviations, we can use a table of standard deviation values (Table 5 in Appendix 1) to tell us what the proportion or probability is. A sample of the values contained in the appendix is shown in Table 6.8.

Table 6.8   Sample of area values for the normal distribution

Z	0.00	0.01	0.02	0.03
1.1	.1357	.1335	.1314	.1292
1.2	.1151	.1131	.1112	.1093
1.3	.0968	.0951	.0934	.0918
1.4	.0808	.0793	.0778	.0764
1.5	**.0668**	.0655	.0643	.0630
1.6	.0548	.0537	.0526	.0516
1.7	.0446	.0436	.0427	.0418

Consulting the table we find that Z = 1.50 has an area value or probability of 0.0668. This value is in fact the area from the tail to the point 503, so to find the area from 500 to 503 we subtract 0.0668 from 0.5 (because the area from 500 to the tail is half of the total area) to arrive at the final answer of .5 – .0668 = .4332. Figure 6.15 depicts this process diagrammatically.

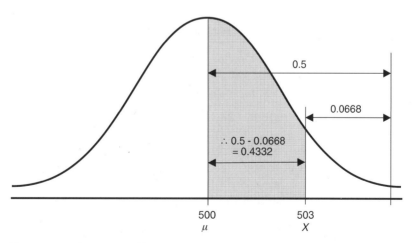

Figure 6.15   Determining the area value for *P*(500 < *X* < 503)

The organisation now know that there is a 43.32 per cent chance that a packet of breakfast cereal will weigh between 500 and 503 grams.

The Excel spreadsheet package can also be used to find the amount of area from the tail to 503. Using the formula paste function to select 'statistical' and then 'normdist', you will find it asks for '(X,MEAN,STANDARD-DEV,CUMU-LATIVE)'. Typing in 503, 500, 2, true, will produce a value of .93317. Taking this away from 1 (i.e. $1 - .93317 = .0668$) provides us with the correct answer of .0668.

Having established that the normal distribution can be used to answer questions that involve a proportion of the area, we can explore a range of other similar questions. The first of these involves determining what proportion of the packets are between 497 and 500 grams. This is very similar to the original question, but as Figure 6.16 shows, it is to the left of the distribution. It is important to remember that the normal distribution is symmetrical, which means that the left-hand side of the distribution is exactly the same as the right-hand side. This is reflected in the Z value being negative, indicating that it is to the left of the mean value. The symmetry of the distribution explains why there are no negative values in Table 5 of Appendix 1: they are exactly the same as the positive Z values.

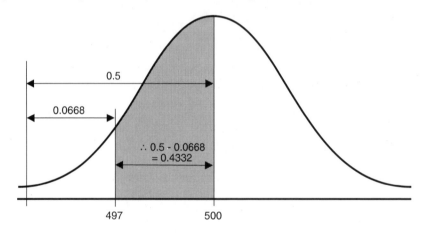

Figure 6.16   Area between 497g and 500g

$$Z = \frac{497 - 500}{2} = -1.5$$

$$.5 - .0668 = .4332$$

As you can see this is exactly the same result as before, because it is the same amount of area, but to the left of the mean. The result tells us that there is a 43.32 per cent chance that a packet will weigh between 497 and 500 grams.

Taking another example, what proportion of the packets are between 501 and 503 grams? Figure 6.17 tells us that this is slightly different from the other two examples because it does not have the mean as one of its boundaries. To find the amount of area in this type of situation we need to determine the Z values for 501 and 503, and then take the area value associated with 503 away from the area value associated with 501. This shows us that there is a 24.17 per cent chance that a packet will weigh between 501 and 503 grams.

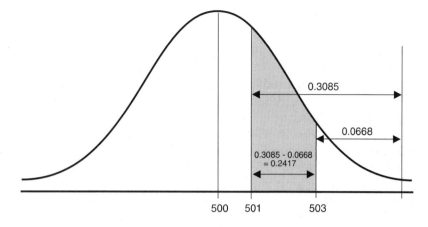

Figure 6.17   Area between 501g and 503g

$$Z_1 = \frac{501 - 500}{2} = .5 = 0.3085$$

$$Z_2 = \frac{503 - 500}{2} = 1.5 = 0.0668$$

$$0.3085 - 0.0668 = 0.2417$$

It is also possible to have an amount of area that is to both sides of the mean value, such as is illustrated in Figure 6.18, where we want to find the amount of area between 498 grams and 503 grams.

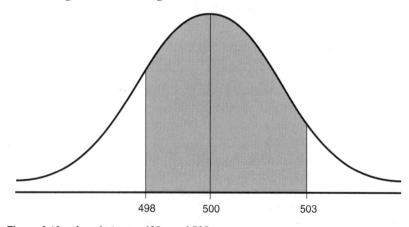

Figure 6.18   Area between 498g and 503g

$$Z_1 = \frac{498 - 500}{2} = -1$$

Area between 498 and 500 is $.5 - .1587 = .3413$

$$Z_2 = \frac{503 - 500}{2} = 1.5$$

Area between 500 and 503 is .5 − .0668 = .4332

.3413 + .4332 = .7745

The procedure adopted in this example is to find the area from 500 to 503 grams and then add it to the area from 498 to 500 grams. This points to a 77.45 per cent probability that a packet of breakfast cereal will weigh between 498 grams and 503 grams.

If we wanted to know the proportion of packets weighing more than 505 grams then we simply find the Z value for 505 and its corresponding area value. There is no need to subtract or add any values because Table 5 in Appendix 1 provides values from the tail to the Z value (*see* Figure 6.19).

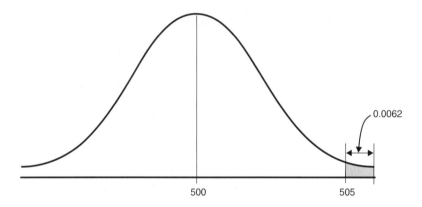

Figure 6.19   Area above 505g

$$Z = \frac{505 - 500}{2} = 2.5 = 0.00621$$

The proportion of the area above 505 is therefore less than 1 per cent (0.621 per cent). The organisation can therefore relax in the sense that it is not greatly overfilling the cereal packets.

A slightly different type of question involves finding the value above which the top 20 per cent of weights lie. This is shown diagrammatically in Figure 6.20, where we are trying to find the missing ? value. The secret to finding this missing value is to first look at Table 5 in Appendix 1 to find an area value that is closest to 20 per cent. The value that comes closest is 0.2005, which has a Z value of 0.84. Putting this into the Z formula gives us a situation where we only have one unknown value, which can be quite easily found by slightly rearranging the formula:

Nearest Z value to 20 per cent is 0.84

$$Z = \frac{X - \mu}{\sigma} \quad 0.84 = \frac{X - 500}{2} \quad X = 500 + (0.84)(2) \quad X = 501.68$$

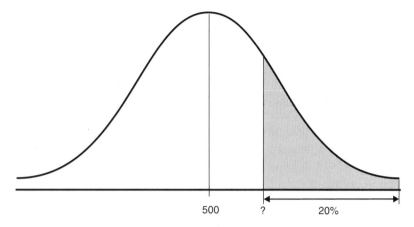

Figure 6.20   The highest 20 per cent of packet weights

The missing X value is therefore 501.68, which enables us to say that 20 per cent of the cereal packets weigh more than 501.68 grams.

The principle of finding a value that corresponds to a proportion can also be used for setting guarantee periods. A manufacturer of television sets, for example, wants to set a guarantee period that will involve no more than 3 per cent of the televisions being returned. The mean life of the television, based on extensive testing, is 6.5 years. The standard deviation is 0.75 years. Figure 6.21 demonstrates that the manufacturer is only really concerned about those television sets that are not in the shaded area, since this area represents the first 3 per cent of the shortest lifespans – the televisions that failed the earliest.

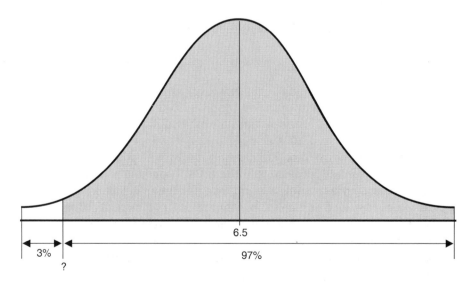

Figure 6.21   Setting a guarantee period for a less than 3 per cent return rate

$$Z = \frac{X - \mu}{\sigma} \quad -1.88 = \frac{X - 6.5}{0.75} \quad X = 6.5 - (1.88)(0.75) \quad X = 5.09$$

Following the previous procedure, the nearest Z value to 3 per cent in Table 5, Appendix 1, is -1.88 (with an area value of 0.0301). Putting -1.88 into the Z formula we are able to find the unknown X value. This tells us that if the television manufacturer sets a guarantee period of 5.09 years it can expect a maximum of 3 per cent to be returned. Put another way, 97 per cent of the television sets are likely to last more than 5.09 years. The boundaries that we have just identified are sometimes called 'percentiles of a normal distribution' because they act in exactly the same way as the percentiles that we looked at in Chapter 4.

Competence Example 6.4

At the end of this section you should now be able to demonstrate how to:

1 **recognise a normal distribution type problem**

2 **ascertain probabilities using an appropriate method**

3 **draw suitable conclusions from the analysis**

To practise and demonstrate these competences complete problems 6.7 and 6.8 at the end of this chapter. To help you to develop these competences a description of the procedure you will need to follow is now given, along with a typical problem format. The problem format is based on a problem that is similar to that previously outlined.

PROCEDURE

❶ Identify normal distribution conditions within the problem.

❷ Determine Z values.

❸ Use the normal distribution table to determine probabilities.

❹ Summarise the outcomes of the analysis.

PROBLEM

A leading manufacturer of batteries has ascertained, through extensive tests, that its best seller, the 1.5 volt HP7 battery, has a mean life of 115 hours and a standard deviation of 20 hours. The lifespan tests also showed that the median and the mode corresponded with the value of 115 hours, and that when the data was plotted as a frequency distribution it formed a bell shaped curve. This segment of the battery market is fiercely competitive, with many claims being made by the manufacturers that their batteries last the longest. Not surprisingly therefore, the manufacturer is interested in knowing the probability that its HP7 battery will last less than 100 hours, the probability that the lifetime of a battery will be between 90 and 130 hours, the probability that the batteries will last longer than 135 hours, and the value above which the top 20 per cent of battery lifetimes lie.

SOLUTION FORMAT

❶ The problem appears to satisfy the normal distribution constraints in that:

  - the data is continuous

● • the data appears to be symmetrical (bell shaped)
    • the data is unimodal in that the mean, mode, and median are the same value

❷❸ Acceptance of these conditions enables us to answer the questions that have been asked in the problem. The first question wanted to know what the probability was that a battery would last for less than 100 hours. A diagrammatic representation of the question is shown in Figure 6.22.

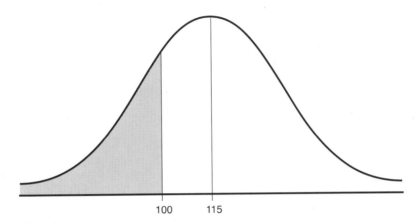

Figure 6.22   Area below 100 hours

The shaded area is equal to:

$$Z = \frac{X - \mu}{\sigma}$$

$$Z = \frac{100 - 115}{20} = -.75 = .2266$$

A similar procedure can be used to find the probability that a battery will last between 90 and 130 hours:

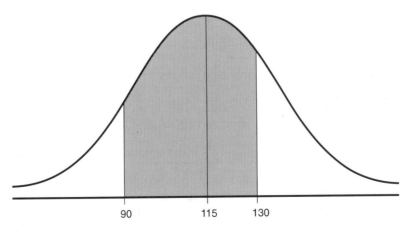

Figure 6.23   Area between 90 and 130 hours

❷ ❸

$$Z_1 = \frac{90 - 115}{20} = -1.25 = .1056$$

$$.5 - .1056 = .3944$$

$$Z_2 = \frac{130 - 115}{20} = 0.75 = .2266$$

$$.5 - .2266 = .2734$$

$$Z_1 + Z_2 = .3944 + .2734 = .6678$$

The number of batteries lasting longer than 135 hours is:

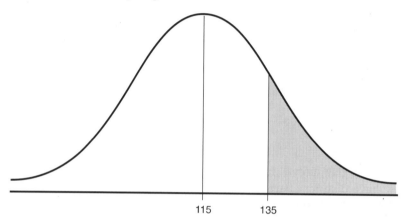

Figure 6.24   Area above 135 hours

$$Z = \frac{135 - 115}{20} = 1 = .1587$$

The fourth and final question involves finding the value beyond which fall the top 20 per cent of batteries (in terms of their lifespan):

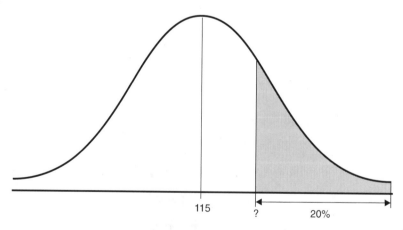

Figure 6.25   The highest 20 per cent of battery lifespans

Nearest Z value to 20 per cent is 0.84.

❸ $$Z = \frac{X - \mu}{\sigma} \quad 0.84 = \frac{X - 115}{20} \quad X = 115 + (0.84)(20) \quad X = 131.8$$

❹ The analysis has shown that 22.66 per cent of the batteries will last less than 100 hours, 66.78 per cent of the batteries will last between 90 and 130 hours, 15.87 per cent will last longer than 135 hours, and 20 per cent of the batteries will last longer than 131.8 hours. This information might be very useful for comparing the company to its competitors, as well as for benchmarking generally. The information may also be of use to the marketing department, in that they could utilise the positive aspects of the analysis. It might also prove useful when lifetime warranties are set and/or reviewed.

Practise your competence now on problems 6.7 and 6.8 at the end of the chapter. When you have demonstrated competence in this area you can use the Lotus disk provided to automate the labour intensive and arithmetic elements. You may choose either a Lotus 1-2-3 or an Excel spreadsheet depending on the package you have access to. The operation of this package was developed in detail in Chapter 2. You may now demonstrate the competence in this area against problems from your own work environment.

Summary

Chapter 6 has shown that there are a number of probability distributions, and that they have distinct characteristics that can be utilised to help solve certain types of problems. More specifically:

- Binomial distributions are used in situations where there are two distinct outcomes, such as buy or do not buy and accept or reject.
- Poisson distributions are used when we want to know about the number of events that are occurring over time or space, such as arrivals and breakdowns.
- Exponential distributions are used when we want to know about the time periods between events or activities, such as the time between arrivals and breakdowns.
- Normal distributions are used to find proportions of area under a normal distribution curve. It has a wide range of applications and is especially important because it underpins many other areas of statistics.

As with previous chapters the methods in Chapter 6 have been explained manually to aid understanding. To reduce the amount of time involved in some of the manual calculations, they have also been shown and solved using the built-in functions of a spreadsheet package.

The competences that have been gained in this chapter are directly transferable to most organisations, and the Lotus 1-2-3 and Excel disk provide an opportunity for you to analyse your own company's data. The following exercises provide an opportunity for you to practise and demonstrate these competences, but again they are no substitute for the data that needs analysing in your organisation.

Problems for Chapter 6

6.1 Students in a quantitative management class are contemplating guessing the answers in a 30 question multiple choice exam. If each question on the exam has five choices, what are the chances of a student getting the correct answer on any single question? What is the probability that a student will get more than half of the questions correct? What is the probability that a student will get more than five correct?

6.2 A market research company has discovered that 30 per cent of the people who earn between £25,000 and £50,000 per year have taken out a PEP (Personal Equity Plan) within the past two years. In a sample of 12 people earning between £25,000 and £50,000 per year, what is the probability that between four and ten people have taken out a PEP within the past two years?

6.3 Research for a high street bank has shown that the average waiting time for customers in local branches ranged from 0.75 minutes to six minutes. A local branch manager feels comfortable in the knowledge that if the bank is checked against this criterion it will be deemed to be performing satisfactorily. This belief is based on the manager's judgement that for any ten minute time interval there will be on average three customers arriving for service, and that an arrival rate of three customers per ten minute time interval can be processed well within the upper limit of six minutes. Assuming that the data conforms to a Poisson distribution:
a. what percentage of the time will the number of arrivals, over a ten minute time period, exceed three?
b. can the arrival of seven or more customers over a ten minute time interval be considered a rare event, given the manager's assumptions?
c. given the answers to (a) and (b), can the manager's beliefs be considered correct?

6.4 During the rush hour cars arrive at a city centre car park at the rate of 35 every 60 minutes. The car park is not automated, and the three car park attendants can just manage this level of arrivals. Looking at this within a time frame of ten minutes, what is the probability of more than four arrivals, exactly five arrivals, and less than three arrivals?

6.5 There has been frequent criticism that reform of the emergency services has resulted in longer response times. A recent study in your local area shows that the average time it takes an ambulance to arrive at a destination is eight minutes, and that the response times are exponentially distributed. Given this information:
a. what is the probability that an ambulance will arrive at a destination in less than eight minutes?
b. what is the probability that an ambulance will take longer than ten minutes to arrive at a destination?

6.6 A maintenance firm estimates that it takes on average six hours to clean and check an air conditioning system. Given that the times are exponentially distributed, what is the probability that a system can be cleaned and checked in less than four hours, and what is the probability that it will take longer than nine hours?

6.7 A manufacturer of car tyres produces a high performance sports tyre that has a mean life of 18,000 miles and a standard deviation of 2,000 miles (the life of the tyres is also normally distributed).
   a. What is the probability that:
      i.   a tyre will last for more than 14,000 miles?
      ii. a tyre life will fall below 15,000 miles?
      iii. a tyre life will be greater than 20,000 miles?
   b. What proportion of tyres will have a life between 17,000 miles and 21,000 miles?
   c. If we are looking at the life expectancy of tyres, what is the value above which will fall the largest 25 per cent of tyre lives?

6.8 The achievement scores of 100 senior managers are normally distributed with a mean of 99.3 and a standard deviation of 13.4.
   a. What proportion of the managers can be expected to have achievement scores:
      i.   greater than 120?
      ii. less than 90?
      iii. between 70 and 130?
   b. What achievement score will be exceeded by:
      i.   1 per cent of managers?
      ii. 0.1 per cent of managers?
      iii. 90 per cent of managers?
   c. Between what limits will 95 per cent of managers' achievement scores lie?

6.9 The weekly output of a production line varies according to a normal distribution with a mean of 1,163 units and a standard deviation of 113 units.
   a. What is the probability that the weekly output will be 1,160 units or less?
   b. What is the probability that the weekly output will exceed 1,170 units?
   c. The production manager wants to know what the production output is for 80 per cent of the time.

6.10 A personnel manager is concerned about absenteeism in the summer months. Records show that absenteeism in the summer months is normally distributed with a mean of 95 days and a standard deviation of 8 days. This being the case, what is the probability that there will be more than 110 people absent during the summer months, and more than 120 people absent during the summer months? The personnel manager, because of a forthcoming order, also wants to know what the probability is that there will be less than 70 people absent during this period.

7 Survey design and sampling
getting to know the customer

7.1 Introduction

Information can be of great value. Politicians, for instance, are very interested in the way their constituents are going to vote at election time and will spend a great deal of time trying to ascertain if it will be for them or not. A social scientist investigating juvenile crime is likely to need information from those committing the crimes before he or she can say what causes juvenile crime. The hospital administrator might require information on patient care before an application for further funds can be made. The marketing people from Lever will be very interested in consumer perceptions following the extensive media coverage given to its main competitor, Procter & Gamble, in its claim that Lever's washing powder can damage clothes after prolonged use. In all these situations there is a need to gather information so that informed judgements or decisions can be made. The consequences of insufficient information are perhaps best illustrated by Perrier, which lost $35 million when it had to recall its worldwide stocks of mineral water due to the presence of the cancer agent benzene. This happened because its quality control procedures did not detect the problem, which subsequently was traced back to poor statistical process control due to insufficient and unreliable information.

In most situations a survey of some kind will be used to collect the required information. Since the information collected is usually only taken from a very small number (a sample) of all the items available for study (the population), many people are suspicious of these findings. Indeed, it is remarkable how a small number of items enable us to make confident predictions about the much larger population.

This chapter is therefore concerned with developing competence in carrying out a survey to collect a representative sample of data so that statements about the wider population can be made with a known degree of accuracy. It also provides the foundations on which much of market research, statistical process control and financial auditing is built. By the end of this chapter you should be able to demonstrate how to:

- outline the stages involved in survey research
- determine an appropriate sampling method
- construct and use a range of sampling methods
- design a questionnaire
- appreciate survey interviewing techniques
- recognise the main problems associated with interpreting surveys
- calculate confidence limits and sample size

The chapter will also use a series of practical examples to develop the underpinning knowledge in the area of survey design and sampling.

At the end of each section the required competence will be specified and described. A typical problem format with the competences highlighted will also be given to help you to demonstrate the competences on the problems at the end of the chapter. At the end of the book a full solution will be given for the first of these problems as well as the answers for the rest.

7.2 The background

The main purpose of surveys is to gather information from a sample so that inferences can be made about the wider population. For the inferences to be accurate we must do our utmost to ensure that the sample is representative of the population, and this can be both difficult and time-consuming. Even when we are sure we have a representative sample it is still possible to go wrong if a question is worded in a leading way or if we place a greater emphasis on a certain part or aspect of a question.

The benefits associated with a representative survey can be substantial. It can make the difference between a product failing or succeeding in the market place (e.g. Clive Sinclair's C5 car) or damages being awarded by a court (e.g. the link between child leukaemia and nuclear power or smoking and lung cancer).

More specifically, samples can have the following advantages:

- They reduce costs.
- They enable information to be gathered quickly.
- They avoid destruction of the entire population (if you are testing car seatbelts for strength you would not want to test each one to destruction to make sure that they met the required standards!).
- They are sometimes the only practical way to get information about the population due to the very large size of the population, the geographical spread of the population, or even the confidentiality of the information.

It is also worth noting that samples are of little use when:

- information is required on every individual member of the population, or when the population is so small that it does not make sense to take a sample.
- a full set of information is required (we would be alarmed if our bank statements were based on a sample of withdrawals).
- the items we are looking at are so rare and/or variable that a sample would be a waste of time and money.
- the people looking at the results of a sample are so sceptical about inferring from a relatively small number of items that decisions will never be made that are based upon them.

It is worth remembering that surveys and samples are a tool for collecting information and that like many tools they can be used to either good or poor effect.

7.3 Types of surveys

Surveys are used to gather information on such things as opinions, attitudes and factual data. There are a number of survey methods, and their suitability and applicability are largely determined by the nature of the problem or market that is being looked at.

Political and commercial polls tend to be the most widely known of the opinion surveys due to the extensive coverage that is given to them by the media at election times. Commercial pollsters such as Gallup and Harris gather people's views on matters ranging from abortion to crime throughout the year, but it is at election time that they go into overdrive and produce an almost endless stream of polls (the media's appetite for such information seems inexhaustible). The high profile status accorded to political polls during an election worries a number of people, for they feel that they unduly focus the political debate. There is even evidence to suggest that opinion polls influence the way people are going to vote, and that they should therefore be banned during the final run-in to an election. The primary purpose of political polls is to inform the general public on the way people are going to vote or on the views of people on specific political issues. They can also be used by political parties to gauge the public's perceptions on the most important political issues, as well as to what they think about specific candidates or opponents etc. Information of this kind can then be used to shape policies and election strategies.

Market research companies carry out surveys for a variety of organisations, from a high street bank seeking information on the types of services it should be offering its customers to a manufacturer wanting information on the strengths and weaknesses of its products. Organisations are likely to use a specialised marketing research company to gather this type of information unless it has the internal capability or confidence to carry out its own survey. The types of difficulties organisations face in carrying out their own surveys vary with the survey method being used and the nature of the target audience. Typical problems include difficulties in reaching and interviewing a geographically diverse sample of people, having staff trained in interviewing, and using statistical tools correctly. On the positive side, an organisation will know its own customers better than an outside agency and may therefore be better equipped at tailoring a survey to meet its needs and in interpreting the data generated by the survey.

Academic surveys normally concentrate on collecting data on people's attitudes to various happenings, events etc. Following the classic scientific tradition, data gathered by surveys is frequently used to formulate or test some hypothesis or theory of human behaviour. The focus on attitudes and the scientific method have traditionally made academic surveys more rigorous than other types of surveys, though this is less marked with the growth in expertise and sophistication now exhibited by the established market research companies.

The demarcation lines between academic and commercial surveys have been reduced by many business schools, with students typically carrying out market research surveys as part of a project or dissertation. Perhaps a greater distinguishing feature is that academic surveys involve a deeper and often more sophisticated level of analysis than commercial surveys, especially if they are going into an academic journal.

Factual information surveys tend to be used by government and public agencies. The most extensive and best-known factual information survey is the ten-yearly **census**. The objective of the census is to ascertain information about every person in every dwelling in the UK, ranging from income to age, sex, race, number of cars, years of education, how we commute to work, etc. It takes two years or longer to analyse the census returns (because of its sheer size), and the information it generates will be seized upon by advertising and direct mail companies in their search for upwardly mobile young families and affluent households. Factual surveys are also extensively used by academics and policy makers to underpin research and provide details on crime, drugs, inflation and a variety of other phenomena.

7.4   The survey process

The processes involved in designing and carrying out a survey are similar to those for modelling generally (this becomes clear in the discussion that follows). Before a survey is carried out there is normally a certain amount of preparatory work, and this work can improve the likelihood of success of the survey if it is conscientiously carried out.

7.4.1   Pre-survey work

The *objectives* of a study or survey should be carefully thought through and explicitly stated before any work is carried out. Although this is an obvious point, our experience tells us that there have been too many occasions when a survey has failed due to the lack of clearly stated objectives. These objectives can range from 'what' is to be studied to a 'proposition' on why a group of people are behaving the way they are. If a proposition is being stated, then consideration needs to be given to how the proposition can be tested. This can then be used as a guide when selecting the respondents to the survey as well as in the selection and wording of appropriate questions. A specific testable proposition is called a hypothesis in scientific and management research. In management research a hypothesis is normally a *causal hypothesis*, in that it states that certain phenomena cause the condition being studied. For example, a hypothesis might state that high absenteeism in women is due to a lack of childcare facilities. The hypothesis can then be tested using an appropriate methodology, which may well include a survey. The important point to remember in all this is that regardless of the type of study being undertaken, time spent carefully formulating and stating objectives in the initial stages of a study or survey can save a great deal of time and effort in the later stages.

If a hypothesis and/or proposition is to be tested then it is essential that they are *operationalised* so that they can be measured. For example, when it is stated in a hypothesis that senior executives have a high internal need for achievement and status, it will be necessary to clearly state the criteria on which a person is deemed to be a senior executive. It will also be necessary to have some sort of measure for achievement and status, otherwise the hypothesis is unmeasurable and untestable.

Before any survey is undertaken it is worthwhile remembering that there are alternative ways of gathering information. A classical approach is to conduct an *experiment*, and the advantage of an experiment compared to a survey is that it allows *control* over events that is impossible in a survey. Teamwork, for example, can be directly observed and measured in an outward bound programme and a laboratory setting. The results of such experiments are often felt to be more valid than the responses to a survey. The problem with experiments is that they can also be highly artificial and do not replicate the nuances and sophistication of the real world.

Another alternative to the survey is to use information that is already available, such as the census that was previously mentioned. The advantage of such information is that it is widely available and very cheap compared to the expense involved in carrying out a survey. The disadvantage in using published statistics is that they may not exactly meet your needs. It is not uncommon to actually use published data in the initial stages of a study, and then move towards a survey once the issues and problems have been clarified by the analysis of the published data.

7.4.2 Steps in the survey process

As a detailed account of the stages that a professionally conducted survey goes through is beyond the scope of this book, only the main steps are shown below:

1. Define the problem and explicitly state what the objectives of the survey are.
2. Identify the conditions under which the survey will be conducted (e.g. what information is needed, what date is the information needed by, what is the degree of accuracy required, etc.).
3. Determine if any or all of the information is already available.
4. If the information is not available, decide on the type and size of sampling method that is going to be used, the method for selecting the items in the sample, and the survey method for collecting the data.
6. Design the *research instrument* that is going to be used to collect the data (frequently a questionnaire).
7. Test the research instrument (in a questionnaire this would normally involve carrying out a pilot survey to see if responses were adequate and meaningful, that the questions were not misleading, that the responses were in a format that could be easily analysed, that the questionnaire was not too short or too long, etc.).
8. Collect the data.
9. If necessary edit the data (if using a questionnaire make sure responses are logical and meaningful).
10. Tabulate and classify the information that has been collected.
11. Analyse the information.

12. Is a follow-up survey necessary? This is not that uncommon, especially in attitude surveys where one wants to know if attitudes have changed since the previous survey.
13. Interpret the findings and report upon them.

7.4.3 Survey methods

The three main information-gathering methods are the mail survey, the phone survey and the personal survey. The most popular of these is the mail survey, which nearly always uses a questionnaire to elicit the required information from the respondent (questionnaires, because of their pivotal place in survey research, will be looked at separately a little further on in the chapter). The mail survey is also normally the cheapest of the survey methods, but suffers from a poor response rate (usually between 10 and 50 per cent, though it is possible to get higher response rates with follow-up surveys). It has also been shown that people who do not respond can have significantly different views from those who do. This criticism obviously applies to all survey methods, and careful consideration should therefore be given to ways of minimising the problem.

An advantage in using a mail survey is that it can be used to obtain data from a wide geographical area, and offers a uniform stimulus to all the respondents. It is also the case that the anonymity that is associated with a mail survey can induce respondents to be more open and truthful. On the other hand it is not possible to clarify a question when using a mail survey, which can then result in an incorrect response or no response at all. A mail survey is also inappropriate if the respondent has a poor command of the English language.

Phone surveys normally get quite high response rates (circa 70 per cent), but are slightly more expensive than a mail survey due to the telephone charges incurred and the cost of hiring a suitably experienced person or persons to ask the questions. Phone interviews can be carried out relatively quickly, and this can be an important consideration if a deadline has to be met. The problem with a phone survey is that it can only reach those people who have a telephone, which can exclude important segments of the population. It can also be difficult to contact respondents at certain times of the day, which in turn affects response rates and increases costs. There are a range of benefits associated with a person actually asking the questions, whether it be on a telephone or in person, and these can be looked at in the context of the third method, the personal survey.

Going to a person's home and asking them questions directly has been shown to be effective in gaining a respondent's trust, though it is clearly the most costly of the survey methods. Personal interviews also have a high response rate and can be used to gather large amounts of information. On the negative side they do necessitate a skilled interviewer, otherwise bias is likely to creep in due to the interviewer leading the respondent. A skilled interviewer is also able to go beyond the constraints of a structured questionnaire in that he or she can let the respondent answer a question in the way he or she wants. This immensely rich information can be very useful, although it is difficult to quantify and analyse in a statistical sense.

Interviews can be structured, semi-structured or even unstructured. In a structured interview a standard set of questions are asked, and as such it appears to offer little additional benefit to a questionnaire. An unstructured interview is non-directive and usually quite informal. The interview cannot of course be completely open ended, otherwise there is no purpose to the interview itself, but within a general purpose framework it is possible to have great flexibility and explore areas that were not previously thought of as core interest. The interviewer can also probe the interviewee if there is an issue worth pursuing. An unstructured interview can be particularly useful during the early stages of a survey, where the emphasis might be on developing a hypothesis or model rather than on testing it.

The disadvantage in using an interview to collect data is that it is more costly, and the cost increases as the interview becomes more unstructured because of the greater skill needed by the interviewer. Great care is also needed to ensure that the interviewer does not lead the interviewee or misinterpret what is being said. It is also difficult to get a uniform format for the responses, which again can lead to problems when it comes to the analysis stage. Table 7.1 summarises and compares the three survey methods, and this can be a useful reference point when you are considering undertaking a survey of some kind.

There has been a trend in recent years to offer some sort of incentive to the target audience in an attempt to increase the response rate. The incentive can range from winning a holiday in the Caribbean to a copy of the final report. Purists would argue that this in itself can distort the type of response that is received, but the evidence suggests that it certainly increases the response rate!

Table 7.1 Comparison of survey methods

Feature	Mail survey	Phone survey	Personal survey
Cost	Cheap – interviews not required	Slightly more expensive – but no transportation	Expensive
Response rate	Low	Good	High
Bias	Some – difference between respondents and non-respondents?	Some – applies to telephone owners only	Some – does it rely on people being at home?
Length of interview	Zero	Short	Long
Interviewer effect	None	Limited	Highest
Ability to handle complex questions	Poor	Good	Excellent
Ability to collect large amounts of data	Fair	Good	Excellent
Accuracy on sensitive questions	Good	Fair	Fair
Ability to sample required population	Good	Fair	Good

7.5 Questionnaire design

Questionnaires are the most frequently used method for gathering information, and the validity of the information that is gained from the questionnaire is affected greatly by its design. There is a great deal of literature on questionnaire design, and this suggests that there are a number of simple rules that should be followed to ensure truthful, meaningful and easy-to-analyse answers:

1. Provide a covering letter explaining why the survey is being carried out.
2. Use terms that can be understood and avoid words that can have several meanings.
3. Avoid ambiguous questions.
4. Be sure that the question can actually be answered correctly.
5. Avoid the double question (two questions within one question).
6. Avoid embarrassing questions.
7. Word questions so that they can be easily tabulated and classified.
8. Avoid leading questions (questions which imply that there is only one answer).
9. List questions in a logical order.
10. Make the questionnaire as short and attractive as possible.
11. Place the sender's name and/or organisation's name and address on each questionnaire.
12. Provide a stamped addressed envelope for returning the questionnaire.

In the light of these guidelines, how could the following questions be interpreted:

a. What is your occupation?
b. How long has your agency published its magazine?
c. What is the most important industry in your town?

The first impression one gets is that the questions can be interpreted in a variety of ways, which is likely to result in a variety of answers. For example, a lecturer might answer to question (a) that he or she is a teacher, college instructor, social scientist or researcher, etc. The second question might also result in answers like 'several years', which is open-ended and non-quantifiable. The word 'long' in the second question is also unclear in that it will have different connotations for different people. It might therefore have been better to have reworded the question as:

How many years has your agency published its magazine?
( ) Under 1
( ) 1–4
( ) 5–9
( ) 10 and over

In the third question the words 'important' and 'industry' again have different potential interpretations. How do you measure the importance of an industry? Is it by volume of output, number of employees, return on investment?

As previously stated, questions should be clear, concise and unambiguous, and should not 'lead' the respondent. It is also possible to structure and repeat questions in a way that reinforces reliability and consistency of the responses. But even with careful planning it is usually beneficial to carry out a trial study (pilot study) so that poorly worded questions are identified. Preparatory work of this kind can only enhance the quality of the questionnaire in terms of the number of returned questionnaires and the accuracy of the responses.

Broadly speaking, there are three types of questions that a questionnaire can contain:

- **Demographic (factual)**: age, sex, income, etc.
- **Behavioural**: reporting on their own behaviour.
- **Attitudes and opinions**: why they behaved in that way, as well as their attitude to specific items (products, services, etc.).

Within these general bands it is possible to ask either open-ended or closed questions. Open-ended questions are good at starting and/or ending questionnaires because they enable the respondents to answer a question in their own way. This can then lead to a more interested and committed respondent. They should not, however, be used too frequently, as they are difficult to analyse and may lead to non-completion due to the effort required. Closed questions on the other hand are easier to answer and result in precise and relevant answers.

Attitude scales are an example of a closed question, and they provide a numerical continuum within which the respondent can rate or categorise his or her answer. A balanced attitude scale is shown in Figure 7.1, and it has an equal list of positive and negative answers. It is possible to have all negative or all positive scales – it depends on the area you are looking at (e.g. price changes). Questions should always include a 'don't know' or 'not relevant' or 'other' category, otherwise they can bias the responses by forcing the respondent to choose a category that is not appropriate or leading to a non-response.

Very Important	Important	Neither important nor unimportant	Unimportant	Very unimportant
①	②	③	④	⑤

Figure 7.1 A balanced attitude scale

Likert and **semantic differential** scales are also widely used, and an example of each is shown in Figures 7.2 and 7.3. In Figure 7.2 there is an even number of response categories, which forces the respondent to choose either a negative or positive category. In Figures 7.1, 7.3 and 7.4 there are an odd number of response categories, which creates a middle response category that respondents may be tempted to score against, as it is a safe option. There are no hard and fast rules on the use of even or odd ranges of response categories – it depends on the type of study that is being undertaken and the questions being asked.

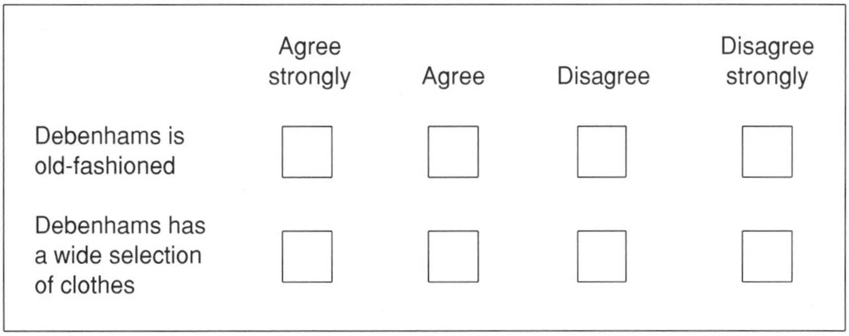

Figure 7.2   Likert scale

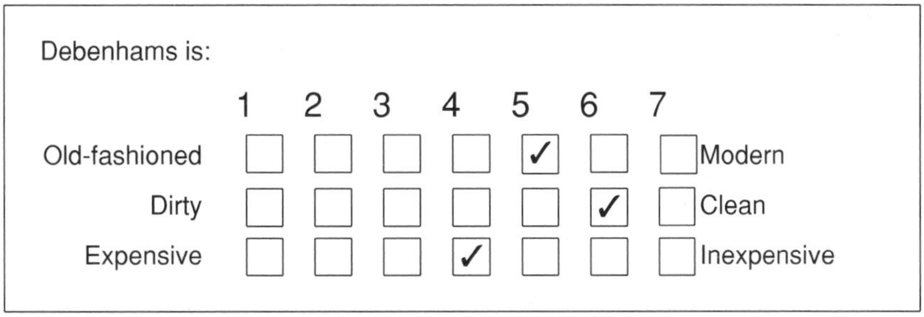

Figure 7.3   Semantic differential scale

(Psychological research has shown that people can make up to seven distinctions reliably, and this is why many attitude scales, like Figure 7.3, have a seven-point scale. Indeed, it has been used so extensively that it is sometimes sarcastically referred to as the magic number seven.)

When responses are in this form it is possible to find the mean response for each element of a question or questions and produce a profile of all the scores, as shown in Figure 7.4.

If the profile scores exhibit a trend, say to the positive side of the scale, then it is possible to identify the overall characteristics of the data easily and quickly using this method.

In general, a questionnaire is well designed if it elicits the information required with maximum efficiency. For those who fill in the questionnaire this means the time and effort they spend on the questionnaire should be kept to a minimum. This in turn implies a minimum number of questions and the achievement of a

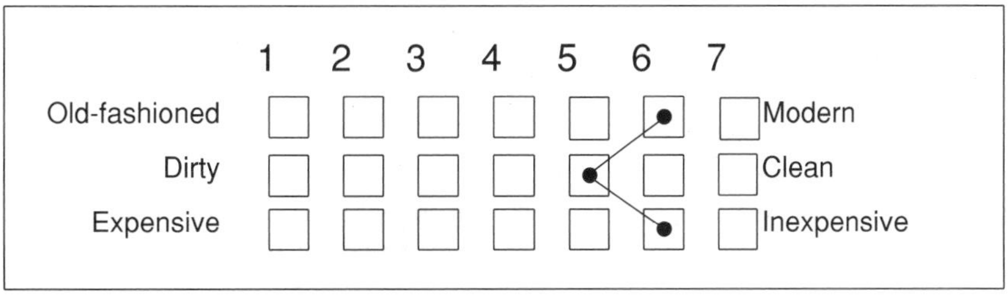

Figure 7.4   Profile scores

high response rate. A well designed questionnaire should also lead to good quality information which should be accurate, complete and unbiased. To support this, questions should be as short and straightforward as possible. It is normally recommended that there be one question asked for each specific piece of information required. In the light of this it might be better to ask:

Do you prefer:
  a. a small diesel car
  b. a small petrol car
  c. a large diesel car
  d. a large petrol car

rather than the broader and less precise question:

Do you prefer a small economy car or a large family car?

When you are wording questions it is also advisable to use words that are likely to be familiar to the respondent and easy to understand. If it is necessary to use technical terms then they should be clearly explained.

A question, unless it is carefully worded, can unwittingly lead to bias. To avoid such bias a question should:

- Avoid leading a respondent by indicating the expected answer to the question (e.g. you should ask, 'Are you in favour of capital punishment?' rather than, 'You are not in favour of capital punishment, are you?').
- Avoid emotive words (e.g. you should ask, 'Are you in favour of donating money to overseas charities?' rather than, 'Do you favour sending money to help the starving children of Ethiopia?').
- Avoid referring to an authority figure (e.g. you should ask, 'Do you support the de-nationalisation programme?' rather than, 'Do you support the Conservative government's de-nationalisation programme?').
- Avoid questions that encourage people to answer in socially acceptable terms (e.g. you should ask, 'Do you read the *Sun*?' or 'Do you read *The Times*?' rather than, 'Which of the following newspapers do you read – the *Sun*, *The Times*, etc.?' because many people will say they read *The Times* when in fact they read the *Sun*).

The way the questions are sequenced is also an important consideration. In general the sequence should be:

- Easy questions should be at the beginning so that the respondent gains confidence in being able to answer the questions.
- Questions that the respondent is likely to find interesting should also be located early on in the sequence.
- Questions should be asked in a logical order, with related questions being in the correct sequence.
- Before there is a change of topic in the questions, an introductory phrase should be used to facilitate a smooth transition for the respondent.
- Personal and/or emotional questions should be towards the end of the questionnaire.
- More complicated questions should also be at the end of the questionnaire.

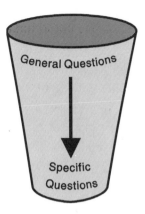

Figure 7.5   Funnel design

These types of guidelines have led people to argue that a questionnaire should follow a 'funnel' design, as shown in Figure 7.5.

It is argued that the superiority of the funnel design rests on the premise that the general questions provide time for the respondents to orientate themselves to the context of the specific questions that follow later. However, an inverted funnel design (from the specific to the general) also has advantages, in that it can be helpful in cases where the specific provides a guide to the general. Instead of asking, 'How much per week do you spend on housekeeping?' you could ask, 'How much per week do you spend on bread/milk/washing power/other items? How much per week do you spend in total?'

Summary of questionnaire design

Questionnaire design is a very important part of the survey process, and time spent on getting it right is normally time well spent. A pilot survey to test the questionnaire has also been shown to be valuable in refining the final layout and shape of the questions asked.

Competence Example 7.1

At the end of this section you should now be able to demonstrate how to:

1 **identify survey type applications and evaluate appropriate survey methods**

2 **follow the survey process**

3 **design and evaluate questionnaires**

To practise and demonstrate these competences complete problems 7.1 and 7.2 at the end of this chapter. To help you to develop these competences a description of the procedure you will need to follow is now given, along with a typical problem format. The problem format is based on a process similar to that previously outlined.

PROCEDURE

❶ Identify an appropriate survey method.

❷ Outline the types of variables that might shape people's attitudes.

❸ Look in detail at the variable 'education' and its various meanings.

❹ Describe the process you would follow in this type of survey.

❺ Provide examples of the types of questions that could be used in ascertaining a person's educational background.

PROBLEM

As a marketing specialist you are interested in the way attitudes vary in relation to different lifestyles. Identify the types of variables that might be important in shaping attitudes, paying particular attention to a person's education, and describe the process you would follow in carrying out such a survey. The term 'education' can have different meanings to different people, and in the light of this write a question or questions that would facilitate an analysis of a person's educational background.

A description of the layout of the solution format is given at the beginning of the book.

SOLUTION FORMAT

❶ The context of the problem suggests that the survey will contain elements of both market research and academic type surveys. Because of the emphasis on people's attitudes and the assumed hypothesis that attitudes significantly affect people's lifestyles, it could be argued that there is a much greater emphasis on an academic type survey than a market research type survey. Regardless of the category that the survey falls into, there are essentially three survey methods available to the researcher: a mail survey, a phone survey or a personal survey. The precise choice will depend upon the time frame within which the survey has to operate, the degree of 'rich' information required, the size of the population and sample, and the costs constraints faced. From the brief information provided, a mail (postal) survey would seem to be appropriate as it is widely used to collect information on people's attitudes, can reach a wide and geographically diverse population, and is relatively cheap to carry out.

❷ A difficulty with looking at the variables that affect/determine people's attitudes is the potential range, variability and interaction of the variables themselves. For example, we might expect a person's age and sex to have some bearing on their attitudes, just as we might expect the area they live in, their personal wealth and their occupation to have some influence too. Careful consideration would have to be given to the variables chosen so that they matched with the objectives of the study and how they fitted with the chosen research instrument (i.e. a questionnaire). To verify that the correct variables have been chosen and are being interpreted as expected a pilot survey would be useful.

❸ Focusing on education as a variable that affects attitudes, it is clear that it can be interpreted and measured in a number of different ways. A person's education, for instance, includes the number of years at school and college, and the types of qualifications gained. It also includes the mode of learning (e.g. part-time, vocational, distance learning, etc.) and the type of institution attended (private or public, large or

⑤ small). There is no single correct way to ask all this, but it is important to get as much as possible for later analysis. The question examples below illustrate the complexity of obtaining even factual data on a person's education:

a. What type of junior school did you attend?
   i. state school
   ii. private school
   iii. religious denomination school (e.g. Roman Catholic)

b. What type of senior school did you attend?
   i. state school
   ii. private school
   iii. religious denomination school (e.g. Roman Catholic)

c. Did you attend a sixth form college or its equivalent?

   Yes.......No......

d. Did you go to university?

   Yes.......No......

e. Have you studied:
   i. part-time
   ii. by distance learning
   iii. by other non-traditional ways?

f. Do you have:
   i. no qualifications
   ii. GCSE qualifications
   iii. a degree
   iv. a professional qualification?
   etc.
   etc.

④ It is important that the ideas and questions outlined above fit in the survey process that was discussed earlier. Some of the steps have been identified, such as explicitly stating what the objectives of the study are and testing the research instrument and questions through a pilot study. The target audience must also be clearly identified, as must the level of accuracy and the types of analysis that will be carried out once the data has been collected. As with all surveys, it is the pre data collection stages of the survey process that are critical to the success of the study itself.

Practise your competence now on problems 7.1 and 7.2 at the end of the chapter and in problems from your own work environment.

7.6 Sampling methods

When the survey method has been decided and the questionnaire designed, consideration must be given to the sampling procedures or methods that are to be followed (though not necessarily in that order). The fundamental issue facing those carrying out a survey is *how do we get a representative sample*? If a sample of data is not truly representative of the population from which it is drawn, that is, if it is a biased sample, then it becomes impossible to make an accurate prediction about the population. There are in fact two main approaches to taking a sample – those that are gathered using non-probability methods and those that are gathered using probability as the selection criterion.

7.6.1 Non-probability based sampling methods

The methods that come under this heading – convenience sampling, judgement sampling and quota sampling – are also referred to as non-scientific sampling methods. The major problem with these methods is that they cannot guarantee that every individual in the population has had an equal chance of being included in the sample, and are therefore more prone to bias than the probability based samples. Yet they can be economical and practical in many instances, and as the remainder of this section will show, the final sampling procedure we adopt is often a compromise between accuracy and economy.

Convenience sampling

This is a very simple and straightforward approach, and it involves selecting items on the basis that they are accessible and easy to measure. It can work quite well if the population you are interested in is homogeneous geographically and structurally. Carrying out a convenience sample in the local high street and asking about crime might, for instance, result in a uniform response that conforms to researchers' expectations (on the other hand, the time of day and the particular location of the high street might lead to different types of responses). The classic example of a convenience sample was that carried out by *Literary Digest* magazine in the USA during the 1920s and 1930s. The magazine sampled large numbers of people from telephone books and car registrations to predict the winner of presidential elections. They predicted a victory for Landon, and lost credibility (and actually went out of business) when Roosevelt romped home with a landslide victory. The reason why they had got it so wrong was that they had missed the large Democratic vote that had no cars or telephones.

A general difficulty that we can encounter with this approach is that we tend to seek out what we perceive to be *typical people* in social and economic terms. There is no guarantee of course that people with typical social and economic backgrounds will have attitudes that are representative of the wider population. Indeed, the evidence suggests that we are likely to seek out people with similar socio-economic backgrounds to our own and/or those from the middle and upper classes. All of these factors suggest that bias will be a problem with convenience samples. They can be used constructively, however, during the pilot study stage of a survey when the main objective is to improve the questionnaire design.

Judgement sampling

The main criterion used in this sampling method is to select items on the basis of expert judgement as to who should or should not be included in the sample. The

Retail Price Index (RPI), for instance, is based upon what economists and government think should be in a 'basket of goods', which in turn is supposed to be reflective of a typical household's expenditure.

Although judgemental sampling is generally considered to be unreliable, there are a number of examples where they have been found to be very accurate. At election time, for instance, it is possible for a few key districts to be selected and for these to be used as a barometer for the rest of the country. In a similar vein, a marketing expert can predict national sales by selecting and testing a very small number of geographical areas. The areas chosen are based upon the expert's judgement, and the resulting predictions are seldom wrong.

Quota sampling

This is based on a known proportion or 'quota' of the population. For instance, if a census indicates that half of the UK is female and one-tenth is Jewish, then interviewers are told to obtain half of their interviews with women and ten per cent with Jews.

The major problem with this approach is that interviewers will again tend to select respondents that they feel comfortable with, which oftens leads to a middle class bias. This bias cannot be eliminated until the decision regarding who to interview is entirely taken away from the interviewer. Probability forms the basis for the elimination of this type of error.

Another of the great gaffs in polling history was the 1948 Gallup prediction that Thomas E. Dewey would have a massive majority and become the next president of the USA. In fact it was Harry S. Truman who became president with a vote of 50 per cent. One of the reasons that Gallup got it so wrong was that they stopped polling three weeks before the election day and thus missed those voters who only made up their minds, or changed their minds, in the last three weeks of the campaign. Another reason was that Gallup was using a quota sample to keep its costs down. It is interesting to note that academic polls using more accurate methods had correctly predicted that Truman would win the election.

7.6.2 Probability based sampling methods

Most surveys are based upon a probability sample, in which the sample is drawn in such a way that each person in the population has a known (generally equal) probability of being included in the sample. This will reduce bias in the selection process and thereby improve the accuracy of the sample data as well as the resultant predictions. There are a number of probability based sampling methods, and one of the most widely known is the **simple random sample**.

Simple random sampling

In simple random sampling each member of the population has an equal chance of being selected. The method involves selecting at random the required number of subjects for the sample. Because the process of selection is random we would expect the sample to mirror the population, in that if the population had some old, some young, some tall, some short, some fit, some unfit, some rich, and some poor, etc., then the sample should have some old, some young, some tall, some short, some fit, some unfit, some rich, and some poor, etc.

We could draw our sample from a container if the population were small enough, but this can be time-consuming due to the time it takes in preparing cards for the container and is potentially biased due to the problems associated with mixing the cards thoroughly. An alternative to this method is to number ten cards from 0 to 9, and then shuffle the cards and randomly draw one, record its number, replace the card, reshuffle the cards, randomly draw a card and record its number etc. This process will generate a random sequence of numbers that are statistically independent of each other. A large table of such numbers would be very time-consuming and tedious to compile, though as we shall shortly see, they are the basis upon which many surveys are based.

In 1955, the Rand Corporation used an electromechanical process of coding digitised electronic impulses that occur randomly to compile a million random digits. This has been extensively tested to ensure that each of the digits in the table has an equal chance of appearing at any location. This means that any one number will appear as often as any other number. For example, if there are ten thousand 10s, there will be ten thousand 20s, and any single digit 0 through 9 will appear at any particular location one tenth of the time.

A computer can also generate random numbers via a **random number generator**. In Lotus 1-2-3 the command is @RAND, while for Excel it is the pasted MATH & TRIG command RAND().

Once we have the random numbers it is normal practice to select at random from a list of the population (this is known as the *sampling frame*) the required number of subjects for the sample. The main problem associated with this is that there might not be such a listing, and if there is no listing it could be very expensive to compile one. The electoral roll is probably the most widely used list, but examples of others include the Medical Council's listing of doctors and the Campas directory on companies. Assuming that we have such a listing, how do we actually select the items using the random numbers?

If we had 2,500 customers and we wanted to carry out a simple random sample, we would first list out the customers from 1 to 2,500. Since the largest number in our population is 2,500, which has four digits, we select random numbers from the table of random numbers in sets or groups of four digits. A small section of the Rand Corporation's million random numbers is shown in Table 7.2 (a larger section is shown in Table 2 in Appendix 1).

While we could select four-digit numbers from any portion of the table, let's start from the top left-hand corner of the table and read off the numbers from left to right:

5732 3997 9310 4049 6963 3472 0063 5613 etc.

Since the numbers are random, the four-digit numbers are all equally likely. With these numbers it is now possible to give each element in the population an equal chance of being included in the sample.

The first number from the table is 5732, which is greater than the population size of 2,500, so it is ignored. As we go through the numbers we find that it is not

Table 7.2   Table of random numbers

5	7	3	2	3	9	9	7	9	3	1	0	4	0	4	9	6	9	6	3
3	4	7	2	0	0	6	3	5	6	1	3	3	0	9	0	4	9	5	8
0	7	5	7	8	6	5	4	1	0	0	0	0	3	5	3	2	6	9	3
4	7	3	7	1	3	7	3	3	6	2	2	9	3	7	5	1	7	3	8
7	5	1	6	5	9	7	5	7	5	8	3	6	1	5	0	7	2	8	1
0	4	8	8	5	8	1	1	3	6	9	0	5	7	4	8	8	2	0	0
8	3	2	3	9	5	4	8	2	6	7	5	0	3	0	7	5	5	2	7
6	6	4	7	4	0	6	2	9	8	3	8	0	9	6	4	4	3	7	6
8	7	3	2	9	3	0	1	5	6	0	1	5	5	1	5	0	2	1	0
7	9	1	5	5	8	4	8	2	9	4	8	0	0	6	3	3	1	4	6

until we reach the seventh number that we find a number that is within the range of 1 to 2,500, which is 0063. This means that the 63rd customer will be the first one in our sample. This process would continue until we got our required sample size (say 30). It is worth re-emphasising that we could have started our selection of random numbers from anywhere in the table, but once we have chosen a starting point we should stick to the system adopted, such as reading along the rows of numbers, rather than suddenly changing and reading down the columns (it is of course perfectly acceptable to start by reading down the columns and then stick to reading down the columns). The layout of the digits into blocks has no significance; they are presented in this format for ease of handling only.

With probability sampling being the basis for most surveys, a perfectly reasonable question to ask is, 'How good are they?'. An alternative way of expressing this would be to ask, 'What is the error associated with using such a sampling method?' Looking at this a little more closely, suppose we have a population of 400 people, with 200 being Catholics and 200 being Protestants, and we take a sample of 100 people and record their religion. In the light of these proportions we would probably expect the ratio in the sample to be close to 50:50. If we continue to take lots of different samples of 100 from the population of 400 we might expect the ratio to stay close to 50:50, although it is of course possible to draw a very unrepresentative sample that was all Catholic, even if we think this is very unlikely. In general we would expect the samples of 100 people to contain numbers of Catholics that were close to 50; say 49, 48, 51, 52, etc.

By using a simple random sample we can actually be much more precise about the accuracy or error of our estimate of the number of Catholics in a sample of 100 people than that discussed above. It will be shown later in the chapter that if the true proportion in the population is 50 per cent, then we would expect a sample of 100 people to be within 9.8 per cent of the 50 per cent most of the time (actually it is 95 per cent of the time). This possible 9.8 per cent of error is called the *sampling error* and is the result of looking at a sample rather than the population (i.e. you would intuitively expect a sample to be slightly different from the population). From what we have said we can expect 95 per cent of the all the possible samples of 100 people to have between 40.2 Catholics (50 per cent – 9.8

per cent = 40.2 per cent) and 59.8 Catholics (50 per cent + 9.8 per cent = 59.8 per cent) in them.

This means that if we only have one sample we hope it is one of the 95 per cent of samples rather than one of the 5 per cent of samples, otherwise the error could be greater than 9.8 per cent. Another way of saying this is that we are taking a 5 per cent chance of drawing a wrong conclusion, which are not bad betting odds. In most situations the 9.8 per cent sampling error would be too high, and the ways that it can be reduced will be looked at later in the chapter when we consider how sample sizes are determined. The important point to bring out here is that the sampling error can be calculated for simple random samples, which provides us with an estimate of the accuracy of the sample. This is the great advantage of probability samples over non-probability based samples.

It is worth pointing out that throughout the remainder of this text the term 'sample' will mean a simple random sample, and that the inferential statistics discussed further on in the text assume a simple random sample. Without the assumption of a simple random sample the inferential statistics are meaningless. There are, however, alternative random sampling plans available that can be more efficient and accurate for certain situations.

Systematic sampling

This method is a modified form of simple random sampling. It involves selecting subjects from a population list in a systematic rather than a random way. A random start is used to choose the first person, and then a fixed amount are skipped to get the next person, and so on.

For example, if an auditor wanted to sample 400 invoices from all the company's invoices, of which there are 20,000, the auditor would select every 50th invoice until she or he had the 400 invoices needed (this is a 1 in 50 sample, as $20,000/400 = 50$). Using this procedure, the auditor would randomly choose the first invoice, which would be 53 if she or he took the first two-digit number, working downwards, from the top left-hand corner of the random number table in Table 2, Appendix 1. Having selected the first number the auditor then uses multiples of 50 to select the full 400 invoices:

53   103   153   203   253   etc.

This procedure makes sample selection very convenient, as long as the list corresponds to the population. Apart from the problems of having such an up-to-date listing, there is a potential problem with periodicity in the list. For example, if your list was of houses, and if you chose the first house and every fifteenth house, you might accidentally obtain a sample containing only houses on corners, which are often more expensive than houses in the rest of the street.

Another example of a systematic sampling scheme, and one which is quite widely used, is when every nth person is selected as they pass through a supermarket or airport etc. Again the first person would be selected for interview randomly, and then every nth person until the sample was complete.

A problem frequently associated with simple random sampling and systematic sampling is that they can be very expensive to carry out. If the sample was based on a national listing, for instance, then the sample could cover the whole of the country, which would be very expensive due to transportation costs etc.

Stratified sampling

Stratified sampling involves dividing the population into homogeneous groups, each group containing subjects with similar characteristics. If you were interested in some aspect of the population of the UK, for example, and know the proportion of the population living in each region, it makes sense to stratify your sample by region so that the proper proportion of interviews can be taken independently within each region. So, if 25 per cent of the population lives in the south-east, then 25 per cent of the interviews can be taken in the south-east. This can actually improve the accuracy in that it assures that certain known population proportions are matched in your sample.

Once the proportions have been determined, the selection of respondents within those proportions is done by simple random sampling – the selection of exact respondents is still left to chance.

Another reason for using stratified samples is that they can be more economical. For instance, if we are interested in contrasting Catholic and Protestant views on abortion, we could obtain more economical estimates of each group's views by sampling them separately than if we sampled the entire nation and then compared the Catholics and Protestants in the sample.

A further example of the value of stratified samples is demonstrated by the fact that if we wanted to determine the average weight of 10,000 students in a university by weighing a representative sample of 100 students, we might assure a more representative average by stratifying the population by sex, as the general weight levels of males and females differ. Therefore, if there are 3,000 female students we would include in our 100 sample a simple random sample of 30 females and a simple random sample of 70 of the 7,000 males.

Some readers may be surprised to learn that they can use as much judgement as they please in setting up the strata. The final sample will be a probability sample so long as a random method of selection is used in drawing the sample units from each of the strata. The better one's judgement in defining the strata, the higher the precision one would expect from the sample. One should also bear in mind that regardless of how homogeneous the elements of each stratum are and how nicely the strata differ from one another, the sample may be invalid unless there is a logical relationship between the strata and the items of information being sought. Thus, one would probably achieve little or no gain in precision in stratifying a group of women according to shoe size if one were attempting to estimate their average annual expenditure on cigarettes. On the other hand, in estimating the average mileage per gallon for motor vehicles it would be logical to stratify these vehicles by type (e.g. trucks, buses, cars, etc.) before sampling. Otherwise we might get a disproportionate number of trucks, which would then distort the results.

Looking at an example in a little more detail, suppose we had an organisation that had the profile shown in Table 7.3, and we wanted to get a representative sample of 400 people from the different strata:

Table 7.3 Example of stratification of employee categories by level of education

	Direct workers	Middle management	Senior management
GCSE qualifications	18,100	136	10
Professional qualifications	2,160	978	24
Degree qualifications	56	310	47

The first step would be to divide the sample size by the total workforce in order to arrive at a sampling fraction that can be used to determine the size of each of the strata in the sample:

$$\text{Sample size} = 400$$
$$\text{Total workforce} = 21,821$$

$$\text{Sampling fraction} = \frac{400}{21,821} = .0183$$

.0183	×	18,100	=	331.23	= 331
.0183	×	2,160	=	39.53	= 40
.0183	×	56	=	1.02	= 1
.0183	×	136	=	2.49	= 2
.0183	×	978	=	17.89	= 18
.0183	×	310	=	5.67	= 6
.0183	×	10	=	0.18	= 1
.0183	×	24	=	0.43	= 1
.0183	×	47	=	0.86	= 1
		21,821		399.3	401

You will have noticed that common sense has been used to round up and down, to ensure that all the segments get represented in the sample.

Stratified sampling once again assumes that we have a listing of the population in order that the strata can be identified and a simple random sample taken. If there is no such listing the only alternative is to use a quota sample, even though this is a non-probability type sample.

Cluster sampling

Cluster sampling, like stratified sampling, investigates sub-populations of the main population. But unlike stratified sampling, which requires investigation of each sub-population or strata, cluster sampling requires only a random selection from a small number of clusters. The procedure therefore involves investigating only a small number of clusters from many clusters.

There are two distinct benefits of cluster sampling. First, it is cheaper to sample a given number of people from the same cluster than to sample the same number of people from a geographically diverse area. Secondly, cluster sampling avoids the need for a complete listing of the population.

Suppose a psychologist wishes to examine levels of neuroticism in British managers and decides to look at managers from a variety of organisations in the public sector, service sector, manufacturing sector and retail sector of the economy. The psychologist also looks at these organisations in four distinct geographical areas, as shown in Table 7.4.

Table 7.4 Cluster table

Cluster	Sector organisations			
A	1	2	3	4
B	5	6	7	8
C	9	10	11	12
D	13	14	15	16

The process followed in cluster sampling is to first randomly select, say, two of the clusters and then to look at all the elements within those clusters. This would ensure that every item in the population had an equal chance (50 per cent) of being included in the sample, but not that every combination of items had an equal chance of being included in the sample. For instance, it is not possible to have items 1, 2, 5, 6, 9, 10, 13, 14 in the sample because of the way that the clusters have been formed. In this way the psychologist would be sure that she or he has the four sectors covered and that all the items in the sample had an even chance of being included.

In general, the most precise results under cluster sampling will be obtained when each cluster contains as varied a mixture as possible, and each cluster is as nearly alike as possible. We noted earlier that stratified sampling is just the reverse – strata should be internally as homogeneous (alike) as possible, but as externally heterogeneous (different) as possible.

While stratification, if performed with at least a little judgement, will usually yield a more precise estimate than a simple random sample, we find that a cluster sample will normally provide a less precise estimate than a simple random sample. The reason for this is that in most practical situations we must accept clusters as they actually exist, which tend to be of a homogeneous kind. People living in the same area for instance tend to share the same demographic characteristics, and children attending a fee-paying school will have similar academic capabilities. Generally speaking we can therefore say that cluster sampling is less precise than simple random sampling and stratified random sampling. But the close proximity of the items in the cluster sample usually makes it cheaper than a simple random sample or a stratified random sample. The relationship between cost and accuracy is referred to as *net efficiency*, and this is normally high for cluster samples, which probably explains their popularity.

Area sampling

An area sample is really a geographically-based cluster sample. It is popular with pollsters because it does not necessarily require a complete listing of the population. If we wanted to carry out some market research on households' TV viewing habits, for instance, we could get a map of a city and divide it into districts (clusters). A simple random sample of districts can then be carried out and every house in the selected district visited. Figure 7.6 shows an example of this diagrammatically, and as can be seen it involves breaking down a city into blocks, which consist of a fixed number of households per block. Suppose, for simplicity, that we have only eight households in each block and we have 35 blocks, giving us

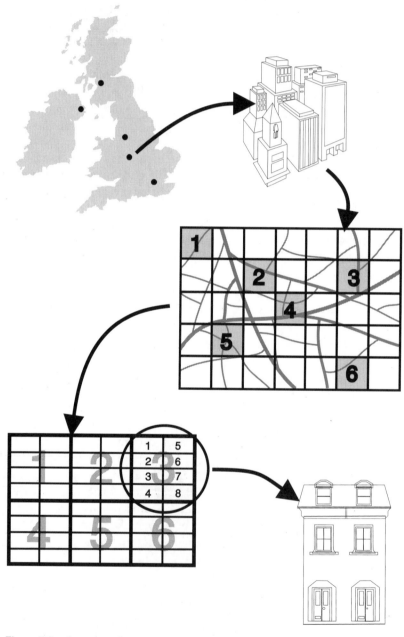

Figure 7.6   Area sampling

a total of 280 households. If we want to random sample eight households, our *sampling ratio* would be $8/280 = 1/35$. This would mean us taking a random sample of one of the 35 blocks (Figure 7.6 only shows six of the 35 blocks because of limited space), which in our illustration is block three, from which every household would be surveyed with respect to their viewing habits. The advantage for the person doing the survey is that everyone is located in the same area, even though it might not be as accurate as a simple random sample or stratified sample due to the possible homogeneity of that block. It is of course possible to have a sampling ratio of any value, such as $1/17.5$, which would involve randomly selecting two blocks from the total of 35 blocks $(16/280 = 1/17.5)$. The maximum number of blocks that we could look at is 35, which would give us a sampling ratio of $1/1$.

Table 7.5 Comparison of sampling methods

Sampling method	Advantages	Disadvantages
Non-Probability	***Cheap***	***No estimate of accuracy***
Convenience sampling	Available sample.	No necessary relation to population.
Judgement sampling	Take advantage of specialist advice and information.	Bias or misrepresentation by using specialists.
Quota sampling	Target known proportions in population. Willing respondents.	Middle class and other biases.
Probability	***Accuracy can be estimated***	***Expensive***
Simple random sample	Sampling error can be estimated.	Sample can be too dispersed and full list required.
Systematic sampling	Convenience.	Periodicity in list.
Stratified sampling	Guarantee adequate representation of different groups.	Sometimes requires weighting to get proper representation. Judgement (bias) used in selecting strata.
Cluster sampling	Lower cost and no listing required.	Less accurate than stratified and simple random sampling.
Area sampling	No listing required. Lower cost. Increase accuracy with two-staged area sampling.	Less accurate than stratified and simple random sampling.

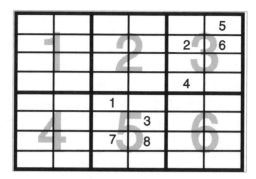

Figure 7.7   Two stage area sample

A way of reducing this homogeneity is to carry out a **two-stage area sample**. This involves taking a simple random sample of two out of the 35 blocks and then randomly selecting four out of the eight households (*see* Figure 7.7). This ensures that we still have a sampling ratio of $1/35$ ($\frac{2}{35} \times \frac{4}{8} = \frac{8}{280} = \frac{1}{35}$), and that it is more representative, even if it is slightly more expensive due to the greater travelling costs involved. Perhaps not surprisingly, most surveys are of this type, and they reflect the compromise between cost and accuracy.

An overview of sampling methods is shown in Table 7.5.

Competence Example 7.2

At the end of this section you should now be able to demonstrate how to:

1 **identify an appropriate sampling method**

2 **show the processes associated with a specific sampling method**

3 **compare the sampling methods**

To practise and demonstrate these competences complete problems 7.3 and 7.4 at the end of this chapter. To help you to develop these competences a description of the procedure you will need to follow is now given, along with a typical problem format. The problem format is based on a process similar to that previously outlined.

PROCEDURE

❶ Identify an appropriate sampling method.

❷ Outline the design features of the chosen sampling method.

❸ Look at the stages involved in the sample design.

❹ Compare the chosen sampling method with another sampling method.

PROBLEM

One of the most widely known sample types is the political opinion poll. Describe how such polls are carried out, paying particular attention to the overall design and stages involved. In addition to this, compare the sampling method that opinion polls are based upon to another sampling method.

SOLUTION FORMAT

❶ Although political opinion polls occur most notably at General Election time, they are in fact carried out on a regular basis by a number of organisations such as Gallup, Harris, NOP, Marplan, Opinion Research Centre, Research Services Ltd, and MORI. Using NOP (National Opinion Polls) as an example, the process and procedures followed in a political opinion poll will be outlined.

The NOP Random Omnibus Survey (this is a weekly opinion survey) has a **proportionate stratified random sample** design. The Electoral Register of Great Britain is taken as the global population (N) for the survey. The population is then sub-divided into mutually exclusive sub-populations or strata with random samples then being taken from each stratum.

❷ The first stage of the sample design involves stratifying the population in the following manner:

> **First** sub-population – stratification by **geographical location**
> **Second** sub-population – stratification by **demographic region**
> **Third** sub-population – order constituencies by **preference in the previous election**

❸ The above design has three main stages associated with it, with several levels in each stage. The stages and levels are:

Stage 1   Stratification

Level 1   Stratify by geographical region – into ten regions.

Level 2   Stratify the ten geographic regions by demography – that is, by Metropolitan Council, Urban Area, Rural Area and Mixed Area.

Level 3   Stratify Level 2 by constituency political preference in the previous General Election.

Stage 2   Systematic sample selection of constituencies

Level 4   List electorate in individual constituencies.

Level 5   Select 180 constituencies and allocate a number to each elector in the 180 constituencies.

Level 6   Randomly select an elector (the constituency to which this elector belongs is thereby considered to be selected into the sample).

Level 7   Determine the remaining 179 sample items (constituencies) by systematic sample selection, using the selection at Level 6 as the starting point (it is worth noting that each constituency has a chance of being selected that is proportional to the size of the electorate).

The 180 systematically selected samples are used to determine the target constituencies carried forward to Stage 3. Each individual on the Electoral Register is represented at the

❸ constituency selection stage and has an equal probability of selection. In this way the ▯2 constituences are represented in proportion to the regional population density and therefore the resultant constituency sample is expected to be proportional to geographical population spread.

Stage 3   Systematic sample selection of the electorate

Level 8   For each target constituency selected in Stage 2, list the electorate and randomly select a single elector. This has identified a particular elector within a particular constituency.

Level 9   The selected elector in Level 8 forms the starting point for selecting a group of electors from the Electoral Register. In practice, every 15th elector on the Register is chosen from this starting point until 18 names have been selected.

The consequences of this method of selection are that the sample contains a representative cross-section of urban and rural seats as well as having a mixture of safe Conservative, safe Labour and marginal seats. It also makes it representative of the people on the Electoral Register within those constituencies.

❹ In comparison to a simple random sample, the NOP Omnibus Survey has the advantage ▯3 that it can target the population much more effectively. As has been demonstrated, randomness is the foundation on which most sample designs are built, and yet a simple random sample from a large population may not be representative of the population as a whole, as it can quite legitimately fail to represent all segments of the population (the larger the proportion in the population, the greater the chance that it will be included in a simple random sample, and conversely, the smaller the proportion the more chance there is that it will not be included in a simple random sample). Methods need to be adopted so that knowledge of the population can be effectively utilised, and the precision of the sample can be correspondingly improved. In the NOP survey, stratification results in a sample that is proportional to the geographical population density and represents the social/political characteristics of the population.

Practise your competence now on problems 7.3 and 7.4 at the end of the chapter and on problems from your own work environment.

7.7   Sampling theory

When decisions have been made on what type of survey and sample to use and the information has been collected, the person conducting the survey must then analyse the sample information to infer what is happening in the wider population. Sampling theory provides the basis from which we are able to use *sample statistics* to estimate *population parameters*. We can more formally describe these two terms:

- A **statistic** is a numerical quantity (such as a proportion or average) which summarises some characteristic of a sample.
- A **parameter** is the corresponding value of that characteristic in the population (such as a proportion or average).

We are able to use sample statistics to estimate population parameters because of what is known as the **Central Limit Theorem** (one of the most important theorems in statistics). It was noted earlier that if we take a number of different samples from the same population, it would be unlikely that they would have identical characteristics – either to each other or to the population. These differences are known as the *sampling error*.

Sampling error is not necessarily due to mistakes in the sampling process (if the candidates or elements of a sample do not have an equal chance of being included in the sample then it is called *sampling bias*), since variations can occur due to the chance selection of different elements. For example, if we take a large number of samples from the population and measure the mean value of each sample, then the sample means will not be identical. Some of the sample means will be relatively high, some will be relatively low, and many will cluster around a mean value of all the sample means. These are important characteristics that will now be explored a little further.

7.7.1 Distribution of sample means

The Central Limit Theorem, which is derived from probability, explains why samples vary in the way just described. The Central Limit Theorem says that if random samples of the same size are repeatedly drawn from a population, then the means of those samples will be normally distributed. In addition to this, the means of the sample means will be the same as the population mean. This is shown diagrammatically in Figure 7.8.

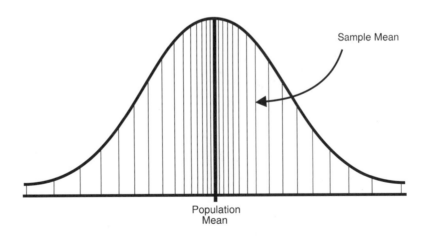

Figure 7.8   Distribution of sample means around the population mean

The statement that the mean of all the sample means equals the population mean can also be shown empirically. Suppose there are five companies and they have the following stock turnover rates (stock turnovers per year):

2   3   6   8   11

The mean of these stock turnover rates is:

$$\mu = \frac{\Sigma X}{N} = \mu = \frac{30}{5} = 6$$

If we now take all possible samples of two companies (there are $\frac{n!}{(n-r)!} = \frac{5!}{(5-2)!} = \frac{5!}{3!} = \frac{120}{6} = 20$ permutations) and list them, as in Table 7.6, we find there are 20 such samples. The means of these samples have been computed and are shown in Table 7.7.

Table 7.6   Twenty equally likely samples of $n = 2$

(2, 3)	(2, 6)	(2, 8)	(2, 11)
(3, 2)	(3, 6)	(3, 8)	(3, 11)
(6, 2)	(6, 3)	(6, 8)	(6, 11)
(8, 2)	(8, 3)	(8, 6)	(8, 11)
(11, 2)	(11, 3)	(11, 6)	(11, 8)

Table 7.7   Sample means

2.5	4	5	6.5
2.5	4.5	5.5	7
4	4.5	7	8.5
5	5.5	7	9.5
6.5	7	8.5	9.5

The mean of these 20 sample means is:

$$\mu_{\overline{X}} = \frac{\Sigma \overline{X}}{N} = \mu_{\overline{X}} = \frac{120}{20} = 6$$

This demonstrates that the mean of all possible sample means equals the population mean. Another way of expressing this is to say that the mean of a sampling distribution equals the population mean.

The variance and standard deviation of the population of five stock turnover rates is:

$$\sigma^2 = \frac{(X-\mu)^2}{N} = \sigma^2 = \frac{(2-6)^2 + (3-6)^2 + (6-6)^2 + (8-6)^2 + (11-6)^2}{5} = \frac{54}{5} = 10.8$$

$$\sigma = \sqrt{\sigma^2} = \sigma = \sqrt{10.8} = 3.29$$

Comparing this to the variance and standard deviation of the sampling distribution (distribution of sample means) we find:

$$\sigma_{\overline{X}}^2 = \frac{(\overline{X}-\mu_{\overline{X}})^2}{N} = \sigma_{\overline{X}}^2 = \frac{(2.5-6)^2 + (4-6)^2 + (5-6)^2 + \ldots\ldots(9.5-6)^2}{20} = \frac{81}{20} = 4.05$$

$$\sigma_{\overline{X}} = \sqrt{\sigma_{\overline{X}}^2} = \sigma_{\overline{X}} = \sqrt{4.05} = 2.01$$

This shows us that:

$$\mu_{\bar{X}} = \mu$$

but that:

$$\sigma_{\bar{X}} \neq \sigma$$

The reason why the standard deviation of the distribution of sample means is less than the standard deviation of the population is simply due to the fact that the sample means are the average of two values, the consequence of which is that the sampling distribution of mean values no longer has the range of values that were in the original 20 samples. However, as we shall shortly demonstrate, it is important that we are able to make an accurate estimate of the standard deviation of the distribution sample means so that we can predict how close a sample mean is to the population mean.

The relationship of the variance (and hence standard deviation) of the distribution of sample means to the variance (and hence standard deviation) of the population is as follows:

$$\sigma_{\bar{X}}^2 = \left(\frac{\sigma^2}{n} \right) \left(\frac{N - n}{N - 1} \right)$$

where N = population size and n = sample size,

$$\sigma_{\bar{X}}^2 = \left(\frac{10.8}{2} \right) \left(\frac{5 - 2}{5 - 1} \right) = 5.4 \times 0.75 = 4.05$$

This shows that the population variance (σ^2) can be used to accurately estimate the distribution of sample means variance ($\sigma_{\bar{X}}^2$). This formula is known as the *finite population correction factor*. It can be shown that as the population size N becomes large relative to the sample size n, the finite population correction factor ratio $(N - n)/(N - 1)$ gets very close to 1, as the following example demonstrates:

$$N = 50, n = 10: \qquad \frac{50 - 10}{50 - 1} = 0.82$$

$$N = 1,000, n = 50: \qquad \frac{1,000 - 50}{1,000 - 1} = 0.95$$

$$N = 10,000, n = 100: \qquad \frac{10,000 - 100}{10,000 - 1} = 0.99$$

This feature enables us to amend the formula slightly for when the population is large relative to the sample size (we no longer need $(N - n)(N - 1)$ when it is very close to 1):

$$\sigma_{\bar{X}}^2 = \frac{\sigma^2}{n}$$

The standard deviation is the square root of the variance, so the standard deviation of the distribution of sample means is:

$$\sqrt{\sigma_{\bar{X}}^2} \quad \text{which is the same as} \quad \sqrt{\frac{\sigma^2}{n}}$$

This standard deviation of the distribution of sample means can be rearranged so that:

$$\sqrt{\frac{\sigma^2}{n}} \quad \text{becomes} \quad \frac{\sigma}{\sqrt{n}}$$

If we are using the finite population correction factor formula the standard deviation of the sample means is:

$$\sqrt{\left(\frac{\sigma^2}{n}\right)\left(\frac{N-n}{N-1}\right)}$$

The standard deviation of the distribution of sample means has been given the special name of the **standard error of the mean**, to distinguish it from other standard deviations Throughout the rest of this text it will be represented as:

$$\sigma_{\bar{X}} = \frac{\sigma}{\sqrt{n}} \quad \text{or} \quad \sigma_{\bar{X}} = \sqrt{\left(\frac{\sigma^2}{n}\right)\left(\frac{N-n}{N-1}\right)}$$

The question we now face is when do we use the $\sigma_{\bar{x}} = \sqrt{\left(\frac{\sigma^2}{n}\right)\left(\frac{N-n}{N-1}\right)}$ formula and when do we use the $\sigma_{\bar{x}} = \frac{\sigma}{\sqrt{n}}$ formula? As a general rule we will use $\sigma_{\bar{x}} = \frac{\sigma}{\sqrt{n}}$ when the population size is at least 20 times the size of the sample size, that is, when the sample size is less than 5 per cent of the population size ($n/N \leqslant .05$). For the example used earlier, $n = 2$ and $N = 5$, consequently $2/5 = .4$, which is more than .05, so we were correct in using the finite population correction factor.

The second important feature of the Central Limit Theorem (the first was that the mean of a distribution of sample means will equal the population mean) relates to the fact that when you take all possible samples of a certain size ($n \geqslant 30$) and plot the means of those samples, you will end up with a normal distribution, regardless of the shape of the original population distribution. Figure 7.9 illustrates the way that various sampling distributions move towards a normal distribution as the sample size is increases, until a normal distribution is reached when the magical sample size of 30 is reached.

Previous chapters have shown that there are certain characteristics when we have a normal distribution, namely that 68.26 per cent of the values lie between ± 1 standard deviations from the mean. It follows from this that for a distribution of sample means, which will conform to a normal distribution as long as the samples consist of 30 items or more (or where samples of less than 30 are drawn from a population that is normally distributed and the population standard deviation σ is

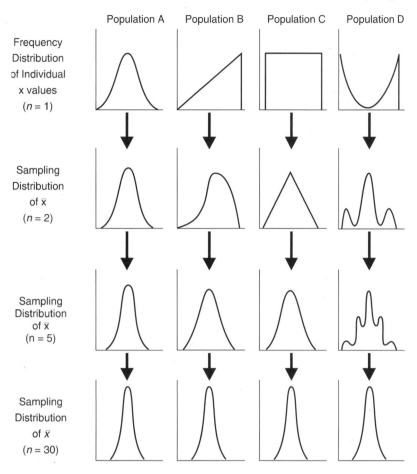

Figure 7.9   Sample size and the movement towards a normal distribution

known – you will always get a normal distribution of sample means, even if the sample size is only two, if the population from which they are derived is normally distributed and σ is known), 68.26 per cent of the sample means will lie between ±1 standard deviations from the population mean. **Put differently, if we take just one sample mean from the total of 20 sample means, we know that it has a 68.26 per cent chance of falling between ±1 standard deviations from the population mean**.

The percentage of values that fall within specified numbers of standard deviations are (as shown in Chapters 4 and 6):

Distance from the mean	Percentage of values falling within distance
$\mu \pm 1\sigma$	68.26
$\mu \pm 2\sigma$	95.44
$\mu \pm 3\sigma$	99.72

It is general practice to talk about 95 per cent and 99 per cent of the values rather than 95.44 per cent and 99.72 per cent, in which case the distances from the mean change from $\mu \pm 2\sigma$ to $\mu \pm 1.96\sigma$ and $\mu \pm 3\sigma$ to $\mu \pm 2.58\sigma$. This being the case, we can talk about a sample mean as having a 95 per cent chance of lying between ± 1.96 standard deviations from the population mean and of having a 99 per cent chance of lying between ± 2.58 standard deviations from the mean.

Clearly, if we can calculate the standard deviation of the distribution of sample means, we will be able to predict, with varying degrees of certainty or confidence, how far our sample mean lies from the population mean. As we have seen, the standard deviation of the distribution of sample means is called the standard error of the mean, and it now enables us to say that we will be:

95 per cent certain or confident that a sample mean is $1.96\sigma_{\bar{x}}$ from μ

99 per cent certain or confident that a sample mean is $2.58\sigma_{\bar{x}}$ from μ

The standard error of the mean formula has the population variance (σ^2) and the population standard deviation (σ) within it, but as we are usually unable to ascertain what the population variance and standard deviation are (because we are only taking a sample!), we use the sample standard deviation instead (when n is large, that is $\geqslant 30$, there is little error incurred by using a sample standard deviation rather than a population standard deviation). As a consequence of this:

$$\sigma_{\bar{X}} = \frac{\sigma}{\sqrt{n}} \quad \text{becomes} \quad \sigma_{\bar{X}} = \frac{s}{\sqrt{n}}$$

This can be demonstrated through the example of a consumer watchdog panel that wanted to know and compare the average time, in days, it takes mail order companies to deliver goods to customers. A random sample of 60 orders are selected from a range of mail order companies, and the sample mean for this set of data is 5.9 days and the sample standard deviation is 1.7 days.

The question we can now ask is, 'How far away do we expect the true population mean to lie from a sample mean of 5.9 when the standard deviation of the sample is 1.7 and the size of the sample is 60?' It can be seen that in this situation the population standard deviation is not known, so we have to use the sample standard deviation instead:

$$\sigma_{\bar{X}} = \frac{s}{\sqrt{n}} = \frac{1.7}{\sqrt{60}} = 0.219$$

Therefore, the population mean has:

a 95 per cent chance of equalling 5.9 days $\pm 1.96 \times 0.219$ days $(\bar{X} \pm 1.96\sigma_{\bar{x}})$, that is, between 5.47 and 6.33 days

Another way of saying this is:

$$\mu = \overline{X} \pm 1.96\,\sigma_{\overline{X}}$$

$$\mu = 5.9 \pm 1.96\,(0.219)$$

$$\mu = 5.9 \pm 0.429 \text{ days}$$

Thus we are 95 per cent sure that the population mean lies somewhere between 5.47 and 6.33 days.

A similar process can be used when we want to be 99 per cent sure of where the population mean lies:

$$\mu = \overline{X} \pm 2.58\,\sigma_{\overline{X}}$$

$$\mu = 5.9 \pm 2.58\,(0.219)$$

$$\mu = 5.9 \pm 0.565 \text{ days}$$

Thus we are 99 per cent sure that the population mean lies somewhere between 5.33 and 6.46 days.

It is worth remembering at this point that a distribution of sample means can be approximated to a normal distribution when:

- the sample size is equal to or greater than 30 ($n \geqslant 30$)
- the sample size is less than 30 ($n < 30$), with the population known or assumed to be normal and the population standard deviation (σ) known

7.7.2 Levels of confidence

The varying degrees of certainty or confidence that we have so far talked about (i.e. 95 per cent and 99 per cent) are called *levels of confidence* (they are also frequently referred to as *confidence limits* and/or *confidence intervals*). As we have seen, these levels tell us the probability of a sample mean being a certain distance from the population mean. Our discussion has tended to describe these levels in terms of percentages, but it is in fact more common to describe them as probabilities, as illustrated in Table 7.8 and Figure 7 10.

When a confidence level is expressed as a probability, it is usually the case that it refers to the probability of a sample mean lying outside the confidence range. In these situations the 5 per cent (.05) or 1 per cent (.01) are called *significance levels*.

Table 7.8 Summary of selected confidence levels

Level	Confidence range (interval)	Probability of sample mean lying within confidence range (interval)	Probability of sample mean lying outside confidence range (interval)
95%	$\mu = \overline{X} \pm 1.96\,\sigma_{\overline{X}}$	0.95	0.05
99%	$\mu = \overline{X} \pm 2.58\,\sigma_{\overline{X}}$	0.99	0.01

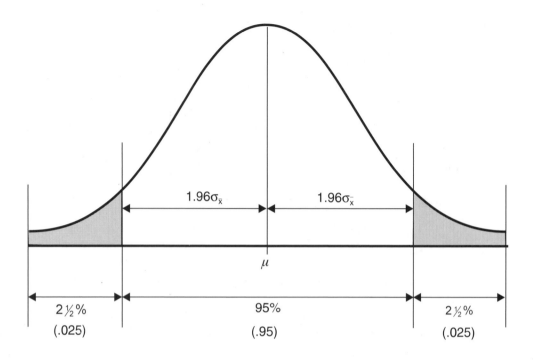

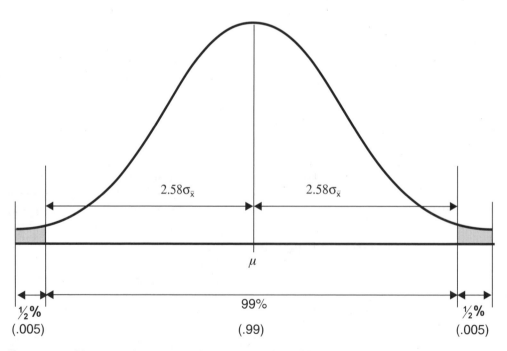

Figure 7.10   Diagrammatic representation of selected confidence levels

For example, the .05 significance level is the one *outside* of which a sample mean has only a 5 in 100 chance of lying. It is worth mentioning at this point that the percentage of values that 1.96 and 2.58 standard deviations represent can be confirmed by looking up the Z values (i.e. standard deviation area values) in Table 5, Appendix 1. For example, the Z value of 1.96 gives an area value of .0250, which is the value from the tail to 1.96. Repeating this for the other tail also gives us .0250. Adding the two values together gives us .05, which when taken away from the total area under the curve provides us with $1 - .05 = .95$.

From our discussion we can now see that the further away a sample mean is from the population mean, the less trust we can place in it. For example, suppose the sample mean lies outside the .01 significance level. What exactly does this tell us about it? It says, in effect, that it only has a 1 in 100 chance of being representative of the population mean. Put differently, that particular sample mean has a 99 in 100 chance of being non-representative.

Competence Example 7.3

At the end of this section you should now be able to demonstrate how to:

1 **recognise a sampling theory type problem**

2 **carry out the necessary calculations**

3 **correctly interpret the results of the analysis**

To practise and demonstrate these competences complete problems 7.5 and 7.6 at the end of this chapter. To help you to develop these competences a description of the procedure you will need to follow is now given, along with a typical problem format. The problem format is based on a problem that is similar to that previously outlined.

PROCEDURE

❶ Formulate the problem.

❷ Calculate the standard error.

❸ Calculate a 95 per cent confidence interval.

❹ Interpret the output of the analysis.

PROBLEM

A snack food vending machine produces a total profit of £1,799 over seven randomly selected months. If the monthly profit from the vending machine is considered to be normally distributed with a standard deviation of £300, what would be a 95 per cent confidence interval for the mean monthly profit from this machine?

SOLUTION FORMAT

❶ The question is asking about the population mean for this particular vending machine. **1** More specifically it is asking what the range or boundaries are within which the population mean lies. It also clearly states that we want to be 95 per cent sure that what we are saying is correct, in which case we are living with a 5 per cent chance of being wrong. This

1 scenario suggests that this is a sampling theory problem and that it entails constructing 95 per cent confidence limits (interval) for the population mean.

2 The mean value has been interpreted to be 1,799/7 = 257 per month.

The standard error formula is:

$$\sigma_{\bar{X}} = \frac{s}{\sqrt{n}} \quad \text{or} \quad \sigma_{\bar{X}} = \sqrt{\left(\frac{\sigma^2}{n}\right)\left(\frac{N-n}{N-1}\right)}$$

As a general rule we will use $\sigma_{\bar{x}} = \frac{s}{\sqrt{n}}$ when the population size is at least 20 times the size of the sample size, that is, when the sample size is less than 5 per cent of the population size ($n/N \leqslant .05$). For the example used earlier, $n = 7$ and $N =$ an unknown number, which can safely be assumed to be three years (156 months). Consequently 7/156 = .04, which is less than .05, so we can use the first of the formulae shown above.

With the sample size being the seven months quoted in the problem, the standard error is:

$$\frac{300}{\sqrt{7}} = \frac{300}{2.646} = 113.38$$

3 The 95 per cent confidence limits (interval) for the population mean can be found as follows:

$$\mu = \bar{X} \pm 1.96\,\sigma_{\bar{X}}$$

$$\mu = 257 \pm 1.96\,(113.38)$$

$$\mu = 257 \pm 222.22$$

Thus we are 95 per cent sure that the population mean lies somewhere between £34.78 and £479.22.

4 The wide width of the confidence interval can be explained by the large standard error when compared to the size of the mean.

Practise your competence now on problems 7.5 and 7.6 at the end of the chapter. The supporting Lotus 1-2-3 or Excel disk will enable you to calculate confidence intervals, and the details on how to operate the package can be found in Chapter two. You may now demonstrate the competence in this area against problems from your own work environment.

7.7.3 Distribution of sample proportions

A proportion can represent any set amount, such as the number of Catholics in a sample or population. A distribution of sample proportions behaves in the same way as a distribution of sample means, in that if you collected all possible samples of a fixed size from the population, and found the mean of all the proportions in those samples (i.e. the proportion that are Catholic), the mean of all those means would equal the population proportion.

If we let P equal the population proportion, $\bar{P}$ equal a sample proportion, and $\mu_{\bar{P}}$ equal the mean of the distribution of sample proportions, we can say that (just as $\mu_{\bar{X}} = \mu$):

$$\mu_{\bar{P}} = P$$

The standard deviation of the distribution of sample proportions, which is referred to as the *standard error of the proportion* again acts like the standard error of the mean, so that (just as $\sigma_{\bar{X}} \neq \sigma$):

$$\sigma_{\bar{P}} \neq \sigma_P$$

When we calculate the standard error of the proportion we can once again use one of two equations, the difference between them being that one uses a finite population correction factor:

$$\sigma_{\bar{P}} = \sqrt{\frac{P(1-P)}{n}} \sqrt{\frac{N-n}{N-1}} \quad \text{or} \quad \sigma_{\bar{P}} = \sqrt{\frac{P(1-P)}{n}}$$

The difference between the two expressions, as with the sample mean, becomes negligible if the size of the population is large compared to the sample size. The rule of thumb also remains the same, the finite population correction factor should be used if $n/N > .05$. When we looked at simple random sampling it was mentioned that a sample of 100 was taken from a population of 400. Testing this we find $100/400 = .25$, which is greater than .05, so the finite population correction factor should be used:

$$\sigma_{\bar{P}} = \sqrt{\frac{P(1-P)}{n}} \sqrt{\frac{N-n}{N-1}} = \sigma_{\bar{P}} = \sqrt{\frac{.5(1-.5)}{100}} \sqrt{\frac{400-100}{400-1}}$$

$$\sigma_{\bar{P}} = \sqrt{.0025} \sqrt{.7519} = .05 \times .867 = .0433$$

where P = population proportion
N = population size
n = sample size

Continuing the comparison of the distribution of sample proportions to the distribution of sample means, we can assume that it conforms to a normal distribution if the sample size is large enough. For the distribution of sample means this was when $n \geqslant 30$; for the distribution of sample proportions it is when the following conditions are met:

$$nP \geqslant 5 \quad \text{and} \quad n(1-P) \geqslant 5$$

For our Catholics example we have $100(.5) = 50$ and $100(.5) = 50$, therefore the sampling distribution of proportions for this set of data can be approximated by a normal distribution.

With this approximation we can once again use the characteristics of the normal distribution to estimate the likely difference between the sample proportion and the population proportion. Using a 95 per cent confidence level, we find:

$$P = \bar{P} \pm 1.96\,\sigma_{\bar{p}}$$

$$P = .5 \pm 1.96\,(.0433)$$

$$P = .5 \pm .085$$

Hence, there is a 95 per cent chance that the population proportion is between .5 ± .085 (i.e. 50 per cent ± 8.5 per cent), that is between .415 and .585. Alternatively, we might prefer to say that the proportion of Catholics is between $(.415 \times 100) = 41.5$ per cent and $(.585 \times 100) = 58.5$ per cent.

It is possible to use any level of confidence, although the 95 per cent confidence level and 99 per cent confidence level are the two that are most frequently used. A summary of these two levels is shown in Table 7.9.

Table 7.9 Summary of selected confidence levels for proportions

Level	Confidence range (interval)	Probability of sample proportion lying within confidence range (interval)	Probability of sample proportion lying outside confidence range (interval)
95%	$\mu = \bar{P} \pm 1.96\,\sigma_{\bar{p}}$	0.95	0.05
99%	$\mu = \bar{P} \pm 2.58\,\sigma_{\bar{p}}$	0.99	0.01

When we looked at the standard error of the mean it was noted that in most situations the standard deviation of the population is unknown, so the standard deviation of the sample is used instead (with very little loss in accuracy):

$$\sigma_{\bar{X}} = \frac{\sigma}{\sqrt{n}} \quad \text{becomes} \quad \sigma_{\bar{X}} = \frac{s}{\sqrt{n}}$$

This very same principle can be applied to the standard error of the proportion:

$$\sigma_{\bar{p}} = \sqrt{\frac{P(1-P)}{n}} \quad \text{becomes} \quad \sigma_{\bar{p}} = \sqrt{\frac{\bar{P}(1-\bar{P})}{n}}$$

Looking at another example, suppose that we collect a random sample of 1,000 electors, and 400 say they will vote Conservative at the next election. Assuming that we have no previous knowledge on the way the electorate vote, how accurate an estimate is this sample proportion with respect to how all electors will vote at the next general election?

Because this sample does not exceed $n/N > .05 (1000/36\,\text{m} = .000027)$ we do not need to use the finite population correction factor. Therefore we can say that:

$$\bar{P} = .4\,(40\%)$$

$$\sigma_{\bar{P}} = \sqrt{\frac{\bar{P}(1 - \bar{P})}{n}} = \sigma_{\bar{P}} = \sqrt{\frac{.4(1 - .4)}{1000}} = \sigma_{\bar{P}} = \sqrt{\frac{.4(.6)}{1000}} = .015$$

At the 95 per cent confidence level, we are therefore sure that the population proportion is:

$$P = \bar{P} \pm 1.96\,\sigma_{\bar{P}}$$

$$P = .4 \pm 1.96\,(.015)$$

$$P = .4 \pm .029 \ \ (\text{i.e. } 40\% \pm 2.94\%)$$

Based upon this sample of data we are 95 per cent confident that between 37.06 per cent and 42.94 per cent of the population will vote Conservative at the next general election.

Competence Example 7.4

At the end of this section you should now be able to demonstrate how to:

1 **recognise a sampling theory type problem**

2 **carry out the necessary calculations**

3 **correctly interpret the results of the analysis**

To practise and demonstrate these competences complete problems 7.7 and 7.8 at the end of this chapter. To help you to develop these competences a description of the procedure you will need to follow is now given, along with a typical problem format. The problem format is based on a problem that is similar to that previously outlined.

PROCEDURE

❶ Formulate the problem.

❷ Calculate the standard error.

❸ Calculate a 99 per cent confidence interval.

❹ Interpret the output of the analysis.

PROBLEM

Fruity Bars is considering withdrawing its Crispy Bar product from the market if it has not captured at least 5 per cent of the snack bar market. A random sample of 250 snack bar buyers was taken, of which ten bought Crispy Bars. Find the 99 per cent confidence limits (interval) for the proportion of the population of snack bar buyers who choose Crispy Bars.

A description of the layout of the solution format is given at the beginning of the book.

SOLUTION FOMAT

❶ The question is asking what proportion of the population of snack bar buyers buy the Crispy Bar product. More specifically, it is asking what the boundaries are within which the population proportion lies. It also clearly states that we want to be 99 per cent sure that what we are saying is correct, in which case we are living with a 1 per cent chance of being wrong. This scenario suggests that this is a sampling theory problem and that it entails constructing 99 per cent confidence limits (interval) for the population proportion.

The sample proportion within the problem is:

$$\bar{P} = .04 \ (4\%)$$

❷ The standard error formula is either:

$$\sigma_{\bar{p}} = \sqrt{\frac{\bar{P}(1 - \bar{P})}{n}} \ \text{or} \ = \sigma_{\bar{p}} = \sqrt{\frac{P(1 - P)}{n}} \sqrt{\frac{N - n}{N - 1}}$$

Because this sample does not exceed $n/N > .05$ ($10/250 = .04$) we do not need to use the finite population correction factor. Therefore we can say that:

$$\sigma_{\bar{p}} = \sqrt{\frac{\bar{P}(1 - \bar{P})}{n}} = \sigma_{\bar{p}} = \sqrt{\frac{.04(1 - .04)}{250}} = \sigma_{\bar{p}} = \sqrt{\frac{.04(.96)}{250}} = .0124$$

❸ At the 99 per cent confidence level, we are therefore sure that the population proportion is:

$$P = \bar{P} \pm 2.58 \sigma_{\bar{p}}$$

$$P = .04 \pm 2.58(0.0124)$$

$$P = .04 \pm .032 \ (\text{i.e. } 4\% \pm 3.2\%)$$

❹ Based upon this sample of data we are 99 per cent confident that the proportion of buyers who will purchase Crispy Bars will be between 0.8 per cent and 7.2 per cent of the snack bar population. This may mean that Fruity Bars will pull out of this market because there is a high probability that it has less than 5 per cent of the market.

Practise your competence now on problems 7.7 and 7.8 at the end of the chapter. The supporting Lotus 1-2-3 or Excel disk will enable you to calculate confidence intervals, and the details on how to operate the package can be found in Chapter 2. You may now demonstrate the competence in this area against problems from your own work environment.

7.7.4 *t* Distributions

The discussion on the way that we can estimate limits within which a population mean or proportion lies, using confidence levels, relies upon the known characteristics of a normal distribution. A sampling distribution will approximate a normal distribution when $n \geqslant 30$, but what happens when the sample size is less than 30 ($n < 30$)?

The 95 per cent confidence level (interval) is situated at ±1.96 standard deviations or standard errors from the mean of the population. It was pointed out earlier that the standard deviations value of 1.96 was taken from the Z values in Table 5, Appendix 1 (a Z score of 1.96 equates to an area or probability value of 95 per cent). Yet this table can only be used, of course, when the distribution of sample means is normal. If the distribution is not normal then the 95 per cent confidence level (or if you prefer, the 0.05 significance level) will not be located at a Z score of ±1.96. This is important because as samples become smaller ($n < 30$), their distributions become flatter and more spread out than a normal distribution (*see* Figure 7.11). These non-normal distributions are called *Student t distributions* after W. S. Gosset, a statistician who worked in the Guinness brewery and who published under the pen name of 'Student'.

There are, as shown in Figure 7.11, a range of distinct and separate *t* distributions. In fact there is a *t* distribution for every size of sample. When we want to set a confidence level for a *t* distribution (such as the 95 per cent confidence level) it is necessary to move further out in standard deviation units

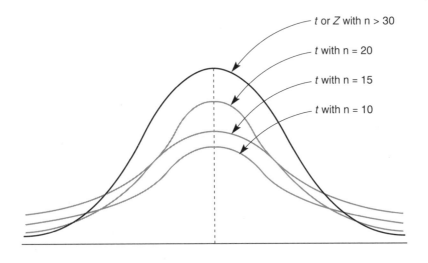

Figure 7.11 Comparison of the normal distribution to *t* distributions

from the mean than was the case for a normal distribution. This is illustrated in Figure 7.12.

Before we look at how we use the *t* distributions it is perhaps appropriate that we outline, more specifically, when a *t* distribution can be used. It should be used when:

- the population is assumed to be normal
- the sample is small ($n < 30$)
- the population standard deviation (σ) is unknown (if it is known we can use the normal distribution approximation)

The way we use the *t* distributions is similar to the way we used the normal distribution. In a normal distribution, the distance between the mean and any point away from the mean, measured in standard deviation units, is expressed as a *Z* value, and this is used to estimate areas under the normal distribution. In a *t* distribution, the distance between the mean and successive points, measured in standard deviation units, is expressed as a *t* value. For a given sample size this *t*

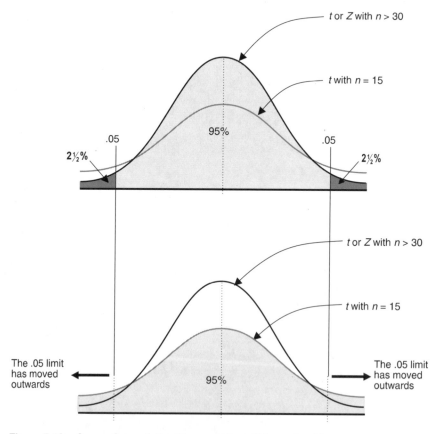

Figure 7.12 Comparison of the 95 per cent confidence level in a normal and *t* distribution

value can be used to estimate the area between a particular point and the mean. A set of t values for different levels of confidence is provided in Table 3, Appendix 1. A portion of these t values is shown in Table 7.10, and to use this table it is necessary to decide on the level of confidence you wish to use and the number of *degrees of freedom* associated with the sample size you are using.

Table 7.10 Portion of t distribution table

Degrees of freedom	Level of significance for one-tailed test				
	0.10	0.05	0.025	0.01	0.005
	Level of significance for two-tailed test				
	0.20	0.10	0.05	0.02	0.01
6	1.440	1.943	2.447	3.143	3.707
7	1.415	1.895	2.365	2.998	3.499
8	1.397	1.860	2.306	2.896	3.355
9	1.383	1.833	2.262	2.821	3.250
10	1.372	1.812	2.228	2.764	3.169
11	1.363	1.796	2.201	2.718	3.106
12	1.356	1.782	2.179	2.681	3.055
13	1.350	1.771	2.160	2.650	3.012
14	1.345	1.761	2.145	2.624	2.977
15	1.341	1.753	2.131	2.602	2.947

In estimating the population mean from a sample mean the degrees of freedom are found by using $n-1$, where n equals the number of items in the sample. For example, if we wanted to establish the 0.05 level of confidence for the mean of a population when the sample size is 12, then we enter the table at 11 degrees of freedom $(12-1=11)$ and at the 0.05 confidence level, to find the t value of 2.201. We can conclude from this that when sample sizes are 12, we can expect 95 per cent of the sample means to lie between ± 2.201 standard deviations from the population mean. This is represented diagrammatically in Figure 7.13.

When we looked at the distribution of sample means and proportions it was shown that when the standard error is determined, it becomes possible to calculate confidence limits within which the population mean or proportion lies. Following exactly the same logic, once we have determined the standard error of a small sample $(n < 30)$ it is possible to estimate limits within which the population mean lies. Looking at the 95 per cent confidence level we find that expression changes from:

$$\mu = \overline{X} \pm 1.96 \sigma_{\overline{X}} \quad \text{to} \quad \mu = \overline{X} \pm (t)(s_{\overline{X}})$$

Notice that instead of multiplying 1.96 (95 per cent) by the standard error of the mean $(\sigma_{\bar{X}})$ we now multiply the appropriate t value by the sample estimate of the standard error of the mean $(s_{\bar{X}})$. The standard error formula therefore changes from:

$$\sigma_{\bar{X}} = \frac{\sigma}{\sqrt{n}} \quad \text{to} \quad s_{\bar{X}} = \frac{s}{\sqrt{n}}$$

because the population standard deviation is unknown (so we use the sample standard deviation instead)[*].

For example, with a sample size of 12, and working to 95 per cent confidence limits, we have:

$$0.05 \ (95\%) \text{ confidence interval} = \mu = \bar{X} \pm (2.201)(s_{\bar{X}})$$

With a sample standard deviation value of 8, we find that the standard error becomes:

$$s_{\bar{X}} = \frac{s}{\sqrt{n}} = s_{\bar{X}} = \frac{8}{\sqrt{12}} = s_{\bar{X}} = 2.309$$

If the mean of the sample had been 45 the confidence limits are:

$$0.05 \ (95\%) \text{ confidence interval} = \mu = 45 \pm (2.201)(2.309)$$
$$0.05 \ (95\%) \text{ confidence interval} = \mu = 45 \pm 5.08$$

Consequently we are 95 per cent sure that the population mean lies between 39.92 and 50.08.

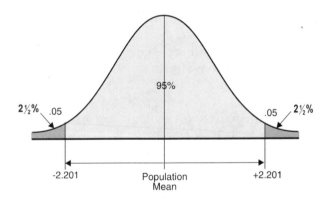

Figure 7.13 *t* distribution for a sample size of 12 and a 95 per cent confidence level

---

[*] This is distinguishable from the standard error of the mean formula that also uses the sample standard deviation rather than the population standard deviation $\left(\sigma_{\bar{X}} = \frac{s}{\sqrt{n}} \right)$ because of the fact that it is dealing with samples of less than 30 ($n < 30$).

The same procedure can be used for estimating 99 per cent confidence levels, with the only difference being that the t value from the table changes from 2.201 to 3.106:

$$0.01 \ (99\%) \ \text{confidence interval} = \mu = 45 \pm (3.106)(2.309)$$
$$0.01 \ (99\%) \ \text{confidence interval} = \mu = 45 \pm 7.17$$

Consequently we are 99 per cent sure that the population mean lies between 37.83 and 52.17.

Competence Example 7.5

At the end of this section you should now be able to demonstrate how to:

1 recognise a sampling theory type problem

2 carry out the necessary calculations

3 correctly interpret the results of the analysis

To practise and demonstrate these competences complete problems 7.9 and 7.10 at the end of this chapter. To help you to develop these competences a description of the procedure you will need to follow is now given, along with a typical problem format. The problem format is based on a problem that is similar to that previously outlined.

PROCEDURE

1 Formulate the problem.

2 Identify and use an appropriate t value.

3 Calculate the standard error.

4 Calculate a 95 per cent confidence interval.

5 Interpret the output of the analysis.

PROBLEM

If the mean life of nine car batteries is 50 months, with a standard deviation of eight months, what is the confidence interval (working at the 95 per cent confidence level) for the mean life of all car batteries?

SOLUTION FORMAT

❶ This is a clearly stated problem, and it differs from Competence Examples 7.3 and 7.4 **1** only in the fact that it is dealing with a sample of less than 30. This suggests that this is a t distribution type problem. More specifically, we are saying that it satisfies the following conditions:

- the population is assumed to be normal
- the sample is small ($n < 30$)
- the population standard deviation (σ) is unknown (if it is known we can use the normal distribution approximation)

❷ ❹ The formula for finding a 95 per cent confidence interval for a population mean is: **2**

$$\mu = \bar{X} \pm (t)(s_{\bar{x}})$$

The appropriate t value can be found in Table 3, Appendix 1, a portion of which is shown in Table 7.11. With $n - 1$ degrees of freedom ($9 - 1 = 8$), working at the 95 per cent confidence level (0.05 significance level) we find that the t table value is 2.306.

❷ **Table 7.11 Portion of t distribution table** **2**

Degrees of freedom	Level of significance for one-tailed test				
	0.10	0.05	0.025	0.01	0.005
	Level of significance for two-tailed test				
	0.20	0.10	0.05	0.02	0.01
6	1.440	1.943	2.447	3.143	3.707
7	1.415	1.895	2.365	2.998	3.499
8	1.397	1.860	2.306	2.896	3.355
9	1.383	1.833	2.262	2.821	3.250
10	1.372	1.812	2.228	2.764	3.169

❸ The standard error is:

$$s_{\bar{x}} = \frac{s}{\sqrt{n}} = s_{\bar{x}} = \frac{8}{\sqrt{9}} = s_{\bar{x}} = 2.67$$

❹ At the 95 per cent confidence level we are therefore sure that the population mean is:

$$\mu = \bar{X} \pm (t)(s_{\bar{x}})$$

$$\mu = 50 \pm (2.306)(2.67)$$

$$\mu = 50 \pm 6.16$$

❺ Based upon the sample data we are therefore 95 per cent sure that the mean life of a **❸**
battery is between 43.84 months and 56.16 months.

Practise your competence now on problems 7.9 and 7.10 at the end of the chapter. The supporting Lotus 1-2-3 or Excel disk will enable you to calculate confidence limits, and the details on how to operate the package can be found in Chapter 2. You may now demonstrate the competence in this area against problems from your own work environment.

7.7.5 Altering the width of the confidence interval

The size of the confidence interval (or if you prefer, the confidence limits) reflects the range within which we expect the population mean to lie. If we can narrow the width of the confidence interval then we can get a closer estimate of where the population mean lies. To narrow the confidence interval we can either *decrease the level of confidence* or *increase the sample size*.

When the confidence level is lowered (say from 99 per cent to 95 per cent), the confidence interval is reduced. This can be demonstrated by referring back to the consumer watchdog panel example, where we found that:

For 95 per cent confidence limits

$$\mu = \overline{X} \pm 1.96\sigma_{\overline{X}}$$

$$\mu = 5.9 \pm 1.96(0.219)$$

$$\mu = 5.9 \pm 0.429 \text{ days}$$

Thus we are 95 per cent sure that the population mean lies somewhere between 5.47 and 6.33 days. For 99 per cent confidence limits:

$$\mu = \overline{X} \pm 2.58\sigma_{\overline{X}}$$

$$\mu = 5.9 \pm 2.58(0.219)$$

$$\mu = 5.9 \pm 0.565 \text{ days}$$

Thus we are 99 per cent sure that the population mean lies somewhere between 5.33 and 6.46 days.

It can be seen from this example that if we reduced the confidence limits from 99 per cent to 95 per cent we would reduce the confidence interval from ±0.565 days to ±0.429 days, a reduction of ±0.136 days. This reduction has, of course, been at the cost of the level of confidence we have in the estimate itself. So although the confidence interval has been reduced by ±0.136 days our confidence in it has been reduced by 4 per cent. The chance of our estimate being wrong has consequently increased from 1 per cent to 5 per cent.

When the confidence interval needs to be reduced with no reduction in the level of confidence then it is necessary to increase the sample size. This is hardly surprising when we consider that as the sample gets larger it gets closer to the size of the population, which in turn means that the sample statistic (e.g. a sample mean or sample proportion) gets closer to the population parameter (e.g. a population mean or population proportion). Looking at the previous example, the consumer watchdog panel was based on a sample of 60 orders, with the 99 per cent confidence limits being ±0.565 days. To reduce the confidence interval while maintaining the level of confidence involves increasing the sample size. If we increase the sample size to 500 orders the standard error will be reduced:

$$\sigma_{\bar{X}} = \frac{s}{\sqrt{n}} = \frac{1.7}{\sqrt{60}} = 0.219$$

$$\sigma_{\bar{X}} = \frac{s}{\sqrt{n}} = \frac{1.7}{\sqrt{500}} = 0.076$$

Applying the reduced standard error to the confidence interval expression has the following effect:

$$\mu = \bar{X} \pm 2.58\sigma_{\bar{x}} \qquad\qquad \mu = \bar{X} \pm 2.58\sigma_{\bar{x}}$$

$$\mu = 5.9 \pm 2.58(0.219) \qquad \mu = 5.9 \pm 2.58(0.076)$$

$$\mu = 5.9 \pm 0.565 \text{ days} \qquad \mu = 5.9 \pm 0.196 \text{ days}$$

It can be seen that to reduce the confidence interval from ±0.565 to ±0.196 (a reduction of 0.369) has necessitated increasing the sample size from 60 to 500. The increase in sample size would increase costs, so it is usually a compromise between the level of accuracy you would like and the amount of money you can afford to spend.

7.7.6 Determining sample size

The main factor that determines sample size is the amount of error that can be tolerated (remembering that the 'error' is the difference between the sample statistic and the population proportion). Suppose that we were measuring the mean weight of cans of beans, and took a sample of 100 cans and found the mean weight to be 15 ounces, with a standard deviation of two ounces. The 95 per cent confidence limits for this would therefore be:

$$\sigma_{\bar{X}} = \frac{s}{\sqrt{n}} = \frac{2}{\sqrt{100}} = 0.2$$

$$\mu = \bar{X} \pm 1.96\sigma_{\bar{x}}$$

$$\mu = 15 \pm 1.96(0.2)$$

$$\mu = 15 \pm 0.392 \text{ ounces}$$

If we were unhappy with the range within which the population mean could lie (14.608 ounces to 15.392 ounces), and therefore stated that we wanted to be 95 per cent sure that the population mean was within ±0.1 ounces of the sample mean, then the sample size would have to increase to provide this level of accuracy. Looking at the example below, we can see that it is the size of the standard error which determines the size of the confidence interval, and that the standard error can only be reduced by increasing the sample size. Restating this, to obtain 95 per cent confidence limits of ±0.1 ounces would require a standard error of:

$$\mu = 15 \pm 1.96(?) \qquad \therefore\ 1.96/0.1 = 0.051 \qquad \mu = 15 \pm 1.96(0.051)$$

$$\mu = 15 \pm 0.1\ \text{ounces} \qquad\qquad\qquad \mu = 15 \pm 0.1\ \text{ounces}$$

With the standard error determined for a confidence interval of ±0.1 ounces, we can determine the required sample size:

$$\text{if}\quad \sigma_{\bar{X}} = \frac{s}{\sqrt{n}} \quad \text{then}\quad 0.051 = \frac{2}{\sqrt{n}} \quad \text{in which case}\quad n = (2/0.051)^2 = 1{,}538$$

To reduce the error to 0.1 ounces at the 95 per cent confidence level has therefore required us to increase the sample size from 100 to 1,538.

An alternative and equivalent way of determining the sample size is to use the following:

$$n = \frac{(CL^2)(s^2)}{L^2}$$

Where CL = confidence level
s = sample standard deviation
L = the required level of accuracy

therefore

$$n = \frac{(1.96^2)(2^2)}{0.1^2}$$

$$n = \frac{(3.84)(4)}{0.01} \cong 1538$$

The same type of procedure can be used for determining sample sizes for proportions. In a previous example it was stated that 400 out of 1,000 voters would vote Conservative at the next election, and that the 95 per cent confidence limits for this were:

$$\bar{P} = .4 \ (40\%)$$

$$\sigma_{\bar{p}} = \sqrt{\frac{\bar{P}(1-\bar{P})}{n}} = \sigma_{\bar{p}} = \sqrt{\frac{.4(1-.4)}{1,000}} = \sigma_{\bar{p}} = \sqrt{\frac{.4(.6)}{1,000}} = .015$$

$$P = \bar{P} \pm 1.96\sigma_{\bar{p}}$$

$$P = .4 \pm 1.96\,(.015)$$

$$P = .4 \pm .029 \ (\text{i.e. } 40\% \pm 2.94\%)$$

If we now wanted to reduce the error from 2.94 per cent to 1 per cent we need to increase the sample size. With a 1 per cent error we find (notice that we have changed the 1 to 100 in the formula so that we can express the numbers as percentages)

$$CL = \sqrt{\frac{\bar{P}(100 - \bar{P})}{n}} = 1$$

Squaring and transposing this provides us with:

$$n = (CL^2\bar{P})(100 - \bar{P})$$

$$n = (1.96^2 \times 40)(100 - 40)$$

$$n = (153.66)(60) = 9,220$$

An equivalent way to determine the sample size is to use:

$$n = \frac{(CL^2\bar{P})(100 - \bar{P})}{L^2}$$

$$n = \frac{(1.96^2 \times 40)(60)}{1^2}$$

$$n = \frac{(153.66)(60)}{1} \cong 9,220$$

As can be seen, to increase the accuracy of the sample estimate from 2.94 per cent to 1 per cent we need to increase the sample size from 1,000 to 9,220. The balance between accuracy and cost is therefore an important consideration, and careful consideration should be given to it.

The procedure for finding the sample size for a proportion requires that we have an estimate of the sample proportion ($\bar{P}$). One way of finding the sample proportion is to take a small pre-sample so that we can identify a preliminary estimate for $\bar{P}$. This can then be used in conjunction with the required level of accuracy and confidence level to determine the sample size. An alternative approach is to assume that $\bar{P} = 50$ per cent, since the maximum sample size occurs when $\bar{P} = 50$ per cent, as the following demonstrates:

If $\overline{P} = 50\%$ then

$n = (CL^2 2\overline{P})(100 - \overline{P})$

$n = (1.96^2 \times 50)(100 - 50)$

$n = (192.08)(50) = 9,604$

If $\overline{P} = 65\%$ then

$n = (1.96^2 \times 65)(100 - 65)$

$n = (249.70)(35) = 8,739$

If $\overline{P} = 30\%$ then

$n = (1.96^2 \times 30)(100 - 30)$

$n = (115.25)(70) = 3,457$

As can be seen, the largest sample size occurs when $\overline{P} = 50$ per cent, which ensures that the sample size is not less than that required for any given level of accuracy. The problem with doing this is that we might be carrying out a much larger survey than is actually needed.

Competence Example 7.6

At the end of this section you should now be able to demonstrate how to:

1 **recognise a sampling theory type problem**

2 **carry out the necessary calculations**

3 **correctly interpret the results of the analysis**

To practise and demonstrate these competences complete problems 7.11 and 7.12 at the end of this chapter. To help you to develop these competences a description of the procedure you will need to follow is now given, along with a typical problem format. The problem format is based on a problem that is similar to that previously outlined.

PROCEDURE

1 Formulate the problem.

2 Use an appropriate sample size formula.

3 Interpret the output of the analysis.

PROBLEM

A manufacturer of microcomputers purchases electronic chips from a supplier that claims its chips are defective only 5 per cent of the time. Determine the sample size that would be required to estimate the true proportion of defective chips if we wanted our estimate of the proportion defective to be within 1.25 per cent of the true proportion, with a 99 per cent level of confidence.

SOLUTION FORMAT

❶ This problem is concerned with finding a sample size for a proportion such that the estimate does not differ from the true population proportion by more than 1.25 per cent. Furthermore, the problem explicitly states that the estimate should have no more than a 1 per cent chance of being wrong (99 per cent confidence level). An appropriate formula for determining a sample size at a required level of accuracy is: **1**

❷

$$n = \frac{(CL^2 \bar{P})(100 - \bar{P})}{L^2}$$

$$n = \frac{(2.58^2 \times 5)(95)}{1.25^2}$$

$$n = \frac{(33.28)(95)}{1.56} \cong 2023$$

2

❸ The problem does not mention previous sample sizes, but as can be seen, to have a level of accuracy of 1.25 at the 95 per cent confidence level does require a large sample. **3**

Practise your competence now on problems 7.11 and 7.12 at the end of the chapter. The supporting Lotus 1-2-3 or Excel disk will enable you to calculate sample sizes, and the details on how to operate the package can be found in Chapter 2. You may now demonstrate the competence in this area against problems from your own work environment.

Summary

Chapter 7 has outlined one of the most important areas of quantitative management. It has purposely brought together survey design, sampling methods and sampling theory, as they are closely linked in many practical areas of business. Many new ideas have been introduced, such as the Central Limit Theorem and the way that we can use confidence levels in a variety of situations.

Although the content of Chapter 7 may at first appear daunting, it is worth persevering because of its importance within both quantitative management and other areas and disciplines generally.

The competences that have been gained in this chapter are directly transferable to most organisations, and the Lotus 1-2-3 and Excel disk provided can be used on the sampling theory side of Chapter 7 and your own company's data. The following exercises provide an opportunity for you to practise and demonstrate these competences, but again they are no substitute for the data that needs analysing in your organisation.

Problems for Chapter 7

7.1 It is very difficult to phrase unbiased questions on emotionally charged issues. Assume that you want to study people's opinions on abortion – more precisely, that you are interested in the circumstances in which people would permit abortion. What are the most basic types of circumstances that should be included in a question? (There are a large number of distinct alternatives, so concentrate on a few major types.) How would you phrase a closed-ended question on this topic?

7.2 Assume that you are an expert in survey research and that you have been asked to evaluate the following survey results:

a. A survey of sixth-formers concluded that the majority of young people experiment with drugs.
b. A poll shows that 75 per cent of British people favour the pulling out of British troops from trouble spots around the world.
c. A survey of Members of Parliament shows that a majority believe they should follow the wishes of their constituents rather than their own attitudes when the two are in conflict.

What would you question about these studies?

7.3 Your organisation has recently introduced a productivity-related bonus scheme and wishes to determine the attitude of the workforce to the new scheme. The personnel department has supplied the following breakdown of workers, by their sex and level of skill:

	Men	Women
Unskilled	734	1,473
Semi-skilled	1,426	1,075
Skilled	2,897	500

Design a sampling scheme to obtain a sample of 500 people taking special care to ensure that the sample is representative of all sections of the workforce.

7.4 A random sample is desirable in each of the four situations listed below. Should a simple random sample, stratified random sample, cluster/area sample or systematic sample be used in each case? Would you recommend a combination of sampling methods? Explain your reasons.

  a. An airline operates 50 flights a week from London to Paris. It wants to know how its passengers feel about the quality of the meals served on this flight sector.
  b. A lecturer wants to know the average number of years of work experience of the students in an MBA evening class. Apart from the class register, the lecturer has no other information on the students.
  c. You want to predict who will be elected as the next parliamentary MP for your constituency.
  d. As part of a marketing survey you are asked to interview members of households. You are told to sample 10 per cent of the homes on a long street, and there are ten such identical streets.

7.5 A sample of 36 tyres from a manufacturer lasted an average of 18,000 miles, with a standard deviation of 1,200 miles. What are the 95 per cent confidence limits for the average life of all tyres supplied by the manufacturer?

7.6 36 samples of a new yarn are tested to breaking point. The average breaking strength is 30 lb with a standard deviation of 4 lb. Calculate 95 per cent and 99 per cent confidence limits for the true average breaking strength of the yarn.

7.7 A random sample of 400 rail passengers is taken and 55 per cent are in favour of proposed new timetables. With 95 per cent confidence, what proportion of all rail passengers are in favour of the timetables?

7.8 A large high street retailer is going to float a new stock issue. Law requires that current stockholders be given the first opportunity to buy any new issue. Management feels that 45 per cent of current stockholders will want to make a purchase. A random sample of 130 stockholders are selected, 63 of whom express a desire to buy. In the light of this information, are management right in their assumption that 45 per cent will purchase?

7.9 The price per month of back orders at Yates Industries is beginning to cause concern to management. A random sample of three randomly selected months yields a mean of £115,320 with a standard deviation of £35,000. Construct a 95 per cent confidence interval for the mean price of back orders per month at Yates Industries.

7.10 An ambulance station is looking at its response times and takes a sample of 16 call outs, and finds that the mean response time was 17 minutes with a standard deviation of five minutes. What are the 99 per cent confidence limits for the mean response time of all call outs?

7.11 In order to evaluate the success of a television advertising campaign for a new product, a company interviewed 400 residents in the television area. 120 of them knew about the product. How accurately does this estimate the percentage of residents in the area who know about the product? How many more interviews must be made in order to establish this percentage to an accuracy of ±2 per cent at the 95 per cent confidence level?

7.12 The average IQ of a sample of 30 MBA students is 120, with a standard deviation of ten. How accurately does this estimate the average IQ of all the MBA students?

How many more students must be stated in order to ensure that the estimate is not more than two points out with 99 per cent confidence?

8 Statements and beliefs

how confident can we be?

8.1 Introduction

Managers frequently have to use their judgement when they make decisions. This often rests on the beliefs which the manager has on the way that an activity or process is proceeding. Although these beliefs are frequently subjective and personal to the individual, they can often be tested in the workplace. The area in statistics and management science which deals with this type of subject matter is 'hypothesis testing', and it has many potential applications. An important aspect or extension of hypothesis testing is the *chi-square technique*, and this will also be looked at in this chapter. The idea of significance testing was introduced in Chapter 7 and it will be extensively used in hypothesis testing and chi-square analysis, as it enables us to test the strength of our beliefs. The general area of hypothesis testing provides a conceptual framework that managers may well find useful when they are faced with difficult issues, problems and decisions within the workplace.

The process of developing an idea or hypothesis and then testing it is also fundamental to quantitative modelling. Chapter 1 provided an introduction to the modelling process, and this will now be extended by incorporating hypothesis formulation and testing. This chapter is therefore concerned with developing a competence in developing a hypothesis and testing it to a known degree of accuracy. It also provides the foundation upon which much management research is based. By the end of this chapter you should be able to demonstrate how to:

- formulate a range of hypotheses
- test a range of hypotheses
- appreciate how hypothesis formulation and testing underpins much of management research
- recognise the main problems associated with hypothesis formulation and interpretation

The chapter will also use a series of practical examples to develop the underpinning knowledge in the area of hypothesis formulation and testing. At the end of the chapter the required competence will be specified and described. A typical problem format with the competences highlighted will also be given to help you demonstrate the competences on the problems at the end of the chapter. At the end of the book a full solution will be given for the first of these problems as well as answers for the rest.

8.2　A way of thinking

Many people flinch at the term 'scientific method', associating it with the sterile and dry collection of data and some obscure method of proving or disproving a theory or statement of some kind. In reality the scientific method has been at the centre of many technological, scientific and psychological developments of the twentieth century. In its broadest sense, scientific method is the setting up and observation of acceptable intellectual standards for rational argument. It is quite possible to follow and observe these standards without collecting large quantities of data and indulging in detailed and sophisticated types of analysis (philosophical debate that rests on the formulation of ideas, constructs and logical argument has been tremendously powerful and productive over the centuries). If this is the case, why do we need quantification and what purpose can it serve?

One line of argument for the use of a quantitative approach is that it forces us to think logically and consistently, a trait that lapses for most people from time to time. Many managers have an intuitive grasp of the scientific method, and although they may use it very constructively, it could be argued that this can be sharpened and refined by a formal analysis of it. A detailed analysis of rational explanation and methodology is beyond the scope of this book, but it is worth pointing out that the sharpest tools within science are mathematics and statistics. Although these tools often get misapplied in management, and there is a widespread lack of understanding of the philosophical and methodological assumptions upon which their use necessarily rests, they can nevertheless be used constructively and creatively, especially in the formulation and testing of hypotheses.

Most scientists regard a hypothesis as being a proposition whose truth or falsity is capable of being tested. Once the truth or falsity of the proposition has been determined the proposition becomes a true or false statement. For example, the hypothesis that Glasgow is north of London can be determined to be true or false by reference to an atlas. The process of proof may well involve collecting evidence (data), and it is against this backdrop that the principles and process of hypothesis testing in management will be explored.

8.3　Hypothesis testing

Part of Chapter 7 was concerned with providing boundaries within which the population proportion or population mean lay. A slightly different approach is to state a hypothesis about the population and then to collect a sample of data and test it to see if the hypothesis is true or not. As has been indicated, a hypothesis in business and management is a statement or belief that is capable of being tested to see if it is true or not. The process can be best explained through an example.

An ambulance service that operates within a large rural and urban region has set itself the goal of responding to emergency calls within a mean time of 15 minutes or less. There has been heated debate within the ambulance service on this performance measure, with some members arguing that the response time was already being achieved. In response to this the senior officer of the service requested that a study be undertaken to determine if the ambulance service was meeting its 15 minutes or less response goal.

8.3.1 Null and alternative hypotheses

The question that is being asked can be looked at from a hypothesis testing point of view. The general hypothesis being stated would concern whether the ambulance service was meeting its response goal or not. Being a little more precise, the procedure we would follow in hypothesis testing would involve stating a *null hypothesis* and an *alternative hypothesis*. The null hypothesis is normally designated by H_0 and it is frequently an initial assumption that no change has occurred. For instance, in testing a new drug it would be assumed that it was no different from current drugs in use. The onus of proof must therefore rest with disproving the null hypothesis – we have to prove beyond reasonable doubt that the drug is better before we can reject the null hypothesis. This replicates the situation in a courtroom, where the proof of evidence rests with the prosecution, in that the accused is innocent unless guilt can be proved beyond reasonable doubt. The alternative hypothesis is designated by H_a and it will be accepted if we reject the null hypothesis. In a courtroom the null hypothesis would be that the accused is innocent and the alternative hypothesis would be that the accused is guilty, but we would only accept the alternative hypothesis if the null hypothesis was proved beyond all reasonable doubt.

8.3.2 Type I and Type II errors

When a hypothesis is tested it is possible to draw both correct and incorrect interpretations from the analysis. The four types of statements and decisions that can be made in hypothesis testing are shown in Table 8.1.

The probability of making a Type I error, designated by alpha (α), actually represents a level of significance. In common with Chapter 7, it is normal practice to have either a 1 per cent or 5 per cent chance of making a Type I error (i.e. .01 or .05 significance level). The level of risk that these alpha values represent is an important aspect of the testing procedure and they should therefore be explicitly stated. The probability of making a Type II error is more difficult to calculate, as we need the true population parameter (remembering that we only have a sample of data on

Table 8.1 Correct and incorrect decisions in hypothesis testing

Statement	Decision
We accept a true hypothesis	Correct decision
We reject a false hypothesis	Correct decision
We reject a true hypothesis (*this is known as a Type I error – designated by α*)	Incorrect decision
We accept a false hypothesis (*this is known as a Type II error – designated by β*)	Incorrect decision

which to test our hypothesis). A Type II error is where we accept H_0 when in fact it is false, and because of the difficulty involved in its calculation it is recommended by many statisticians that it is wiser to say 'do not reject H_0' instead of 'accept H_0' – never directly concluding that H_0 is true stops us making a Type II error! This conservatism has, in the main, been disregarded through the rest of the chapter.

8.3.3 Developing a decision rule

If we let μ equal the mean response time for all emergency trips that the ambulance service carries out, then it is possible to develop the decision rules shown in Table 8.2.

Table 8.2 Decision rules for emergency ambulance service

Possible outcome	Conclusion and action
$\mu > 15$	Trip time exceeds target mean response time; follow-up action needed to improve response time
$\mu = 15$	Trip time equals the target mean response time; no action required
$\mu < 15$	Trip time is less than target mean response time; no action required

The hypothesis for the ambulance service can now be formally stated and it includes a null and alternative hypothesis and their respective decision rules:

Hypothesis	*Conclusion and action*
H_0: $\mu \leqslant 15$	Ambulance service meeting response goal; no action needed
H_a: $\mu > 15$	Ambulance service not meeting the response goal; corrective action needed

Once the hypothesis has been formulated the data can be collected and the null hypothesis tested. The ambulance service took a random sample of 60 emergency calls and found that the mean response time was 16.7 minutes, with a standard deviation of 4.5 minutes.

As can be seen, the sample mean of 16.7 minutes exceeds the target response time of 15 minutes, so do we reject the null hypothesis and accept the alternative hypothesis? The problem we face is similar to that encountered in Chapter 7, namely that the sample mean time of 16.7 minutes could have occurred by chance and is not representative of the true population mean. Indeed, we would expect all sample means to fluctuate around the population mean, in which case the question now changes to that of at what point do we accept or reject the null hypothesis. Do we reject at 16 minutes, 17 minutes or 18 minutes etc.? The point at which we accept or reject the null hypothesis is known as the *critical value*, and this is designated by the letter c. Applying this to the null hypothesis we can formulate the following decision rule:

Accept H_0 if $\bar{x} \leqslant c$
Reject H_0 if $\bar{x} > c$

The critical value we actually use is normally based upon the probability that we are prepared to accept of making a Type I error (remembering that a Type I error is when we reject a true hypothesis). If we assume that the population mean (μ) equals 15, then the sampling distribution of means for all samples of size 60 would be as shown in Figure 8.1. If the critical value in our decision rule was 15, we would effectively be saying that we are prepared to live with a 50 per cent chance of making a Type I error. This is represented graphically in Figure 8.2, and it shows that with a critical value of 15 we would find that for 50 per cent of the time any sample mean collected from that population would have a value greater than 15 minutes, which would result in the rejection of the null hypothesis. The important point to remember is that the population mean is 15 minutes and that we would *expect* the sample means to fluctuate either side of it, and therefore that it is normal to find, for 50 per cent of the time, sample means greater than 15 minutes when in fact the population mean is 15 minutes. Consequently the setting of a critical value of 15 minutes would be quite inappropriate because we would have far too high a probability of rejecting the null hypothesis when in fact it is true. This line of argument is based on the known characteristics of the

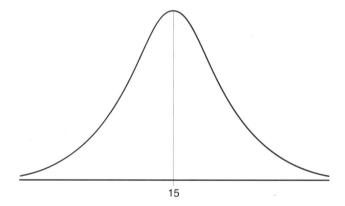

15

Figure 8.1   Sample distribution of means for samples of size 60 (with $\mu = 15$)

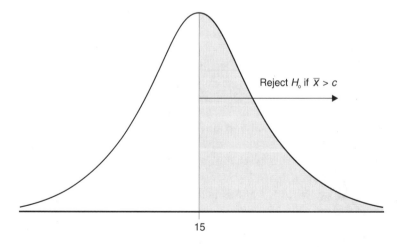

Reject H_o if $\overline{X} > c$

15

Figure 8.2   Probability of making a Type I error when μ and $c = 15$ minutes

sampling distribution of $\bar{x}$, which demands that we have samples of at least 30 items (i.e. $n \geqslant 30$). It is normal practice to allow a .05 or .01 probability of making a Type I error. This means that we must prove beyond reasonable doubt (the level of doubt or error is thus 5 per cent or 1 per cent) that the ambulance service is not meeting its response goal. This is shown in Figure 8.3, and the shaded area represents the chance of rejecting the null hypothesis when in fact it is true, but as can be seen, there is now only a 5 per cent chance of making such an error. The actual value of c can be determined by finding the Z value that corresponds to the top 5 per cent of the distribution (the concept of Z values and the area they represent can be found in Chapter 6), and then positioning the 5 per cent through the following formula:

$$c = \mu + (Z_{.05} \times \sigma_{\bar{x}})$$

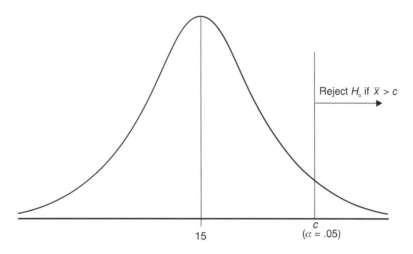

Figure 8.3 Type I error with $a = .05$

This says that the critical value lies to the right of the population mean (in practice it may well be what people expect the population mean to be or what they hypothesise it to be), and that its exact location can be found by multiplying the Z value that corresponds to 5 per cent by the standard error. If the problem was concerned with the left-hand side of the distribution, the formula would change slightly in that the addition would change to a subtraction (e.g. $c = 15 - (Z_{.05} \times \sigma_{\bar{x}})$)

The standard error ($6\bar{x}$) is:

$$n = 60$$

$$\bar{x} = 16.7$$

$$s = 4.5$$

$$\sigma_{\bar{x}} = \frac{s}{\sqrt{n}} = \frac{4.5}{\sqrt{60}} = 0.58$$

Applying this to our sample data the Z value that corresponds to 5 per cent can be found from Table 5 in Appendix 1, and it is 1.645.

Therefore

$$c = 15 + (Z_{.05} \times \sigma_{\bar{x}})$$

$$c = 15 + (1.645 \times 0.58)$$

$$c = 15 + (0.9541) = 15.95$$

The decision rule therefore becomes:

Accept H_0 if $\bar{x} \leqslant 15.95$

Reject H_0 if $\bar{x} > 15.95$

Since the sample mean was 16.7, we are able to reject the null hypothesis and say that we are 95 per cent sure that the ambulance service is failing to meet its response goal of 15 minutes or less.

Testing at the .01 significance level ($Z_{.01} = 2.33$) provides us with the following:

$$c = 15 + (Z_{.01} \times \sigma_{\bar{x}})$$

$$c = 15 + (2.33 \times 0.58)$$

$$c = 15 + (1.35) = 16.35$$

Again, the sample mean of 16.7 exceeds the critical value of 16.35, and we are now 99 per cent sure that the ambulance service is not meeting its response goal of 15 minutes or less. This last example also demonstrates that as we reduce the size of the significance level (increase our confidence level) the stiffer the test becomes because it results in a higher critical value.

Competence Example 8.1

At the end of this section you should now be able to demonstrate how to:

1 **formulate a hypothesis**

2 **develop a decision rule**

3 **test a hypothesis**

4 **interpret the results of the hypothesis test**

To practise and demonstrate these competences complete problems 8.1 and 8.2 at the end of this chapter. To help you to develop these competences a description of the procedure you will need to follow is now given, along with a typical problem format. The problem format is based on a process similar to that previously outlined.

PROCEDURE

❶ Specify a null and alternative hypothesis.

❷ Identify the critical value.

❸ Construct a decision rule.

❹ Compare the sample mean to the decision rule.

❺ Interpret the results of the analysis.

PROBLEM

A health clinic claims that members who follow its diet programme will lose, on average, at least 8 kilograms during the first month of the programme. A random sample of 40 members participating in the programme showed a sample mean weight loss of 7 kilograms. The sample standard deviation was 3.2 kilograms. Using an alpha value of .05, can the claims of the health clinic be substantiated?

SOLUTION FORMAT

❶ The development of the null hypothesis in this situation is somewhat open-ended, in that it ▮ is conceivable that it could take two forms. One line of argument proclaims that it must be assumed that the diet has no effect, and that the null hypothesis should therefore state that the diet has no effect unless it can be disproved beyond reasonable doubt. The opposite view is that it is the claim of the health clinic that has to be assumed to be true and that it is the purpose of the analysis to try to disprove it. It is the latter view that has been adopted here.

The null and alternative hypotheses are therefore as follows:

Hypothesis	**Conclusion and action**
$H_0: \mu \geqslant 8$	Health clinic claim substantiated; no action needed
$H_a: \mu < 8$	Health clinic claim is unsubstantiated; corrective action needed

❷

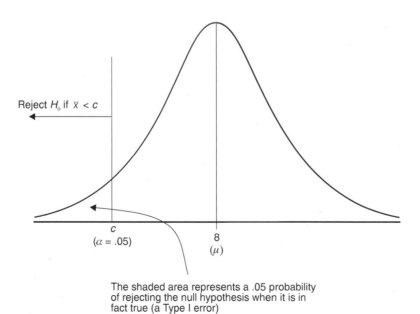

Reject H_0 if $\bar{x} < c$

c
$(\alpha = .05)$

8
(μ)

The shaded area represents a .05 probability of rejecting the null hypothesis when it is in fact true (a Type I error)

Figure 8.4　Critical value of the health clinic claim

❷ Working to a .05 significance level is equivalent to saying that we are going to live with an ▣2 $a = .05$ probability of making a Type I error. Integrating this into the critical value formula provides us with a critical value of:

$$c = \mu - (Z_{.05} \times \sigma_{\bar{x}})$$

The reason why there is a minus sign in this formula can be best explained by reference to Figure 8.4. The critical value has to be to the left of the hypothesised value as otherwise we would increase the likelihood of rejecting the claim when in fact it is true.

With $n = 40$ $\bar{x} = 7$ $s = 3.2$

$$\sigma_{\bar{x}} = \frac{s}{\sqrt{n}} = \frac{3.2}{\sqrt{40}} = 0.506$$

$$c = 8 - (1.645 \times 0.506)$$

$$c = 8 - (0.832) = 7.168$$

❸ The decision rule is therefore:

Accept H_0 if $\bar{x} \geqslant 7.168$

Reject H_0 if $\bar{x} < 7.168$

❹ ❺ Since the sample was 7 kilograms, we reject the null hypothesis and state that we are 95 ▣4 per cent sure that the claim made by the health clinic is untrue.

Practise your competencies now on problems 8.1. and 8.2. at the end of this chapter. When you have demonstrated competence in this area you can use the computer disk provided to automate the arithmetic elements of the competences. You may choose either a Lotus or an Excel spreadsheet depending on the package you have access to. The operation of the spreadsheets is developed in more detail in Chapter 2. You may now demonstrate the competences in this area against problems from your own work environment.

8.3.4 Two-tailed tests

The previous hypotheses were based on one-tailed tests, and as might be expected, hypothesis testing applies equally well to two-tailed tests. The following example demonstrates a typical application of a two-tailed test.

P & C Ltd. produces a variety of health and beauty products, including *Glow Toothpaste*. The production line for Glow Toothpaste is designed to fill tubes of toothpaste with a mean weight of 165 grams. Available data also shows that the fill weight has a standard deviation of 12 grams. Periodically a sample of 30 tubes will be selected in order to check the filling operation. Quality assurance procedures call for the continuation of the production operation if the sample results are consistent with the assumption that the mean filling weight for the population of tubes of toothpaste is 165 grams. However, if the sample results indicate that overfilling ($\mu > 165$) or underfilling ($\mu < 165$) exists, then the production line will have to be stopped and the filling mechanism adjusted.

Letting μ equal the mean weight of all the tubes of toothpaste, we can develop the null and alternative hypotheses:

Hypothesis	*Conclusion*
H_0: $\mu = 165$	The production line is operating satisfactorily; continue operation
H_a: $\mu \neq 165$	The production line is overfilling or underfilling; stop the production and adjust the filling mechanism

It is clearly a two-tailed test as it is looking at both underfilling, which will be in the left-hand side of the distribution, and overfilling, which will be in the right-hand side of the distribution. A portion of the rejection region will therefore be in each tail of the distribution, which means that if we have $\alpha = .05$, there will be a .025 rejection zone in each tail, as shown in Figure 8.5. For the null hypothesis to be rejected, the sample mean must accordingly exceed a critical value of $Z_{.025} = 1.96$.

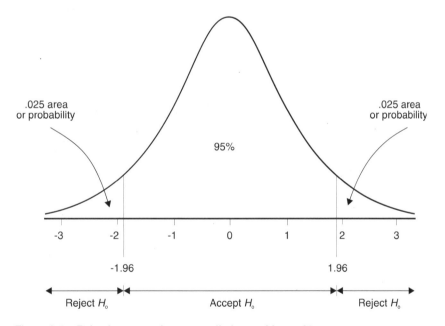

Figure 8.5 **Rejection zones for a two-tailed test with $a = .05$**

The decision rule now becomes:

Reject H_0 if $Z < -1.96$ or if $Z > 1.96$
Accept H_0 otherwise

The Z value of 1.96 can be converted to an actual value as follows:

$$c = \mu + (Z_{.025} \times \sigma_{\bar{x}})$$

If a sample of 30 tubes of toothpaste is taken and the sample mean is 167 grams with a standard deviation of 11 grams, the critical is:

$$\sigma_{\bar{x}} = \frac{s}{\sqrt{n}} = \frac{11}{\sqrt{30}} = 2$$

$$c = 165 + (1.96 \times 2)$$

$$c = 165 + (3.92) = 168.92$$

The critical value on the left-hand side of the distribution is:

$$c = \mu - (Z_{.025} \times \sigma_{\bar{x}})$$

$$c = 165 - (1.96 \times 2)$$

$$c = 165 - (3.92) = 161.08$$

The decision rule is therefore:

Reject H_0 if $\bar{x} < 161.08$ or if $\bar{x} > 168.92$
Accept H_0 otherwise

Since the sample mean is 167 grams we are unable to disprove the null hypothesis and do not stop the production process to adjust the filling mechanism.

Competence Example 8.2

At the end of this section you should now be able to demonstrate how to:

1 **formulate a two-tailed hypothesis**

2 **develop a two-tailed decision rule**

3 **test a two-tailed hypothesis**

4 **interpret the results of the hypothesis test**

To practise and demonstrate these competences complete problems 8.3 and 8.4 at the end of this chapter. To help you to develop these competences a description of the procedure you will need to follow is now given, along with a typical problem format. The problem format is based on a process similar to that previously outlined.

PROCEDURE

1 Specify a null and alternative hypothesis.

2 Identify the critical value.

3 Construct a decision rule.

4 Compare the sample mean to the decision rule.

5 Interpret the results of the analysis.

PROBLEM

A recently constructed by-pass has a speed limit of 60 mph. In response to local residents' concerns on the actual speed of vehicles on the by-pass, the Department of Transport has stated that the average speed of vehicles using the by-pass is 55 mph. To verify this claim the residents have taken a random sample of 70 vehicles using the by-pass and found that the average speed was 59.5 mph with a standard deviation of 8 mph. Using a .05 level of significance, test the Department of Transport's claim that the average speed is 55 mph.

SOLUTION FORMAT

❶ The null and alternative hypotheses for this problem are:

Hypothesis	Conclusion
$H_0: \mu = 55$	Vehicles are travelling at the expected average speed; no action required
$H_a: \mu \neq 55$	Vehicles are not travelling at the expected average speed; action required

❷ Working to a .05 significance level is equivalent to saying that we are going to live with an $a = .05$ probability of making a Type I error. Integrating this into the critical value formula for a two-tailed test provides us with a critical value of:

$$c = \mu + (Z_{.025} \times \sigma_{\bar{x}})$$

If a sample of 70 vehicles is taken and the sample mean is 59.5 mph with a standard deviation of 8 mph, the critical is:

$$\sigma_{\bar{x}} = \frac{s}{\sqrt{n}} = \frac{8}{\sqrt{70}} = 0.956$$

$$c = 55 + (1.96 \times 0.956)$$

$$c = 55 + (1.874) = 56.87$$

The critical value on the left-hand side of the distribution is:

$$c = \mu - (Z_{.025} \times \sigma_{\bar{x}})$$

$$c = 55 - (1.96 \times 0.956)$$

$$c = 55 - (1.874) = 53.13$$

❸ The decision rule is therefore:

Reject H_0 if $\bar{x} < 53.13$ or if $\bar{x} > 56.87$
Accept H_0 otherwise

❹ ❺ Since the sample mean is 59.5 mph we reject the null hypothesis and the claim made by the Department of Transport and demand that remedial action be taken.

Practise your competences now on problems 8.3. and 8.4. at the end of this chapter. When you have demonstrated competence in this area you can use the computer disk provided to automate the arithmetic elements of the competences. You may choose either a Lotus or an Excel spreadsheet depending on the package you have access to. The operation of the spreadsheets is developed in more detail in Chapter 2. You may now demonstrate the competences in this area against problems from your own work environment.

8.3.5 Hypothesis testing of proportions

This is a very similar procedure to that previously outlined, as the following example demonstrates. During the Christmas and New Year holiday period the European Commission for Road Safety estimate that 500 individuals would be killed and 25,000 injured on Member States' roads. They also claim that 50 per cent of these accidents would be caused by drunk driving. A sample of 120 accidents showed that 67 were caused by drunk driving. Use this data to test the European Commission's claim, using a .05 significance level.

The hypothesis for this problem can be stated as follows:

Hypothesis	Conclusion
$H_0: P = .50$	Proportion equals 50%; hypothesis is true
$H_a: P \neq .50$	Proportion does not equal 50%; reject hypothesis

Because this is a two-tailed test and $\alpha = .05$, the decision rule is:

Reject H_0 if $Z < -1.96$ or if $Z > 1.96$
Accept H_0 otherwise

The Z value of 1.96 represents 2½ per cent of the total area, with 2½ per cent being in the left-hand side of the distribution and 2½ per cent being in the right-hand side of the distribution. The Z value of 1.96 can be converted to an actual value as follows:

$$c = P + (Z_{.025} \times \sigma_{\bar{p}})$$

$$\sigma_{\bar{p}} = \sqrt{\frac{P(1-P)}{n}} = \sqrt{\frac{.50(1-.50)}{120}} = .0456$$

$$c = P + (Z_{.025} \times \sigma_{\bar{p}})$$

$$c = .50 + (1.96 \times .0456)$$

$$c = .50 + (.0894) = .59$$

The critical value on the left-hand side of the distribution is:

$$c = P - (Z_{.025} \times \sigma_{\bar{p}})$$

$$c = .50 - (1.96 \times .0456)$$

$$c = .50 - (.0894) = .41$$

The decision rule is therefore:

> Reject H_0 if $\bar{P} < .41$ or if $\bar{P} > .59$
> Accept H_0 otherwise

Since the sample proportion is $\bar{P} = 67/120 = .56$, the hypothesis that 50 per cent of the accidents are caused by drunk driving cannot be rejected on available sample evidence.

8.4 Chi-square tests

The *chi-square test* is an important extension of hypothesis testing and is used when we wish to compare an actual or observed set of data with an expected or hypothesised set of data. Because chi-square involves the comparison of an actual set of data to what we might expect to be there, it is often referred to as a *goodness of fit test*.

The chi-square test is distinctly different from the other types of tests so far looked at, in that it is not concerned with population parameters (e.g. means, proportions etc.). Instead, it concentrates on how the individual items in the sample are distributed, which is why it is known as a 'non-parametric' test. There are a number of non-parametric tests, but chi-square is the most widely known and used non-parametric test.

To demonstrate the principles of the chi-square technique, suppose a random sample of a 1000 households reveals the following data on TV viewing preferences:

Channel	Channel 4	ITV	BBC 2	BBC 1	Satellite
Preference	187	221	193	204	195

Because ITV has the highest preference, are we justified in saying that ITV is the most popular channel? From our previous discussions we would be sceptical of this claim, as we know that samples vary, and if we took another sample the distribution of preferences could well have been different. Perhaps the question we should ask is, 'At what point do we say that the differences between the channels are sufficiently large that we are sure that there are distinct differences in viewing preferences?' To test this a hypothesis has been formulated such that the null hypothesis states that the channels are watched equally, with no differences in viewing behaviour. With a sample of a 1,000 we would therefore expect the following distribution:

Channel	Channel 4	ITV	BBC 2	BBC 1	Satellite
Preference	200	200	200	200	200

The difference between the observed values and the hypothesised values can now be compared to see if the difference is significant or not.

Looking carefully at the data it is clear that we do not have complete freedom in assigning the expected frequencies, for if the sample size is 1,000 and we assign 200 to the first four channels, which gives us a sub-total of 800, then the fifth and last channel must be 200 if it is to add up to 1,000. This means that we have four degrees of freedom (notation for degrees of freedom is v, pronounced new, which would be shown as $v = 4$) in assigning the expected values. Generalising, if we have n observed values, then we have $v = n - 1$ degrees of freedom in assigning expected values.

The chi-square test which compares the observed values to those expected is designated by x^2 and the formula used in its calculation is:

$$x^2 = \sum \frac{(O - E)^2}{E}$$

where

O = the observed frequency
E = the expected frequency

The first step in the calculation of chi-square is to measure the deviations of the observed from the expected frequencies:

Channel	Observed (O)	Expected (E)	($O - E$)
Channel 4	187	200	−13
ITV	221	200	21
BBC 2	193	200	−7
BBC 1	204	200	4
Satellite	195	200	−5

Because the totals of the observed and expected frequencies must equal 1,000 apiece, the total of the differences between the observed and expected frequencies always equals zero ($\Sigma (O - E) = 0$). In response to this we square the deviations ($\Sigma (O - E)^2$). It is also necessary to divide $\Sigma (O - E)^2$ by E, and this can be explained by the following example:

Observed	Expected	($O - E$)	($O - E$)²
150	200	−50	2500
150	100	50	2500

The deviation of 50 is twice as significant on an expected value of 100 as it is on an expected value of 200. To cater for this we weight the $(O - E)^2$ values by dividing by E:

Observed	Expected	$(O-E)$	$(O-E)^2$	$\dfrac{(O-E)^2}{E}$
150	200	−50	2500	12.5
150	100	50	2500	25

Returning to the original problem, the calculated chi-square value will therefore be:

Channel	Observed	Expected	$(O-E)$	$(O-E)^2$	$\dfrac{(O-E)^2}{E}$
Channel 4	187	200	−13	169	0.845
ITV	221	200	21	441	2.205
BBC 2	193	200	−7	49	0.245
BBC 1	204	200	4	16	0.080
Satellite	195	200	−5	25	0.125
			$\Sigma(O-E)=0$		$\Sigma\dfrac{(O-E)^2}{E}=3.5$

As the calculated chi-square shows, the total of the differences between the observed and the expected frequencies equals 3.5. If our null hypothesis is true then we might expect the calculated chi-square value to be zero, with no difference between the expected and the observed values. But as we are sampling, the actual value of x^2 will fluctuate from sample to sample, in which case we must state the point at which we are prepared to accept or reject the calculated x^2 value.

The x^2 distribution is like the t distribution, there is a different x^2 distribution for each degree of freedom. In line with hypothesis testing it is normal practice to work to either a .05 or .01 significance level. With the degrees of freedom being $v=4$ and working to a significance level of $\alpha=.05$, it is possible to refer to Table 4 in Appendix 1, a portion of which is shown in Table 8.3, and identify the critical value of 9.488.

Table 8.3 Portion of chi-square distribution values

$a=$	.05	.025	.02	.01
$v=1$	3.841	5.024	5.412	6.635
2	5.991	7.378	7.824	9.210
3	7.815	9.348	9.837	11.345
4	**9.488**	11.143	11.668	13.277
5	11.070	12.832	13.388	15.086
6	12.592	14.449	15.033	16.812
7	14.067	16.013	16.622	18.475

Figure 8.6 illustrates that the critical value of 9.488 is to the far right of this chi-square distribution, and that this value is unlikely to have occurred by chance (there is in fact a .05 probability of a calculated x^2 value exceeding 9.488 by chance). Since the calculated x^2 value is 3.5, which is to the left of the critical value of 9.488, we are unable to disprove the null hypothesis that there is no difference in viewing preference between the channels.

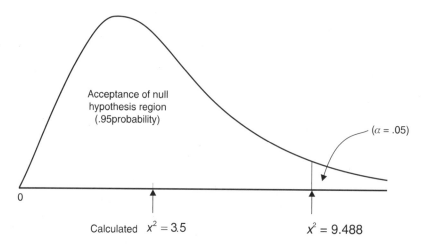

Figure 8.6   Chi-square distribution based on a critical value = $v = 4$ and $a = 0.05$

The decision rule for this problem would have been:

Accept H_0 and reject H_a if calculated $x^2 < 9.488$

Thus the null hypothesis is accepted. Before the chi-square technique is developed further, it is important to note that it should only be used when the expected frequencies are 5 or more. If the expected frequencies are less than 5 a large calculated chi-square value can be obtained erroneously, leading us to reject a true hypothesis, which is a Type I error.

8.4.1   Chi-square test of independence

The chi-square test outlined above is constrained in that it can only deal with *one* variable, which in the last example was the different types of channels. If we want to analyse *two* variables simultaneously then we have to use a chi-square test of independence, which as the name suggests, enables us to determine if the two variables are independent or not. The chi-square test of independence is also known as contingency table analysis or contingency analysis.

A random sample of 200 purchasers are classified by sex and product preference, as shown in Table 8.4.

The company carrying out the survey want to know if there is any connection or relationship between the products that are being bought and the sex of the

Table 8.4 Comparison of sex of purchaser and product buying behaviour

	Product A	Product B	Product C	Product D	Row totals
Male	26	48	21	25	120
Female	8	48	7	17	80
Column totals	34	96	28	42	200

connection between the purchaser's sex and the products that they buy.

H_0: the two variables or classifications are independent (there is no connection or relationship between them)

H_a: the two variables or classifications are not independent

The reader should note that rejection of the null hypothesis does not automatically mean that the two variables are related (dependent). Before any such cause and effect statements are possible it is necessary to investigate the variables a great deal more closely.

The first stage in the analysis of the data is to calculate the expected frequencies for each cell of the contingency table and to then compare them with the actual or observed frequencies. The expected frequencies are normally derived from the row totals, column totals, and the grand total. The reason for this is that the row totals are used to estimate the overall proportion of buyers in each sex category. We have, out of a grand total of 200 buyers, 120 in the *male* category, which equates to 60 per cent ($120/200 = 0.6$). Since 34 of the buyers have purchased product A, we would, on a straight percentage basis, expect 60 per cent of them to be male. The expected frequency for the first cell of the table is therefore 60 per cent of 34, which is 20.4, and as can be seen this differs from the observed frequency of 26.

The calculation of the expected frequencies can also be gained by using the following simple formula:

$$\text{Expected frequency of cell} = \frac{\text{Row total} \times \text{Column total}}{\text{Grand total}}$$

For the first cell this provides us with a value of $\frac{120 \times 34}{200} = 20.4$. The full set of expected frequencies are shown in Table 8.5.

purchaser. To evaluate this a hypothesis has been stated, namely that there is no

Table 8.5 Actual and expected frequencies

	Product A	Product B	Product C	Product D	Totals
Male	26	48	21	25	120
	(20.4)	(57.6)	(16.8)	(25.2)	
Female	8	48	7	17	80
	(13.6)	(38.4)	(11.2)	(16.8)	
Totals	34	96	28	42	200

The next step is to calculate x^2 as shown previously:

Observed	Expected	$(O-E)$	$(O-E)^2$	$\dfrac{(O-E)^2}{E}$
26	20.4	5.6	31.36	1.54
8	13.6	−5.6	31.36	2.31
48	57.6	−9.6	92.16	1.60
48	38.4	9.6	92.16	2.40
21	16.8	4.2	17.64	1.05
7	11.2	−4.2	17.64	1.57
25	25.2	−0.2	0.04	0.00
17	16.8	0.2	0.04	0.00
		$\Sigma(O-E)=0$		$\Sigma\dfrac{(O-E)^2}{E} = 10.47$

Before we test the calculated x^2 value it is necessary to identify the number of degrees of freedom associated with the data. The contingency table had eight cells. However, in order to calculate the expected frequencies, we made use of the row and column totals. The fixing of each row total uses up one degree of freedom in that row. In the first row for instance, once the first three cells have been filled, the fourth is automatically determined because the row total must be 120. The same remark applies to the columns. The first column total must be 34, which means that only one of the cells in that column is free. If you check through the table you will see that we only have three degrees of freedom. In general, if the table contains r rows and c columns, the number of degrees of freedom is obtained by:

$$v = (r-1)(c-1)$$

$$v = (2-1)(4-1)$$

$$v = 3$$

Referring to Table 4 in Appendix 1, we find that the critical value at $v = 3$ and $a = .05$ is 7.815. The decision rule for this problem can now be formulated as:

Accept H_0 and reject H_a if calculated $x^2 < 7.815$

Since the calculated x^2 value is 10.47 we are able to reject the null hypothesis that there is no relationship between the sex of the buyer and the product types that are purchased.

Competence Example 8.3

At the end of this section you should now be able to demonstrate how to:

1 **formulate a chi-square hypothesis**

2 **develop chi-square decision rule**

3 test the chi-square hypothesis

4 interpret the results of the hypothesis test

To practise and demonstrate these competences complete problems 8.5 and 8.6 at the end of this chapter. To help you to develop these competences a description of the procedure you will need to follow is now given, along with a typical problem format. The problem format is based on a process similar to that previously outlined.

PROCEDURE

❶ Specify a null and alternative hypothesis.

❷ Identify the expected frequencies.

❸ Calculate the chi-square value.

❹ Identify the critical chi-square value.

❺ Develop a decision rule.

❻ Test the decision rule and interpret the results.

PROBLEM

A survey by a regional sports agency has identified the following sporting preferences by men and women:

	Swimming	Basketball	Football
Men	19	15	24
Women	16	18	16

With $a = .05$, test the data to see if there is any similarity between the preferences of men and women.

SOLUTION FORMAT

❶ The null and alternative hypotheses for this problem are:

1

H_0: the two variables or classifications are independent (there is no connection or relationship between them).

H_a: the two variables or classifications are not independent.

❷ The contingency table for this set of data, with the expected frequencies, is shown below:

3

	Swimming	Basketball	Football	Totals
Men	19	15	24	58
	(18.80)	(17.72)	(21.48)	
Women	16	18	16	50
	(16.20)	(15.28)	(18.52)	
Totals	35	33	40	108

③ The calculated x^2 value is:

Observed	Expected	$(O-E)$	$(O-E)^2$	$\dfrac{(O-E)^2}{E}$
19	18.80	0.2	0.04	0.002
16	16.20	−0.2	0.04	0.002
15	17.72	−2.72	7.398	0.417
18	15.28	2.72	7.398	0.484
24	21.48	2.52	6.35	0.296
16	18.52	−2.52	6.35	0.343
		$\Sigma(O-E)=0$		$\Sigma \dfrac{(O-E)^2}{E} = 1.544$

④ The degrees of freedom associated with this problem are:

$$v = (r-1)(c-1)$$
$$v = (2-1)(3-1)$$
$$v = 2$$

Referring to Table 4 in Appendix 1, we find that the critical value at $v=2$ and $a=.05$ is 5.991. The decision rule for this problem can now be formulated as:

⑤   Accept H_0 and reject H_a if calculated $x^2 < 5.991$

⑥ Since the calculated x^2 value is 1.544 we are unable to reject the null hypothesis that the sex of the individual is independent of the three sporting areas identified.

Practise your competences now on problems 8.5. and 8.6. at the end of this chapter. When you have demonstrated competence in this area you can use the computer disk provided to automate the arithmetic elements of the competences. You may choose either a Lotus 1-2-3 or an Excel spreadsheet depending on the package you have access to. The operation of the spreadsheets is developed in more detail in Chapter 2. You may now demonstrate the competences in this area against problems from your own work environment.

Summary

Hypothesis testing is an important component of the scientific method, and its power lies in the methodology and discipline it demands of its practitioners, as well as in the general conceptual framework it provides for asking and testing beliefs and statements. The chi-square test is an important extension of the hypothesis area, and it has proven an important tool for analysing relationships between two variables.

As with other areas of statistics and quantitative management, it is quite possible to draw the wrong conclusions from hypothesis testing. The benefit of hypothesis testing is that it explicitly states what the probability is of making such wrong conclusions. This enables us to be much more precise in the way that we interpret and portray information.

The scientific method and hypothesis testing have a major role to play in model building. They provide a vehicle for simplifying and testing the real world, and these are fundamental traits for any analysis of the complex and dynamic world of business and management.

Problems for Chapter 8

8.1 Royale Marketing Research (RMR) bases its charges to clients on the assumption that telephone surveys can be completed with a mean time of 15 minutes or less. If a greater mean survey time is required, a premium rate is charged to the client. Does a sample of 35 surveys that shows a sample mean of 17 minutes and a sample standard deviation of 4 minutes justify the premium rate? Test at a .01 level of significance.

8.2 New tyres manufactured by a leading supplier are claimed to have an average life of at least 28,000 miles. Tests with 30 tyres show a sample mean of 27,000 miles with a sample standard deviation of 1,000 miles. Working with a .05 significance level, test to see if there is sufficient evidence to reject the claim of a mean life of at least 28,000 miles.

8.3 Historically, long-distance phone calls from a particular city have averaged 15.20 minutes per call. In a random sample of 35 calls, the sample mean time was 14.30 minutes per call, with a sample standard deviation of 5 minutes. Use this sample information to test whether or not there has been a change in the average duration of long-distance phone calls. Use a .05 level of significance.

8.4 A study of the operation of a city centre car park shows a historical mean parking time of 220 minutes per car. The car park has recently been modernised and the parking charges have been increased. The owners of the car park would like to know if these changes have had any effect on the mean parking time of the car park customers. Test the hypotheses $H_0: \mu = 220$ and $H_a: \mu \neq 220$ at a .05 level of significance. What is your conclusion if a sample of 50 cars showed a mean of 208 and a standard deviation of 80?

8.5 A study of educational levels of voters and their political affiliations showed the following results:

	Conservative	Labour	Green
No GCSEs	40	20	10
Up to 3 'A' levels	30	35	15
Degree	30	45	25

Use a .01 significance level to test to see if party affiliation is independent of the educational level of voters.

8.6 Articles made from three different kinds of plastic are subjected to a series of tests to compare the relative strengths of the materials. The results are shown in the following table. Is the true percentage of items falling into each category the same for all three plastics (test at the .05 level)?

	1	2	3
Undamaged	30	40	45
Slight damage	50	30	45
Heavy damage	20	10	30

8.7 The number of units sold of three products by three salespeople over a five-month period are:

	A	B	C
Smith	14	12	8
Brown	21	16	18
Jones	15	7	10

Using $a = .05$, test for independence of salesperson and type of product sold.

9 Regression and correlation
relationships and their importance

9.1 Introduction

This chapter is concerned with the related modelling approaches of regression analysis and correlation. Regression analysis is an approach that will fit a straight line through data sets of two variables, such as a company's advertising budget against the level of sales achieved. Regression analysis is sometimes referred to as *the method of least squares*, which gives a clue as to the method the approach uses. It minimises the square of the difference between the points and the proposed line. This line is called *the line of best fit*. Correlation is a method of testing how good a relationship exists between the two variables on which the line of best fit has been made.

By the end of this chapter you should be able to demonstrate how to:

- identify the dependent and independent variable for the data set
- calculate the correlation coefficient
- interpret the significance of this correlation coefficient
- calculate the line of best fit for the data set
- produce a scatter graph
- calculate predictions
- interpret the confidence in these predictions

The chapter will also provide the underpinning knowledge in the area of linear regression and correlation.

At the end of the chapter the required competence will be specified and described. A typical problem format with the competences highlighted will also be given to help you to demonstrate the competences on the problems at the end of the chapter. At the end of the book a full solution will be given for the first of these problems as well as answers for the rest.

Let us now expand the area of regression and correlation through an example. Given the strong links between regression and correlation, competence in both will be demonstrated through the same example. The following example is concerned with the sale and marketing of a major consumer product in the domestic washing powder industry. The sales of the product have been examined and there are no cyclic variations and the underlying sales are constant. Table 9.1 gives a sample of weekly sales figures and the associated expenditure on advertising. You may take these weeks as a representative sample.

Table 9.1 Sample of weekly sales figures and advertising expenditure

Expenditure on advertising (£000s)	0.8	2.7	1.9	2.5	1.4	1.2	1.9
Sales (£ millions)	1.3	2.7	2.2	2.3	1.6	2.0	1.8

To ensure that effective decisions are made when setting the advertising budget, management would like to know if there is a relationship between the sales and the expenditure on advertising.

9.2 Correlation

The first step in answering management's query is to determine if there is a relationship between the two variables, and to carry this out the approach of correlation will be used. If the two variables are independent of each other (i.e one variable cannot affect the other or vice versa), then no relationship can exist between them. If the mathematics of correlation show a relationship then this is a spurious relationship (*spurious correlation*). Mathematics alone is not enough to suggest a relationship – there needs to be further evidence to add to the mathematics. Like all areas of modelling, correlation requires a good understanding of the context of the data to which the mathematics is to be applied. If, however, one of the variables is dependent on the other and a relationship can be shown mathematically then a relationship is strongly suggested. In such a situation the *independent variable* will be the *x* variable, sometimes referred to as the *controlled variable*, and the *dependent variable* will be the *y* variable. It is important to identify which variable is independent and which is dependent.

In the example being considered, the independent variable will be the expenditure spent on advertising. This is the variable that can be controlled and will affect the sales. The sales are therefore dependent on the expenditure. Other examples are:

- time spent on training (independent variable) against level of skill achieved (dependent variable)

- a person's height (independent variable) against a person's weight (dependent variable)

- time (independent variable) against Retail Price Index (dependent variable)

- time (independent variable) against number of leavers (dependent variable)

- time (independent variable) against sales (dependent variable)

It is important to identify the independent and dependent variables, and an easy way to do this is to say to yourself that each of the variables are dependent on each other in turn.

For example:

- A person's height is independent and their weight is dependent on their height ✓ OR
- A person's weight is independent and their height is dependent on their weight ✗

You should then consider each alternative and one will make sense and the other will not. For example, the next time you feel you are overweight for your height you may consider that you are not overweight but you are in fact not tall enough. This may make you feel a little better temporarily but is obviously not possible. In business examples which involve time, then time will be the independent variable.

The mathematics that we are going to use to determine the correlation coefficient and regression line uses the following underlying assumptions:

- That the dependent variable (y) will be normally distributed for each value of the independent variable (x).
- That the variance of y within these distributions across the x values will not be significantly different (i.e. the variability of these distributions is the same).
- There is little or no error on the independent variable (x).

These assumptions will be valid for the vast majority of business or management examples you may be tempted to try regression and correlation on.

9.2.1 Calculation of the correlation coefficient

The measure that correlation uses to indicate the 'goodness of fit' of a linear line through the data points of the variables is called the **correlation coefficient**. The correlation coefficient will be a number between -1 and $+1$. The closer the value is to $+1$ or -1 then the better the fit of the line. The closer the value is to zero then the poorer the fit of the line. The difference between the -1 and the $+1$ is the slope of the line. The $+1$ would indicate a relationship on an upward sloping line and the -1 would indicate a relationship on a downwards sloping line. Figure 9.1 shows a series of data patterns and the type of correlation coefficient that would be calculated from them.

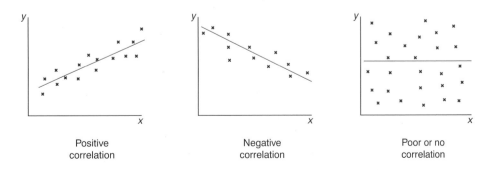

Positive correlation

Negative correlation

Poor or no correlation

Figure 9.1   Correlation coefficient examples

The following formula is used to calculate the correlation coefficient and the symbol r is used to represent it.

$$r = \frac{\sum xy - \frac{(\sum x)(\sum y)}{n}}{\sqrt{\left(\sum x^2 - \frac{(\sum x)^2}{n}\right)\left(\sum y^2 - \frac{(\sum y)^2}{n}\right)}}$$

where x = the independent variable
y = the dependent variable
n = the number of data pairs of the variables
r = the correlation coefficient
$\sum$ = the sum of, i.e. $\sum x$ = the sum of all the x values

To calculate the correlation coefficient a table needs to be produced to determine the summation values. By examining the formula it can be identified that five summation values are required, these being $\sum x$, $\sum y$, $\sum xy$, $\sum x^2$ and $\sum y^2$. This means that our calculation table will contain the following columns: x, y, xy, x^2 and y^2, Having identified the columns that are required the summations for our advertising and sales example are shown in Table 9.2.

Table 9.2   Summation values

x	y	xy	x^2	y^2
0.8	1.3	1.04	0.64	1.69
2.7	2.7	7.29	7.29	7.29
1.9	2.2	4.18	3.61	4.84
2.5	2.3	5.75	6.25	5.29
1.4	1.6	2.24	1.96	2.56
1.2	2.0	2.40	1.44	4.00
1.9	1.8	3.42	3.61	3.24
12.4	13.9	26.32	24.80	28.91

Therefore the summations are as follows:

$\sum x = 12.4$
$\sum y = 13.9$
$\sum xy = 26.32$
$\sum x^2 = 24.80$
$\sum y^2 = 28.91$
The number of data pairs = $n = 7$

These values can now be put into the formula to calculate the correlation coefficient:

$$r = \frac{\sum xy - \frac{(\sum x)(\sum y)}{n}}{\sqrt{\left(\sum x^2 - \frac{(\sum x)^2}{n}\right)\left(\sum y^2 - \frac{(\sum y)^2}{n}\right)}}$$

$$= \frac{26.2 - \dfrac{12.4 \times 13.9}{7}}{\sqrt{\left(24.8 - \dfrac{(12.4)^2}{7}\right)\left(28.91 - \dfrac{(13.9)^2}{7}\right)}}$$

$$= \frac{26.32 - 24.62}{\sqrt{(24.8 - 21.97)(28.91 - 27.6)}}$$

$$= \frac{1.70}{\sqrt{2.83 \times 1.31}} = \frac{1.70}{\sqrt{3.71}} = \frac{1.70}{1.93} = 0.88$$

Table 9.3 can be used to determine the significance of this value in the same manner as you have used the tables for significance testing. The degrees of freedom are given by the symbol γ and are calculated by subtracting 2 from the number of data pairs.

$\gamma = n - 2$

For the example we are considering, the following values have been calculated:

$r = 0.88 \quad \gamma = 7 - 2 = 5$

Table 9.3

γ	Level 1 ←0.05→	Level 2 ←0.01→
3	0.88	0.96
4	0.81	0.92
5	0.75	0.87
6	0.71	0.83
7	0.66	0.80
8	0.63	0.76
9	0.60	0.73
10	0.58	0.71
11	0.55	0.68
12	0.53	0.66
13	0.51	0.64
14	0.50	0.62
15	0.48	0.61
20	0.42	0.54
25	0.38	0.49
30	0.35	0.45
40	0.30	0.39
50	0.27	0.35

The line from Table 9.3 we are interested in is as follows:

γ	Level 1	Level 2
	$\leftarrow 0.05 \rightarrow$	$\leftarrow 0.01 \rightarrow$
5	0.75	0.87

The value we have calculated for the correlation coefficient (if it is a negative value then assume for the table it is positive) is then compared with this line:

- If it is below the table value of level 1 then the correlation coefficient value is not significant and we can draw the conclusion that no significant relationship exists between expenditure on advertising and sales.
- If it is between or on the table values of level 1 and level 2 then the correlation coefficient value is significant and we can draw the conclusion that a significant relationship exists between expenditure on advertising and sales (providing other evidence of a relationship exists).
- If it is above the table value of level 2 then the correlation coefficient value is highly significant and we can draw the conclusion that a relationship exists between expenditure on advertising and sales (providing other evidence of a relationship exists).

In the case of our example the r value is greater than the table value for level 2. Therefore the correlation coefficient is highly significant and we can draw the conclusion that a relationship exists between expenditure on advertising and sales. It should be remembered that on its own the mathematics *does not* prove a relationship. There should be other evidence to confirm the relationship, such as research into the reaction of the consumer to the advertising. There should also be evidence to show this effect is not caused by other factors such as variations in sales patterns. This does mean that you should fully understand the data you apply correlation to – you should not just use it as a mathematical technique. Understanding of the situation the data is concerned with is vital.

You should remember that the line that correlation tests will be linear, and this will mean that if the relationship is non-linear the mathematics will probably tell you there is no relationship. What this means is there is no linear relationship.

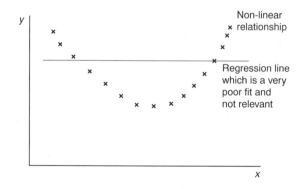

Figure 9.2   Non-linear relationship and correlation

Figure 9.2 demonstrates a non-linear relationship that occurs in a number of cost relationships (*see* Chapter 12 for an example of a non-linear cost relationship).

Although in this case the correlation coefficient and straight line approximation do not indicate a relationship there clearly exists a non-linear relationship in this data. To avoid this misinterpretation it is recommended that you always examine the data graphically before carrying out any calculations. This should be part of ensuring you understand the data and its context. If you suspect there is a non-linear relationship then you may still be able to use linear regression, but you need to transform the non-linear relationship into a linear one. The process of this is dealt with in more detail in the section on non-linear trends in Chapter 10.

9.3 Regression analysis

Having determined that we have a good relationship between expenditure on advertising and the sales we must now calculate the relationship itself.

9.3.1 Calculation of the regression line

The calculation of the regression line is carried out using the following summation values from the table we have calculated previously.

$$\Sigma x = 12.4$$
$$\Sigma y = 13.9$$
$$\Sigma xy = 26.32$$
$$\Sigma x^2 = 24.80$$
$$\Sigma y^2 = 28.91$$

The following formulae are used to determine the straight line relationship.

$$y = a + b(x - \bar{x})$$

where $\quad a = \dfrac{\Sigma y}{n} \quad \bar{x} = \dfrac{\Sigma x}{n}$

$$b = \dfrac{\Sigma xy - \dfrac{(\Sigma x)(\Sigma y)}{n}}{\Sigma x^2 - \dfrac{(\Sigma x)^2}{n}}$$

and

x = the independent variable
y = the dependent variable
n = the number of data pairs of the variables
r = the correlation coefficient
Σ = the sum of i.e. Σx = the sum of all the x values
$\bar{x}$ = the arithmetic mean of the independent variable

If we enter the summations from the example we are considering into the formulae we can determine the line of best fit.

$$a = \frac{\Sigma y}{n} = \frac{13.9}{7} = 1.99$$

$$\bar{x} = \frac{\Sigma x}{n} = \frac{12.4}{7} = 1.77$$

$$b = \frac{\Sigma xy - \dfrac{(\Sigma x)(\Sigma y)}{n}}{\Sigma x^2 - \dfrac{(\Sigma x)^2}{n}}$$

$$= \frac{26.32 - \dfrac{12.4 \times 13.9}{7}}{24.8 - \dfrac{(12.4)^2}{7}}$$

$$= \frac{26.32 - 24.62}{24.80 - 21.97} = \frac{1.70}{2.83} = 0.6$$

These figures can now be substituted into the straight line relationship:

$$y = a + b(x - \bar{x})$$
$$y = 1.99 + 0.6(x - 1.77)$$

This can now be simplified to the usual $y = mx + c$ form of the straight line.

$$y = 1.99 + 0.6(x - 1.77)$$
$$y = 1.99 + 0.6x - 1.06$$
$$y = 0.93 + 0.6x$$

We have already determined that there is a very good association between the two variables, expenditure on advertising (x) and sales (y). This relationship can now be given in a symbolic format as:

$$y = 0.6x + 0.93$$

where x = the expenditure on advertising

y = the expected level of sales for the given expenditure on advertising

It is also useful to represent the relationship in a more visual format. This type of graph is called a scatter graph and shows both the line of best fit and the data points that have been used to determine the line. The graph is plotted from the smallest to the largest x value in the data pairs and this should also be the length of the straight line. You may wish to extend this to show predictions, but you should clearly differentiate between the calculated line and the extended predictions. A scatter graph for this example is given in Figure 9.3.

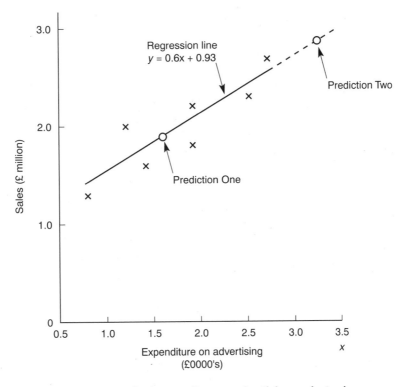

Figure 9.3   Scatter graph of expenditure on advertising against sales

9.4   Predictions and confidence limits using regression analysis

Having calculated the best line of fit and the significance of the fit we can now produce predictions. Care needs to be exercised when using the line for predictions. The correlation coefficient will obviously be important when considering the quality of the predictions. The more significant the correlation value the better the predictions will be. It would be dangerous and simplistic just to take the correlation coefficient as the only measure. Figure 9.4 illustrates the confidence limits on a typical regression line.

From Figure 9.4 it can be seen that if predictions are being made around the middle of the values over which the calculations were made (the limit of the regression – this is the smallest x value to the largest x value) then confidence in the predictions can be high provided the correlation value is significant or better. As the predictions move out towards the ends of the limits of the regression then confidence reduces progressively as they get closer to the ends. Once the predictions start to move outside the limit of the regression then greater and greater caution should be taken with predictions. It is here that a thorough understanding of the underlying context of the data is required. It is important that an assessment is made as to whether the data pattern is likely to be changing

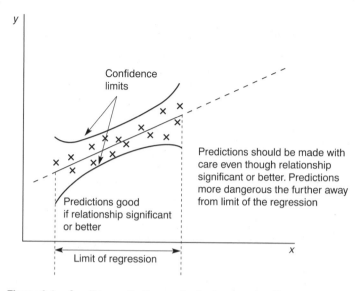

Figure 9.4 Confidence limits on a typical regression line

away from a linear pattern where the predictions are being made. The 65 mph dinosaur prediction in Chapter 1 is an example where predictions have been made far outside the limit of the regression. This was certainly 'a prediction too far'.

In the example based on advertising and sales the management in budget decision making require a prediction of sales for the following levels of advertising – £16,000 and £32,000. They would also like to know how confident they can be of the predictions.

Prediction One (£16,000)
Take 1.6 on the prediction line to represent £16,000 figure for advertising.

$$y = 0.6x + 0.93$$

where x = the expenditure on advertising
y = the expected level of sales for the given expenditure on advertising

therefore
$$y = 0.6 \times 1.6 + 0.93$$
$$= 0.96 + 0.93$$
$$= 1.89$$

With an advertising expenditure of £16,000, a sales value of £1.89 million would be expected. This is a value of average sales for weeks when an advertising expenditure of £16,000 is used. The actual values will be normally distributed around this mean. Given that the correlation coefficient is highly significant and that the prediction is inside the limit of the regression, then management can be very confident of this prediction.

Prediction Two (£32,000)
Take 3.2 on the prediction line to represent £32,000 figure for advertising.

$$y = 0.6x + 0.93$$

where x = the expenditure on advertising
y = the expected level of sales for the given expenditure on advertising

therefore
$$y = 0.6 \times 3.2 + 0.93$$
$$= 1.92 + 0.93$$
$$= 2.85$$

With an advertising expenditure of £32,000, a sales value of £2.85 million would be expected. This is a value of average sales for weeks when an advertising expenditure of £32,000 is used. The actual values will be normally distributed around this mean. Even given that the correlation coefficient is highly significant, the prediction is outside the limit of the regression, therefore management needs to be careful of this prediction. This will need detailed knowledge of the context of this data pattern to ensure it is still valid at the value the predictions are being made.

Summary

The approach of regression and correlation is a very powerful and useful technique. It should only be applied when you are familiar with the context of the data concerned. Always graph and examine the data before you start. Regression and correlation will determine the relationship and its significance. Care should be taken when using the relationship outside the limit of the regression.

Competence Example 9.1

At the end of this chapter you should now be able to demonstrate how to:

1 **identify the dependent and independent variable for the data set**

2 **calculate the correlation coefficient**

3 **interpret the significance of this correlation coefficient**

4 **calculate the line of best fit for the data set**

5 **produce a scatter graph**

6 **calculate predictions**

7 **interpret the confidence in these predictions**

To practise and demonstrate these competences complete problems 9.1 to 9.4 at the end of this chapter. To help you develop these competences a description of the procedure you will need to follow is now given, along with a typical problem format. This problem format is based on the example we have just considered.

PROCEDURE

❶ Identify the independent and dependent variable.

❷ Produce the calculation table.

❸ Calculate the correlation coefficient.

❹ Determine the significance of the correlation coefficient.

❺ Calculate the relationship.

❻ Produce the scatter graph.

❼ Calculate the predictions.

❽ Comment on the confidence of the predictions.

PROBLEM

The example is concerned with the sale and marketing of a major consumer product in the domestic washing powder industry. The sales of the product have been examined and there are no cyclic variations and the underlying sales are constant. The following table gives a sample of weekly sales figures and the associated expenditure on advertising You may take these weeks as a representative sample.

Expenditure on advertising (£0000)	0.8	2.7	1.9	2.5	1.4	1.2	1.9
Sales (£ million)	1.3	2.7	2.2	2.3	1.6	2.0	1.8

To ensure that effective decisions are made when setting the advertising budget management would like to know if there is a relationship between the sales and the expenditure on advertising.

Management in budget decision making require a prediction of sales for the following levels of advertising: £16,000 and £32,000. They would also like to know how confident they can be of the predictions.

SOLUTION FORMAT

❶ In this example the independent variable will be the expenditure spent on advertising. This is the variable that can be controlled and will affect the sales. The sales are therefore dependent on the expenditure.

❷

x	y	xy	x^2	y^2
0.8	1.3	1.04	0.64	1.69
2.7	2.7	7.29	7.29	7.29
1.9	2.2	4.18	3.61	4.84
2.5	2.3	5.75	6.25	5.29
1.4	1.6	2.24	1.96	2.56
1.2	2.0	2.40	1.44	4.00
1.9	1.8	3.42	3.61	3.24
12.4	13.9	26.32	24.80	28.91

❸ Therefore the summations are as follows:

$$\Sigma x = 12.4$$
$$\Sigma y = 13.9$$
$$\Sigma xy = 26.32$$
$$\Sigma x^2 = 24.80$$
$$\Sigma y^2 = 28.91$$

The number of data pairs $= n = 7$

These values can now be put into the formula to calculate the correlation coefficient.

$$r = \frac{\Sigma\, xy - \dfrac{(\Sigma\, x)(\Sigma\, y)}{n}}{\sqrt{\left(\Sigma\, x^2 - \dfrac{(\Sigma\, x)^2}{n}\right)\left(\Sigma\, y^2 - \dfrac{(\Sigma\, y)^2}{n}\right)}}$$

$$= \frac{26.2 - \dfrac{12.4 \times 13.9}{7}}{\sqrt{\left(24.8 - \dfrac{(12.4)^2}{7}\right)\left(28.91 - \dfrac{(13.9)^2}{7}\right)}}$$

$$= \frac{26.32 - 24.62}{\sqrt{(24.8 - 21.97)(28.91 - 27.6)}}$$

$$= \frac{1.70}{\sqrt{2.83 \times 1.31}} = \frac{1.70}{\sqrt{3.71}} = \frac{1.70}{1.93} = 0.88$$

❹ For this example the following values have been calculated:

$$r = 0.88 \qquad \gamma = 7 - 2 = 5$$

The line from the table we are therefore interested in is as follows:

γ	Level 1	Level 2
	$\leftarrow 0.05 \rightarrow$	$\leftarrow 0.01 \rightarrow$
5	0.75	0.87

In the case of this example the r value is greater than the table value for level 2. Therefore the correlation coefficient is highly significant and we can draw the conclusion that a highly significant relationship exists between expenditure on advertising and sales. It should be remembered that on its own the mathematics does not prove a relationship. There should be other evidence to confirm the relationship such as research into the reaction of the consumer to the advertising. There should also be evidence to show this effect is not caused by other factors such as variations in sales patterns. The calculation of the regression line can now be carried out using the following summation values from the calculation table.

❺
$$\Sigma x = 12.4$$
$$\Sigma y = 13.9$$
$$\Sigma xy = 26.32$$

5

$$\Sigma x^2 = 24.80$$
$$\Sigma y^2 = 28.91$$

$$a = \frac{\Sigma y}{n} = \frac{13.9}{7} = 1.99$$

$$x = \frac{\Sigma x}{n} = \frac{12.4}{7} = 1.77$$

$$b = \Sigma xy - \frac{(\Sigma x)(\Sigma y)}{n}$$

$$\Sigma x^2 - \frac{(\Sigma x)^2}{n}$$

$$= 26.32 - \frac{12.4 \times 13.9}{7}$$

$$24.8 - \frac{(12.4)^2}{7}$$

$$= \frac{26.32 - 24.62}{24.80 - 21.97} = \frac{1.70}{2.83} = 0.6$$

These figures can now be substituted into to the straight line relationship.

$$y = a + b(x - \bar{x})$$
$$y = 1.99 + 0.6(x - 1.77)$$

This can now be simplified to the usual $y = mx + c$ form of the straight line.

$$y = 1.99 + 0.6(x - 1.77)$$
$$y = 1.99 + 0.6x - 1.06$$
$$y = 0.93 + 0.6x$$

5 We have already determined with the correlation coefficient that there is a very good association between the two variables, expenditure on advertising (x) and sales (y). This relationship can now be given in a symbolic format as:

$$y = 0.6x + 0.93$$

where x = the expenditure on advertising
y = the expected level of sales for the given expenditure on advertising

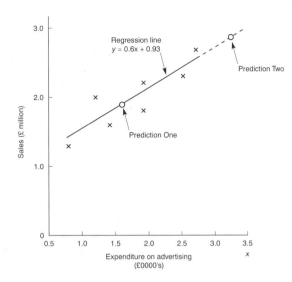

❼ Prediction One (£16,000)

Take 1.6 on the prediction line to represent £16,000 figure for advertising.

$$y = 0.6x + 0.93$$

where x = the expenditure on advertising
y = the expected level of sales for the given expenditure on advertising

therefore

$$y = 0.6 \times 1.6 + 0.93$$
$$= 0.96 + 0.93$$
$$= 1.89$$

❽ With an advertising expenditure of £16,000 then a sales value of £1.89 million of sales would be expected. This is a value of average sales for weeks when an advertising expenditure of £16,000 is used. The actual values will be normally distributed around this mean. Given that the correlation coefficient is highly significant and the prediction is inside the limit of the regression then management can be very confident of this prediction.

❼ Prediction Two (£32,000)

Take 3.2 on the prediction line to represent £32,000 figure for advertising.

$$y = 0.6x + 0.93$$

where x = the expenditure on advertising
y = the expected level of sales for the given expenditure on advertising

therefore

$$y = 0.6 \times 3.2 + 0.93$$
$$= 1.92 + 0.93$$
$$= 2.85$$

⑧ With an advertising expenditure of £32,000 then a sales value of £2.85 million of sales **7** would be expected. This is a value of average sales for weeks when an advertising expenditure of £32,000 is used. The actual values will be normally distributed around this mean. Even given the correlation coefficient is highly significant the prediction is outside the limit of the regression, therefore management needs to be careful of this prediction. This will need a careful and detailed knowledge of the context of this data pattern to ensure it is still valid at the value the predictions are being made.

Practise your competence now on problems 9.1 to 9.4 at the end of this chapter. When you have demonstrated competence in this area you can use the computer disk provided to automate the arithmetic elements of the competences. You may choose either a Lotus or an Excel spreadsheet depending on the package you have access to. With this disk you will input the number of data pairs and then the x and y values. The spreadsheet will then calculate the correlation coefficient and the regression line; you will then need to evaluate these values. The operation of the spreadsheet is developed in more detail in Chapter 2. You may now demonstrate the competences in this area against problems from your own work environment.

Problems for Chapter 9

9.1 The following table gives the sales of houses by a chain of estate agents. Figures are given for the first five months of 1994.

Month	1	2	3	4	5
House sales	152	164	160	178	185

Use regression and correlation to determine if there is a relationship between the sales and time; also produce a forecast for months six and seven. Comment on the confidence of these forecasts.

9.2 The following table shows the number of visitors at a city museum per month and the publicity budget spent in that month.

Month	1	2	3	4	5	6
Visitors (000s)	150	180	125	143	189	156
Publicity budget (£0s)	120	150	110	119	148	133

Determine if there is a relationship between visitors and the publicity budget and discuss its significance.

Predict the number of visitors with a budget of £1,600 and comment on its validity.

9.3 A record has been kept in the machine shop of a manufacturer of parts for the automotive industry. They are concerned with the maintenance costs for seven computer numerical-controlled machines of different ages.

Age of machine in years	Average weekly maintenance costs
6	120
2	50
7	180
5	60
3	110
1	20
6	90

Determine if there is a relationship between the age of the machine and its maintenance cost, commenting on the significance of the relationship. Predict the maintenance cost of a four-year-old machine and comment on its validity.

9.4 The following figures are amounts spent per year in a particular area of your budget.

Year	1988	1989	1990	1991	1992	1993	1994
Amount spent (£)	150	200	180	350	500	400	450

Use regression and correlation to determine relationship of the amount spent and produce a forecast for the five-year period 1995 to 1999. Comment on the confidence of these forecasts.

Note: To ease the amount of calculation on this example you will find it easier to number the years i.e. 1988 becomes year 1, 1989 becomes year 2 and so on.

10 Forecasting

predicting the future

10.1 Introduction

Forecasting is one of the most difficult tasks for managers, and this is particularly true when predicting the future trends of sales and markets in today's changing technological and economic environment. Sales and market trends will be used as the main example within this chapter, but you must remember that there are many other needs for forecasting. Many approaches to forecasting have been tried with varying success from very early times. Two thousand years ago the Romans used to foretell the future by examining the patterns on a sacrificed goat's liver. This approach, besides making a terrible mess on the boardroom carpet, along with other mystical, magical, astrological or pure guess approaches, is not to be recommended. All these approaches are random in nature. This chapter will explore a variety of more logical approaches to the setting of forecasts.

At the end of each section of the chapter the required competence will be specified and described. A typical problem format with the competences highlighted will also be given to help you to demonstrate the competences on the problems at the end of the chapter. At the end of the book a full solution will be given for the first of these problems as well as answers for the rest.

Before examining the approaches to forecasting, the objectives must be first considered. Figure 10.1 shows a typical data pattern.

The data pattern shown in Figure 10.1 is typical in that it is made up of random variations around an underlying trend. The random variations are small fluctuations that occur in the sales and market data. These fluctuations are due to a whole range of factors that will affect any sales or market data. It is often difficult, if not impossible, to associate particular factors with fluctuations or to predict when they will occur again. Next, an important question. Should the objective of the forecasting be to follow the underlying average or to try and follow the random variations? It will almost certainly be best for the company as a whole to produce forecasts that follow the underlying average. Such an approach will allow effective planning of the company's resources with the peaks balancing out the troughs.

If the underlying average of the data is found, this will mean that the majority of forecasts will be wrong; half too high and half too low. Therefore it would be wrong to measure the success of the forecasting system by how many times it is correct. The best measure is that the total error of the forecasts remains around zero. This will show the system is finding the underlying average and balancing out the peaks and troughs.

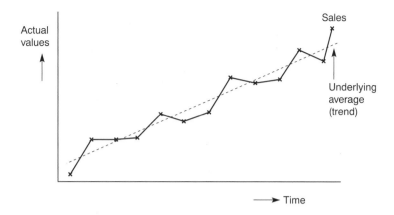

Figure 10.1   A typical data pattern

Forecasting systems will be made up of two parts: first, the **smoothing method** which will find the underlying average of the data to date. This will then be followed by the **forecasting method** that will extend this into the future and produce the forecast model. A standard forecast symbol will be used in many of the forecast models given in this chapter.

$$\hat{Y}_{t-T} = \text{forecast calculated in time } t \text{ for } T \text{ time periods ahead}$$

The actual data is referred to with the symbol Y and the forecast is differentiated by the $\hat{}$ symbol. An important consideration in forecasting is time, and this is shown in the symbol with the suffix fixing the point on the time scale. In using this symbol the t and T must be shown separately and not added together. It is necessary to know the time period in which the forecast is calculated (t) and how far ahead the forecast is for (T).

The many mathematically-based forecasting approaches that are available produce forecasts to many decimal places. This can cause problems of reality if a large number of decimal places are used. It is difficult to sell 265.35678 washing machines in a week – not many people want to buy 0.35678 of a washing machine. It also gives a false level of accuracy to the forecasting. All sales and market forecasts should be rounded into units that can actually be sold.

10.2 Data patterns

This section of Chapter 10 will enable you to:

- identify the main patterns that occur in forecast data
- recognise the main data problems that can occur in data patterns

The section will also provide underpinning knowledge in the area of data pattern recognition.

An important part of forecasting is to recognise the pattern that exists in the data from which a forecast is to be drawn. This is needed to determine the forecasting method or model best suited to the data. The data pattern will be one of three or a combination of these. The three data patterns are as follows:

a) *Constant data pattern with random variation.* With this data pattern the underlying average is more or less constant with random variations. These random variations are the small fluctuations that occur in the data. These variations, because of the many factors that affect sales and markets, are difficult and sometimes impossible to explain. This makes it difficult to predict the exact future values. An example of this type of data pattern is given in Figure 10.2.

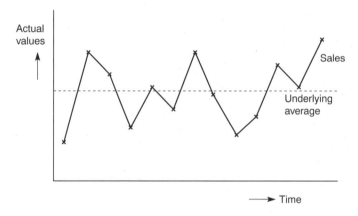

Figure 10.2 Constant data pattern with random variation

b) *Trend data pattern with random variation.* In this data pattern the underlying average is increasing or decreasing with time in a trend. Again it is difficult to predict random variation around this trend. The trend line can be in the form of a straight line or it can be in some form of curve. An example of this type of data pattern is given in Figure 10.3. Illustrated in this figure is a rising straight line trend.

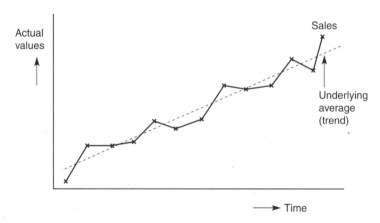

Figure 10.3 Trend data pattern with random variation

c) *Cyclic data pattern with random variation.* In this data pattern there will be a repeatable pattern over time. The pattern could have a cycle that is less or more than a year. The pattern may repeat itself over a year (weekly, monthly or quarterly) and in this case it would be called seasonal. Good examples of seasonal sales patterns are found with the sales of ice-cream, sunglasses or umbrellas. The cycle will be subject to random variation like the other data patterns and this can sometimes make it difficult to identify the cycle. The underlying average of the cycle could be constant or trend and the cycle itself could be increasing or decreasing in size. An example of this type of data pattern is given in Figure 10.4. Illustrated in this example is a four part cycle with a constant underlying average and with the size of the cycle remaining constant.

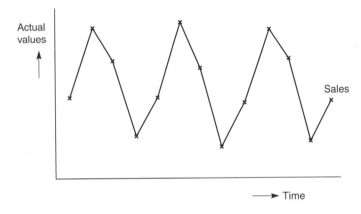

Figure 10.4   Cyclic data pattern with random variation

The data for both sales and the market will follow one of these three patterns or some combination of them. It is also possible for the data to change from pattern to pattern over time. This is particularly so with the constant and trend data patterns.

There are many problems that can occur with data patterns but two main ones cause the most trouble when forecasting. These problems can occur with any of the data patterns – either a **spike** or a **step** in the data.

10.2.1 Spike

This is where the data stream is suddenly interrupted with a spike either upwards or downwards. Such a spike can be one or two time periods. An example of this type of problem is shown in Figure 10.5. Illustrated in this figure is an upward spike within a constant data pattern but remember that the spike can occur in any of the data patterns. A typical spike could occur with bus transport if there was a rail strike. Another example is umbrella sales on a rainy day.

If it is possible to determine why the spike occurred and when a similar spike is likely to occur then this can be built into later forecasts – however, the spike should normally be taken out of present calculations and considerations. A most annoying type of spike is one where the reason for it is known but it is difficult or impossible to tell when it will occur again. With some spikes it will not be possible to determine why or when it will occur again.

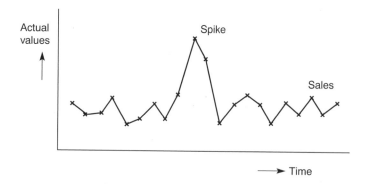

Figure 10.5   A spike in a data pattern

10.2.2 Step

This is where the data steps upwards or downwards suddenly. A step can take one or two periods: many more than this and it is probably a trend and not a step. An example of this type of problem is given in Figure 10.6. Illustrated in this figure is an upward step taking place within a constant data pattern. An example of a step can sometimes be seen when a company goes out of business and the demand is shared between its competitors, thus causing a step.

When a step occurs in a data pattern the forecast must be moved up or down to the new data pattern as soon as possible after the step has occurred. The old data before the step must be ignored in the calculations or consideration of the forecast.

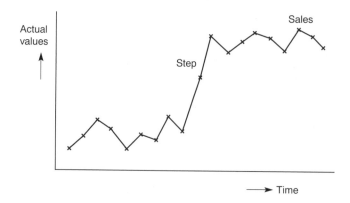

Figure 10.6   A step in a data pattern

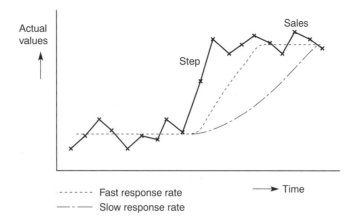

Figure 10.7 Response rates and steps

10.3 Forecast response rates

An important factor of forecasting systems is the response rate of the system. The response rate is the speed at which the forecast system responds to changes in the actual data. Figure 10.7 shows a step in a constant data pattern.

The forecasting system with the faster response rate shows a major advantage in this situation. It moves to the new level in the data at a faster rate, which will significantly reduce the build up of errors. Figure 10.8. shows a data pattern which has high variability.

The forecast system with the high response rate is responding to all the fluctuations in the data. This makes the system too variable and so it poorly identifies the true underlying trend of the data. In this situation the best forecast system is the one with the slow response rate – it truly identifies the underlying average of the data.

The two examples show how varying response rates are required under different conditions. With any data and forecasting system combination, various response

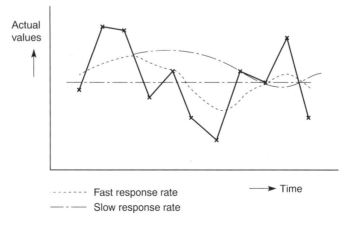

Figure 10.8 Response rates and high variability

rates should be tried until the one that best suits the objectives required of the forecast system is found. Given that the data may change with time, the response rate may also need to be changed. With all the forecasting approaches in the text the factors that control the response rate will be identified.

Competence Example 10.1

At the end of this section you should now be able to demonstrate how to:

1 **identify the main patterns that occur in forecast data**

2 **recognise the main data problems that can occur in data patterns**

To practise and demonstrate these detailed competences complete example problems 10.1 to 10.8 at the end of the chapter. To help you to develop these competences a description of the procedure you will need to follow is now given. A typical problem format is not given in this section because the procedure involved is one of inspection of graphs. An example of the data patterns is given.

PROCEDURE (IDENTIFICATION OF DATA PATTERNS)

1 Produce a graph of the data pattern (you may find the Lotus or Excel spreadsheet useful for this).

2 Inspect the graph and using the examples given identify the data patterns.

3 Identify if any of the problems are occurring with the data pattern.

DATA PATTERNS AND PROBLEMS

Constant data pattern with random variation

Trend data pattern with random variation

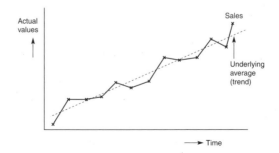

Cyclic data pattern with random variation

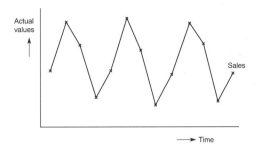

A spike in a data pattern

A step in a data pattern

Practise your competence now on problems 10.1 to 10.8 at the end of the chapter. Attempt all of these problems as they will give you a range of patterns and will all be used for forecasting later in this chapter. There is no formal part of the computer disk on data patterns but you may find it useful to use Lotus or Excel to plot the graphs for you. You may now demonstrate the competence in this area against problems from your own work environment.

10.4 Forecasting approaches

This section of Chapter 10 will enable you to:

- identify the main components of forecast data patterns
- estimate future forecasts from these components.

The section will also provide underpinning knowledge in the area of simple data pattern recognition forecasting, using visual methods.

A quick versatile and easy way of producing one-off forecasts is to make use of the considerable pattern recognition ability that the human brain possesses. This means producing a graph of the existing data with space for the forecast values to be added later. Do remember that spreadsheets like Lotus or Excel help considerably in the production of graphs. The next step is to determine the pattern of the data, and to see if either of the problems have occurred (spike or step). Then you must estimate the average line through the data. This can be carried out by placing a piece of cotton or string through the centre of the data. The cotton or string is much more versatile than a rule because it allows all the points to be viewed while the line is being balanced on the data average. It is also more useful when dealing with any form of curve trends.

The process of balancing the average line can be helped with simple calculations. If the constant data pattern is being considered then a series of arithmetical averages can be plotted on the graph to help the positioning of the cotton. If the trend pattern is being considered then semi-averages can be calculated. To calculate a semi-average, split the data into two halves, calculate the average of each half and then plot the two averages on the graph. These two points will then give a guide of where to place the cotton. Once the cotton has been placed on the existing data it can then be used to extrapolate the pattern into the future. These cotton forecasts can be added to the graph and the forecast values read off. Cyclic forecasting needs to be approached slightly differently. The cycle needs to be split into its component parts (e.g. months). Each part of the cycle is forecast as a pattern separately, each of these parts then making up the total forecast.

The graphical approach is a suitable way of producing one-off forecasts but it becomes unworkable in situations where many forecasts are required or when a forecasting system is required. Forecasting systems are needed with most products because they need to be updated regularly on either a daily, weekly, quarterly or yearly basis.

With the present trends in information technology the growing majority of forecasts are carried out on some type of computer-based system. To carry out smoothing and forecasting in this way requires a more formal mathematical-based approach. There are a vast range of formal mathematical smoothing and forecasting systems that can be used today, but it is beyond the scope of this chapter to outline every approach that could be used. What will be given is a series of the most popular approaches. Many of these are best suited to certain data patterns so these will be presented as such. However, remember that these formal approaches are for use mainly on computers.

Competence Example 10.2

At the end of this section you should now be able to demonstrate how to:

1 identify the main components of forecast data patterns

2 estimate future forecasts from these components

To practise and demonstrate these competences complete example problems 10.9 to 10.16 at the end of the chapter. To help you to develop these competences a description of the procedure you will need to follow is now given. A typical problem format is not given in this section because the procedure involved is one of inspection of graphs. An example of the data patterns is given.

PROCEDURE (GRAPHICAL FORECASTING)

Note: You have already completed procedure elements 1 to 3 in the first part of this chapter.

❶ Produce a graph of the data pattern (you may find the Lotus or Excel spreadsheet useful for this).

❷ Inspect the graph and using the examples given identify the data patterns.

❸ Identify if any of the problems are occurring with the data pattern.

❹ Identify the components of the data patterns.

❺ Use the components of the data pattern to estimate the forecasts required.

DATA PATTERNS AND PROBLEMS

Constant data pattern with random variation

Trend data pattern with random variation

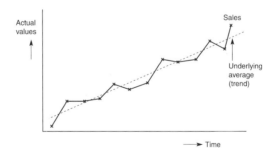

Cyclic data pattern with random variation

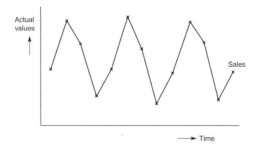

A spike in a data pattern

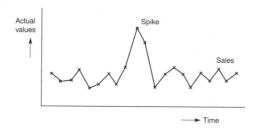

A step in a data pattern

Practise your competence now on problems 10.9 to 10.16 at the end of the chapter. Attempt all of these problems as they will give you a range of patterns and they will all be used for more formal forecasting approaches later in this chapter. There is no formal part of the package on graphical forecasting but you may find it useful to use Lotus or Excel to plot the graphs for you. You may now demonstrate the competence in this area against problems from your own work environment.

10.5 Constant data pattern forecasting approaches

Two methods which work well for the constant data pattern are **moving averages** and **exponential smoothing**. Both of these approaches also form the basis of a number of other forecasting approaches. The following example will develop these forecasting approaches.

The following data gives the sales pattern for bookcases at a furniture wholesaler for the first five months of the year. Looking over the past sales figures the data pattern is fairly constant, with no seasonal variations.

Month	1	2	3	4	5
Actual sales (Y_t)	101	142	91	133	115

We now need to produce a forecast for month 6.

10.5.1 Moving average

This section of Chapter 10 will enable you to:

- produce a table to calculate moving averages
- calculate the moving averages
- use the moving averages for forecasting

The section will also provide underpinning knowledge in the area of moving averages and their use in forecasting.

The moving average approach is the simplest of the more formal forecasting approaches. A moving average is simply an average that moves with time. As a new time period advances then the new data point is added into the average calculation and the oldest data point is dropped out of the average calculation, the length of the average remaining fixed.

The following example shows how a moving average is calculated. A three period moving average is calculated on this example and the symbol M_t is used for the moving average calculated in time period t.

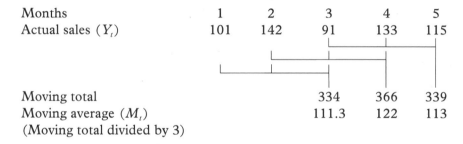

Months	1	2	3	4	5
Actual sales (Y_t)	101	142	91	133	115
Moving total			334	366	339
Moving average (M_t)			111.3	122	113
(Moving total divided by 3)					

As can be seen from the above example the average moves with time. The length of the moving average is the factor that controls the response rate of this smoothing approach. A three period moving average gives a fast response rate which can become unstable under some conditions. A medium response rate will be given with a moving average of around six time periods in length. Where moving averages are used in practice this is a common length to find in use. A slow response rate will be given with a moving average of around twelve time periods in length.

There are two forms of the moving average. One type is illustrated in the example where the moving average that is calculated is written in the last time period of the average. This type is used when the moving average is the main device of the forecasting approach. An alternative type of moving average is to write the moving average in the middle time period of the moving average calculation (best to have an uneven length to the average in this situation). This type can be used when the moving average is part of a more complicated forecasting approach for other data patterns.

The forecast model for moving average is as follows:

$$\hat{Y}_{t+T} = M_t$$

where $\hat{Y}_{t+T}$ = forecast calculated in time period t for T time periods ahead.

The forecast is the most up-to-date value of the moving average calculations. In the case of the example the forecasts are as follows:

$$\hat{Y}_{5+1} = M_5 = 113 \text{ bookcases}$$

Competence Example 10.3

At the end of this section you should now be able to demonstrate how to:

1 produce a table to calculate moving averages

2 calculate the moving averages

3 use the moving averages for forecasting

To practise and demonstrate these competences complete example problems 10.17 and 10.18 at the end of this chapter. To help you to develop these competences a description of the procedure you will need to follow is now given, along with a typical problem format. This problem format is based on the example we have just considered.

PROCEDURE

❶ Identify data pattern to be constant.

❷ Determine the response rate (length of the moving average).

❸ Produce the moving average data table.

❹ Calculate the moving average.

❺ Identify the required forecast.

PROBLEM

The following data gives the sales pattern for bookcases at a furniture wholesaler for the first five months of the year. Looking over the past sales figures the data pattern is fairly constant with no seasonal variations.

Month	1	2	3	4	5
Actual sales (Y_t)	101	142	91	133	115

You are required to produce a forecast for month 6.

SOLUTION FORMAT

❶ ❷ Response rate required is fast, therefore a three period moving average has been chosen. **1 2**

❸ ❹

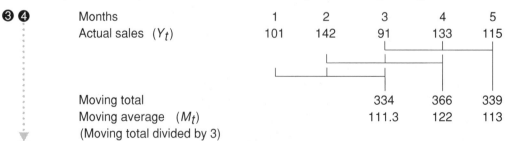

Months	1	2	3	4	5
Actual sales (Y_t)	101	142	91	133	115
Moving total			334	366	339
Moving average (M_t)			111.3	122	113
(Moving total divided by 3)					

$$\hat{Y}_{t+T} = M_t$$
$$\hat{Y}_{5+1} = M_5 = 113 \text{ bookcases}$$

Practise your competence now on problems 10.17 and 10.18 at the end of this chapter. When you have demonstrated competence in this area you can use the computer disk provided to automate the arithmetic elements. You may choose either a Lotus or Excel spreadsheet. With this disk you will be able to input the data to be forecasted and specify the length of the moving average. The spreadsheet will then calculate the moving average. You will then be able to identify the required forecast. You may now demonstrate the competence in this area against problems from your own work environment.

10.5.2 Exponential smoothing

This section of Chapter 10 will enable you to:

- produce a table to calculate exponential smoothing
- calculate the exponentially smoothed values
- use the exponentially smoothed values for forecasting

The section will also provide underpinning knowledge in the area of exponential smoothing and its use in forecasting.

This approach allows us to produce a smoothed average through the data and is a widely-used approach with constant data patterns and as a basis for a number of later approaches. The exponentially smoothed average (U_t) will be given by the following expression:

$$U_t = \alpha Y_t + (1 - \alpha) U_{t-1}$$

where U_t = exponentially smoothed average of time period t
$\quad U_{t-1}$ = exponentially smoothed average of time period $t - 1$
$\qquad$ i.e. the previous exponentially smoothed value
$\quad Y_t$ = actual value in time period t
$\quad \alpha$ = smoothing constant (number between 0 and 1)

An alternative way of presenting exponential smoothing would be:

This period's smoothed = $[\alpha \times$ this period's actual $]$ + $[(1 - \alpha) \times$ last period's smoothed$]$

There are two ways to initialise an exponential smoothing calculation:

1. When no previous data is available. In this case the first value of the actuals is taken to be the first exponential smoothed value. Calculation then proceeds from the second time period.
2. Where previous data exists. When previous data exists then an average should be taken of the most recent data (generally four or five time periods). This average can then be used in the initial time period for the previous smoothed value.

Wherever possible the second approach of averaging should be used to initialise an exponential smoothing system. This approach will take the smoothing system directly to the underlying average in the initial periods (*see* Figure 10.9).

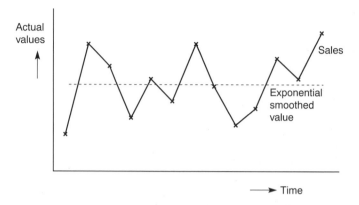

Figure 10.9   Initialising exponential smoothing by averaging

The approach of taking the first value to initialise can lead to an extreme value being taken. This can mean that it takes several time periods for the smoothed value to settle to the underlying average (*see* Figure 10.10).

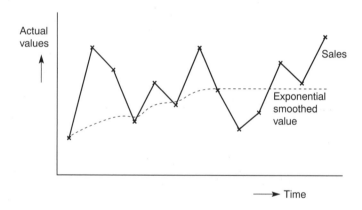

Figure 10.10   Initialising exponential smoothing by taking the first value

The following example shows how exponential smoothing is calculated. In this example the initialisation value has been calculated from previous data to be 112 and a smoothing constant of 0.2 used.

Months		1	2	3	4	5
Actual sales Y_t		101	142	91	133	115
$0.2 \times Y_t$		20.2	28.4	18.2	26.6	23
$0.8 \times U_{t-1}$		89.6	87.84	92.99	88.95	92.44
U_t	112 (initial)	109.8	116.24	111.19	115.55	115.44

The smoothing constant is the factor that controls the response rate of the exponential smoothing approach. It can be any number between 0 and 1 but in practice the value should not go above 0.3. Any value above 0.3 would make the smoothing system unstable. The higher the smoothing constant the greater the response rate. The most common value used in practice is 0.1. The procedure for the selection of the smoothing constant is trial and change. Different values of the smoothing constant should be tried with typical data from which forecasts are to be drawn. The value of the smoothing constant is then chosen that best meets the smoothing and forecasting objectives. It should also be remembered that the characteristics of the data may change with time and therefore the smoothing constant may need to be changed to still meet the objectives.

The forecast model for exponential smoothing is as follows:

$$\hat{Y}_{t+T} = U_t$$

where $\hat{Y}_{t+T}$ = forecast calculated in time period t for T time periods ahead.

The forecast is the most up-to-date value of the exponential smoothing calculations.

The forecast for the example for month 6 is as follows:

$$\hat{Y}_{5+1} = U_5 = 115.44 \cong 115 \text{ bookcases}$$

When selecting a method for use with the constant data pattern, exponential smoothing has a number of advantages over moving averages:

1. Less data needs to be stored.
2. Only one initial estimate is required to start the method.
3. The rate of response can be changed easily by only changing the smoothing constant.
4. Past data is rejected gradually rather than suddenly and more account is taken of the more recent information, both important to more effective smoothing.

The first three advantages are administrative and have more of an effect within computerised systems. The fourth advantage is more fundamental to the way in which the method smoothes the data.

Competence Example 10.4

At the end of this section you should now be able to demonstrate how to:

1 **produce a table to calculate exponential smoothing**

2 **calculate the exponentially smoothed values**

3 **use the exponentially smoothed values for forecasting**

To practise and demonstrate these competences complete example problems 10.19 and 10.20 at the end of this chapter. To help you to develop these competences a description of the procedure you will need to follow is now given, along with a typical problem format. This problem format is based on the example we have just considered.

PROCEDURE (EXPONENTIAL SMOOTHING)

❶ Identify data pattern to be constant.

❷ Determine the response rate (the α which will be in the range 0.1 to 0.3) and the method to be used to initialise the data.

❸ Produce the exponential smoothing data table.

❹ Calculate the exponentially smoothed values.

❺ Identify the required forecast.

PROBLEM

The following data gives the sales pattern for bookcases at a furniture wholesaler for the first five months of the year. Looking over the past sales figures the data pattern is fairly constant with no seasonal variations.

Month	1	2	3	4	5
Actual sales (Y_t)	101	142	91	133	115

You are required to produce a forecast for month 6.

SOLUTION FORMAT

❶ ❷ In this example the initialisation value has been calculated from previous data to be 112 **1** **2** and a smoothing constant of 0.2 is to be used (a medium response rate).

❸ ❹

Months		1	2	3	4	5
Actual sales Y_t		101	142	91	133	115
$0.2 \times Y_t$		20.2	28.4	18.2	26.6	23
$0.8 \times U_{t-1}$		89.6	87.84	92.99	88.95	92.44
U_t	112	109.8	116.24	111.19	115.55	115.44
	Initial					

❺ $$\hat{Y}_{t+T} = U_t$$ **3**

The forecast for the example for month 6 is as follows:

$$\hat{Y}_{5+1} = U_5 = 115.44 \approx 115 \text{ bookcases}$$

Practise your competence now on problems 10.19 and 10.20 at the end of this chapter. When you have demonstrated competence in this area you can use the computer disk provided to automate the arithmetic elements. You may choose either a Lotus or Excel spreadsheet depending on the package you have access to. With this disk you will be able to input the data to be forecasted and specify the smoothing constant $\propto$. The spreadsheet will then calculate the exponentially smoothed values. You will then be able to identify the required forecast. You may now demonstrate the competence in this area against problems from your own work environment.

Summary of constant data pattern approaches

Both moving averages and exponential smoothing are important building blocks for other more complex forecasting approaches for the other data patterns. If a forecasting approach for the constant data pattern is required then exponential smoothing is likely to be the best. Moving averages will only be superior to exponential smoothing if a very high degree of smoothing is required.

Moving averages and exponential smoothing will not provide successful forecasts if they are derived from a trend data pattern or from a cyclic data pattern. Both approaches will always lag a trend which could lead to lost sales or overstocking. Also, neither approach will follow a cycle closely enough to give realistic forecasts.

10.6 Trend data pattern forecasting approaches

Three methods are now illustrated which work well for the trend data pattern. First the **exponential double smoothing**, an approach that shows how the disadvantage of single exponential smoothing lagging a trend can be turned to an advantage. The second approach is that of **regression analysis**, a technique familiar to those of you who have worked through Chapter 8. The third approach is that of the mathematically sophisticated technique of **Box Jenkins**. This third approach is one that should only be seriously considered for use in a computerised system. This section concludes by considering non-linear trends. The following example will be used to develop the trend forecasting approaches.

The following data gives the recorded crime for aggravated burglary in a particular division of a police force.

Year	1989	1990	1991	1992	1993
Actual crime (Y_t)	152	164	160	178	185

The pattern of this particular crime has been growing over time and requires a trend method. Police managers require a forecast of this particular crime for 1994.

10.6.1 Exponential double smoothing

This section of Chapter 10 will enable you to:

- produce a table to calculate double exponential smoothing
- calculate the double exponentially smoothed values
- use the double exponentially smoothed values for forecasting

The section will also provide underpinning knowledge in the area of double exponential smoothing and its use in forecasting.

Exponential double smoothing turns a disadvantage of single exponential smoothing to an advantage. Single exponential smoothing will always lag a trend. If the value obtained by smoothing is exponentially smoothed again this will lag the first exponentially smoothed value by the same amount as the first exponentially smoothed value lags the underlying average of the data. This is shown graphically in Figure 10.11.

The lag can be determined by differencing the single exponential smoothing and the double exponential smoothing values. The lag can then be added back to the single exponential smoothed value to bring it to the underlying average. This approach will also work for downward trends but the lag will be negative. The following expressions give the method for producing a **double smoothed system**:

$$U_t = \alpha Y_t + (1 - \alpha) U_{t-1}$$
$$\overline{U}_t = \alpha U_t + (1 - \alpha) \overline{U}_{t-1}$$

where U_t = single exponential smoothed value in time period t
Y_t = actual value in time period t
α = smoothing constant (same for both single and double smoothing)
$\overline{U}_t$ = double exponential smoothed value in time period t
lag = $U_t - \overline{U}_t$
$\overline{Y}_t$ = underlying average of the data

The underlying average will then be given by the following expression; the lag added to the single exponentially smoothed value:

$$\overline{Y}_t = U_t + (U_t - \overline{U}_t)$$

This is best rewritten:

$$\overline{Y}_t = 2U_t - \overline{U}_t$$

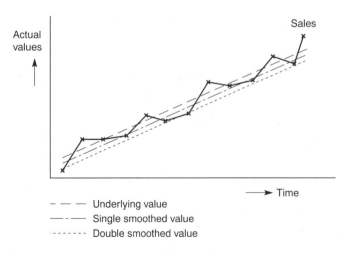

Figure 10.11 Exponential double smoothing

Like all exponential smoothing, double smoothing needs to be initialised. The single exponentially smoothed part can be initialised like any other exponentially smoothed method – it is the double smoothing that requires a slightly different approach. There are two ways to initialise the double smoothing element:

1. When no previous data is available. In this case the first single smoothed estimate is taken to be the initialisation value of the double smoothing. Given this assumes no lag it will take several time periods to settle down.
2. Where previous data exists. Carry out exponential smoothing on some previous data. The last exponentially smoothed value will then be used to initialise the single exponentially smoothed element. Determine the average lag from the underlying average of this previous data (best carried out graphically). Then subtract (add if negative) the lag from the value used to initialise the single smoothing and use this value to initialise the double smoothing.

The following example shows how exponential double smoothing is calculated. In this example the initialisation values have been calculated from previous data and a smoothing constant of 0.2 used.

Year	Initial	1989	1990	1991	1992	1993
Actual Crime Y_t		152	164	160	178	185
$0.2 \times Y_t$		30.4	32.8	32	35.6	37
$0.8 \times U_{t-1}$		116	117.12	119.94	121.55	125.72
U_t	145	146.4	149.92	151.94	157.15	162.72
$0.2 \times U_t$		29.28	29.98	30.39	31.43	32.54
$0.8 \times \bar{U}_{t-1}$		100	103.42	106.72	109.69	112.90
$\bar{U}_t$	125	129.28	133.40	137.11	141.12	145.44
$\bar{Y}_t = 2U_t - \bar{U}_t$		163.52	166.44	166.77	173.18	180.0

The underlying average cannot be used directly for a forecast as with constant data methods; there needs to be an incremental change with time to take account of the trend. The forecast model for exponential double smoothing is as follows.

$$\hat{Y}_{t+T} = 2U_t - \bar{U}_t + \frac{\alpha}{1-\alpha}(U_t - \bar{U}_t)T$$

which simplifies for a one period ahead forecast (i.e. $T+1$):

$$\hat{Y}_{t+1} = \frac{(2-\alpha)U_t - \bar{U}_t}{1-\alpha}$$

For the example previously calculated, the general forecasting model calculated in time period 1993 for forecasting T time periods ahead can be produced as follows:

$$\hat{Y}_{1993+T} = 2U_{1993} - \bar{U}_{1993} + \frac{0.2}{0.8}(U_{1993} - \bar{U}_{1993})T$$

$$= 2 \times 162.72 - 145.44 + 0.25(162.72 - 145.44)T$$
$$= 325.44 - 145.44 + 0.25(17.28)T$$
$$= 180 + 4.32T$$

Forecasts for any time period in the future can now be calculated using this model. For example:

Forecast for time period 1995
$$\hat{Y}_{1993+2} = 180 + (4.32 \times 2)$$
$$= 180 + 8.64$$
$$= 188.64 \cong 189 \text{ crimes}$$

If only forecasts for one period ahead are required then the general forecast model could still be used or the simplified version of the forecast model:

$$\hat{Y}_{1993+1} = \frac{(2-\alpha)U_{1993} - \bar{U}_{1993}}{1-\alpha}$$

$$= \frac{(2-0.2)162.72 - 145.44}{1-0.2}$$

$$= \frac{1.8 \times 162.72 - 145.44}{0.8}$$

$$= \frac{292.90 - 145.44}{0.8}$$

$$= \frac{147.46}{0.8} = 184.33 \cong 184 \text{ crimes}$$

Competence Example 10.5

At the end of this section you should now be able to demonstrate how to:

1 produce a table to calculate double exponential smoothing

2 calculate the double exponentially smoothed values

3 use the double exponentially smoothed values for forecasting

To practise and demonstrate these competences complete example problems 10.21 and 10.22 at the end of this chapter. To help you to develop these competences a description of the procedure you will need to follow is now given, along with a typical problem format. This problem format is based on the example we have just considered.

PROCEDURE

❶ Identify data pattern to be a trend.

❷ Determine the response rate (the α which will be in the range 0.1 to 0.3) and the method to be used to initialise the data.

❸ Produce the double exponential smoothing data table.

❹ Calculate the double exponentially smoothed values.

❺ Calculate the required forecast.

PROBLEM

The following data gives the recorded crime for aggravated burglary in a particular division of a police force.

Year	1989	1990	1991	1992	1993
Actual crime (Y_t)	152	164	160	178	185

The pattern of this particular crime has been growing over time and requires a trend method. Police managers require a forecast of this particular crime for 1994.

SOLUTION FORMAT

❶ ❷ In this example the initialisation values have been calculated from previous data and a ▮1 ▮2 smoothing constant of 0.2 is to be used.

❸ ❹

Year	Initial	1989	1990	1991	1992	1993
Actual crime Y_t		152	164	160	178	185
$0.2 \times Y_t$		30.4	32.8	32	35.6	37
$0.8 \times U_{t-1}$		116	117.12	119.94	121.55	125.72
U_t	145	146.4	149.92	151.94	157.15	162.72
$0.2 \times U_t$		29.28	29.98	30.39	31.43	32.54
$0.8 \times \bar{U}_{t-1}$		100	103.42	106.72	109.69	112.90
$\bar{U}_t$	125	129.28	133.40	137.11	141.12	145.44
$\bar{Y}_t = 2U_t - \bar{U}_t$		163.52	166.44	166.77	173.18	180.0

❺ ▮3

$$\hat{Y}_{1993+1} = \frac{(2-a)U_{1993} - \bar{U}_{1993}}{1-a}$$

$$= \frac{(2-0.2)162.72 - 145.44}{1-0.2}$$

$$= \frac{1.8 \times 162.72 - 145.44}{0.8}$$

$$= \frac{292.90 - 145.44}{0.8}$$

$$= \frac{147.46}{0.8} = 184.33 \cong 184 \text{ crimes}$$

Practise your competence now on problems 10.21 and 10.22 at the end of this chapter. When you have demonstrated competence in this area you can use the computer disk provided to automate the arithmetic elements. You may choose either a Lotus or an Excel spreadsheet depending on the package you have access to. With this disk you will be able to input the data to be forecasted and specify the smoothing constant a. The spreadsheet will then calculate the exponentially smoothed values (single and double). You will then be able to identify the required forecast. You may now demonstrate the competence in this area against problems from your own work environment.

10.6.2 Regression analysis

From working through Chapter 9 you should now be familiar with the approach of regression analysis. This approach can also be used in forecasting. The approach used so far in regression analysis could only be used for a one-off forecast, so it needs to be modified if it is to be used in a forecast system and updatable as time periods advance. New time periods cannot just be added and then the regression recalculated or too much account will be taken of old data.

The solution to making regression analysis into a forecast system is to turn it into a moving regression in the same manner as moving averages. When a new data point is reached the new data point is added and the oldest data point removed and then the regression is recalculated.

The length of the moving regression is best kept around ten data points. If the length of the regression is too short the process becomes unstable and forecasts can then fluctuate wildly. If the length of the regression is too long it will be unresponsive and take too much account of old data.

10.6.3 Box Jenkins

The **Box Jenkins** approach is a sophisticated mathematical approach that owes its development to control theory. The approach is based on building into the forecast a measure of the error to ensure the forecast is more effective. Unlike exponential double smoothing, which is a single parameter system (a), Box Jenkins is a three parameter system. This makes it a complicated approach to use. It requires a degree of skill in setting the parameters and it is highly recommended that the calculations are carried out on a computer.

Box Jenkins is an approach that has found considerable favour in a large number of computerised forecasting systems. The approaches so far given in the text can easily be used by the manager. However, it is recommended that Box Jenkins should only be considered by the manager if there exists the support of a specialist, unless the approach is part of an automated computerised system.

Due to the complications of using this approach independently to computerised systems a detailed example will not be given. Box Jenkins is however a powerful and effective forecasting approach for dealing with trend data.

10.6.4 Non-linear trends

Not all trends will be underlying straight line trends. Double smoothing and regression both fit trends that are straight lines, therefore some alternative approach is needed to smooth these non-linear trends. The following sales data illustrates a non-linear trend and this is shown graphically in Figure 10.12.

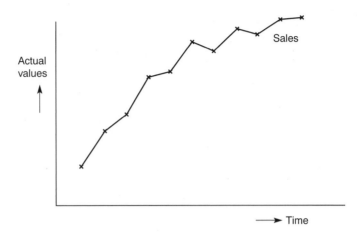

Figure 10.12   A non-linear sales trend

If regression analysis is applied to this data the straight line produced will not smooth successfully, nor will the forecasts be successful. Double smoothing and Box Jenkins will have more success at smoothing this data, but both will have the problem that forecasts will be made in a straight line. Forecasts one period ahead will be reasonably successful but the further into the future forecasts are made the more the straight line will deviate from the curve of the data.

There is a simple procedure so that all the methods will operate successfully with non-linear trends. The procedure is to transform the data into a straight line. For the majority of sales and market non-linear trends this will be achieved by taking logarithms of the sales value. This will transform the relationship into a straight line and this is shown in Figure 10.13.

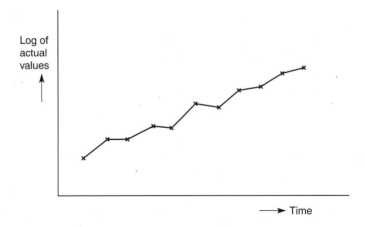

Figure 10.13   A transformed sales trend

Once the transformation has been carried out then the chosen forecasting approach can be used. It must be remembered to transform back when the forecast has been produced, i.e. to take anti-logarithms.

Summary of trend data pattern approaches

Three forecasting approaches are illustrated in this trend section. Exponential double smoothing is a single parameter forecasting approach. This approach builds back the amount that single exponential smoothing produces when it lags a trend. The double smoothing approach will not be very successful with constant data as it is likely to become unstable. Regression analysis is a statistical approach that will be familiar to many managers. By making it move with time, like moving averages, it will provide a useful forecasting approach. It will also work reasonably well with the constant data pattern but will only directly work successfully on linear trends. The final approach is that of Box Jenkins – a mathematically sophisticated three parameter forecasting approach. To use Box Jenkins it is recommended that it is set up in conjunction with a specialist. All of these trend forecasting approaches do not work totally successfully with non-linear trends but this problem can be overcome by transforming the data.

Trend forecasting becomes more arithmetical than the constant data pattern approaches and therefore it is recommended that it is carried out on a computer. The cost of a modern personal computer (PC) brings computing within the price of all companies and therefore all sales and marketing departments.

10.7 Cyclic data pattern forecasting approaches

This section of Chapter 10 will enable you to:

- identify the elements of the cycle
- calculate the basic elements of the cycle
- use these elements to construct a forecast

The section will also provide underpinning knowledge in the area of cyclic forecasting methods.

Cyclic or **seasonal** forecasting is the most complicated of forecasting approaches. Many approaches are produced directly for the computer, and these packages have been produced and marketed by a variety of organisations from individuals to companies, who have developed the package for their own use and now sell the successful result.

Although many of the modern cyclic forecasting approaches are complicated, the basic principles are quite simple. The first step is to find the underlying trend of the cycle. The second step is to determine cyclic or seasonal factors. This is the difference between the points on the cycle and the underlying trend. The third and final step is to use the underlying trend and cyclic factors to build forecasts of the future. This process can be illustrated with a simplified approach to cyclic forecasting used on the following example. Table 10.1 gives the sales of a particular brand of electric jug kettle given in thousand units.

Table 10.1   Sales of an electric jug kettle

Year	1990	1991	1992	1993
1st quarter	100	101	98	99
2nd quarter	56	57	54	57
3rd quarter	68	67	69	68
4th quarter	151	148	150	152
Year total	375	373	371	376

The first stage is to find the underlying trend of the overall data pattern. This can be achieved with this data by using moving averages. The length of the moving average should be equal to the length of the cycle or in multiples of the cycle. With this example a four year period moving average will be used. The seasonal or cyclic differences can then be calculated by determining the difference between the actual value and the de-seasonalised line calculated in the first stage.

Year	Quarter	Actual	Moving average	Seasonal value
1990	1	100		
	2	56		
	3	68		
	4	151	93.75	57.25
1991	1	101	94	7
	2	57	94.25	−37.25
	3	67	94	−27
	4	148	93.25	54.75
1992	1	98	92.5	5.5
	2	54	91.75	−37.75
	3	69	92.25	−23.25
	4	150	92.75	57.25
1993	1	99	93	6
	2	57	93.75	−36.75
	3	68	93.5	−25.5
	4	152	94	58

The seasonal values now need to be brought together into a single seasonal factor for each part of the cycle (i.e. quarter in this case). With this example a simple average will be taken but on an ongoing basis either moving average or exponential smoothing should be used.

Table 10.2   Average seasonal factors

Year	1990	1991	1992	1993	Ave seasonal factor
1st quarter		7	5.5	6	6.17
2nd quarter		−37.25	−37.75	−36.75	−37.25
3rd quarter		−27	−23.25	−25.5	−25.25
4th Quarter	57.25	54.75	57.25	58	56.81

The calculation of a forecast for 1994 is made by extending the deseasonalised line (i.e. the moving average) into the future. This will be the most up-to-date moving average value (i.e. $M_{1993\ 4th\ Qtr} = 94$). The forecast is then completed by adding to this value the seasonal factor appropriate to the quarter.

$$1994\ \text{FORECAST}\qquad \begin{aligned}&\text{1st quarter} = 94 + 6.17 = 100.17\\&\text{2nd quarter} = 94 - 37.25 = 56.75\\&\text{3rd quarter} = 94 - 25.25 = 68.75\\&\text{4th quarter} = 94 + 56.81 = 150.81\end{aligned}$$

All the values in this example are measured in thousands, therefore the forecast for 1994 is:

1st quarter = 100,170 units
2nd quarter = 56,750 units
3rd quarter = 68,750 units
4th quarter = 150,810 units

Many of the more complicated cyclic forecasting approaches will be similar to the approach used in the example. One forecasting system is used to remove the cyclic effects. Then separate forecasting systems are used to forecast each of the cyclic factors, one for each element of the cycle. Any of these separate systems can be constant or trend, may contain spikes or steps and may require different response rates. All of this makes cyclic forecasting complicated, involving a large number of calculations.

Competence Example 10.6

At the end of this section you should now be able to demonstrate how to:

1 **identify the elements of the cycle**

2 **calculate the basic elements of the cycle**

3 **use these elements to construct a forecast**

To practise and demonstrate these competences complete example problems 10.23 and 10.24 at the end of this chapter. To help you to develop these competences a description of the procedure you will need to follow is now given, along with a typical problem format. This problem format is based on the example we have just considered.

PROCEDURE (CYCLIC FORECASTING)

❶ Identify data pattern to be a cycle.

❷ Identify the elements of the cycle.

❸ Calculate the underlying trend of the cycle.

❹ Calculate cyclic elements.

❺ Calculate the required forecast using the underlying trend and cyclic elements.

THE PROBLEM

The following table gives the sales of a particular brand of electric jug kettle given in thousand units. A forecast is required for the next year (1994).

Year	1990	1991	1992	1993
1st quarter	100	101	98	99
2nd quarter	56	57	54	57
3rd quarter	68	67	69	68
4th quarter	151	148	150	152
Year Total	375	373	371	376

A description of the layout of the solution format is given at the beginning of the book.

SOLUTION FORMAT

❶ ❷ In this example a four year period moving average will be used given that the cycle is made up of four quarters. The underlying average is constant as are the cyclic elements.

❷ ❸

Year	Quarter	Actual	Moving average	Seasonal value
1990	1	100		
	2	56		
	3	68		
	4	151	93.75	57.25
1991	1	101	94	7
	2	57	94.25	−37.25
	3	67	94	−27
	4	148	93.25	54.75
1992	1	98	92.5	5.5
	2	54	91.75	−37.75
	3	69	92.25	−23.25
	4	150	92.75	57.25
1993	1	99	93	6
	2	57	93.75	−36.75
	3	68	93.5	−25.5
	4	152	94	58

❹

Year	1990	1991	1992	1993	Ave seasonal factor
1st quarter		7	5.5	6	6.17
2nd quarter		−37.25	−37.75	−36.75	−37.25
3rd quarter		−27	−23.25	−25.5	−25.25
4th quarter	57.25	54.75	57.25	58	56.81

⑤   1994 FORECAST   1st quarter = 94 + 6.17 = 100.17   **3**
                                            2nd quarter = 94 − 37.25 = 56.75
                                            3rd quarter = 94 − 25.25 = 68.75
                                            4th quarter = 94 + 56.81 = 150.81

All the values in this example are measured in thousands, therefore the forecast for 1994 is:

1st quarter = 100,170 units
2nd quarter = 56,750 units
3rd quarter = 68,750 units
4th quarter = 150,810 units

Practise your competence now on problems 10.23 and 10.24 at the end of this chapter. When you have demonstrated competence in this area you can use the computer disk provided to automate the arithmetic elements. You may choose a Lotus or Excel spreadsheet depending on which package you have access to. With this disk you will be able to input the data to be forecasted and specify the elements of the cycle. The spreadsheet will then calculate the forecast. You may now demonstrate the competence in this area against problems from your own work environment.

10.8   Control of forecast models

It is important when building any forecast model to ensure that the model can check on its own consistency. Consistency in a forecasting situation means that the forecasts are taking the middle or average line through the data.

This section of Chapter 10 will enable you to:

- identify the forecast (or smoothed value) and the actual data
- calculate the cumulative sum of the errors (CUSUM)
- use the CUSUM to interpret the errors

The section will also provide underpinning knowledge in the area of using the CUSUM to control forecasting systems.

The simplest approach for carrying out this check is to use a procedure called CUSUM (cumulative sum). This procedure is to produce a running total of the error of the forecasting system.

Week number	1	2	3	4	5	6	7	8	9	10
Actual values	151	151	148	149	150	148	153	151	152	154
Forecast	150	150	150	150	150	150	150	150	150	150
Error	−1	−1	+2	+1	0	+2	−3	−1	−2	−4
CUSUM	−1	−2	0	+1	+1	+3	0	−1	−3	−7

Figure 10.14   CUSUM example

Error = Forecast value – Actual

The error will be positive and negative and if the forecast model is performing correctly the sum of all errors will stay around zero. If the value of the CUSUM rises or falls significantly then the forecasts are not being produced correctly and therefore corrective action should be taken. Figure 10.14. shows how a CUSUM can be calculated from a series of actuals and forecasts. The graphical presentation of the CUSUM is shown in Figure 10.15.

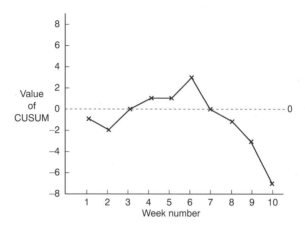

Figure 10.15   CUSUM chart

This shows how at first the forecasts work well when the data follows a constant data pattern but they fail towards the end because the underlying average has changed. This failure is shown effectively on the CUSUM with the dramatic movement to week ten. The CUSUM is a simple to operate error tracking routine that works well for the simpler and more heuristic approaches to forecasting. Problems arise with the decision of when the forecast is out of control. With experience individuals can quickly decide when this has occurred – it is a little more difficult to transfer this experience onto the computer.

Competence Example 10.7

At the end of this section you should now be able to demonstrate how to:

1 identify the forecast (or smoothed value) and the actual data

2 calculate the cumulative sum of the errors (CUSUM)

3 use the CUSUM to interpret the errors

To practise and demonstrate these competences complete example problems 10.25 and 10.26 at the end of this chapter. To help you to develop these competences a description of the procedure you will need to follow is now given, along with a typical problem format. This problem format is based on the example we have just considered.

PROCEDURE (CUSUM)

❶ Identify forecast (or smoothed) and actual values.

❷ Calculate the error.

❸ Calculate the cumulative sum (CUSUM).

❹ Interpret the CUSUM to control the forecast system.

PROBLEM

The following table gives the forecast and actual values for the sale of a particular design of folder at a stationery wholesaler.

Week number	1	2	3	4	5	6	7	8	9	10
Actual sales	151	151	148	149	150	148	153	151	152	154
Forecast	150	150	150	150	150	150	150	150	150	150

Management of the stationery wholesaler requires to know if the forecasting system is operating correctly.

SOLUTION FORMAT

❶ ❷ ❸

Week number	1	2	3	4	5	6	7	8	9	10
Actual values	151	151	148	149	150	148	153	151	152	154
Forecast	150	150	150	150	150	150	150	150	150	150
Error	−1	−1	+2	+1	0	+2	−3	−1	−2	−4
CUSUM	−1	−2	0	+1	+1	+3	0	−1	−3	−7

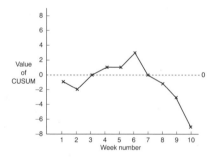

❹ This shows how at first the forecasts work well when the data follows a constant data pattern but they fail towards the end because the underlying average has changed This failure is shown effectively on the CUSUM with the dramatic movement to week 10.

Practise your competence now on problems 10.25 and 10.26 at the end of this chapter. When you have demonstrated competence in this area you can use the computer disk provided to automate the arithmetic elements. You may choose either a Lotus or Excel spreadsheet depending on which you have access to. With this disk you will be able to input the actual data and the forecast. The spreadsheet will then calculate the CUSUM and produce the graph. You may now demonstrate the competence in this area against problems from your own work environment.

10.9 Computerised tracking signal

This section of Chapter 10 will enable you to:

- identify the forecast (or smoothed value) and the actual data
- calculate the computerised tracking signal on the errors
- use the computerised tracking signal to interpret the errors

The section will also provide underpinning knowledge in the area of using the computerised tracking signal to control forecasting systems.

A widely used tracking system used in computerised forecasting systems is one based on the forecast error and exponential smoothing. The first step is to create an exponentially smoothed error (E_t). This will be given by the following expression:

$$E_t = \alpha e_t + (1 - \alpha)E_{t-1}$$

where e_t = forecast error in time period t

The second step is to create an exponentially smoothed absolute error: this is referred to as the mean absolute deviation (MAD_t). The term absolute refers to the taking of all errors to be positive, therefore this gives a weighted average of errors irrespective of the sign. The MAD_t will be given by the following expression:

$$MAD_t = \alpha \mid e_t \mid + (1 - \alpha)\ MAD_t$$

where $\mid e_t \mid$ = the absolute value of the forecast error in time period t (i.e. by taking all the errors to be positive)

The smoothing constant (α) must be the same for both the exponentially smoothed error (E_t) and the mean absolute deviation (MAD_t). The tracking signal (TS_t) is created with the following expression:

$$TS_t = \frac{E_t}{MAD_t}$$

The tracking signal can be calculated as shown in Table 10.3 using an α value of 0.1.

Like all exponentially based systems there are two ways to start up the calculations:

1. When no previous data is available. Take the first error (e_t) and this will become an initialisation value to the exponentially smoothed error (E_t). To initialise the mean absolute deviation (MAD_t) a value of at least twice the initialisation value for the exponentially smoothed error must be used. This is to stop the tracking signal going out of limits in the first periods. This approach could pick an extreme value and therefore take several periods to settle to steady state (this is shown in the calculated example).

Table 10.3 Calculating the tracking signal

Month	Initial	1	2	3	4	5
Actual sales		6	17	12	9	10
Forecast sales		10	12	11	12	11
Error (e_t)		4	−5	−1	3	1
$0.1 \times e_t$		0.4	−0.5	−0.1	0.3	0.1
$0.9 \times e_{t-1}$		3.6	3.6	2.8	2.4	2.4
E_t	4	4	3.1	2.7	2.7	2.5
$0.1 \times \mid e_t \mid$		0.4	0.5	0.1	0.3	0.1
$0.9 \times MAD_{t-1}$		9	8.5	8.1	7.4	6.9
MAD_t	10	9.4	9.0	8.2	7.7	7.0
TS_t		0.43	0.34	0.33	0.35	0.36

2. Where previous data exists. From several recent past actuals and forecasts calculate the errors. From these errors calculate the average using this to initialise the exponentially smoothed error (E_t). Recalculate the average, but now taking all errors to be positive, and use this average to initialise the mean absolute deviation (MAD_t). This approach will place the values at a correct level and will ensure the tracking signal settles to steady state quickly in the initial periods. Wherever possible this is the approach to use.

The value of the tracking signal can be examined in each time period to see if it is within limits. Table 10.4 gives the cumulative probabilities for $a = 0.1$ and $a = 0.2$ assuming the errors to be normally distributed, which in most cases they will. Therefore for $a = 0.2$ then a value of $TS_t \geqslant 0.74$ would indicate with 95 per cent confidence that the forecasting system being monitored is out of control for reasons other than random fluctuations. Table 10.4 gives the cumulative probability limits of the tracking signal. The limits normally used are the 0.90 level to act as a warning limit and 0.95 or 0.98 to act as an action limit. The system would allow procedures to continue if the warning limit is passed but produce an exception list of any such items for investigation. If the action limit is passed then all procedures for that item would be stopped for immediate investigation.

Table 10.4 Limits of tracking signal

Cumulative probability	Tracking signal $a = 0.1$	$a = 0.2$
0	0	0
0.50	0.21	0.32
0.70	0.30	0.46
0.80	0.36	0.54
0.90	0.45	0.66
0.95	0.51	0.74
0.98	0.60	0.81
1.00	1.00	1.00

Competence Example 10.8

At the end of this section you should now be able to demonstrate how to:

1 **identify the forecast (or smoothed value) and the actual data**

2 **calculate the computerised tracking signal on the errors**

3 **use the computerised tracking signal to interpret the errors**

To practise and demonstrate these competences complete example problems 10.27 and 10.28 at the end of this chapter. To help you to develop these competences a description of the procedure you will need to follow is now given, along with a typical problem format. This problem format is based on the example we have just considered.

PROCEDURE (COMPUTERISED TRACKING SIGNAL)

1 Identify forecast (or smoothed) and actual values.

2 Calculate the error.

3 Identify the smoothing constant α and the initialisation values.

4 Calculate the exponentially smoothed error.

5 Calculate the mean absolute deviation.

6 Calculate the tracking signal.

7 Interpret the tracking signal to control the forecasting system.

PROBLEM

The following table gives the sales figures and forecast for customised computer systems for a medium-sized software house:

Month	1	2	3	4	5
Actual sales	6	17	12	9	10
Forecast sales	10	12	11	12	11

Management of the software house want to know if their forecasting system is operating correctly.

SOLUTION FORMAT

3 The tracking signal can be calculated as follows using an α value of 0.1. and initialisation values calculated from previous data:

1 2

Month	Initial	1	2	3	4	5
Actual sales		6	17	12	9	10
Forecast sales		10	12	11	12	11
Error (e_t)		4	−5	−1	3	1
4 $0.1 \times e_t$		0.4	−0.5	−0.1	0.3	0.1
$0.9 \times e_{t-1}$		3.6	3.6	2.8	2.4	2.4
E_t	4	4	3.1	2.7	2.7	2.5

339

⑤	$0.1 \times \mid e_t \mid$		0.4	0.5	0.1	0.3	0.1	**2**
	$0.9 \times MAD_{t-1}$		9	8.5	8.1	7.4	6.9	
	MAD_t	10	9.4	9.0	8.2	7.7	7.0	
⑥	TS_t		0.43	0.34	0.33	0.35	0.36	

⑦ The tracking system has stayed within both warning and action limit, therefore the forecast **3**
system is operating well.

Practise your competence now on problems 10.27 and 10.28 at the end of this chapter. When you have demonstrated competence in this area you can use the computer disk provided to automate the arithmetic elements. You may choose either a Lotus or Excel spreadsheet depending on which package you have access to. With this disk you will be able to input the actual data and the forecast. The package will then calculate the computerised tracking signal and check it against limits. You may now demonstrate the competence in this area against problems from your own work environment.

Summary of tracking methods

The first of the tracking methods, CUSUM, is best used on manual, graphical or heuristic forecasting methods. The second tracking method is for use in computerised systems, having fixed limits to determine when forecasts are out of control.

10.10 Adaptive forecasting approaches

Adaptive forecasting approaches combine the ideas of control into the forecasting approach. The idea of adaptive approaches is that the control element monitors the basic forecast approach and this is then fed back into the forecasting approach by changing the response rate.

If for example there is a constant data pattern that is susceptible to steps, adaptive forecasting will prove very successful. When the data is in the constant pattern the errors will balance around zero and this will feed back into the forecast system by keeping the response rate low and so achieving efficient smoothing. When the step occurs the error will build in the direction of the step. This will be picked up by the control system which in turn will feed back into the forecasting system by increasing the response rate. This increased response rate will mean the forecasts will move up to the new level quickly. Once the forecasts reach the new level the errors will balance around zero and the response rate will fall to a level that smoothes effectively.

The main advantage to adaptive forecasting systems is that they can be built into automatic computerised forecasting systems. The system will then deal with many problems automatically rather than needing human intervention. This can significantly improve the efficiency of forecasting large independent product ranges.

10.11 Forecasting in practice

This section is concerned with the application of the forecasting approaches so far considered. The first part of the section looks at the importance of measuring the variability of forecasts in a sensitivity analysis. The second part of the section looks at passive and dynamic forecasting. The forecasts produced so far are passive because they assume that the future will be the same as the past. Therefore we will also examine how these can be made to react to the changing environment. The final part of the section looks at estimation and how this skill can be developed in managers.

10.11.1 Sensitivity analysis

The idea of sensitivity analysis is an important concept for any form of management model building, not least forecasting. It has already been said at the beginning of this section on forecasting that the majority of forecasts will be wrong. The measure of a good forecasting system is that the forecast error will stay around zero. In some situations how much these values will vary from the underlying average can be important. This variation can be measured by some form of sensitivity analysis. Figure 10.16 shows how sensitivity analysis can be applied to a series of forecasts. This shows an upper and lower limit in which the forecast will lie with the most likely value being an extension of the underlying average.

The limits will be a measure of the variability that has occurred in the past but it must also take account of the stability of the product or market. The more unstable the product or market the more the limits will widen as the forecasts move forward in time.

Sensitivity analysis is important when using forecasts at a strategic level. Strategic plans should not only be suitable for a series of single point forecasts. If an organisation is to maximise its chance of survival and growth in today's changeable environment then strategic plans should be able to cope with change, but it would

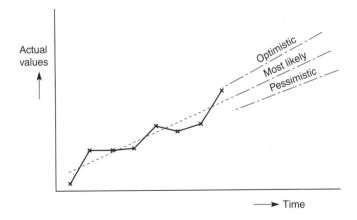

Figure 10.16   Sensitivity analysis

be unreasonable to expect strategic plans to cope with all change without requiring major revisions. Sensitivity analysis will put limits on the forecast that most of the time (99 per cent) the forecast will be within. Strategic plans that can deal with situations within the limits of sensitivity analysis will make the organisation more able to cope with change effectively and quickly.

It is not just at the strategic level that some measure of variability is important. Many operational level decisions need a measure of the variability of forecasts such as stock control. Some forecasts feed into stock control systems (some completely automatically). When this occurs it is important that a measure of variability is also fed into the system.

The measure of the variability can be made by statistical means and in the short term this will work satisfactorily. In the long term the stability of the product needs to be built into the limits. This is not so easy to carry out mechanistically and will owe more to heuristics and estimation.

10.11.2 Passive against dynamic forecasting

All the forecasting approaches so far used are passive in nature. That is to say they assume that the future will be similar to the past. There will of course be a degree of similarity in the future and the past but it must be remembered that business operates within a dynamic situation. The company, competitors, governments, etc., can all affect the future.

Most business situations do not depend completely on the past but on changing conditions in the present. The oil crisis of the early 1970s was a dramatic example of this. The oil-producing countries put a steep increase onto the price of oil and then the world changed. This crisis had an effect on the sales of new motor vehicles, the sales of which were less than expected. This was just one factor which could have had an effect on car sales; others could have been government legislation (taxation changes, vehicle testing), social changes (disposable income changes, reduction in public transport), environmental issues (exhaust emissions) etc. An alternative approach to producing a single component forecast is to carry out a *multivariate* analysis. With multivariate analysis the effect of each factor is estimated individually. This has the advantage that when a forecast is produced each factor can be varied individually. This makes the forecast sensitive to changes in individual factors. The problem with this approach is the separation of the total effect into individual effects. The approach also still assumes that the effect of each factor will be similar to the past.

The previous case concerns external changes but it is also possible for the company to make changes. For example, if the company has just launched an advertising campaign which it would expect to boost sales by ten per cent then the passive forecasts for the period of the campaign would be calculated as normal and then increased by ten per cent to take account of the advertising – so making them *dynamic* in nature. In this case it is clear by how much the forecasts should be changed. However, in many cases the informal information, the collection of which has been described in previous chapters, needs to be built into the forecast. To build much of this information in will require the experience and skill of management to estimate the effect it will have. Estimation will be considered in more detail in the next section.

The need to apply some form of modification to the passive forecast will become more likely the further into the future that forecasts are made. It will also become more necessary the more unstable the product is. This will mean that modifications will be quite common with forecasts being used at the strategic level, but will still be an occasional possibility for forecasts at the operational level.

The modification of passive forecasting needs the intervention of management into the forecasting system. If the forecast has been produced using a graph or a manual calculation by the manager then this is no problem.

If the forecast is being used at the strategic level in a company any modification to the passive forecast can be made as part of the strategic planning, therefore it makes little difference if the original passive forecasts are produced manually or on a computer-based system.

Problems can arise when modification is required on a computer-based system. Problems particularly arise with operational level systems where the forecasts are automatically linked into systems in the organisation. All of these systems should have control and checking measurements that check forecast errors and check all the numbers for validity. Any problems would then be reported to managers by some form of exception reporting system. This form of interaction should be part of any computerised forecasting system and not be considered an optional extra.

Also, with any automated computerised forecasting system it should be possible (on rare occasions) to intervene and modify the passive forecasts produced in the system. This type of intervention is not readily available in all computerised forecasting systems.

There can be dangers in having forecasting systems that can be 'tinkered' with. The changing of passive forecasts should only be undertaken when there is good reason. Unthought-through changes and too frequent changes can destabilise forecast systems and seriously affect their efficiency.

10.12 Estimation

This section of Chapter 10 will enable you to:

- set subjective forecasts using heuristics
- ensure the subjective forecasts are estimates and not guesses
- take account of statistical theory using these heuristics
- use techniques like cumulative density function (CDF) to improve estimates

The section will also provide the underpinning knowledge in the area of subjective forecasts and ways of improving their accuracy.

The approach of estimating forecasts should not be underrated neither should it degenerate into an uninformed guess. The estimation of forecasts must use all the experience and ability of the manager along with all the data that is available about the situation. When estimating values for forecasts managers will use one of two basic heuristics: (1) representativeness and availability and (2) anchoring and adjustment.

1 The heuristic of representativeness and availability works by considering how representative the estimate is of the availability of experience of the

manager. This method of determining forecast estimates needs to take account of other factors and if these are ignored the following problems could arise:

(a) Not allowing for all prior information. There is a danger when estimating forecasts not to allow all the relevant information to take its effect on the forecast. This can be a system problem in that all the information is not put before the decision maker. The estimation process can be further confused by poorly presented information.

(b) Misconception of regression. Applying incorrect causal relationships can lead to bias and error in the representative heuristic. The following example illustrates an incorrectly assumed relationship: in a discussion of salesmen motivation some experienced sales managers noted that praise for an exceptionally high sales achievement would typically be followed by a lower sales achievement next time, while harsh criticism after a low sales achievement would be followed by an improvement in sales achievement next time. The sales managers concluded that verbal punishments are beneficial and praise detrimental to motivation, which is contrary to well accepted motivational theory.

This is in fact a spurious relationship. Whatever comments are made to the salesman, the results are likely to be the same. This is due to the fact that sales achievements are distributed about a mean for each salesman and will vary about that mean; some better, some worse. Therefore when a high sales value is achieved the probability will be great that the next result will be lower and vice versa. The acceptance of spurious relationships can lead to inaccuracies in the estimation of forecasts. This type of mistake is not only made by people with no statistical or modelling training but is all too common among people with this training.

(c) The retrievability of instances. Many problems of retrievability are created by the way in which events arrived at the brain and the recentness of such events. If one actually experiences an event oneself the impact and therefore the retrievability is usually much greater than if one records or is told of such an event. Also the source of one's information (whether read or told) can affect the impact of the information; the more 'reliable' the information, the more the impact. Retrievability can therefore be affected by many things and will of course vary considerably from individual to individual.

(d) Biases due to the effectiveness of a search set. Biases may be due to the ineffectiveness of certain sets of events stored by people. Due to social, economic, business or other reasons people form different sets of events due to their different experiences and this could form an element of bias. The search set of managers (i.e. their experience) will vary from manager to manager depending upon such factors as the length of time the person has been a manager, the types of management roles carried out, the management ability of the person, etc.

(e) Biases of imaginability. There can be a great difficulty in imagining and conceiving all the factors involved and all the possible outcomes of events.

2　The heuristic of adjustment and anchoring starts from an initial value and then adjusts this value in the light of experience or knowledge. In forecasting, the initial forecast will be set by using one of the formal mathematical forecasting approaches, this being the anchoring stage. This initial value would then be adjusted by managers to take account of such factors as increased amounts of advertising by either their company or competitors, the present economic climate, etc., this being the adjustment stage.

Where a manager is estimating a forecast it is unlikely that just one of the heuristics will be used. It is far more likely that some combination of the two will be used. These heuristics can give reasonable results and will be improved further by combining them with some other techniques.

A technique that can be used successfully to supplement the heuristics is the cumulative density function (CDF). This has the advantage that a range of values can be created instead of individual values. To create a CDF five percentiles have to be estimated: the 1st, 25th, 50th, 75th and 99th percentiles. Training may need to be given as to what percentiles are and most people will need some experience at setting them which can be obtained by using gaming simulation. In most people there will be a tendency to set the percentiles too close together and to give a CDF with too little range because the majority of people fail to appreciate the uncertainty associated with situations. With training this natural conservatism can be overcome. The percentiles required are as follows:

1st percentile is a value such that in the assessor's opinion there is a one per cent chance that the forecast being assessed will be below it and a 99 per cent chance it will be above it (this value could almost be considered the lower limit of the forecast).

25th percentile is a value such that in the assessor's opinion there is a 25 per cent chance that the forecast being assessed will be below it and a 75 per cent chance it will be above it.

50th percentile is a value such that in the assessor's opinion there is a 50 per cent chance that the forecast being assessed will be below it and a 50 per cent chance it will be above it.

75th percentile is a value such that in the assessor's opinion there is a 75 per cent chance that the forecast being assessed will be below it and a 25 per cent chance it will be above it.

99th percentile is a value such that in the assessor's opinion there is a 99 per cent chance that the forecast being assessed will be below it and a one per cent chance it will be above it (this value could almost be considered the upper limit of the forecast).

A procedure for the setting of these percentiles is as follows:

1　Select a value for the 50th percentile. This can be called the most likely forecast.
2.　Select the values for the 1st and 99th percentile (i.e. the upper and lower limit). These can be called the pessimistic and optimistic forecasts.

3. The values for the 25th and 75th percentiles now need to be set. These can be arrived at by dividing the halves of the distribution already obtained. This division must be carried out by dividing probability of forecasts by two and not the distance along the distribution. The value arrived at by this division will be approximately one third of the way along the scale from the 50th percentile (one standard deviation limit). An alternative approach to the setting at these two percentiles is to produce a range within a range. When the 1st and 99th percentile are set the range of all values is set. The second range is then set within the first range but now containing 50 per cent of values. Individual managers may have a preference for either of these methods depending on their statistical knowledge and training.

Such a procedure is useful when used in conjunction with the heuristics and basic knowledge of statistics. The procedure can be simplified, but it will not be quite as powerful. It can be simplified into three estimates: the most likely, pessimistic and optimistic forecast. Whether the simplified or the full version of the CDF is used to estimate forecasts it will have the added advantage of building sensitivity analysis directly into the forecasts.

Gaming simulation can also be very useful in training managers in the estimation of forecasts because it allows individuals to gain experience and allows them to get over some of the problems outlined without any dangers to the organisation of incorrect or biased results. It also gives the organisation and the individual the chance to assess the ability of managers in setting forecast estimates.

Computers will obviously be of value for gaming simulation. Some companies have taken the use of the computer into an interactive role, providing a series of on-line packages. Initially the packages provide a tutorial system so that the manager gains knowledge and experience in the estimation of forecasts. They then go on to assist the manager in the production of actual forecast estimates, also providing built-in consistency checks. The experience of many companies has been that managers prefer the computer interaction as opposed to a person providing the consistency checks.

Groups of managers may become involved with estimating forecasts. One major problem with the use of groups is the bandwagon effect – the group will tend to follow the individual or sub-group of individuals with the stronger personality and/or most power. This particular effect is very likely to be felt in the business environment when estimates are set by the managing director or a technical specialist whom other personnel would be reluctant to challenge. This would be fine if these were the people who were best at setting these forecast estimates but unfortunately this is not necessarily the case. A way to overcome this effect is to use techniques like **Delphi** where individual managers are asked to fill in questionnaires and the results are used to produce the next questionnaire. This procedure is continued until a consensus opinion is reached.

Another approach that can be used either in conjunction with Delphi or just to improve group estimates is to produce a weighted average of the individuals' estimates. Four methods used in such weightings are:

1. *Equal weights to each individual.* This approach will reduce the dominance of one or a small group of individuals. However, it will average across all individuals equally and take no account of ability or experience.

2. *Self weighting.* This should take account of ability or experience. The problem is that an individual's view of his or her ability and experience is not always accurate.

3. *Subjective weighting by a third party.* This can be by members of the group or by an 'expert unbiased individual'. Given that the last type of individual is difficult to find the group would seem the best.

4. *A weighting based on past ability and experience in estimating forecasts.* This approach can be supported by a computer based system that would record past estimates and then the actual results that occurred.

A combination of these approaches has given the best results in practice. The first approach is used to start off the process and then the weights are modified, taking into account past experience and ability in the estimating of forecasts. This modification will be a mixture of self and group changes and based on computer recording systems of past performance.

Estimation can be an important part of forecast systems. However, it is vital that consistency checks are kept on individuals' success and failure at estimation. This needs to be returned to individuals so that they can improve and maintain abilities in this area.

Competence Example 10.9

At the end of this section you should now be able to demonstrate how to:

1 set subjective forecasts using heuristics

2 ensure that the subjective forecasts are estimates and not guesses

3 take account of statistical theory using these heuristics

4 use techniques like cumulative density function (CDF) to improve estimates

To practise and demonstrate these competences you will need to use examples from your own work environment. With subjective forecasts it is important that the forecast setters have experience and knowledge of the background of these forecasts. You are much more likely to have this knowledge in your own area of business than in any examples we could simulate in this text.

Summary of forecasting

Forecasting future sales and markets can be one of the more difficult tasks facing managers. It is also of critical importance to the future of the organisation.

When judging a forecasting system it is important to use the right criteria. The most important criterion is that it finds the underlying average. This should be carried out to give a smooth line. The best measure of a forecasting system's effectiveness is that the forecast errors will balance around zero (the peaks will balance out the troughs).

The first stage of the forecasting process is to find the data pattern of the information. This will determine the forecasting approach that will be most appropriate for the information. It could vary from the simple graphical approach to more formal mathematical forecasting approaches based on computers.

Whatever approach is used it is of great importance that some form of control system is used to ensure that the forecast errors are within acceptable limits. Control systems are absolutely vital with automatic computerised forecast systems.

It is also important to consider forecasts not to be single point values but to be a range of values. These values will go from a pessimistic forecast to an optimistic forecast.

These forecasting approaches are passive in nature because they assume that the future will be similar in nature to the past. The world of business and commerce operates in a changing technological, economic and social environment. Forecasting therefore needs to be more dynamic to be able to react to the action that can be taken by the company or others (competitors, governments, etc.). It is important that all modifications are recorded along with the resultant actual value. This should be fed back to the managers making the modification. This will help to ensure that managers improve their estimation.

Computers are likely to form an important part of any forecasting system and care should be used in choosing such a system. If it is a packaged computer system then it should be inspected actually in a company environment. It should also be tested with some typical company data and the results examined to see if they match the company's forecasting objectives. If a supplier will not arrange this, particularly if it is an expensive system, then be suspicious – this is a reasonable request.

If a computer forecasting system is being custom built or bought as a package, the following features should be expected:

- It should be versatile enough to be able to deal with the types of data patterns that will be expected from the application being considered.
- It should clearly state the forecasting approaches used in the system.
- The system should be able to cope effectively with such problems as steps and spikes.
- It should have a control system monitoring the forecast error.
- It should be possible for managers to intervene in the forecasting process to modify forecasts based on additional knowledge.
- It should be possible to modify the response rate of the forecast system to deal with different data conditions. In some adaptive systems this will change automatically.

If these features are part of a forecasting system it cannot guarantee success but it does show a good practical base. If these factors are missing it could create problems when trying to use the system.

Problems for Chapter 10

10.1 Examine the following data and determine its underlying data pattern. This data is taken from the sales of a particular specification of glass display cabinet of a major national quality manufacturer of reproduction furniture. The sales are in 100s.

	1991	1992	1993	1994
Jan, Feb, March	20	19	21	20
April, May, June	15	16	14	16
July, Aug, Sept	28	30	31	29
Oct, Nov, Dec	25	23	26	24

10.2 Examine the following data and determine its underlying data pattern. This data is taken from the weekly sales total of the Ipswich branch of a national chain of stores.

Week	1	2	3	4	5	6	7	8
Sales (£000)	54	48	51	50	55	53	58	62

10.3 Examine the following data and determine its underlying data pattern. This data is taken from the enrolment of first year pupils at Middle Town High School.

Year	1989	1990	1991	1992	1993	1994
Number of pupils	380	348	365	358	346	340

10.4 Examine the following data and determine its underlying data pattern. This data is taken from water consumption figures for a particular district (given in million gallon units) over the last eight years.

Year	1987	1988	1989	1990	1991	1992	1993	1994
Demand	350	298	320	340	318	385	340	345

10.5 Examine the following data and determine its underlying data pattern. This data is taken from the sales of wood-cased wall clocks made by a specialist clock manufacturer.

	1991	1992	1993	1994
1st quarter	15	18	16	15
2nd quarter	83	86	82	84
3rd quarter	128	124	126	126
4th quarter	136	133	132	133

10.6 Examine the following data and determine its underlying data pattern. This data is taken from the number of complaints received by a building society on the behaviour of its counter staff.

Year	1989	1990	1991	1992	1993	1994
Complaints	163	158	159	165	161	162

10.7 Examine the following data and determine its underlying data pattern. This data is taken from the incidence of quality faults in a production process after the introduction of a quality programme within the department.

Week number	1	2	3	4	5	6	7
Number of faults	28	23	26	22	15	16	12

10.8 Examine the following data and determine its underlying data pattern. This data is taken from the expenses of the sales staff in a small pottery manufacturing company.

Year	1988	1989	1990	1991	1992	1993	1994
Expenses (£s)	1,000	1,150	930	1,010	1,090	980	1,060

10.9 Using the data in problem 10.1, apply the graphical estimation approach and produce a forecast for the year of 1995.

10.10 Using the data in problem 10.2, apply the graphical estimation approach and produce a forecast for week 9.

10.11 Using the data in problem 10.3, apply the graphical estimation approach and produce a forecast for 1995.

10.12 Using the data in problem 10.4, apply the graphical estimation approach and produce a forecast for the year 1995.

10.13 Using the data in problem 10.5, apply the graphical estimation approach and produce a forecast for the year of 1995.

10.14 Using the data in problem 10.6, apply the graphical estimation approach and produce a forecast for the years 1995 and 1996.

10.15 Using the data in problem 10.7, apply the graphical estimation approach and produce a forecast for week 6.

10.16 Using the data in problem 10.8, apply the graphical estimation approach and produce a forecast for the year 1995.

10.17 Using the data in problem 10.2, apply the smoothing technique of moving averages. Use a four period moving average and calculate a forecast for week 9.

10.18 Using the data in problem 10.4, apply the smoothing technique of moving averages. Use a four period moving average and calculate a forecast for the year 1995.

10.19 Using the data in problem 10.6, apply the smoothing technique of exponential smoothing and calculate a forecast for 1995. Use an $\alpha = 0.2$ and a smoothed value of 160 for 1988 (U_0).

10.20 Using the data in problem 10.8, apply the smoothing technique of exponential smoothing and calculate a forecast for 1995. Use an $\alpha = 0.2$ and a smoothed value of £9,800 for 1987 (U_0).

10.21 Using the data in problem 10.3, apply the smoothing technique of double exponential smoothing and calculate a forecast for 1995. Use an $\alpha = 0.2$ and a smoothed value of 375 pupils for 1988 (U_0) and a double smoothed value of 365 pupils for 1988 (U_0).

10.22 Using the data in problem 10.7, apply the smoothing technique of double exponential smoothing and calculate a forecast for week 8. Use an $\alpha = 0.2$ and a smoothed value of 26 faults for week 0 (U_0) and a double smoothed value of 28 faults for week 0 (U_0).

10.23 Using the data in problem 10.1, apply the technique of cyclic forecasting. Use a moving average of four periods long to deseasonalise the data and produce a forecast for the year of 1995.

10.24 Using the data in problem 10.5, apply the technique of cyclic forecasting. Use a moving average of four periods long to deseasonalise the data and produce a forecast for the year of 1995.

10.25 If for the data pattern given in problem 10.7 normal exponential smoothing was to be used then the following smoothed values would have been calculated:

Week number	1	2	3	4	5	6	7
Number of faults	28	23	26	22	15	16	12
Smoothed values	26.4	25.7	25.8	25	23	21.6	19.7

Use the control technique of CUSUM to track this forecasting system and demonstrate when the forecasting system is going out of control.

10.26 The following data is taken from the sales of bookcases from a furniture wholesaler for the first seven months of the year. Single exponential smoothing has been used to smooth the data.

Month	1	2	3	4	5	6	7
Bookcase sales	101	142	91	133	115	152	191
Smoothed value	109.8	116.2	111.2	115.6	115.4	122.8	136.4

Use the control technique of CUSUM to track this forecasting system and demonstrate when the forecasting system is going out of control.

10.27 Apply the computerised tracking signal to the problem given in 10.25 using $\alpha = 0.2$. For the period prior to week one the exponentially smoothed error should be taken as 0.6 (E_0) and the mean absolute deviation should be taken as 2.4 (MAD_0).

10.28 Apply the computerised tracking signal to the problem given in 10.26 using $\alpha = 0.2$. For the period prior to month 1 the exponentially smoothed error should be taken as -8 (E_0) and the mean absolute deviation should be taken as 20 (MAD_0).

11 Performance indicators
a helping hand

11.1 Introduction

This chapter is concerned with the use of performance indicators and performance measurement. We will examine first the way in which we may need to indicate or measure more operational factors and here we will use sales figures and the performance of sales personnel as examples. These examples will allow the pitfalls and problems of performance indicators to be identified. The chapter will then develop the general characteristics of performance indicators and conclude by relating these to the ideas of benchmarking.

By the end of this chapter you should be able to:

- understand and interpret performance indicators
- set up performance indicators
- identify the limitation of a performance indicator
- set up baskets of performance indicators
- relate performance indicators to benchmarking

The chapter will also provide the underpinning knowledge in the area of performance indicators and benchmarking.

11.2 Examples of the use of performance indicators

The first problem area that will be considered is that of how to measure the performance of sales. Care should be taken in the collection and collation of sales data so that reasonable forecasts and decisions can be produced from it. Chapter 10 has shown you how to produce forecasts from the sales figures. It is important that the sales analysis is used to its best advantage in making decisions and planning the business or organisation, and the choice of units of how the sales are to be measured should be given careful consideration. A common mistake is to produce sales data in monetary units. In this form the data is useful for working out cash flows and other accounting modelling approaches; unfortunately, it is not very stable for the production of reasonable trends for use in decision making and planning. The problem lies in money itself. It is not a stable commodity: at home inflation is but one factor constantly affecting its value; in the export market fluctuating exchange rates are a further complication.

This leads to two major problems. First, it can give a false impression of growth. For example, if sales volume in money terms has increased by 3 per cent over a particular year this may appear to be a healthy growth. However, if inflation for that year was 4 per cent or greater the company will in fact have seen a contraction in real terms. The second problem can occur when a business is achieving growth in real terms: coupled with inflation it can give an apparently astronomical growth rate. This can give a false picture of the company's potential if it is not corrected. It can also provide an unstable relationship between time and sales, which can make it difficult to produce realistic trends.

Given that monetary units of sales are not very useful in determining trends, what units should be used? The best unit for use in forecasting is some physical measure of sales, i.e. number, weight, volume sold, etc. These measures do not suffer from the unstabilising influences of inflation or fluctuating exchange rates and therefore provide a stable set of figures to determine trends from. Most businesses find it possible to use such units but may face problems. Those companies or organisations dealing with products that are one-offs or small specialised batches will have the most problems. The problem lies in the apparent incompatibility in the comparison of the products. In most cases some common unit can be found, such as production hours, or some common link between batches. In a small number of cases it may not be possible to find a suitable physical unit and in these cases monetary units will have to be used – with care.

In cases where monetary units have to be used, the monetary values first need to be stabilised. This is done by removing the effect of inflation. There can be problems in actually determining the rate of inflation. If asked, most managers would quote the government's figure for inflation, the Retail Price Index (RPI). Unfortunately, this figure may not be relevant to the company in question. The RPI gives a weighted average inflation for a 'typical' family budget in the country; it includes things like food, mortgage payments, electrical consumer goods, etc., all given a weighting to reflect the average shopping basket. In any particular business the figure may be totally different, reflecting higher increases in fuel charges, raw materials, etc. The inflation rate will therefore need to be determined for each company by the accounts section, with regard to all the price rises for the previous year. Having achieved this difficult task, the effect of inflation is removed and the trend produced. To make this trend meaningful it must be used in planning the future. This leads to another formidable task: forecasting the inflation rate for the future. For these reasons this approach should only be used as a last resort, when no suitable physical measure can be found. It will always be easier and more sensible to use some form of unit measurement.

There will be other things we need to consider before these measurements indicate what is happening to the sales. It is important to know what the history of past sales is. This will enable managers to know if the general trend for sales is increasing, static or decreasing. The way sales are reacting will significantly affect the decision making of managers. The examination of sales history will enable the sales measurement to be put into the perspective of time. It is on this data that you will be able to use the competences you developed in Chapter 3 on the presentation of the sales figures and in Chapter 10 on producing forecasts. Having placed the sales measurement into the perspective of time it is also important to place it into the perspective of its environment. What is meant by this is to compare it to the performance of the market. If the sales are *increasing* against a market that is *increasing* then it will require different decisions on advertising, promotion offers, etc. than if the sales are rising against a falling market. The sales figures can be the same – it is their relationship with the environment that requires different decisions. By placing the sales measurement into the perspective of time and its environment then we have produced performance indicators that will enable better decision making concerning sales. This type of analysis may need to be carried out for each product or service, geographical area or sales personnel. Information technology will enable such a large analysis to be carried out at an acceptable cost given the value of the analysis.

There are still other factors that should be taken into account when making decisions based on the performance indicators so far produced. When taking decisions on products or service it is important to know the margin or contribution to profit of the product or service. It is not sufficient simply to identify patterns of sales; it is also vital to know how much the product has cost to 'produce' and therefore what the margin is. 'Produce' needs to be taken in its widest context to cover manufacturing and service industries.

Traditional costing approaches will not identify the cost in sufficient detail to give accurate costing down to product level. Again, information technology can help with the collection of accurate costing data. The use of bar code readers and hand-held computers makes it possible to record the resources needed to produce the product. With such detailed information it is possible to arrive at a detailed product costing and therefore a reasonably accurate view of margin.

It is important to examine the product mix of an organisation in terms of margin. Loss leaders are a strategy used by some organisations; what is very dangerous is where traditional costing systems are hiding products with very low or negative margins. Margins are likely to be different across the product range of an organisation. It is important to match this true reflection on margins with the sales analysis. The changes taking place in the product mix need to be mapped carefully on to the analysis of margins. It is important to know when high margin products are moving into decline and to know the margin on growth products and new products. High margin products in decline and new growth products on a low or negative margin are a dangerous combination. An organisation using traditional costing methods could find that by the time this is discovered it is too late. By using information technology and good practice in information management, forewarning of these events can be obtained and strategies to counteract them developed.

Margin analysis should also be applied to other parts of the sales analysis. It may also reveal interesting information if applied to different divisions of the organisation or different sales personnel.

What has been produced by having indicators over time, against the environment, and indicating margins, is a **basket of indicators**. The idea of a broad-based basket of indicators is important when using indicators in decision making and planning, to ensure that poor decisions are not made because of a narrow view of the information available.

Information technology can make both the detailed product costing and the detailed sales analysis possible. By using performance indicators provided by information technology to best advantage at both operational and strategic levels it is possible for an organisation to gain a competitive edge over its competitors.

We will now consider what sort of performance indicators we can use to manage a sales force of representatives operating over a wide area of the UK selling a series of industrial components to small to medium-sized manufacturing companies. Before you read on any further produce a list of the indicators you think could be used in the case of this sales force. Having listed these identify what you think they will tell you about the sales force and what the dangers might be.

You may have produced a list similar to the one below, or you may have thought of more or less indicators than those on our list. The list given is meant to be illustrative and not exhaustive, but it does contain the main indicators that could be used for this example:

- Monetary value of sales
- Unit based amount of sales
- Number of customers visited each week
- Average size of orders per week
- Margin on products sold
- Range of products sold
- Number of orders from existing customers per week
- Number of new customers per month
- Mileage travelled per week
- Expenses per week
- Number of order mistakes made per month
- Number of complaints from customers
- Number of congratulations from customers

Let us now consider each of the indicators and identify the main indication concerning the sales force of each and any problems they will have. The way in which indicators can be linked together will also be considered.

11.2.1 Monetary value of sales

Indication: This is a traditional way of looking at the performance of a sales force. It can be very easily measured and is normally available from existing information sources of the organisation.

Problems: There are some problems with using this indicator. The value of money is not stable as we have already considered. It also takes no account of margins and it can be easier to sell products with lower margins than ones with high margins. This indicator does not give any direct measure of how the sales force is maintaining or developing sales opportunity, its efficiency or the quality of sales care. If it is used on its own then it is possible that the sales force may change their behaviour to improve this indicator to the possible detriment of the other factors.

11.2.2 Unit based amount of sales

Indication: This is also a traditional way of looking at the performance of a sales force in some organisations. It can be easily measured and is normally available from existing information sources of the organisation. This indicator does not suffer from the problem of the unstable nature of the value of money.

Problems: There are some problems with using this indicator. It will work with organisations where there is a small or common product range but it can be difficult to make any meaning of it when the product range is large and/or variable. The sale of an item costing £1 does not compare with the sale of an item costing £100. It also takes no account of margins, and it can be easier to sell products with lower margins than ones with high margins. Again this indicator does not give any direct measure of how the sales force is maintaining or developing sales opportunity, its efficiency or the quality of sales care. Again if it is used on its own then it is possible that the sales force may change their behaviour to improve this indicator to the possible detriment of the other factors.

11.2.3 Number of customers visited each week

Indication: This indicator is one connected with the efficiency of the sales force. It will give an indication of the use they are making of their time. Linking this indicator to the amount of sales to give the ratio of sales per visit will improve its ability to indicate the efficiency of the visits. The indicator can be also linked to success and failure by indicating the number of visits where an order is made.

Problems: Like the previous indicators it could be dangerous to use it on its own as it could change the behaviour of the sales force. They could end up being dominated by the number of visits rather than the real end game of selling products. This information will be available within organisations that have a reasonably sophisticated sales visit reporting system. It will be difficult to obtain from an organisation that has a rudimentary or non-existent sales visit reporting system.

11.2.4 Average size of orders per week

Indication: The average size of orders per week will again provide an efficiency indicator of the sales force. It can be used in conjunction with the number of visits per week to ensure that if the number of visits is rising the efficiency of the visits in terms of sales is not falling.

Problems: Like the previous indicators it could be dangerous to use it on its own as it could change the behaviour of the sales force. This information will be available within organisations that have a reasonably sophisticated order processing and reporting system. It will be difficult to obtain from an organisation that has a rudimentary or non-existent order reporting system.

11.2.5 Margin on products sold

Indication: This indicator will give an important indication of the amount of margin each of the sales personnel is bringing into the organisation.

Problems: Like the previous indicators it could be dangerous to use it on its own as it could change the behaviour of the sales force. This information will be available within organisations that have a reasonably sophisticated accounting and reporting system in addition to a sophisticated order processing and reporting system. It will be difficult to obtain from an organisation that has a rudimentary or non-existent accounting and order reporting system.

11.2.6 Range of products sold

Indication: This indicator will look at the range of products that the sales personnel are selling to customers. It will indicate if the sales staff have 'favourite' products they sell more of or 'disliked' products they sell little of.

Problems: Like the previous indicators it could be dangerous to use it on its own as it could change the behaviour of the sales force. Care should be taken because different products in a range will have different popularity. This information will be available within organisations that have a reasonably sophisticated order processing and reporting system. It will be difficult to obtain from an organisation that has a rudimentary or non-existent order reporting system. With organisations with a very sophisticated information technology system it should be possible to produce this indicator down to separate customers.

11.2.7 Number of orders from existing customers per week

Indication: This indicator will monitor the way in which the sales force are maintaining and developing the existing customers of the organisation.

Problems: Like the previous indicators it could be dangerous to use it on its own as it could change the behaviour of the sales force. This information will be available within organisations that have a reasonably sophisticated order processing and reporting system. It will be difficult to obtain from an organisation that has a rudimentary or non-existent order reporting system.

11.2.8 Number of new customers per month

Indication: This indicator will monitor the way in which the sales force are using prospects and turning these into new customers for the organisation.

Problems: Like the previous indicators it could be dangerous to use it on its own as it could change the behaviour of the sales force. This information will be available within organisations that have a reasonably sophisticated order processing and reporting system. It will be difficult to obtain from an organisation that has a rudimentary or non-existent order reporting system.

11.2.9 Mileage travelled per week

Indication: This indicator can be used to monitor one of the cost elements of the sales force, but it can be dangerous to monitor this with the wrong attitude. It is important that travel is seen as an important part of the process to ensure the representative visits the customer enough to ensure the best order pattern. It can be useful to link this to the number of customers visited and amount of sales achieved.

Problems: Like the previous indicators it could be dangerous to use it on its own as it could change the behaviour of the sales force. This information will be available within organisations that have a reasonably sophisticated accounting and reporting system. It will be difficult to obtain from an organisation that has a rudimentary or non-existent accounting and reporting system.

11.2.10 Expenses per week

Indication: This indicator can be used to monitor one of the cost elements of the sales force but it can be dangerous to monitor this with the wrong attitude. The way customers are treated can be an influencing factor in the sales. There are however ethical issues connected with this factor.

Problems: Like the previous indicators it could be dangerous to use it on its own as it could change the behaviour of the sales force. This information will be available within organisations that have a reasonably sophisticated accounting and reporting system. It will be difficult to obtain from an organisation that has a rudimentary or non-existent accounting and reporting system.

11.2.11 Number of order mistakes made per month

Indication: This indicator can be used to indicate part of the efficiency of the sales force and the quality of parts of the ordering process for the customer.

Problems: Like the previous indicators it could be dangerous to use it on its own as it could change the behaviour of the sales force. This information will be available within organisations that have a reasonably sophisticated order processing and reporting system. It will be difficult to obtain from an organisation that has a rudimentary or non-existent order reporting system.

11.2.12 Number of complaints from customers

Indication: This is a quality indicator that will indicate the quality of parts of the ordering process for the customer. A measure of customer satisfaction that would indicate satisfaction with both product and process could be built into the sales visit report.

Problems: Like the previous indicators it could be dangerous to use it on its own as it could change the behaviour of the sales force. This information will be available within organisations that have a reasonably sophisticated customer information and reporting system. It will be difficult to obtain from an organisation that has a rudimentary or non-existent customer information reporting system.

11.2.13 Number of congratulations from customers

Indication: This is a quality indicator that will indicate the quality of parts of the ordering process for the customer. Human nature being as it is, these will occur much more infrequently than complaints.

Problems: Like the previous indicators it could be dangerous to use it on its own as it could change the behaviour of the sales force. This information will be available within organisations that have a reasonably sophisticated customer information and reporting system. It will be difficult to obtain from an organisation that has a rudimentary or non-existent customer information reporting system.

By examining the different indicators it can be seen that it would be very dangerous just to use a single indicator to try to monitor and plan the sales force. Performance indicators will normally affect the behaviour of the individuals within an organisation and therefore the direction of the organisation. With single indicators the direction of the organisation may not be quite what is expected. To monitor and plan the sales force effectively it is important to have a broad base of indicators that will indicate sales, margin, visits, cost and quality. The indicators should not be taken individually but treated as a *basket of indicators*. This way it will be possible to influence the organisation in a more complex and balanced way.

11.3 Definition of performance indicators

A performance indicator can be defined as any information either quantitative or qualitative:

- that is used on an historical and/or predictive basis
- that will evaluate and lead towards the achievement of an organisation's goals
- that will allow timely corrective action

Quantitative indicators can be such things as return on investment, profit, return on equity, pupil teacher ratio and crime figures. **Qualitative indicators** can be such things as market dominance, quality of service and fear of crime. Qualitative indicators are usually about perceptions and often we will use a quantitative indicator (or *basket* of quantitative indicators) to act as a proxy measure for a qualitative indicator. Examples of this are where a number of complaints can be used as an indicator of quality or staff turnover can be used as an indicator of staff morale.

It is important to know what the indicator is measuring and what is being indicated. Crime figures are a good example of this, as they are an important indicator to police managers. When these figures are released there are often headlines of 'Crime rise in UK'. This is not necessarily the case because these crime figures only measure crime that has been reported to the police and they may be mistakenly considered an indicator of crime itself. There can be cases where figures become unreliable as an indicator. An example of this occurred in a crime prevention initiative on a north-east England housing estate.

The initiative was concerned with the introduction of community policing on a housing estate suffering high levels of burglary and car crime. The community policing meant the establishment of a small police station at the centre of the estate and several beat officers to build a better relationship with the residents of the estate. The performance indicator selected to monitor the project was the crime figures for the beat area of the estate. After the first few weeks of the project the crime figures for the beat area started to rise significantly and from the point of the indicators seemed to be a spectacular failure. However, the officers on the project claimed it to be a great success. Which of the two was right? On examining the crime figures in more detail, the number of burglaries and car crime had in fact fallen significantly. What had occurred was an increase in the reporting of much smaller crime. An example of this was the loss of a garden gnome from a resident's garden. Such small crimes were being reported due to a rising confidence in the police and the closer proximity of a police station. Other indicators such as a fall in the value of property stolen also confirmed the success of the project. Strangely, it is in fact the case that rising overall crime figures can be an indication that the project is a success. What it does show clearly is the danger of relying on single or limited indicators, and that the idea of *baskets of indicators* is a more reliable approach. It also shows the importance of linking the indicators to the objectives that the indicators are concerned with. In this case one of the objectives was the reduction of burglary and car crime and the indicators should have reflected this. As a footnote to this example the gnome was later recovered from another part of the estate where the abductor had dumped it.

If a company has produced a 10 per cent return on investment is this a useful indicator on company performance? On its own it is a poor indication of performance. It will need to be put into the context of time. This will give the long term trend of increase, decrease or stability and the rate of change if appropriate. The figure also needs to be put into the perspective of the environment of the company. The rate of return needs to be compared against what is the norm for the industry the company is in. This will vary from industry to industry. This example shows the need to place the indicators into the perspective of time and environment to ensure a reasonable historic perspective. This good historic perspective is important to give a base for predictions. However, remember that history is not the only perspective to be taken into account when producing predictions (*see* Chapter 10).

It is important that the indicators allow timely corrective action to take place. There is little point in having indicators that will tell the company it is bankrupt as it happens. Good indicators will provide warnings early on to allow changes to be made to ensure the solvency of the company.

11.4 Characteristics of performance indicators

The following is a list of characteristics of performance indicators:

- **Mission related** – the indicators need to be related clearly to the objectives of the part of the organisation they are to indicate the performance of.
- **Comprehensive but minimal** – this is a balancing act to ensure that the indicators give a correct indication but with the minimum number of indicators. It is important to ensure that the indication does not cost more than its value.

- **Reliable but simple** – this is also a balancing act to ensure that the indicators are reliable (and therefore likely to be more complex) while being kept as simple as possible to ensure suitability.
- **Quantitative and qualitative** – indicators will be a mix of quantitative and qualitative. Care should be taken when quantitative indicators are used as a proxy for qualitative measures or an indicator is used as a proxy for another measure.
- **Indicative not absolute** – the role of performance indicators is to act as an indication of performance and not an absolute measure of performance.
- **Timely** – any indicator must provide this indication in time to allow corrective action to take place.
- **Acceptable** – it is important that any indicators that are used are acceptable to both the people or organisations that are being monitored as well as to those carrying out the monitoring.
- **Baskets of indicators** – it is important to produce baskets of indicators for two main reasons. First, to provide a broad-based provision of indicators and second, to reduce the chance of unexpected or incorrect behavioural changes brought about by using performance indicators.

11.5 The QUEST criteria

The following criteria may be a useful memory aid when you are thinking about performance indicators. It is the QUEST for good performance indicators:

- **Q**uick – to calculate and use
- **U**nderstandable – and acceptable
- **E**ffective – cost of obtaining indicator is less than value
- **S**imple – to use and understand
- **T**imely – to allow timely correction

11.6 Benchmarking and performance indicators

Benchmarking can be a very useful principle to link to performance indicators. The ideas of benchmarking are concerned with the comparison of performance against a reference. Given the idea is concerned with performance it is a natural extension and use of performance indicators. A benchmark is a standard reference which performance is compared against. The benchmark is a 'measure' of best practice and this can be from within or outside the organisation. Care should be taken when using an external benchmark to ensure that it is applicable to the organisation. There can be nothing more demoralising than a benchmark that is unattainable. The idea of benchmarking is to achieve a continuous improvement through attempting to match best practice. Benchmarking can also create and maintain high levels of competitiveness. To be most effective the setting of benchmarks should also include the identification of why best practice is an improvement on normal practice. The changing and modification of methods and procedures to achieve this best practice should then be seen as an integral part of the process. Again it can be demoralising just to be given new target performance levels and to receive no help in trying to achieve them.

Competence Example 11.1

At the end of this chapter you should now be able to demonstrate how to:

1 understand and interpret performance indicators

2 set up performance indicators

3 identify the limitation of a performance indicator

4 set up baskets of performance indicators

5 relate performance indicators to benchmarking

To practise and demonstrate these competences you will need to use examples from your own work environment. With performance indicators and benchmarking it is important that the person setting up such indicators has experience and knowledge of the areas in which they are to operate. You are much more likely to have this knowledge in your own area of business than in any example we could simulate in this text.

12 Stock control

keeping the customer happy

12.1 Introduction

This chapter is concerned with the control of stocks. Within the area of stocks there exist approaches like **Materials Requirements Planning** (MRP). MRP is a stock *evasion* approach rather than a *control*. MRP's main theme is to get the right quantity of supply and components to the right place at the right time, and it is principally an approach best suited to manufacturing, construction etc. Also linked in with this are **Just In Time** (JIT) ideas. Even within MRP systems there exist items that are required to be kept in stock. Stocks are needed to be kept in many areas of industry, retailing and the public sector where it is not applicable to use MRP type systems on all stock items. MRP is based on systems work and is beyond the scope of this book. This chapter will concentrate on the control of stocks that must be kept. It will examine the costs involved in stock control and then develop your competence in the setting up of simple and effective stock control systems.

At the end of each section the required competence will be specified and described. A typical problem format with the competences highlighted will also be given to help you to demonstrate the competences on the problems at the end of the chapter. At the end of the book a full solution will be given for the first of these problems as well as the answers for the rest.

This first section of Chapter 12 will enable you to:

- identify the various costs involved in stocking items
- calculate Economic Order Quantity (EOQ)
- calculate the order level
- calculate the total yearly operating cost
- carry out a sensitivity analysis on the stock control scheme

The section will also provide the underpinning knowledge in the area of stock costs and setting up fixed order quantity stock control schemes.

12.2 Costs involved in the control of stocks

There are five main areas of cost involved with the control of stocks – the cost of holding stock, the set up cost of an order, the shortage cost of running out of stock, the purchase price of the stock and the operating cost of the stock control system itself. Each of these areas of cost will have different impacts on the type of stock control system designed. These five areas will now be considered in more detail.

12.2.1 Cost of holding stock

This will be the costs that are incurred during the time that goods are kept in stock and for any particular stock item it could include the following items:

Cost of capital

This is the cost of the capital tied up in keeping the item in stock. At a minimum this will be the interest cost of the capital employed in keeping the stock. At the maximum this will be the opportunity cost of the capital tied by keeping items in stock. This is the opportunity lost by not using this capital in other profitable aspects of the business. It is possible in times of recession and high interest rates for these two elements to be reversed.

Obsolescence

This is the cost that is concerned with redundant stock due to obsolescence. An example of this can be found in the retailing of personal computers. When a new model is released this will mean that competing existing models will be to a degree made obsolete. The cost of this could vary from the need to discount existing products to sell them through to the need to write off the products completely due to the complete obsolescence of the product.

Deterioration

This will be the cost that will occur due to deterioration while the products are kept in stock. This cost will vary considerably depending on the item being considered. Some items like petrol will deteriorate over time through evaporation while others like fresh cream cakes will be considered to have deteriorated completely when they have passed their sell-by date. However, many items will not deteriorate significantly during the time they are kept in stock.

Insurance

This will be the cost to insure the goods in stock. This will be a cost that will vary depending on the risk of the item. For example petrol will have a high risk due to its explosive nature while precious metal will have a high risk due to its attraction to thieves.

Cost of space

This will be the cost of the space taken up by the items kept in stock. This will include all the costs of providing the space for the stock items including the cost of operating the space. It may be very expensive space such as a cold store for storing food products or relatively low cost space such as a yard for storing steel bars. This cost of space will include the cost of any personnel operating the space.

Inflation

The cost of inflation also needs to be taken into account. The value of money will deteriorate in time. If an item is purchased and kept in stock for a time and then only its purchase price is recovered this will be a loss to the organisation. The money recovered will be worth less, due to inflation, than the money recovered. This loss would of course be made worse by all the other costs incurred in keeping items in stock. There is another possible impact of inflation – it is possible that due to fluctuations in the commodity markets the value of commodity items in stock can *rise* significantly. This rise can pay for all the holding costs and turn stock holding into a profitable activity. However, it must be remembered that commodity markets can fall and this will further increase holding costs.

Taking into account all these elements a cost for holding the items in stock can be derived. If a number of items are kept in a store area it is likely that most organisations will only be able to produce average costs across all items kept in the area. An average item kept in stock is likely to incur a holding cost of 20 per cent to 30 per cent of the purchase price of the item for each year it is kept in stock. The holding cost is unlikely to fall much below this value, but due to special storage conditions (i.e. cold stores) it is possible that it may rise significantly.

There are two ways that the holding cost may be represented in symbolic terms. First, the following symbol may be used:

C_2 = cost of holding stock (£/item/year)

Second, it is possible to separate the holding cost into two elements. The purchase price is one element and the proportion that the holding costs are of this price is the second. This will then give the following:

$C_2 = i_p$

where p = purchase price of the item

i = the proportion the holding costs are of the purchase price (if you have a percentage then divide by 100)

This second approach is probably more useful in practice given that most organisations calculate and think of stock holding cost as a proportion or percentage of the purchase price.

12.2.2 Cost of ordering stock (set up cost)

This will be costs that are incurred each time a replenishment order is raised. This cost will be the same no matter how many items are ordered. This means that the more items that are ordered the smaller the proportion of this cost that needs to be allocated to each item ordered. The cost of ordering stock will vary depending on whether the items are being bought in or are to be manufactured within the organisation.

Items being bought in

The cost of ordering bought in items will include all the administrative costs involved in the placing and receiving of the order. This will include any procurement costs which may vary considerably depending on whether the item needs new suppliers or whether it has existing satisfactory suppliers. The other costs will include administrative costs of placing and receiving the order, paying for the goods, etc.

Items manufactured in the organisation

The cost of ordering items manufactured in the organisation will contain similar administrative costs to the first type, i.e. the placing of internal orders etc. There may be some procurement costs if the internal organisation has to compete with external competition. The main difference is that there will be some dislocation costs due to changes in the manufacturing process. An example that demonstrates this well is a machine for the mixing and packing of paint in plastic 'tins'. If the machine is packing one litre cans of red paint and the machine is required to pack one litre cans of white paint then the machine will need to be thoroughly cleaned out before packing can restart. Cleaning the machine will cost money in chemicals, operator time and in lost production, so all of this needs to be added to the ordering cost (set up cost). The more cynical among you may consider that the whites with a hint of another colour in them was first 'developed' when somebody failed to clean out the machine properly ... However, such failures will add to the set up cost. This cost will be the same whether one tin of white is packed or 10,000 tins of white are packed. Obviously, the set up cost for each tin will fall the more tins that are packed.

The following symbol is used for the cost of ordering (set up cost):

$$C_1 = \text{cost of ordering stock } (\text{£/order})$$
$$\text{(set up cost)}$$

Information technology is beginning to have a significant effect on the administrative costs of ordering through the use of such things as Electronic Data Interchange (EDI). EDI is where the computers of the organisations in the supply chain communicate directly. This means that the costs of order exchange being reduced very significantly.

12.2.3 Cost of running out of stock

This will be costs that are incurred each time there is a shortage of a stock item. The composition of this cost will depend very considerably on the item being stocked. With items like consumer goods then there may be the cost of lost orders or the more difficult to measure loss of goodwill. With items like machine spares then no stock could mean stopped production machines and all the dislocation associated with such stoppages. With items that are to become part of another item or service then shortage could lead to loss of orders, loss of goodwill, dislocation expenses, extra charges for express delivery, etc. Many contracts today contain penalty clauses which can add considerably to the cost of running out of stock. With some items, such as life-saving drugs in a hospital, then the consequences of running out of stock can be life threatening. It is difficult to measure such costs but an estimate needs to be made. This cost of running out of stock needs to be taken into account when setting the acceptable stock out risk discussed later in this chapter.

12.2.4 Purchase price of the item

It may seem a little strange to put the purchase price of the item down as a cost of stocking goods. However, the price can have an effect on the cost of holding stocks. This occurs when discounts are offered if the items are bought in certain quantities. These are called **price breaks** and it is important to know if the extra stock the discount will incur will be worth the money saved by the discount. Later in this chapter your competence in evaluating if price breaks are worthwhile will be developed.

12.2.5 Operating cost of the stock control system

This will be the cost of actually controlling the stocks. This will be contained in the first cost area because it is a holding cost so we do not have to take it into account again. However, it is important to identify this cost to ensure that the stock control system itself does not cost more than it saves. I remember an example of a stock control system I came across in a company. The system was to control the office consumable supplies. To obtain any office consumables (pens, pencils, paper, etc.) a requisition was required, which had to be signed by a senior manager and then presented to the office manager's secretary who personally issued the required consumables. The cost of operating this system was considerable in terms of time to get the requisitions signed and time to issue the items. In fact, when this was costed it was found that the cost was more than the value of consumables used. It was therefore decided to place these office consumables on free issue, but to provide a steadying influence it was decided to keep the stationery cupboard in sight of the office manager's secretary. There was still the reordering system to ensure stock outs were at an acceptable level. When the items went onto free issue there was naturally the 'bonanza' period but the items were still kept on free issue. Here the 'bonanza' period staff had built their own stocks of supplies and so demand on central stocks fell away to very little. Demand then rose slowly to pre-free issue days and no significant difference in demand patterns. As a matter of interest, the demand pattern of office consumables was cyclic, with three peaks that occurred around the start of school terms. It was of interest to note that there was no significant difference between the peaks from the highly controlled scheme to the free issue scheme. The only real difference was the saving in staff time. It is therefore important to ensure that the cost of controlling the stocks do not exceed the benefits in controlling them. If this is the case then alternative methods of control need to be considered.

12.3 Fixed order quantity stock control scheme

Having now considered the various costs let us consider their effect on the stock control schemes and develop your competence in the construction of one of the more widely used stock control schemes.

Let us now consider the following problem which we need to develop an efficient stock control scheme for. The problem concerns the sale of a particular brand of low power lightbulbs (long-life environmentally-friendly) at the Stoke-on-Trent branch of a large electrical superstore. The following information has been obtained from the records of the organisation:

- average demand of 9,000 per year
- purchase price of the item is £4
- cost of working capital is 15 per cent per year
- insurance on goods held in stock is $2\frac{1}{2}$ per cent per year
- miscellaneous storage charges are $7\frac{1}{2}$ per cent per year
- cost of placing an order is £5

The stock control scheme being considered is one that has a fixed order level and when the stock falls below this level then an order is placed for a fixed order quantity. This type of scheme is illustrated diagrammatically in Figure 12.1.

Figure 12.1 shows how over time items are taken from stock and the stock level falls until it reaches the **order level**. If the stock level fails to fall or falls very slowly then these items should be examined carefully as demand for them may have ceased or be falling way. However, it is possible that some items will be naturally slow moving and are not a cause for concern. Once the order level is reached then an order will be placed but this order will not arrive immediately. The time between placing the order and the order arriving in stock is called the **lead time**. The lead time is variable and an average value for it can be determined from past records. Like all forecasts it may need to be modified to take more account of future trends (*see* Chapter 10). At the base of the diagram is the **buffer stock**. This is part of the order level and its size will be determined by the stock out risk that is acceptable within the stock control scheme. It is possible to have negative stocks in the scheme – this is when orders are placed and then these items will go out of stock as soon as the ordered quantity arrives. If orders are lost when there are no stocks then negative stocks are not allowed. These are usually items where there are substitutes or little brand loyalty and therefore the customer will either buy a substitute product or switch brands.

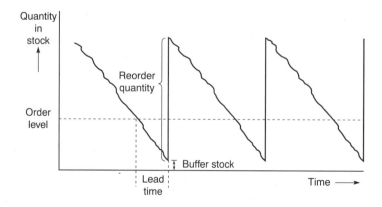

Figure 12.1   Fixed order quantity scheme

The following symbols will be used to develop the fixed order quantity stock control scheme:

d = demand for the item per year
Q = order quantity
EOQ = economic order quantity (this is to be determined by the scheme)
C_2 = holding cost ($£$/item/year)
C_1 = cost incurred when an order is placed
p = purchase price of the item
i = proportion that the holding cost is of price (note $C_2 = ip$)
B = buffer stock
Z = total yearly operating cost

Let us start by considering the order quantity. To obtain a cost efficient scheme two costs will need to balanced. The first of these costs will be the holding cost. The effect of this cost will be to try to reduce the amount held in stock to a minimum and therefore the order quantity to a minimum. The second cost is the cost of ordering. The effect of this cost will be to try to increase the order quantity as much as possible. The greater the order quantity then the more items the order cost can be spread over. The order cost is fixed whether one item or 1,000 items are ordered. If these two costs are balanced so that the minimum operating cost is determined then the order quantity will be the **economic order quantity** (EOQ). You may find other names used for this, such as **economic batch quantity** or **optimum order quantity** or a variety of combinations of these words.

To obtain a balance between these two costs the relationship between them needs to be modelled. This relationship will be made up of three elements, the sum of which will give total yearly operating cost. The three elements of cost are the cost of placing orders over the year, the cost of holding stock over the year and cost of purchasing the items over the year.

Cost of placing orders

This will be based on the number of orders placed over the year. This can be calculated by dividing the total demand by the order quantity and this will give the number of orders placed each year. To obtain the cost this frequency of ordering can be multiplied by the cost of ordering. This can be represented symbolically as follows:

$$\text{Cost of placing orders} = \frac{C_1 d}{Q}$$

Cost of holding stock

This will be based on the average amount held in stock. If Figure 12.1 is examined then one element of the stock level will be the order quantity. To obtain the average of this element of the stock then the order quantity needs to be divided by two. The other element of the stock that needs to be considered is the buffer stock. Unlike the first element this is not an average but there all the time. Therefore the average stock is half the order quantity plus the buffer stock. To obtain the cost this average is multiplied by the holding cost. This can be represented symbolically as follows:

$$\text{Cost of holding stock} = C_2\left(\frac{Q}{2} + B\right) = ip\left(\frac{Q}{2} + B\right)$$

Cost of purchasing items

The cost of purchasing items for the year will be the price of the item multiplied by the yearly demand. The importance of this element will become more apparent later in this chapter when discounts are taken into account. This can be represented symbolically as follows:

$$\text{Cost of purchasing items} = p\,d$$

These three elements can now be added together to give the expression for the total yearly operating cost (Z):

$$Z = pd + \frac{C_1 d}{Q} + C_2\left(\frac{Q}{2} + B\right)$$

OR

$$Z = pd + \frac{C_1 d}{Q} + ip\left(\frac{Q}{2} + B\right)$$

If this expression is calculated for a series of values for Q then the type of graph that will be produced is shown in Figure 12.2.

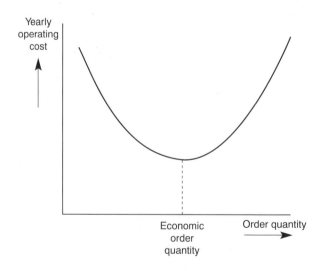

Figure 12.2 Graph of yearly operating cost against order quantity

Figure 12.2 is produced from the combination of the falling cost element, as the order quantity rises due to the cost of ordering, and the rising cost element, as the order quantity rises due to the cost of holding stock. The bottom of this graph is the point that shows the order quantity that gives the minimum yearly operating cost. This is called the **economic order quantity**. This point can be determined mathematically by using differential calculus. This form of mathematics is beyond the scope of this book. Here we are interested in the result. The following expressions can be used to determine the economic order quantity:

$$EOQ = \sqrt{\frac{2C_1 d}{C_2}}$$

OR

$$EOQ = \sqrt{\frac{2C_1 d}{ip}}$$

Both of these approaches will calculate the EOQ but the second is probably the more common given that the holding costs are normally given as a percentage of the purchase price in many organisations. We will now go back to the example and calculate the EOQ. In this example we will use the second expression.

The first step is to identify the holding cost. In this example it will be made up of the cost of working capital, the insurance on goods held in stock and the miscellaneous storage charges.

$$
\begin{aligned}
\text{Holding} &= 15\ \% + 2\tfrac{1}{2}\ \% + 7\tfrac{1}{2}\ \% \text{ of purchase price} \\
&= 25\% \text{ of purchase price}
\end{aligned}
$$

therefore $i = 0.25$
$$C_1 = 5$$
$$d = 9{,}000$$
$$p = 4$$

$$EOQ = \sqrt{\frac{2C_1 d}{ip}}$$

$$EOQ = \sqrt{\frac{2 \times 5 \times 9000}{0.25 \times 4}}$$

$$= \sqrt{\frac{90000}{1}}$$

$$= \sqrt{90000}$$

$$= 300 \text{ items}$$

Therefore the EOQ for this item has been calculated at 300 items. Does this mean that exactly 300 items need to be ordered or will it make a great deal of difference if 290 or 310 are ordered? To answer this we need to carry out a sensitivity analysis on the EOQ. Before this sensitivity analysis is carried out we need to address the other element of the stock control scheme – the order level.

The EOQ calculation is based on a balancing of costs. The order level is calculated in a different manner based on the statistical work used in earlier chapters concerning statistical distributions. The expression for calculating the order level is as follows:

$$\text{Order level} = L\bar{R} + k\sqrt{L}\ \sigma_R$$

where

L = length of lead time
$\bar{R}$ = average demand in the time unit of the lead time
σ_R = standard deviation of demand in the time unit of the lead time
k = a constant that will determine the chance of running out of stock

The first part of this expression (LR) calculates the average demand used in the lead time. The second part of this expression ($k\sqrt{L}\sigma_R$) is based on a similar calculation to the confidence limits of the normal distribution. Demand in lead times normally conform to a **Gamma** distribution. This is a different distribution to the ones covered in the book and hence the slightly different form of the expression. This element of the expression is also the buffer stock in the scheme.

$$\text{Buffer stock} = B = k\sqrt{L}\sigma_R$$

These expressions can now be used on the example to calculate the order level and buffer stock. To carry this out some further information about the problem is needed. From past records the lead time was found to be four days. This has now fixed the unit of the lead time and care needs to be taken to ensure that the demand is calculated per day and that the standard deviation is on daily demand. For the example the store operates for 300 days per year and given that the yearly demand is 9,000 by dividing by the number of days operating it can be calculated that the daily demand is 30 items. From past records the standard deviation of daily demand was found to be five items. There is only one more value to find and that is the constant (k). This constant is to fix the level of stock out risk that is acceptable to the organisation. This will be discussed in more detail later in this chapter but for the moment it will be assumed that the stock out risk required is 1 in 100 (0.01) – this will give a k value of 2.33.

$$\begin{aligned}
\text{Order level} &= L\bar{R} + k\sqrt{L}\ \sigma_R \\
&= (4 \times 30) + (2.33 \times \sqrt{4} \times 5) \\
&= 120 + 23 \\
&= 143
\end{aligned}$$
$$\text{Buffer stock} = 23$$

Having now calculated the order level a sensitivity analysis needs to be carried out and for this a more detailed table of stock out risk values is given in Table 12.1.

Table 12.1   Stock out risk values

Stock out risk		k value
5 in 1,000	0.005	2.58
1 in 100	0.01	2.33
2.5 in 100	0.025	1.96
5 in 100	0.05	1.65
10 in 100	0.10	1.28
20 in 100	0.20	0.84
30 in 100	0.30	0.53
40 in 100	0.40	0.25
50 in 100	0.50	0.00

The determination of stock out risk is carried out by balancing the cost of the increased buffer stock against the cost of running out of stock. This is carried out with a sensitivity analysis on the k values. This will give a range of buffer stocks from which the cost of increased stock holding for the reduced risk of stock out can be calculated. This range of risks should then be compared with the cost of stock outs to find the stock out risk that can be afforded.

Having now determined the order level and buffer stocks, a sensitivity analysis on the order quantity can be carried out. This will give the sensitivity of the EOQ. The sensitivity analysis is carried out by calculating the yearly operating cost for a range of order quantities. The sensitivity analysis is tabulated in Table 12.2. To help you to understand how the three elements of yearly cost relate together these have been kept separate in the table. A graph of the sensitivity analysis is given in Figure 12.3.

This sensitivity analysis shows an important point about the vast majority of calculated EOQs. The vast majority, if not all the EOQs you will calculate will be relatively insensitive. This is important in the practical use of EOQs. I have seen such stock systems used slavishly with people not willing to move away from the calculated value. The EOQ is calculated using costs only and takes no account of distribution logistics. There may exist distribution logistic constraints such as minimum delivery amounts, economic delivery loads or packaging constraints on numbers of items. By

Table 12.2   Sensitivity analysis of order quantity

Order quantity	Purchase of items	Order cost	Holding cost	Yearly cost	
50	36000	900	48	36948	
100	36000	450	73	36523	
150	36000	300	98	36398	
200	36000	225	123	36348	
250	36000	180	148	36328	
300	36000	150	173	36323	**EOQ**
350	36000	129	198	36327	
400	36000	113	223	36336	

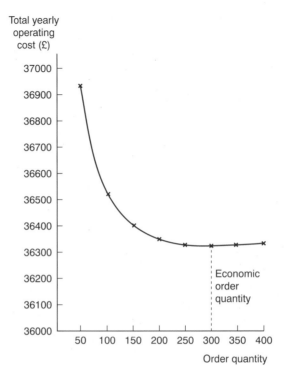

Figure 12.3   Graph of sensitivity analysis of order quantity

applying a sensitivity analysis to the EOQ constraints can be taken into account and their cost can be compared with the cost of changing the EOQ. In the example being considered the order quantity can vary between 250 and 350 with a maximum penalty cost of £5 in a total yearly operating cost of over £36,000. It is important that you do not become dominated by the right answer and that you see this approach as a range of possible answers taking into account other constraints.

Competence Example 12.1

At the end of this section you should now be able to demonstrate how to:

1 **identify the various costs involved in stocking items**

2 **calculate economic order quantity (EOQ)**

3 **calculate the order level**

4 **calculate the total yearly operating cost**

5 **carry out a sensitivity analysis on the stock control scheme**

To practise and demonstrate these competences complete example problems 12.1 to 12.3 at the end of this chapter. To help you develop these competences a description of the procedure you will need to follow is now given, along with a typical problem format. This problem format is based on the example we have just considered.

PROCEDURE

❶ Identify the cost elements of the stocks.

❷ Use the costs to set the EOQ.

❸ Use the statistical information to set the order level.

❹ Use the EOQ, order level and other costs to determine the total yearly operating cost.

❺ Carry out a sensitivity analysis on the EOQ by calculating the total yearly operating costs for a range of order quantities around the EOQ.

PROBLEM

The problem concerns the sale of a particular brand of low power lightbulbs (long-life environmentally-friendly) at the Stoke-on-Trent branch of a large electrical superstore. The following information has been obtained from the records of the organisation:

- average demand of 9,000 per year
- purchase price of the item is £4
- cost of working capital is 15 per cent per year
- insurance on goods held in stock is 2½ per cent per year
- miscellaneous storage charges are 7½ per cent per year
- cost of placing an order is £5

The stock control scheme being considered is one that has a fixed order level and when the stock falls below this level then an order is placed for a fixed order quantity.

SOLUTION FORMAT

❶ The first step is to identify the holding cost. In this example it will be made up of the cost of working capital, the insurance on goods held in stock and the miscellaneous storage charges. **1**

$$\text{Holding cost} = 15\% + 2\tfrac{1}{2}\% + 7\%$$
$$= 25\% \text{ of purchase price}$$
$$\text{therefore } i = 0.25$$
$$C_i = 5$$
$$d = 9,000$$
$$p = 4$$

❷ **2**

$$EOQ = \sqrt{\frac{2C_i d}{ip}}$$

$$EOQ = \sqrt{\frac{2 \times 5 \times 9,000}{0.25 \times 4}}$$

$$= \sqrt{\frac{90,000}{1}}$$

$$= \sqrt{90,000}$$

$$= 300 \text{ items}$$

Therefore the EOQ for this item has been calculated at 300 items.

❸ To calculate the order level further information about the problem is needed. From past **3** records the lead time was found to be four days. This has now fixed the unit of the lead

③ time and care needs to be taken to ensure that the demand is calculated per day and that **3**
the standard deviation is on daily demand. For the example the store operates for 300
days per year and given that the yearly demand is 9,000, by dividing by the number of
days operating it can be calculated that the daily demand is 30 items. From past records
the standard deviation of daily demand was found to be five items. The stock out risk
required is 1 in 100 (0.01) this will give a k value of 2.33.

$$\text{Order level} = L\bar{R} + k\sqrt{L}\ \sigma_R$$
$$= (4 \times 30) + (2.33 \times \sqrt{4} \times 5)$$
$$= 120 + 23$$
$$= 143$$

Buffer stock $= 23$

⑤ Sensitivity analysis of order quantity. **5**

Order quantity	Purchase of items	Order cost	Holding cost	Yearly cost	
50	36,000	900	48	36,948	
100	36,000	450	73	36,523	
150	36,000	300	98	36,398	
200	36,000	225	123	36,348	
250	36,000	180	148	36,328	
300	36,000	150	173	36,323	**EOQ**
350	36,000	129	198	36,327	
400	36,000	113	223	36,336	

④ **4**

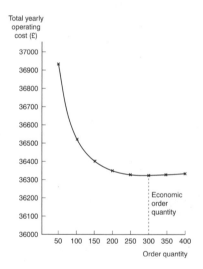

In this example being considered the order quantity can vary between 250 and 350 with a
maximum penalty cost of £5 in a total yearly operating cost of over £36,000. This shows
this is not particularly sensitive over a range of order quantities.

Practise your competence now on problems 12.1 to 12.3 at the end of this chapter. When
you have demonstrated competence in this area you can use the computer disk provided to

automate the arithmetic elements. You may choose either a Lotus or an Excel spreadsheet depending on the package to which you have access. With this disk you will be able to input the cost and statistical elements and the spreadsheet will calculate the EOQ and order level and allow you to carry out a sensitivity analysis on order quantities. The spreadsheet will allow you to carry out 'what if' calculations to produce a sensitivity analysis on other costs or values. The operation of this package is developed in more detail in Chapter 2. You may now demonstrate the competence in this area against problems from your own work environment.

12.4 Discounts and the fixed order quantity stock control scheme

By the end of this section of Chapter 12 you should be able to demonstrate basic competence in:

- evaluating the economic advantage of discounts (price breaks)

The section will also provide the underpinning knowledge in the area of discounts and their effect on fixed order quantity stock control schemes.

The procedure for taking account of discounts or price breaks can be considered in a special type of sensitivity analysis. If the supplier offered a discount of 5 per cent if 1,000 or more items are purchased and 10 per cent if 3,000 items are purchased, there are two stages to the evaluation of discounts. The first stage is to calculate the EOQ for each of the price breaks. If the EOQ is greater than the quantity to gain the price break then it is economic to take the price break. In most situations this will not be the case and the process moves to the second stage. The second stage is to calculate the yearly operating cost for each of the price breaks. If these are lower than the normal price yearly cost then it is economic to take advantage of the price break. If they are higher then it is not economic to take advantage of the price break. Let us now work through this process with the example:

$$\text{Normal price} = p_1 \quad \text{1st price break} = p_2 \quad \text{2nd price break} = p_3$$

Economic order quantities and order quantities will also use a suffix to denote the price break being used:

$$EOQ_1 = \sqrt{\frac{2C_1 d}{i p_1}} = \sqrt{\frac{2 \times 5 \times 9000}{0.25 \times 4}} = 300 \text{ items}$$

$$EOQ_2 = \sqrt{\frac{2C_1 d}{i p_2}} = \sqrt{\frac{2 \times 5 \times 9000}{0.25 \times 3.8}} = 308 \text{ items}$$

$$EOQ_3 = \sqrt{\frac{2C_1 d}{i p_3}} = \sqrt{\frac{2 \times 5 \times 9000}{0.25 \times 3.6}} = 316 \text{ items}$$

On the basis of EOQ then none of the price breaks are economic. Hopefully you can see from this calculation that it would need a massive change to the price to move an EOQ past its price break. We now move to the second part of the procedure to calculate the total yearly operating cost for each of the price breaks:

Normal price

$$Z_1 = p_1 d + \frac{C_1 d}{EOQ_1} + ip_1 \left(\frac{EOQ_1}{2} + B \right)$$

$$= 4 \times 9,000 + \frac{5 \times 9,000}{300} + 0.25 \times 4 \left(\frac{300}{2} + 23 \right)$$

$$= 36,000 + 150 + 173$$

$$= 36,323 \text{ total yearly operating cost for } p_1$$

The EOQ_1 has been used in the case of the normal price given that it is the most economic quantity to use when there is no minimum quantity to order.

1st price break (5 per cent for 1,000 items or more)

$$Z_2 = p_2 d + \frac{C_1 d}{Q_2} + ip_2 \left(\frac{Q_2}{2} + B \right)$$

$$= 3.8 \times 9,000 + \frac{5 \times 9,000}{1,000} + 0.25 \times 3.8 \left(\frac{1,000}{2} + 23 \right)$$

$$= 34,200 + 45 + 496.85$$

$$= 34,741.85 \text{ total yearly operating cost for } p_2$$

The order quantity used for the first price break is the minimum quantity that will attract the discount price, i.e. 1,000 items.

2nd price break (10 per cent for 3,000 items or more)

$$Z_3 = p_3 d + \frac{C_1 d}{Q_3} + ip_3 \left(\frac{Q_3}{2} + B \right)$$

$$= 3.6 \times 9,000 + \frac{5 \times 9,000}{3,000} + 0.25 \times 3.6 \left(\frac{3,000}{2} + 23 \right)$$

$$= 32,400 + 15 + 1,370.7$$

$$= 33,785.7 \text{ total yearly operating cost for } p_3$$

The order quantity used for the second price break is the minimum quantity that will attract the discount price, i.e. 3,000 items.

Both the price breaks have a lower total yearly operating cost than the normal price and are therefore economically worth taking. Before any decision is taken on these discounts then other factors like the cash flow of the organisation and limitation of storage space need to be taken into account. It is also worth noting that the relative reduction in operating cost is greater for the first price break than for the second price break. This may make the first price break more attractive if there are limitations on storage space and/or cash flow.

Competence Example 12.2

At the end of this section you should now be able to demonstrate how to:

1 evaluate the economic advantage of discounts (price breaks)

To practise and demonstrate this competence complete example problems 12.4 and 12.5 at the end of this chapter. To help you to develop this competence a description of the procedure you will need to follow is now given, along with a typical problem format. This problem format is based on the example we have just considered.

PROCEDURE (DISCOUNT EVALUATION)

❶ Calculate the EOQ for each price break.

❷ Evaluate if price breaks are worth taking on EOQs.

❸ If not, calculate total yearly operating cost for each price break.

❹ Evaluate if price breaks are worth taking on total yearly operating cost.

PROBLEM

The problem is the one already considered and concerns the sale of a particular brand of low power lightbulbs (long-life environmentally-friendly) at the Stoke-on-Trent branch of a large electrical superstore. The following information has been obtained from the records of the organisation.

- average demand of 9,000 per year
- purchase price of the item is £4
- cost of working capital is 15 per cent per year
- insurance on goods held in stock is 2½ per cent per year
- miscellaneous storage charges are 7½ per cent per year
- cost of placing an order is £5

The stock control scheme that has already been considered is one that has a fixed order level and when the stockfalls below this level then an order is placed for a fixed order quantity.

If the supplier now offers a discount of 5 per cent if an order of 1000 or more items is placed and 10 per cent if an order of 3,000 items is placed, should these discounts be accepted?

SOLUTION FORMAT

❶   Normal price = p_1 1st price break = p_2 2nd price break = p_3 **1**

1 Economic order quantities and order quantities will also use a suffix to denote the price
break being used.

$$EOQ_1 = \sqrt{\frac{2C_1d}{ip_1}} = \sqrt{\frac{2 \times 5 \times 9000}{0.25 \times 4}} = 300 \text{ items}$$

$$EOQ_2 = \sqrt{\frac{2C_1d}{ip_2}} = \sqrt{\frac{2 \times 5 \times 9000}{0.25 \times 3.8}} = 308 \text{ items}$$

$$EOQ_3 = \sqrt{\frac{2C_1d}{ip_3}} = \sqrt{\frac{2 \times 5 \times 9000}{0.25 \times 3.6}} = 316 \text{ items}$$

2 On the basis of EOQ then none of the price breaks are economic.

3 **Normal price**

$$Z_1 = p_1d + \frac{C_1d}{EOQ_1} + ip_1\left(\frac{EOQ_1}{2} + B\right)$$

$$= 4 \times 9,000 + \frac{5 \times 9,000}{300} + 0.25 \times 4\left(\frac{300}{2} + 23\right)$$

$$= 36,000 + 150 + 173$$
$$= 36,323 \text{ total yearly operating cost for } p_1$$

1st price break (5% for 1,000 items or more)

$$Z_2 = p_2d + \frac{C_1d}{Q_2} + ip_2\left(\frac{Q_2}{2} + B\right)$$

$$= 3.8 \times 9,000 + \frac{5 \times 9,000}{1,000} + 0.25 \times 3.8\left(\frac{1,000}{2} + 23\right)$$

$$= 34,2000 + 45 + 496.85$$
$$= 34,741.85 \text{ total yearly operating cost for } p_2$$

2nd price break (10 % for 3,000 items or more)

$$Z_3 = p_3d + \frac{C_1d}{Q_3} + ip_3\left(\frac{Q_3}{2} + B\right)$$

$$= 3.6 \times 9,000 + \frac{5 \times 9,000}{3,000} + 0.25 \times 3.6\left(\frac{3,000}{2} + 23\right)$$

$$= 32,400 + 15 + 1,370.7$$
$$= 33,785.7 \text{ total yearly operating cost for } p_3$$

4 Both the price breaks have a lower total yearly operating cost than the normal price and
are therefore economically worth taking. Before any decision is taken on these discounts
then other factors like the cash flow of the organisation and limitation on storage space
need to be taken into account. It is also worth noting that the relative reduction in operating

❹ cost is greater for the first price break than for the second price break. This may make the 🔳
first price break more attractive if there are limitations on storage space and/or cashflow.

Practise your competence now on problems 12.4 and 12.5 at the end of this chapter. When you have demonstrated competence in this area you can use the computer disk provided to automate the arithmetic elements. You may choose either a Lotus or an Excel spreadsheet depending on which package you have access to. With this disk you will be able to input the cost, statistical elements and discounts and the package will calculate the EOQs and total yearly operating cost. The spreadsheet will allow you to carry out 'what if' calculations to produce a sensitivity analysis on, for example, costs or discounts. The operation of this spreadsheet is developed in more detail in Chapter 2. You may now demonstrate the competence in this area against problems from your own work environment.

12.5 Coverage analysis

This final section of Chapter 12 will enable you to:

- determine order quantities for large numbers of stock items
- evaluate the savings

This section will also provide the underpinning knowledge in the area of setting order quantities where there are large numbers of stock items in a stocklist.

If an organisation has a large list of stock items in store then it may face a problem when calculating an EOQ for each item on its stocklist. When there is a large list of stock items there are two main problems. First, there would be a considerable amount of work in setting each order level using the standard approach of EOQ. Second, there is usually a problem in determining the cost of holding items in stock and the cost of ordering stock items. In large stock lists these costs are usually averaged across the stocklist and it would be a very considerable cost to identify these costs down to the individual items. For these reasons the normal EOQ is no longer as effective in such large stocklists. Table 12.3 is a shortened case of a large stocklist to demonstrate and develop the technique of coverage analysis. The following is a representative list of stock items from a company that supplies the engineering industry with self-lubricated bearings.

Table 12.3   Stocklist to demonstrate coverage analysis

Part number	Price (£)	Usage items/year	Average quantity of stock held (items)
54/001	0.50	1200	210
54/002	1.00	50	3
54/003	2.00	500	60
54/004	50.00	50	6
54/005	4.0	25	2
54/006	0.25	800	80
54/007	40.0	20	2

The operating conditions are such that replenishment can be taken as occurring when supplies are practically exhausted. Management require the order quantities to be reset in a more efficient way.

The approach of coverage analysis is based on two assumptions. First, that the annual usage values of the stock items follows a **parato distribution** – that is, approximately 20 per cent of the items account for 80 per cent of the usage. The vast majority, if not all, large lists of stock items follow a parato distribution. Second, that the number of orders is usually fixed by the capability of the organisation. Coverage analysis is a way of redistributing these orders through the stock items so that the high usage items are ordered more frequently. This will make the stock holding more efficient and reduce the capital tied up in stock. The following procedure is used to reallocate the orders.

12.5.1 Set order levels

1. Construct a table of item number (i), annual yearly demand (d_i) and price (p_i) for each item on the stocklist.
2. Calculate the annual usage by multiplying the price by the demand ($p_i d_i$) for each item on the stocklist.
3. Calculate the next column which is the square root of the $p_i d_i$ column ($\sqrt{p_i d_i}$) determining the total of the column to give $\Sigma\sqrt{p_i d_i}$.
4. Determine the total number of orders that are placed in a year over all the items in the stocklist. This can be determined from past records and can be increased or decreased depending on the capability of the organisation to place orders. This number of orders is a useful value to carry out a sensitivity analysis on. The cost of extra orders can then be compared to the savings in capital employed.
5. Calculate the constant K such that

$$K = \frac{\text{Total number of orders per year}}{\Sigma\sqrt{p_i d_i}}$$

6. Reallocate the orders and determine the new frequency of ordering (f^*_i) for each item on the stock list such that

$$f^*_i = K \times \sqrt{p_i d_i}$$

   Note: check f^*_i adds to total number of orders per year.
7. Determine the new order quantities Q^*_i for each stock item

$$Q^*_i = \frac{d_i}{f^*_i}$$

   Note: this figure must be rounded to whole items.

12.5.2 Calculate savings on capital employed

8. Determine the present capital employed.
   a) Calculate the average amount in stock for each item on the list using the present order quantity:

$$\text{Average amount in stock} = \frac{\text{Present order quantity}}{2}$$

   b) Convert this to a monetary value by multiplying by the price of each item and sum to obtain present capital employed.

9. Determine the new capital employed.
   a) Calculate the average amount in stock for each item on the list using the new order quantity:

$$\text{Average amount in stock} = \frac{\text{New order quantity}}{2}$$

   b) Convert this to a monetary value by multiplying by the price of each item and sum to obtain new capital employed.

10. Determine the percentage saving on capital employed:

$$\text{Saving on capital employed} = \frac{\text{Present capital employed} - \text{New capital employed}}{\text{Present average capital employed}} \times 100$$

This procedure can now be applied to the example:

Set order levels

Item number (i)	Price p_i	d_i	$p_i d_i$	$\sqrt{p_i d_i}$	f^*_i	Q^*_i
54/001	0.5	1,200	600	24.5	5.3	226
54/002	1.0	50	50	7.1	1.5	33
54/003	2.0	500	1,000	31.6	6.9	72
54/004	50.0	50	2,500	50	10.9	5
54/005	4.0	25	100	10	2.2	11
54/006	0.25	800	200	14.1	3.1	258
54/007	40.0	20	800	28.3	6.1	3
				165.6	36	

$$K = \frac{\text{Total number of orders}}{\Sigma \sqrt{p_i d_i}} = \frac{36}{165.6} = 0.217$$

Calculate savings on capital employed

Item number (i)	Price p_i £	Q^*_i	Average stock $Q^*_i/2$	New value Ave Stk × p_i £	Old ave stock	Old value £
54/001	0.5	226	113	56.5	210	105
54/002	1.0	33	16.5	16.5	3	3
54/003	2.0	72	36	72	60	120
54/004	50.0	5	2.5	125	6	300
54/005	4.0	11	5.5	22	2	8
54/006	0.25	258	129	32.25	80	20
54/007	40.0	3	1.5	60	2	80
				384.25		636

Old capital employed = £636
New capital employed = £384.25

$$\text{Percentage saving in capital employed} = \frac{636 - 384.25}{636} \times 100$$

$$= \frac{251.75}{636} \times 100 = 39.6 \cong 40\%$$

By using coverage analysis to reset the order quantities there will be a saving on capital employed of 40 per cent.

Competence Example 12.3

At the end of this final section you should now be able to demonstrate how to:

1 **determine order quantities for large numbers of stock items**

2 **evaluate the savings**

To practise and demonstrate these competences complete example problems 12.6 and 12.7 at the end of this chapter. To help you to develop these competences a description of the procedure you will need to follow is now given, along with a typical problem format. This format is based on the example we have just considered.

PROCEDURE

❶ Construct a table of item number, yearly demand and price.

❷ Calculate the annual usage.

❸ Reallocate the orders based on usage.

❹ Calculate the order quantity from the frequency of ordering.

❺ Determine the savings on capital employed.

PROBLEM

The following is a representative list of stock items from a company that supplies the engineering industry with self-lubricated bearings.

Part number	Price £	Usage items/year	Average quantity of stock held (items)
54/001	0.50	1,200	210
54/002	1.00	50	3
54/003	2.00	500	60
54/004	50.00	50	6
54/005	4.0	25	2
54/006	0.25	800	80
54/007	40.0	20	2

The operating conditions are such that replenishment can be taken as occurring when supplies are practically exhausted. Management require the order quantities to be reset in a more efficient way.

SOLUTION FORMAT

❶❷❸❹

Item number (i)	Price p_i £	d_i	$p_i d_i$	$\sqrt{p_i d_i}$	f^*_i	Q^*_i
54/001	0.5	1,200	600	24.5	5.3	226
54/002	1.0	50	50	7.1	1.5	33
54/003	2.0	500	1,000	31.6	6.9	72
54/004	50.0	50	2,500	50	10.9	5
54/005	4.0	25	100	10	2.2	11
54/006	0.25	800	200	14.1	3.1	258
54/007	40.0	20	800	28.3	6.1	3
				165.6	36	

$$K = \frac{\text{Total number of orders}}{\Sigma \sqrt{p_i d_i}} = \frac{36}{165.6} = 0.217$$

❺

Item number (i)	Price p_i £	Q^*_i	Average stock $Q^*_i/2$	New value Ave Stk $\times p_i$	Old Ave stock	Old value
54/001	0.5	226	113	56.5	210	105
54/002	1.0	33	16.5	16.5	3	3
54/003	2.0	72	36	72	60	120
54/004	50.0	5	2.5	125	6	300
54/005	4.0	11	5.5	22	2	8
54/006	0.25	258	129	32.25	80	20
54/007	40.0	3	1.5	60	2	80
				384.25		636

1

2

⑤   Old capital employed = £636
        New capital employed = £384.25

$$\text{Percentage saving in capital employed} = \frac{636 - 384.25}{636} \times 100$$

$$= \frac{251.75}{636} \times 100 = 39.6 \cong 40\%$$

By using coverage analysis to reset the order quantities there will be a saving on capital employed of 40 per cent.

Practise your competence now on problems 12.6 and 12.7 at the end of this chapter. When you have demonstrated competence in this area you can use the computer disk provided to automate the arithmetic elements. You may choose either a Lotus or an Excel spreadsheet depending on which package you have access to. With this disk you will be able to input the information on the stocklist and the package will calculate the coverage analysis, re-setting the order quantities and determining the savings on capital employed. The spreadsheet will allow you to carry out 'what if' calculations to produce a sensitivity analysis on elements of the coverage analysis such as the number of orders placed. The operation of this spreadsheet is developed in more detail in Chapter 2. You may now demonstrate the competence in this area against problems from your own work environment.

Summary of stock control

This chapter has developed your basic skills and competence in the development of stock control models. You should now be able to build models to set order levels and order quantities for both individual items and large lists of stock items and be aware of a procedure for dealing with the acceptance or not of discounts. Stock models are important due to the fact that there are many areas where stocks need to be kept. This is still the case even with MRP systems. The setting up of MRP systems is beyond the scope of a book concerned with modelling as it is more to do with systems.

Problems for Chapter 12

12.1 A certain ingredient is used regularly in the catering section of a motorway service area at an average rate of 5,000 cans per year. This particular item is priced at £6 per can. The cost of working capital is 10 per cent per annum, insurance on goods held in stock 8½ per cent per annum and a miscellaneous storage charge of 6½ per cent per annum. The cost of placing an order is £10. On average 13.7 items per day are used (365 days working per year) with a standard deviation of 1.8 items and from past records the lead time is three days. Management is willing to accept a 1 in 100 chance of running out of stock. Use this information to set up a fixed order quantity stock control scheme. Carry out a sensitivity analysis on the elements of this stock control scheme.

12.2 The following information relates to a type of pen that is stocked in the central consumable stores of a large retail company:

Demand per year   2,400 items (48 working weeks per year)
Cost of holding stock   15% of price per year
Lead time   2 weeks
Cost of placing an order   £10
Standard deviation of weekly demand   12 items
Purchase price   £0.30 per item

If management accept a 1 in 100 chance of running out of stock, set up a fixed order quantity stock control scheme. Carry out a sensitivity analysis on the elements of this stock control scheme.

12.3 The following information relates to the stocking of a raw material in the building maintenance department of a district council.

Average demand   2,010 units per week
Standard deviation of daily demand   570 units per week
Cost of holding stock   £0.80 per unit per year (50 weeks)
Cost of ordering stock   £200 per occasion (due to a set up cost passed on by the manufacturer)
Lead time for supply   1 week

Set up a fixed order quantity stock control scheme for the above situation. Management is not sure if it needs a 95 per cent or a 99 per cent level of service, so advise on the result and cost of each. If the supplier advises that due to production difficulties the lead time will rise to three weeks, how will this affect the stock control scheme?

Note: Care needs to be taken over units and costs in this example and price does not need to be taken into account in the sensitivity analysis.

12.4 A certain type of security lock is used by a manufacturer of desks at an average rate of 900 per year. The lock is being purchased at a price of £4.00 per item.
Given the following information:

Cost of working capital   15% per annum
Insurance on goods held in stock   2½% per annum
Miscellaneous storage charges   7½% per annum
Cost of placing an order   £5.00

what quantity should be ordered if the following discounts are offered?

Quantity	Discount
0–200	0%
200–500	2½%
500+	5%

Note: Given the cost of the buffer stock is fixed across all the price breaks you may assume the buffer stock to be zero.

12.5 If the supplier of the items for problem 12.1 offers the following discounts would it be profitable to accept any of these price breaks?

Quantities	Discount
0–500	0%
500–1,000	3%
1,000+	4%

12.6 The following stocklist is representative of a stocklist of a small retail store selling provisions:

Item number	Demand/year	Price (£)	Present order quantity
1	300	0.95	25
2	150	0.03	50
3	200	0.15	25
4	50	0.60	25
5	250	2.50	50

There are in total 30 orders placed per year. Use the technique of coverage analysis to reset the order quantities and estimate the savings in capital employed.

12.7 The following items are representative of small items kept in an engineering store by a manufacturer of electrical switchgear. There are 28 orders placed per year. Use the technique of coverage analysis to reset the order quantities and estimate the savings in capital employed.

Item number	Demand/year	Price (£)	Present order quantity
1	100	0.68	20
2	150	0.04	50
3	200	0.20	20
4	250	0.01	50
5	300	0.05	60

13 Simulation

imitating the real thing

13.1 Introduction

Simulation modelling is one of the most widely used of the modelling areas. The area is sometimes referred to as **Monte Carlo simulation**, and the reason for such a name will be clearly seen later in this chapter.

This chapter will develop important competences in the structuring and building of simulation models.

By the end of this chapter you should be able to demonstrate how to:

- identify problems for solution by simulation models
- define and analyse systems when building simulation models
- construct simulation models
- verify and validate simulation models
- use simulation models in prediction

The chapter will also provide the underpinning knowledge of the basic theory of simulation modelling. WIthin the chapter a single case study is used to develop the underpinning knowledge and demonstrate the specific competence required.

To demonstrate and practise these competences it is recommended that you work through problem 13.1 (given at the end of this chapter). You may wish to undertake this problem in one of two ways. One approach is to attempt each part of the problem when prompted in the text, competence by competence. The second approach is to work through the whole chapter and then complete the problem in one attempt. At the end of the chapter the required competence will be specified and described. A typical problem format with the competences highlighted will also be given to help you to demonstrate the competences on the problems at the end of the chapter. At the end of the book a full solution will be given for the first of these problems and the answers, where appropriate, for the rest.

The reasons for using simulation are those for all modelling. Simulation provides an inexpensive way to make predictions for varying conditions for a wide range of management processes. The approach of simulation is very general and makes it applicable to a wide range of problems from queuing problems to corporate modelling. The best way to see simulation in action is through an example.

13.2 Construction of a simulation model

The case chosen to introduce the area of simulation concerns the use made of a type of hand-controlled road rolling machine used by a county council in road repairs. The machines are kept at one of its northern depots and are sent out to road repair sites as and when required. The council want to determine the number of rolling machines required at the depot to provide a reasonable service at an economic cost. The council has a number of such depots containing specialised equipment around the county.

The processes involved in the construction of a simulation model are the same for the building of any model and are best considered in five stages, these being:

1. Define the problem.
2. Define the system.
3. Analyse the system.
4. Build the model.
5. Verify and validate the model.

These five stages will now be considered in more detail.

13.2.1   Define the problem

The first stage in the construction of a simulation model is that of determining the problem to be solved. This is extremely important as it will influence the later stages in the construction of the model. One difficulty in defining problems is that usually only consequences of problems are discovered and not the problems themselves. In the case of this example, the council officials are likely to consider the problem to be that jobs are waiting for road rollers. This is only a consequence of the real problems, which could be that there are not enough machines or that the machines are not run efficiently. In building a model it is vital to know the problem. In a model in which it is easy to change the number of machines it may not be as easy to change the mode of operating the machines and vice versa.

If the wrong problem is identified and a model built then it can cause considerable expense to modify the model to enable other predictions to be made. It should also be remembered that it would be extremely expensive to produce a model that will allow all the types of predictions to be made in any situation. In this particular case the problem is that the council have found that the three machines they have are not sufficient to give the service level required. The model is required to predict how many machines they need to give the required service, taking into account the economics of more machines. It is also useful at this stage to try to consider possible future uses of the simulation to improve the economic viability of the work. Given that the council has a range of specialist equipment used in the same way as the road rolling machines being simulated, this may mean that the simulation can be used in other situations. Therefore it would be of advantage to make this simulation as flexible as possible to allow it to be used in similar situations. Given this statement of the problem the model can now be constructed.

You may now want to define the problem for problem 13.1

13.2.2   Define the system

The next stage is to define the system that is to be modelled. A system can be described as a series of entities (components), either physical or non-physical, that exhibit a set of inter-relations among themselves and interact towards one or more goals, objectives or ends. These goals, objectives or ends may or may not be achieved and the end could be intentional or accidental. The entities can be physical entities such as men, machines, etc., or they may be non-physical such as jobs. Some of the entities could also be other systems, i.e. sub-systems making up a larger complex system.

This definition of a system will help with the later analysis but initially a more simplistic definition of a system can be used. The system can initially be defined by the boundary drawn around it. Everything inside the boundary is the 'system'; everything outside the boundary is the 'environment'. The drawing of this boundary can be difficult. Too wide a boundary and the simulation will be large, difficult to construct and possibly uneconomic; too small a boundary and the simulation is easy to construct but is unlikely to represent the situation correctly. The boundary should therefore be drawn as small as possible for economic reasons but wide enough to allow as accurate as possible a representation of the factors affecting the problem. This definition of the system may change as the situation is analysed in more detail.

Examining the case, let us consider some of the elements involved in the process to be modelled. Obvious elements involved will be road rolling machines and the jobs requiring road rolling machines. Also involved will be other road work jobs, the state of the economy and government spending right through to the state of the world economy. If the system boundary was drawn around all these it would be prohibitively expensive and would mean producing a world model just to find out how many road rollers to base at a depot. To build an efficient simulation model we require only the entities of the total system needed to predict the number of road rollers at the depot. The remaining entities of the total system can be considered as parts of the environment. These entities placed into the environment will not be ignored and will have an effect on the model. The effect they will have though will be aggregated together; they will not be modelled individually. In the case of the example being considered a reasonable definition of the system would appear to be the sets of the equipment and the jobs on which they are used. This will give two different entities as part of the model sets of road rolling equipment and jobs requiring road rolling equipment.

You may now want to define the system for problem 13.1

13.2.3 Analyse the system

Having defined the system the next step is to analyse it and to decide how detailed the simulation needs to be. How detailed the simulation is to be is a similar problem to that of defining the system. The more highly detailed the model the more it will reproduce the real system; it will however be large, cumbersome and expensive. A model with little detail will be general in nature and it will be relatively inexpensive but the results obtained from it will have a wider margin of error. Within the example do we need to create a separate entity for the operator? This will depend upon the relationship between the operator and equipment. If the operator comes with the equipment or if anybody can operate the equipment then no. The operator is not a constraining factor and therefore can be considered part of the equipment (models do not have behavioural problems although they can be built in if they are required). If there are only a limited number of operators within the organisation all operating any of the sets of the equipment then it may be possible that they could affect the utilisation of the machine. If so then it would be necessary to create separate entities for the operators and machines. In the case of the example it will be assumed that the equipment can be operated by any individual, so such a model will require two sets of entities, one to represent the sets of equipment (three initially but these will need to be increased when the model is used for prediction), and the other to represent the jobs requiring the equipment (number unknown but dependent on the length of time the simulation is run).

Continuing the analysis of the system the entities need to be described further. This is carried out in simulation by describing for each entity type the states in which the entities can be found, the relationship between these states and the rules of transition between the states. Taking the example, we must first describe the entity of road rolling machines.

ENTITY: Set of road rolling equipment (three such sets initially, more needed as predictions are made)

The first part of the analysis is to describe the possible states of the entity. This is a list of the ways in which the equipment can be found:

STATE 0 Not in use, waiting at depot
STATE 1 In use, at road repair site

Note: In an actual situation there would be far more states, such as broken down, waiting transport, etc. These have not been included so as not to overcomplicate the case, but you will see that they would be easy to add into the simulation.

The second part of the analysis is to describe the relationship between the states of the entity. This is best produced in the form of a flowchart. The flowchart of the relationships between the states of the road rolling equipment is given in Figure 13.1.

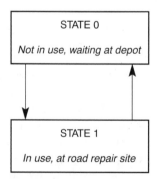

Figure 13.1   Relationship flowchart for the states of entity of road rolling equipment

Figure 13.1 shows that the relationship between the states of the machine entity is a closed loop as the entity stays in the system all the time.

The third and final stage of the analysis is to describe the rules of transition between the stages. The rules of transition will be of two types. Some transitions are due to logic, but the majority occur because of the progression of time. The rule of transition between State 0 (not in use) and State 1 (in use) is a logical transition. It will occur when a job enters the system requiring a road rolling machine. Or if there is a queue of jobs, a job moves from the head of the queue when the machine becomes free. The transition between State 1 (in use) and State 0 (not in use) will be a time progression. The transition will take place when the time taken to complete the job has elapsed. If each job took exactly two days then this would be a fixed time transition. The more common situation is that time transitions are variable. In the case of the example, times will only be in whole days but the average job time is 2.84 days. The distribution of time taken to complete jobs is given in Table 13.1.

Table 13.1 Distribution of time taken to complete jobs

Job time (days)	Occurrence (percentage)
1	33
2	19
3	13
4	12
5	12
6	11

The distribution will be derived from examining past records (*see* Chapters 2 and 3 for details of how this is carried out). When collecting the job time data it is necessary to ensure that only the time a road roller is on site is counted and that waiting time is not included. This now completes the analysis of the entity set of road rolling equipment.

The other entity that needs to be analysed is the **job entity** and this will then complete the analysis of the system.

ENTITY: Job (requiring the use of hand road roller)
Number dependent on the length of simulation run

There will be four states for the job entity, these being:

STATE 0 Job arrived
STATE 1 Waiting for piece of equipment to become vacant
STATE 2 Job being carried out by equipment
STATE 3 Job completed

The relationship between these states is given in the flowchart in Figure 13.2.

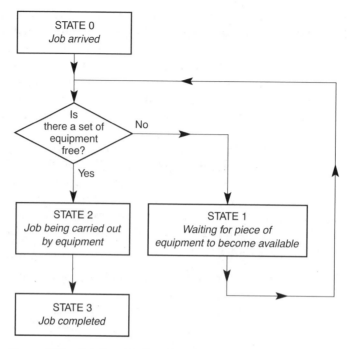

Figure 13.2   Relationship flowchart for the states of entity of jobs

The job entity is not a closed loop like the machine entity. This entity is transient – it arrives in the system and when completed leaves the system. An important element of the analysis of this entity is the rate at which jobs requiring road rolling machines occur. Requests for road rolling machines occur at the beginning of each day. The average number of jobs arising in a day is 0.96 jobs. The distribution of the number of new arrivals of jobs is given in Table 13.2.

The rules of transition between State 0 (job arrived) and State 2 (job being carried out) and State 1 (job waiting) will be a transition depending upon the availability of road rolling machines. The transition between State 2 (job being carried out) and State 3 (job completed) will be a time progression, and this has already been given in Table 13.1.

Table 13.2   Distribution of new job arrivals each day

Number of new jobs (per day)	Occurrence (percentage)
0	39
1	36
2	17
3	6
4	2

The analysis of the system is now completed. If the average number of job arrivals is multiplied by the average time each job takes (0.96×2.84) it will give a measure of the average number of road rolling machines required. This produces an average number of machines required of $2.73 \cong 3$. This is a very simplistic and dangerous method of determining the number of machines required, because it takes no account of queues. The simulation model will allow a more sophisticated approach that takes account of waiting time and costs it against the cost of additional machines.

You may now want to analyse the system for problem 13.1.

13.2.4 Build the model

The detailed construction of the model can now proceed. The general rules of the model first need to be laid down to replicate the real world problem. A flowchart of the general rules of operation for the simulation are given in Figure 13.3.

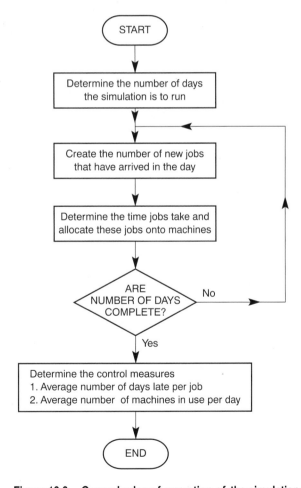

Figure 13.3   General rules of operation of the simulation

The first step of the simulation is to determine the number of days the simulation is to run. This will be discussed in more detail later in this section. For each day the simulation is to run the number of new jobs arriving in each day is created. These jobs are then allocated onto the free machines or queue until a machine becomes free. When all the day's jobs are allocated the simulation moves on to the next day until all the days required in the simulation are completed. At the end of the simulation model a range of control measures need to be calculated so that the predictions can be related together. In this example two measures are used. First, the average number of days late per job – this will give a measure of the problems created with jobs queuing. Second, the average number of machines in use per day – this will be used to give a measure of the machine utilisation.

Part of the process of the model is to create the number of new jobs arriving each day and allocate job times to each of them. Let's start with the number of new jobs arriving in each day. If the same number of jobs arriving each day were constant this would not cause any problems within the model, but unfortunately real life has a considerable amount of variability in it. This is the case with the road roller example – on average 0.96 jobs will arrive per day with a distribution of values already given in Table 13.2. The average value cannot be used, otherwise this will underestimate the queuing problems, i.e. 2 per cent of the days when four jobs will arrive. Therefore a method that gives the same distribution of values that occur in reality is required.

One approach to reproduce the same distribution of values as the real world is to use the actual daily arrival rate of jobs used to create the distribution in Table 13.2. The disadvantage with this technique is the length of time the simulation model will need to run to give all the required predictions. This will certainly mean that there will not be sufficient up-to-date daily job arrival figures available. A method of creating job arrivals is required to create an unlimited amount of daily figures.

The ideas of sampling developed in Chapter 7 will provide a method suitable for creating daily job arrivals. Table 13.2 shows the percentage distribution of daily arrival figures. To represent these percentage points 100 counters are needed. 39 per cent of days there will be no jobs arising, so 39 of the counters should be marked with no jobs. 36 should be marked with one job to represent the 36 per cent of days there will be with one job arising. This will be continued until all the counters are allocated: 17 with two jobs, 6 with three jobs and 2 with four jobs. All the counters are placed in a bag and then drawn out at random to create as many daily job arrivals as needed. The counters chosen must be returned to the bag and the counters randomised (shaken) between each selection. Another approach is to take a disc of a roulette wheel and to segment this in the same way as a pie chart (*see* Chapter 3). By spinning the wheel against a pointer, daily job arrivals can be created. Because of the use of roulette wheels this form of manual simulation modelling used to be called **Monte Carlo simulation**. Both of these approaches are physical and so do not allow themselves to be computerised.

For modern simulation a method is required that will work in both manual and computerised simulations. To carry this out random numbers as already discussed in Chapter 7 will be used. If a random number stream of two digits is taken from 00 to 99 this will give the equivalent of 100 counters. Table 13.2. gives the distribution of daily job arrivals. 39 per cent of these represent no jobs arriving. In the same way as the counters were given a number of jobs, the random numbers will be associated with a number of jobs. The first 39 numbers in the range will be associated with no jobs, i.e. numbers 00 to 38. The next 36 numbers in the range will be associated with one job, i.e. numbers 39 to 74, and so on till random number 99. This can be shown in table form in Table 13.3. These tables are referred to as **look-up charts**.

Table 13.3   Look-up chart for number of new arrivals each day

Random number	Number of jobs per day
00–38	0
39–74	1
75–91	2
92–97	3
98–99	4

By taking a stream of random numbers (*see* Table 2 in the Appendix) as many daily new arrival figures as required can be created by determining the number of new jobs by the position of the random number in Table 13.3. This procedure will replicate the real world distribution. The model will also need a similar look-up chart to create job times. The distribution of job times is given in Table 13.1 and this can be turned into the look-up chart given in Table 13.4.

Table 13.4   Look-up chart for job times (in days)

Random number	Job time (in days)
00–32	1
33–51	2
52–64	3
65–76	4
77–88	5
89–99	6

Having charts that will create both random elements of the model, a more detailed flowchart will be required to operate the model. This detailed flowchart is given in Figure 13.4. The counters are used in the flowchart to record the operation of the model.

M = number of days simulation is to run
i = number of days simulation has been run (i will equal M at the end of the simulation run)
n = main job number counter
j = daily job counter

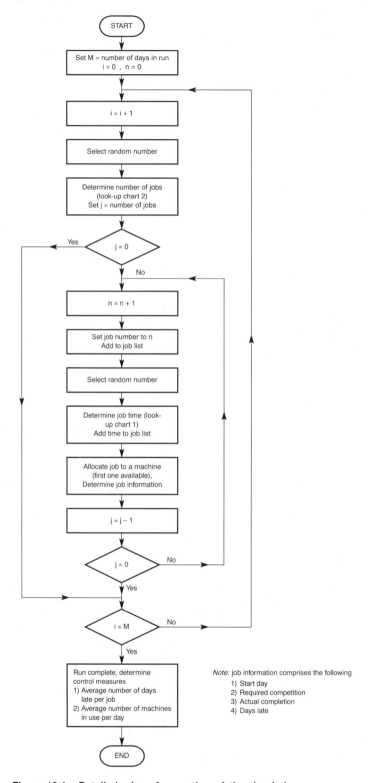

START

Set M = number of days in run
i = 0 , n = 0

i = i + 1

Select random number

Determine number of jobs
(look-up chart 2)
Set j = number of jobs

j = 0   Yes

No

n = n + 1

Set job number to n
Add to job list

Select random number

Determine job time (look-
up chart 1)
Add time to job list

Allocate job to a machine
(first one available),
Determine job information

j = j − 1

j = 0   No

Yes

i = M   No

Yes

Run complete, determine
control measures
1) Average number of days
late per job
2) Average number of machines
in use per day

Note: job information comprises the following
1) Start day
2) Required competition
3) Actual completion
4) Days late

END

Figure 13.4   Detailed rules of operation of the simulation

The detailed flowchart in Figure 13.4 now gives sufficient detail to run the model either manually or on a computer. Initially a manual model will be operated to demonstrate the processes of the model. Before the tables to operate the instructions can be produced the method for determining time needs to be derived. The simulation needs a clock, this usually being a simple counter because the simulation operates in its own time rather than real time. Within the design of the simulation the tick of the clock is influenced by the need to make it as large as possible to be economic and yet to be as detailed as possible so as to measure the parameters of the simulation. This is a balancing act to ensure the simulation is economic but is still effective. In the case of the road roller example things occur in day units, therefore this would seem an appropriate 'tick'. If time units of an hour were used then there would be many with no changes occurring in them and this would be a waste. If time units of a week were used then many things would be missed by the simulation. Therefore a day is the best unit of time to measure the simulation. It will be the case in parts of the simulation that the clock will move more than one time unit at a time.

Table 13.5 Simulation operating (machine recording)

Run No __1__ Sheet No __1__ No of Days __15__

Time Days	Number of jobs		M/C 1	M/C 2	M/C 3	No of M/Cs in use
	R N	Jobs				
1	09	0				0
2	54	1[1]				1
3	01	0				1
4	80	2[2][3]				2
5	26	0				0
6	57	1[4]				1
7	52	1[5]				2
8	45	1[6]				3
9	59	1[7]				3
10	12	0				3
11	35	0				3
12	91	2[8][9]				3
13	33	0				2
14	10	0				1
15	55	1[10]				2
16						
17						
18						
19						

Now the time scale has been determined, the tables to carry out these rules can be constructed. In this case we need one to record the machines and one to record the jobs. These tables are shown with the simulation being run for 15 days. Table 13.5 shows the main simulation operating table which records the machine operations. The days shown on this table are only working days. Non-working days need not be shown as jobs will not arrive or be worked on during them. Table 13.6 shows the second operating table of the simulation which records the information about each job. Also given, in Table 13.7, are the random numbers used in this example. More are given in Table 2 of the Appendix.

The operation of these charts is as follows. At the start of day one the number of jobs is determined on Table 13.5 by taking the first random number from Table 13.7, which is 09. Then, using Table 13.3 (the look-up chart for arrivals) we can see that this gives 0 new jobs arriving in day one. With no jobs to allocate this means that day one is completed, so the model moves on to day two. The job arrivals for day two need to be determined and the next random number is 54. Using Table 13.3 this gives one job arriving in day two. This job is now transferred onto Table 13.6 to determine the job time. The next random number, 42, is used in conjunction with Table 13.4 (the look-up chart for job times) to determine that this first job will take two days. Job number one can now be allocated onto machines. The first machine available is machine one, the job starts at the beginning of day two and it will take two days to be completed. This means that machine one cannot now be used until after the end of day three (this is shown with the arrow on Table 13.5). The job information is now added to Table 13.6 (the start day and completion days). There was only one job on day two and this has now been allocated to a machine, therefore day two is now complete. The model moves on to day three. Similarly the remaining days are operated to day 15.

On completion of the number of days required the control measure can be calculated. The average number of machines in use per day is calculated from Table 13.5 by summing all machines in use (the figures from the end column) and

Table 13.6 Simulation operating (job recording)

Run No __1__ Sheet No __1__ No of Days __15__

Job number	Number of days		Start day	Req compltn (end of day)	Actual compltn (end of day)	Days late
	R N	Days				
1	42	2	2	3	3	
2	06	1	4	4	4	
3	06	1	4	4	4	
4	79	5	6	10	10	
5	80	5	7	11	11	
6	68	4	8	11	11	
7	48	2	11	10	12	2
8	89	6	12	17	17	
9	49	2	12	13	13	
10	60	3	15	17	17	

Table 13.7   Random numbers for the simulation example

09	49	09	99		52	98	05	19		45	89	27	98
54	54	62	47		02	49	03	36		27	75	35	38
42	96	32	08		14	42	14	45		89	76	42	81
01	80	91	76		14	29	39	41		34	85	93	93
80	05	69	21		49	46	06	96		20	70	07	68
06	17	48	57		19	66	86	53		24	27	61	22
06	23	07	77		48	73	87	89		05	22	68	52
26	56	64	54		62	13	17	64		89	56	24	52
57	15	69	96		04	17	17	37		42	92	56	53
79	86	44	02		33	94	77	15		89	03	70	72
52	08	72	73		05	54	66	07		37	74	47	08
80	18	11	76		53	07	14	57		11	00	86	84
45	95	37	56		29	91	68	05		75	53	77	09
68	73	35	98		70	36	26	32		47	74	80	07
59	20	99	68		17	97	85	52		16	07	84	86
48	26	31	05		05	06	11	90		24	75	49	96
12	90	80	45		02	30	16	80		94	40	09	03
35	79	88	45		35	38	26	28		38	88	80	15
91	57	90	19		53	94	95	50		01	63	72	47
89	01	46	37		67	26	67	51		47	18	91	50
49	97	54	93		31	32	97	46		50	80	85	06
33	33	51	04		34	06	73	72		67	72	76	92
10	64	43	52		00	76	75	40		73	09	68	48
55	01	62	85		48	64	64	25		27	92	79	78
60	50	51	62		74	19	26	22		18	74	20	07
19	29	10	83		35	09	45	47		16	87	44	32
47	34	25	24		17	80	01	94		54	60	77	83
55	46	68	76		03	34	87	15		96	81	99	01
48	11	89	53		05	45	20	10		56	02	43	69
52	43	25	83		23	02	01	50		82	15	87	50

dividing by the 15 days (the length of the simulation run). The average number of days late per job is calculated from Table 13.6 by summing all the days late and dividing by the number of jobs.

Over the 15 day run of the simulation:

$$\text{Average number of days late per job} = \frac{2}{10} = 0.2 \text{ days}$$

$$\text{Average number of M/Cs in use per day} = \frac{27}{15} = 1.8 \text{ m/cs}$$

Models will usually have two modes of operation – an initialisation phase and then a steady state. The initialisation phase of the example is when all the sets of equipment are in the depot and there are no jobs waiting to be processed, i.e. the start up after an annual shut down providing all jobs are completed before the shut down and the machines withdrawn to the depot. The steady state will be reached in a few days of operation, with the possibility of machines being out and jobs waiting. Depending upon the application it may be necessary to have an initialisation stage. To remove this initialisation stage from the model the first few days are taken out of the calculation. This should be taken into account at the verification and validation stages and also when the model is used for prediction.

An important element of simulation modelling is the length the simulation is to run. This a sample size problem. The same procedure for determining sample size is carried out on the control measures using confidence limits (*see* Chapter 7). Before the model can be used in prediction it is necessary to determine that it is truly modelling the real situation within the limits of accuracy acceptable.

You may now want to construct the model for problem 13.1.

13.2.5 Verify and validate the model

The verification of the simulation model is to ensure that the model is behaving in the manner intended by the modeller. This involves testing the mechanics of the simulation, and testing things like the random number generator or the random numbers to ensure they are random. In the majority of simulations pseudo-random number generators are in fact used. They produce random numbers but after a few million they tend to repeat themselves. This stage is like a program test ensuring that all the sub-systems operate as intended. In the road roller example this is a relatively easy stage. The simulation uses a set of standard random number tables and the rules of operation are relatively simple. Within a large complex simulation carried out on a computer this can be a difficult and time-consuming stage. The programs (normally written in a special computer simulation language) as well as the systems need to be debugged.

Having verified the simulation and decided it is following the rules set down by the modeller it must now be validated. Validation is the process where the similarity between the model and the real system is tested. The model is run with parameters for which there are known results from the real system and then checked to ensure that there is no significant difference between the model and the real system. Not only should various means be tested but so should the variance of the measures to ensure similarity between the model and the real system. To carry this out there are various statistical tests, and these have been explored in Chapter 8. In the case of the road rolling example measures such as average number of days late per job and average number of machines in use and their variability would be taken from the model and compared with the real system, using the appropriate significance tests. If the tests show no significant difference the model is valid but if they show significant differences then the model requires modification to make it valid. This stage of verification and validation can be likened to the testing of a scientific instrument. It can be very important when it comes to the implementation stage of the simulation results.

13.3 Using simulation models for prediction

Once the model has been tested it can be used to predict by running with different parameters to obtain the information required. This information used with data such as cost information can then be used in the decision process. It must be remembered that this is the principal reason for building the model. Care should be taken to ensure that the relationships used within the simulation are valid over the range of the parameters used in the predictions. However, it is unlikely that the whole range can be statistically validated.

In the example being considered, runs (the length of which would be determined using sample size procedures) would be carried out to determine the number of machines required, i.e. with different numbers of machines. The results of these runs would then be used with such costs as the cost of operating road rolling machines and the cost of days late on jobs in conjunction with the council's strategies and policies. This will assist the public sector management and councillors in determining a solution to the problem of waiting time.

In this particular example it has been found that ten runs of 500 days each are needed to bring the confidence limits within acceptable limits (*see* Chapter 7 for sample size calculation method). To work out the number of machines needed will require a run to be carried out with three, four, five and six machines. It has been seen that each of these runs will require 10×500 days simulations each, i.e. 5,000 days each. This gives a grand total of 20,000 days of simulation to give the results to predict the number of machines required. This number of days would take a long time to produce on the manual simulation so far developed in this chapter. It would also provide a severe test of the sanity of the person operating such a model.

With all but the simplest simulation this does mean that the main calculations of the simulation are best carried out with the use of a computer. Managers may need to get specialist help to write the computer programs (normally in a special computer simulation language) required to operate the model. The increased computing power of personal computers also means that the powerful simulation languages previously only available on large machines are now available on personal computers. These simulation languages, such as HOCUS or SIMSCRIPT, provide easy-to-use languages for managers to build their own models although it would probably be more efficient to bring in a specialist to build the model. More details of spreadsheets and their role in modelling are given in Chapter 2.

The more complex the simulation and the more runs required of the model, the more likely it will be economic to computerise it. Computer models have the advantage of speed and accuracy, but are difficult to conceptualise and understand by the non-specialist. Therefore, when it comes to presenting the results of the simulations to management and unions it may be necessary to employ an analogue model to assist their understanding of the operation of the simulation.

A computer model has been built of the road roller model to show how the prediction process operates. Given in Table 13.8 are the results obtained by operating the simulation for 10×500 days for each machine configuration.

Table 13.8   Simulation model results for different machine configurations

No. of M/Cs	Average no. of Days late	Average no. of M/Cs in use	M/C utilisation
3	6.29	2.73	91%
4	0.76	2.78	70%
5	0.19	2.78	56%
6	0.05	2.78	46%

The table of results from the model will need some additional data before it can be used to predict the number of machines. The cost of delaying jobs will need to be calculated not just for one job but for the average number of jobs passing through the system. Multiplying this by the average number of days late per job will give the cost of delays for each of the machine configurations. This cost will then be added to the cost of operating the different machine configurations to give the total cost of operating the machines. The cost of days late will reduce as the number of machines increase but the cost of machines will increase. The resulting total cost of operation is shown in Figure 13.5.

Figure 13.5 also shows the optimum number of machines required to balance these two costs. It is usually safer to round up the number of machines where it does not fall on an integer solution. The model once produced can be used to predict other situations. The effect of working Saturday could be found. Different scheduling rules could also be experimented with, such as keeping one machine for all the small jobs. Sensitivity analysis should also be carried out on job arrivals. Job arrivals can be changed by varying the distribution of job arrivals. Also, if it were possible to improve the efficiency of the road rolling machines this could be modelled by modifying the distribution of job times. The variety of predictions that can be produced shows the power of simulation modelling.

Simulations are of considerable value in the provision of prediction information and data to management both at the operational and strategic level.

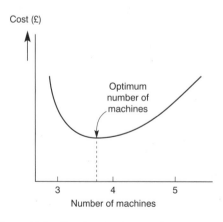

Figure 13.5   Total cost of operating different numbers of the machines

Summary

Simulation provides a method of experimenting with processes which it would be impossible or very uneconomical to experiment with in real life. Models can be used in demonstration or can be used to make predictions which can then be used by managers in decision making and planning.

Simulation can be applied to a wide range of problems including queuing problems, stock control, production line balancing, production planning and scheduling through to market and corporate planning. Simulation provides predictions for many other areas of quantitative modelling like business forecasting and decision analysis. For example, in Chapter 12 which deals with the control of stock, simulation modelling is one of the methods that can be used to help. Simulation modelling can also be used to help in the implementation of other modelling areas. It can be used to demonstrate the success of the other modelling areas before they are applied to the real world.

Competence Example 13.1

At the end of this chapter you should be able to demonstrate how to:

1 identify problems for solution by simulation models

2 define and analyse systems when building simulation models

3 construct simulation models

4 verify and validate simulation models

5 use simulation models in prediction

To practise and demonstrate these competences complete the problems at the end of this chapter. To help you to develop these competences a description of the procedure you will need to follow is now given, along with a typical problem format. This problem format is based on the case we have just considered.

PROCEDURE

❶ Identify and define the problem.

❷ Define the system by drawing a boundary around the entities of the system.

❸ Analyse the system by defining the states of the entities and the rules of transition between these states.

❹ Build the simulation model by constructing the rules of operation, the look-up charts and the operating charts.

❺ Verify and validate the model.

❻ Use the model for predictions.

THE PROBLEM

The case concerns the use made of a type of hand-controlled road rolling machine used by a large shire county council in road repairs. The machines are kept at one of its northern depots and are sent out to road repair sites as and when required. The council want to determine the number of rolling machines required at the depot to provide a reasonable service at an economic cost. The council has a number of such depots containing specialised equipment around the county. In this example the council officials consider the problem to be that jobs are waiting for road rollers. There are three road rolling machines currently based at this northern depot. From past records it has been found that jobs arrive in a daily pattern, at the start of each day, according to the following distribution. A distribution is also given of the time taken to complete jobs.

Distribution of new job arrivals each day

Number of new jobs (per day)	Occurrence (percentage)
0	39
1	36
2	17
3	6
4	2

Distribution of time taken to complete jobs

Job time (days)	Occurrence (percentage)
1	33
2	19
3	13
4	12
5	12
6	11

Construct a simulation model of this situation.

SOLUTION FORMAT

❶ In the case of this example the council officials consider the problem to be that jobs are waiting for road rollers. This is only a consequence of the real problems, which are that there are not enough machines or that the machines are not run efficiently. **1**

❷ In the case of the example being considered a definition of the system will contain the sets of the equipment and the jobs on which they are used. This will give two different entities as part of the model, that is sets of road rolling equipment and jobs requiring road rolling equipment. **2**

❸ ENTITY: Set of road rolling equipment (three such sets initially, more needed as predictions are made)

List of states:

STATE 0 Not in use, waiting at depot

STATE 1 In use, at road repair site

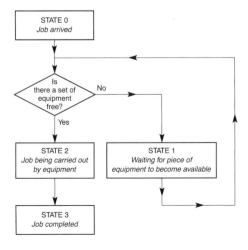

```
STATE 0
Not in use, waiting at depot
```

```
STATE 1
In use, at road repair site
```

The rule of transition between State 0 (not in use) and State 1 (in use) is a logical transition. It will occur when a job enters the system requiring a road rolling machine. Or if there is a queue of jobs, a job moves from the head of the queue when the machine becomes free. The transition between State 1 (in use) and State 0 (not in use) will be a time progression. The transition will take place when the time taken to complete the job has elapsed. This transition will be given by look-up chart 1.

Look-up chart 1 (number of new arrivals each day)

Random number	Number of jobs per day
00–38	0
39–74	1
75–91	2
92–97	3
98–99	4

ENTITY: Job (requiring the use of hand road roller)
          Number dependent on the length of simulation run

List of states:

STATE 0   Job arrived
STATE 1   Waiting for piece of equipment to become vacant
STATE 2   Job being carried out by equipment
STATE 3   Job is completed

Relationship flowchart for the states of entity of jobs:

```
STATE 0
Job arrived
    |
    v
Is there a set of equipment free? --No--> STATE 1
    |                                      Waiting for piece of
   Yes                                     equipment to become available
    |
    v
STATE 2
Job being carried out
by equipment
    |
    v
STATE 3
Job completed
```

❸ This entity is transient: it arrives in the system and when completed leaves the system. An important element of the analysis of this entity is the rate at which jobs requiring road rolling machines occur. Requests for road rolling machines occur at the beginning of each day. The average number of jobs arising in a day is 0.96 jobs. The arrival rate of new jobs is given by look-up chart 2.

Look-up chart 2 (number of new arrivals each day)

Random number	Number of jobs per day
00–38	0
39–74	1
75–91	2
92–97	3
98–99	4

❹ The flowchart records the operation of the model based on the following counters:

M = number of days simulation is to run
i = number of days simulation has been run (i will equal M at the end of the simulation run)
n = main job number counter
j = daily job counter

Detailed rules of operation of the simulation:

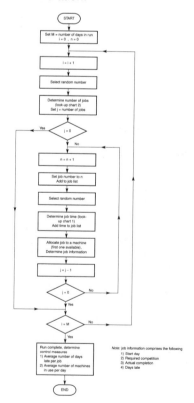

(Please refer back to Fig 13.4 on page 398 for actual diagram)

❹ Simulation operating (Machine recording):

Table 13.5 Simulation operating (machine recording)

Run No _1_ Sheet No _1_ No of Days _15_

Time Days	Number of jobs R N	Number of jobs Jobs	M/C 1	M/C 2	M/C 3	No of M/Cs in use
1	09	0				0
2	54	1 [1]				1
3	01	0				1
4	80	2 [2][3]				2
5	26	0				0
6	57	1 [4]				1
7	52	1 [5]				2
8	45	1 [6]				3
9	59	1 [7]				3
10	12	0				3
11	35	0				3
12	91	2 [8][9]				3
13	33	0				2
14	10	0				1
15	55	1 [10]				2
16						
17						
18						
19						

Simulation operating (job recording):

Table 13.6 Simulation operating (job recording)

Run No _1_ Sheet No _1_ No of Days _15_

Job number	Number of days R N	Number of days Days	Start day	Req compltn (end of day)	Actual compltn (end of day)	Days late
1	42	2	2	3	3	
2	06	1	4	4	4	
3	06	1	4	4	4	
4	79	5	6	10	10	
5	80	5	7	11	11	
6	68	4	8	11	11	
7	48	2	11	10	12	2
8	89	6	12	17	17	
9	49	2	12	13	13	
10	60	3	15	17	17	

❹ Random numbers for the simulation example:

Table 13.7   Random numbers for the simulation example

09	49	09	99	52	98	05	19	45	89	27	98
54	54	62	47	02	49	03	36	27	75	35	38
42	96	32	08	14	42	14	45	89	76	42	81
01	80	91	76	14	29	39	41	34	85	93	93
80	05	69	21	49	46	06	96	20	70	07	68
06	17	48	57	19	66	86	53	24	27	61	22
06	23	07	77	48	73	87	89	05	22	68	52
26	56	64	54	62	13	17	64	89	56	24	52
57	15	69	96	04	17	17	37	42	92	56	53
79	86	44	02	33	94	77	15	89	03	70	72
52	08	72	73	05	54	66	07	37	74	47	08
80	18	11	76	53	07	14	57	11	00	86	84
45	95	37	56	29	91	68	05	75	53	77	09
68	73	35	98	70	36	26	32	47	74	80	07
59	20	99	68	17	97	85	52	16	07	84	86
48	26	31	05	05	06	11	90	24	75	49	96
12	90	80	45	02	30	16	80	94	40	09	03
35	79	88	45	35	38	26	28	38	88	80	15
91	57	90	19	53	94	95	50	01	63	72	47
89	01	46	37	67	26	67	51	47	18	91	50
49	97	54	93	31	32	97	46	50	80	85	06
33	33	51	04	34	06	73	72	67	72	76	92
10	64	43	52	00	76	75	40	73	09	68	48
55	01	62	85	48	64	64	25	27	92	79	78
60	50	51	62	74	19	26	22	18	74	20	07
19	29	10	83	35	09	45	47	16	87	44	32
47	34	25	24	17	80	01	94	54	60	77	83
55	46	68	76	03	34	87	15	96	81	99	01
48	11	89	53	05	45	20	10	56	02	43	69
52	43	25	83	23	02	01	50	82	15	87	50

Over the 15 day run of the simulation:

$$\text{Average number of days late per job} = \frac{2}{10} = 0.2 \text{ days}$$

$$\text{Average number of M/Cs in use per day} = \frac{27}{15} = 1.8 \text{ m/cs}$$

❺ For the verification and validation stage see the relevant section in the text on p. 402.

❻

Simulation model results for different machine configurations

No. of M/Cs	Average number of days late	Average number of M/Cs in use	M/C utilisation
3	6.29	2.73	91%
4	0.76	2.78	70%
5	0.19	2.78	56%
6	0.05	2.78	46%

6 A computer model has been built of the road roller model to show how the prediction **5** process operates. Given above are the results obtained by operating the simulation for 10 × 500 days for each machine configuration.

The resulting total cost of operation and optimum number of machines is shown below:

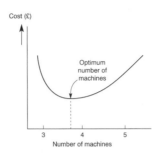

Practise your competence now on problems 13.1 to 13.6 at the end of this chapter. Simulation is not contained on the computer disk provided with this book because it is not possible to provide a single spreadsheet that will cover all simulations you need to construct. It is possible that those of you who have competence in using spreadsheets will be able to automate your operating tables on either a Lotus or an Excel spreadsheet and so save time on calculation. If you are to use the idea of simulation modelling to a significant degree then we would recommend that you develop competence in one of the more formal simulation languages discussed in the text. Simulation modelling is one of the more straightforward of the techniques developed in this book and you can apply your competence in this area on problems from your own work environment. However, you must always remember to validate your models against the real world before carrying out predictions.

Problems for Chapter 13

Simulation models concerning real business situations are usually complex and take a considerable amount of time to construct. Therefore, so you can practise and demonstrate the competences in this area in a reasonable amount of time, two types of problems have been given. First, there are highly structured problems (13.1, 13.2, 13.3 and 13.5) and with these problems you should practise and demonstrate the competences concerned with the actual construction of simulation models (for example, look-up and operating charts). Second, there are more general problems (13.4 and 13.6) to allow you to practise the full range of competences in this area (in fact you will need almost the full range of competences in this book). These examples include areas that all readers should have some experience of, but you may choose to replace these with examples from your own business environment.

13.1 Given below is the demand pattern and the lead time for a spare part for a production machine.

The production manager suggests that a reorder level of 13 parts and a reorder quantity of 20 parts will be sufficient. Build a simulation of the situation and run for 60 days. Make recommendations to the production manager about the reorder level and reorder quantity.

Demand per day	Probability	Observed lead time in days	Probability
0	0.20	5	0.30
1	0.30	6	0.45
2	0.15	7	0.20
3	0.13	8	0.05
4	0.09		
5	0.07		
6	0.06		

Notes:
i) Negative stocks are allowed because the machine broken down will require the spare part as soon as it arrives; production will of course be lost during this period.
ii) The lead time starts the day after the order is sent out and the parts arrive at the beginning of the last day of the lead time (weekends are worked and included in the lead time).
iii) The initial stock should be taken as 15 parts.

13.2 A car hire company has produced the following distributions from past data for the hire of Ford Escort cars:

No. of new hiring jobs arising in any one day	Probability	Length of hire in days	Probability
1	0.10	1	0.20
2	0.18	2	0.35
3	0.32	3	0.22
4	0.26	4	0.14
5	0.14	5	0.07
		6	0.02

Given that the company has eight Ford Escort cars for hire, construct a simulation model to enable them to predict the amount of custom lost for different fleet sizes.
Notes:
i) Customers only hire cars in whole day units.
ii) The hire office is open for six days (Monday to Saturday) and therefore jobs only arise on these days.
iii) The length of hire includes Sunday where this occurs.

13.3 Given below are the demand pattern and the lead time for a particular brand of fridge freezer stocked in a large electrical superstore.

The experienced store manager has set the reorder level to 48 fridge freezers and the reorder quantity to 130. Build a simulation of the situation and run for 60 days. Make recommendations to the store manager about the reorder level and reorder quantity.

Demand per day	Probability	Observed lead time in days	Probability
5	0.05	5	0.30
6	0.15	6	0.40
7	0.18	7	0.20
8	0.35	8	0.10
9	0.20		
10	0.07		

Notes:

i) Negative stocks are not allowed. If items are not in stock the demand is lost – the customer will take custom elsewhere.

ii) The lead time starts the day after the order is sent out and the items arrive at the beginning of the last day of the lead time (Sundays are not worked but are not counted in the lead time).

iii) The initial stock should be taken as 69 items.

13.4 Construct a simulation model for a typical high street bank counter system. The aim of the model is to determine the number of service points required. This will also include the type of service, i.e. automatic teller machines, foreign currency, etc. In your model identify the data you would require to operate your model in any particular high street bank.

13.5 A district council employs three carpenters but feels this may not be enough to give the level of service required. Given below is the arrival rate of job distribution (jobs only arrive at the beginning of a working day) and the time taken to complete jobs (jobs will occur in half day units but will only be taken as late if they are not started within the day they arrive). Jobs will only arrive on Monday to Friday and the carpenters will only work Monday to Friday.

Number of new job arrivals per day	Probability	Time taken to complete job	Probability
0	0.13	½ day	0.18
1	0.18	1 day	0.33
2	0.36	1½ days	0.30
3	0.18	2 days	0.19
4	0.10		
5	0.05		

Construct a simulation model of this situation to allow the council to predict the number of carpenters required. Build your model so you can experiment with the possibility of using premium work time on Saturday morning.

13.6 Construct a simulation model for a typical petrol station forecourt. The aim of the model is to determine the number of pumps required. This will also include the grade of petrol, leaded, unleaded or diesel. Identify the data you would require to operate your model in any particular petrol station situation.

14 The future

This chapter will examine the future of modelling. It will also consider how modelling is likely to affect you. There are no extra competences in this chapter.

The changes that are taking place in information technology are likely to have the greatest impact on the future of modelling, and the following example illustrates the impact of such changes. This example concerns the way in which the larger supermarkets operate their check out systems. Some years ago the price would have been entered on the old style till and at the end of the day the only information in any usable form would have been the totals of goods sold. The valuable data of exactly *which* goods had been sold was lost as if it had fallen through the till. With the advent of recent information technology, such as light pens and bar coding, it is now possible to capture all the data directly on to the computer system of the supermarket. This data can then be used to create information which, in the first instance, created a competitive edge for some supermarkets and certainly now creates a competitive disadvantage for supermarkets not using these approaches. The data and information produced by such systems can be used to improve the organisation's performance in the following areas:

- **Stock control** – it allows the supermarket to carry out a much more sophisticated stock recording approach. The system will remove all items as they are purchased. This will then allow the store to place orders for replacement goods more effectively. It should also reduce the chance of stock out by ensuring the system flags up stock levels, and it does not rely on store management walking the store and checking shelves.

- **Buying patterns** – this system will allow a much more sophisticated analysis to be carried out on the buying patterns of customers. On a global level it will provide store management with information on the way goods are selling by time of day and by the day of the week. Buying patterns will vary and such information will enable store management to ensure the right amount of stocks are on the shelves at the right times. This is particularly important with goods of short shelf life like fresh food. At the more detailed level it is possible to examine the make-up of individual shopping baskets. This will provide a more detailed analysis that can help with decision making on, for example, the relative positioning of items on the supermarket shelves. Some supermarkets sell this information as market research information to their suppliers.

- **Sales point efficiency** – the electronic point of sales systems (EPOS) are more efficient than the older sales tills. They also provide performance monitoring of the till operators for both speed and errors (although errors are less on the new EPOS systems).

Data capture systems such as these are now becoming very common in industry, commerce and the public sector. Information technology also means that with communication networks and database management systems this vast array of data is available to the manager. By taking full advantage of this data and using models to turn it into information, organisations can gain a competitive advantage and individual managers can succeed within their organisations.

This book has been designed to ensure you have the basic skills and knowledge in the area of modelling in business and management. The best way to test these competences is to carry them out on problems in your own work environment. The evidence you collect from this work can be used against the MCI management standards if you are working on these, or the use of the competences should improve your standing within your own organisation. The text has helped you to develop these basic competences but to extend these you will need to study further texts and probably take advice from a specialist in the area of modelling. We will now briefly examine the various areas of the book and consider the way in which you may need to develop your skills.

- *Mathematical programming.* In the text we have developed basic competences in the area of linear programming with the use of graphs. This has limited use in practice but has been used because it provides an excellent introduction into the area of modelling. You will now have the competence to formulate problems for use in computer-based linear programming packages. These LP packages can be obtained with the facility to produce integer solutions. LP would still be limited in practice because not all the functions involved are linear. This wider view is mathematical programming and to develop into these areas you will need to be able to understand and use a variety of non-linear approaches. Most applications of mathematical programming are in the area of production management and particularly in flow production areas such as the chemical industry. The approach is best suited to these areas.
- *Spreadsheets.* This book has discussed the basic skills needed for the construction of spreadsheets. The development of further skills in this area is best done by prolonged use and practice. It is useful to find a mentor in your organisation with greater spreadsheet skills to help you with this development.
- *Data presentation.* The book has developed sophisticated presentation competences. You may wish to develop more data presentation skills through computer presentation packages, e.g. Free Lance or Harvard Graphics. It would be a good idea to increase your experience in presenting data from your own work environment.
- *Averages and variability.* The book has developed your competence in an area that managers are likely to be involved in on a daily basis, and the development of further competence is best carried out by looking at further examples from your work environment. This chapter also introduced the very important characteristic of the normal distribution and the idea of using Z values to answer certain types of questions.
- *Probability.* The book has also looked at the area of probability and decision analysis. Further development in the area of decision analysis and subjective

probability may be gained through practice. Further development of probability may be undertaken by the more confident into the area of Bayesian probabilities, which will take account of prior probabilities.

- *Probability distributions.* This is the most common of the distributions and can be further developed with practice. An understanding of the normal distribution, Poisson distribution, binomial distribution and exponential distribution will ensure you are able to tackle a wide range of problems within the workplace.

- *Survey design and sampling.* The book has developed your competence in this area and the development of further competence is best carried out by looking at further examples from your work environment. The chapter also outlined a limited range of significance tests. A competence in these tests will give you the confidence to search out and develop competence in the wide range of significance tests that are available.

- *Hypothesis testing and chi-square analysis.* The book has developed your competence in a rational methodology for testing statistical statements and beliefs. There are many potential applications within the workplace, but care should be taken in not necessarily inferring cause and effect on the basis of rejecting or accepting a null hypothesis. Chi-square analysis is a very robust technique that can be used in a wide range of situations. Again, you should develop your competence by finding suitable examples within the workplace.

- *Regression and correlation.* You should now be competent in the areas of linear regression and correlation. The natural extension of this for the more confident is the area of multiple regression. Multiple regression is best developed with the aid of a computer-based package.

- *Forecasting.* The book has developed your competence in forecasting and the evaluation of different forecasting techniques, giving you a limited range of forecasting techniques. There is a very wide range available to you and the competence developed in this book should enable you to understand and choose from this wide selection.

- *Performance indicators.* The development of further competence in performance indicators is best carried out by looking at further examples from your work environment.

- *Stock control.* The book has developed your competence in stock control and the evaluation of different stock control techniques, giving you a limited range of stock control techniques. There is a wide range available to you and you should be able to choose from this selection.

- *Simulation.* The area of simulation modelling has also been covered. Because of its flexibility simulation modelling will provide the solution to many of your future modelling applications. To develop further in this area you need to look at computer-based simulation language. You may choose a package like WITNESS, which is very easy to learn how to use but is limited in how far you can develop it for more sophisticated modelling. Or you may choose a more sophisticated package like HOCUS or SUPERSIM, both of which are more difficult to learn how to use but will allow the development of very sophisticated models.

The main aim of this book has been to develop real competence and understanding in the area of quantitative modelling. By applying these skills against real problems from your own work environment you should have discovered that they are of *real* value to you. Given the changes that are taking place in IT and the greater array of data that will be available, you should now be in a position to make more sense of this data for your organisation.

Hopefully you now see quantitative modelling not just as a subject you need to pass to gain a qualification but as an area that can really help you in your job and your future.

15 Solutions to the chapter problems

This part of the book contains the solutions to the problems given at the end of the chapters. A full solution is given to the first problem in an area of the book. If your evidence matches the solution you may judge yourself *competent* and you will then find brief answers for the other problems in the area. If you find your evidence does not match the solution in this section, *don't panic* – this does not mean you have failed. What it does mean is that you are *not yet competent* in one or more of the elements of competence. To help you to gain competence in the areas you are not yet competent in you need to refer to the text and look again at the underpinning knowledge. If you look down the right side of the complete competent solution given in this section you will find the page number you need to refer back to. When you have done this, attempt to produce the evidence of competence for the problem again and then check against the complete competent solution. If you find after repeated attempts that you are still not producing competent evidence then you should contact your tutor or somebody in your organisation who has quantitative management skills.

Solutions to Chapter 1

1.1 To produce a particular product there exist two elements of cost, a fixed cost of £2,000 and a variable cost of £50 for each unit produced. The revenue for each unit sold is £70. Carry out a break-even analysis for this product. It has also been estimated that the variable cost could be as low as £42 or as high as £64. Carry out a sensitivity analysis on the effect of this variability on the break-even analysis.

A description of the layout of the solution format is given at the beginning of the book.

Solution format

❶ Let y_1 = the total cost of production
Let y_2 = the total revenue of items produced
and x = the number of units produced

1

❷ This will give the following cost model:

$$y_1 = 2,000 + 50x$$

2

② This will give the following revenue model:

$$y_2 = 70x$$

③ The break-even point will occur when the total revenue will equal the total cost.

$$\therefore y_1 = y_2$$

knowing that $y_1 = 2,000 + 50x$ and $y_2 = 70x$:
then $2,000 + 50x = 70x$
$$2,000 = 70x - 50x$$
$$2,000 = 20x$$
$$\frac{2,000}{20} = x$$
$$100 = x$$

Therefore the break-even point occurs at a production level of 100. To determine the revenue and cost at which this break-even point occurs the production level of 100 can be substituted into either equation of the model. Therefore:

$$y_2 = 70x = 70 \times 100 = £7,000$$
$$\therefore \text{ break-even point occurs at production of } 100$$
with a revenue of £7,000
and a cost of £7,000

④

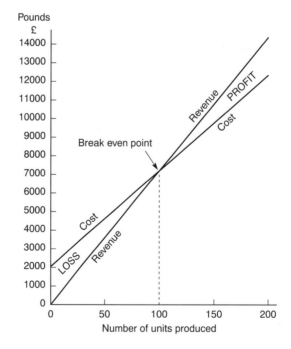

Pounds
£

Break even point

Revenue PROFIT
Cost

Cost
LOSS Revenue

Number of units produced

Figure 15.1.1   Break-even chart for Problem 1.1

The £70 is considered to be the best estimate of the future variable cost. But the cost may fall as low as £42 if there is a low pay award and the cost could rise as high as £64 commodity prices rise more than anticipated.

Variable cost	Modified cost equation	Break-even point
42	$y_1 = 2{,}000 + 42x$	$= 71.43 \cong 72$
50	$y_1 = 2{,}000 + 50x$	$= 100$
50	$y_1 = 2{,}000 + 55x$	$= 113.33 \cong 114$
60	$y_1 = 2{,}000 + 60x$	$= 200$
64	$y_1 = 2{,}000 + 64x$	$= 333.33 \cong 334$

1.2 Solution

Break-even point = 48,125

Sensitivity analysis

For variable cost £10, break-even point = 29,616
For variable cost £20, break-even point = 128,334

1.3 A light engineering firm has the following material available: 16 square metres of sheet steel, 11 square metres of sheet copper and 15 square metres of sheet brass. The firm produces high quality barbecues in two varieties: the 'old Western' style (Rawhide) and the 'old Spanish' style (Seville). The Rawhide requires two square metres of steel, one square metre of copper and one square metre of brass. A Seville requires one square metre of steel, two square metres of copper and three square metres of brass. The Rawhide returns a profit of £30 and the Seville returns a profit of £50 for each item.

a) How many of each product should the firm make to obtain the maximum profit?

b) If an unlimited amount of sheet copper is available would it pay the firm to buy more and if so how much more would be required?

Solution format

Let x = the number of Rawhide barbecues produced
y = the number of Seville barbecues produced

Materials	RAWHIDE (x)	SEVILLE Requirements (y)	Available
Steel	2	1	16
Copper	1	2	11
Brass	1	3	15
Profit	£30	£50	

Maximise $Z = 30x + 50y$
subject to $2x + y \leqslant 16$ steel constraint
$\qquad x + 2y \leqslant 11$ copper constraint
$\qquad x + 3y \leqslant 15$ brass constraint
$\qquad x$ and $y \geqslant 0$

Determine intersections with the x and y axis

Cut x	Cut y	Constraint
8	16	Steel
11	5.5	Copper
15	5	Brass

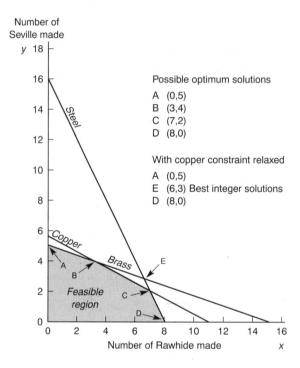

Figure 15.1.2   Graph for Problem 1.3

Evaluation of possible optimum solution:

$A \quad Z_A = 30 \times 0 + 50 \times 5 = 0 + 250 = £250$
$B \quad Z_B = 30 \times 3 + 50 \times 4 = 90 + 200 = £290$
$C \quad Z_C = 30 \times 7 + 50 \times 2 = 210 + 100 = £310$ (maximum value)
$D \quad Z_D = 30 \times 8 + 50 \times 0 = 240 + 0 = £240$

Therefore the optimum solution is C, to make seven Rawhide barbecues and two Seville barbecues giving a maximum profit of £310.

Suppose that it would be possible to obtain further supplies of copper. Would this increase profits? Remove copper constraint and evaluate new solutions.

To find the integer solution to represent point E evaluate possible integer solutions against the objective function:

$$Z = 30x + 50y$$
$$\delta(6,3) \quad Z_\delta = 30 \times 6 + 50 \times 3 = 180 + 150 = £330$$
$$\gamma(7,2) \quad Z_\gamma = 30 \times 7 + 50 \times 2 = 210 + 100 = £310$$

The best of these integer solutions (6,3) can now be used to represent point E. The evaluation of the new situation can now be carried out. With the relaxed copper constraint there are three feasible solutions to be evaluated to determine the new optimum solution: A(0,5), D(8,0) and E(6,3).

$$A \quad Z_A = 30 \times 0 + 50 \times 5 = 0 + 250 = £250$$
$$D \quad Z_D = 30 \times 8 + 50 \times 0 = 240 + 0 = £240$$
$$E \quad Z_E = 30 \times 6 + 50 \times 3 = 180 + 150 = £330$$

Therefore the new optimum solution if more copper is available will be to produce six Rawhides and three Sevilles at a maximum profit of £330. The profit on this new solution is £20 more than that of the first solution, therefore a more profitable solution does exist if more copper can be obtained. It can be calculated that 12 square metres of copper will now be needed as opposed to 11 square metres of copper in the previous optimum solution.

1.4 Solution

a) Optimum solution make   5.5 loads of small taper pins
5.6 loads of large taper pins
at maximum profit of £834

b) New optimum solution make   6 loads of small taper pins
5.6 loads of large taper pins
with a loss of profit of £6

1.5 Solution

a) Optimum solution operate   Dunsmoor facility for 40 days
Hillhouse facility for 20 days
at a minimum cost of £1,200 k

b) Road salt of 400 tons

c) New optimum solution operate   Dunsmoor facility for 30 days
Hillhouse facility for 25 days
reducing operating cost by £100 k

1.6 Solution

a)   Optimum solution make   30 of Product A
70 of Product B
with maximum profit of £5,400

b) New optimum solution make 60 of Product A
60 of Product B
improving profit by £600

Solutions to Chapter 3

The first five questions from Chapter 3 are based on the company data contained in Table 3.1, which really necessitates the use of a spreadsheet package (Lotus 123 and/or Excel) The data in Table 3.1 is available on the disk that accompanies this book, under the file name of TABLE31.WK1 if you are using Lotus 123 or TABLE31.XLS if you are using Excel. The remainder of the questions in Chapter 3 can be answered without the use of a spreadsheet package

3.1 For the absenteeism (Absent variable) data in Table 3.1 construct a relative frequency distribution and a bar graph, and report upon your findings.

Solution format

❶

$$\frac{\text{largest data value} - \text{smallest data value}}{\text{class width}}$$

$$\frac{27 - 0}{5} = 5.4 \quad \text{It was decided to round this up to 6 classes}$$

❷ ❸

Table 15.3.1 Frequency distribution for absenteeism variable

Absent Class	Frequency
0 to 4	59
5 to 9	57
10 to 14	25
15 to 19	7
20 to 24	2
25 to 29	2
	152

The frequencies in Table 15.3.1 were obtained from Lotus 123, using the 'DATA' and then 'DISTRIBUTION' command. They can also be generated from Excel using the 'FORMULA', 'PASTFUNCTION', 'STATISTICAL', and then 'FREQUENCY' command. Lotus 123 and Excel were also used to calculate the relative frequencies shown in Table 15.3.2 and to create the bar graph in Figure 15.3.1.

(pp 54–56)

❷ ❸

Table 15.3.2   Relative frequency distribution for absenteeism variable

Absent Class	Relative Frequency
0 to 4	38.81
5 to 9	37.5
10 to 14	16.45
15 to 19	4.6
20 to 24	1.32
25 to 29	1.32
	100.00

1

❹

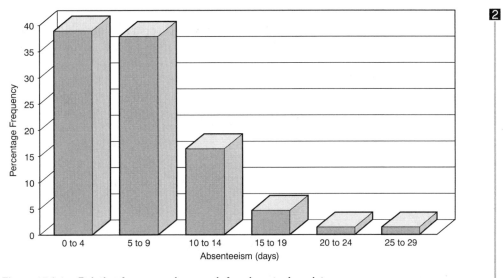

Figure 15.3.1   Relative frequency bar graph for absenteeism data

2

(pp 57–58)

❺   It can be seen that the majority of absenteeism (76.31%) is between 0 and 9 days. Although it is encouraging to note that absenteeism is relatively short term in nature, careful consideration needs to be given as to why so many employees have up to 9 days off. In this respect it could be argued that the simple bar graph, using actual numbers rather than percentages, would have been better, as it enables us to see more easily the number of employees who had up to 9 days absenteeism.

3

(p 63)

3.2 Solution

Overall, the data suggests that absenteeism and sickness follow each other very closely, and that there appears to be a real problem within the organisation due to the very high number of employees who have 10 days or less off work.

3.3 For the Service variable in Table 3.1 (pp 49–53), estimate via a cumulative frequency distribution and a cumulative frequency curve the following:

a. the number of employees who have had 12 years service or less

b. the number of employees who have had 18 years service or less

c. the number of employees who have had at least 8 years service but less than 14 years service

Solution Format

❶ The frequency distribution for the length of service data is shown in Table 15.3.3, **1** and this was obtained from Lotus 123 using the 'DATA' and then 'DISTRIBUTION' command. From this it is possible to construct a cumulative frequency distribution, as depicted in Table 15.3.4.

Table 15.3.3 Frequency distribution of Length of Service data

Length of Service Class	Frequency
5	86
10	39
15	22
20	2
25	2
30	0
35	1
	152

Table 15.3.4 Cumulative frequency distribution for Length of Service data

Length of Service (years)	Cumulative Frequency
Less than or equal to 5	86
Less than or equal to 10	125
Less than or equal to 15	147
Less than or equal to 20	149
Less than or equal to 25	151
Less than or equal to 30	151
Less than or equal to 35	152

(p 69)

❷ With Lotus 123 we can convert the cumulative frequency distribution into a **2** cumulative frequency curve and estimate the required values, as shown in Figure 15.3.2.

❷

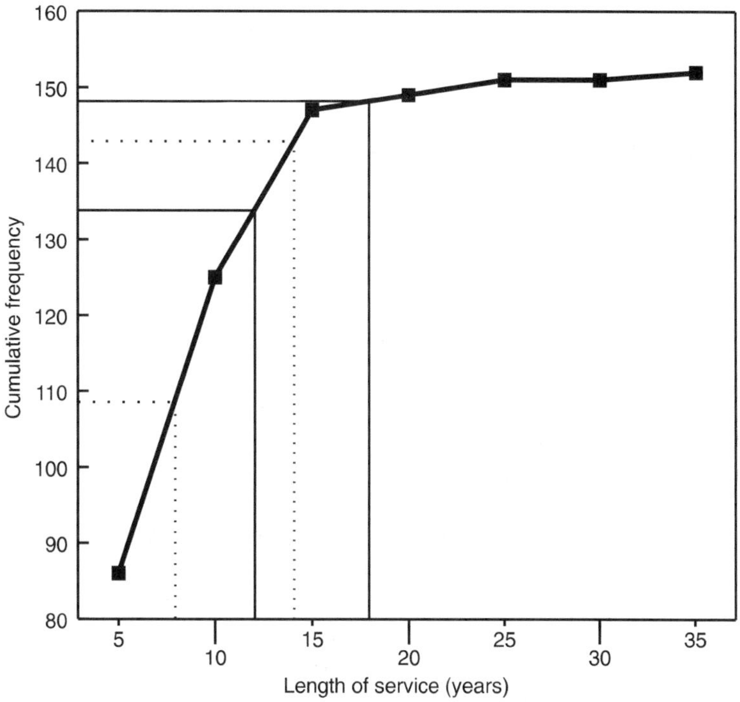

Figure 15.3.2   Cumulative frequency curve for Length of Service data

② (page 70)

③ (page 69)

❸ Estimating from the cumulative frequency curve we find:

a. 12 years or less = 134
b. 18 years or less = 148
c. at least 8 years and less than 14 years is 144 – 109 = 35

3.4 Solution

The estimated answers from the 'or more' cumulative frequency distribution are as follows:

a. 5 years or more = 92
b. 13 years or more = 18
c. at least 7 years but less than 16 years = 58 – 5 = 53

3.5 Solution

Five classes, with an interval width of 4, were used for the frequency distribution. The bar chart that was developed from this frequency distribution clearly shows that the highest frequency of accidents per week is between 0 and 4 accidents. While the company might feel reassured by this, it is worrying to see such high frequencies against the 5 to 8 and the 9 to 12 classes and every effort should be made to identify the causes of the accidents and reduce their frequency.

3.6 Solution

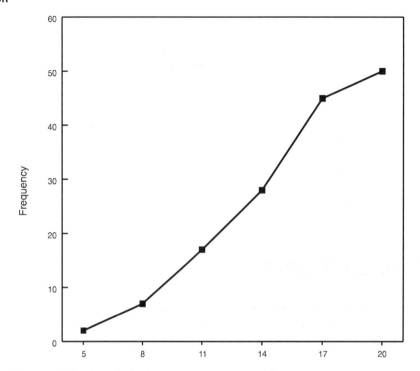

Figure 15.3.3 Cumulative frequency curve for problem 3.6

3.7 Solution

The pie chart for consumer spending data shows that the housing slice is the largest, and that it is twice as large as the next largest slice, the food slice. The pie chart is particularly good at showing the major segments, but is less successful at differentiating the smaller slices.

3.8 Solution

The bar graph for the UK balance of trade data clearly highlights the downward trend that occurred from the high of 1984 to the low of 1992. The graph has an advantage over the table of data in that it allows the viewer to get a very good appreciation of the overall situation in a glance, which is why they are used so frequently and to such good effect in the media.

3.9 Solution

Class	Frequency	Relative Frequency (%)	Cumulative Frequency	Relative Cumulative Frequency (%)
10 to 15	3	15	3	15
16 to 20	9	45	12	60
21 to 25	2	10	14	70
26 to 30	4	20	18	90
31 to 35	2	10	20	100
	20	100		

Solutions to Chapter 4

4.1 The following daily temperatures (°F) were recorded in the cold room of a large market garden that supplies fresh vegetables to a number of the national food retailers.

9	10	6	7	4	8
7	5	4	7	7	5
12	6	5	9	8	6
4	4	6	8	6	4
5	3	8	4	5	6

a) Calculate the mean, median and standard deviation for this set of data

b) The recommended temperature for the cold room is 6°F, which is strictly monitored by the food retailers. In light of this, comment on the summary statistics calculated above and their possible implications.

Solution format

a) The sample mean for this set of temperatures is:

$$\bar{X} = \frac{\sum X}{n}$$

$n = 30$

❶

1

$$\sum X = 9 + 10 + 6 + 7 + 4 + 8 + 7 + 5 + 4 + 7 + 7 + 5 + 12 + 6 + 5$$

$$+ 9 + 8 + 6 + 4 + 4 + 6 + 8 + 6 + 4 + 5 + 3 + 8 + 4 + 5 + 6 = 188$$

$$\bar{X} = \frac{\sum X}{n} = \bar{X} = \frac{188}{30} = 6.27$$

(pp 85–87)

❷ The median for this set of temperatures is:

... arranging the data in ascending order we get

3 4 4 4 4 4 4 5 5 5 5 5 6 6 6 6 6 6 7 7 7 7 8 8 8 8 9 9 10 12

... and finding the location of the median

$$\frac{n + 1}{2} = \frac{30 + 1}{2} = 15.5$$

... tells us that the median is the mean of 15th and 16th items $\left(\frac{6+6}{2}\right)$, which provides a mean value of 6.

❸ The sample variance and standard deviation, using the shortcut formula, for this set of data are:

3

(pp 95–100)

sample variance $\quad s^2 = \dfrac{\sum X^2 - \dfrac{\left(\sum X\right)^2}{n}}{n - 1}$

sample standard deviation $\quad s = \sqrt{s^2}$

The data with the necessary calculations is shown in Table 15.4.1

$$s^2 = \frac{\sum X^2 - \dfrac{\left(\sum X\right)^2}{n}}{n - 1} \quad s^2 = \frac{1304 - \dfrac{(188)^2}{30}}{29} \quad s^2 = \frac{1304 - 1178.13}{29}$$

$$s^2 = \frac{125.87}{29} = 4.34$$

$$s = \sqrt{s^2} \quad s = \sqrt{4.34} = 2.08$$

❸

Table 15.4.1   Cold room temperature data

X	X²
9	81
10	100
6	36
7	49
4	16
8	64
7	49
5	25
4	16
7	49
7	49
5	25
12	144
6	36
5	25
9	81
8	64
6	36
4	16
4	16
6	36
8	64
6	36
4	16
5	25
3	9
8	64
4	16
5	25
6	36
$\Sigma X = 188$	$\Sigma X^2 = 1304$

3

❷ ❹ ❻   b. The mean and median are in line with the recommended temperature of 6°F. The standard deviation value of 2.08 indicates that there is some variation around this recommended temperature. Indeed, it says that on average the temperatures will vary from 3.92 to 8.08°F. This may lead to problems with the retailers, and it is likely that the size of the standard deviation will need to be reduced as well as a reduction in the size of the mean.

2 4

(pp 96–99)

4.2 Solution

A summary of the information obtained for each sales region is shown below:

Area	$\bar{X}$	s
A	110.5	65.11
B	173.17	161.93
C	47.5	31.56
D	155.67	59.25

Very briefly, Area B has the the highest mean and standard deviation, which suggests that there is a high degree of variability around the mean. Area D on the other hand has the second highest mean but a smaller standard deviation. The great variability associated with Area B perhaps explains why it had the lowest average rate of commission of the four areas. Interestingly, Area C, which has the lowest mean and standard deviation, has the highest average rate of commission. This suggests that Area C was able to target the higher commission products but had difficulty in achieving the volume, while Area D had the volume but was slightly more ineffective in targeting the high commission products. Overall it seems that Area D performed most satisfactorily.

4.3 The management of a large hospital are aware that public expectations have changed with the introduction of the Citizens Charter. Since the maternity outpatients unit has always been a major part of the hospital's activities it seemed sensible to monitor how long outpatients had to wait to see a paediatrician before any corrective action was taken and public statements made. A sample of waiting times was taken over a four week period and these revealed the following information:

Time (minutes)	Frequency
0–19	25
20–39	74
40–59	158
60–79	131
80–99	92
100–119	33
120–139	17
140–159	4

Calculate the mean waiting time and its standard deviation and comment on your findings.

Solution Format

❶ The formula for computing the mean from a sample of grouped data is:

$$\bar{X} = \frac{\sum fM}{n}$$

where f = class frequency
M = midpoint of class
n = sample frequencies

❶

Table 15.4.2   Mean from grouped data table

Time (minutes)	Frequency f	Midpoint M	fM
0 to 19	25	9.5	237.5
20 to 39	74	29.5	2183
40 to 59	158	49.5	7821
60 to 79	131	69.5	9104.5
80 to 99	92	89.5	8234
100 to 119	33	109.5	3613.5
120 to 139	17	129.5	2201.5
140 to 159	4	149.5	598
	$n = 534$		$\Sigma fM = 33993$

The grouped mean waiting time is therefore:

$$\bar{X} = \frac{\sum fM}{n} = \frac{33993}{534} = 63.66 \text{ minutes}$$

❸ The standard deviation using the shortcut formula is:

sample variance (grouped data) $\qquad s^2 = \dfrac{\sum fM - \dfrac{\left(\sum fM\right)^2}{n}}{n-1}$

sample standard deviation (grouped data) $\quad s = \sqrt{s^2}$

Table 15.4.3   Standard deviation from grouped data table

Age Class	Frequency f	Midpoint M	fM	fM²
0 to 19	25	9.5	237.5	2256.25
20 to 39	74	29.5	2183	64398.5
40 to 59	158	49.5	7821	387139.5
60 to 79	131	69.5	9104.5	632762.75
80 to 99	92	89.5	8234	736943
100 to 119	33	109.5	3613.5	395678.25
120 to 139	17	129.5	2201.5	285094.25
140 to 159	4	149.5	598	89401
	$n = 534$		$\Sigma fM = 33993$	$\Sigma fM^2 = 2593673.5$

(pp 103–106)

❸

$$s^2 = \frac{\sum fM^2 - \frac{(\sum fM)^2}{n}}{n-1} = \frac{2593673.5 - \frac{(33993)^2}{534}}{533} = \frac{2593673.5 - 2163902.7}{533}$$

$$= \frac{429770.8}{533} = 806.32$$

$$s = \sqrt{s^2} = \sqrt{806.32} = 28.39$$

❹ ❻ The mean waiting time of 63.66 minutes and the standard deviation of 28.39 ❸ minutes indicate a high average waiting time with a wide degree of variability. One would assume that the management would want to reduce both the size of the mean and the spread of the data so that a better and more consistent service can be provided.

4.4 Solution

a. The mean size of an account receivable is:

$$\overline{X} = \frac{\sum fM}{n} \quad \overline{X} = \frac{46200}{100} = 462$$

The median size of an account receivable is:

$$\text{median} = L + \frac{f_1}{f_2} W = 100 + \frac{15}{18} 100 = 183.32$$

b. The mean value of 462 is much higher than the median value of 183 and this suggests that the shape of the 'Accounts Receivable Percentage' distribution is skewed to the left.

c. The median is the more appropriate of the averages to use because it is not distorted by the fewer unusually high account receivable items. As previously pointed out, the size of the accounts receivable is skewed to the left and this shows that the majority of the accounts are of a lower value. The standard deviation is 784.22, which would indicate a high level of variation in the type of accounts receivable. The problem with the standard deviation is that it has been distorted by the very high number generated in the 1000 to under 5000 class. The percentage overdue frequencies are not uniform in the sense that they do not mirror the accounts receivable frequencies. There might be some concern that the higher value accounts have overdue frequencies, since they presumably would be a priority target for collection.

4.5 In a civil servants' capability profiling assessment, 12 candidates obtained fewer than 10 marks, 25 obtained 10 to under 25 marks, 51 obtained 25 to under 40 marks, 48 obtained 40 to under 50 marks, 46 obtained 50 to under 60 marks, 54 obtained 60 to under 80 marks, and only 8 obtained 80 marks or more. Marks were out of 100.

The results for previous candidates were:

Marks	No. of candidates
0 to under 15	40
15 to under 30	80
30 to under 45	150
40 to under 60	480
60 to under 75	190
75 to under 90	50
90 and over	10

a. Compare these two sets of marks by way of a five number summary and a box and whiskers plot. In light of this what can you deduce about the two sets of data?

b. By using Z values, describe and compare the performance of a candidate who scored 64 points, to both groups of scores.

Solution Format

❷ a. A five number summary consists of the following measures:

　　Median
　　Lower Quartile
　　Upper Quartile
　　Minimum Value
　　Maximum Value

❶ For the civil servants' *previous* capability profiling assessment marks these measures are:

Median

$N/2 = 1000/2 = 500$th item

$$\text{median} = L + \frac{f_1}{f_2} W = 45 + \frac{230}{480} 15 = 52.19$$

　　where L = The lower limit of the median class
　　　　　f_1 = The frequency of items interpolated into the median class
　　　　　f_2 = The median class frequency
　　　　　W = The width of the median class

Lower Quartile

The lower quartile is the same as the 25th percentile, and when data is presented as a grouped frequency distribution, then a similar computational procedure to that

1

(pp 116–117)

2

(pp 113–117)

❶ for determining the median can be used:

$$n\text{th percentile} = L + \frac{f_1}{f_2}\, W$$

where L = The lower limit of the nth percentile class
$\quad f_1$ = The frequency of items interpolated into the nth percentile class
$\quad f_2$ = The nth percentile class frequency
$\quad W$ = The width of the nth percentile class

The 25th percentile is the $(N)(.25) = 1000(.25) =$ the 250th item in the distribution.

Substituting into the formula in the same way as the median we find:

$$\text{The 25th percentile} = 30 + \frac{130}{150}\, 15 = 43$$

Upper Quartile

The upper quartile is the 75th percentile:

$$(N)(.75) = 1000(.75) = 750\text{th item}$$

$$\text{Therefore the 75th percentile} = 60 + \frac{0}{190}\, 15 = 60$$

❷ *Minimum Value*

The minimum value is taken to be the midpoint of the lowest class, which is 7.5.

Maximum Value

The maximum value is taken to be the midpoint of the highest class. The problem with this is that the highest class has no upper limit, but since we know that the marks are out of a maximum of 100, the midpoint value must 95.

❶ For the *new* set of marks we have the following distribution:

Marks	No. of Candidates
0 to under 10	12
10 to under 25	25
25 to under 40	51
40 to under 50	48
50 to under 60	46
60 to under 80	54
80 and over	8

❶ The values associated with a five number summary for this set of data are: **2**

Median

$$N/2 = 244/2 = 122\text{nd item}$$

$$\text{median} = L + \frac{f_1}{f_2} W = 40 + \frac{34}{48} 10 = 47.08$$

Lower Quartile

The 25th percentile is the $(N)(.25) = 244(.25) =$ the 61st item

$$\text{The 25th percentile} = 25 + \frac{24}{51} 15 = 32.06$$

Upper Quartile

The 75th percentile is the $(N)(.75) = 244(.75) = 183\text{rd item}$

$$\text{Therefore the 75th percentile} = 60 + \frac{1}{54} 20 = 60.37$$

❷ *Minimum Value*

The minimum value is taken to be the midpoint of the lowest class, which is 5.

Maximum Value

The maximum value is taken to be the midpoint of the highest class. The problem with this is that the highest class has no upper limit, but since we know that the marks are out of a maximum of 100, the midpoint value must 90.

A comparison of the two frequency distributions using the five number **1** summary is shown below:

	Previous Candidates	Current Candidates
Median	52.19	47.08
Lower Quartile	43	32.06
Upper Quartile	60	60.37
Minimum Value	7.5	5
Maximum Value	95	90

A box and whisker plot based upon the five number summaries is shown below in Figure 15.4.1.

(pp 113–117)

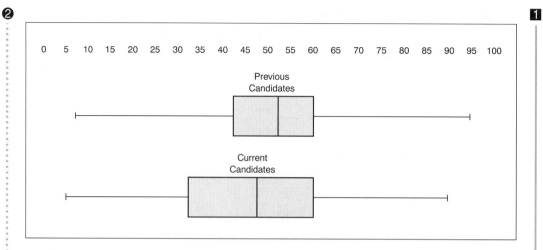

Figure 15.4.1 Box and whisker plot for question 4.5

The comparison of previous and current candidates' marks indicates that although there is a broad similarity between the marks, there are a number of differences. The current candidates have a slightly lower median value and a much lower quartile value. This suggests that although the median and upper quartile values are very close, there is a proportion of the current candidates that have performed more poorly than previous candidates.

b. By using Z values describe and compare the performance of a candidate who scored 64 points, to both groups of scores.

The Z value formula $z = \frac{X - \mu}{\sigma}$ entails finding the mean and standard deviation before the actual Z value can be calculated. The mean and standard deviation values for previous and current candidates are:

Marks	Previous Candidates f	Midpoint M	fM	fM^2
0 to under 15	40	7.5	300	2250
15 to under 30	80	22.5	1800	40500
30 to under 45	150	37.5	5625	210937.5
45 to under 60	480	52.5	25200	1323000
60 to under 75	190	67.5	12825	865687.5
75 to under 90	50	82.5	4125	340312.5
90 and over	10	95	950	90250
	$n = 1000$		$\Sigma\, fM = 50825$	$\Sigma\, fM^2 = 2872937.5$

$$\bar{X} = \frac{\sum fM}{n} \qquad \bar{X} = \frac{50825}{1000} = 50.82$$

(pp 120–121)

❹

❸

$$s^2 = \frac{\sum fM^2 - \frac{\left(\sum fM\right)^2}{n}}{n-1} = \frac{2872937.5 - \frac{(50825)^2}{1000}}{999} = \frac{2872937.5 - 2583180.6}{999}$$

$$= \frac{289756.9}{999} = 290.05$$

$$s = \sqrt{s^2} = \sqrt{290.05} = 17.03$$

Marks	Current Candidates f	Midpoint M	fM	fM²
0 to under 10	12	5	60	300
10 to under 25	25	17.5	437.5	7656.25
25 to under 40	51	32.5	1657.5	53868.75
40 to under 50	48	45	2160	97200
50 to under 60	46	55	2530	139150
60 to under 80	54	70	3780	264600
80 and over	8	90	720	64800
	n = 244		Σ fM = 11345	Σ fM² = 627575

$$\bar{X} = \frac{\sum fM}{n} \qquad \bar{X} = \frac{11345}{244} = 46.49$$

$$s^2 = \frac{\sum fM^2 - \frac{\left(\sum fM\right)^2}{n}}{n-1} = \frac{627575 - \frac{(11345)^2}{244}}{243} = \frac{627575 - 527496}{243}$$

$$= \frac{100079}{243} = 411.85$$

$$s = \sqrt{s^2} = \sqrt{411.85} = 20.29$$

The Z values with a score of 64 against the previous and current candidates can now be be calculated:

Previous candidates $\quad Z = \frac{X - \mu}{\sigma} \qquad Z = \frac{64 - 50.82}{17.03} = 0.77$

Current candidates $\quad Z = \frac{X - \mu}{\sigma} \qquad Z = \frac{64 - 46.49}{20.29} = 0.86$

⑤ The *Z* values show that the candidate has scored better against the current ③
candidates than against the previous candidates, which supports the conclusion
arrived at in part (a).

4.6 Solution

a. Determine the average time per customer and the standard deviation

The grouped mean waiting time is:

$$\bar{X} = \frac{\sum fM}{n} = \frac{2428}{348} = 6.97 \text{ minutes}$$

The standard deviation using the shortcut formula is:

$$s^2 = \frac{\sum fM^2 - \frac{\left(\sum fM\right)^2}{n}}{n-1} = \frac{19964 - \frac{(2428)^2}{348}}{347} = \frac{19964 - 16940}{347} = \frac{3024}{347} = 8.71$$

$$s = \sqrt{s^2} = \sqrt{8.71} = 2.95$$

b. Calculate the 30th and 60th percentiles

The computational formula for grouped data is:

$$n\text{th percentile} = L + \left(\frac{f_1}{f_2}\right)W$$

$$\text{The 30th percentile} = 4 + \left(\frac{49.4}{69}\right)2 = 5.43$$

This means that 30% of the customers had to wait for 5.43 minutes or less

$$\text{The 60th percentile} = 6 + \left(\frac{84.8}{107}\right)2 = 7.58$$

This means that 60% of the customers had to wait for 7.58 minutes or less

c. Explain how the Office Manager should use the measures determined in (a) and (b) to monitor the efficiency of the customer service system.

The mean time can be used as a benchmark, in that the office manager will be able to compare the mean time for any given week and thus monitor efficiency and the effects of any changes in personnel etc. The standard deviation can also be used as a benchmark, for it enables the office manager to monitor the spread of the service times about the mean. Similarly it can be used to monitor the effects of any changes that have taken place within the office. The mean and standard deviation can also be used to set targets and again monitored to see if they have been achieved or reduced.

4.7 A friend's investment of £1,000 was invested over a six year period and was valued over that period as:

Year	Value (£)
1990	1000
1991	1273
1992	1539
1993	1855
1994	2281
1995	2640

  a. Find the value of the geometric mean.
  b. What would be the expected return if you invested £4,500 at the geometric mean value over an 8 year period?

Solution Format

❶ a. Find the value of the geometric mean

Using the geometric mean formula:

$$GM = \sqrt[n]{X_1 X_2 X_3 \ldots X_n}$$

we find that the geometric mean is:

$$GM = \sqrt[6]{(1000)(1273)(1539)(1855)(2281)(2640)} = 1672.46$$

❷ b. What would be the expected return if you invested £4,500 at the geometric mean value over an 8 year period?

The first step is to determine what the existing average growth rate has been:

Year	Value (£)	Performance (proportional increase over previous year)
1990	1000	–
1991	1273	1.273
1992	1539	1.209
1993	1855	1.205
1994	2281	1.230
1995	2640	1.157

(pp 92–94)

❸ The next step is to then calculate what the average rate of growth has been using the geometric mean:

$$GM = \sqrt[5]{(1.273)(1.209)(1.205)(1.230)(1.157)} = 1.214$$

The growth factor can now be used to determine the expected return on £4,500 over an 8 year period:

Year	Investment Amount		Growth Factor		Investment return
1	£4,500	×	1.214	=	£5,463
2	£5,463	×	1.214	=	£6,632.08
3	£6,632.08	×	1.214	=	£8,051.34
4	£8,051.34	×	1.214	=	£9,774.33
5	£9,774.33	×	1.214	=	£11,866.04
6	£11,866.04	×	1.214	=	£14,404.37
7	£14,405.37	×	1.214	=	£17,488.12
8	£17,488.12	×	1.214	=	**£21,230.58**

The expected return of £4,500 over an 8 year period is therefore £21,230.58.

4.8 Solution

A five number summary and a box and whisker plot were used to compare the three different stocks. The box and whisker plot shows that stock B has the least amount of risk associated with it, although it has the lowest median value of the three stocks. An attractive feature of stock B is that it has the highest lowest number, so even in the worst scenario situation it would perform better than the lower quartile of stocks A and C.

4.9 Solution

a. Calculate the mean and standard deviation.

$$\bar{X} = \frac{50}{7} = 7.14$$

The standard deviation of the journey times is:

$$s^2 = \frac{104.86}{6} = 17.48$$

b. What is the 90th percentile value?

$$\text{The 90th percentile} = 22 + \left(\frac{1}{4}\right)1 = 22.25$$

This means that 90 per cent of the journeys between the two production sites took 22.25 minutes or less.

4.10 A university finance officer has looked at the number of MBA students who are still owing money, and as part of this analysis has found that the mean payment of fees is 46 days with a standard deviation of 12 days. Armed with this information is it possible to say how many MBA students paid between 34 and 58 days?

The finance officer also noted that the number of MBA students had increased steadily over the last four years:

Year	Number of MBA students	Growth rate
1992	27	–
1993	36	33.33
1994	58	61.11
1995	75	29.31

In light of this the finance officer would like you to calculate the average annual compounded rate of growth and to estimate the number of MBA students there will be in 1996.

Solution Format

❶ Since 68.26 per cent of a population lies between plus and minus one standard deviation of a population mean, and the mean equals 46 days and the standard deviation equals 12 days for the MBA students, we can say that 68.26 per cent of the MBA students will take from 34 to 58 days to pay their bills.

❷ The average annual compounded rate of growth, using the geometric mean formula, is:

The first step is to determine what the existing average growth rate has been:

Year	Number of MBA Students	Performance (proportional increase over previous year)
1992	27	–
1993	36	1.333
1994	58	1.611
1995	75	1.293

(pp 92–94)

❸ The next step is to then calculate what the average rate of growth has been using the geometric mean:

$$GM = \sqrt[n]{X_1 X_2 X_3 \ldots X_n}$$

$$\boldsymbol{GM} = \sqrt[3]{(1.333)(1.611)(1.293)} = 1.405$$

❸ Assuming that the average rate of growth continues we would expect 🔳🔳
75 × 1.405 = 105 students in 1996.

Solutions to Chapter 5

5.1 The Highways Committee of a county council has a decision to make concerning three independent road projects. Before the meeting to help with future planning, the chief engineer has estimated the following probabilities:

Project A   a road widening scheme   Probability of acceptance   0.9
Project B   a bridge modernisation scheme   Probability of acceptance   0.6
Project C   a new by-pass scheme   Probability of acceptance   0.7

You can assume there is sufficient cash for all three projects. Construct a probability tree and determine the following probabilities:

a) all projects will be accepted
b) at least one project will be accepted
c) at least two projects will be accepted
d) all the projects will be rejected

Solution Format

❶

	Acceptance	Non-acceptance
Project A (a road widening scheme)	0.9	0.1
Project B (a bridge modernisation scheme)	0.6	0.4
Project C (a new by-pass scheme)	0.7	0.3

🔳

a) To obtain the probability, the probability tree needs to be inspected and all the branches that give all projects accepted need to be identified. These are marked on the tree with a * symbol.

$$P(\text{all projects accepted}) = 0.378$$

b) To obtain the probability, the probability tree needs to be inspected and all the branches that give at least one project accepted need to be identified. These are marked on the tree with a † symbol.

$$P(\text{at least one project accepted}) = 0.378 + 0.162 + 0.252 + 0.108 + 0.042$$
$$+ 0.018 + 0.028 = 0.988$$

An alternative way of calculating this probability is to identify from the tree that the only branch on the tree that does not give at least one project accepted can be found at the bottom.

$$P(\text{at least one project accepted}) = 1 - P(\text{no project accepted})$$
$$= 1 - 0.012$$
$$= 0.988$$

(pp 134–137)

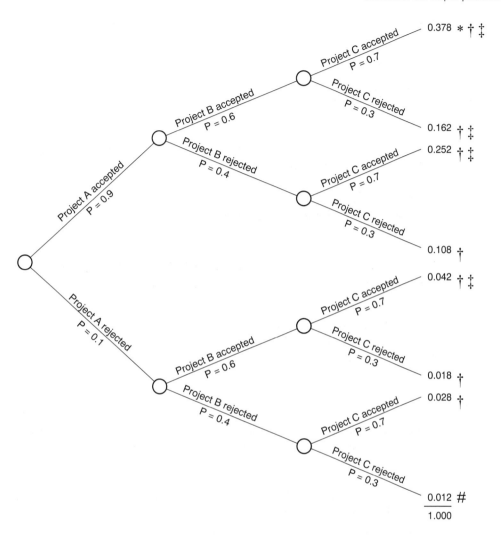

Figure 15.5.1   Probability tree for problem 5.1

c) To obtain the probability, the probability tree needs to be inspected and all the branches that give at least two projects accepted need to be identified. These are marked on the tree with a ‡ symbol.

$$P(\text{at least two projects accepted}) = 0.378 + 0.162 + 0.252 + 0.042$$
$$= 0.834$$

d) To obtain the probability, the probability tree needs to be inspected and all the branches that give all projects rejected need to be identified. These are marked on the tree with a # symbol.

$$P(\text{all projects rejected}) = 0.012$$

5.2. Solution

a) P(both jobs offered) = 0.0168

b) P(at least one job offered) = 0.692

c) P(no job offered) = 0.308

5.3 Solution

a) P(all project accepted) = 0.3024

b) P(projects in group one accepted) = 0.72

c) P(projects in group two accepted) = 0.42

d) P(at least one project accepted) = 0.96

e) P(at least two projects accepted) = 0.87

f) P(at least three projects accepted) = 0.5076

5.4 A manufacturer of plastic toys has to decide whether or not to produce and market a new Christmas novelty toy. The life of the product is only expected to be one year in the highly volatile toy business. If the manufacturer decides to produce the toy a special plastic mould will need to be purchased. You can assume that the retirement costs will be balanced out by the scrap value. There exists a choice of moulds to buy: a normal quality mould costing £1,500 and with a cost of manufacturing, distribution, advertising, etc., of £1.50 per unit (this cost includes all costs other than the cost of purchase of the mould); or a high quality mould costing £2,000 could be purchased with a cost of manufacturing, distribution, advertising, etc., of £1 per unit (this cost includes all costs other than the cost of purchase of the mould). This mould produces good items to the same quality as the first mould but it is more efficient and has a lower scrap rate and this is reflected in the cost structure. The selling price is £5 per unit and the following probabilities of sales have been estimated.

Sales	400	1,000	2,000
Probability	0.4	0.3	0.3

Produce a decision analysis of this situation and advise the manufacturer in connection with the alternative decisions.

Solution format

❶ Management has three possible actions it can take:

Strategy 1   To produce the new novelty toy using the normal quality mould
Strategy 2   To produce the new novelty toy using the high quality mould
Strategy 3   Not to produce the new novelty toy

The probabilities after Strategies 1 and 2 are then as follows:

Sell 400 items with a probability of 0.4
Sell 1,000 items with a probability of 0.3
Sell 2,000 items with a probability of 0.3

(pp 149–150)

❷ ❸

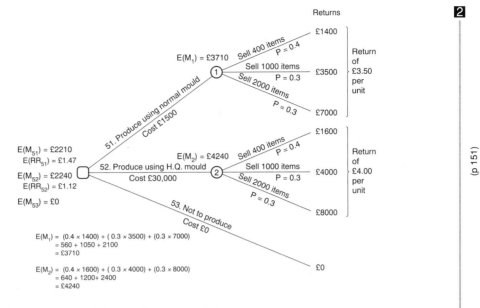

Figure 15.5.2   Decision tree for problem 5.4

❹   Using classical statistical decision theory the decision giving the greatest return is that of producing the new Christmas novelty toy using the high quality mould with an expected return of £2,240 (i.e. Strategy 1).

You should also show in your solution the use of other financial criteria. An example of this is to use a rate of return. If this is done then the best strategy is to produce the novelty toy using the normal quality mould which gives a rate of return of £1.47 per pound invested (i.e. Strategy 2). If the company wishes to minimise risk then there is only one route that will not give a loss and that is not to produce the novelty toy (i.e. Strategy 3).

Company policy could well affect the decision. Your solution should demonstrate this. For example, if the company wishes to maximise the amount and rate of return then this is not possible and management will need to determine which of these two is the dominant company policy. This is where policy identifies the decision for the company to take. It is also possible that company policy may eliminate the feasibility of routes. For example, the company may have a policy of no redundancies for its employees, therefore the not to produce route may no longer be feasible given that it may mean redundancies. The cost of such policies can be determined from the tree.

The decision maker must add into the decision-making process the effects of factors which may be difficult to quantify. In this example it may be that the higher quality mould uses new technology and although this will have been taken into account in the calculation of the figures the higher risks involved need to be highlighted to the decision maker.

❺   Finally it must be recognised that most of the figures used in a decision tree of this nature are estimated. Your solution should reflect this in a sensitivity analysis on the elements in the tree. The best way of carrying this out is to use a

⑤ spreadsheet to produce the calculations for you. One way of presenting this **3** analysis is to produce three trees:

1. An optimistic tree showing all the values at their best possible, i.e. costs at the lowest, returns at the highest, etc.
2. A pessimistic tree showing all the values at their worst possible, i.e. cost at the highest, returns at the lowest, etc.
3. An expected tree showing all the values at their expected or average value.

(pp 159–164)

5.5 Solution

Buy one disk drive with the computer	then expected cost of £4,990.50
Buy two disk drives with the computer	then expected cost of £4,129.50
Buy three disk drives with the computer	then expected cost of £4,389
Buy four disk drives with the computer	then expected cost of £5,520

5.6 Solution

Undertake standard improvement project	a return of £295,000
Undertake a high risk development project	a return of £676,000
Undertake no development project	a return of £90,000

Solutions to Chapter 6

6.1 Students in a quantitative management class are contemplating guessing the answers in a 30 question multiple choice exam. If each question on the exam has five choices, what are the chances of a student getting the correct answer on any single question? What is the probability that a student will get exactly half of the questions correct? What is the probability that a student will get five correct?

Solution format

❶ It is important that any problem that is tackled using the binomial distribution **1** meets the following conditions:

- the problem has a number of trials (an activity or experiment, denoted by n, that is repeatable) that are known and fixed.
- each trial has only two possible outcomes, often identified as success or failure, and the probability of success or failure in one trial is totally independent of any other trial.
- the probability of success (p) and failure ($1 - p$) remains constant from one trial to the next.

(p 176)

In respect to problem 6.1 we find that the following binomial conditions apply:

- There are 30 identical trials, in that there are 30 questions with 5 possible answers per question. It could of course be argued that the 30 questions vary in

❶ difficulty, in which case they are not identical. For the purposes of this **1**
question it is assumed that they are identical.

- A trial results in a correct answer or an incorrect answer, and these are
independent because the probability of success or failure in one question is
independent of success or failure in any other question. Again it could be
argued that the questions are not totally independent, in that there might be a
number of questions that have a common underpinning skill, and that a
competence in that underpinning skill would therefore invalidate the claim that
success or failure is independent from one question to the next. This potential
complication is conveniently put to one side and it is assumed that success or
failure is independent between questions.
- The probability of a correct answer or an incorrect answer is the same for each
question, with $p = .2$ and $1 - p = .8$.

❷ The first part of problem 6.1 asks what the probability is of getting a correct **2**
answer on any single question assuming that pure guesswork is used in the
selection of the answer. Because there are five possible answers for each question,
the probability of getting the correct answer is $p = \frac{1}{5} = .2$

The middle part of question 6.1 looks at the probability of a student getting
exactly half of the questions correct. Since the problem satisfies the binomial
conditions we can now use the binomial probability function to answer the
question.

$$\text{Binomial Probability Function: } P(x) = \frac{n!}{x!(n-x)!} \, p^x (1-p)^{n-x} = {}_nC_x(p)^x(1-p)^{n-x}$$

where $x = $ a particular outcome
$P(x) = $ the probability of that outcome
$n = $ number of trials
$p = $ probability of success
$1 - p = $ probability of failure
${}_nC_x = $ the number of combinations of n trials taken x at a time, which is
computed from $\frac{n!}{x!(n-x)!}$

Using the binomial formula, with $p = .2$, $n = 30$, and $x = 15$, we find:

$$ {}_{30}C_{15} = \frac{30!}{15!(30-15)!} = \frac{30!}{15!15!} = \frac{2.6525k + 32}{(1.3077k + 12)(1.3077k + 12)}$$

$$ = \frac{2.6525k + 32}{1.71001k + 2} = 155117520 $$

$$155117520\,(.2)^{15}\,(.8)^{15} = 155117520\,(.00000000003)\,(.035184372) = .0002$$

❺ According to our calculations there is less than a 1 per cent chance of a student **3 3**
getting exactly 50 per cent of the questions correct by guessing. The answer could

449

(pp 176–180)
(p 180)

❷ have also been obtained by following the Excel commands shown below:

3

- Paste Function
- Statistical
- Binomdist

and then entering '=Binomdist (15, 30, 0.2, false)' will produce the answer of .0001788.

❸ ❺ The other way of determining the binomial probability is to use the binomial probability table, which is Table 1 in Appendix 1. With $n = 30$, $x = 15$, and $p = .2$, we find the value of .0002.

The final part of the question asks what the probability is that a student will get five correct answers. Using the Excel function Binomdist or Table 1 in Appendix 1, with $n = 30$, $x = 5$, and $p = .2$, we find that the binomial probability is .1723. It is therefore possible to say that there is a 17.23 per cent chance that a student will get five correct answers out of the 30 questions by guessing alone.

3

(p 180)

6.2 Solution

The binomial probabilities for between 4 and 10 people taking out a PEP within a two year period are:

x-value	Binomial Value
$x = 4$	0.2311
$x = 5$	0.1584
$x = 6$	0.0792
$x = 7$	0.0291
$x = 8$	0.0077
$x = 9$	0.0014
$x = 10$	0.0001
	0.507

This tells us that there is a 50.7 per cent chance that between 4 and 10 people will take out a PEP within the next two years.

6.3 Research for a high street bank has shown that the average waiting time for customers in local branches ranged from 0.75 minutes to 6 minutes. A local branch manager feels comfortable in the knowledge that if the bank is checked against this criterion it will be deemed to be performing satisfactorily. This belief is based on the manager's judgement that for any 10 minute time interval there will be on average 3 customers arriving for service, and that an arrival rate of 3 customers per 10 minute time interval can be processed well within the upper limit of 6 minutes. Assuming that the data conforms to a Poisson distribution:

a. What percentage of the time will the number of arrivals, over a 10 minute time period, exceed three?

b. Can the arrival of seven or more customers over a 10 minute time interval be considered a rare event, given the manager's assumptions?

c. Given the answers to a and b, can the manager's beliefs be considered correct?

Solution format

❶ **a.** What percentage of the time will the number of arrivals, over a 10 minute time period, exceed three? **1**

The constraints in using the Poisson distribution are that the problem must:

- have discrete data.
- ensure that the discrete data is contained within discrete time or space periods (intervals).
- have occurrences that are independent of each other.
- ensure that the occurrences remain constant in each time or space interval.

In respect to problem 6.3 we find that the following Poisson conditions apply:

- the arrival of customers are discrete individual occurrences
- there are discrete 10 minute time intervals
- the arrival of customers in any one time interval is independent of any other arrival of customers in other time intervals.
- the 10 minute time intervals are constant over time

(p 183)

❷ A Poisson formula that determines the probability of occurrence of an event for a particular lambda value is: **2**

$$P(x) = \frac{\lambda^x e^{-\lambda}}{x!}$$

where: x = the number of times the event occurs
λ = long-run average (mean)
e = 2.718282, the base of the natural logarithm system

Using the Poisson formula we find that the probability of 4 customers arriving within a 10 minute time interval is:

$$P(4) = \frac{(3^4)(e^{-3})}{4!} = \frac{(81)(0.0497871)}{24} = \frac{4.0327551}{24} = 0.1680$$

(p 184–186)

❸   It is possible to simplify this process by using Table 7 in Appendix 1, which is a table of Poisson probability values. With λ at 3 and x at 4 the table provides us with a Poisson probability value of 0.1680. The Poisson probability value can also be obtained quite simply by using the 'Poisson' command in Excel. The instruction ' = Poisson (4, 3, false)' produces the answer of 0.168031.

Because the question in part **a** is a '4 or more' type problem, we have to find all the values of x greater than 3 and add them up. Since theoretically there is no upper limit to the number of x values (i.e., $x = 4, 5, 6, 7, 8, \ldots \infty$) we use

451

❸ common sense and stop adding the probability values once they get close to zero. **2**
Using the values from Table 7 in Appendix 1 we find:

$$P(4) = \frac{(3^4)(e^{-3})}{4!} = .1680$$

$$P(5) = \frac{(3^5)(e^{-3})}{5!} = .1008$$

$$P(6) = \frac{(3^6)(e^{-3})}{6!} = .0504$$

$$P(7) = \frac{(3^7)(e^{-3})}{7!} = .0216$$

$$P(8) = \frac{(3^8)(e^{-3})}{8!} = .0081$$

$$P(9) = \frac{(3^9)(e^{-3})}{9!} = .0027$$

$$P(10) = \frac{(3^{10})(e^{-3})}{10!} = .0008$$

$$P(11) = \frac{(3^{11})(e^{-3})}{11!} = .0002$$

$$P(12) = \frac{(3^{12})(e^{-3})}{12!} = .0000$$

$$\text{Total} = .3527$$

❺ This tells us that there is a 35.27 per cent chance of more than 3 customers **3**
arriving in a 10 minute time period. (p 185)

❸ **b.** Can the arrival of 7 or more customers over a 10 minute time interval be **2**
considered a rare event, given the manager's assumptions?

The Poisson probabilities for 7 or more customers arriving over a 10 minute time (p 184–186)
period are:

$$P(7) = \frac{(3^7)(e^{-3})}{7!} = .0216$$

$$P(8) = \frac{(3^8)(e^{-3})}{8!} = .0081$$

❸

$$P(9) = \frac{(3^9)(e^{-3})}{9!} = .0027$$

$$P(10) = \frac{(3^{10})(e^{-3})}{10!} = .0008$$

$$P(11) = \frac{(3^{11})(e^{-3})}{11!} = .0002$$

$$P(12) = \frac{(3^{12})(e^{-3})}{12!} = .0000$$

$$\text{Total} = .0334$$

❺ The probability value of .0334 (3.34%) suggests that it is unlikely that seven or more customers will arrive within any 10 minute time period.

c. Given the answers to a and b, can the manager's beliefs be considered correct?

❺ With a 35.27 per cent chance of more than 3 customers arriving within any 10 minute time period it would appear that the branch manager is living dangerously in the belief that there is little chance of more than 3 customers arriving within a 10 minute time interval. It should also be noted that although the probabilities get much smaller as the number of arrivals increases, there is still a 3.34 per cent chance of 7 or more customers arriving within a 10 minute time period.

② (p 185)

③ (p 185)

6.4 Solution

There are three parts to question 6.4:

a. What is the probability of more than 4 arrivals over a 10 minute time period?

There is a .6914 probability (69.14% chance) of more than 4 cars arriving in a 10 minute time period. Since the average is 5.83 arrivals in a 10 minute time interval, it is highly likely that there will be periods when the car park attendant will be unable to process all the arriving cars.

b. What is the probability of exactly 5 cars arriving in a 10 minute time interval?

There is a .1648 probability (16.48% chance) of 5 cars arriving within a 10 minute time interval.

c. What is the probability of less than three cars arriving within a 10 minute time interval?

There is a .0668 probability (6.68% chance) of less than 3 cars arriving within a 10 minute time interval.

6.5 There has been frequent criticism that reform of the emergency services has resulted in longer response times. A recent study in your local area shows that the average time it takes an ambulance to arrive at a destination is 8 minutes, and that the response times are exponentially distributed. Given this information:

a. What is the probability that an ambulance will arrive at a destination in less than 8 minutes?

b. What is the probability that an ambulance will take longer than 10 minutes to arrive at a destination?

Solution format

❶ **a.** What is the probability that an ambulance will arrive at a destination in less than 8 minutes? **1**

To use an exponential distribution the problem must fit within the exponential constraints:

- the data is continuous.
- there is a distinct distribution for every value of λ (λ is the mean number of events per time period).
- x values go from 0 to ∞.

The problem appears to satisfy the exponential constraints in that:

- the data is continuous in that a response time can take on any value.
- there is a distinct distribution for every value of λ (λ is the mean number of events per time period), for there will be a distinct distribution when the mean arrival time is 8 minutes, a distinct distribution if the mean arrival time is 10 minutes, 13 minutes etc.
- the number of arrivals can go from 0 to ∞.

❷ The formula for the exponential probability function is: **2**

$$f(x) = \lambda e^{-\lambda x}$$
where x = number of time intervals
$\quad\quad \lambda$ = mean number of events per time period
$\quad\quad e = 2.71828$
$\quad\quad f(x)$ = the probability density function represented by the height of the curve

It is possible to find answers to problems that involve an amount of area of the exponential distribution by rearranging this formula (using calculus) so that it becomes:

$$P(x > x_1) = e^{-\lambda x_1}$$

Using Figure 15.6.1 as a guide, we want to find the area to the left of $x_1 = 8$ minutes. With an average arrival period of 8 minutes for an ambulance to reach a destination we get a λ value of $1/8 = .125$ per 1 minute time interval (another way of expressing this is $60/8 = 7.5$; $\lambda = 7.5/60 = 0.125$). This provides us with the

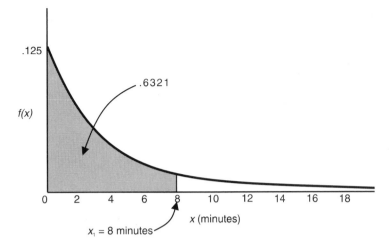

Figure 15.6.1   Exponential distribution for $x<8$ minutes

information to determine the probability that the arrival rate will be less than 8 minutes:

$$P(x<x_1) = 1 - e^{-\lambda x_1}$$
$$P(x<8) = 1 - e^{-(1.25)(8)} = 1 - e^{-1} = 1 - .36788 = .63212$$

This tells us that there is a .6321 (63.21% chance) probability that an ambulance will arrive at a destination in less than 8 minutes. The $e^{-\lambda x_1}$ value can be obtained from Table 3 in Appendix 1 and the exponential value that corresponds to 1 is 0.6321. The exponential distribution value can also be obtained from the Excel spreadsheet package by using the 'EXPONDIST' function from the 'Past Formula' facility (e.g. = EXPONDIST $(x$, lambda, cumulative) – which for our example would be = EXPONDIST (8, 0.125, true) = 0.63212).

b. What is the probability that an ambulance will take longer than 10 minutes to arrive at a destination?

Using Figure 15.6.2 and following the previous procedure, we find:

$$P(x>x_1) = e^{-\lambda e_1}$$
$$P(x>10) = e^{-\lambda x_1} = e^{-(.125)(10)} = e^{-1.25} = 0.2865$$

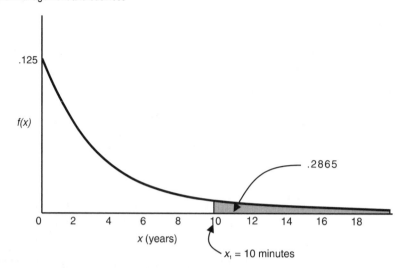

Figure 15.6.2 Exponential distribution for $x > 10$ minutes

This tells us that there is a .2865 probability (28.65% chance) that an ambulance will take longer than 10 minutes to arrive at a destination. Again the answer could have been obtained by using an exponential distribution table or the Excel command 'EXPONDIST'.

6.6 Solution

a. What is the probability that a system will be cleaned and checked in less than 4 hours?

$$P(x < x_1) = 1 - e^{-\lambda x_1}$$
$$P(x < 4) = 1 - e^{-(.1666)(4)} = 1 - e^{-.6664} = 1 - .5135 = .4865$$

This tells us that there is a .4865 (48.65% chance) probability that an air conditioning system will be cleaned and checked in less than 4 hours.

b. What is the probability that the cleaning and checking of an air conditioning system will take longer than 9 hours?

$$P(x > x_1) = e^{-\lambda e_1}$$
$$P(x > 9) = e^{-\lambda x_1} = e^{-(.1666)(9)} = e^{-1.499} = 0.2233$$

This tells us that there is a .2233 probability (22.33% chance) that the cleaning and checking of an air conditioning system will take longer than 9 hours.

6.7 A manufacturer of car tyres produces a high performance sports tyre that has a mean life of 18,000 miles and a standard deviation of 2,000 miles (the life of the tyres is also normally distributed).

a. What is the probability that a tyre will last for more than 14,000 miles?
b. What is the probability that the life of a tyre will be below 15,000 miles?
c. What is the probability that the life of a tyre will be greater than 20,000 miles?
d. What proportion of tyres will last between 17,000 miles and 21,000 miles?
e. What is the value above which will fall the largest 25 per cent of tyre lives?

❶ ❷ **Solution format** 🟦🟦

a. What is the probability that a tyre will last for more than 14,000 miles?

The probability of a tyre lasting more than 14,000 miles is represented by the shaded area in Figure 15.6.3.

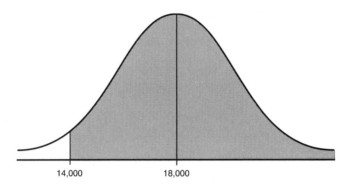

Figure 15.6.3   Area above 14,000 miles

The value of 14,000 can be converted in a standard deviation value by using:

$$Z = \frac{X - \mu}{\sigma} \quad \text{or} \quad Z = \frac{x - \bar{x}}{s}$$

The Z value that corresponds to 14,000 miles is:

$$Z = \frac{x - \bar{x}}{s} \qquad Z = \frac{14,000 - 18,000}{2,000} = -2$$

❸ Using Table 5 in Appendix 1 we find that a Z value of -2 provides us with a probablility/area value of .02275. Since this is the probability/area value from the

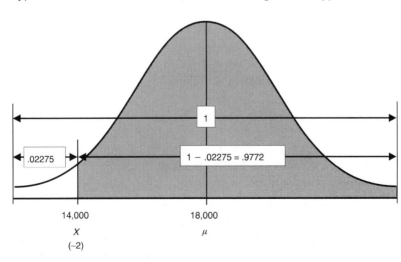

Figure 15.6.4   Process used in determining the probability of a tyre lasting more than 14,000 miles

(pp 199–204)

❸ end of the left-sided tail to the value of 14,000, we must take .02275 from 1 to determine the probability/area from 14,000 to the end of the right-sided tail:

$$1 - .02275 = .9772$$

This process is represented in Figure 15.6.4.

❹ There is therefore a .9772 probability (97.72% chance) of a tyre lasting more than 14,000 miles. The Excel spreadsheet package can also be used to find the amount of area from the tail to 14,000. Using the formula paste function, select 'statistical' and then 'normdist', at which point it asks for '(x, mean, standard-dev, cumulative)'. Typing **14,000, 18,000, 2,000, true** produces the value .02275, which then needs to be taken away from 1 to get the answer of .9772.

❶ b. What is the probability that the life of a tyre will be below 15,000 miles?

Following the same procedure as in part **a** we find:

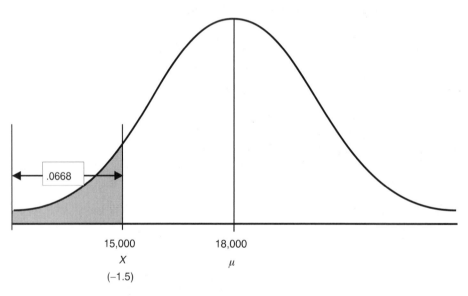

.0668

15,000
X
(−1.5)

18,000
μ

Figure 15.6.5   Area below 15,000 miles

❷ The Z value that corresponds to 15,000 miles is:

$$Z = \frac{x - \bar{x}}{s} \qquad Z = \frac{15,000 - 18,000}{2,000} = -1.5$$

❸ Using Table 4 in Appendix 1 we find that a Z value of -1.5 provides us with a probablility/area value of .0668. Since this is the probability/area value from the end of the left-sided tail to the value of 15,000, no further action is required. There is thus a .0668 probability (6.68% chance) of a tyre lasting less than 15,000 miles.

(pp 199–204)

❶ c. What is the probability that the life of a tyre will be greater than 20,000 miles? 🔳🔳

Following the same procedure as in part **a** we find:

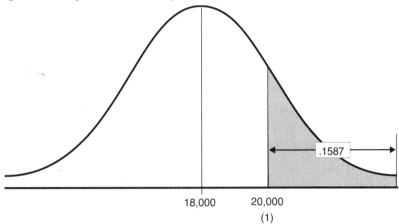

18,000 20,000

(1)

Figure 15.6.6   Area above 20,000 miles

❷   The *Z* value that corresponds to 20,000 miles is:

$$Z = \frac{x - \bar{x}}{s} \qquad Z = \frac{20,000 - 18,000}{2,000} = 1$$

❸ Using Table 4 in Appendix 1 we find that a *Z* value of 1 provides us with a probablility/area value of .1587. Since this is the probability/area value from the ❹ end of the right-sided tail to the value of 20,000, no further action is required. There is thus a .1587 probability (15.87% chance) of a tyre lasting longer than 20,000 miles.

❷ d. What proportion of tyres will last between 17,000 miles and 21,000 miles? 🔳🔳

Following the same procedure as in part **a** we find:

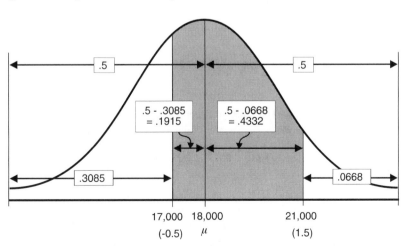

17,000 18,000   21,000

(-0.5) μ (1.5)

Figure 15.6.7   Area between 17,000 and 21,000 miles

(pp 199–204)

(pp 203–4)

② The Z value that corresponds to 17,000 miles is:

$$Z = \frac{x - \bar{x}}{s} \qquad Z_1 = \frac{17,000 - 18,000}{2,000} = -.5$$

$$Z = \frac{x - \bar{x}}{s} \qquad Z_2 = \frac{21,000 - 18,000}{2,000} = 1.5$$

(pp 199–204)

❸ Using Table 4 in Appendix 1 we find that a Z value of $-.5$ provides us with a probablility/area value of .3085 and a Z value of 1.5 a probability/area value of .0668. Since these are the probability/area values from the end of the tails we need to take them away from .5 and then add them together:

$$Z_1 = .5 - .3085 = .1915$$
$$Z_2 = .5 - .0668 = .4332$$
$$.6247$$

❹ There is thus a .6247 probability (62.47% chance) of a tyre lasting between 17,000 and 21,000 miles. **3**

❶ **e.** What is the value above which will fall the largest 25 per cent of tyre lives? **1 2**

The top 25 per cent of the normal distribution is shown in Figure 15.6.8.

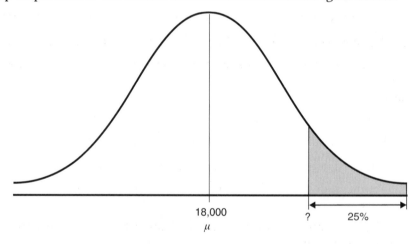

Figure 15.6.8 **The highest 25 per cent of tyre lives**

❷ ❸ The nearest Z value to .2500 (25%) in Table 4, Appendix 1, is .67. With this information we are now able to find the missing value:

$$Z = \frac{x - \bar{x}}{s} \qquad Z = \frac{? - 18,000}{2,000} = .67$$

Therefore $18,000 + (2,000 \times .67) = 19,340$

❹ We can now say that 25 per cent of the tyres will last for 19,340 or more miles. **3**

(pp 199–204)

6.8 Solution

a. What proportion of the managers can be expected to have achievement scores

  i. **greater than 120?**

      6.18 per cent of the managers will have an achievement score greater than 120.

  ii. **less than 90?**

      24.51 per cent of the managers will have an achievement score of less than 90.

  iii. **between 70 and 130?**

      97.47 per cent of the managers will have an achievement score that lies between 70 and 130.

b. What achievement score will be exceeded by

  i. **1 per cent of managers?**

      1 per cent of the managers will have a score of 130.52 or more.

  ii. **0.1 per cent of managers?**

      0.1 per cent (1 in a 100) of the managers will have a score of 140.84 or more.

  iii. **90 per cent of managers?**

      90 per cent of the managers will have a score of 82.1 or more.

c. Between what limits will 95 per cent of managers achievement scores lie?

   95 per cent of the managers will have a score between 73.1 and 125.5.

6.9 Solution

a. What is the probability that the weekly output will be 1160 units or less?

There is a 48.8 per cent chance of the weekly output being 1160 units or less.

b. What is the probability that the weekly output will exceed 1170 units?

The analysis shows that 47.61 per cent of the weekly output will exceed 1170 units.

c. The production manager wants to know what the production output is for 80 per cent of the time.

The analysis shows us that 80 per cent of the weekly output will be between 1025.14 and 1300.86 units.

6.10 Solution

a. What is the probability that there will be more than 110 people absent during the summer months?

There is only a 3.07 per cent chance that more than 110 people will be absent in the summer months.

b. What is the probability that there will be more than 120 people absent during the summer months?

There is less than a 1 per cent chance (0.09%) of more than 120 people being absent in the summer months.

c. What is the probability that there will be less than 70 people absent during the summer period?

There is less than a 1 per cent chance (0.09%) of less than 70 people being absent in the summer months.

Solutions to Chapter 7

7.1 It is very difficult to phrase unbiased questions on emotionally charged issues. Assume that you want to study people's opinions on abortion – more precisely, that you are interested in the circumstances in which people would permit abortion. What are the most basic types of circumstances that should be included in a question? There are a large number of distinct alternatives, so concentrate on a few major types. How would you phrase a closed-ended question on this topic?

Solution format

❸ There are many possible ways to phrase a question on this topic. Some major distinctions are between permitting abortion (a) under no circumstances, (b) only for medical reasons, and (c) under all circumstances.

❺ What is most important is to avoid emotionally charged terms (such as 'killing foetuses' or 'the woman should control her own body') so that the question wording does not bias the answers. An example of a typical question might be:

There has been some discussion about abortion during recent years. Which one of these opinions best agrees with your view?

   a. Abortion should never be permitted
   b. Abortion should be permitted only if the life and health of the woman is in danger
   c. Abortion should be permitted if, due to personal reasons, the woman would have difficulty in caring for the child
   d. Abortion should never be forbidden, since one should not require a woman to have a child she doesn't want.

This example could be criticised in that it is very general, with no questions relating to rape etc. On the other hand it does focus the response, for the respondent has to choose one of the four scenarios. It might be argued, though, that the respondents should be able to choose more than one scenario from a wider range of choices since this would provide a richer picture about what respondents actually felt.

(pp 217–222)

7.2 Solution

a. A survey of sixth formers concluded that the majority of young people experiment with drugs.

It is wrong to assume that you can generalize about 'young people' from a sample of sixth formers (at best it could only provide conclusions about sixth formers themselves). The answers themselves might also be suspect as some sixth formers may be unwilling to admit to drug use while others may boast about drug use when in fact they do not take drugs. Drugs is also a very broad term that could include anything from marijuana to crack or aspirin to alcohol.

b. A poll shows that 75 per cent of British people favour the pulling out of troops from trouble spots around the world.

This assumes that 75 per cent of British people know about the trouble spots that its troops are involved in. It is quite usual on questions like this to use filter questions on the respondents to ensure that they understand the question that is being asked. The question is also very broad and could therefore induce negative responses.

c. A survey of Members of Parliament shows that a majority believe they should follow the wishes of their constituents rather than their own attitudes when the two are in conflict.

This survey gave Members of Parliament a very abstract and hypothetical choice. It is very easy for them to claim that they follow their constituents' wishes, and their answers may therefore not be predictive of how they behave when they have real conflict. Presenting Members of Parliament with an actual conflict may therefore yield more meaningful answers.

7.3 Your organisation has recently introduced a productivity related bonus scheme and wishes to determine the attitude of the workforce to the new scheme. The Personnel Department has supplied the following breakdown of workers, by their sex and level of skill:

	Men	Women
Unskilled	734	1473
Semi-skilled	1426	1075
Skilled	2897	500

Design a sampling scheme to obtain a sample of 500 people, taking special care to ensure that the sample is representative of all sections of the workforce.

Solution format

Total workforce = 8105

Sampling fraction (S.F.) = $\dfrac{500}{8105}$ = .0617

❷❸
Unskilled Women	$= .0617 \times 1473 =$	91
Unskilled Men	$= .0617 \times 734 \ \ =$	45
Semi-skilled Women	$= .0617 \times 1075 =$	66
Semi-skilled Men	$= .0617 \times 1426 =$	88
Skilled Women	$= .0617 \times 500 \ \ =$	31
Skilled men	$= .0617 \times 2897 =$	179
		500

(pp 229–230)

❶❹ The above sampling strata in association with a sampling technique that ensures that people within the strata are selected randomly will ensure a representative and unbiased sample of the workforce.

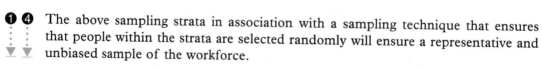

7.4 Solution

a. An airline operates fifty flights a week from London to Paris. It wants to know how its passengers feel about the quality of the meals served on this flight sector.

Combination of systematic sampling and simple random sampling.

b. A lecturer wants to know the average years of work experience of the students in an MBA evening class. Apart from the class register, the lecturer has no other information on the students.

Simple random sampling or systematic random sampling.

c. You want to predict who will be elected as the next parliamentary MP for your constituency.

Combination of stratified sampling, systematic sampling, and simple random sampling (proportionate stratified random sample).

d. As part of a marketing survey you are asked to interview members of households. You are told to sample 10 per cent of the homes on a long street, and there are ten such identical streets.

Area sampling followed by simple random sampling or systematic sampling.

7.5 A sample of 36 tyres from a manufacturer lasted an average of 18,000 miles, with a standard deviation of 1,200 miles. What are the 95 % confidence limits for the average life of all tyres supplied by the manufacturer?

Solution format

❶ The formula for determining 95% confidence limits is:

$$\mu = X \pm 1.96\,\sigma_{\bar{X}}$$

(p 243)

❷ with the standard error formula being:

$$\sigma_{\bar{X}} = \frac{s}{\sqrt{n}}$$

❷ The standard error for this problem is:

$$\sigma_{\bar{X}} = \frac{s}{\sqrt{n}} = \frac{1200}{\sqrt{36}} = 200$$

❸ The 95% confidence limits are:

$$\mu = \bar{X} \pm 1.96 - \sigma_{\bar{X}}$$
$$\mu = 18,000 \pm 1.96\,(200)$$
$$\mu = 18,000 \pm 392 \text{ miles}$$

❹ We are therefore 95 per cent sure that the population mean lies somewhere between 17,608 and 18,392 miles.

(pp 242–243)

(p 243)

7.6 Solution

We are 95 per cent sure that the population mean lies somewhere between 28.71 and 31.29 lbs and 99 per cent sure that it lies somewhere between 28.3 and 31.70 lbs.

7.7 A random sample of 400 rail passengers is taken and 55 per cent are in favour of proposed new timetables. With 95% confidence limits, what proportion of all rail passengers are in favour of the timetables?

Solution format

❶ The formula for determining 95% confidence limits is:

$$P = \bar{P} \pm 1.96\sigma_{\bar{p}}$$

(p 245)

❸ with the standard error formula being:

$$\sigma_{\bar{p}} = \sqrt{\frac{\bar{P}(1 - \bar{P})}{n}}$$

The standard error for this problem is:

$$\bar{P} = .55 \ (55\%)$$

$$\sigma_{\bar{p}} = \sqrt{\frac{\bar{P}(1 - \bar{P})}{n}} = \sqrt{\frac{.55(1 - .55)}{400}} = \sqrt{\frac{.55(.45)}{400}} = .025$$

(pp 247–249)

❸ At the 95% confidence level, we are therefore sure that the population proportion is:

$$P = \bar{P} \pm 1.96\sigma_{\bar{p}}$$
$$P = .55 \pm 1.96\,(0.25)$$
$$= .55 \pm .049 \ (\text{i.e. } 55\% \pm 4.9\%)$$

❹ We are therefore 95 per cent confident that between 50.1% and 59.9% of the
▼ railway passengers are in favour of the timetables.

3 (p 249)

7.8 Solution

We are 95 per cent confident that between 39.4% and 56.6% of stockholders will
purchase the shares. Although management's assumption that 45% will purchase is
within these limits, it is clear that it is quite possible that less than 45% will
purchase as the 95% confidence limits go down to 39.4%.

7.9 The price per month of back orders at Yates Industries is beginning to cause
concern to management. A random sample of 3 randomly selected months yields a
mean of £115,320 with a standard deviation of £35,000. Construct a 95%
confidence interval for the mean price of back orders per month at Yates
Industries.

Solution format

❶ The t distribution formula for finding 95% confidence limits for a population
mean is:

1 (p 253)

$$\mu = \overline{X} \pm (t)(s_{\overline{X}})$$

❷ The appropriate t value can be found in Table 5, Appendix 1. With $n-1$ degrees
of freedom $(3-1=2)$, working at the 95% confidence level (0.05 significance
level), we find that the t table value is 4.303.

2 (p 254)

❸ The standard error is:

$$s_{\overline{X}} = \frac{s}{\sqrt{n}} = s_{\overline{X}} = \frac{35,000}{\sqrt{3}} = 20,207.26$$

❹ At the 95% confidence level, we are therefore sure that the population mean is:

$$\mu = \overline{X} \pm (t)(s_{\overline{X}})$$
$$\mu = 115,320 \pm (4.303)(20,207.26)$$
$$\mu = 115,320 \pm 86,952$$

❺ Based upon the sample data we are therefore 95 per cent sure that the mean price
▼ of back orders is between £28,368 and £202,272.

3 (p 254)

7.10 Solution

Based upon the sample data we are 99 per cent sure that the mean response time
for ambulances is between 13.32 and 20.68 minutes.

7.11 In order to evaluate the success of a television advertising campaign for a new product, a company interviewed 400 housepersons in the television area. 120 of them knew about the product. How accurately does this estimate the percentage of housepersons in the area who know about the product? How many more interviews must be made in order to establish this percentage to an accuracy of ±2% at the 95% confidence level?

Solution format

❶ The formula for determining 95% confidence limits is:

$$P = \bar{P} \pm 1.96\sigma_{\bar{p}}$$

1

(p 248)

❷ with the standard error formula being:

$$\sigma_{\bar{p}} = \sqrt{\frac{\bar{P}(1-\bar{P})}{n}}$$

2

The standard error for this problem is:

$$\bar{P} = .3 \ (30\%)$$

$$\sigma_{\bar{p}} = \sqrt{\frac{\bar{P}(1-\bar{P})}{n}} = \sigma_{\bar{p}} = \sqrt{\frac{.3(1-.3)}{400}} = \sigma_{\bar{p}} = \sqrt{\frac{.3(.7)}{400}} = .023$$

(pp 247–249)

At the 95% confidence level, we are therefore sure that the population proportion is:

$$P = \bar{P} \pm 1.96\sigma_{\bar{p}}$$
$$P = .3 \pm 1.96(.023)$$
$$P = .3 \pm .045 \ (\text{i.e. } 30\% \pm 4.5\%)$$

❸ We are therefore 95 per cent confident that between 25.5% and 34.5% of the housepersons know about the product.

3

(p 248)

❷ To reduce the boundaries from 4.5% to 2% (to increase the level of accuracy of our estimate) will entail increasing the sample size to:

4

$$n = \frac{(\text{CL}^2\bar{P})(100 - \bar{P})}{\text{L}^2}$$

Where CL = confidence level
    L = the required level of accuracy

(pp 259–261)

$$n = \frac{(1.96^2 \times 30)(70)}{2^2}$$

❷
$$n = \frac{(115.25)(70)}{4}$$

$$n = \frac{8067.5}{4} \cong 2017$$

2

❸ As can be seen, to increase the accuracy of the sample estimate from 4.5% to 2% entails increasing the sample size from 400 to 2017.

3 (p 261)

7.12 Solution

The analysis shows that we are 95 per cent sure that the population mean (the average I.Q. of MBA students) lies somewhere between 116.41 and 123.59 points. The 99% confidence limits show that the population mean (the average I.Q. of MBA students) lies somewhere between 115.28 and 124.72.

To reduce the confidence limits from 4.72 to 2 (at the 99% confidence level) has necessitated increasing the sample size from 30 to 166.

Solutions to Chapter 8

8.1 Royale Marketing Research (RMR) bases its charges to clients on the assumption that telephone surveys can be completed with a mean time of 15 minutes or less. If a greater mean survey time is required, a premium rate is charged to the client. Does a sample of 35 surveys that shows a sample mean of 17 minutes and a sample standard deviation of 4 minutes justify the premium rate? Test at a .01 level of significance.

Solution format

❶ The null and alternative hypotheses are therefore as follows:

1

Hypothesis	*Conclusion and Action*
H_0: $\mu \leqslant 15$	RMR telephone survey within normal time period; standard rate charge.
H_a: $\mu > 15$	RMR telephone survey exceeds normal time period; premium rate charge.

(p 269)

❷ Working to a .01 significance level is equivalent to saying that we are going to live with an $\alpha = .01$ probability of making a Type I error. Integrating this into the critical value formula provides us with a critical value of:

2

$$c = \mu + (Z_{.01} \times \sigma_{\bar{x}})$$

The position of the critical value is shown diagrammatically in Figure 15.8.1, and the shaded area represents the probability of rejecting the null hypothesis when in fact it is true (we charge a premium rate when we should have charged a standard rate).

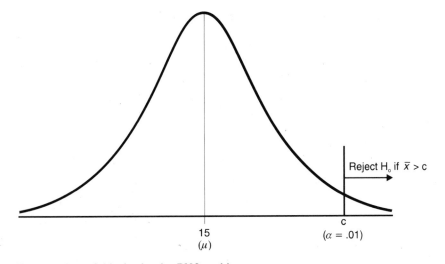

Figure 15.8.1 Critical value for RMC problem

with $n = 35$, $\bar{x} = 17$, $s = 4$

$$\sigma_{\bar{x}} = \frac{s}{\sqrt{n}} = \frac{4}{\sqrt{35}} = 0.676$$

$$c = \mu + (Z_{.01} \times \sigma_{\bar{x}})$$
$$c = 15 + (2.33 \times 0.676)$$
$$c = 15 + (1.575) = 16.575$$

The decision rule is therefore:

Accept H_0 if $\bar{x} \leqslant 16.575$
Reject H_0 if $\bar{x} > 16.575$

Since the sample mean was 17 minutes we reject the null hypothesis and state that we are 99 per cent sure that the premium rate should be charged.

8.2 Solution

The decision rule is:

Accept H_0 if $\bar{x} \geqslant 27,699.67$
Reject H_0 if $\bar{x} < 27,699.67$

Since the sample mean was 27,500 miles we reject the null hypothesis and state that we are 95 per cent sure that the tyres are not lasting on average to 28,000 miles.

8.3 Historically, long-distance phone calls from a particular city have averaged 15.20 minutes per call. In a random sample of 35 calls, the sample mean time was 14.30

minutes per call, with a sample standard deviation of 5 minutes. Use this sample information to test whether or not there has been a change in the average duration of long-distance phone calls. Use a .05 level of significance.

Solution format

❶ The null and alternative hypotheses for this two-tailed test are therefore as follows:

Hypothesis	Conclusion and Action
H_0: $\mu = 15.20$	Duration of long-distance phone calls is as expected; no action required.
H_a: $\mu \neq 15.20$	Duration of long-distance phone calls not as expected; action required.

❷ Working to a .05 significance level is equivalent to saying that we are going to live with an $\alpha = .05$ probability of making a Type I error. Integrating this into the critical value formula for a two-tailed test provides us with a critical value of:

$$c = \mu + (Z_{.025} \times \sigma_{\bar{x}})$$

The position of the critical values is shown diagrammatically in Figure 15.8.2, and the shaded area represents the probability of rejecting the null hypothesis when in fact it is true (we say the duration time is not an average of 15.20 minutes when in fact it is).

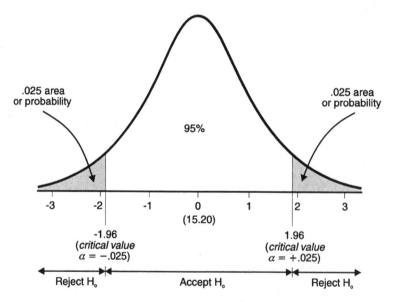

Figure 15.8.2 Critical value for long-distance telephone calls

The critical value on the right hand side of the distribution is:

with $n = 35$, $\bar{x} = 14.30$, $s = 5$

$$\sigma_{\bar{x}} = \frac{s}{\sqrt{n}} = \frac{5}{\sqrt{35}} = 0.845$$

❷
$$c = \mu + (Z_{.025} \times \sigma_{\bar{x}})$$
$$c = 15.20 + (1.96 \times 0.845)$$
$$c = 15.20 + (1.656) = 16.856$$

The critical value on the left hand side of the distribution is:

$$c = \mu - (Z_{.025} \times \sigma_{\bar{x}})$$
$$c = 15.20 - (1.96 \times 0.845)$$
$$c = 15.20 - (1.656) = 13.544$$

❸ The decision rule is therefore:

> Reject H_0 if $\bar{x} < 13.54$ or if $\bar{x} > 16.86$
> Accept H_0 otherwise

❹ ❺ Since the sample mean is 14.30 minutes we are unable to reject the null hypothesis, and can say with 95 per cent confidence that long-distance phone calls are still averaging 15.20 minutes (the sample data does not provide evidence that there has been a change).

(p 276)

8.4 Solution

The decision rule is:

> Reject H_0 if $\bar{x} < 197.83$ or if $\bar{x} > 242.17$
> Accept H_0 otherwise

Since the sample mean is 208 minutes we are unable to reject the null hypothesis, and can say with 95 per cent confidence that the car parking times are still averaging 220 minutes (the sample data does not provide evidence that there has been a change).

8.5 A study of educational levels of voters and their political affiliations showed the following results:

	Conservative	Labour	Green
No 'O' levels	40	20	10
Up to 3 'A' levels	30	35	15
Degree	30	45	25

Use a .01 significance level to test to see if party affiliation is independent of the educational level of voters.

Solution format

❶ The null and alternative hypotheses for this problem are:

1

H_0: Education and party affiliation are independent (there is no connection or relationship between them).

H_a: Education and party affiliation are not independent.

❷ The contingency table for this set of data, with the expected frequencies, is shown below:

2

	Conservative	Labour	Green	Totals
No 'O' Levels	40	20	10	70
'O' Levels	(28)	(28)	(14)	
Up to 3 'A'	30	35	15	80
Levels	(32)	(32)	(16)	
Degree	30	45	25	100
	(40)	(40)	(20)	
Totals	100	100	50	250

❸ The calculated x^2 value is:

Observed	Expected	$(O-E)$	$(O-E)^2$	$\dfrac{(O-E)^2}{E}$
40	28	12	144	5.143
30	32	−2	4	0.125
30	40	−10	100	2.5
20	28	−8	64	2.286
35	32	3	9	0.281
45	40	5	25	0.625
10	14	−4	16	1.143
15	16	−1	1	0.062
25	20	5	254	1.25
		$\Sigma(O-E)=0$		$\dfrac{\Sigma(O-E)^2}{E}=13.41$

(pp 283–284)

❹ The degrees of freedom associated with this problem are:

$$v = (r-1)(c-1)$$
$$v = (3-1)(3-1)$$
$$v = 4$$

Referring to Table 6 in Appendix 1, we find that the critical value at $v = 4$ and $\alpha = .01$ is 13.28. The decision rule for this problem can now be formulated as:

❺

Accept H_0 and reject H_a if calculated $x^2 < 13.28$

6 Since the calculated x^2 value is 13.41 we reject the null hypothesis that education and party affiliation are independent.

(p 284)

8.6 Solution

The decision rule for this problem is:

Accept H_0 and reject H_a if calculated $x^2 < 9.49$

Since the calculated x^2 value is 10.88 we reject the null hypothesis that the level of damage and type of material are independent (there are significant differences between the materials).

8.7 Solution

The decision rule for this problem can now be formulated as:

Accept H_0 and reject H_a if calculated $x^2 < 9.49$

Since the calculated x^2 value is 6.276 we accept the null hypothesis that the salesperson and the product type are independent (there are no significant differences between the salespersons and products).

Solutions to Chapter 9

9.1 The following gives the sales of houses by a chain of estate agents. Figures are given for the first five months of 1994.

Month	1	2	3	4	5
House sales	152	164	160	178	185

Use regression and correlation to determine the relationship of the sales and produce a forecast for months 6 and 7. Comment on the confidence of these forecasts.

Solution format

1 In this example the independent variable will be time measured in months. This is the variable that can be controlled and will affect the sales of houses. The sales of houses are therefore dependent on time.

(p 291)

❷ *Calculation table*

x	y	xy	x^2	y^2
1	152	152	1	23,104
2	164	358	4	26,896
3	160	480	9	25,600
4	178	712	16	31,684
5	185	925	25	34,225
15	839	2,597	55	141,509

❸ Therefore the summations are as follows:

$$\Sigma x = 15$$
$$\Sigma y = 839$$
$$\Sigma xy = 2,597$$
$$\Sigma x^2 = 55$$
$$\Sigma y^2 = 141,509$$

The number of data pairs $= n = 5$

These values can now be put into the formula to calculate the correlation coefficient.

$$r = \frac{\Sigma xy - \dfrac{(\Sigma x)(\Sigma y)}{n}}{\sqrt{\left(\Sigma x^2 - \dfrac{(\Sigma x)^2}{n}\right)\left(\Sigma y^2 - \dfrac{(\Sigma y)^2}{n}\right)}}$$

$$= \frac{2,597 - \dfrac{15 \times 839}{5}}{\sqrt{\left(55 - \dfrac{(15)^2}{5}\right)\left(141509 - \dfrac{(839)^2}{5}\right)}}$$

$$= \frac{2,597 - 2517}{\sqrt{55 - 45)(141509 - 140784.2)}}$$

$$= \frac{80}{\sqrt{10 \times 724.8}} = \frac{80}{\sqrt{7,248}} = \frac{80}{85.14} = 0.94$$

❹ For this example the following values have been calculated:

$$r = 0.94 \quad \gamma = 5 - 2 = 3$$

❹ The line from the table 9.3 in Chapter 9 (page 28) we are therefore interested in **3**
is as follows:

γ	Level 1	Level 2
	← 0.05 →	← 0.01 →
5	0.88	0.96

(p 294)

In the case of this example the r value is greater than the table value for Level 1
but less than the table value for Level 2. Therefore the correlation coefficient is
significant and we can draw the conclusion that a significant relationship exists
between time and sales of houses. It should be remembered that on its own the
mathematics does not prove a relationship. There should be other evidence to
confirm the relationship form other sources. The calculation of the regression line
can now be carried out using the following summation values from the calculation
table:

❺

$\Sigma x = 15$

$\Sigma y = 839$

$\Sigma xy = 2{,}597$

$\Sigma x^2 = 55$

$\Sigma y^2 = 141{,}509$

4

$$a = \frac{\Sigma y}{n} = \frac{839}{5} = 167.8$$

$$\bar{x} = \frac{\Sigma x}{n} = \frac{15}{5} = 3$$

$$b = \frac{\Sigma xy - \frac{(\Sigma x)(\Sigma y)}{n}}{\Sigma x^2 - \frac{(\Sigma x)^2}{n}}$$

$$= \frac{2{,}597 - \frac{15 \times 839}{5}}{5 - \frac{(15)^2}{5}}$$

$$= \frac{2597 - 2517}{55 - 45} = \frac{80}{10} = 8$$

(pp 294–297)

These figures can now be substituted into to the straight line relationship.

$y = a + b(x - \bar{x})$

$y = 167.8 + 8\ (x - 3)$

5

This can now be simplified to the usual $y = mx + c$ form of the straight line.

$$y = 167.8 + 8(x - 3)$$
$$y = 167.8 + 8x - 24$$
$$y = 143.8 + 8x$$

We have already determined with the correlation coefficient that there is a good association between the two variables, time (x) and sales of houses (y). This relationship can now be given in a symbolic format as:

$$y = 8x + 143.8$$

where x = time in months
y = sales of houses

4

6

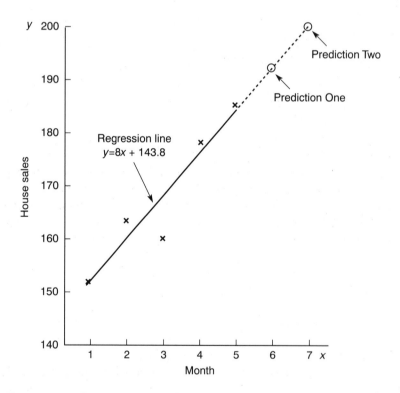

Figure 15.9.1   Scatter graph for problem 9.1

5

7

Prediction One (Month 6)
Substitute the value of time, Month 6, which for the prediction line stays 6:

$$y = 8x + 143.8$$

where x = time in months
y = the sales of houses

5

(p 297)

(p 296)

7

therefore
$$y = 8 \times 6 + 143.8$$
$$= 48 + 143.8$$
$$= 191.8$$

6

8 For Month 6 then a sales value of 191.8 houses would be expected. The actual value of sales achieved will be normally distributed around this mean. The correlation coefficient is significant but the prediction is outside the limit of the regression. Although this is only by one time period, management can therefore be reasonably confident of this prediction.

7

(p 297)

7 *Prediction Two (Month 7)*

Substitute the value of time, Month 7, which for the prediction line stays 7:

$$y = 8x + 143.8$$

where x = time in months
y = sales of houses

therefore
$$y = 8 \times 7 + 143.8$$
$$= 56 + 143.8$$
$$= 199.8$$

6

(pp 297–298)

8 For Month 7 then a sales value of 199.8 houses would be expected. The actual value of sales achieved will be normally distributed around this mean. The correlation coefficient is significant but the prediction is outside the limit of the regression. Although this is only by two time periods, management can therefore be reasonably confident of this prediction although less so than for Month 6.

7

(pp 297–299)

9.2 Solution

$$y = 1.4x - 24.8$$

where x = the expenditure on publicity
y = the expected number of visitors for the given expenditure on publicity

With a publicity expenditure of £1,600 then 199,200 visitors would be expected.

9.3 Solution

$$y = 18.15x + 12.14$$

where x = the age of the machine
y = the expected cost of maintenance given the age of the machine

With an age of the machine of four years then a maintenance cost of £84.74 would be expected.

9.4 Solution

$$y = 57.9x + 87$$

where x = time measured in years (1 representing 1988)
y = the expected level of the budget

For year 1995 a budget value of £550.20 would be expected.
For year 1996 a budget value of £608.10 would be expected.
For year 1997 a budget value of £666.00 would be expected.
For year 1998 a budget value of £723.90 would be expected.
For year 1999 a budget value of £781.80 would be expected.

Solutions to Chapter 10

10.1 The pattern that this data follows is cyclic with random variation.

10.2 The pattern that this data follows is constant with random variation, although the last two weeks' figures may be suggesting there is a change or a problem taking place in the data pattern.

10.3 The pattern that this data follows is a trend with random variation.

10.4 The pattern that this data follows is constant with random variation. The consumption for 1992 would need to be investigated – this may be a spike.

10.5 The pattern that this data follows is cyclic with random variation.

10.6 The pattern that this data follows is constant with random variation.

10.7 The pattern that this data follows is a trend with random variation although this is likely to change when the fault rate reaches a steady state.

10.8 The pattern that this data follows is constant with random variation.

10.9 Your forecast should be 8,900 cabinets for the year of 1995 with a breakdown as follows:

1st quarter – 2,000 cabinets
2nd quarter – 1,500 cabinets
3rd quarter – 3,000 cabinets
4th quarter – 2,400 cabinets

10.10 Your forecast should be £55,000.

10.11 Your forecast should be 140 pupils.

10.12 Your forecast should be 340 million gallons if the effect of the 1992 peak is reduced.

10.13 Your forecast should be 358 clocks for the year of 1995 with a breakdown as follows:

1st quarter – 16 clocks
2nd quarter – 84 clocks
3rd quarter – 125 clocks
4th quarter – 133 clocks

10.14 Your forecast should be 161 complaints for 1995 and 1996.

10.15 Your forecast should be 14 faults for week 8.

10.16 Your forecast should be £10,200 in expenses for 1995.

10.17 This data is taken from the weekly sales total of the Ipswich branch of a national chain of stores.

Week	1	2	3	4	5	6	7	8
Sales (£000)	54	48	51	50	55	53	58	62

Using this data apply the smoothing technique of moving averages. Use a four period moving average and calculate a forecast for week 9.

Solution Format

❶ ❷ Response rate required is a four period moving average.

1 2 (p 317)

❸ ❹

Week	1	2	3	4	5	6	7	8
Actual sales (Y_t)	54	48	51	50	55	53	58	62
Moving total				203	204	209	216	228
Moving average (M_t)				50.75	51	52.25	54	57
(Moving total divided by 4)								

❺

$$\hat{Y}_{t+T} = M_t$$

$$\hat{Y}_{8+1} = M_8 = £57,000$$

3 (pp 317–318)

This forecast should be treated with care given the last two weeks' figures may suggest a change is taking place in the data pattern. If the data pattern is still found to be constant then a lower figure should be used (around £55,000). The sales at this branch should be investigated and further information should be sought.

10.18 Solution

Year	1990	1991	1992	1993	1994
Moving average (M_t)	327	319	340.8	345.8	347

10.19 This data is taken from the number of complaints received by a building society on the behaviour of its counter staff.

Year	1989	1990	1991	1992	1993	1994
Complaints	163	158	159	165	161	162

Using the data in problem 10.6 apply the smoothing technique of exponential smoothing and calculate a forecast for 1995. Use an $\alpha = 0.2$ and a smoothed value of 160 for 1988 (U_0).

Solution format

❶ ❷ In this example the initialisation value has been calculated from previous data to be 160 and a smoothing constant of 0.2 is to be used (a medium response rate).

1 2 (pp 319–321)

❸ ❹

Years	Initial	1989	1990	1991	1992	1993	1994
Complaints Y_t		163	158	159	165	161	162
$0.2 \times Y_t$		32.6	31.6	31.8	33	32.2	32.4
$0.8 \times U_{t-1}$		128	128.5	128.1	127.9	128.7	128.7
U_t	160	160.6	160.1	159.9	160.9	160.9	161.1

⑤
$$\hat{Y}_{t+T} = U_t$$

3

(p 321)

The forecast for 1995 is as follows:

$$\hat{Y}_{1994+1} = U_{1994} = 161.1 \cong 161 \text{ complaints}$$

The forecast for 1996 is as follows:

$$\hat{Y}_{1994+2} = U_{1994} = 161.1 \cong 161 \text{ complains}$$

10.20 Solution

The forecast for 1995 is as follows:

$$\hat{Y}_{1994+1} = U_{1994} = 102.1 \cong £10,210 \text{ in expenses}$$

10.21 This data is taken from the enrolment of first year pupils at Middle Town High School:

Year	1989	1990	1991	1992	1993	1994
Number of pupils	380	348	365	358	346	340

Using the data in problem 10.3 apply the smoothing technique of double exponential smoothing and calculate a forecast for 1995. Use an $\alpha = 0.2$ and a smoothed value of 365 pupils for 1988 (U_0) and a double smoothed value of 375 pupils for 1988 (U_0).

Solution format

❶ ❷ In this example the initialisation values have been calculated from previous data and a smoothing constant of 0.2 is to be used.

1 2

(pp 323–325)

❸ ❹

Year	Initial	1989	1990	1991	1992	1993	1994
Number of pupils Y_t		380	348	365	358	346	340
$0.2 \times Y_t$		766	69.6	73	71.6	69.2	68
$0.8 \times U_{t-1}$		292	294.4	291.2	291.4	290.4	287.7
U_t	365	368	364	364.2	363	359.6	355.7
$0.2 \times U_t$		73.6	72.8	72.8	72.6	71.9	71.1
$0.8 \times U_{t-1}$		300	298.9	297.4	296.2	295	293.5
U_t	375	373.6	371.7	370.2	368.8	366.9	364.6
$Y_t = 2U_t - U_t$		362.4	356.3	358.2	357.2	352.3	346.8

5

$$\hat{Y}_{1995+1} = \frac{(2-\alpha)U_{1994} - \bar{U}_{1994}}{1-a}$$

$$= \frac{(2-0.2)355.7 - 364.6}{1-0.2}$$

$$= \frac{1.8 \times 355.7 - 364.6}{0.8}$$

$$= \frac{640.26 - 364.6}{0.8}$$

$$= \frac{275.66}{0.8} = 344.6 \cong 345 \text{ pupils}$$

3

(p 326)

10.22 Solution

Forecast for week 8 calculated in week 7 = $14.45 \cong 14$ faults.

10.23 This data is taken from the sales of a particular specification of glass display cabinet of a major national quality manufacturer of reproduction furniture. The sales are in 100s.

	1991	1992	1993	1994
Jan, Feb, March	20	19	21	20
April, May, June	15	16	14	16
July, Aug, Sept	28	30	31	29
Oct, Nov, Dec	25	23	26	24

Using this data apply the technique of cyclic forecasting. Use a moving average of four periods long to deseasonalise the data and produce a forecast for the year of 1995.

Solution format

❶ ❷ In this example a four year period moving average will be used given the cycle is made up of four quarters. The underlying average is constant as are the cyclic elements.

1

(pp 330–331)

❷ ❸

Year	Quarter	Actual	Moving average	Seasonal value
1991	1	20		
	2	15		
	3	28		
	4	25	22	3

2

❷ ❸

1992	1	19	21.75	−2.75
	2	16	22	−6
	3	30	22.5	7.5
	4	23	22	1
1993	1	21	22.5	−1.5
	2	14	22	−8
	3	31	22.25	8.75
	4	26	23	3
1994	1	20	22.25	−2.75
	2	16	23.25	−7.25
	3	29	22.75	6
	4	24	22.25	1.75

❷ (pp 331–332)

❹

Year	1991	1992	1993	1994	Ave seasonal factor
1st quarter		−2.75	−1.5	−2.75	−2.33
2nd quarter		−6	−8	−7.25	−7.10
3rd quarter		7.5	8.75	6.25	7.50
4th quarter	3	1	3	1.75	2.20

❺ 1995 FORECAST

1st quarter = 22.25 − 2.33 = 19.92
2nd quarter = 22.25 − 7.10 = 15.15
3rd quarter = 22.25 + 7.50 = 29.75
4th quarter = 22.25 + 2.20 = 24.45

❸ (p 332)

All the values in this example are measured in hundreds, therefore forecast 1995:

1st quarter = 1,992 ≅ 2,000 cabinets
2nd quarter = 1,515 ≅ 1,500 cabinets
3rd quarter = 2,975 ≅ 3,000 cabinets
4th quarter = 2,445 ≅ 2,400 cabinets

10.24 Solution

Forecast 1995:

1st quarter = 15.9 ≅ 16 clocks
2nd quarter = 83.5 ≅ 84 clocks
3rd quarter = 125 ≅ 125 clocks
4th quarter = 133.2 ≅ 133 clocks

10.25 If for the data pattern given in problem 10.7 normal exponential smoothing was to be used then the following smoothed values would have been calculated.

Week number	1	2	3	4	5	6	7
Number of faults	28	23	26	22	15	16	12
Smoothed values	26.4	25.7	25.8	25	23	21.6	19.7

Use the control technique of CUSUM to track this forecasting system and demonstrate when the forecasting system is going out of control.

Solution format

❶❷❸

Week number	1	2	3	4	5	6	7
Number of faults	28	23	26	22	15	16	12
Smoothed values	26.4	25.7	25.8	25	23	21.6	19.7
Error		−1.6	2.7	−0.2	3	8	5.6	7.7
CUSUM		−1.6	1.1	0.9	3.9	11.9	17.5	25.2

1 2 (p 374)

❹ This shows how at first the forecasts work well when the data follows a constant data pattern but they fail towards the end because the underlying average has changed. This failure is shown effectively on the CUSUM with the dramatic movement in weeks 5, 6 and 7.

3 (pp 334–335)

10.26 Solution

The final CUSUM value for month 7 = 97.6.

10.27 Apply the computerised tracking signal to the problem given in 10.25 using $\alpha = 0.2$. For the period prior to week 1 the exponentially smoothed error should be taken as 0.6 (E_0) and the mean absolute deviation should be taken as 2.4 (MAD$_0$).

Solution format

❸ The tracking signal can be calculated as follows using an α value of 0.2 and initialisation values calculated from previous data.

1 (pp 337–338)

❶❷

Week	Initial	1	2	3	4	5	6	7
Actual faults		28	23	26	22	15	16	12
Smoothed faults		26.4	25.7	25.8	25	23	21.6	19.7
Error (e_t)		−1.6	2.7	−0.2	3	8	5.6	7.7
$0.2 \times e_t$		−0.32	0.54	−0.04	0.6	1.6	1.12	1.54
$0.8 \times e_{t-1}$		0.48	0.13	0.54	0.4	0.8	1.92	2.43
E_t	0.6	0.16	0.67	0.50	1.0	2.4	3.04	3.97
$0.2 \times | e_t |$		0.32	0.54	0.04	0.6	1.6	1.12	1.54
$0.8 \times \mathrm{MAD}_{t-1}$		1.92	1.79	1.86	1.52	1.7	2.64	3.01
MAD_t	2.4	2.24	2.33	1.90	2.12	3.3	3.76	4.55
TS_t		0.07	0.29	0.26	0.47	0.73	0.81	0.87

❹ ❺ ❻

❼ The tracking signal has passed the warning limit in week 5 and the action limit in week 6. This indicates that the forecasting system is not working with the data. The forecasting system is for constant data whereas this data is a trend.

3 (p 338)

10.28 Solution

Month	1	2	3	4	5	6	7
Tracking signal	−0.46	−0.07	−0.26	−0.03	−0.04	0.29	0.60

Solutions to Chapter 12

12.1 A certain ingredient is used regularly in the catering section of a motorway service station at an average rate of 5,000 cans per year. This particular item is priced at £6 per can. The cost of working capital is 10 per cent per annum, insurance on goods held in stock is 8½ per cent per annum and there's a miscellaneous storage charge of 6½ per cent per annum. The cost of placing an order is £10. On average 13.7 items per day are used (365 days working per year) with a standard deviation of 1.8 items and from past records the lead time is three days. Management is willing to accept a 1 in 100 chance of running out of stock. Use this information to set up a fixed order quantity stock control scheme. Carry out a sensitivity analysis on the elements of this stock control scheme.

Solution format

❶ The first step is to identify the holding cost. In this example it will be made up of **1** the cost of working capital, the insurance on goods held in stock and the miscellaneous storage charges.

$$\text{Holding cost} = 10\% + 8\tfrac{1}{2}\% + 6\tfrac{1}{2}\% \text{ of purchase price}$$
$$= 25\% \text{ purchase price}$$

therefore $i = 0.25$
$$C_1 = 10$$
$$d = 5,000$$
$$p = 6$$

❷

$$\text{EOQ} = \sqrt{\frac{2C_1 d}{ip}}$$

$$\text{EOQ} = \sqrt{\frac{2 \times 10 - 5,000}{0.25 \times 6}}$$

$$= \sqrt{\frac{100,000}{1.5}}$$

$$= \sqrt{66,666.66'}$$

$$= 258.2 \text{ items} \cong 258$$

Therefore the EOQ for this item has been calculated at 258 item.

(pp 365–367)

(pp 367–371)

❸

Lead time = 3 days
Average demand per day = 13.7 per day
Stock out risk required is 1 in 100 (0.01) – this will give a k value of 2.33
Standard deviation of daily demand = 1.8 items

$$Order\ level = LR + k\sqrt{L}\ \sigma_R$$
$$= (3 \times 13.7) + (2.33 \times \sqrt{3} \times 1.8)$$
$$= 41.1 + 7.3$$
$$= 48.4 \cong 48$$

Buffer stock = 7.3

3

(p 372)

❺

Sensitivity analysis of order quantity:

5

(p 373)

Order quantity	Purchase of items £	Order cost £	Holding cost £	Yearly cost £	
50	30,000	1,000	54	31,054	
100	30,000	500	91	30,591	
150	30,000	333	129	30,462	
200	30,000	250	166	30,416	
258	30,000	194	210	30,404	EOQ
300	30,000	167	241	30,408	
350	30,000	143	279	30,422	
400	30,000	125	316	30,441	

❹

4

In this example being considered the order quantity can vary between 200 and 300 with a maximum penalty cost of £12 in a total yearly operating cost of over £30,000. This shows this is not particularly sensitive over a range of order quantities.

12.2 Solution

EOQ = 1,033
Order level = 140

Sensitivity:

Order quantity = 750   Yearly operating cost = £769
Order quantity = 1,033   Yearly operating cost = £766
Order quantity = 1,250   Yearly operating cost = £767

Therefore not particularly sensitive over a range of order quantities.

12.3 Solution

EOQ = 7,089

Lead time one week:

    99% stock out risk   Order level = 3,338
    95% stock out risk   Order level = 2,951

Cost difference between the 95 per cent and 99 per cent stock out risks = £309.60 per year.

Lead time three weeks:

    99% Stock out risk   Order level = 7,358
    95% Stock out risk   Order level = 6,971

Cost difference between the one week and three weeks lead times = £1,608 per year.

12.4 A certain type of security lock is used by a manufacturer of desks at an average rate of 900 per year. The lock being purchased is £4.

Given the following information:

- cost of working capital is 15 per cent per annum.
- insurance on goods held in stock is 2½ per cent per annum.
- miscellaneous storage charges are 7½ per cent per annum.
- cost of placing an order is £5.

What quantity should be ordered if the following discounts are offered:

Quantity	Discount
0–200	0%
200–500	2½%
500+	5%

Note: Given the cost of the buffer stock is fixed across all the price breaks you may assume the buffer stock to be zero.

Solution format

❶   Normal price = p_1 1st price break = p_2 2nd price break = p_3 ◳

Economic order quantities and order quantities will also use a suffix to denote the price break being used:

$$EOQ_1 = \sqrt{\frac{2C_1d}{ip_1}} = \sqrt{\frac{2 \times 5 \times 900}{0.25 \times 4}} = 95 \text{ items}$$

$$EOQ_2 = \sqrt{\frac{2C_1d}{ip_2}} = \sqrt{\frac{2 \times 5 \times 900}{0.25 \times 3.9}} = 96 \text{ items}$$

$$EOQ_3 = \sqrt{\frac{2C_1d}{ip_3}} = \sqrt{\frac{2 \times 5 \times 900}{0.25 \times 3.8}} = 97 \text{ items}$$

❷ On the basis of EOQ then none of the price breaks are economic.

1

❸ *Normal price*

$$Z_1 = p_1 d + \frac{C_1 d}{EOQ_1} + ip_1\left(\frac{EOQ_1}{2} + B\right)$$

$$= 4 \times 900 + \frac{5 \times 900}{95} + 0.25 \times 4\left(\frac{95}{2}\right)$$

$$= 3600 + 47.37 + 47.5$$

$$= 3694.87 \text{ total yearly operating cost for } p_1$$

1st price break (2½ per cent for 200 items or more):

$$Z_2 = p_2 d + \frac{C_1 d}{Q_2} + ip_2\left(\frac{Q_2}{2} + B\right)$$

$$= 3.90 \times 900 + \frac{5 \times 900}{200} + 0.25 \times 3.90 \frac{(200)}{2}$$

$$= 3{,}510 + 22.50 + 97.50$$

$$= 3{,}630 \text{ total yearly operating cost for } p_2$$

2nd price break (5 per cent for 500 items or more):

$$Z_2 = p_3 d + \frac{C_1 d}{Q_3} + ip_3\left(\frac{Q_3}{2} + B\right)$$

$$= 3.80 \times 900 + \frac{5 \times 900}{500} + 0.25 \times 3.80 \frac{(500)}{2}$$

$$= 3{,}420 + 9 + 237.5$$

$$= 3{,}666.5 \text{ total yearly operating cost for } p_3$$

❹ Both the price breaks have a lower total yearly operating cost than the normal price and are therefore economically worth taking. The optimum policy would be to order 200 units at a discount of 2½ per cent.

12.5 Solution

P_1	$EOQ_1 = 258$	$Z_1 = 30{,}398.25$
P_2	$EOQ_2 = 262$	$Z_2 = 29{,}574.40$
P_3	$EOQ_3 = 258$	$Z_3 = 29{,}580.50$

(pp 377–379)

Price breaks not accepted on EOQs but on total yearly operating costs optimum policy is to order 500 cans at a discount of 3 per cent.

12.6 The following stocklist is representative of a stocklist of a small retail store selling provisions:

Item number	Demand/Year	Price (£)	Present order quantity
1	300	0.95	25
2	150	0.03	50
3	200	0.15	25
4	50	0.60	25
5	250	2.50	50

There are 30 orders placed per year. Use the technique of coverage analysis to reset the order quantities and estimate the savings in capital employed.

Solution format

❶❷❸❹

Item number (i)	Price p_i	d_i	$p_i d_i$	$\sqrt{p_i d_i}$	f^*_i	Q^*_i
1	0.95	300	285	16.9	9.3	32
2	0.03	150	4.5	2.1	1.2	125
3	0.15	200	30	5.5	3.0	67
4	0.60	50	30	5.5	3.0	17
5	2.50	250	625	25	13.8	18
				55.0	30.3	

$$K = \frac{\text{Total number of orders}}{\sqrt{p_i d_i}} = \frac{30}{55} = 0.55$$

1 (p 383)

❺

Item number (i)	Price p_i	Q^*_i	Average stock $Q^*_{i/2}$	New value ave stk $\times p_i$	Old ave stock	Old value
1	0.95	32	16	15.2	12.5	11.88
2	0.03	125	62.5	1.9	25	0.75
3	0.15	67	33.5	5	12.5	1.88
4	0.60	17	8.5	5.1	12.5	7.50
5	2.50	18	9	22.5	25	62.5
				49.7		84.51

2 (p 284)

Old capital employed = £84.51
New capital employed = £49.70

⑤

$$\text{Percentage saving in capital employed} = \frac{84.51 - 49.70}{84.51} \times 100$$

$$= \frac{34.81}{84.51} \times 100 = 41.19 \cong 41\%$$

2

By using coverage analysis to reset the order quantities there will be a saving on capital employed of 41 per cent.

12.7 Solution

Item Number	New order quantity
1	10
2	50
3	25
4	125
5	61

Old capital employed = £11.55
New capital employed = £9.06
∴ 22% saving on capital employed

Solutions to Chapter 13

13.1 Given below are the demand pattern and the lead time for a spare part for a production machine.

Demand per day	Probability	Observed lead time in days	Probability
0	0.20	5	0.30
1	0.30	6	0.45
2	0.15	7	0.20
3	0.13	8	0.05
4	0.09		
5	0.07		
6	0.06		

The production manager suggests that a reorder level of 13 parts and a reorder quantity of 20 parts will be sufficient. Build a simulation of the situation and run for 60 days. Make recommendations to the production manager about the reorder level and reorder quantity.

Notes:

i) Negative stocks are allowed because the machine broken down will require the spare part as soon as it arrives; production will of course be lost during this period.

ii) The lead time starts the day after the order is sent out and the parts arrive at the beginning of the last day of the lead time (weekends are worked and included in the lead time).

iii) The initial stock should be taken as 15 parts.

Solution format

❶ ❷ In this simulation model there will be two look-up charts, one to create daily demands for the spare part and the second to create lead times when an order is made. The simulation model will follow the basic order level stock control scheme and this needs to be varied to test different order levels and order quantities. The operating chart will need to record the starting stock for the day and the demand for the day. It will also need to record lead times and when the order quantity should be added to the daily stock figure. The performance indicators that can be used to measure this model need to be concerned with two areas, first the stock levels (average quantity in stock) and second the negative stocks (average negative stocks and average negative stocks per day).

1 (pp 396–397)

2 (p 397)

❸ **Look-up chart for demand**:

Random number	Demand per day
00–19	0
50–64	2
65–77	3
78–86	4
87–93	5
94–99	6

Look-up chart for lead time:

Random number	Lead time (days)
00–29	5
30–74	6
75–94	7
95–99	8

3

❹ **Operating chart:**

Order level = 13 parts   Order quantity = 20 parts

Time days	Starting stock	Daily RN	demand	Lead RN	time days	Quantity in stock	Negative stocks
1	15	09	0				
2	15	54	2				
3	13	42	1				
4	12	80	4	01	5		
5	8	06	0			1	
6	8	06	0			2	
7	8	26	1			3	
8	7	57	2			4	
9	25 (5 + 20)	79	4			5	20
10	21	52	2				

	Order level = 13 parts			Order quantity = 20 parts			
Time days	Starting stock	Daily RN	demand	Lead RN	time days	Quantity in stock	Negative stocks
11	19	80	4				
12	15	45	1				
13	14	68	3				
14	11	48	1	59	6		
15	10	12	0			1	
16	10	35	1			2	
17	9	91	5			3	
18	4	89	5			4	
19	−1	49	1			5	−1
20	$18^{(-2 + 20)}$	33	1			6	−1
21	17	10	0				20
22	17	55	2				
23	15	60	2				
24	13	19	0				
25	13	47	1	55	6		
26	12	52	2			1	
27	10	48	1			2	
28	9	49	1			3	
29	8	54	2			4	
30	6	96	6			5	
31	$20^{(0 + 20)}$	80	4			6	20
32	16	05	0				
33	16	17	0				
34	16	23	1				
35	15	56	2				
36	13	15	0				
37	13	86	4	18	5		
38	9	08	0			1	
39	9	95	6			2	
40	3	73	3			3	
41	0	20	1			4	−1
42	$19^{(-1 + 20)}$	26	1			5	20
43	18	90	5				
44	13	79	4	01	5		
45	9	57	2			1	
46	7	97	6			2	
47	1	33	1			3	
48	0	64	2			4	−2
49	$18^{(-2 + 20)}$	01	0			5	20
50	18	50	2				
51	16	29	1				
52	15	34	1				
53	14	11	0				
54	14	43	1				
55	13	09	0				
56	13	62	2	32	6		
57	11	91	5			1	
58	6	48	1			2	
59	5	69	3			3	
60	2	07	0			4	

$$\text{Average quantity in stock} = \frac{703}{60} = 11.7$$

$$\text{Average negative stock} = \frac{5}{4} = 1.25$$

$$\text{Average negative stock per day} = \frac{5}{60} = 0.08$$

(pp 396–402)

❺ ❻ It would be dangerous to make conclusions from a simulation run of only 60 days. ❹❺
To draw conclusions the cost of running out of stock should be balanced against
the cost of increased stock holding. The simulation model would need to be run
for more days and with different order levels. By varying the order quantity the
cost of ordering can be balanced against the cost of holding stocks. The order
quantity will need to be varied against a fixed order level.

(p 402)

13.2 Solution

With simulation modelling it is difficult to give a short solution due to the variable
nature of the models. Your solution will depend on the random number stream
and the number of time periods the model is operated. The following is the result
we achieved and can be used as a guide.

Average number of cars in use per day = 5.2
Average days hire lost per week = 1.5

13.3 Solution

With simulation modelling it is difficult to give a short solution due to the variable
nature of the models Your solution will depend on the random number stream and
the number of time periods the model is operated The following is the result we
achieved and can be used as a guide.

Average quantity in stock = 66.6
Average negative stock = 8
Average negative stock per day = 0.13

13.4 Solution

With this type of general simulation modelling problem it is not possible to give a
short solution.

13.5 Solution

With simulation modelling it is difficult to give a short solution due to the variable
nature of the models. Your solution will depend on the random number stream
and the number of time periods the model is operated. The following is the result
we achieved and can be used as a guide.

Average number of carpenters in use per day = 2.3
Average days late per week = 0.5

13.6 Solution

With this type of general simulation modelling problem it is not possible to give a
short solution.

Glossary

Alternative Hypothesis is a statement that is accepted if the null hypothesis is disproved in hypothesis testing. It normally signifies that a change has occurred.

Analogue model a model that uses one set of properties to describe another set of properties. An example is a map that uses lines and symbols to describe roads and features.

Area Sampling is a random sampling method that is, for all intents and purposes, a geographically based cluster sample. It involves breaking down a large geographical area into smaller geographical areas and then selecting items in a random way.

Balanced Attitude Scale is a closed type of question, where the possible response is typically limited to very important to very unimportant.

Bar Graph is a graphical representation of a frequency distribution, with the height of the columns representing the frequency of a class/interval.

Benchmarking an approach to reference performance indicators to good practice, either internal or external. It looks for gradual improvement towards the best practice.

Bimodal is where there are two or more modes in a set of data.

Binomial Distribution is a discrete probability distribution that has many potential applications. It is based on situations where there are only two possible outcomes, such as success and failure. It is constructed by determining the probabilities of x successes in n trials.

Binomial Probability Function is the formula for determining the number of x successes in n trials in a binomial distribution.

Box Jenkins a sophisticated forecasting system for use on trend data patterns with random variation.

Box and Whisker Plot is a graphical representation of a five number summary, and it is very useful when you want to compare one set of data against another set of data.

Break-even Analysis a simple but powerful model that compares the cost against the revenue of a product. It allows a decision to be made on the minimum numbers of a product that can break even.

Capability "... is an all round human quality, an integration of knowledge, skills and personal qualities used effectively and appropriately in response to varied, familiar and unfamiliar circumstances".

Central Limit Theorem is one of the most important theorems in statistics, and it states that as long as samples are large (30+) then the distribution of sample means or proportions will be normally distributed regardless of the shape of the original population.

Chebyshev's Theorem acts in a similar way to the normal distribution, but has the advantage that it applies to any set of data rather than to data that conforms to a normal distribution. Chebyshev's Theorem is more conservative than the normal distribution in that $\mu \pm 2\sigma = 75\%$ of the area of a distribution, $\mu \pm 3\sigma = 89\%$ of the area of a distribution, and $\mu \pm 4\sigma = 94\%$ of the area of a distribution.

Chi-Square Test is a statistical test that compares expected frequencies with actual frequencies.

Chi-Square Test of Independence is a statistical test that compares the frequencies of two variables to see if the two variables are independent.

Class Midpoint is the middle point of a class/interval (i.e., the mean of the class endpoints).

Cluster Sampling is a random sampling method that involves dividing a population into nonoverlaping clusters and then selecting items from those clusters.

Coefficient of Variation is a relative measure (ratio) that is particularly useful for comparing the spreads of different sets of data. It works by saying how many times the mean of a set of data goes into the standard deviation of that set of data. The higher the number of times that it goes, the higher the ratio. When comparing two sets of data with different means and standard deviations, the set of data that has the highest coefficient of variation ratio has the highest relative spread around the mean.

Competence is a measurable skill in carrying out an activity and/or process. The measurement criterion is one of either being competent or not yet competent. The national standards that have been laid down by MCI (Management Charter Initiative) cover a number of levels, i.e., Level I and Level II (NVQ 4 and 5). The principles of the competence movement have been adopted in this text, with competence based problems and solutions and the associated procedure steps and competencies being a major component of the book.

Confidence Limits are also known as confidence intervals, levels of confidence, confidence levels, and significance levels. They are used extensively in statistics and they tell us with a known degree of accuracy what the difference is between a sample statistic and its corresponding population parameter.

Contingency Tables are used for summarising and comparing two or more variables simultaneously.

Convenience Sampling is a nonrandom sampling technique where the items within the sample are selected on the basis of the convenience of the researcher.

Correlation a technique that will determine the significance of the relationship determined in a regression analysis.

Correlation Coefficient a value between −1 to +1 which is calculated within correlation to determine the significance of a relationship.

Coverage Analysis a stock control scheme that applies to stocklists and takes account of the parato distribution by ordering items with high usage more frequently and items with low usage less frequently.

Critical value is the point at which we reject or accept a null hypothesis.

Cumulative Frequency Distributions are used to represent the frequencies of a frequency distribution in a cumulative fashion. A 'less than' cumulative frequency distribution adds one set of class frequencies to the next set of class frequencies to get an increasing cumulative total. An 'or more' cumulative frequency distribution accumulates from the highest to the lowest class. Both types of cumulative frequency distribution can be used for estimating values.

CUSUM a simple approach to track errors in forecasting and other systems. It produces a cumulative sum of the errors to indicate when systems are out of control.

Deciles are names given to the 10th, 20th, 30th etc. percentiles. They are used to describe sets of data.

Decision Rule is a numerical measure that is used as a benchmark in accepting or rejecting a null hypothesis.

Decision analysis a complete analysis of a decision situation which will normally include a decision tree.

Decision tree a graphical way of presenting a decision situation. A decision tree combines probability trees with decision boxes.

Discounted cash flow an accounting method to allow for the change in the value of money over time.

Economic order quantity the optimum order quantity determined by balancing the cost of ordering against the cost of holding stock.

Empirical Distribution Function is similar to a cumulative frequency curve, but differs in that it deals with every individual item in the data set. The empirical distribution function can be used for determining percentile positions and for estimating values.

Excel is a pioneering window based spreadsheet package (see 'Spreadsheets') that is used extensively within the educational sector and is gaining an increasing share of the business sector. It's user friendly icon driven interface provides an easy route into its powerful functions and features.

Expected Value is the long-run average of occurrences in a probability based experiment/distribution.

Exponential Distribution is a continuous probability distribution that describes (measures) the time between random occurrences. It is closely related to the Poisson Distribution, which measures the arrival rate of events, because it measures the time between those events.

Exponential Double Smoothing a forecasting method for use with trend data patterns with random variation.

Exponential Smoothing a forecasting method for use with constant data patterns with random variation.

Finite Population Correction Factor is an adjustment that is made to accurately estimate the variance of a distribution of sample means or proportions.

Five Number Summary is used to describe a set of data. It uses the median, the lower and upper quartiles, the minimum value and the maximum value in its description of the set of data. It is particularly useful when one wants to compare a number of sets of data.

Fixed Order Quantity Stock Control Scheme a stock control scheme that orders a fixed order quantity when an order level trigger is reached as the quantity in stock falls.

Forecast Response Rate the speed at which forecasting systems respond to changing data. A high response rate will quickly take account of changing data but will not effectively smooth the forecast. A low response rate will smooth the forecast effectively but will not respond quickly to changing data.

Frequency Distribution is a method by which a set of data is summarised. It involves creating a range of classes or intervals into which the data can fall and then recording the data (frequencies) against those classes.

Funnel Design is a term that describes the way that questionnaires move from general and closed questions to more specific and open ended questions.

Geometric Mean is like the median in that it reduces the distortion of high or low values. Its main use though is in calculating compounded rates of growth.

Histogram is a graphical representation of a frequency distribution that is very similar to a bar graph. The distinguishing feature of a histogram is that the columns are not separated as with a bar graph and that the boundaries of the columns are based on the real class limits as opposed to the apparent class limits.

Hypothesis Testing is the process by which hypotheses are developed and tested. It involves setting up a null and alternative hypothesis and testing to see which is accepted or rejected.

Iconic Model a model that is an exact representation of the entity being modelled, although the scale will be increased or decreased. An example of an iconic model is a scale model of a plane in a wind tunnel.

Integer a whole number.

Interquartile Range is the distance from the lower quartile to the upper quartile. It is used to describe the central half of a set of data.

Judgement Sampling is a nonrandom sampling technique where items selected for the sample are chosen on the basis of the judgement of the researcher.

Likert Scale is a closed question format that typically asks a question that ranges from agree strongly to disagree strongly over a number of closely related areas.

Line Graph is an alternative to the bar graph and histogram for graphically representing a frequency distribution. The mid-point of the top of the class frequencies are used to provide the points for the line graph. It is a useful method for portraying longer time periods.

Linear programming a mathematical programming technique to optimise resource constrained problems. In simple cases it can be carried out graphically, but for most examples it will require the use of a computer model. The relationships need to be linear.

Lotus 1-2-3 is one of the original spreadsheet packages (see 'Spreadsheets'), and it developed into a market leader, especially within the business sector. Lotus 1-2-3 is still extensively used, with the latest versions having full windows capability and flexibility.

Mail (Postal) Survey normally involves sending a questionnaire through the post to obtain responses on a range of questions. It has the advantage that it can reach a wide geographical area, although it does suffer from a poor response rate.

Mean is the most widely used averaging method, and it represents the most typical and representative value of a set of data. Technically known as the 'arithmetic mean', it is used extensively in statistics, even though it suffers from the handicap that it can be distorted by extremely high or low values.

Mean Absolute Deviation is a measure of the spread of a set of data. It is the average of the individual deviations (i.e., differences) of each data value against the mean. What distinguishes this from other measures is that it ignores the sign of the deviations.

Median is a widely used averaging method, and it represents the most typical and representative value of a set of data. It is locationally in the middle of a set of data and consequently does not get distorted by high or low values. It is for this reason that it is normally used to represent average salaries.

Mode is the weakest of the averaging methods, and it represents the most frequently occurring number.

Moving Average forecasting method for use with constant data patterns with random variation.

Normal Distribution is the most typical and widely used probability distribution in statistics. It typifies many aspects of the physical and human world, such as peoples height and weight. The normal distribution has the important characteristic that its area can be described by standard deviations. More specifically, $\mu \pm 1\sigma = 68$. 26% of the area of a normal distribution,

$\mu \pm 2\sigma = 95.44\%$ of the area of a normal distribution, and $\mu \pm 3\sigma = 99.72\%$ of the area of a normal distribution. These characteristics can be used in determining the probability of certain types of events occurring.

Null Hypothesis is an integral part of hypothesis testing, and it is a statement that says that nothing has changed. Normally one is looking to see if the null hypothesis can be disproved.

Objective Function a term used in optimisation modelling to give the aim of the model that will be either maximised or minimised.

One-Tailed Test is a test that only looks at one side of a distribution.

Optimisation an aim in modelling to achieve the best result for a given set of conditions. It does not mean a good solution but the best possible solution.

Parameter is the equivalent of a sample statistic in a population.

Parato Distribution a distribution used in many areas but usually in stock control. Means that 20 per cent of the items on a stocklist will account for 80 per cent of the usage of the items.

Percentiles are used to split a set of data into given amounts/proportions. As an example, the 67th percentile says that 67% of the data are equal to or less than the value that the 67th percentile equates to.

Personal Survey is where the interviewer asks the questions of a survey directly to the respondent. It obtains a very high response rate and the interviewer can elicit very rich and detailed information from the respondent. On the negative side it can be very expensive, especially if it is carried out over a wide geographical area.

Phone Survey uses the telephone system to obtain information from respondents. It is more expensive than mail surveys but has a higher response rate. Assumes that all respondents have a phone and can be contacted through a phone.

Pictograms are used extensively in the media and they can be very effective at capturing peoples attention and getting the message across in an easily understandable form. They typically use pictures to represent the columns of a bar chart etc. Care has to be taken in their use because they can quite easily miss-represent a situation.

Pie Chart is an effective means of summarising a set of data when you want to show the size of different proportions and how those proportions relate to each other.

Poisson Distribution is a discrete probability distribution that is used to determine the occurrence of rare events over time or space.

Probability a way of measuring the uncertainty of an event using a scale of zero to one. Zero is certainty that an event will not occur and one is certainty that an event will occur.

Probability Distributions can take a number of forms, but their primary characteristic is that they represent all the items within the population and the corresponding likelihood of an event happening.

Probability Tree a graphical way of presenting a complex probability situation of multiple events. It uses nodes to represent events and lines coming from these nodes to denote the alternative outcomes that can occur in each event.

Quantiles correspond to the 25th and 75th percentiles. Used in association with the median (the 50th percentile) they split a set of data into four quarters.

QUEST Criteria the QUEST for good performance indicators. **Q**uick, **U**nderstandable, **E**ffective, **S**imple, **T**imely.

Questionnaires are a medium for asking questions in order to elicit information on a particular topic or area. Can be used via mail, telephone or personal surveys. Careful thought has to be given to the design and structure of the questions to ensure a good and valid level of response.

Quota Sampling is a nonrandom sampling method where known proportions in the population are matched in the sample. It is nonrandom because the items within the sample proportions are selected in a nonrandom way.

Range is used to measure the spread of a set of data. It is the difference between the lowest and the highest value and thus measures how wide a set of data is. Its main limitation as a measure of spread is that it can be distorted by high or low values, and this greatly reduces it usefulness in statistics.

Random Variable is a variable that contains the outcomes of a chance experiment.

Regression Analysis a technique that fits a straight line equation through a set of data points.

Relative Frequency Distribution is the same as a frequency distribution but with the frequencies expressed as percentages.

Scatter Graph a presentation method used in regression and correlation. It is a graph that shows the line of the regression and the points on which the line was calculated.

Semantic Differential Scale is a closed question format that is used on a range of characteristics on a specific area.

Sensitivity Analysis an approach that should be applied to all models. Modelling does not give an answer but should give a range of possibilities for different conditions. Sensitivity analysis is this approach of 'what if' modelling.

Simple Random Sampling is the most basic of the random sampling methods, and it necessitates having a complete list of the population which is then numbered. Items from this numbered list are then selected using random numbers.

Spreadsheet a computer based package that will allow you to carry out calculations at considerable speed. A spreadsheet is like a large piece of squared paper with rows and columns on to which you would write down numbers and carry out calculations on them. The advantage is that the computer does all the work and provides a very powerful 'what if' calculation device.

Standard Deviation is the most widely used measure of the spread of a set of data. It is the square root of the variance (taking the square root of a number is the reverse of taking the square of a number, so taking the square root of the variance brings the average back in line with the magnitude of the original deviations). The standard deviation is used extensively in statistics.

Standard Error of the Mean is the standard deviation of a distribution of sample means.

Standard Error of a Proportion is the standard deviation of a distribution of sample proportions.

Statistic is a numerical quantity (such as the mean) of a sample.

Stem-and-Leaf Display is a bar graph/histogram based upon actual values, with the stem being composed of 10's, 100's etc., and the leafs being composed of units (1,2,3 etc.). It is a useful technique for quickly summarising a set of data.

Stratified Sampling is a popular random sampling method that involves dividing the population into strata (the strata are distinguishable by some characteristic, such as age, education, social status etc.) and then selecting items from the strata in a random way.

Subjective Probability when probabilities cannot be calculated but need to be estimated. It is important that subjective probabilities do not degenerate into a guess but are based on the best information available and are carried out using the best estimation techniques.

Survey is the process by which data is collected and collated on a particular topic or area of interest. Examples include political, social and market research surveys.

Symbolic Model a model that represents the entity being modelled with a mathematical equation or a set of such equations and mathematical rules.

Systematic Sampling is a nonrandom sampling method which is similar to simple random sampling, but it differs in that the first item of the sample is selected by random numbers and then every nth item thereafter until the required sample size is obtained.

***t* Distribution** is a distribution that is able to deal with samples that are less than 30 and where the population variance is unknown.

Two-Tailed Test is a test that looks at both sides of a distribution.

Type I Error is an error committed by rejecting a true null hypothesis.

Type II Error is an error committed by failing to reject a false null hypothesis.

Validation of a Model a process for testing the model with actual data and in actual conditions. It is a process of calibrating the model against the situation it has been constructed to model.

Variance is a widely used measure of the spread of a set of data. It is the average of the individual deviations (i.e., differences) of each individual data value against the mean. It resolves the problem of negative and positive deviations by taking the square of the deviations. The problem with this measure is that the average is of a higher magnitude than the deviations themselves due to the deviations being squared. The square root of the variance is the standard deviation.

Verification of a Model a process for testing that the model is behaving in the way in which the modeller intends. It can be likened to a program test in computing.

Weighted mean is similar to the mean, but the values are weighted so that the average represents the true impact of one set of values on another set of values.

Z Scores represent a number as a standard deviation, and can be used in conjunction with the normal distribution to determine the probability of an event occuring.

Appendix 1   Statistical tables

Table 1: table of binomial probabilities

n	x					p				
		.05	.10	.15	.20	.25	.30	.35	.40	.45
1	0	.9500	.9000	.8500	.8000	.7500	.7000	.6500	.6000	.5500
	1	1.0000	1.0000	1.0000	1.0000	1.0000	1.0000	1.0000	1.0000	1.0000
2	0	.9025	.8100	.7225	.6400	.5625	.4900	.4225	.3600	.3025
	1	.9975	.9900	.9775	.9600	.9375	.9100	.8775	.8400	.7975
	2	1.0000	1.0000	1.0000	1.0000	1.0000	1.0000	1.0000	1.0000	1.0000
3	0	.8574	.7290	.6141	.5120	.4219	.3430	.2746	.2160	.1664
	1	.9928	.9720	.9392	.8960	.8438	.7840	.7182	.6480	.5748
	2	.9999	.9990	.9966	.9920	.9844	.9730	.9571	.9360	.9089
	3	1.0000	1.0000	1.0000	1.0000	1.0000	1.0000	1.0000	1.0000	1.0000
4	0	.8145	.6561	.5220	.4096	.3164	.2401	.1785	.1296	.0915
	1	.9860	.9477	.8905	.8192	.7383	.6517	.5630	.4752	.3910
	2	.9995	.9963	.9880	.9728	.9492	.9163	.8735	.8208	.7585
	3	1.0000	.9999	.9995	.9984	.9961	.9919	.9850	.9744	.9590
	4	1.0000	1.0000	1.0000	1.0000	1.0000	1.0000	1.0000	1.0000	1.0000
5	0	.7738	.5905	.4437	.3277	.2373	.1681	.1160	.0778	.0503
	1	.9774	.9185	.8352	.7373	.6328	.5282	.4284	.3370	.2562
	2	.9988	.9914	.9734	.9421	.8965	.8369	.7648	.6826	.5931
	3	1.0000	.9995	.9978	.9933	.9844	.9692	.9460	.9130	.8688
	4	1.0000	1.0000	.9999	.9997	.9990	.9976	.9947	.9898	.9815
	5	1.0000	1.0000	1.0000	1.0000	1.0000	1.0000	1.0000	1.0000	1.0000
6	0	.7351	.5314	.3771	.2621	.1780	.1176	.0754	.0467	.0277
	1	.9672	.8857	.7765	.6554	.5339	.4202	.3191	.2333	.1636
	2	.9978	.9842	.9527	.9011	.8306	.7443	.6471	.5443	.4415
	3	.9999	.9987	.9941	.9830	.9624	.9295	.8826	.8208	.7447
	4	1.0000	.9999	.9996	.9984	.9954	.9891	.9777	.9590	.9308
	5	1.0000	1.0000	1.0000	.9999	.9998	.9993	.9982	.9959	.9917
	6	1.0000	1.0000	1.0000	1.0000	1.0000	1.0000	1.0000	1.0000	1.0000
7	0	.6983	.4783	.3206	.2907	.1335	.0824	.0490	.0280	.0152
	1	.9556	.8503	.7166	.5767	.4449	.3294	.2338	.1586	.1024
	2	.9962	.9743	.9262	.8520	.7564	.6471	.5323	.4199	.3164
	3	.9998	.9973	.9879	.9667	.9294	.8740	.8002	.7102	.6083
	4	1.0000	.9998	.9988	.9953	.9871	.9712	.9444	.9037	.8471
	5	1.0000	1.0000	.9999	.9996	.9987	.9962	.9910	.9812	.9643
	6	1.0000	1.0000	1.0000	1.0000	.9999	.9998	.9994	.9984	.9963
	7	1.0000	1.0000	1.0000	1.0000	1.0000	1.0000	1.0000	1.0000	1.0000
8	0	.6634	.4305	.2725	.1678	.1001	.0576	.0319	.0168	.0084
	1	.9428	.8131	.6572	.5033	.3671	.2553	.1691	.1064	.0632
	2	.9942	.9619	.8948	.7969	.6785	.5518	.4278	.3154	.2201
	3	.9996	.9950	.9786	.9437	.8862	.8059	.7064	.5941	.4770
	4	1.0000	.9996	.9971	.9896	.9727	.9420	.8939	.8263	.7396
	5	1.0000	1.0000	.9998	.9988	.9958	.9887	.9747	.9502	.9115
	6	1.0000	1.0000	1.0000	.9999	.9996	.9987	.9964	.9915	.9819
	7	1.0000	1.0000	1.0000	1.0000	1.0000	.9999	.9998	.9993	.9983
	8	1.0000	1.0000	1.0000	1.0000	1.0000	1.0000	1.0000	1.0000	1.0000

							p				
n	x	.50	.55	.60	.65	.70	.75	.80	.85	.90	.95
1	0	.5000	.4500	.4000	.3500	.3000	.2500	.2000	.1500	.1000	.0500
	1	1.0000	1.0000	1.0000	1.0000	1.0000	1.0000	1.0000	1.0000	1.0000	1.0000
2	0	.2500	.2025	.1600	.1225	.0900	.0625	.0400	.0225	.0100	.0025
	1	.7500	.6975	.6400	.5775	.5100	.4375	.3600	.2775	.1900	.0975
	2	1.0000	1.0000	1.0000	1.0000	1.0000	1.0000	1.0000	1.0000	1.0000	1.0000
3	0	.1250	.0911	.0640	.0429	.0270	.0156	.0080	.0034	.0010	.0001
	1	.5000	.4252	.3520	.2818	.2160	.1562	.1040	.0608	.0280	.0072
	2	.8750	.8336	.7840	.7254	.6570	.5781	.4880	.3859	.2710	.1426
	3	1.0000	1.0000	1.0000	1.0000	1.0000	1.0000	1.0000	1.0000	1.0000	1.0000
4	0	.0625	.0410	.0256	.0150	.0081	.0039	.0016	.0005	.0001	.0000
	1	.3125	.2415	.1792	.1265	.0837	.0508	.0272	.0120	.0037	.0005
	2	.6875	.6090	.5248	.4370	.3483	.2617	.1808	.1095	.0523	.0140
	3	.9375	.9085	.8704	.8215	.7599	.6836	.5904	.4780	.3439	.1855
	4	1.0000	1.0000	1.0000	1.0000	1.0000	1.0000	1.0000	1.0000	1.0000	1.0000
5	0	.0312	.0185	.0102	.0053	.0024	.0010	.0003	.0001	.0000	.0000
	1	.1875	.1312	.0870	.0540	.0308	.0156	.0067	.0022	.0005	.0000
	2	.5000	.4069	.3174	.2352	.1631	.1035	.0579	.0266	.0086	.0012
	3	.8125	.7438	.6630	.5716	.4718	.3672	.2627	.1648	.0815	.0226
	4	.9688	.9497	.9222	.8840	.8319	.7627	.6723	.5563	.4095	.2262
	5	1.0000	1.0000	1.0000	1.0000	1.0000	1.0000	1.0000	1.0000	1.0000	1.0000
6	0	.0156	.0083	.0041	.0018	.0007	.0002	.0001	.0000	.0000	.0000
	1	.1094	.0692	.0410	.0223	.0109	.0046	.0016	.0004	.0001	.0000
	2	.3438	.2553	.1792	.1174	.0705	.0376	.0170	.0059	.0013	.0001
	3	.6562	.5585	.4557	.3529	.2557	.1694	.0989	.0473	.0158	.0022
	4	.8906	.8364	.7667	.6809	.5798	.4661	.3446	.2235	.1143	.0328
	5	.9844	.9723	.9533	.9246	.8824	.8220	.7379	.6229	.4686	.2649
	6	1.0000	1.0000	1.0000	1.0000	1.0000	1.0000	1.0000	1.0000	1.0000	1.0000
7	0	.0078	.0037	.0016	.0006	.0002	.0001	.0000	.0000	.0000	.0000
	1	.0625	.0357	.0188	.0090	.0038	.0013	.0004	.0001	.0000	.0000
	2	.2266	.1529	.0963	.0556	.0288	.0129	.0047	.0012	.0002	.0000
	3	.5000	.3917	.2898	.1998	.1260	.0706	.0333	.0121	.0027	.0002
	4	.7734	.6836	.5801	.4677	.3529	.2436	.1480	.0738	.0257	.0038
	5	.9375	.8976	.8414	.7662	.6706	.5551	.4233	.2834	.1497	.0444
	6	.9922	.9848	.9720	.9510	.9176	.8665	.7903	.6794	.5217	.3017
	7	1.0000	1.0000	1.0000	1.0000	1.0000	1.0000	1.0000	1.0000	1.0000	1.0000
8	0	.0039	.0017	.0007	.0002	.0001	.0000	.0000	.0000	.0000	.0000
	1	.0352	.0181	.0085	.0036	.0013	.0004	.0001	.0000	.0000	.0000
	2	.1445	.0885	.0498	.0253	.0113	.0042	.0012	.0002	.0000	.0000
	3	.3633	.2604	.1737	.1061	.0580	.0273	.0104	.0029	.0004	.0000
	4	.6367	.5230	.4059	.2936	.1941	.1138	.0563	.0214	.0050	.0004
	5	.8555	.7799	.6846	.5722	.4482	.3215	.2031	.1052	.0381	.0058
	6	.9648	.9368	.8936	.8309	.7447	.6329	.4967	.3428	.1869	.0572
	7	.9961	.9916	.9832	.9861	.9424	.8999	.8322	.7275	.5695	.3366
	8	1.0000	1.0000	1.0000	1.0000	1.0000	1.0000	1.0000	1.0000	1.0000	1.0000

(Table of binomial probabilities continued)

n	x	.05	.10	.15	.20	.25	.30	.35	.40	.45
						p				
9	0	.6302	.3874	.2316	.1342	.0751	.0404	.0207	.0101	.0046
	1	.9288	.7748	.5995	.4362	.3003	.1960	.1211	.0705	.0385
	2	.9916	.9470	.8591	.7382	.6007	.7628	.3373	.2318	.1495
	3	.9994	.9917	.9661	.9144	.8343	.7297	.6089	.4826	.3614
	4	1.0000	.9991	.9944	.9804	.9511	.9012	.8283	.7334	.6214
	5	1.0000	.9999	.9994	.9969	.9900	.9747	.9464	.9006	.8342
	6	1.0000	1.0000	1.0000	.9997	.9987	.9957	.9888	.9750	.9502
	7	1.0000	1.0000	1.0000	1.0000	.9999	.9996	.9986	.9962	.9909
	8	1.0000	1.0000	1.0000	1.0000	1.0000	1.0000	.9999	.9997	.9992
	9	1.0000	1.0000	1.0000	1.0000	1.0000	1.0000	1.0000	1.0000	1.0000
10	0	.5987	.3487	.1969	.1074	.0563	.0282	.0135	.0060	.0025
	1	.9139	.7361	.5443	.3758	.2440	.1493	.0860	.0464	.0233
	2	.9885	.9298	.8202	.6778	.5256	.3828	.2616	.1673	.0996
	3	.9990	.9872	.9500	.8791	.7759	.6496	.5138	.3823	.2660
	4	.9999	.9984	.9901	.9672	.9219	.8497	.7515	.6331	.5044
	5	1.0000	.9999	.9986	.9936	.9803	.9527	.9051	.8338	.7384
	6	1.0000	1.0000	.9999	.9991	.9965	.9894	.9740	.9452	.8980
	7	1.0000	1.0000	1.0000	.9999	.9996	.9984	.9952	.9877	.9726
	8	1.0000	1.0000	1.0000	1.0000	1.0000	.9999	.9995	.9983	.9955
	9	1.0000	1.0000	1.0000	1.0000	1.0000	1.0000	1.0000	.9999	.9997
	10	1.0000	1.0000	1.0000	1.0000	1.0000	1.0000	1.0000	1.0000	1.0000
11	0	.5688	.3138	.1673	.0859	.0422	.0198	.0088	.0036	.0014
	1	.8981	.6974	.4922	.3221	.1971	.1130	.0606	.0302	.0139
	2	.9848	.9104	.7788	.6174	.4552	.3127	.2001	.1189	.0652
	3	.9984	.9815	.9306	.8396	.7133	.5696	.4256	.2963	.1911
	4	.9999	.9972	.9841	.9496	.8854	.7897	.6683	.5328	.3971
	5	1.0000	.9997	.9973	.9883	.9657	.9218	.8513	.7535	.6331
	6	1.0000	1.0000	.9997	.9980	.9924	.9784	.9499	.9006	.8262
	7	1.0000	1.0000	1.0000	.9998	.9988	.9957	.9878	.9707	.9390
	8	1.0000	1.0000	1.0000	1.0000	.9999	.9994	.9980	.9941	.9852
	9	1.0000	1.0000	1.0000	1.0000	1.0000	1.0000	.9998	.9993	.9978
	10	1.0000	1.0000	1.0000	1.0000	1.0000	1.0000	1.0000	1.0000	.9998
	11	1.0000	1.0000	1.0000	1.0000	1.0000	1.0000	1.0000	1.0000	1.0000
12	0	.5404	.2824	.1422	.0687	.0317	.0138	.0057	.0022	.0008
	1	.8816	.6590	.4435	.2749	.1584	.0850	.0424	.0196	.0083
	2	.9804	.8891	.7358	.5583	.3907	.2528	.1513	.0834	.0421
	3	.9978	.9744	.9078	.7946	.6488	.4925	.3467	.2253	.1345
	4	.9998	.9957	.9761	.9274	.8424	.7237	.5833	.4382	.3044
	5	1.0000	.9995	.9954	.9806	.9456	.8822	.7873	.6652	.5269
	6	1.0000	.9999	.9993	.9961	.9857	.9614	.9154	.8418	.7393
	7	1.0000	1.0000	.9999	.9994	.9972	.9905	.9745	.9427	.8883
	8	1.0000	1.0000	1.0000	.9999	.9996	.9983	.9944	.9847	.9644
	9	1.0000	1.0000	1.0000	1.0000	1.0000	.9998	.9992	.9972	.9921
	10	1.0000	1.0000	1.0000	1.0000	1.0000	1.0000	.9999	.9997	.9989
	11	1.0000	1.0000	1.0000	1.0000	1.0000	1.0000	1.0000	1.0000	.9999
	12	1.0000	1.0000	1.0000	1.0000	1.0000	1.0000	1.0000	1.0000	1.0000

							p				
n	*x*	.50	.55	.60	.65	.70	.75	.80	.85	.90	.95
9	0	.0020	.0008	.0003	.0001	.0000	.0000	.0000	.0000	.0000	.0000
	1	.0195	.0091	.0038	.0014	.0004	.0001	.0000	.0000	.0000	.0000
	2	.0898	.0498	.0250	.0112	.0043	.0013	.0003	.0006	.0001	.0000
	3	.2539	.1658	.0994	.0536	.0253	.0100	.0031	.0056	.0009	.0000
	4	.5000	.3786	.2666	.1717	.0988	.0489	.0196	.0339	.0083	.0006
	5	.7461	.6386	.5174	.3911	.2703	.1657	.0856	.1409	.0530	.0084
	6	.9102	.8505	.7682	.6627	.5372	.3993	.2618	.4005	.2252	.0712
	7	.9805	.9615	.9295	.8789	.8040	.6997	.5638	.7684	.6126	.3698
	8	.9980	.9954	.9899	.9793	.9596	.9249	.8658	1.0000	1.0000	1.0000
	9	1.0000	1.0000	1.0000	1.0000	1.0000	1.0000	1.0000			
10	0	.0010	.0003	.0001	.0000	.0000	.0000	.0000	.0000	.0000	.0000
	1	.0107	.0045	.0017	.0005	.0001	.0000	.0000	.0000	.0000	.0000
	2	.0547	.0274	.0123	.0048	.0016	.0004	.0001	.0000	.0000	.0000
	3	.1719	.1020	.0548	.0260	.0106	.0035	.0009	.0001	.0000	.0000
	4	.3770	.2616	.1662	.0949	.0473	.0197	.0064	.0014	.0001	.0000
	5	.6230	.4956	.3669	.2485	.1503	.0781	.0328	.0099	.0016	.0001
	6	.8281	.7340	.6177	.4862	.3504	.2241	.1209	.0500	.0128	.0010
	7	.9453	.9004	.8327	.7384	.6172	.4744	.3222	.1798	.0702	.0115
	8	.9893	.9767	.9536	.9140	.8507	.7560	.6242	.4557	.2639	.0861
	9	.9990	.9975	.9940	.9865	.9718	.9437	.8926	.8031	.6513	.4013
	10	1.0000	1.0000	1.0000	1.0000	1.0000	1.0000	1.0000	1.0000	1.0000	1.0000
11	0	.0005	.0002	.0000	.0000	.0000	.0000	.0000	.0000	.0000	.0000
	1	.0059	.0022	.0007	.0002	.0000	.0000	.0000	.0000	.0000	.0000
	2	.0327	.0148	.0059	.0020	.0006	.0001	.0000	.0000	.0000	.0000
	3	.1133	.0610	.0293	.0122	.0043	.0012	.0002	.0000	.0000	.0000
	4	.2744	.1738	.0994	.0501	.0216	.0076	.0020	.0003	.0000	.0000
	5	.5000	.3669	.2465	.1487	.0782	.0343	.0117	.0027	.0000	.0000
	6	.7256	.6029	.4672	.3317	.2103	.1146	.0504	.0159	.0003	.0001
	7	.8867	.8089	.7037	.5744	.4304	.2867	.1611	.0694	.0028	.0016
	8	.9673	.9348	.8811	.7999	.6873	.5448	.3826	.2212	.0896	.0152
	9	.9941	.9861	.9698	.9394	.8870	.8029	.6779	.5078	.3026	.1019
	10	.9995	.9986	.9964	.9912	.9802	.9578	.9141	.8327	.6862	.4312
	11	1.0000	1.0000	1.0000	1.0000	1.0000	1.0000	1.0000	1.0000	1.0000	1.0000
12	0	.0002	.0001	.0000	.0000	.0000	.0000	.0000	.0000	.0000	.0000
	1	.0032	.0011	.0003	.0001	.0000	.0000	.0000	.0000	.0000	.0000
	2	.0193	.0079	.0028	.0008	.0002	.0000	.0000	.0000	.0000	.0000
	3	.0730	.0356	.0153	.0056	.0017	.0004	.0001	.0000	.0000	.0000
	4	.1938	.1117	.0573	.0255	.0095	.0028	.0006	.0001	.0000	.0000
	5	.3872	.2607	.1582	.0846	.0386	.0143	.0039	.0007	.0001	.0000
	6	.6128	.4731	.3348	.2127	.1178	.0544	.0194	.0046	.0005	.0002
	7	.8062	.6956	.5618	.4167	.2763	.1576	.0726	.0239	.0043	.0022
	8	.9270	.8655	.7747	.6533	.5075	.3512	.2054	.0922	.0256	.0196
	9	.9807	.9579	.9166	.8487	.7472	.6093	.4417	.2642	.1109	.1184
	10	.9968	.9917	.9804	.9576	.9150	.8416	.7251	.5565	.3410	.4596
	11	.9998	.9992	.9978	.9943	.9862	.9683	.9313	.8578	.7176	1.0000
	12	1.0000	1.0000	1.0000	1.0000	1.0000	1.0000	1.0000	1.0000	1.0000	

(Table of binomial probabilities continued)

n	x	.05	.10	.15	.20	.25	.30	.35	.40	.45
									p	
13	0	.5133	.2542	.1209	.0550	.0238	.0097	.0037	.0013	.0004
	1	.8646	.6213	.3983	.2336	.1267	.0637	.0296	.0126	.0049
	2	.9755	.8661	.9620	.5017	.3326	.2025	.1132	.0579	.0269
	3	.9969	.9658	.8820	.7473	.5843	.4206	.2783	.1686	.0929
	4	.9997	.9935	.9658	.9009	.7940	.6543	.5005	.3530	.2279
	5	1.0000	.9991	.9925	.9700	.9198	.8346	.7159	.5744	.4268
	6	1.0000	.9999	.9987	.9930	.9757	.9376	.8705	.7712	.6437
	7	1.0000	1.0000	.9998	.9988	.9944	.9818	.9538	.9023	.8212
	8	1.0000	1.0000	1.0000	.9998	.9990	.9960	.9874	.9679	.9302
	9	1.0000	1.0000	1.0000	1.0000	.9999	.9993	.9975	.9922	.9797
	10	1.0000	1.0000	1.0000	1.0000	1.0000	.9999	.9997	.9987	.9959
	11	1.0000	1.0000	1.0000	1.0000	1.0000	1.0000	1.0000	.9999	.9995
	12	1.0000	1.0000	1.0000	1.0000	1.0000	1.0000	1.0000	1.0000	1.0000
	13	1.0000	1.0000	1.0000	1.0000	1.0000	1.0000	1.0000	1.0000	1.0000
14	0	.4877	.2288	.1028	.0440	.0178	.0068	.0024	.0008	.0002
	1	.8470	.5846	.3567	.1979	.1010	.0475	.0205	.0081	.0029
	2	.9699	.8416	.6479	.4481	.2811	.1608	.0839	.0398	.0170
	3	.9958	.9559	.8535	.6982	.5213	.3552	.2205	.1243	.0632
	4	.9996	.9908	.9533	.8702	.7415	.5842	.4227	.2793	.1672
	5	1.0000	.9985	.9885	.9561	.8883	.7805	.6405	.4859	.3373
	6	1.0000	.9998	.9978	.9884	.9617	.9067	.8164	.6925	.5461
	7	1.0000	1.0000	.9997	.9976	.9897	.9685	.9247	.8499	.7414
	8	1.0000	1.0000	1.0000	.9996	.9978	.9917	.9757	.9417	.8811
	9	1.0000	1.0000	1.0000	1.0000	.9997	.9983	.9940	.9825	.9574
	10	1.0000	1.0000	1.0000	1.0000	1.0000	.9998	.9989	.9961	.9886
	11	1.0000	1.0000	1.0000	1.0000	1.0000	1.0000	.9999	.9994	.9978
	12	1.0000	1.0000	1.0000	1.0000	1.0000	1.0000	1.0000	.9999	.9997
	13	1.0000	1.0000	1.0000	1.0000	1.0000	1.0000	1.0000	1.0000	1.0000
	14	1.0000	1.0000	1.0000	1.0000	1.0000	1.0000	1.0000	1.0000	1.0000
15	0	.4633	.2059	.0874	.0352	.0134	.0047	.0016	.0005	.0001
	1	.8290	.5490	.3186	.1671	.0802	.0353	.0142	.0052	.0017
	2	.9638	.8159	.6042	.3980	.2361	.1263	.0617	.0271	.0107
	3	.9945	.9444	.8227	.6482	.4613	.2969	.1727	.0905	.0424
	4	.9994	.9873	.9383	.8358	.6865	.5155	.3519	.2173	.1204
	5	.9999	.9978	.9832	.9389	.8516	.7216	.5643	.4032	.2608
	6	1.0000	.9997	.9964	.9819	.9434	.8689	.7548	.6098	.4522
	7	1.0000	1.0000	.9994	.9958	.9827	.9500	.8868	.7869	.6535
	8	1.0000	1.0000	.9999	.9992	.9958	.9848	.9578	.9050	.8182
	9	1.0000	1.0000	1.0000	.9999	.9992	.9963	.9876	.9662	.9231
	10	1.0000	1.0000	1.0000	1.0000	.9999	.9993	.9972	.9907	.9745
	11	1.0000	1.0000	1.0000	1.0000	1.0000	.9999	.9995	.9981	.9937
	12	1.0000	1.0000	1.0000	1.0000	1.0000	1.0000	.9999	.9997	.9989
	13	1.0000	1.0000	1.0000	1.0000	1.0000	1.0000	1.0000	1.0000	.9999
	14	1.0000	1.0000	1.0000	1.0000	1.0000	1.0000	1.0000	1.0000	1.0000
	15	1.0000	1.0000	1.0000	1.0000	1.0000	1.0000	1.0000	1.0000	1.0000

							p				
n	x	.50	.55	.60	.65	.70	.75	.80	.85	.90	.95
13	0	.0001	.0000	.0000	.0000	.0000	.0000	.0000	.0000	.0000	.0000
	1	.0017	.0005	.0001	.0000	.0000	.0000	.0000	.0000	.0000	.0000
	2	.0112	.0041	.0013	.0003	.0001	.0000	.0000	.0000	.0000	.0000
	3	.0461	.0203	.0078	.0025	.0007	.0001	.0000	.0000	.0000	.0000
	4	.1334	.0698	.0321	.0126	.0040	.0010	.0002	.0000	.0000	.0000
	5	.2905	.1788	.0977	.0462	.0182	.0056	.0012	.0002	.0000	.0000
	6	.5000	.3563	.2288	.1295	.0624	.0243	.0070	.0013	.0001	.0000
	7	.7095	.5732	.4256	.2841	.1654	.0802	.0300	.0075	.0009	.0000
	8	.8666	.7721	.6470	.4995	.3457	.2060	.0991	.0342	.0065	.0000
	9	.9539	.9071	.8314	.7217	.5794	.4157	.2527	.1180	.0342	.0003
	10	.9888	.9731	.9421	.8868	.7975	.6674	.4983	.3080	.1339	.0031
	11	.9983	.9951	.9874	.9704	.9363	.8733	.7664	.6017	.3787	.1354
	12	.9999	.9996	.9987	.9963	.9903	.9762	.9450	.8791	.7458	.4867
	13	1.0000	1.0000	1.0000	1.0000	1.0000	1.0000	1.0000	1.0000	.1.000	1.0000
14	0	.0001	.0000	.0000	.0000	.0000	.0000	.0000	.0000	.0000	0000
	1	.0009	.0003	.0001	.0000	.0000	.0000	.0000	.0000	.0000	.0000
	2	.0065	.0022	.0006	.0001	.0000	.0000	.0000	.0000	.0000	.0000
	3	.0287	.0114	.0039	.0011	.0002	.0000	.0000	.0000	.0000	.0000
	4	.0898	.0426	.0175	.0060	.0017	.0003	.0000	.0000	.0000	.0000
	5	.2120	.1189	.0583	.0243	.0083	.0022	.0004	.0000	.0000	.0000
	6	.3953	.2586	.1501	.0753	.0315	.0103	.0024	.0003	.0000	.0000
	7	.6047	.4539	.3075	.1836	.0933	.0383	.0116	.0022	.0002	.0000
	8	.7880	.6627	.5141	.3595	.2195	.1117	.0439	.0115	.0015	.0000
	9	.9102	.8328	.7207	.5773	.4158	.2585	.1298	.0467	.0092	.0004
	10	.9713	.9368	.8757	.7795	.6448	.4787	.3018	.1465	.0441	.0042
	11	.9935	.9830	.9602	.9161	.8392	.7189	.5519	.3521	.1584	.0301
	12	.9991	.9971	.9919	.9795	.9525	.8990	.8021	.6433	.4154	.1530
	13	.9999	.9998	.9992	.9976	.9932	.9822	.9560	.8972	.7712	.5123
	14	1.0000	1.0000	1.0000	1.0000	1.0000	1.0000	1.0000	1.0000	1.0000	1.0000
15	0	.0000	.0000	.0000	.0000	.0000	.0000	.0000	.0000	.0000	.0000
	1	.0005	.0001	.0000	.0000	.0000	.0000	.0000	.0000	.0000	.0000
	2	.0037	.0011	.0003	.0001	.0000	.0000	.0000	.0000	.0000	.0000
	3	.0176	.0063	.0019	.0005	.0001	.0000	.0000	.0000	.0000	.0000
	4	.0592	.0255	.0093	.0028	.0007	.0001	.0000	.0000	.0000	.0000
	5	.1509	.0769	.0333	.0124	.0037	.0008	.0001	.0000	.0000	.0000
	6	.3036	.1818	.0950	.0422	.0152	.0042	.0008	.0001	.0000	.0000
	7	.5000	.3465	.2131	.1132	.0500	.0173	.0042	.0006	.0000	.0000
	8	.6964	.5478	.3902	.2452	.1311	.0566	.0181	.0036	.0003	.0000
	9	.8491	.7392	.5968	.4357	.2784	.1484	.0611	.0168	.0022	.0001
	10	.9408	.8796	.7827	.6481	.4845	.3135	.1642	.0617	.0127	.0006
	11	.9824	.9576	.9095	.8273	.7031	.5387	.3518	.1773	.0556	.0055
	12	.9963	.9893	.9729	.9383	.8732	.7639	.6020	.3958	.1841	.0362
	13	.9995	.9983	.9948	.9858	.9647	.9198	.8329	.6814	.4510	.1710
	14	1.0000	.9999	.9995	.9984	.9953	.9866	.9648	.9126	.7941	.5367
	15	1.0000	1.0000	1.0000	1.0000	1.0000	1.0000	1.0000	1.0000	1.0000	1.0000

(Table of binomial probabilities continued)

						p				
n	x	.05	.10	.15	.20	.25	.30	.35	.40	.45
16	0	.4401	.1853	.0743	.0281	.0100	.0033	.0010	.0003	.0001
	1	.8108	.5147	.2839	.1407	.0635	.0261	.0098	.0033	.0010
	2	.9571	.7892	.5614	.3518	.1971	.0994	.0451	.0183	.0066
	3	.9930	.9316	.7899	.5981	.4050	.2459	.1339	.0651	.0281
	4	.9991	.9830	.9209	.7982	.6302	.4499	.2892	.1666	.0853
	5	.9999	.9967	.9765	.9183	.8103	.6598	.4900	.3288	.1976
	6	1.0000	.9995	.9944	.9733	.9204	.8247	.6881	.5272	.3660
	7	1.0000	.9999	.9989	.9930	.9729	.9256	.8406	.7161	.5629
	8	1.0000	1.0000	.9998	.9985	.9925	.9743	.9329	.8577	.7441
	9	1.0000	1.0000	1.0000	.9998	.9984	.9929	.9771	.9417	.8759
	10	1.0000	1.0000	1.0000	1.0000	.9997	.9984	.9938	.9809	.9514
	11	1.0000	1.0000	1.0000	1.0000	1.0000	.9997	.9987	.9951	9851
	12	1.0000	1.0000	1.0000	1.0000	1.0000	1.0000	.9998	.9991	.9965
	13	1.0000	1.0000	1.0000	1.0000	1.0000	1.0009	1.0000	.9999	.9994
	14	1.0000	1.0000	1.0000	1.0000	1.0000	1.0900	1.0000	1.0000	.9999
	15	1.0000	1.0000	1.0000	1.0000	1.0000	1.0000	1.0000	1.0000	1.0000
	16	1.0000	1.0000	1.0000	1.0000	1.0000	1.0000	1.0000	1.0000	1.0000
17	0	.4181	.1668	.0631	.0225	.0075	.0023	.0007	.0002	.0000
	1	.7922	.4818	.2525	.1182	.0501	.0193	.0067	.0021	.0006
	2	.9497	.7618	.5198	.3096	.1637	.0774	.0327	.0123	.0041
	3	.9912	.9174	.7556	.5489	.3530	.2019	.1028	.0464	.0184
	4	.9988	.9779	.9013	.7582	.5739	.3887	.2348	.1260	.0596
	5	.9999	.9953	.9681	.8943	.7653	.5968	.4197	.2639	.1471
	6	1.0000	.9992	.9917	.9623	.8929	.7752	.6188	.4478	.2902
	7	1.0000	.9999	.9983	.9861	.9598	.8954	.7872	.6405	.4743
	8	1.0000	1.0000	.9997	.9974	.9876	.9597	.9006	.8011	.6626
	9	1.0000	1.0000	1.0000	.9995	.9969	.9873	.9617	.9081	.8166
	10	1.0000	1.0000	1.0000	.9999	.9994	.9968	.9880	.9652	.9174
	11	1.0000	1.0000	1.0000	1.0000	.9999	.9993	.9970	.9894	.9699
	12	1.0000	1.0000	1.0000	1.0000	1.0000	.9999	.9994	.9975	.9914
	13	1.0000	1.0000	1.0000	1.0000	1.0000	1.0000	.9999	.9995	.9981
	14	1.0000	1.0000	1.0000	1.0000	1.0000	1.0000	1.0000	.9999	.9997
	15	1.0000	1.0000	1.0000	1.0000	1.0000	1.0000	1.0000	1.0000	1.0000
	16	1.0000	1.0000	1.0000	1.0000	1.0000	1.0000	1.0000	1.0000	1.0000
	17	1.0000	1.0000	1.0000	1.0000	1.0000	1.0000	1.0000	1.0000	1.0000

							p				
n	x	.50	.55	.60	.65	.70	.75	.80	.85	.90	.95
16	0	.0000	.0000	.0000	.0000	.0000	.0000	.0000	.0000	.0000	.0000
	1	.0003	.0001	.0000	.0000	.0000	.0000	.0000	.0000	.0000	.0000
	2	.0021	.0006	.0001	.0000	.0000	.0000	.0000	.0000	.0000	.0000
	3	.0106	.0035	.0009	.0002	.0003	.0000	.0000	.0000	.0000	.0000
	4	.0384	.0149	.0049	.0013	.0016	.0003	.0000	.0000	.0000	.0000
	5	.1051	.0486	.0191	.0062	.0071	.0016	.0002	.0000	.0000	.0000
	6	.2272	.1241	.0583	.0229	.0257	.0075	.0015	.0002	.0000	.0000
	7	.4018	.2559	.1423	.0671	.0744	.0271	.0070	.0011	.0001	.0000
	8	.5982	.4371	.2839	.1594	.1753	.0796	.0267	.0056	.0005	.0000
	9	.7728	.6340	.4728	.3119	.3402	.1897	.0817	.0235	.0033	.0001
	10	.8949	.8024	.6712	.5100	.5501	.3698	.2018	.0791	.0170	.0009
	11	.9616	.9147	.8334	.7108	.7541	.5950	.4019	.2101	.0684	.0070
	12	.9894	.9719	.9349	.8661	.9006	.8029	.6482	.4386	.2108	.0429
	13	.9979	.9934	.9817	.9549	.9739	.9365	.8593	.7161	.4853	.1892
	14	.9997	.9990	.9967	.9902	.9967	.9900	.9719	.9257	.8147	.5599
	15	1.0000	.9999	.9997	.9990	1.0000	1.0000	1.0000	1.0000	1.0000	1.0000
	16	1.0000	1.0000	1.0000	1.0000						
17	0	.0000	.0000	.0000	.0000	.0000	.0000	.0000	.0000	.0000	.0000
	1	.0001	.0000	.0000	.0000	.0000	.0000	.0000	.0000	.0000	.0000
	2	.0012	.0003	.0001	.0000	.0000	.0000	.0000	.0000	.0000	.0000
	3	.0064	.0019	.0005	.0001	.0000	.0000	.0000	.0000	.0000	.0000
	4	.0245	.0086	.0025	.0006	.0001	.0001	.0000	.0000	.0000	.0000
	5	.0717	.0301	.0106	.0030	.0007	.0006	.0001	.0000	.0000	.0000
	6	.1662	.0826	.0348	.0120	.0127	.0031	.0005	.0000	.0000	.0000
	7	.3145	.1834	.0919	.0383	.0403	.0124	.0026	.0003	.0000	.0000
	8	.5000	.3374	.1989	.0994	.1046	.0402	.0109	.0017	.0001	.0000
	9	.6855	.5257	.3595	.2128	.2248	.1071	.0377	.0083	.0008	.0000
	10	.8338	.7098	.5522	.3812	.4032	.2347	.1057	.0319	.0047	.0001
	11	.9283	.8529	.7361	.5803	.6113	.4261	.2418	.0987	.0221	.0012
	12	.9755	.9404	.8740	.7652	.7981	.6470	.4511	.2444	.0826	.0088
	13	.9936	.9816	.9536	.8972	.9226	.8363	.6904	.4802	.2382	.0503
	14	.9988	.9959	.9877	.9673	.9807	.9499	.8818	.7475	.5182	.2078
	15	.9999	.9994	.9979	.9933	.9977	.9925	.9775	.9369	.8332	.5819
	16	1.0000	1.0000	.9998	.9993	1.0000	1.0000	1.0000	1.0000	1.0000	1.0000
	17	1.0000	1.0000	1.0000	1.0000						

(Table of binomial probabilities continued)

n	x	.05	.10	.15	.20	.25	.30	.35	.40	.45
						p				
18	0	.3972	.1501	.0536	.0180	.0056	.0016	.0004	.0001	.0000
	1	.7735	.4503	.2241	.0991	.0395	.0142	.0046	.0013	.0003
	2	.9419	.7338	.4797	.2713	.1353	.0600	.0236	.0082	.0025
	3	.9891	.9018	.7202	.5010	.3057	.1646	.0783	.0328	.0120
	4	.9985	.9718	.8794	.7164	.5187	.3327	.1886	.0942	.0411
	5	.9998	.9936	.9581	.8671	.7175	.5344	.3550	.2088	.1077
	6	1.0000	.9988	.9882	.9487	.8610	.7217	.5491	.3743	.2258
	7	1.0000	.9998	.9973	.9837	.9431	.8593	.7283	.5634	.3915
	8	1.0000	1.0000	.9995	.9957	.9807	.9404	.8609	.7368	.5778
	9	1.0000	1.0000	.9999	.9991	.9946	.9790	.9403	.8653	.7473
	10	1.0000	1.0000	1.0000	.9998	.9988	.9939	.9788	.9424	.8720
	11	1.0000	1.0000	1.0000	1.0000	.9998	.9986	.9938	.9797	.9463
	12	1.0000	1.0000	1.0000	1.0000	1.0000	.9997	.9986	.9942	.9817
	13	1.0000	1.0000	1.0000	1.0000	1.0000	1.0000	.9997	.9987	.9951
	14	1.0000	1.0000	1.0000	1.0000	1.0000	1.0000	1.0000	.9998	.9990
	15	1.0000	1.0000	1.0000	1.0000	1.0000	1.0000	1.0000	1.0000	.9999
	16	1.0000	1.0000	1.0000	1.0000	1.0000	1.0000	1.0000	1.0000	1.0000
	17	1.0000	1.0000	1.0000	1.0000	1.0000	1.0000	1.0000	1.0000	1.0000
	18	1.0000	1.0000	1.0000	1.0000	1.0000	1.0000	1.0000	1.0000	1.0000
19	0	.3774	.1351	.0456	.0144	.0042	.0011	.0003	.0001	.0000
	1	.7547	.4203	.1985	.0829	.0310	.0104	.0031	.0008	.0002
	2	.9335	.7054	.4413	.2369	.1113	.0462	.0170	.0055	.0015
	3	.9868	.8850	.6841	.4551	.2631	.1332	.0591	.0230	.0077
	4	.9980	.9648	.8556	.6733	.4654	.2822	.1500	.0696	.0280
	5	.9998	.9914	.9463	.8369	.6678	.4739	.2968	.1629	.0777
	6	1.0000	.9983	.9837	.9324	.8251	.6655	.4812	.3081	.1727
	7	1.0000	.9997	.9959	.9767	.9225	.8180	.6656	.4878	.3169
	8	1.0000	1.0000	.9992	.9933	.9713	.9161	.8145	.6675	.4940
	9	1.0000	1.0000	.9999	.9984	.9911	.9674	.9125	.8139	.6710
	10	1.0000	1.0000	1.0000	.9997	.9977	.9895	.9653	.9115	.8159
	11	1.0000	1.0000	1.0000	1.0000	.9995	.9972	.9886	.9648	.9129
	12	1.0000	1.0000	1.0000	1.0000	.9999	.9994	.9969	.9884	.9658
	13	1.0000	1.0000	1.0000	1.0000	1.0000	.9999	.9993	.9969	.9891
	14	1.0000	1.0000	1.0000	1.0000	1.0000	1.0000	.9999	.9994	.9972
	15	1.0000	1.0000	1.0000	1.0000	1.0000	1.0000	1.0000	.9999	.9995
	16	1.0000	1.0000	1.0000	1.0000	1.0000	1.0000	1.0000	1.0000	.9999
	17	1.0000	1.0000	1.0000	1.0000	1.0000	1.0000	1.0000	1.0000	1.0000
	18	1.0000	1.0000	1.0000	1.0000	1.0000	1.0000	1.0000	1.0000	1.0000
	19	1.0000	1.0000	1.0000	1.0000	1.0000	1.0000	1.0000	1.0000	1.0000

						p					
n	x	.50	.55	.60	.65	.70	.75	.80	.85	.90	.95
18	0	.0000	.0000	.0000	.0000	.0000	.0000	.0000	.0000	.0000	.0000
	1	.0001	.0000	.0000	.0000	.0000	.0000	.0000	.0000	.0000	.0000
	2	.0007	.0001	.0000	.0000	.0000	.0000	.0000	.0000	.0000	.0000
	3	.0038	.0010	.0002	.0000	.0000	.0000	.0000	.0000	.0000	.0000
	4	.0154	.0049	.0013	.0003	.0003	.0000	.0000	.0000	.0000	.0000
	5	.0481	.0183	.0058	.0062	.0014	.0000	.0000	.0000	.0000	.0000
	6	.1189	.0537	.0203	.0212	.0014	.0002	.0002	.0000	.0000	.0000
	7	.2403	.1280	.0576	.0597	.0061	.0054	.0009	.0001	.0000	.0000
	8	.4073	.2527	.1347	.1391	.0210	.0193	.0043	.0005	.0000	.0000
	9	.5927	.4222	.2632	.2717	.0596	.0569	.0163	.0027	.0002	.0000
	10	.7597	.6085	.4366	.4509	.1407	.1390	.0513	.0118	.0012	.0000
	11	.8811	.7742	.6257	.6450	.2783	.2825	.1329	.0419	.0064	.0002
	12	.9519	.8923	.7912	.8114	.4656	.4813	.2836	.1206	.0282	.0015
	13	.9846	.9589	.9058	.9217	.6673	.6943	.4990	.2798	.0982	.0109
	14	.9962	.9880	.9672	.9764	.8354	.8647	.7287	.5203	.2662	.0581
	15	.9993	.9975	.9918	.9954	.9400	.9605	.9009	.7759	.5497	.2265
	16	.9999	.9997	.9987	.9996	.9858	.9944	.9820	.9464	.8499	.6028
	17	1.0000	1.0000	.9999	1.0000	.9984	1.0000	.9820	.9464	.8499	.6028
	18	1.0000	1.0000	1.0000	1.0000	1.0000	1.0000	1.000	1.0000	1.0000	1.0000
19	0	.0000	.0000	.0000	.0000	.0000	.0000	.0000	.0000.	.0000	.0000
	1	.0000	.0000	.0000	.0000	.0000	.0000	.0000	.0000	.0000	.0000
	2	.0004	.0001	.0000	.0000	.0000	.0000	.0000	.0000	.0000	.0000
	3	.0022	.0005	.0001	.0000	.0000	.0000	.0000	.0000	.0000	.0000
	4	.0096	.0028	.0006	.0001	.0001	.0000	.0000	.0000	.0000	.0000
	5	.0318	.0109	.0031	.0007	.0006	.0001	.0000	.0000	.0000	.0000
	6	.0835	.0342	.0116	.0114	.0028	.0005	.0000	.0000	.0000	.0000
	7	.1796	.0871	.0352	.0347	.0105	.0023	.0003	.0000	.0000	.0000
	8	.3238	.1841	.0885	.0875	.0326	.0089	.0016	.0001	.0000	.0000
	9	.5000	.3290	.1861	.1855	.0839	.0287	.0067	.0008	.0000	.0000
	10	.6762	.5060	.3325	.3344	.1820	.0775	.0233	.0041	.0003	.0000
	11	.8204	.6831	.5122	.5188	.3345	.1749	.0676	.0163	.0017	.0000
	12	.9165	.8273	.6919	.7032	.5261	.3322	.1631	.0537	.0086	.0002
	13	.9682	.9223	.8371	.8500	.7178	.5346	.3267	.1444	.0352	.0020
	14	.9904	.9720	.9304	.9409	.8668	.7369	.5449	.3159	.1150	.0132
	15	.9978	.9923	.9770	.9830	.9538	.8887	.7631	.5587	.2946	.0665
	16	.9996	.9985	.9945	.9969	.9896	.9690	.9171	.8015	.5797	.2453
	17	1.0000	.9998	.9992	.9997	.9989	.9958	.9856	.9544	.8649	.6226
	18	1.0000	1.0000	.9999	1.0000	1.0000	1.0000	.9856	.9544	.8649	.6226
	19	1.0000	1.0000	1.0000	1.0000	1.0000	1.0000	1.0000	1.0000	1.0000	1.0000

(Table of binomial probabilities continued)

						p				
n	x	.05	.10	.15	.20	.25	.30	.35	.40	.45
20	0	.3585	.1216	.0388	.0115	.0032	.0008	.0002	.0000	0000
	1	.7358	.3917	.1756	.0692	.0243	.0076	.0021	.0005	.0001
	2	.9245	.6769	.4049	.2061	.0913	.0355	.0121	.0036	.0009
	3	.9841	.8670	.6477	.4114	.2252	.1071	.0444	.0160	.0049
	4	.9974	.9568	.8298	.6296	.4148	.2375	.1182	.0510	.0189
	5	.9997	.9887	.9327	.8042	.6172	.4164	.2454	.1256	.0553
	6	1.0000	.9976	.9781	.9133	.7858	.6080	.4166	.2500	.1299
	7	1.0000	.9996	.9941	.9679	.8982	.7723	.6010	.4159	.2520
	8	1.0000	.9999	.9987	.9900	.9591	.8867	.7624	.5956	.4143
	9	1.0000	1.0000	.9998	.9974	.9861	.9520	.8782	.7553	.5914
	10	1.0000	1.0000	1.0000	.9994	.9961	.9829	.9468	.8725	.7507
	11	1.0000	1.0000	1.0000	.9999	.9991	.9949	.9804	.9435	.8692
	12	1.0000	1.0000	1.0000	1.0000	.9998	.9987	.9940	.9790	.9420
	13	1.0000	1.0000	1.0000	1.0000	1.0000	.9997	.9985	.9935	.8692
	14	1.0000	1.0000	1.0000	1.0000	1.0000	1.0000	.9997	.9984	.9936
	15	1.0000	1.0000	1.0000	1.0000	1.0000	1.0000	1.0000	.9997	.9985
	16	1.0000	1.0000	1.0000	1.0000	1.0000	1.0000	1.0000	1.0000	.9997
	17	1.0000	1.0000	1.0000	1.0000	1.0000	1.0000	1.0000	1.0000	1.0000
	18	1.0000	1.0000	1.0000	1.0000	1.0000	1.0000	1.0000	1.0000	1.0000
	19	1.0000	1.0000	1.0000	1.0000	1.0000	1.0000	1.0000	1.0000	1.0000
	20	1.0000	1.0000	1.0000	1.0000	1.0000	1.0000	1.0000	1.0000	1.0000
21	0	.3406	.1094	.0329	.0092	.0024	.0006	.0001	.0000	.0000
	1	.7170	.3647	.1550	.0576	.0190	.0056	.0014	.0003	.0001
	2	.9151	.6484	.3705	.1787	.0745	.0271	.0086	.0024	.0006
	3	.9811	.8480	.6113	.3704	.1917	.0856	.0331	.0110	.0031
	4	.9968	.9478	.8025	.5860	.3674	.1984	.0924	.0370	.0126
	5	.9996	.9856	.9173	.7693	.5666	.3627	.2009	.0957	.0389
	6	1.0000	.9967	.9713	.8915	.7436	.5505	.3567	.2002	.0964
	7	1.0000	.9994	.9917	.9569	.8701	.7230	.5365	.3495	.1971
	8	1.0000	.9999	.9980	.9856	.9439	.8523	.7059	.5237	.3413
	9	1.0000	1.0000	.9996	.9959	.9794	.9324	.8377	.6914	.5117
	10	1.0000	1.0000	.9999	.9990	.9936	.9736	.9228	.8256	.6790
	11	1.0000	1.0000	1.0000	.9998	.9983	.9913	.9687	.9151	.8159
	12	1.0000	1.0000	1.0000	1.0000	.9996	.9976	.9892	.9648	.9092
	13	1.0000	1.0000	1.0000	1.0000	.9999	.9994	.9969	.9877	.9621
	14	1.0000	1.0000	1.0000	1.0000	1.0000	.9999	.9993	.9964	.9868
	15	1.0000	1.0000	1.0000	1.0000	1.0000	1.0000	.9999	.9992	.9963
	16	1.0000	1.0000	1.0000	1.0000	1.0000	1.0000	1.0000	.9998	.9992
	17	1.0000	1.0000	1.0000	1.0000	1.0000	1.0000	1.0000	1.0000	.9999
	18	1.0000	1.0000	1.0000	1.0000	1.0000	1.0000	1.0000	1.0000	1.0000
	19	1.0000	1.0000	1.0000	1.0000	1.0000	1.0000	1.0000	1.0000	1.0000
	20	1.0000	1.0000	1.0000	1.0000	1.0000	1.0000	1.0000	1.0000	1.0000
	21	1.0000	1.0000	1.0000	1.0000	1.0000	1.0000	1.0000	1.0000	1.0000

							p				
n	x	.50	.55	.60	.65	.70	.75	.80	.85	.90	.95
20	0	.0000	.0000	.0000	.0000	.0000	.0000	.0000	.0000	.0000	.0000
	1	.0000	.0000	.0000	.0000	.0000	.0000	.0000	.0000	.0000	.0000
	2	.0002	.0000	.0000	.0000	.0000	.0000	.0000	.0000	.0000	.0000
	3	.0013	.0003	.0000	.0000	.0000	.0000	.0000	.0000	.0000	.0000
	4	.0059	.0015	.0003	.0000	.0000	.0000	.0000	.0000	.0000	.0000
	5	.0207	.0064	.0016	.0003	.0000	.0000	.0000	.0000	.0000	.0000
	6	.0577	.0214	.0065	.0015	.0003	.0000	.0000	.0000	.0000	.0000
	7	.1316	.0580	.0210	.0060	.0013	.0002	.0000	.0000	.0000	.0000
	8	.2517	.1308	.0565	.0196	.0051	.0009	.0001	.0000	.0000	.0000
	9	.4119	.2493	.1275	.0532	.0171	.0039	.0006	.0000	.0000	.0000
	10	.5881	.4086	.2447	.1218	.0480	.0139	.0026	.0002	.0000	.0000
	11	.7483	.5857	.4044	.2376	.1133	.0409	.0100	.0013	.0001	.0000
	12	.8684	.7480	.5841	.3990	.2277	.1018	.0321	.0059	.0004	.0000
	13	.9423	.8701	.7500	.5834	.3920	.2142	.0867	.0219	.0024	.0000
	14	.9793	.9447	.8744	.7546	.5836	.3828	.1958	.0673	.0113	.0003
	15	.9941	.9811	.9490	.8818	.7625	.5852	.3704	.1702	.0432	.0026
	16	.9987	.9951	.9840	.9556	.8929	.7748	.5886	.3523	.1330	.0159
	17	.9998	.9991	.9964	.9879	.9645	.9087	.7939	.5951	.3231	.0755
	18	1.0000	.9999	.9995	.9979	.9924	.9757	.9308	.8244	.6083	.2642
	19	1.0000	1.0000	1.0000	.9998	.9992	.9968	.9885	.9612	.8784	.6415
	20	1.0000	1.0000	1.0000	1.0000	1.0000	1.0000	1.0000	1.0000	1.0000	1.0000
21	0	.0000	.0000	.0000	.0000	.0000	.0000	.0000	.0000	.0000	.0000
	1	.0000	.0000	.0000	.0000	.0000	.0000	.0000	.0000	.0000	.0000
	2	.0001	.0000	.0000	.0000	.0000	.0000	.0000	.0000	.0000	.0000
	3	.0007	.0001	.0000	.0000	.0000	.0000	.0000	.0000	.0000	.0000
	4	.0036	.0008	.0002	.0000	.0000	.0000	.0000	.0000	.0000	.0000
	5	.0133	.0037	.0008	.0001	.0000	.0000	.0000	.0000	.0000	.0000
	6	.0392	.0132	.0036	.0007	.0001	.0000	.0000	.0000	.0000	.0000
	7	.0946	.0379	.0123	.0031	.0006	.0001	.0000	.0000	.0000	.0000
	8	.1917	.0908	.0352	.0108	.0024	.0004	.0000	.0000	.0000	.0000
	9	.3318	.1841	.0849	.0313	.0087	.0017	.0002	.0000	.0000	.0000
	10	.5000	.3210	.1744	.0772	.0264	.0064	.0010	.0001	.0000	.0000
	11	.6682	.4883	.3086	.1623	.0676	.0206	.0041	.0004	.0000	.0000
	12	.8083	.6587	.4763	.2941	.1477	.0561	.0144	.0020	.0001	.0000
	13	.9054	.8029	.6505	.4635	.2770	.1299	.0431	.0083	.0006	.0000
	14	.9608	.9036	.7998	.6433	.4495	.2564	.1085	.0287	.0033	.0000
	15	.9867	.9611	.9043	.7991	.6373	.4334	.2307	.0827	.0144	.0004
	16	.9964	.9874	.9630	.9076	.8016	.6326	.4140	.1975	.0522	.0032
	17	.9993	.9969	.9890	.9669	.9144	.8083	.6296	.3887	.1520	.0189
	18	.9999	.9994	.9976	.9914	.9729	.9255	.8213	.6295	.3516	.0849
	19	1.0000	.9999	.9997	.9986	.9944	.9810	.9424	.8450	.6353	.2830
	20	1.0000	1.0000	1.0000	.9999	.9994	.9976	.9908	.9671	.8906	.6594
	21	1.0000	1.0000	1.0000	1.0000	1.0000	1.0000	1.0000	1.0000	1.0000	1.0000

(Table of binomial probabilities continued)

n	x	.05	.10	.15	.20	.25	.30	.35	.40	.45
22	0	.3235	.0985	.0280	.0074	.0018	.0004	.0001	.0000	.0000
	1	.6982	.3392	.1367	.0480	.0149	.0041	.0010	.0002	.0000
	2	.9052	.6200	.3382	.1545	.0606	.0207	.0061	.0016	.0003
	3	.9778	.8281	.5752	.3320	.1624	.0681	.0245	.0076	.0020
	4	.9960	.9379	.7738	.5429	.3235	.1645	.0716	.0266	.0083
	5	.9994	.9818	.9001	.7326	.5168	.3134	.1629	.0722	.0271
	6	.9999	.9956	.9632	.8670	.6994	.4942	.3022	.1584	.0705
	7	1.0000	.9991	.9886	.9439	.8385	.6713	.4736	.2898	.1518
	8	1.0000	.9999	.9970	.9799	.9254	.8135	.6466	.4540	.2764
	9	1.0000	1.0000	.9993	.9939	.9705	.9084	.7916	.6244	.4350
	10	1.0000	1.0000	.9999	.9984	.9900	.9613	.8930	.7720	.6037
	11	1.0000	1.0000	1.0000	.9997	.9971	.9860	.9526	.8793	.7543
	12	1.0000	1.0000	1.0000	.9999	.9993	.9957	.9820	.9449	.8672
	13	1.0000	1.0000	1.0000	1.0000	.9999	.9989	.9942	.9785	.9383
	14	1.0000	1.0000	1.0000	1.0000	1.0000	.9998	.9984	.9930	.9757
	15	1.0000	1.0000	1.0000	1.0000	1.0000	1.0000	.9997	.9981	.9920
	16	1.0000	1.0000	1.0000	1.0000	1.0000	1.0000	.9999	.9996	.9979
	17	1.0000	1.0000	1.0000	1.0000	1.0000	1.0000	1.0000	.9999	.9995
	18	1.0000	1.0000	1.0000	1.0000	1.0000	1.0000	1.0000	1.0000	.9999
	19	1.0000	1.0000	1.0000	1.0000	1.0000	1.0000	1.0000	1.0000	1.0000
	20	1.0000	1.0000	1.0000	1.0000	1.0000	1.0000	1.0000	1.0000	1.0000
	21	1.0000	1.0000	1.0000	1.0000	1.0000	1.0000	1.0000	1.0000	1.0000
	22	1.0000	1.0000	1.0000	1.0000	1.0000	1.0000	1.0000	1.0000	1.0000
23	0	.3074	.0886	.0238	.0059	.0013	.0003	.0000	.0000	.0000
	1	.6794	.3151	.1204	.0398	.0116	.0030	.0007	.0001	.0000
	2	.8948	.5920	.3080	.1332	.0492	.0157	.0043	.0010	.0002
	3	.9742	.8073	.5396	.2965	.1370	.0538	.0181	.0052	.0012
	4	.9951	.9269	.7440	.5007	.2832	.1356	.0551	.0190	.0055
	5	.9992	.9774	.8811	.6947	.4685	.2688	.1309	.0540	.0186
	6	.9999	.9942	.9537	.8402	.6537	.4399	.2534	.1240	.0510
	7	1.0000	.9988	.9848	.9285	.8037	.6181	.4136	.2373	.1152
	8	1.0000	.9998	.9958	.9727	.9037	.7709	.5860	.3884	.2203
	9	1.0000	1.0000	.9990	.9911	.9592	.8799	.7408	.5562	.3636
	10	1.0000	1.0000	.9998	.9975	.9851	.9454	.8575	.7129	.5278
	11	1.0000	1.0000	1.0000	.9994	.9954	.9786	.9318	.8364	.6865
	12	1.0000	1.0000	1.0000	.9999	.9988	.9928	.9717	.9187	.8164
	13	1.0000	1.0000	1.0000	1.0000	.9997	.9979	.9900	.9651	.9063
	14	1.0000	1.0000	1.0000	1.0000	.9999	.9995	.9970	.9872	.9589
	15	1.0000	1.0000	1.0000	1.0000	1.0000	.9999	.9992	.9960	.9847
	16	1.0000	1.0000	1.0000	1.0000	1.0000	1.0000	.9998	.9990	.9952
	17	1.0000	1.0000	1.0000	1.0000	1.0000	1.0000	1.0000	.9998	.9988
	18	1.0000	1.0000	1.0000	1.0000	1.0000	1.0000	1.0000	1.0000	.9998
	19	1.0000	1.0000	1.0000	1.0000	1.0000	1.0000	1.0000	1.0000	1.0000
	20	1.0000	1.0000	1.0000	1.0000	1.0000	1.0000	1.0000	1.0000	1.0000
	21	1.0000	1.0000	1.0000	1.0000	1.0000	1.0000	1.0000	1.0000	1.0000
	22	1.0000	1.0000	1.0000	1.0000	1.0000	1.0000	1.0000	1.0000	1.0000
	23	1.0000	1.0000	1.0000	1.0000	1.0000	1.0000	1.0000	1.0000	1.0000

						p					
n	x	.50	.55	.60	.65	.70	.75	.80	.85	.90	.95
22	0	.0000	.0000	.0000	.0000	.0000	.0000	.0000	.0000	.0000	.0000
	1	.0000	.0000	.0000	.0000	.0000	.0000	.0000	.0000	.0000	.0000
	2	.0001	.0000	.0000	.0000	.0000	.0000	.0000	.0000	.0000	.0000
	3	.0004	.0001	.0000	.0000	.0000	.0000	.0000	.0000	.0000	.0000
	4	.0022	.0005	.0001	.0000	.0000	.0000	.0000	.0000	.0000	.0000
	5	.0085	.0021	.0004	.0001	.0000	.0000	.0000	.0000	.0000	.0000
	6	.0262	.0080	.0019	.0003	.0000	.0000	.0000	.0000	.0000	.0000
	7	.0669	.0243	.0070	.0016	.0002	.0000	.0000	.0000	.0000	.0000
	8	.1431	.0617	.0215	.0058	.0011	.0001	.0000	.0000	.0000	.0000
	9	.2617	.1328	.0551	.0180	.0043	.0007	.0001	.0000	.0000	.0000
	10	.4159	.2457	.1207	.0474	.0140	.0029	.0003	.0000	.0000	.0000
	11	.5841	.3963	.2280	.1070	.0387	.0100	.0016	.0001	.0000	.0000
	12	.7383	.5650	.3756	.2084	.0916	.0295	.0061	.0007	.0000	.0000
	13	.8569	.7236	.5460	.3534	.1865	.0746	.0201	.0030	.0001	.0000
	14	.9331	.8482	.7102	.5264	.3287	.1615	.0561	.0114	.0009	.0000
	15	.9738	.9295	.8416	.6978	.5058	.3006	.1330	.0368	.0044	.0001
	16	.9915	.9729	.9278	.8371	.6866	.4832	.2674	.0999	.0182	.0006
	17	.9978	.9917	.9734	.9284	.8355	.6765	.4571	.2262	.0621	.0040
	18	.9996	.9980	.9924	.9755	.9319	.8376	.6680	.4248	.1719	.0222
	19	.9999	.9997	.9984	.9939	.9793	.9394	.8455	.6618	.3800	.0948
	20	1.0000	1.0000	.9998	.9990	.9959	.9851	.9520	.8633	.6608	.3018
	21	1.0000	1.0000	1.0000	.9999	.9996	.9982	.9926	.9720	.9015	.6765
	21	1.0000	1.0000	1.0000	1.0000	1.0000	1.0000	1.0000	1.0000	1.0000	1.0000
23	0	.0000	.0000	.0000	.0000	.0000	.0000	.0000	.0000	.0000	.0000
	1	.0000	.0000	.0000	.0000	.0000	.0000	.0000	.0000	.0000	.0000
	2	.0000	.0000	.0000	.0000	.0000	.0000	.0000	.0000	.0000	.0000
	3	.0002	.0000	.0000	.0000	.0000	.0000	.0000	.0000	.0000	.0000
	4	.0013	.0002	.0000	.0000	.0000	.0000	.0000	.0000	.0000	.0000
	5	.0053	.0012	.0002	.0000	.0000	.0000	.0000	.0000	.0000	.0000
	6	.0173	.0048	.0010	.0002	.0000	.0000	.0000	.0000	.0000	.0000
	7	.0466	.0153	.0040	.0008	.0001	.0000	.0000	.0000	.0000	.0000
	8	.1050	.0411	.0128	.0030	.0005	.0001	.0000	.0000	.0000	.0000
	9	.2024	.0937	.0349	.0100	.0021	.0003	.0000	.0000	.0000	.0000
	10	.3388	.1836	.0813	.0283	.0072	.0012	.0001	.0000	.0000	.0000
	11	.5000	.3135	.1636	.0682	.0214	.0046	.0006	.0000	.0000	.0000
	12	.6612	.4722	.2871	.1425	.0546	.0149	.0025	.0002	.0000	.0000
	13	.7976	.6364	.4438	.2592	.1201	.0408	.0089	.0010	.0000	.0000
	14	.8950	.7797	.6116	.4140	.2291	.0963	.0273	.0042	.0002	.0000
	15	.9534	.8848	.7627	.5864	.3819	.1963	.0715	.0152	.0012	.0000
	16	.9827	.9490	.8760	.7466	.5601	.3463	.1598	.0463	.0058	.0001
	17	.9947	.9814	.9460	.8691	.7312	.5315	.3053	.1189	.0226	.0008
	18	.9987	.9945	.9810	.9449	.8644	.7168	.4993	.2560	.0731	.0049
	19	.9998	.9988	.9948	.9819	.9462	.8630	.7035	.4604	.1927	.0258
	20	1.0000	.9998	.9990	.9957	.9843	.9508	.8668	.6920	.4080	.1052
	21	1.0000	1.0000	.9999	.9993	.9970	.9884	.9602	.8796	.6849	.3206
	22	1.0000	1.0000	1.0000	1.0000	.9997	.9987	.9941	.9762	.9114	.6926
	23	1.0000	1.0000	1.0000	1.0000	1.0000	1.0000	1.0000	1.0000	1.0000	1.0000

(Table of binomial probabilities continued)

						p				
n	x	.05	.10	.15	.20	.25	.30	.35	.40	.45
24	0	.2920	.0798	.0202	.0047	.0010	.0002	.0000	.0000	.0000
	1	.6608	.2925	.1059	.0331	.0090	.0022	.0005	.0001	.0000
	2	.8841	.5643	.2798	.1145	.0398	.0119	.0030	.0007	.0001
	3	.9702	.7857	.5049	.2639	.1150	.0424	.0133	.0035	.0008
	4	.9940	.9149	.7134	.4599	.2466	.1111	.0422	.0134	.0036
	5	.9990	.9723	.8606	.6559	.4222	.2288	.1044	.0400	.0127
	6	.9999	.9925	.9428	.8111	.6074	.3886	.2106	.0960	.0364
	7	1.0000	.9983	.9801	.9108	.7662	.5647	.3575	.1919	.0863
	8	1.0000	.9997	.9941	.9638	.8787	.7250	.5257	.3279	.1730
	9	1.0000	.9999	.9985	.9874	.9453	.8472	.6866	.4891	.2991
	10	1.0000	1.0000	.9997	.9962	.9787	.9258	.8167	.6502	.4539
	11	1.0000	1.0000	.9999	.9990	.9928	.9686	.9058	.7870	.6151
	12	1.0000	1.0000	1.0000	.9998	.9979	.9885	.9577	.8857	.7580
	13	1.0000	1.0000	1.0000	1.0000	.9995	.9964	.9836	.9465	.8659
	14	1.0000	1.0000	1.0000	1.0000	.9999	.9990	.9945	.9783	.9352
	15	1.0000	1.0000	1.0000	1.0000	1.0000	.9998	.9984	.9925	.9731
	16	1.0000	1.0000	1.0000	1.0000	1.0000	1.0000	.9996	.9978	.9905
	17	1.0000	1.0000	1.0000	1.0000	1.0000	1.0000	.9999	.9995	.9972
	18	1.0000	1.0000	1.0000	1.0000	1.0000	1.0000	1.0000	.9999	.9993
	19	1.0000	1.0000	1.0000	1.0000	1.0000	1.0000	1.0000	1.0000	.9999
	20	1.0000	1.0000	1.0000	1.0000	1.0000	1.0000	1.0000	1.0000	1.0000
	21	1.0000	1.0000	1.0000	1.0000	1.0000	1.0000	1.0000	1.0000	1.0000
	22	1.0000	1.0000	1.0000	1.0000	1.0000	1.0000	1.0000	1.0000	1.0000
	23	1.0000	1.0000	1.0000	1.0000	1.0000	1.0000	1.0000	1.0000	1.0000
	24	1.0000	1.0000	1.0000	1.0000	1.0000	1.0000	1.0000	1.0000	1.0000
25	0	.2774	.0718	.0172	.0038	.0008	.0001	.0000	.0000	.0000
	1	.6424	.2712	.0931	.0274	.0070	.0016	.0003	.0001	.0000
	2	.8729	.5371	.2537	.0982	.0321	.0090	.0021	.0004	.0001
	3	.9659	.7636	.4711	.2340	.0962	.0332	.0097	.0024	.0005
	4	.9928	.9020	.6821	.4207	.2137	.0905	.0320	.0095	.0023
	5	.9988	.9666	.8385	.6167	.3783	.1935	.0826	.0294	.0086
	6	.9998	.9905	.9305	.7800	.5611	.3407	.1734	.0736	.0258
	7	.0466	.9977	.9745	.8909	.7265	.5118	.3061	.1536	.0639
	8	1.0000	.9995	.9920	.9532	.8506	.6769	.4668	.2735	.1340
	9	1.0000	.9999	.9979	.9827	.9287	.8106	.6303	.4246	.2424
	10	1.0000	1.0000	.9995	.9944	.9703	.9022	.7712	.5858	.3843
	11	1.0000	1.0000	.9999	.9985	.9893	.9558	.8746	.7323	.5426
	12	1.0000	1.0000	1.0000	.9996	.9966	.9825	.9396	.8462	.6937
	13	1.0000	1.0000	1.0000	.9999	.9991	.9940	.9745	.9222	.8173
	14	1.0000	1.0000	1.0000	1.0000	.9998	.9982	.9907	.9656	.9040
	15	1.0000	1.0000	1.0000	1.0000	1.0000	.9995	.9971	.9868	.9560
	16	1.0000	1.0000	1.0000	1.0000	1.0000	.9999	.9992	.9957	.9826
	17	1.0000	1.0000	1.0000	1.0000	1.0000	1.0000	.9998	.9988	.9942
	18	1.0000	1.0000	1.0000	1.0000	1.0000	1.0000	1.0000	.9997	.9984
	19	1.0000	1.0000	1.0000	1.0000	1.0000	1.0000	1.0000	.9999	.9996
	20	1.0000	1.0000	1.0000	1.0000	1.0000	1.0000	1.0000	1.0000	.9999
	21	1.0000	1.0000	1.0000	1.0000	1.0000	1.0000	1.0000	1.0000	1.0000
	22	1.0000	1.0000	1.0000	1.0000	1.0000	1.0000	1.0000	1.0000	1.0000
	23	1.0000	1.0000	1.0000	1.0000	1.0000	1.0000	1.0000	1.0000	1.0000
	24	1.0000	1.0000	1.0000	1.0000	1.0000	1.0000	1.0000	1.0000	1.0000
	25	1.0000	1.0000	1.0000	1.0000	1.0000	1.0000	1.0000	1.0000	1.0000

n	x	.50	.55	.60	.65	.70	.75	.80	.85	.90	.95
											p
24	0	.0000	.0000	.0000	.0000	.0000	.0000	.0000	.0000	.0000	.0000
	1	.0000	.0000	.0000	.0000	.0000	.0000	.0000	.0000	.0000	.0000
	2	.0000	.0000	.0000	.0000	.0000	.0000	.0000	.0000	.0000	.0000
	3	.0001	.0000	.0000	.0000	.0000	.0000	.0000	.0000	.0000	.0000
	4	.0008	.0001	.0000	.0000	.0000	.0000	.0000	.0000	.0000	.0000
	5	.0033	.0007	.0001	.0000	.0000	.0000	.0000	.0000	.0000	.0000
	6	.0113	.0028	.0005	.0001	.0000	.0000	.0000	.0000	.0000	.0000
	7	.0320	.0095	.0022	.0004	.0000	.0000	.0000	.0000	.0000	.0000
	8	.0758	.0269	.0075	.0016	.0002	.0000	.0000	.0000	.0000	.0000
	9	.1537	.0648	.0217	.0055	.0010	.0001	.0000	.0000	.0000	.0000
	10	.2706	.1341	.0535	.0164	.0036	.0005	.0000	.0000	.0000	.0000
	11	.4194	.2420	.1143	.0423	.0115	.0021	.0002	.0000	.0000	.0000
	12	.5806	.3849	.2130	.0942	.0314	.0072	.0010	.0001	.0000	.0000
	13	.7294	.5461	.3498	.1833	.0742	.0213	.0038	.0003	.0000	.0000
	14	.8463	.7009	.5109	.3134	.1528	.0547	.0126	.0015	.0001	.0000
	15	.9242	.8270	.6721	.4743	.2750	.1213	.0362	.0059	.0003	.0000
	16	.9680	.9137	.8081	.6425	.4353	.2338	.0892	.0199	.0017	.0000
	17	.9887	.9636	.9040	.7894	.6114	.3926	.1889	.0572	.0075	.0001
	18	.9967	.9873	.9600	.8956	.7712	.5778	.3441	.1394	.0277	.0010
	19	.9992	.9964	.9866	.9578	.8889	.7534	.5401	.2866	.0851	.0060
	20	.9999	.9992	.9965	.9867	.9576	.8850	.7361	.4951	.2143	.0298
	21	1.0000	.9999	.9993	.9970	.9881	.9602	.8855	.7202	.4357	.1159
	22	1.0000	1.0000	.9999	.9995	.9978	.9910	.9669	.8941	.7075	.3392
	23	1.0000	1.0000	1.0000	1.0000	.9998	.9990	.9953	.9798	.9202	.7080
	24	1.0000	1.0000	1.0000	1.0000	1.0000	1.0000	1.0000	1.0000	1.0000	1.0000
25	0	.0000	.0000	.0000	.0000	.0000	.0000	.0000	.0000	.0000	.0000
	1	.0000	.0000	.0000	.0000	.0000	.0000	.0000	.0000	.0000	.0000
	2	.0000	.0000	.0000	.0000	.0000	.0000	.0000	.0000	.0000	.0000
	3	.0001	.0000	.0000	.0000	.0000	.0000	.0000	.0000	.0000	.0000
	4	.0005	.0001	.0000	.0000	.0000	.0000	.0000	.0000	.0000	.0000
	5	.0020	.0004	.0001	.0000	.0000	.0000	.0000	.0000	.0000	.0000
	6	.0073	.0016	.0003	.0000	.0000	.0000	.0000	.0000	.0000	.0000
	7	.0216	.0058	.0012	.0002	.0000	.0000	.0000	.0000	.0000	.0000
	8	.0539	.0174	.0043	.0008	.0001	.0000	.0000	.0000	.0000	.0000
	9	.1148	.0440	.0132	.0029	.0005	.0000	.0000	.0000	.0000	.0000
	10	.2122	.0960	.0344	.0093	.0018	.0002	.0000	.0000	.0000	.0000
	11	.3450	.1827	.0778	.0255	.0060	.0009	.0001	.0000	.0000	.0000
	12	.5000	.3063	.1538	.0604	.0175	.0034	.0004	.0000	.0000	.0000
	13	.6550	.4574	.2677	.1254	.0442	.0107	.0015	.0001	.0000	.0000
	14	.7878	.6157	.4142	.2288	.0978	.0297	.0056	.0005	.0000	.0000
	15	.8852	.7576	.5754	.3697	.1894	.0713	.0173	.0021	.0001	.0000
	16	.9461	.8660	.7265	.5332	.3231	.1494	.0468	.0080	.0005	.0000
	17	.9784	.9361	.8464	.6939	.4882	.2735	.1091	.0255	.0023	.0000
	18	.9927	.9742	.9264	.8266	.6593	.4389	.2200	.0695	.0095	.0002
	19	.9980	.9914	.9706	.9174	.8065	.6217	.3833	.1615	.0334	.0012
	20	.9995	.9977	.9905	.9680	.9095	.7863	.5793	.3179	.0980	.0072
	21	.9999	.9995	.9976	.9903	.9668	.9038	.7660	.5289	.2364	.0341
	22	1.0000	.9999	.9996	.9979	.9910	.9679	.9018	.7463	.4629	.1271
	23	1.0000	1.0000	.9999	.9997	.9984	.9930	.9726	.9069	.7288	.3576
	24	1.0000	1.0000	1.0000	1.0000	.9999	.9992	.9962	.9828	.9282	.7226
	25	1.0000	1.0000	1.0000	1.0000	1.0000	1.0000	1.0000	1.0000	1.0000	1.0000

(Table of **binomial probabilities** continued)

n	x					p				
		.05	.10	.15	.20	.25	.30	.35	.40	.45
26	0	.2635	.0646	.0146	.0030	.0006	.0001	.0000	.0000	.0000
	1	.6241	.2513	.0817	.0227	.0055	.0011	.0002	.0000	.0000
	2	.8614	.5105	.2296	.0841	.0258	.0067	.0015	.0003	.0000
	3	.9613	.7409	.4385	.2068	.0802	.0260	.0070	.0016	.0003
	4	.9915	.8882	.6505	.3833	.1844	.0733	.0242	.0066	.0015
	5	.9985	.9601	.8150	.5775	.3371	.1626	.0649	.0214	.0058
	6	.9998	.9881	.9167	.7474	.5154	.2965	.1416	.0559	.0180
	7	1.0000	.9970	.9679	.8687	.6852	.4605	.2596	.1216	.0467
	8	1.0000	.9994	.9894	.9408	.8195	.6274	.4106	.2255	.1024
	9	1.0000	.9999	.9970	.9768	.9091	.7705	.5731	.3642	.1936
	10	1.0000	1.0000	.9993	.9921	.9599	.8747	.7219	.5213	.3204
	11	1.0000	1.0000	.9998	.9977	.9845	.9397	.8384	.6737	.4713
	12	1.0000	1.0000	1.0000	.9994	.9948	.9745	.9168	.8007	.6257
	13	1.0000	1.0000	1.0000	.9999	.9985	.9906	.9623	.8918	.7617
	14	1.0000	1.0000	1.0000	1.0000	.9996	.9970	.9850	.9482	.8650
	15	1.0000	1.0000	1.0000	1.0000	.9999	.9991	.9948	.9783	.9326
	16	1.0000	1.0000	1.0000	1.0000	1.0000	.9998	.9985	.9921	.9707
	17	1.0000	1.0000	1.0000	1.0000	1.0000	1.0000	.9996	.9975	.9890
	18	1.0000	1.0000	1.0000	1.0000	1.0000	1.0000	.9999	.9993	.9965
	19	1.0000	1.0000	1.0000	1.0000	1.0000	1.0000	1.0000	.9999	.9991
	20	1.0000	1.0000	1.0000	1.0000	1.0000	1.0000	1.0000	1.0000	.9998
	21	1.0000	1.0000	1.0000	1.0000	1.0000	1.0000	1.0000	1.0000	1.0000
	22	1.0000	1.0000	1.0000	1.0000	1.0000	1.0000	1.0000	1.0000	1.0000
	23	1.0000	1.0000	1.0000	1.0000	1.0000	1.0000	1.0000	1.0000	1.0000
	24	1.0000	1.0000	1.0000	1.0000	1.0000	1.0000	1.0000	1.0000	1.0000
	25	1.0000	1.0000	1.0000	1.0000	1.0000	1.0000	1.0000	1.0000	1.0000

							p				
n	x	.50	.55	.60	.65	.70	.75	.80	.85	.90	.95
26	0	.0000	.0000	.0000	.0000	.0000	.0000	.0000	.0000	.0000	.0000
	1	.0000	.0000	.0000	.0000	.0000	.0000	.0000	.0000	.0000	.0000
	2	.0000	.0000	.0000	.0000	.0000	.0000	.0000	.0000	.0000	.0000
	3	.0000	.0000	.0000	.0000	.0000	.0000	.0000	.0000	.0000	.0000
	4	.0003	.0000	.0000	.0000	.0000	.0000	.0000	.0000	.0000	.0000
	5	.0012	.0002	.0000	.0000	.0000	.0000	.0000	.0000	.0000	.0000
	6	.0047	.0009	.0001	.0000	.0000	.0000	.0000	.0000	.0000	.0000
	7	.0145	.0035	.0007	.0001	.0000	.0000	.0000	.0000	.0000	.0000
	8	.0378	.0110	.0025	.0004	.0002	.0000	.0000	.0000	.0000	.0000
	9	.0843	.0293	.0079	.0015	.0002	.0000	.0000	.0000	.0000	.0000
	10	.1635	.0674	.0217	.0052	.0009	.0001	.0000	.0000	.0000	.0000
	11	.2786	.1350	.0518	.0150	.0030	.0004	.0000	.0000	.0000	.0000
	12	.4225	.2383	.1082	.0377	.0094	.0015	.0001	.0000	.0000	.0000
	13	.5775	.3743	.1993	.0832	.0255	.0052	.0006	.0001	.0000	.0000
	14	.7214	.5287	.3263	.1616	.0603	.0155	.0023	.0002	.0000	.0000
	15	.8365	.6796	.4787	.2781	.1253	.0401	.0079	.0007	.0000	.0000
	16	.9157	.8064	.6358	.4269	.2295	.0909	.0232	.0030	.0001	.0000
	17	.9622	.8976	.7745	.5894	.3726	.1805	.0592	.0106	.0006	.0000
	18	.9855	.9533	.8784	.7404	.5395	.3148	.1313	.0321	.0030	.0000
	19	.9953	.9820	.9441	.8584	.7035	.4846	.2526	.0833	.0119	.0002
	20	.9988	.9942	.9786	.9351	.8374	.6629	.4225	.1850	.0399	.0015
	21	.9997	.9985	.9934	.9758	.9267	.8156	.6167	.3495	.1118	.0085
	22	1.0000	.9997	.9984	.9930	.9740	.9198	.7932	.5615	.2591	.0387
	23	1.0000	1.0000	.9997	.9985	.9933	.9742	.9159	.7704	.4895	.1386
	24	1.0000	1.0000	1.0000	.9998	.9989	.9945	.9973	.9183	.7487	.3759
	25	1.0000	1.0000	1.0000	1.0000	.9999	.9994	.9970	.9854	.9354	.7365
	26	1.0000	1.0000	1.0000	1.0000	1.0000	1.0000	1.0000	1.0000	1.0000	1.0000

(Table of binomial probabilities continued)

n	x	.05	.10	.15	.20	.25	.30	.35	.40	.45
27	0	.2503	.0581	.0124	.0024	.0004	.0001	.0000	.0000	.0000
	1	.6061	.2326	.0716	.0187	.0042	.0008	.0001	.0000	.0000
	2	.8495	.4846	.2074	.0718	.0207	.0051	.0010	.0002	.0000
	3	.9563	.7179	.4072	.1823	.0666	.0202	.0051	.0011	.0002
	4	.9900	.8734	.6187	.3480	.1583	.0591	.0182	.0046	.0009
	5	.9981	.9529	.7903	.5387	.2989	.1358	.0507	.0155	.0038
	6	.9997	.9853	.9014	.7134	.4708	.2563	.1148	.0421	.0125
	7	1.0000	.9961	.9602	.8444	.6427	.4113	.2183	.0953	.0338
	8	1.0000	.9991	.9862	.9263	.7859	.5773	.3577	.1839	.0774
	9	1.0000	.9998	.9958	.9696	.8867	.7276	.5162	.3087	.1526
	10	1.0000	1.0000	.9989	.9890	.9472	.8434	.6698	.4585	.2633
	11	1.0000	1.0000	.9998	.9965	.9784	.9202	.7976	.6127	.4034
	12	1.0000	1.0000	1.0000	.9990	.9922	.9641	.8894	.7499	.5562
	13	1.0000	1.0000	1.0000	.9998	.9976	.9857	.9464	.8553	.7005
	14	1.0000	1.0000	1.0000	1.0000	.9993	.9950	.9771	.9257	.8185
	15	1.0000	1.0000	1.0000	1.0000	.9998	.9985	.9914	.9663	.9022
	16	1.0000	1.0000	1.0000	1.0000	1.0000	.9996	.9972	.9866	.9536
	17	1.0000	1.0000	1.0000	1.0000	1.0000	.9999	.9992	.9954	.9807
	18	1.0000	1.0000	1.0000	1.0000	1.0000	1.0000	.9998	.9986	.9931
	19	1.0000	1.0000	1.0000	1.0000	1.0000	1.0000	1.0000	.9997	.9979
	20	1.0000	1.0000	1.0000	1.0000	1.0000	1.0000	1.0000	.9999	.9995
	21	1.0000	1.0000	1.0000	1.0000	1.0000	1.0000	1.0000	1.0000	.9999
	22	1.0000	1.0000	1.0000	1.0000	1.0000	1.0000	1.0000	1.0000	1.0000
	23	1.0000	1.0000	1.0000	1.0000	1.0000	1.0000	1.0000	1.0000	1.0000
	24	1.0000	1.0000	1.0000	1.0000	1.0000	1.0000	1.0000	1.0000	1.0000
	25	1.0000	1.0000	1.0000	1.0000	1.0000	1.0000	1.0000	1.0000	1.0000
	26	1.0000	1.0000	1.0000	1.0000	1.0000	1.0000	1.0000	1.0000	1.0000
	27	1.0000	1.0000	1.0000	1.0000	1.0000	1.0000	1.0000	1.0000	1.0000

						p					
n	x	.50	.55	.60	.65	.70	.75	.80	.85	.90	.95
27	0	.0000	.0000	.0000	.0000	.0000	.0000	.0000	.0000	.0000	.0000
	1	.0000	.0000	.0000	.0000	.0000	.0000	.0000	.0000	.0000	.0000
	2	.0000	.0000	.0000	.0000	.0000	.0000	.0000	.0000	.0000	.0000
	3	.0000	.0000	.0000	.0000	.0000	.0000	.0000	.0000	.0000	.0000
	4	.0002	.0000	.0000	.0000	.0000	.0000	.0000	.0000	.0000	.0000
	5	.0008	.0001	.0000	.0000	.0000	.0000	.0000	.0000	.0000	.0000
	6	.0030	.0005	.0001	.0000	.0000	.0000	.0000	.0000	.0000	.0000
	7	.0096	.0021	.0003	.0000	.0000	.0000	.0000	.0000	.0000	.0000
	8	.0261	.0069	.0014	.0002	.0000	.0000	.0000	.0000	.0000	.0000
	9	.0610	.0193	.0046	.0008	.0001	.0000	.0000	.0000	.0000	.0000
	10	.1239	.0464	.0134	.0028	.0004	.0000	.0000	.0000	.0000	.0000
	11	.2210	.0978	.0337	.0086	.0015	.0002	.0000	.0000	.0000	.0000
	12	.3506	.1815	.0743	.0229	.0050	.0007	.0000	.0000	.0000	.0000
	13	.5000	.2995	.1447	.0536	.0143	.0024	.0002	.0000	.0000	.0000
	14	.6494	.4438	.2501	.1106	.0359	.0078	.0010	.0000	.0000	.0000
	15	.7790	.5966	.3873	.2024	.0798	.0216	.0035	.0002	.0000	.0000
	16	.8761	.7367	.5415	.3302	.1566	.0528	.0110	.0011	.0000	.0000
	17	.9390	.8474	.6913	.4838	.2724	.1133	.0304	.0042	.0002	.0000
	18	.9739	.9226	.8161	.6423	.4227	.2141	.0737	.0138	.0009	.0000
	19	.9904	.9662	.9047	.7817	.5887	.3573	.1556	.0398	.0039	.0000
	20	.9970	.9875	.9579	.8852	.7437	.5292	.2866	.0986	.0147	.0003
	21	.9992	.9962	.9845	.9493	.8642	.7011	.4613	.2097	.0471	.0019
	22	.9998	.9991	.9954	.9818	.9409	.8417	.6520	.3813	.1266	.0100
	23	1.0000	.9998	.9989	.9949	.9798	.9334	.8177	.5928	.2821	.0437
	24	1.0000	1.0000	.9998	.9990	.9949	.9793	.9282	.7926	.5154	.1505
	25	1.0000	1.0000	1.0000	.9999	.9992	.9958	.9813	.9284	.7674	.3939
	26	1.0000	1.0000	1.0000	1.0000	.9999	.9996	.9976	.9876	.9416	.7497
	27	1.0000	1.0000	1.0000	1.0000	1.0000	1.0000	1.0000.	1.0000	1.0000	1.0000

(Table of binomial probabilities continued)

n	x	.05	.10	.15	.20	.25	.30	.35	.40	.45
							p			
28	0	.2378	.0523	.0106	.0019	.0003	.0000	.0000	.0000	.0000
	1	.5883	.2152	.0627	.0155	.0033	.0006	.0001	.0000	.0000
	2	.8373	.4594	.1871	.0612	.0166	.0038	.0007	.0001	.0000
	3	.9509	.6946	.3772	.1602	.0551	.0157	.0037	.0007	.0001
	4	.9883	.8579	.5869	.3149	.1354	.0474	.0136	.0032	.0006
	5	.9977	.9450	.7646	.5005	.2638	.1128	.0393	.0111	.0025
	6	.9996	.9821	.8848	.6784	.4279	.2202	.0923	.0315	.0086
	7	1.0000	.9950	.9514	.8182	.5997	.3648	.1821	.0740	.0242
	8	1.0000	.9988	.9823	.9100	.7501	.5275	.3089	.1485	.0578
	9	1.0000	.9998	.9944	.9609	.8615	.6825	.4607	.2588	.1187
	10	1.0000	1.0000	.9985	.9851	.9321	.8087	.6160	.3986	.2135
	11	1.0000	1.0000	.9996	.9950	.9706	.8972	.7529	.5510	.3404
	12	1.0000	1.0000	.9999	.9985	.9888	.9509	.8572	.6950	.4875
	13	1.0000	1.0000	1.0000	.9996	.9962	.9792	.9264	.8132	.6356
	14	1.0000	1.0000	1.0000	.9999	.9989	.9923	.9663	.8975	.7654
	15	1.0000	1.0000	1.0000	1.0000	.9997	.9975	.9864	.9501	.8645
	16	1.0000	1.0000	1.0000	1.0000	.9999	.9993	.9952	.9785	.9304
	17	1.0000	1.0000	1.0000	1.0000	1.0000	.9998	.9985	.9919	.9685
	18	1.0000	1.0000	1.0000	1.0000	1.0000	1.0000	.9996	.9973	.9875
	19	1.0000	1.0000	1.0000	1.0000	1.0000	1.0000	.9999	.9992	.9957
	20	1.0000	1.0000	1.0000	1.0000	1.0000	1.0000	1.0000	.9998	.9988
	21	1.0000	1.0000	1.0000	1.0000	1.0000	1.0000	1.0000	1.0000	.9997
	22	1.0000	1.0000	1.0000	1.0000	1.0000	1.0000	1.0000	1.0000	.9999
	23	1.0000	1.0000	1.0000	1.0000	1.0000	1.0000	1.0000	1.0000	1.0000
	24	1.0000	1.0000	1.0000	1.0000	1.0000	1.0000	1.0000	1.0000	1.0000
	25	1.0000	1.0000	1.0000	1.0000	1.0000	1.0000	1.0000	1.0000	1.0000
	26	1.0000	1.0000	1.0000	1.0000	1.0000	1.0000	1.0000	1.0000	1.0000
	27	1.0000	1.0000	1.0000	1.0000	1.0000	1.0000	1.0000	1.0000	1.0000
	28	1.0000	1.0000	1.0000	1.0000	1.0000	1.0000	1.0000	1.0000	1.0000

		p									
n	x	.50	.55	.60	.65	.70	.75	.80	.85	.90	.95
28	0	.0000	.0000	.0000	.0000	.0000	.0000	.0000	.0000	.0000	.0000
	1	.0000	.0000	.0000	.0000	.0000	.0000	.0000	.0000	.0000	.0000
	2	.0000	.0000	.0000	.0000	.0000	.0000	.0000	.0000	.0000	.0000
	3	.0000	.0000	.0000	.0000	.0000	.0000	.0000	.0000	.0000	.0000
	4	.0001	.0000	.0000	.0000	.0000	.0000	.0000	.0000	.0000	.0000
	5	.0005	.0001	.0000	.0000	.0000	.0000	.0000	.0000	.0000	.0000
	6	.0019	.0003	.0000	.0000	.0000	.0000	.0000	.0000	.0000	.0000
	7	.0063	.0012	.0002	.0000	.0000	.0000	.0000	.0000	.0000	.0000
	8	.0178	.0043	.0012	.0001	.0000	.0000	.0000	.0000	.0000	.0000
	9	.0436	.0125	.0043	.0004	.0000	.0000	.0000	.0000	.0000	.0000
	10	.0925	.0315	.0125	.0015	.0002	.0000	.0000	.0000	.0000	.0000
	11	.1725	.0696	.0315	.0048	.0007	.0001	.0000	.0000	.0000	.0000
	12	.2858	.1355	.0696	.0136	.0025	.0003	.0000	.0000	.0000	.0000
	13	.4253	.2346	.1355	.0337	.0077	.0011	.0001	.0000	.0000	.0000
	14	.5747	.3644	.2345	.0736	.0208	.0038	.0004	.0000	.0000	.0000
	15	.7142	.5125	.3644	.1428	.0491	.0112	.0015	.0001	.0000	.0000
	16	.8275	.6596	.5125	.2471	.1028	.0294	.0050	.0004	.0000	.0000
	17	.9075	.7865	.6596	.3840	.1913	.0679	.0149	.0015	.0000	.0000
	18	.9564	.8813	.7865	.5393	.3175	.1385	.0391	.0056	.0002	.0000
	19	.9822	.9422	.8813	.6911	.4725	.2499	.0900	.0177	.0012	.0000
	20	.9937	.9758	.9422	.8179	.6352	.4003	.1818	.0486	.0050	.0000
	21	.9981	.9914	.9758	.9077	.7798	.5721	.3216	.1152	.0179	.0004
	22	.9995	.9975	.9914	.9607	.8872	.7362	.4995	.2354	.0550	.0023
	23	.9999	.9994	.9975	.9864	.9526	.8646	.6851	.4131	.1421	.0117
	24	1.0000	.9999	.9994	.9963	.9843	.9449	.8398	.6228	.3054	.0491
	25	1.0000	1.0000	.9999	.9993	.9962	.9834	.9388	.8129	.5406	.1627
	26	1.0000	1.0000	1.0000	.9999	.9994	.9967	.9845	.9373	.7848	.4117
	27	1.0000	1.0000	1.0000	1.0000	1.0000	.9997	.9981	.9894	.9477	.7622
	28	1.0000	1.0000	1.0000	1.0000	1.0000	1.0000	1.0000	1.0000	1.0000	1.0000

(Table of binomial probabilities continued)

						p				
n	x	.05	.10	.15	.20	.25	.30	.35	.40	.45
29	0	.2259	.0471	.0090	.0015	.0002	.0000	.0000	.0000	.0000
	1	.5708	.1989	.0549	.0128	.0025	.0004	.0001	.0000	.0000
	2	.8249	.4350	.1684	.0520	.0133	.0028	.0005	.0001	.0000
	3	.9452	.6710	.3487	.1404	.0455	.0121	.0026	.0005	.0001
	4	.9864	.8416	.5555	.2839	.1153	.0379	.0101	.0022	.0004
	5	.9973	.9363	.7379	.4634	.2317	.0932	.0303	.0080	.0017
	6	.9995	.9784	.8667	.6429	.3868	.1880	.0738	.0233	.0059
	7	.9999	.9938	.9414	.7903	.5568	.3214	.1507	.0570	.0172
	8	1.0000	.9984	.9777	.8916	.7125	.4787	.2645	.1187	.0427
	9	1.0000	.9997	.9926	.9507	.8337	.6360	.4076	.2147	.0913
	10	1.0000	.9999	.9978	.9803	.9145	.7708	.5617	.3427	.1708
	11	1.0000	1.0000	.9995	.9931	.9610	.8706	.7050	.4900	.2833
	12	1.0000	1.0000	.9999	.9978	.9842	.9348	.8207	.6374	.4213
	13	1.0000	1.0000	1.0000	.9994	.9944	.9707	.9022	.7659	.5689
	14	1.0000	1.0000	1.0000	.9999	.9982	.9883	.9524	.8638	.7070
	15	1.0000	1.0000	1.0000	1.0000	.9995	.9959	.9794	.9290	.8199
	16	1.0000	1.0000	1.0000	1.0000	.9999	.9987	.9921	.9671	.9008
	17	1.0000	1.0000	1.0000	1.0000	1.0000	.9997	.9973	.9865	.9514
	18	1.0000	1.0000	1.0000	1.0000	1.0000	.9999	.9992	.9951	.9790
	19	1.0000	1.0000	1.0000	1.0000	1.0000	1.0000	.9998	.9985	.9920
	20	1.0000	1.0000	1.0000	1.0000	1.0000	1.0000	1.0000	.9996	.9974
	21	1.0000	1.0000	1.0000	1.0000	1.0000	1.0000	1.0000	.9999	.9993
	22	1.0000	1.0000	1.0000	1.0000	1.0000	1.0000	1.0000	1.0000	.9998
	23	1.0000	1.0000	1.0000	1.0000	1.0000	1.0000	1.0000	1.0000	1.0000
	24	1.0000	1.0000	1.0000	1.0000	1.0000	1.0000	1.0000	1.0000	1.0000
	25	1.0000	1.0000	1.0000	1.0000	1.0000	1.0000	1.0000	1.0000	1.0000
	26	1.0000	1.0000	1.0000	1.0000	1.0000	1.0000	1.0000	1.0000	1.0000
	27	1.0000	1.0000	1.0000	1.0000	1.0000	1.0000	1.0000	1.0000	1.0000
	28	1.0000	1.0000	1.0000	1.0000	1.0000	1.0000	1.0000	1.0000	1.0000
	29	1.0000	1.0000	1.0000	1.0000	1.0000	1.0000	1.0000	1.0000	1.0000

n	x	.50	.55	.60	.65	.70	.75	.80	.85	.90	.95
							p				
29	0	.0000	.0000	.0000	.0000	.0000	.0000	.0000	.0000	.0000	.0000
	1	.0000	.0000	.0000	.0000	.0000	.0000	.0000	.0000	.0000	.0000
	2	.0000	.0000	.0000	.0000	.0000	.0000	.0000	.0000	.0000	.0000
	3	.0000	.0000	.0000	.0000	.0000	.0000	.0000	.0000	.0000	.0000
	4	.0001	.0000	.0000	.0000	.0000	.0000	.0000	.0000	.0000	.0000
	5	.0003	.0000	.0000	.0000	.0000	.0000	.0000	.0000	.0000	.0000
	6	.0012	.0002	.0000	.0000	.0000	.0000	.0000	.0000	.0000	.0000
	7	.0041	.0007	.0001	.0000	.0000	.0000	.0000	.0000	.0000	.0000
	8	.0121	.0026	.0004	.0000	.0000	.0000	.0000	.0000	.0000	.0000
	9	.0307	.0080	.0015	.0002	.0000	.0000	.0000	.0000	.0000	.0000
	10	.0680	.0210	.0049	.0008	.0001	.0000	.0000	.0000	.0000	.0000
	11	.1325	.0486	.0135	.0027	.0003	.0000	.0000	.0000	.0000	.0000
	12	.2291	.0992	.0329	.0079	.0013	.0001	.0000	.0000	.0000	.0000
	13	.3555	.1801	.0710	.0206	.0041	.0005	.0000	.0000	.0000	.0000
	14	.5000	.2930	.1362	.0476	.0117	.0018	.0001	.0000	.0000	.0000
	15	.6445	.4311	.2341	.0978	.0293	.0056	.0006	.0000	.0000	.0000
	16	.7709	.5787	.3626	.1793	.0652	.0158	.0022	.0001	.0000	.0000
	17	.8675	.7167	.5100	.2950	.1294	.0390	.0069	.0005	.0000	.0000
	18	.9320	.8292	.6573	.4383	.2292	.0855	.0197	.0022	.0001	.0000
	19	.9693	.9087	.7853	.5924	.3640	.1663	.0493	.0074	.0003	.0000
	20	.9879	.9573	.8813	.7355	.5213	.2875	.1084	.0223	.0016	.0000
	21	.9959	.9828	.9430	.8493	.6786	.4432	.2097	.0586	.0062	.0001
	22	.9988	.9941	.9767	.9262	.8120	.6132	.3571	.1333	.0216	.0005
	23	.9997	.9983	.9920	.9697	.9068	.7683	.5366	.2621	.0637	.0027
	24	.9999	.9996	.9978	.9899	.9621	.8847	.7161	.4445	.1584	.0136
	25	1.0000	.9999	.9995	.9974	.9879	.9545	.8596	.6513	.3290	.0548
	26	1.0000	1.0000	.9999	.9995	.9972	.9867	.9480	.8316	.5650	.1751
	27	1.0000	1.0000	1.0000	.9999	.9996	.9975	.9872	.9451	.8011	.4292
	28	1.0000	1.0000	1.0000	1.0000.	1.0000	.9998	.9985	.9910	.9529	.7741
	29	1.0000	1.0000	1.0000	1.0000	1.0000	1.0000.	1.0000	1.0000	1.0000	1.0000

(Table of binomial probabilities continued)

n	x	.05	.10	.15	.20	.25	.30	.35	.40	.45
							p			
30	0	.2146	.0424	.0076	.0012	.0002	.0000	.0000	.0000	.0000
	1	.5535	.1837	.0480	.0105	.0020	.0003	.0000	.0000	.0000
	2	.8122	.4114	.1514	.0442	.0106	.0021	.0003	.0000	.0000
	3	.9392	.6474	.3217	.1227	.0374	.0093	.0075	.0003	.0000
	4	.9844	.8245	.5245	.2552	.0979	.0302	.0233	.0015	.0002
	5	.9967	.9268	.7106	.4275	.2026	.0766	.0586	.0057	.0011
	6	.9994	.9742	.8474	.6070	.3481	.1595	.1238	.0172	.0040
	7	.9999	.9922	.9302	.7608	.5143	.2814	.2247	.0435	.0121
	8	1.0000	.9980	.9722	.8713	.6736	.4315	.3575	.0940	.0312
	9	1.0000	.9995	.9903	.9389	.8034	.5888	.5078	.1763	.0694
	10	1.0000	.9999	.9971	.9744	.8943	.7304	.6548	.2915	.1350
	11	1.0000	1.0000	.9992	.9905	.9493	.8407	.7802	.4311	.2327
	12	1.0000	1.0000	.9998	.9969	.9784	.9155	.8737	.5785	.3592
	13	1.0000	1.0000	1.0000	.9991	.9918	.9599	.9348	.7145	.5025
	14	1.0000	1.0000	1.0000	.9998	.9973	.9831	.9699	.8246	.6448
	15	1.0000	1.0000	1.0000	.9999	.9992	.9936	.9876	.9029	.7691
	16	1.0000	1.0000	1.0000	1.0000	.9998	.9979	.9955	.9519	.8644
	17	1.0000	1.0000	1.0000	1.0000	.9999	.9994	.9986	.9788	.9286
	18	1.0000	1.0000	1.0000	1.0000	1.0000	.9998	.9996	.9917	.9666
	19	1.0000	1.0000	1.0000	1.0000	1.0000	1.0000	.9999	.9971	.9862
	20	1.0000	1.0000	1.0000	1.0000	1.0000	1.0000	1.0000	.9991	.9950
	21	1.0000	1.0000	1.0000	1.0000	1.0000	1.0000	1.0000	.9998	.9984
	22	1.0000	1.0000	1.0000	1.0000	1.0000	1.0000	1.0000	1.0000	.9996
	23	1.0000	1.0000	1.0000	1.0000	1.0000	1.0000	1.0000	1.0000	.9999
	24	1.0000	1.0000	1.0000	1.0000	1.0000	1.0000	1.0000	1.0000	1.0000
	25	1.0000	1.0000	1.0000	1.0000	1.0000	1.0000	1.0000	1.0000	1.0000
	26	1.0000	1.0000	1.0000	1.0000	1.0000	1.0000	1.0000	1.0000	1.0000
	27	1.0000	1.0000	1.0000	1.0000	1.0000	1.0000	1.0000	1.0000	1.0000
	28	1.0000	1.0000	1.0000	1.0000	1.0000	1.0000	1.0000	1.0000	1.0000
	29	1.0000	1.0000	1.0000	1.0000	1.0000	1.0000	1.0000	1.0000	1.0000
	30	1.0000	1.0000	1.0000	1.0000	1.0000	1.0000	1.0000	1.0000	1.0000

		p									
n	x	.50	.55	.60	.65	.70	.75	.80	.85	.90	.95
30	0	.0000	.0000	.0000	.0000	.0000	.0000	.0000	.0000	.0000	.0000
	1	.0000	.0000	.0000	.0000	.0000	.0000	.0000	.0000	.0000	.0000
	2	.0000	.0000	.0000	.0000	.0000	.0000	.0000	.0000	.0000	.0000
	3	.0000	.0000	.0000	.0000	.0000	.0000	.0000	.0000	.0000	.0000
	4	.0000	.0000	.0000	.0000	.0000	.0000	.0000	.0000	.0000	.0000
	5	.0002	.0000	.0000	.0000	.0000	.0000	.0000	.0000	.0000	.0000
	6	.0007	.0000	.0000	.0000	.0000	.0000	.0000	.0000	.0000	.0000
	7	.0026	.0004	.0000	.0000	.0000	.0000	.0000	.0000	.0000	.0000
	8	.0081	.0016	.0002	.0000	.0000	.0000	.0000	.0000	.0000	.0000
	9	.0214	.0050	.0009	.0001	.0000	.0000	.0000	.0000	.0000	.0000
	10	.0494	.0138	.0029	.0004	.0000	.0000	.0000	.0000	.0000	.0000
	11	.1002	.0334	.0083	.0014	.0002	.0000	.0000	.0000	.0000	.0000
	12	.1808	.0714	.0212	.0045	.0006	.0001	.0000	.0000	.0000	.0000
	13	.2923	.1356	.0481	.0124	.0021	.0002	.0000	.0000	.0000	.0000
	14	.4278	.2309	.0971	.0301	.0064	.0008	.0001	.0000	.0000	.0000
	15	.5722	.3552	.1754	.0652	.0169	.0027	.0002	.0000	.0000	.0000
	16	.7077	.4975	.2855	.1263	.0401	.0082	.0009	.0000	.0000	.0000
	17	.8192	.6408	.4215	.2198	.0845	.0216	.0031	.0002	.0000	.0000
	18	.8998	.7673	.5689	.3452	.1593	.0507	.0095	.0008	.0000	.0000
	19	.9506	.8650	.7085	.4922	.2696	.1057	.0256	.0029	.0001	.0000
	20	.9786	.9306	.8237	.6425	.4112	.1966	.0611	.0097	.0005	.0000
	21	.9919	.9688	.9060	.7753	.5685	.3264	.1287	.0278	.0020	.0000
	22	.9974	.9879	.9565	.8762	.7186	.4857	.2392	.0698	.0078	.0001
	23	.9993	.9960	.9828	.9414	.8405	.6519	.3930	.1526	.0258	.0006
	24	.9998	.9989	.9943	.9767	.9235	.7974	.5725	.2894	.0732	.0033
	25	1.0000	.9998	.9985	.9925	.9698	.9021	.7448	.4755	.1755	.0156
	26	1.0000	1.0000	.9997	.9981	.9907	.9626	.8773	.6783	.3526	.0608
	27	1.0000	1.0000	1.0000	.9997	.9979	.9894	.9558	.8486	.5886	.1878
	28	1.0000	1.0000	1.0000	1.0000	.9997	.9980	.9895	.9520	.8163	.4465
	29	1.0000	1.0000	1.0000	1.0000	1.0000	.9998	.9988	.9924	.9576	.7854
	30	1.0000	1.0000	1.0000	1.0000	1.0000	1.000	1.0000	1.0000	1.0000	1.0000.

Table 2: table of random numbers

57323	99793	10404	96963	94149	09436	81289	21954	61399	86562
34720	06356	13309	04958	72741	75575	56567	21262	77996	05409
07578	65410	00035	32693	98319	68032	28659	80408	27007	63030
47371	37336	22937	51738	37503	89855	45893	74636	29767	52720
75165	97575	83615	07281	58542	36009	59936	18517	73157	11300
04885	81136	90574	88200	34719	33343	91636	24256	34494	31587
83239	54826	75030	75527	97006	47758	42133	19846	64341	70126
66474	06298	38096	44376	26037	63524	62251	88179	23447	34741
87329	30156	01551	50210	65238	34063	01982	09946	32295	47462
79155	84829	48006	33146	60458	69990	05107	28048	82959	22878
78986	67245	27473	25972	56124	65964	78422	24307	21716	11185
48528	89326	57091	61161	30877	68643	23416	46300	38171	39607
81006	92708	24803	09953	06949	38763	85506	28271	16774	23654
46570	62179	45157	39433	70012	25561	44522	58486	16495	91575
82073	60459	92791	53955	11120	36410	14834	22564	11477	07221
33835	66284	64182	70403	76105	01726	62048	19155	27851	22094
12640	75442	76862	68499	33486	57958	09867	95452	61593	64290
21169	93933	69194	76324	89108	02521	47389	88952	84196	61334
96268	83080	76688	17712	67108	43603	49754	11134	25733	26622
23625	85536	27462	62992	88022	75867	83873	65408	17795	82751
94668	37558	66240	14759	16472	23333	50819	06367	95422	45043
31377	07132	84367	03961	31082	64493	72267	82722	61919	77949
27290	95250	76361	89702	08367	88061	08887	26817	77449	64561
96474	56573	07318	94244	11211	39106	85678	68921	37696	15046
19982	08416	70690	39842	54764	43373	62609	51968	73501	33840
93680	47532	69086	33632	42387	56096	93777	48942	13020	41687
15320	75898	21162	37786	66961	86425	54004	75370	47379	26955
25188	10433	98394	63340	13059	51567	99759	15205	97136	06467
35857	05881	56987	67626	91552	65227	25956	35367	98342	70449
65755	72241	90415	98071	53962	59714	72801	40823	24553	85828
28153	19407	16237	91592	01375	95309	71852	40520	81157	79864
97688	55671	01053	92304	64759	91865	19165	06674	99502	17278
47573	93053	59381	38182	99692	00201	59267	32347	46673	61985
49038	88784	39307	20261	89987	52459	35632	58977	97722	37701
02450	49641	34841	62921	63491	14884	41721	16410	88097	69795
76620	26203	80035	11163	84709	83234	40610	84462	20074	77735
55556	75074	34125	11814	44923	44702	13899	81894	79284	90456
81869	36582	26227	03448	59866	96840	35803	64665	98711	28603
29137	18688	97870	41342	19480	19071	37891	76719	00339	40151
81493	16953	62106	93856	84084	64161	46975	29936	14002	56781
87941	85345	66034	98019	05113	98087	44807	38114	54473	58202
51450	05667	89494	20117	45306	61000	10529	05306	88764	08546
96684	16409	13041	63794	72479	01423	40060	13694	50569	50620
10961	80756	60878	21433	41310	53493	87731	31789	04235	98404
05772	62112	43024	00738	50512	01421	68758	32132	73638	26087

Table 3: table of *t* distribution values

		Level of significance for one-tailed test			
		0.05	0.025	0.01	0.005
		Level of significance for two-tailed test			
		0.10	0.05	0.02	0.01
d.f. (ν) =	1	6.314	12.706	31.821	63.657
	2	2.920	4.303	6.965	9.925
	3	2.353	3.182	4.541	5.841
	4	2.132	2.776	3.747	4.604
	5	2.015	2.571	3.365	4.032
	6	1.943	2.447	3.143	3.707
	7	1.895	2.365	2.998	3.499
	8	1.860	2.306	2.896	3.355
	9	1.833	2.262	2.821	3.250
	10	1.812	2.228	2.764	3.169
	11	1.796	2.201	2.718	3.106
	12	1.782	2.179	2.681	3.055
	13	1.771	2.160	2.650	3.012
	14	1.761	2.145	2.624	2.977
	15	1.753	2.131	2.602	2.947
	16	1.746	2.120	2.583	2.921
	17	1.740	2.110	2.567	2.898
	18	1.734	2.101	2.552	2.878
	19	1.729	2.093	2.539	2.861
	20	1.725	2.086	2.528	2.845
	21	1.721	2.080	2.518	2.831
	22	1.717	2.074	2.508	2.819
	23	1.714	2.069	2.500	2.807
	24	1.711	2.064	2.492	2.797
	25	1.708	2.060	2.485	2.787
	26	1.706	2.056	2.479	2.779
	27	1.703	2.052	2.473	2.771
	28	1.701	2.048	2.467	2.763
	29	1.699	2.045	2.462	2.756
	30	1.697	2.042	2.457	2.750
	40	1.684	2.021	2.423	2.704
	60	1.671	2.000	2.390	2.660
	120	1.658	1.980	2.358	2.617

Table 4: table of chi-square distribution values

a =	.25	.20	.10	.05	.025	.02	0.01	.005	.001
v = 1	1.323	1.642	2.706	3.841	5.024	5.412	6.635	7.879	10.827
2	2.773	3.219	4.605	5.991	7.378	7.824	9.210	10.597	13.815
3	4.108	4.642	6.251	7.815	9.348	9.837	11.345	12.838	16.268
4	5.385	5.989	7.779	9.488	11.143	11.668	13.277	14.860	18.465
5	6.626	7.289	9.236	11.070	12.832	13.388	15.086	16.750	20.517
6	7.841	8.558	10.645	12.592	14.449	15.033	16.812	18.548	22.457
7	9.037	9.803	12.071	14.067	16.013	16.622	18.475	20.278	24.322
8	10.219	11.030	13.362	15.507	17.535	18.168	20.090	21.955	26.125
9	11.389	12.242	14.684	16.919	19.023	19.679	21.666	23.589	27.877
10	12.549	13.442	15.987	18.307	20.483	21.161	23.209	25.188	29.588
11	13.701	14.631	17.275	19.675	21.920	22.618	24.725	26.757	31.264
12	14.845	15.812	18.549	21.026	23.337	24.054	26.217	28.300	23.909
13	15.984	16.985	19.812	22.362	24.736	25.472	27.688	29.819	34.528
14	17.117	18.151	21.064	23.685	26.119	26.873	29.141	31.319	36.123
15	18.245	19.311	22.307	24.996	27.488	28.259	30.578	32.801	37.697
16	19.369	20.465	23.542	26.296	28.845	29.633	32.000	34.267	39.252
17	20.489	21.615	24.769	27.587	30.191	30.995	33.409	35.718	40.790
18	21.605	22.760	25.989	28.869	31.526	32.346	34.805	37.156	42.312
19	22.718	23.900	27.204	30.144	32.852	33.687	36.191	38.582	43.820
20	23.828	25.038	28.412	31.410	34.170	35.020	37.566	39.997	45.315
21	24.935	26.171	29.615	32.671	35.479	36.343	38.932	41.401	46.797
22	26.039	27.301	30.813	33.924	36.781	37.659	40.289	42.796	48.268
23	27.141	28.429	32.007	35.172	38.076	38.968	41.638	44.181	49.728
24	28.241	29.553	33.196	36.415	39.364	40.270	42.980	45.558	51.179
25	29.339	30.675	34.382	37.652	40.646	41.566	44.314	46.928	52.620
26	30.434	31.795	35.563	38.885	41.923	42.856	45.642	48.290	54.052
27	31.528	32.912	36.741	40.113	43.194	44.140	46.963	49.645	55.476
28	32.620	34.027	37.916	41.337	44.461	45.419	48.278	50.993	56.893
29	33.711	35.139	39.087	42.557	45.722	46.693	49.588	52.336	58.302
30	34.800	36.250	40.256	43.773	46.979	47.962	50.892	53.672	59.703
40	45.616	47.269	51.805	55.759	59.342	60.436	63.691	66.766	73.402
50	56.334	58.164	63.167	67.505	71.420	72.613	76.154	79.490	86.661
60	66.981	68.972	74.397	79.082	83.298	84.580	88.379	91.952	99.607
70	77.577	79.715	85.527	90.531	95.023	96.388	100.425	104.215	112.317
80	88.130	90.405	96.578	101.880	106.629	108.069	112.329	116.321	124.839
90	98.650	101.054	107.565	113.145	118.136	119.648	124.116	128.299	137.208
100	109.141	111.667	118.498	124.342	129.561	131.142	135.807	140.170	149.449

Table 5: table of areas in tail of the normal distribution

$\dfrac{(\chi-\sigma)}{\sigma}$	0.00	0.01	0.02	0.03	0.04	0.05	0.06	0.07	0.08	0.09
0.0	0.5000	0.4960	0.4920	0.4880	0.4840	0.4801	0.4761	0.4721	0.4681	0.4641
0.1	0.4602	0.4562	0.4522	0.4483	0.4443	0.4404	0.4364	0.4325	0.4286	0.4247
0.2	0.4207	0.4168	0.4129	0.4090	0.4052	0.4013	0.3974	0.3936	0.3897	0.3859
0.3	0.3821	0.3783	0.3745	0.3707	0.3669	0.3632	0.3594	0.3557	0.3520	0.3483
0.4	0.3446	0.3409	0.3372	0.3336	0.3300	0.3264	0.3228	0.3192	0.3156	0.3121
0.5	0.3085	0.3050	0.3015	0.2981	0.2946	0.2912	0.2877	0.2843	0.2843	0.2810
0.6	0.2743	0.2709	0.2676	0.2643	0.2611	0.2578	0.2546	0.2514	0.2483	0.2451
0.7	0.2420	0.2389	0.2358	0.2327	0.2296	0.2266	0.2236	0.2206	0.2177	0.2148
0.8	0.2119	0.2090	0.2061	0.2033	0.2005	0.1977	0.1949	0.1922	0.1894	0.1867
0.9	0.1841	0.1814	0.1788	0.1762	0.1736	0.1711	0.1685	0.1660	0.1635	0.1611
1.0	0.1587	0.1562	0.1539	0.1515	0.1492	0.1469	0.1446	0.1423	0.1401	0.1379
1.1	0.1357	0.1335	0.1314	0.1292	0.1271	0.1251	0.1230	0.1210	0.1190	0.1170
1.2	0.1151	0.1131	0.1112	0.1093	0.1075	0.1056	0.1038	0.1020	0.1003	0.0985
1.3	0.0968	0.0951	0.0934	0.0918	0.0901	0.0885	0.0869	0.0838	0.0853	0.0823
1.4	0.0808	0.0793	0.0778	0.0764	0.0749	0.0735	0.0721	0.0708	0.0694	0.0681
1.5	0.0668	0.0655	0.0643	0.0630	0.0618	0.0606	0.0594	0.0582	0.0571	0.0559
1.6	0.0548	0.0537	0.0526	0.0516	0.0505	0.0495	0.0485	0.0475	0.0465	0.0455
1.7	0.0446	0.0436	0.0427	0.0418	0.0409	0.0401	0.0392	0.0384	0.0375	0.0367
1.8	0.0359	0.0351	0.0344	0.0336	0.0329	0.0322	0.0314	0.0307	0.0301	0.0294
1.9	0.0287	0.0281	0.0274	0.0268	0.0262	0.0256	0.0250	0.0244	0.0239	0.0233
2.0	0.02275	0.02222	0.02169	0.02118	0.02068	0.02018	0.01970	0.01923	0.01876	0.01831
2.1	0.01786	0.01743	0.01700	0.01659	0.01618	0.01578	0.01539	0.01500	0.01463	0.01426
2.2	0.01390	0.01355	0.01321	0.01287	0.01255	0.01222	0.01191	0.01160	0.01130	0.01101
2.3	0.01072	0.01044	0.01017	0.00990	0.00964	0.00939	0.00914	0.00889	0.00866	0.00842
2.4	0.00820	0.00798	0.00776	0.00755	0.00734	0.00714	0.00695	0.00676	0.00657	0.00639
2.5	0.00621	0.00604	0.00587	0.00570	0.00554	0.00539	0.00523	0.00508	0.00494	0.00480
2.6	0.00466	0.00453	0.00440	0.00427	0.00415	0.00402	0.00391	0.00379	0.00368	0.00357
2.7	0.00347	0.00336	0.00326	0.00317	0.00307	0.00298	0.00289	0.00280	0.00272	0.00264
2.8	0.00256	0.00248	0.00240	0.00233	0.00226	0.00219	0.00212	0.00205	0.00199	0.00193
2.9	0.00187	0.00181	0.00175	0.00169	0.00164	0.00159	0.00154	0.00149	0.00144	0.00139
3.0	0.00135									
3.1	0.00097									
3.2	0.00069									
3.3	0.00048									
3.4	0.00034									
3.5	0.00023									
3.6	0.00016									
3.7	0.00011									
3.8	0.00007									
3.9	0.00005									
4.0	0.00003									

Table 6: table of cumulative exponential probabilities

λ_{x1}	.00	.01	.02	.03	.04	.05	.06	.07	.08	.09
0.0	0.0000	0.0100	0.0198	0.0296	0.0392	0.0488	0.0582	0.0676	0.0769	0.0861
0.1	0.0952	0.1042	0.1131	0.1219	0.1306	0.1393	0.1479	0.1563	0.1647	0.1730
0.2	0.1813	0.1894	0.1975	0.2055	0.2134	0.2212	0.2289	0.2366	0.2442	0.2517
0.3	0.2592	0.2666	0.2739	0.2811	0.2882	0.2953	0.3023	0.3093	0.3161	0.3229
0.4	0.3297	0.3363	0.3430	0.3495	0.3560	0.3624	0.3687	0.3750	0.3812	0.3874
0.5	0.3935	0.3995	0.4055	0.4114	0.4173	0.4231	0.4288	0.4345	0.4401	0.4457
0.6	0.4512	0.4566	0.4621	0.4674	0.4727	0.4780	0.4831	0.4883	0.4934	0.4984
0.7	0.5034	0.5084	0.5132	0.5181	0.5229	0.5276	0.5323	0.5370	0.5416	0.5462
0.8	0.5507	0.5551	0.5596	0.5640	0.5683	0.5726	0.5768	0.5810	0.5852	0.5893
0.9	0.5934	0.5975	0.6015	0.6054	0.6094	0.6133	0.6171	0.6209	0.6247	0.6284
1.0	0.6321	0.6358	0.6394	0.6430	0.6465	0.6501	0.6535	0.6570	0.6604	0.6638
1.1	0.6671	0.6704	0.6737	0.6770	0.6802	0.6834	0.6865	0.6896	0.6927	0.6958
1.2	0.6988	0.7018	0.7048	0.7077	0.7106	0.7135	0.7163	0.7192	0.7220	0.7247
1.3	0.7275	0.7302	0.7329	0.7355	0.7382	0.7408	0.7433	0.7459	0.7484	0.7509
1.4	0.7534	0.7559	0.7583	0.7607	0.7631	0.7654	0.7678	0.7701	0.7724	0.7746
1.5	0.7769	0.7791	0.7813	0.7835	0.7856	0.7878	0.7899	0.7920	0.7940	0.7961
1.6	0.7981	0.8001	0.8021	0.8041	0.8060	0.8080	0.8099	0.8118	0.8136	0.8155
1.7	0.8173	0.8191	0.8209	0.8227	0.8245	0.8262	0.8280	0.8297	0.8314	0.8330
1.8	0.8347	0.8363	0.8380	0.8396	0.8412	0.8428	0.8443	0.8459	0.8474	0.8489
1.9	0.8504	0.8519	0.8534	0.8549	0.8563	0.8577	0.8591	0.8605	0.8619	0.8633
2.0	0.8647	0.8660	0.8673	0.8687	0.8700	0.8713	0.8725	0.8738	0.8751	0.8763
2.1	0.8775	0.8788	0.8800	0.8812	0.8823	0.8835	0.8847	0.8858	0.8870	0.8881
2.2	0.8892	0.8903	0.8914	0.8925	0.8935	0.8946	0.8956	0.8967	0.8977	0.8987
2.3	0.8997	0.9007	0.9017	0.9027	0.9037	0.9046	0.9056	0.9065	0.9074	0.9084
2.4	0.9093	0.9102	0.9111	0.9120	0.9128	0.9137	0.9146	0.9154	0.9163	0.9171
2.5	0.9179	0.9187	0.9195	0.9203	0.9211	0.9219	0.9227	0.9235	0.9242	0.9250
2.6	0.9257	0.9265	0.9272	0.9279	0.9286	0.9293	0.9301	0.9307	0.9314	0.9321
2.7	0.9328	0.9335	0.9341	0.9348	0.9354	0.9361	0.9367	0.9373	0.9380	0.9386
2.8	0.9392	0.9398	0.9404	0.9410	0.9416	0.9422	0.9427	0.9433	0.9439	0.9444
2.9	0.9450	0.9455	0.9461	0.9466	0.9471	0.9477	0.9482	0.9487	0.9492	0.9497
3.0	0.9502	0.9507	0.9512	0.9517	0.9522	0.9526	0.9531	0.9536	0.9540	0.9545
3.1	0.9550	0.9554	0.9558	0.9563	0.9567	0.9571	0.9576	0.9580	0.9584	0.9588
3.2	0.9592	0.9596	0.9600	0.9604	0.9608	0.9612	0.9616	0.9620	0.9624	0.9627
3.3	0.9631	0.9635	0.9638	0.9642	0.9646	0.9649	0.9653	0.9656	0.9660	0.9663
3.4	0.9666	0.9670	0.9673	0.9676	0.9679	0.9683	0.9686	0.9689	0.9692	0.9695
3.5	0.9698	0.9701	0.9704	0.9707	0.9710	0.9713	0.9716	0.9718	0.9721	0.9724
3.6	0.9727	0.9729	0.9732	0.9735	0.9737	0.9740	0.9743	0.9745	0.9748	0.9750
3.7	0.9753	0.9755	0.9758	0.9760	0.9762	0.9765	0.9767	0.9769	0.9772	0.9774
3.8	0.9776	0.9779	0.9781	0.9783	0.9785	0.9787	0.9789	0.9791	0.9793	0.9796
3.9	0.9798	0.9800	0.9802	0.9804	0.9806	0.9807	0.9809	0.9811	0.9813	0.9815
4.0	0.9817	0.9834	0.9850	0.9864	0.9877	0.9889	0.9899	0.9909	0.9918	0.9926
5.0	0.9933	0.9939	0.9945	0.9950	0.9955	0.9959	0.9963	0.9967	0.9970	0.9973
6.0	0.9975	0.9978	0.9980	0.9982	0.9983	0.9985	0.9986	0.9988	0.9989	0.9990
7.0	0.9991	0.9992	0.9993	0.9993	0.9994	0.9994	0.9995	0.9995	0.9996	0.9996
8.0	0.9997	0.9997	0.9997	0.9998	0.9998	0.9998	0.9998	0.9998	0.9998	0.9999
9.0	0.9999	0.9999	0.9999	0.9999	0.9999	0.9999	0.9999	0.9999	0.9999	0.9999

Table 7: table of Poisson probabilities

λ

X	0.005	0.01	0.02	0.03	0.04	0.05	0.06	0.07	0.08	0.09
0	.9950	.9900	.9802	.9704	.9608	.9512	.9418	.9324	.9231	.9139
1	.0050	.0099	.0192	.0291	.0384	.0476	.0565	.0653	.0738	.0823
2	.0000	.0000	.0002	.0004	.0008	.0012	.0017	.0023	.0030	.0037
3	.0000	.0000	.0000	.0000	.0000	.0000	.0000	.0001	.0001	.0001

X	0.1	0.2	0.3	0.4	0.5	0.6	0.7	0.8	0.9	1.0
0	.9048	.8187	.7408	.6703	.6065	.5488	.4966	.4493	.4066	.3679
1	.0905	.1637	.2222	.2681	.3033	.3293	.3476	.3595	.3659	.3667
2	.0045	.0164	.0333	.0536	.0758	.0988	.1217	.1438	.1647	.1839
3	.0002	.0011	.0033	.0072	.0126	.0198	.0284	.0383	.0494	.0613
4	.0000	.0001	.0002	.0007	.0016	.0030	.0050	.0077	.0111	.0153
5	.0000	.0000	.0000	.0001	.0002	.0004	.0007	.0012	.0020	.0031
6	.0000	.0000	.0000	.0000	.0000	.0000	.0001	.0002	.0003	.0005
7	.0000	.0000	.0000	.0000	.0000	.0000	.0000	.0000	.0000	.0001

X	1.1	1.2	1.3	1.4	1.5	1.6	1.7	.18	1.9	2.0
0	.3392	.3012	.2725	.2466	.2231	.2019	.1827	.1653	.1496	.1353
1	.3662	.3614	.3543	.3452	.3347	.3230	.3106	.2975	.2842	.2707
2	.2014	.2169	.2303	.2417	.2510	.2584	.2640	.2678	.2700	.2707
3	.0738	.0867	.0998	.1128	.1255	.1378	.1496	.1607	.1710	.1804
4	.0203	.0260	.0324	.0395	.0471	.0551	.0636	.0723	.0812	.0902
5	.0045	.0062	.0084	.0111	.0141	.0176	.0216	.0260	.0309	.0361
6	.0008	.0012	.0018	.0026	.0035	.0047	.0061	.0078	.0098	.0120
7	.0001	.0002	.0003	.0005	.0008	.0011	.0015	.0020	.0027	.0034
8	.0000	.0000	.0001	.0001	.0001	.0002	.0003	.0005	.0006	.0009
9	.0000	.0000	.0000	.0000	.0000	.0000	.0001	.0001	.0001	.0002

X	2.1	2.2	2.3	2.4	2.5	2.6	2.7	2.8	2.9	3.0
0	.1225	.1108	.1003	.0907	.0821	.0734	.0672	.0608	.0050	.0498
1	.2572	.2438	.2306	.2177	.2052	.1931	.1815	.1703	.1596	.1494
2	.2700	.2681	.2652	.2613	.2565	.2510	.2450	.2384	.2314	.2240
3	.1890	.1966	.2033	.2090	.2138	.2176	.2205	.2225	.2237	.2240
4	.0992	.1082	.1169	.1254	.1336	.1414	.1488	.1557	.1622	.1680
5	.0417	.0476	.0538	.0602	.0735	.0775	.0804	.0872	.0940	.1008
6	.0146	.0174	.0206	.0241	.0278	.0319	.0362	.0407	.0455	.0504
7	.0044	.0055	.0068	.0083	.0099	0118	.0139	.0163	.0188	.0216
8	.0011	.0015	.0019	.0025	.0031	.0038	.0047	.0057	.0068	.0081
9	.0003	.0004	.0005	.0007	.0009	.0011	.0014	.0018	.0022	.0027
10	.0001	.0001	.0001	.0002	.0002	.0003	.0004	.0005	.0006	.0008
11	.0000	.0000	.0000	.0000	.0000	.0000	.0001	.0001	.0002	.0002
12	.0000	.0000	.0000	.0000	.0000	.0000	.0000	.0000	.0000	.0001

X	3.1	3.2	3.3	3.4	3.5	3.6	3.7	3.8	3.9	4.0
0	.0450	.0408	.0369	.0334	.0302	.0273	.0247	.0224	.0202	.0183
1	.1397	.1304	.1217	.1135	.1057	.0984	.0915	.0850	.0789	.0733
2	.2165	.2087	.2008	.1929	.1850	.1771	.1692	.1615	.1539	.1465
3	.2237	.2226	.2209	.2186	.2158	.2125	.2087	.2046	.2001	.1954
4	.1734	.1781	.1823	.1858	.1888	.1912	.1931	.1944	.1951	.1954
5	.1075	.1140	.1203	.1264	.1322	.1377	.1429	.1477	.1522	.1563
6	.0555	.0608	.0662	.0716	.0771	.0826	.0881	.0936	.0989	.1042
7	.0246	.0278	.0312	.0348	.0385	.0425	.0466	.0508	.0551	.0595
8	.0095	.0111	.0129	.0148	.0169	.0191	.0215	.0241	.0269	.0298
9	.0033	.0040	.0047	.0056	.0066	.0076	.0089	.0102	.0116	.0132
10	.0010	.0013	.0016	.0019	.0023	.0028	.0033	.0039	.0045	.0053
11	.0003	.0004	.0005	.0006	.0007	.0009	.0011	.0013	.0016	.0019
12	.0001	.0001	.0001	.0002	.0002	.0003	.0003	.0004	.0005	.0006
13	.0000	.0000	.0000	.0000	.0001	.0001	.0001	.0001	.0002	.0002
14	.0000	.0000	.0000	.0000	.0000	.0000	.0000	.0000	.0000	.0001

X	4.1	4.2	4.3	4.4	4.5	4.6	4.7	4.8	4.9	5.0
0	.0166	.0151	.0136	.0123	.0111	.0101	.0091	.0082	.0074	.0067
1	.0679	.0630	.0583	.0540	.0500	.0462	.0427	.0395	.0365	.0337
2	.1393	.1323	.1254	.1188	.1125	.1063	.1005	.0948	.0894	.0842
3	.1904	.1852	.1798	.1743	.1687	.1631	.1574	.1517	.1460	.1404
4	.1951	.1944	.1933	.1917	.1898	.1875	.1849	.1820	.1789	.1755
5	.1600	.1633	.1662	.1687	.1708	.1725	.1738	.1747	.1753	.1755
6	.1093	.1143	.1191	.1237	.1281	.1323	.1362	.1398	.1432	.1462
7	.0640	.0686	.0732	.0778	.0824	.0869	.0914	.0959	.1002	.1044
8	.0328	.0360	.0393	.0428	.0463	.0500	.0537	.0575	.0614	.0653
9	.0150	.0168	.0188	.0209	.0232	.0255	.0280	.0307	.0334	.0363
10	.0061	.0071	.0081	.0092	.0104	.0118	.0132	.0147	.0164	.0181
11	.0023	.0027	.0032	.0037	.0043	.0049	.0056	.0064	.0073	.0082
12	.0008	.0009	.0011	.0014	.0016	.0019	.0022	.0026	.0030	.0034
13	.0002	.0003	.0004	.0005	.0006	.0007	.0008	.0009	.0011	.0013
14	.0001	.0001	.0001	.0001	.0002	.0002	.0003	.0003	.0004	.0005
15	.0000	.0000	.0000	.0000	.0001	.0001	.0001	.0001	.0001	.0002

X	5.1	5.2	5.3	5.4	5.5	5.6	5.7	5.8	5.9	6.0
0	.0061	.0055	.0050	.0045	.0041	.0037	.0033	.0030	.0027	.0025
1	.0311	.0287	.0265	.0244	.0225	.0207	.0191	.0176	.0162	.0149
2	.0793	.0746	.0701	.0659	.0618	.0580	.0544	.0509	.0477	.0446
3	.1348	.1293	.1239	.1185	.1133	.1082	.1033	.0985	.0938	.0892
4	.1719	.1681	.1641	.1600	.1558	.1515	.1472	.1428	.1383	.1339
5	.1753	.1748	.1740	.1728	.1714	.1697	.1678	.1656	.1632	.1606
6	.1490	.1515	.1537	.1555	.1571	.1584	.1594	.1601	.1605	.1606
7	.1086	.1125	.1163	.1200	.1234	.1267	.1298	.1326	.1353	.1377
8	.0692	.0731	.0771	.0810	.0849	.0887	.0925	.0962	.0998	.1033
9	.0392	.0423	.0454	.0486	.0519	.0552	.0586	.0620	.0654	.0688
10	.0200	.0220	.0241	.0262	.0285	.0309	.0334	.0359	.0386	.0413
11	.0093	.0104	.0116	.0129	.0143	.0157	.0173	.0190	.0207	.0225
12	.0039	.0045	.0051	.0058	.0065	.0073	.0082	.0092	.0102	.0113
13	.0015	.0018	.0021	.0024	.0028	.0032	.0036	.0041	.0046	.0052
14	.0006	.0007	.0008	.0009	.0011	.0013	.0015	.0017	.0019	.0022
15	.0002	.0002	.0003	.0003	.0004	.0005	.0006	.0007	.0008	.0009
16	.0001	.0001	.0001	.0001	.0001	.0002	.0002	.0002	.0003	.0003
17	.0000	.0000	.0000	.0000	.0000	.0001	.0001	.0001	.0001	.0001

Table of Poisson Probabilities continued

X	6.1	6.2	6.3	6.4	6.5	6.6	6.7	6.8	6.9	7.0
0	.0022	.0020	.0018	.0017	.0015	.0014	.0012	.0011	.0010	.0009
1	.0137	.0126	.0116	.0106	.0098	.0090	.0082	.0076	.0070	.0064
2	.0417	.0390	.0364	.0340	.0318	.0296	.0276	.0258	.0240	.0223
3	.0848	.0806	.0765	.0726	.0688	.0652	.0617	.0584	.0552	.0521
4	.1294	.1269	.1205	.1162	.1118	.1076	.1034	.0992	.0952	.0912
5	.1579	.1549	.1519	.1487	.1454	.1420	.1385	.1349	.1314	.1277
6	.1605	.1601	.1595	.1586	.1575	.1562	.1546	.1529	.1511	.1490
7	.1399	.1418	.1435	.1450	.1462	.1472	.1480	.1486	.1489	.1490
8	.1066	.1099	.1130	.1160	.1188	.1215	.1240	.1263	.1284	.1304
9	.0723	.0757	.0791	.0825	.0858	.0891	.0923	.0954	.0985	.1014
10	.0441	.0469	.0498	.0528	.0558	.0588	.0618	.0649	.0679	.0710
11	.0245	.0265	.0285	.0307	.0330	.0353	.0377	.0401	.0426	.0452
12	.0124	.0137	.0150	.0164	.0179	.0194	.0210	.0227	.0245	.0264
13	.0058	.0065	.0073	.0081	.0089	.0098	.0108	.0119	.0130	.0142
14	.0025	.0029	.0033	.0037	.0041	.0046	.0052	.0058	.0064	.0071
15	.0010	.0012	.0014	.0016	.0018	.0020	.0023	.0026	.0029	.0033
16	.0004	.0005	.0005	.0006	.0007	.0008	.0010	.0011	.0013	.0014
17	.0001	.0002	.0002	.0002	.0003	.0003	.0004	.0004	.0005	.0006
18	.0000	.0001	.0001	.0001	.0001	.0001	.0001	.0002	.0002	.0002
19	.0000	.0000	.0000	.0000	.0000	.0000	.0000	.0001	.0001	.0001

X	7.1	.7.2	7.3	7.4	7.5	7.6	7.7	7.8	7.9	8.0
0	.0008	.0007	.0007	.0006	.0006	.0005	.0005	.0004	.0004	.0003
1	.0059	.0054	.0049	.0045	.0041	.0038	.0035	.0032	.0029	.0027
2	.0208	.0194	.0180	.0167	.0156	.0145	.0134	.0125	.0116	.0107
3	.0492	.0464	.0438	.0413	.0389	.0366	.0345	.0324	.0305	.0286
4	.0874	.0836	.0799	.0764	.0729	.0696	.0663	.0632	.0602	.0573
5	.1241	.1204	.1167	.1130	.1094	.1057	.1021	.0986	.0951	.0916
6	.1468	.1445	.1420	.1394	.1367	.1339	.1311	.1282	.1252	.1221
7	.1489	.1486	.1481	.1474	.1465	.1454	.1442	.1428	.1413	.1396
8	.1321	.1337	.1351	.1363	.1373	.1382	.1388	.1392	.1395	.1396
9	.1042	.1070	.1096	.1121	.1144	.1167	.1187	.1207	.1224	.1241
10	.0740	.0770	.0800	.0829	.0858	.0887	.0914	.0941	.0967	.0993
11	.0478	.0504	.0531	.0558	.0585	.0613	.0640	.0667	.0695	.0722
12	.0283	.0303	.0323	.0344	.0366	.0388	.0411	.0434	.0457	.0481
13	.0154	.0168	.0181	.0196	.0211	.0227	.0243	.0260	.0278	.0296
14	.0078	.0086	.0095	.0104	.0113	.0123	.0134	.0145	.0157	.0169
15	.0037	.0041	.0046	.0051	.0057	.0062	.0069	.0075	.0083	.0090
16	.0016	.0019	.0021	.0024	.0026	.0030	.0033	.0037	.0041	.0045
17	.0007	.0008	.0009	.0010	.0012	.0013	.0015	.0017	.0019	.0021
18	.0003	.0003	.0004	.0004	.0005	.0006	.0006	.0007	.0008	.0009
19	.0001	.0001	.0001	.0002	.0002	.0002	.0003	.0003	.0003	.0004
20	.0000	.0000	.0001	.0001	.0001	.0001	.0001	.0001	.0001	.0002
21	.0000	.0000	.0000	.0000	.0000	.0000	.0000	.0000	.0001	.0001

X	8.1	8.2	8.3	8.4	8.5	8.6	8.7	8.8	8.9	9.0
0	.0003	.0003	.0002	.0002	.0002	.0002	.0002	.0002	.0001	.0001
1	.0025	.0023	.0021	.0019	.0017	.0016	.0014	.0013	.0012	.0011
2	.0100	.0092	.0086	.0079	.0074	.0068	.0063	.0058	.0054	.0050
3	.0269	.0252	.0237	.0222	.0208	.0195	.0183	.0171	.0160	.0150
4	.0544	.0517	.0491	.0466	.0443	.0420	.0398	.0377	.0357	.0337
5	.0882	.0849	.0816	.0784	.0752	.0722	.0692	.0663	.0635	.0607
6	.1191	.1160	.1128	.1097	.1066	.1034	.1003	.0972	.0941	.0911
7	.1378	.1358	.1338	.1317	.1294	.1271	.1247	.1222	.1197	.1171
8	.1395	.1392	.1388	.1382	.1375	.1366	.1356	.1344	.1332	.1318
9	.1256	.1269	.1280	.1290	.1299	.1306	.1311	.1315	.1317	.1318
10	.1017	.1040	.1063	.1084	.1104	.1123	.1140	.1157	.1172	.1186
11	.0749	.0776	.0802	.0828	.0853	.0878	.0902	.0925	.0948	.0970
12	.0505	.0530	.0555	.0579	.0604	.0629	.0654	.0679	.0703	.0728
13	.0315	.0334	.0354	.0374	.0395	.0416	.0438	.0459	.0481	.0504
14	.0182	.0196	.0210	.0225	.0240	.0256	.0272	.0289	.0306	.0324
15	.0098	.0107	.0116	.0126	.0136	.0147	.0158	.0169	.0182	.0194
16	.0050	.0055	.0060	.0066	.0072	.0079	.0086	.0093	.0101	.0109
17	.0024	.0026	.0029	.0033	.0036	.0040	.0044	.0048	.0053	.0058
18	.0011	.0012	.0014	.0015	.0017	.0019	.0021	.0024	.0026	.0029
19	.0005	.0005	.0006	.0007	.0008	.0009	.0010	.0011	.0012	.0014
20	.0002	.0002	.0002	.0003	.0003	.0004	.0004	.0005	.0005	.0006
21	.0001	.0001	.0001	.0001	.0001	.0002	.0002	.0002	.0002	.0003
22	.0000	.0000	.0000	.0000	.0001	.0001	.0001	.0001	.0001	.0001

X	9.1	9.2	9.3	9.4	9.5	9.6	9.7	9.8	9.9	10.0
0	.0001	.0001	.0001	.0001	.0001	.0001	.0001	.0001	.0001	.0000
1	.0010	.0009	.0009	.0008	.0007	.0007	.0006	.0005	.0005	.0005
2	.0046	.0043	.0040	.0037	.0034	.0031	.0029	.0027	.0025	.0023
3	.0140	.0131	.0123	.0115	.0107	.0100	.0093	.0087	.0081	.0076
4	.0319	.0302	.0285	.0269	.0254	.0240	.0226	.0213	.0201	.0189
5	.0581	.0555	.0530	.0506	.0483	.0460	.0439	.0418	.0398	.0378
6	.0881	.0851	.0822	.0793	.0764	.0736	.0709	.0682	.0656	.0631
7	.1145	.1118	.1091	.1064	.1037	.1010	.0982	.0955	.0928	.0901
8	.1302	.1286	.1269	.1251	.1232	.1212	.1191	.1170	.1148	.1126
9	.1317	.1315	.1311	.1306	.1300	.1293	.1284	.1274	.1263	.1251
10	.1198	.1210	.1219	.1228	.1235	.1241	.1245	.1249	.1250	.1251
11	.0991	.1012	.1031	.1049	.1067	.1083	.1098	.1112	.1125	.1137
12	.0752	.0776	.0799	.0822	.0844	.0866	.0888	.0908	.0928	.0948
13	.0526	.0549	.0572	.0594	.0617	.0640	.0662	.0685	.0707	.0729
14	.0342	.0361	.0380	.0399	.0419	.0439	.0459	.0479	.0500	.0521
15	.0208	.0221	.0235	.0250	.0265	.0281	.0297	.0313	.0330	.0347
16	.0118	.0127	.0137	.0147	.0157	.0168	.0180	.0192	.0204	.0217
17	.0063	.0069	.0075	.0081	.0088	.0095	.0103	.0111	.0119	.0128
18	.0032	.0035	.0039	.0042	.0046	.0051	.0055	.0060	.0065	.0071
19	.0015	.0017	.0019	.0021	.0023	.0026	.0028	.0031	.0034	.0037
20	.0007	.0008	.0009	.0010	.0011	.0012	.0014	.0015	.0017	.0019
21	.0003	.0003	.0004	.0004	.0005	.0006	.0006	.0007	.0008	.0009
22	.0001	.0001	.0002	.0002	.0002	.0002	.0003	.0003	.0004	.0004
23	.0000	.0001	.0001	.0001	.0001	.0001	.0001	.0001	.0002	.0002
24	.0000	.0000	.0000	.0000	.0000	.0000	.0000	.0001	.0001	.0001

Appendix 2 Listing of selected formulae

Guideline for determining number of classes

$$\frac{\text{Largest Data Value} - \text{Smallest Data Value}}{\text{Class Width}}$$

Relative frequency of a class

$$\frac{\text{Frequency of the class}}{n} \times 100$$

Sample Mean

$$\bar{X} = \frac{\sum X}{N}$$

Population Mean

$$\mu = \frac{\sum X}{N}$$

Location of Median

$$\frac{n+1}{2}$$

Weighted mean

$$\bar{X}w = \frac{\sum XW}{\sum W}$$

Geometric mean

$$GM = \sqrt[n]{X_1 X_2 X_3 \ldots X_n}$$

Mean Absolute Deviation (M.A.D)

$$\text{M.A.D.} = \frac{\sum |X - \bar{X}|}{n}$$

Sample variance

$$s^2 = \frac{\sum (X - \bar{X})^2}{n-1}$$

Population variance

$$\sigma^2 = \frac{\sum (X - \mu)^2}{N}$$

Sample standard deviation

$$s = \sqrt{\frac{\sum (X - \bar{X})^2}{n-1}} \quad \text{or} \quad s = \sqrt{s^2}$$

Population standard deviation

$$\sigma = \sqrt{\frac{\sum (X - \mu)^2}{N}} \quad \text{or} \quad \sigma = \sqrt{\sigma^2}$$

Shortcut (computational) formulae

Sample Variance

$$s^2 = \frac{\sum X^2 - \frac{(\sum X)^2}{n}}{n-1}$$

Sample Standard Deviation

$$s = \sqrt{s^2}$$

Population Variance

$$\sigma^2 = \frac{\sum X^2 - \frac{(\sum X)^2}{N}}{N}$$

Population Standard Deviation

$$\sigma = \sqrt{\sigma^2}$$

Sample mean for grouped data

$$\bar{X} = \frac{\sum fM}{N}$$

Population mean for grouped data

$$\mu = \frac{\sum fM}{N}$$

Sample variance for grouped data

$$s^2 = \frac{\sum f(M - \bar{X})^2}{n - 1}$$

Sample standard deviation for grouped data

$$s = \sqrt{s^2}$$

Population variance for grouped data

$$\sigma^2 = \frac{\sum f(M - \mu)^2}{N}$$

Population standard deviation for grouped data

$$\sigma = \sqrt{\sigma^2}$$

Shortcut (computational) formulae for grouped data

Sample Variance

$$s^2 = \frac{\sum fM^2 - \dfrac{(\sum fM)^2}{n}}{n - 1}$$

Sample Standard Deviation

$$s = \sqrt{s^2}$$

Population Variance

$$\sigma^2 = \frac{\sum fM^2 - \dfrac{(\sum fM)^2}{N}}{N}$$

Population Standard Deviation

$$\sigma = \sqrt{\sigma^2}$$

Median for grouped data

$$\text{median} = L + \frac{f_1}{f_2} W$$

Sample coefficient of variation

$$\frac{s}{\bar{X}} (100)$$

Population coefficient of variation

$$\frac{\sigma}{\mu} (100)$$

Finding a percentile location

$$i = \frac{P}{100} (n)$$

Percentiles for grouped data

$$n\text{th percentile} = L + \frac{f_1}{f_2} W$$

Z scores

$$Z = \frac{X - \mu}{\sigma}$$

Addition law of probability

$$P(A \text{ or } B) = P(A) + P(B)$$

Multiplication law of probability

$$(A \text{ and } B) = P(A \mid B)$$
$$= P(A) \times P(B \mid A)$$

Independent events law of probability

$$P(A \text{ and } B) = P(A) \times P(B)$$

Expected monetary return

$$\begin{aligned}E(M) = \;&(\text{probability of } Z_1 \times M_1) + \ldots \\ &+ (\text{probability of } Z_2 \times M_2) + \ldots \\ &+ (\text{probability of } Z_n \times M_n)\end{aligned}$$

Present value and discounting factor

$$\text{Present Value} = \frac{M}{(1+I)^n}$$

$$\text{Discounting Factor} = \frac{1}{(1+I)^n}$$

Mean of sampling distribution of sample means

$$\mu_{\bar{X}} = \frac{\sum \bar{X}}{N}$$

Variance of sampling distribution of sample means

$$\sigma_{\bar{X}}^2 = \frac{(\bar{X} - \mu_{\bar{X}})^2}{N}$$

Standard deviation of sampling distribution of sample means

$$\sigma_{\bar{X}} = \sqrt{\sigma_{\bar{X}}^2}$$

Finding the variance of a sampling distribution of sample means using the population variance when $n/N > .05$ (finite population correction factor formula).

$$\sigma_{\bar{X}}^2 = \left(\frac{\sigma^2}{n}\right)\left(\frac{N-n}{N-1}\right)$$

Finding the variance of a sampling distribution of sample means using the population variance when $n/N \leqslant .05$.

$$\sigma_{\bar{X}}^2 = \frac{\sigma^2}{n}$$

Finding the standard deviation of a sampling distribution of sample means using the population variance when $n/N > .05$ (finite population correction factor formula). To distinguish it from other standard deviations it is called the finite population correction factor standard error formula.

$$\sigma_{\bar{X}} = \sqrt{\left(\frac{\sigma^2}{n}\right)\left(\frac{N-n}{N-1}\right)}$$

Finding the standard deviation of a sampling distribution of sample means using the population variance when $n/N \leqslant .05$. To distinguish it from other standard deviations it is called the standard error formula.

$$\sigma_{\bar{X}} = \sqrt{\frac{\sigma^2}{n}}$$

which is the same as $\sigma_{\bar{X}} = \frac{\sigma}{\sqrt{n}}$ and which becomes $\sigma_{\bar{X}} = \frac{s}{\sqrt{n}}$ when we do not know the value of σ.

Finding the standard deviation of a sampling distribution of sample proportions using the population variance when $n/N > .05$ (finite population correction factor formula for proportions).

$$\sigma_{\bar{P}} = \sqrt{\frac{P(1-P)}{n}}\sqrt{\frac{N-n}{N-1}}$$

Finding the standard deviation of a sampling distribution of sample means using the population variance when $n/N \leqslant .05$. To distinguish it from other standard deviations it is called the standard error formula for proportions.

$$\sigma_{\bar{P}} = \sqrt{\frac{P(1-P)}{n}}$$

which becomes $\sigma_{\bar{P}} = \sqrt{\frac{P(1-\bar{P})}{n}}$ when we do not know the value of P.

Normal distribution assumption for distribution of sample means when:

$$n \geqslant 30$$

Normal distribution assumption for distribution of sample proportions when:

$$nP \geqslant 5 \text{ and } (1 - P) \geqslant 5$$

Standard error formula for t distributions is represented as follows because it deals with samples of less than 30:

$$s_{\bar{X}} = \frac{s}{\sqrt{n}}$$

95 per cent confidence level for distribution of sample means

$$\mu = \bar{X} \pm 1.96\sigma_{\bar{x}}$$

99 per cent confidence level for distribution of sample means

$$\mu = \bar{X} \pm 2.58\sigma_{\bar{x}}$$

95 per cent confidence level for distribution of sample proportions

$$P = \bar{P} \pm 1.96\sigma_{\bar{p}}$$

99 per cent confidence level for distribution of sample proportions

$$P = \bar{P} \pm 2.58\sigma_{\bar{p}}$$

Confidence levels for t distributions

$$\mu = \bar{X} \pm (t)(s_{\bar{x}})$$

Determining sample size for sample means:

$$n = \frac{(CL^2)(s^2)}{L^2}$$

Determining sample size for sample proportions:

$$n = \frac{(CL^2 \bar{P})(100 - \bar{P})}{L^2}$$

Determining critical value in hypothesis testing (two tailed test at .05 significance level)

$$c = \mu + (Z_{.025} \times \sigma_{\bar{x}})$$

Determining critical value for proportions in hypothesis testing (two tailed test at .05 significance level)

$$c = P + (Z_{.025} \times \sigma_{\bar{x}})$$

Chi-square

$$\chi^2 = \sum \frac{(O - E)^2}{E}$$

Estimated regression line

$$y = a + b(x - \bar{x})$$

where

$$a = \frac{\sum y}{n} \qquad x = \frac{\sum x}{n}$$

$$b = \frac{\sum xy - \frac{(\sum x)(\sum y)}{n}}{\sum x^2 - \frac{(\sum x)^2}{n}}$$

Correlation coefficient

$$r = \frac{\sum xy - \frac{(\sum x)(\sum y)}{n}}{\sqrt{\left(\sum x^2 - \frac{(\sum x)^2}{n}\right)\left(\sum y^2 - \frac{(\sum y)^2}{n}\right)}}$$

Moving average forecast

$$\hat{Y}_{t+T} = M_t$$

Exponential smoothing

$$U_t = \alpha Y_t + (1 - \alpha) U_{t-1}$$

Exponential double smoothing

$$\overline{Y}_t = 2 U_t - \overline{U}_t$$

Exponential smoothed error

$$E_t = \alpha e_t + (1 - \alpha) E_{t-1}$$

Mean absolute deviation

$$M.A.D._t = \alpha \mid e_t \mid + (1 - \alpha) M.A.D._t$$

Tracking signal

$$T.S._t = \frac{E_t}{M.A.D._t}$$

Cost of ordering (set-up cost)

$$C_1 = \frac{\text{Cost of Ordering}}{\text{Set-up cost}}$$

Cost of placing orders

$$\frac{C_1 d}{Q}$$

Cost of holding stock

$$C_2 \left(\frac{Q}{2} + B \right) = ip \left(\frac{Q}{2} + B \right)$$

Cost of purchasing items

$$pd$$

Total operating cost

$$Z = pd + \frac{C_1 d}{Q} + C_2 \left(\frac{Q}{2} + B \right)$$

or

$$Z = pd + \frac{C_1 d}{Q} + ip \left(\frac{Q}{2} + B \right)$$

Economic order quantity

$$EOQ = \sqrt{\frac{2C_1 d}{C_2}}$$

or

$$EOQ = \sqrt{\frac{2C_1 d}{ip}}$$

Order level

$$L\overline{R} + k\sqrt{L}\sigma_r$$

Buffer stock

$$B = k\sqrt{L}\sigma_r$$

Total annual usage

$$\sum \sqrt{p_i d_i}$$

K constant

$$K = \frac{\text{Total number of orders per year}}{\sum \sqrt{p_i d_i}}$$

Frequency of ordering

$$f_i^* = K \times \sqrt{p_i d_i}$$

Order quantities

$$Q_i^* = \frac{d_i}{f_i^*}$$

Index